STRATEGIC
MARKETING

THE IRWIN SERIES IN MARKETING

STRATEGIC MARKETING

David W. Cravens

M. J. Neeley School of Business

Texas Christian University

Fifth Edition

IRWIN

Chicago • Bogotá • Boston • Buenos Aires • Caracas
London • Madrid • Mexico City • Sydney • Toronto

To Sue and Karen

Cover art by Artist Charles Schorre

© The McGraw-Hill Companies, Inc., 1982, 1987, 1991, 1994, and 1997

Irwin Book Team

Publisher: *Rob Zwettler*
Executive editor: *Stephen M. Patterson*
Editorial coordinator: *Andrea Hlavacek*
Marketing manager: *Colleen Suljic*
Project supervisor: *Jim Labeots*
Production supervisor: *Pat Frederickson*
Designer: *Larry J. Cope*
Prepress buyer: *Jon Christopher*
Compositor: *Carlisle Communications, Ltd.*
Typeface: *10/12 Times Roman*
Printer: *R. R. Donnelley & Sons Company*

Library of Congress Cataloging-in-Publication Data

Cravens, David W.
    Strategic marketing / David W. Cravens.—5th ed.
      p. cm.—(Irwin series in marketing)
    Includes index.
    ISBN 0-256-21438-7
    1. Marketing—Decision making. 2. Marketing—Management.
    3. Marketing—Management—Case studies. I. Title. II. Series.
    HF5415.135.C72   1997
    658.8′02—dc20   96–12050

Printed in the United States of America
3 4 5 6 7 8 9 0 DOC 3 2 1 0 9 8 7

Preface

The pivotal role of strategic marketing in business performance is demonstrated in the market-driven strategies of successful organizations competing in a wide array of product and market situations. The escalating importance of providing customer satisfaction, responding to diversity in the marketplace, developing really new products, and recognizing global competition challenges require effective marketing strategies for gaining and keeping a competitive edge. *Strategic Marketing* examines the concepts and processes for gaining competitive advantage in the marketplace.

THE MARKET-ORIENTED ORGANIZATION

Becoming market-oriented is a key objective in many companies. The driving force is the reality that the route to competitive advantage is delivering superior value to customers, which is what becoming market-oriented is all about. Several aspects of the competitive challenge are apparent:

- Marketing strategy provides concepts and processes for gaining competitive advantage through superior customer value.
- Marketing is a major stakeholder in key organizational core processes—new product development, sales and fulfillment, and customer support.

- The use of flexible, multifunctional teams to manage core business processes is changing the role and structure of the traditional hierarchical organization.

- Changes in how organizations are designed place new priorities on forging collaborative relationships with customers, suppliers, marketing channel members, and even competitors.

- Understanding customers, competitors, and the market environment requires the active involvement of the entire organization.

- Developing processes that enable the organization to continually learn from customers, competitors, and other sources is vital to sustaining a competitive edge.

- The environmental and ethical aspects of business practice are critical concerns, requiring active involvement by the entire organization.

Managing effectively in the constantly changing business environment is a requirement for success. Developing and implementing dynamic business and marketing strategies that are adaptable to changing conditions are critical success factors. These challenges mandate that organizations develop the skills essential to anticipating and responding to the constantly changing needs of customers and markets.

Customer diversity and new forms of competition create impressive growth and performance opportunities for those firms in which management applies strategic marketing concepts and analyses into business strategy development and implementation. The market-driven challenge is apparent in a variety of industries in the United States and around the world. Strategic marketing is an essential contributor to companies' survival and growth in the rapidly changing business environment of the 21st century. Analyzing market behavior and matching strategies to changing conditions require a hands-on approach to marketing planning and strategy implementation. Due to the frequent need to alter strategies for goods and services and markets, decision-based planning is critical. Penetrating financial analysis is an important skill of the marketing professional. Seat-of-the-pants approaches to marketing strategy are poorly focused and often ineffective in the current environment.

Strategic Marketing examines marketing strategy using a combination of the text and case materials to develop relevant concepts and their application to business situations. This book is designed for use in undergraduate capstone strategy marketing courses and in the MBA marketing core and advanced strategy courses.

NEW AND EXPANDED SCOPE

Competing in any market today requires a global perspective. This emphasis is expanded in the fifth edition. The shrinking time-and-access boundaries of global markets establish new competitive requirements. This issue is far too important to devote to a single chapter. The global dimensions of marketing strategy are integrated throughout the chapters of the book and also considered in various cases.

Several contemporary strategy topics are discussed throughout the text. These include market orientation, relationship marketing, organizational learning, strategic alliances, competitive benchmarketing, competing on capabilities, and new organizational forms. Competitive advantage is a major dimension that spans the entire book.

THE TEXT

Strategic Marketing examines the key concepts and issues in selecting a strategy. Our discussions with various instructors indicate a desire to provide a strategy perspective and emphasis that extends beyond the traditional focus on managing the marketing mix. Emphasis on services as well as products is expanded in the fifth edition. The length of the book has been shortened to provide flexibility in the use of the text material and cases or as a resource in multifunctional team-based courses.

The book is designed around a marketing planning approach with a clear emphasis on how to do strategic analysis and planning. Part I examines business and marketing strategies. Part II discusses marketing situation analysis. Part III covers designing marketing strategy. Part IV treats marketing program development. Finally, Part V examines implementing and managing marketing strategy. How-to guides, provided throughout the book, assist the reader in applying the analysis and planning approaches developed in the text.

THE CASES

Three-fourths of the cases are new to the fifth edition. Short, application-focused cases are placed at the end of each part of the book. These cases are useful in applying the concepts and methods discussed in the chapters. The cases can be used for class discussion, hand-in assignments, formal presentations, and examinations. The cases consider a wide variety of business environments, both domestic and international. They include goods and services, organizations at different distribution channel levels, and small, medium, and large enterprises.

Part VI is a group of comprehensive cases that offer students a variety of marketing strategy application opportunities. Each case considers several important strategy issues. The cases represent several different competitive situations for consumer and business products and domestic and international markets. A video supplement is available for six of the cases. The videos are useful in generating student interest and providing additional information on the companies.

A major effort has been made to expand the international scope of end-of-part cases and the comprehensive cases. The cases include companies competing in several countries around the world.

CHANGES IN THE FIFTH EDITION

The basic design of *Strategic Marketing* from prior editors is retained in the fifth edition. Nevertheless, the revision incorporates many significant changes, additions, and updated examples. Every chapter includes new material and expanded treatment of important topics.

The first chapter discusses marketing strategy and planning. These topics were moved from Chapter 4. Market analysis and competitor analysis have been combined into one chapter (Chapter 3). The discussion of marketing research and information systems (Chapter 5) has been repositioned to focus more on continuous learning about markets. The chapter on relationship strategies (Chapter 7) is in Part III. The material from the chapter on strategies for different situations is now in the chapter on targeting and positioning strategy (Chapter 6). The discussion of promotion strategy is expanded to two chapters to include coverage of direct marketing strategy. Several chapters discuss current topics, including competing on capabilities, superior customer value, new organization forms, teamwork, mass customization, databases, and market trends. Every chapter includes Application Features.

Additionally, each chapter has been revised to incorporate new concepts and examples, improve readability and flow, and generate reader interest and involvement. Topical coverage has been expanded (or reduced), where appropriate, to better position the book for teaching and learning in the rapidly changing business environment. Financial analysis guidelines will be found in the Chapter 1 Appendix, and sales forecasting materials are in the Chapter 3 Appendix.

INSTRUCTOR'S MANUAL

A complete and expanded teaching–learning package is available in the Instructor's Manual. It includes course planning suggestions, answers to end-of-chapter questions, instructor's notes for cases, a multiple-choice question bank, and transparency masters. Videos are available for six of the cases.

This edition of the manual has been substantially revised and expanded to improve its effectiveness in supporting course planning, case discussion, and examination preparation. Detailed instructor's notes concerning the use of the cases is provided, including epilogues when available.

The text, cases, and instructor's manual offer considerable flexibility in course design, depending on the instructor's objectives and the course in which the book is used.

ACKNOWLEDGMENTS

The book has benefited from the contributions and experiences of many people and organizations. Business executives and colleagues at universities in many countries have influenced the development of *Strategic Marketing*. While space does not permit thanking each person, a sincere note of appreciation is extended to all. I shall identify several individuals whose assistance was particularly important. A special note of appreciation is extended to Gilbert A. Churchill, Jr., of the University of Wisconsin, who was the consulting editor for the previous editions of the book.

A special thank you is extended to the reviewers of prior editions and to colleagues that have offered many suggestions and ideas. Throughout the development of the fifth edition, a number of reviewers have made many important suggestions for improving the book. I appreciate very much the assistance of the following professors in guiding the development of this edition of *Strategic Marketing:*

James Littlefield, Virginia Tech University

Robert Allerheiligen, Colorado State University

Rick Lytle, Abilene Christian University

Mary Jane Sheffet, Michigan State University

Cathy Trower, Johns Hopkins University

Tom Massey, University of Missouri-Kansas City

Kris Bellur, California State-Bakersfield

James M. Snyder, North Adams State College

I am also indebted to the case authors who gave me permission to use their cases. Each author is specifically identified at the beginning of each case. Karen S. Cravens, University of Tulsa, prepared Chapter 5. Her contribution is also very much appreciated.

A special note of thanks is due to the management and professional staff of Richard D. Irwin, Inc., for their support and encouragement on this and prior editions of *Strategic Marketing*. Rob Zwettler, as publisher, has provided an important editorial leadership role. As sponsoring editor, Steve Patterson and his assistant, Andrea Hlavacek, have been a constant source of valuable assistance and encouragement. Colleen Suljic provided important marketing direction for the project. Pat Frederickson and Jim Labeots guided the book through the various stages of production while Larry Cope polished the design.

Many students provided various kinds of support that were essential to completing the revision. In particular, I appreciate the excellent contributions to this edition made by Derek DeCross and Kate O'Rourke. I also appreciate the helpful comments and suggestions offfered by many students in my classes.

I greatly appreciate the support and encouragement provided by Dean H. Kirk Downey and William C. Moncrief, chair of the Marketing Department. Special thanks are due to Linda Blundell and Jana Wright for typing the manuscript and for their assistance in other aspects of the project. Finally, I want to express appreciation to Eunice West and her late husband, James L. West, for the endowment that supports my position and enables me to work on projects like this book.

David W. Cravens

Contents in Brief

Contents

BUSINESS AND MARKETING STRATEGIES

Marketing Strategy and Planning

The market-oriented organization understands buyers' needs and wants and effectively combines and directs the skills and resources of the *entire* organization to provide high levels of satisfaction to its customers. "That model of competing, which links R&D, technology, innovation, production, and finance—integrated through marketing's drive to own a market—is the approach that all competitors will take to succeed in the 1990s."[1] Rather than a specialized function within the organization, marketing is a central process of the entire business. Marketing includes all of the various actions of the organization that are aimed at providing customers with superior value.

The success of Intuit, Inc.'s Quicken personal finance software is an impressive example of how management vision, an obsession about customer service, and employee teamwork can transform an organization into a powerful competitor.[2] The Quicken software helps consumers and small businesses to write checks and manage their finances. Under the leadership of Scott Cook, Intuit's founder, the entire organization strives enthusiastically to satisfy its software users. Making the software simple to use requires sensing market needs, extensive testing, customer feedback, and continuous product improvement. Launched in the 1980s, Quicken owns the market. Intuit's sales increased from $25 million in 1990 to over $240 million in 1994. Microsoft made an offer to acquire Intuit in 1994 for $1.3 billion, but the U.S. government did not approve the purchase because of antitrust concerns. Bill Gates, Microsoft's CEO, viewed Quicken's customer base as a promising avenue for expanding into financial services systems.

This chapter—and this book—begins with a discussion of how companies compete in the business environment of the late 1990s. Then we will look closely at the process of becoming market-oriented. Next, we will describe and illustrate the steps in developing marketing strategy. Finally, we will discuss how the marketing plan is prepared.

DECIDING HOW TO COMPETE

Switzerland's SMH Group (SMH) is an interesting example of how an executive's vision for reviving the Swiss watchmaking industry enabled it to compete with Hattori Seiko for the title of the world's No. 1 watchmaker.[3] The initial strategy was to launch the Swatch watch in 1983. SMH's brands now include Blancpain, Omega, Longines, Rado, Tissot, Certina, Mido, Hamilton, Balmain, Swatch, Flik Flak, and Endura.

We cite SMH's strategy for regaining competitive advantage in the global watch industry throughout this discussion of deciding how to compete. We examine the critical responsibility of management vision in selecting a competitive strategy and discuss how companies gain competitive advantage.

Strategic Vision

Strategic vision involves decisions by the top management of a company about *where* to compete, *when* to compete, and *how* to compete. It may also involve deciding *not* to compete. These decisions require knowledge of market needs and trends, competition, and the strengths (and weaknesses) of the organization. Rapidly changing markets and competitive threats call for high levels of executive skill in charting the course of an organization through a constantly changing business environment. Assessing that environment and deciding the future product and market direction of the corporation are critical to the performance of the enterprise. Top management must anticipate and deal proactively with future threats and opportunities; it must select the product and market area in which the corporation can compete best and then develop market-driven strategies for gaining competitive advantage.

SMH's management was not complacent in deciding how the company should compete in the watch industry. The game plan used by management included a portfolio of watch brands covering a range of prices from inexpensive to expensive. Finding competitive advantage and improving organizational effectiveness are important issues in selecting business strategies.

Finding Competitive Advantage

Companies obtain competitive advantage by offering superior value to the customer through (1) lower prices than competitors for equivalent benefits and/or (2) unique benefits that more than offset a higher price.[4] Several important considerations enter into achieving customer satisfaction and gaining competitive advantage.[5]

1. The process should be customer-focused.

2. Analysis of needs/wants (requirements) should look at groups of buyers with similar preferences.

3. Opportunities for advantage occur when gaps exist between what customers want and competitors' efforts to satisfy them.

4. Opportunities are created by finding buyers' requirements which are not being satisfied.

5. Customer satisfaction analysis should look for the best opportunities for the organization to create superior value.

SMH achieves its competitive advantage in the watch market using both value and cost strategies. Its expensive brands offer unique value derived from high quality and prestigious image. Meanwhile, management has lowered the costs of all brands by using automated production processes.[6] For example, the Swatch watch sells today at a price very similar to its price over a decade ago.

Although several factors contribute to the effectiveness of an organization, competitive advantage is a core requirement. "Chief executives must take the lead in moving their institutions toward strategic management by designing organizations and developing management systems that look forward and look out."[7] Several elements are influencing change in organization structure. The relationships among business functions such as manufacturing, marketing, research and development, finance, and human resources are becoming more integrated in many companies. Teams of people from different functions are working together to design new products and improve customer service. Causes of these changes include (1) a turbulent business environment that is global in scope and (2) the availability of an impressive array of information technology that can be used to improve the effectiveness of workers.

Organizational change occurred in a wide range of companies during the last decade. Many companies reduced the size of professional staff and the number of management levels. "Holding up the latest ideal in organizational design, the flat organization, many companies have already cut the layers of management between the chief executive and front-line supervisors from a dozen to six or fewer."[8] Such changes drastically alter the span of control of managers and require new management and control systems. For example, information technology performs many of the functions traditionally handled by middle-level managers. The increased scope of management also requires executives to have a better understanding of work functions than in the past.

SMH's chief executive, Nicolas G. Hayek, implemented several actions to turn around the poor performance of Switzerland's two largest watchmakers (which were combined in 1983 to create SMH).[9] He streamlined operations, replaced weak managers, strengthened marketing capabilities, and gained direct control of distribution. When the banks financing SMH wanted out of the watch business, insiders took over the company with support from investors. The inexpensive Swatch line was introduced and production costs reduced to facilitate a low-price strategy. Efforts continue toward producing quality at the lowest cost. Innovation generates a regular stream of new products. SMH acquired the primary producer of expensive Swiss mechanical movements in 1992.

MARKET ORIENTATION

Market orientation is a business perspective that makes the customer the focal point of a company's total operations. "A business is market-oriented when its culture is systematically and entirely committed to the continuous creation of superior customer value."[10] Market orientation involves the use of superior organizational skills in understanding and satisfying customers.[11]

Becoming market-oriented requires the support of the entire workforce. Executives must identify rapidly changing customer needs and wants, determine the impact of these changes on customer satisfaction, increase the rate of product/service innovation in business strategies, and develop strategies that build the organization's competitive advantage. We first look at the characteristics and features of market orientation and discuss the importance of becoming market-oriented. Next, several issues in making the transition to a market-oriented organization are discussed.

What Is Market Orientation?

Becoming market-oriented involves obtaining information about customers, competitors, and markets; viewing the information from a total business perspective; deciding how to deliver superior customer value; and taking actions to provide value to customers (Exhibit 1–1). Market orientation is both a culture committed to customer value and a process of continuously creating superior value for buyers. Market orientation requires a customer focus, competitor intelligence, and coordination among the business functions.

Customer Focus.   The marketing concept was first articulated by a General Electric executive in the 1950s. There are many similarities between the marketing concept and market orientation. The marketing concept advocates starting with customer needs/wants, deciding which needs to meet, and involving everyone in the process of satisfying customers. The important difference is that market orientation is more than a philosophy since it provides a process for delivering customer value. The market-oriented organization understands customers' preferences and requirements and effectively combines and directs the skills and resources of the entire organization to satisfy customers. Becoming customer-oriented requires finding out what values buyers want to help them meet their purchasing objectives. Buyers' buying decisions are guided by the attributes and features of the brand that offers the best value for the buyers' use situation. The buyer's experience in using the brand is compared to expectations to determine customer satisfaction.[12]

Competitor Intelligence.   Market orientation recognizes the importance of understanding competition as well as the customer:

> The key questions are which competitors, and what technologies, and whether target customers perceive them as alternate satisfiers. Superior value requires that the seller identify and

EXHIBIT 1–1   Components of Market Orientation

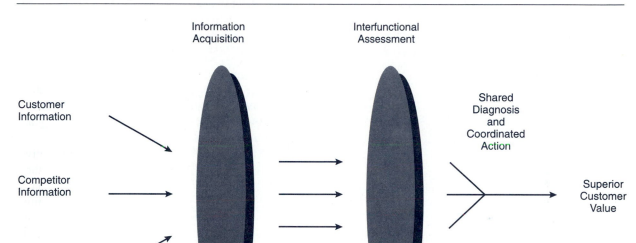

Source: Reprinted from Stanley F. Slater and John C. Narver, "Market Orientation, Customer Value, and Superior Performance," *Business Horizons,* March/April 1994, p. 23. Copyright 1994 by the Foundation for the School of Business at Indiana University.

understand the principal competitors' short-term strengths and weaknesses and long-term capabilities and strategies.[13]

Failure to identify and respond to competitive threats can create serious consequences for a company. For example, Western Union failed to define its competitive area as telecommunications, concentrating instead on its telegraph services, and eventually was outflanked by fax technology. Had Western Union been a market-oriented company its management might have better understood the changes taking place, seen the competitive threat, and developed strategies to counter the threat.

Interfunctional Coordination.   An important characteristic of market-oriented companies is that they are effective in getting all business functions working together to provide customer value. They are successful in removing the walls between business functions—marketing talks with manufacturing and finance. Interfunctional teamwork is how customer value targets are achieved.

As shown in Exhibit 1–2, Rubbermaid Inc. uses teams of people from various business functions to plan, develop, and market new household products. The teams work closely together to define customer needs and develop products to meet the needs.

EXHIBIT 1–2 How Rubbermaid Inc. Is Successful with 90 Percent of Its New Products

---

Rubbermaid introduced over 365 new products in 1992. Sales and earnings grew at an average rate of 15 percent yearly in the past decade. These are the core examples of Rubbermaid's new-product planning:

- The company has an impressive record of spotting trends and bringing innovative products to market.
- Entrepreneurial teams made up of a product manager, research and manufacturing engineers, and financial, sales, and marketing executives conceive new-product ideas and move them from the design stage to the marketplace.
- The innovations are incremental product improvements such as a new mailbox that is large enough for magazines, doesn't leak when opened, is rustproof, and shows a flag when the mail is delivered.

- Rubbermaid's differentiated products are premium priced to reflect their good value and quality. The design team is responsible for pricing.
- The company's relationships with retailers like Wal-Mart and Kmart help to move new products through the distribution channels.
- Product designs incorporate the needs of retailers (e.g., easy stacking on shelves) as well as end-users.
- The design teams relentlessly work on the details that improve products like brooms, mops, or lunchboxes.

Source: Valerie Reitman, "Rubbermaid Turns Up Plenty of Profit in the Mundane," *The Wall Street Journal,* March 27, 1992, p. B3. Reprinted by permission of *The Wall Street Journal,* © 1992 Dow Jones & Company, Inc. All Rights Reserved Worldwide.

Becoming a Market-Oriented Organization

As shown in Exhibit 1–1, becoming a market-oriented company involves several interrelated requirements. These include information acquisition, interfunctional assessment, shared diagnosis, and coordinated action.

Information Acquisition. Becoming a learning organization provides an important capability for building competitive advantage. Learning organizations encourage open-minded inquiry, widespread information dissemination, and the use of mutually informed managers' visions about the current market and how it is likely to change in the future.[14] Intuit's obsession toward customer service gives its managers revealing insights about the problems users encounter with Quicken and the preferences they have concerning software features. "A company can be market-oriented only if it completely understands its markets and the people who decide whether to buy its products or services."[15]

Interfunctional Assessment. Rubbermaid has overcome the hurdles of getting people from different functions to develop shared visions about the market and to work together to develop innovative products. Delivering customer satisfaction involves all business functions. Rubbermaid's entrepreneurial teams are able to resolve conflicting functional objectives and other turf differences. The team members' shared vision about customers and competition center attention on critical business issues. They are able to identify the relevant questions and jointly answer the questions.

Shared Diagnosis and Action. The remaining part of becoming market-oriented is deciding what actions to take to provide superior customer value. This involves shared discussions among company personnel and analysis of trade-offs in meeting customer needs.[16] An effective multifunctional team approach to decision making aids diagnosis and coordinated action. Rubbermaid's teams are empowered to make decisions and are responsible for results.

Becoming market-oriented requires making major changes in the culture, processes, and structure of the traditional pyramid organization organized into functional units. Nonetheless, mounting evidence suggests that the market-oriented organization has an important competitive advantage in providing customer value and achieving superior performance.

Business Strategy and Marketing

Before work can start on marketing strategy, management's objectives and plans for the business must be clearly understood. The discussion in Chapter 2 considers these decisions and activities. An understanding of business purpose, scope, objectives, and strategy is essential to making strategic marketing decisions that are consistent with the corporate and business unit plan of action.

The chief marketing executive's business strategy responsibilities include (1) participating in strategy formulation and (2) developing marketing strategies that follow business strategy priorities. Since these two areas are closely interrelated, it is important to examine marketing's role and functions in both areas to gain more insight into marketing's responsibilities and contributions. Peter F. Drucker describes this role:

> Marketing is so basic that it cannot be considered a separate function (i.e., a separate skill or work) within the business, on a par with others such as manufacturing or personnel. Marketing requires separate work, and a distinct group of activities. But it is, first, a central dimension of the entire business. It is the whole business seen from the point of view of its final result, that is, from the customer's point of view.[17]

Frederick E. Webster describes the role of the marketing manager: "At the corporate level, marketing managers have a critical role to play as advocates for the customer and for a set of values and beliefs that put the customer first in the firm's decision making, and to communicate the value proposition as part of that culture throughout the organization, both internally and in its multiple relationships and alliances."[18] This role includes assessing market attractiveness in the markets available to the firm, providing a customer orientation, and communicating the firm's specific value advantages.

Strategic Marketing

Marketing strategy is defined as the analysis, strategy development, and implementation activities in

> selecting market target strategies for the product-markets of interest to the organization, setting marketing objectives, and developing, implementing, and managing the marketing program positioning strategies designed to meet the needs of customers in each market target.[19]

Strategic marketing is a market-driven process of strategy development, taking into account a constantly changing business environment and the need to achieve high levels of customer satisfaction. Strategic marketing focuses on organizational performance rather than the traditional concern about increasing sales. Marketing strategy builds competitive advantage by combining the customer-influencing strategies of the business into an integrated array of market-focused actions. Strategic marketing links the organization with the environment and views marketing as a responsibility of the entire business rather than a specialized function.

Because of marketing's boundary orientation between the organization and its customers, channel members, and competition, marketing processes are central to the business strategy planning process.[20] Strategic marketing provides the expertise for environmental monitoring, for deciding what customer groups to serve, for setting product specifications, and for selecting which competitors to position against. Successfully integrating multifunctional strategies is critical to providing high levels of customer satisfaction. Customer preferences for product attributes must be transformed into product design and production guidelines. Success in achieving high-quality products and services requires finding out which attributes of product and service quality drive customer satisfaction.

The analysis, planning, implementation, and management process that we follow in this book is described in Exhibit 1–3. The activities that are described correspond to Parts II through V of the book. The situation analysis considers market and competitor analysis, market segmentation, and continuous learning about markets. Designing marketing strategy examines customer targeting and positioning strategies, marketing relationship strategies, and planning for new products. Marketing program development consists of product, distribution, price, and promotion strategies designed and implemented to meet the needs of targeted buyers. Strategy implementation and management look at organizational design and marketing strategy implementation and control. We describe each aspect of the strategy process in the rest of the chapter.

MARKETING SITUATION ANALYSIS

Marketing management needs the information provided by the marketing situation analysis to guide the design of a new strategy or to change an existing strategy. The situation analysis is conducted on a regular basis after the strategy is underway to guide strategy changes.

Analyzing Markets and Competition

Markets need to be defined so that the right buyers and competition are analyzed. For a market to exist, there must be people with particular needs and wants and one or more products that can satisfy these needs. Also, the buyers must be both willing and able to purchase a product that satisfies their needs and wants.

Market Analysis.   A product-market consists of a specific product (or line of related products) that can satisfy a set of needs and wants for the people (or organizations) willing and able to purchase it. We use the term *product* to refer to either a physical good

EXHIBIT 1–3   The Strategic Marketing Process

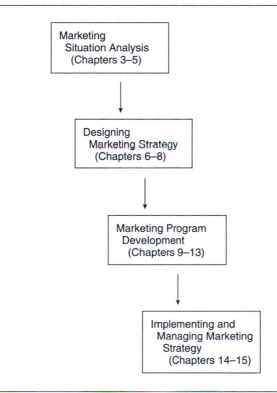

or an intangible service. This definition matches people or organizations with a particular set of similar needs and wants to a product category that can satisfy those needs and wants.

Analyzing product-markets and forecasting how they will change in the future are vital to business and marketing planning. Decisions to enter new product-markets, how to serve existing product-markets, and when to exit from unattractive product-markets are critical strategic marketing choices. Our objective is to identify and describe the buyers, understand their preferences for products, estimate the size and rate of growth of the market, and find out what companies and products are competing in the market.

Analyzing Competition.   Evaluation of competitors' strategies, strengths, limitations, and plans is also a key aspect of the situation analysis. It is important to identify both existing and potential competitors. Typically, a few of the firms in the industry comprise the organization's key competitors. Competitor analysis includes evaluating each key competitor. The analyses highlight the competition's important strengths and weaknesses. A key issue is trying to figure out what the competition is likely to do in the future.

SMH's experience in the U.S. inexpensive-watch market illustrates the importance of sensing what is happening in the marketplace. By 1995 it was apparent that SMH had

EXHIBIT 1–4 Caribbean Cruise Market Size and Competition

The Growing Market . . .

Number of U.S. and Canadian cruise passengers, in millions

*Estimate

And the Major Players

1991 market share of the passenger cruise business, by capacity

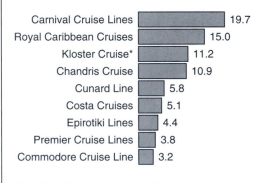

Carnival Cruise Lines	19.7
Royal Caribbean Cruises	15.0
Kloster Cruise*	11.2
Chandris Cruise	10.9
Cunard Line	5.8
Costa Cruises	5.1
Epirotiki Lines	4.4
Premier Cruise Lines	3.8
Commodore Cruise Line	3.2

*Includes Norwegian Cruise Line

Note: 22 other cruise lines make up the remaining 17.7% of the market.

Source: Cruise Liners International Association

Source: Laurie M. Grossman, "Cruise Lines Enjoy Smooth Sailing Despite Recession," *The Wall Street Journal*, February 10, 1992, p. B4. Reprinted by permission of *The Wall Street Journal*, © 1992 Dow Jones & Company, Inc. All Rights Reserved Worldwide.

underestimated buyers' preferences for metal watches with leather bands.[21] Competitors offered buyers new options, stressing both fashion and precision quality to attack Swatch's dominant market position. Timex's successful Guess line racked up $75 million in sales in 1994. Fossil, the market leader, had $100 million, while Swatch's sales declined to less than $30 million. SMH implemented an aggressive counter strategy with new designs and advertising (see the accompanying advertisement).

An example of market size and competitor identification for the Caribbean cruise market is shown in Exhibit 1–4. The cruise ship companies are targeting various customer groups (segments) with their marketing efforts. Revenues for 1991 increased nearly 10 percent to $6 billion. The top 4 companies, out of a total of 32, account for nearly 60 percent of the market. The domination of a market by a few competitors is characteristic of many mature markets.

Segmenting Markets

Market segmentation looks at the nature and extent of diversity of buyers' needs and wants in a market. It offers an opportunity for an organization to focus its business capabilities on the requirements of one or more groups of buyers. The objective of

Courtesy of Swatch/SMH (USA), Inc.

segmentation is to examine differences in needs and wants to identify the segments within the product-market of interest. Each segment contains buyers with similar needs and wants for the product category of interest to management. The subgroups are described using the various characteristics of people, the reasons that they buy or use certain products, and their preferences for certain brands of products. Likewise, segments of industrial product-markets may be formed according to the type of industry, the uses for the product, frequency of product purchase, and various other factors.

Each segment may vary quite a bit from the average characteristics of the entire product-market. The similarities of buyers' needs within a segment enable better targeting of the marketing program. Factors such as age, income, lifestyle, and reason for purchase may be useful in segmenting the Caribbean cruise market. For example, cruises are popular for newlyweds and retired couples, and are used by business firms as incentives for salespeople.

Continuous Learning about Markets

One of the major realities of achieving business success today is the necessity of understanding markets and competition. Sensing what is happening and is likely to occur in the future is complicated by competitive threats beyond traditional industry boundaries. For example, microwave dinners compete with McDonald's, CD-ROMs compete with books, and fax transmission competes with overnight letter delivery.

Our objective is to learn how market-driven firms are able to sense what is happening in their markets, to develop business and marketing strategies to seize opportunities and counter threats, and to anticipate what the market will be like in the future.[22] As illustrated by Intuit, everyone in the organization must be wired into customers and competition. There are several market-sensing methods available to guide the collection and analysis of information.

DESIGNING MARKETING STRATEGY

The situation analysis identifies market opportunities, defines market segments, evaluates competition, and assesses the organization's strengths and weaknesses. This information plays a key role in designing marketing strategy, which includes market targeting and positioning analysis, building marketing relationships, and developing and introducing new products. The Strategy Feature describes the market targeting and positioning strategies employed for the successful soap brand, Lever 2000.

Market Targeting and Positioning Strategy

Marketing advantage is influenced by several situational factors including industry characteristics, type of firm (e.g., size), extent of differentiation in buyers' needs, and the specific competitive advantage(s) of the company designing the marketing strategy. The essential issue is deciding how, when, and where to compete, given a firm's environment.

Market Target Strategy.   The purpose of market targeting is to select the people (or organizations) that management wishes to serve in the product-market. When buyers' needs and wants vary, the market target is usually one or more segments of the product-market. Once the segments are identified and their relative importance to the firm determined, management selects the targeting strategy. This decision is the focal point of marketing strategy since targeting guides the setting of objectives and developing a positioning strategy. The options range from targeting most of the segments to targeting one or a few segments in a product-market. The targeting strategy may be influenced by the market's maturity, the diversity of buyers' needs and preferences, the firm's size

STRATEGY FEATURE   Lever's All-in-One Brand—Lever 2000

Lever Brothers, a New York unit of the Anglo-Dutch Unilever Group, has been competing with Procter & Gamble in the soap market for 100 years. In 1991, for the first time, Lever's toilet-soap market share ($) exceeded P&G's share (see insert). The Lever 2000 brand was a major contributor to Lever's share gain. It accounted for $113 million in sales out of a market total of $1.6 billion. The targeting and positioning of Lever 2000 were major factors in the brand's successful performance.

Targeting Strategy

- Entire family rather than different soaps for men, women, and children.

Positioning Strategy

- Positioned as "the mildest antibacterial soap ever created," "a soap for 2000 body parts." Heavy use of advertising ($25 million), sampling, and coupons to convince households that one soap will meet all of their needs. Premium priced compared to Ivory and Dove.

Source: Valerie Reitman, "Buoyant Sales of Lever 2000 Soap Bring Sinking Sensation to Procter & Gamble," *The Wall Street Journal*, March 19, 1992, pp. B1 and B8. Reprinted by permission of *The Wall Street Journal*, © 1992 Dow Jones & Company, Inc. All Rights Reserved Worldwide.

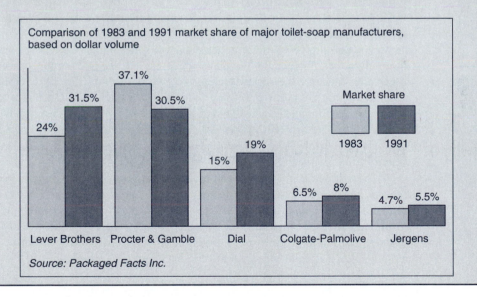

Comparison of 1983 and 1991 market share of major toilet-soap manufacturers, based on dollar volume

Market share: 1983, 1991

	Lever Brothers	Procter & Gamble	Dial	Colgate-Palmolive	Jergens
1983	24%	37.1%	15%	6.5%	4.7%
1991	31.5%	30.5%	19%	8%	5.5%

Source: Packaged Facts Inc.

compared to competition, corporate resources and priorities, and the volume of sales required to achieve favorable financial results.

Deciding the objectives for each market target spells out the results expected by management. Examples of market target objectives are sales, market share, customer retention, profit contribution, and customer satisfaction. Marketing objectives may also be set for the entire company and for specific marketing activities such as advertising.

The targeting and positioning strategies used by ConAgra Inc. for the Healthy Choice frozen food line helped the new brand successfully enter the market in the early 1990s. The low-calorie, low-cholesterol, low-sodium frozen food line quickly gained a strong market position.[23] Frozen food is a very competitive supermarket category because freezer space in stores is limited. Healthy Choice was introduced into the stagnant male-oriented frozen dinner segment of the market. It was positioned as a "health product." This positioning was successful even though it conflicts with conventional marketing guidelines: the female-oriented frozen food is the rapid growth segment and health positioning had been used to describe poor-tasting, low-calorie brands. Health is an issue of great concern to men and the taste of Healthy Choice is appealing to consumers who tried the brand. The new line of frozen foods gained an impressive 25 percent market share in the $700 million frozen dinner market. The line was extended in the early 1990s to include breakfast items, deli meats, and soups. By 1992 intense price competition, new products, and promotion actions of the competition eroded Healthy Choice's position in the frozen dinner market, demonstrating the realities of competing against experienced food marketers.

Positioning Strategy.   The marketing program positioning strategy is the combination of product, channel of distribution, price, and promotion strategies a firm uses to position itself against its key competitors in meeting the needs and wants of the market target. This strategy is also called the "marketing mix" or the "marketing program." The positioning strategy seeks to position the product in the eyes and mind of the buyer and distinguish the product from the competition. The concerns of General Motors Corp. (GMC) about positioning illustrate the strategic importance of positioning. In 1995, GMC launched a major marketing effort to reposition its automobile brands. The objective is to identify the market segment targeted by each brand and to develop a positioning strategy appropriate for the target. The problem is that GM's car brands are perceived by many buyers to be very similar. The objective of GM's new strategy is to give each brand a distinct identity geared to the preferences of the brand's market target.

Positioning indicates how the firm would like its product or brand to be perceived in the eyes and minds of the market target customers. For example, GM wants the buyers in Pontiac's target market to think of it as a sporty brand reflecting youth and spirit. The positioning strategy is intended to help position a product or brand with the buyer. The product, distribution, price, and promotion strategy components make up a bundle of actions that are used to influence buyers' positioning of a brand.

Marketing Relationship Strategies

Marketing relationship strategies seek to achieve high levels of customer satisfaction through collaboration of the parties involved. Marketing relationship partners may include end-user customers, marketing channel members, suppliers, competitor alliances, and internal teams. The driving force underlying these relationships is that a company may enhance its ability to satisfy customers and cope with a rapidly changing business environment through partnering. Relationship marketing gained new importance in the

1990s as customers became more demanding and competition became more intense. Building long-term relationships with customers offers companies a way to build competitive advantage. Similarly, forging relationships with suppliers, channel of distribution members, and sometimes competitors help to provide superior customer value. Although building collaborative relationships may not always be the best course of action, this avenue for gaining a competitive edge is increasing in popularity.

Calyx and Corolla (C&C) markets fresh flowers by phone and mail order. Marketing relationships are the lifeblood of this innovative business. C&C has formed a network of relationships with flower growers, Federal Express, and the buyers of its wide variety of flower arrangements and floral designs. C&C creates the arrangements, portrays them in its catalog, and provides over 25 growers with attractive packaging materials. The growers receive orders and pick up and delivery information via the Federal Express information system. Federal Express delivers the fresh-cut flowers much faster than using the grower-to-wholesaler-to-retail shop distribution channel. Fast delivery of fresh flower arrangements and innovative designs enables C&C to provide superior customer value.

New-Product Strategies

New products are needed to replace old products because of declining sales and profits. Strategies for developing and positioning new market entries involve all functions of the business. Closely coordinated new-product planning is essential to satisfy customer requirements and produce products with high quality at competitive prices. New-product decisions include finding and evaluating ideas, selecting the most promising for development, designing marketing programs, market testing the products, and introducing them to the market.

Listening to the customer is critical to identifying the important product features that influence customer satisfaction. The new-product planning process starts by identifying gaps in customer satisfaction. The differences between existing product attributes and those desired by customers offer opportunities for new and improved products. One of the leaders in product innovation is Minnesota Mining and Manufacturing (3M). It has a reputation of developing products faster and better than most companies.[24] The new-product success guidelines 3M follows include: (1) keeping business units small, (2) encouraging experimentation and risk taking, (3) motivating and rewarding innovators, (4) staying close to the customer, (5) sharing technology with other firms, and (6) avoiding killing the projects of staff advocates.

MARKETING PROGRAM DEVELOPMENT

Market targeting and positioning strategies for new and existing products guide the choice of strategies for the marketing mix components. Product, distribution, price, and promotion strategies are combined to form the positioning strategy selected for each market target. The relationship of the positioning components to the market target is shown in Exhibit 1–5.

EXHIBIT 1–5   Positioning Strategy Development

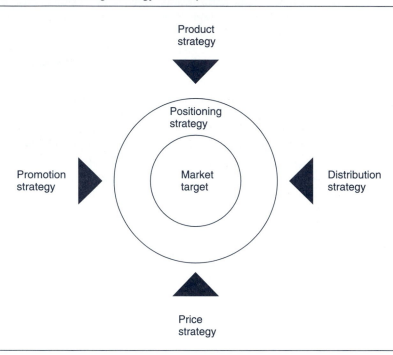

The marketing mix decisions help implement the positioning strategy.[25] The objective is to achieve favorable positioning while allocating financial, human, and production resources to markets, customers, and products as effectively and efficiently as possible.

Product/Service Strategy

Management needs the following information on current and anticipated performance of the products (services) to guide the product strategy decisions.

1. Consumer evaluation of the company's products, particularly their strengths and weaknesses vis-á-vis competition (i.e., product positioning by market segment information).

2. "Objective" information on actual and anticipated product performance on relevant criteria such as sales, profits, and market share.[26]

Typically, products are the focal point of positioning strategy, particularly when companies or business units adopt organizational approaches emphasizing product or brand management. Product strategy includes: (1) developing plans for new products, (2)

GLOBAL FEATURE   How Nestlé Builds Its Brands Throughout the World

- Global brand strategy.
  Largest branded food company in Mexico, Brazil, Chile, and Thailand—building rapidly in Vietnam and China.
  Builds both manufacturing and a political presence.
  Negotiated over a decade to get into China.
- Owns nearly 8,000 brands worldwide—but only 750 are registered in more than one country—only 80 in 10 countries.
  The ingredients or processing technology are adapted for local conditions—often using the local brand name.

  Moves into a new market with a handful of labels—from its 11 strategic brand groups.
  Nestlé is the market leader in instant coffee in Australia (71%), France (67%), Japan (74%), and Mexico (85%).

- Nestlé's Thailand manager has worked there for 30 years.
  The 100 managers worldwide stay in only one region of the world (a key competitive advantage because they know local markets, competition, and governmental requirements). Coffee sales in Thailand were $25 million (1987) to $100 million (1994).
- Developed an entire milk distribution system in China from the farmer to the factory—produced 10,000 tons of powdered milk in 1994 ($700 million in sales by 2000).
- Nestlé is importing sales team and brand management techniques to supermarket chains in Thailand and other countries in the region.

Source: Carla Rapoport, "Nestlé's Brand Building Machine," *Fortune,* September 19, 1994, pp. 147–48, 150, 154, and 156.

managing programs for successful products, and (3) deciding what to do about problem products (e.g., reduce costs or improve the product).

Nestlé, the Swiss branded food company, has a very successful product strategy for competing in world markets. As described in the Global Feature, the company's brand strategy includes favoring local preferences, providing career tracks to keep managers in the same regional areas, and applying global food processing technology to gain cost and quality advantages.

Distribution, Price, and Promotion Strategies

One of the major issues in managing the marketing mix is deciding how to blend together the components of the mix. Product, distribution, price, and promotion strategies are shaped into a coordinated plan of action. Each component helps to influence buyers in their positioning of products. If the activities of these mix components are not coordinated, the actions may conflict and resources may be wasted. For example, if the advertising messages for a company's brand stress quality and performance, but salespeople emphasize low price, buyers will be confused and brand image may be affected.

Distribution Strategy.   Market target buyers may be contacted on a direct basis using the firm's sales force or, instead, through a distribution channel of marketing intermediaries (e.g., wholesalers, retailers, or dealers). Distribution channels are often used in linking producers with end-user household and business markets. Decisions that are made include the type of channel organizations to use, the extent of channel management performed by the firm, and the intensity of distribution appropriate for the product or service. The choice of distribution channels influences buyers' positioning of the brand. For example, expensive watches like SMH's Omega brand are available from a limited number of retailers with prestigious images. Such retailers help to reinforce the brand's image.

Price Strategy.   Price also plays an important role in positioning a product or service. Customer reaction to alternative prices, the cost of the product, the prices of the competition, and various legal and ethical factors establish the extent of flexibility management has in setting prices. Price strategy involves choosing the role of price in the positioning strategy, including the desired positioning of the product or brand as well as the margins necessary to satisfy and motivate distribution channel participants. Price may be used as an active (visible) component of marketing strategy, or, instead, marketing emphasis may be on other marketing mix components (e.g., product quality).

Promotion Strategy.   Advertising, sales promotion, the sales force, direct marketing, and public relations help the organization to communicate with its customers, cooperating or-ganizations, the public, and other target audiences. These activities make up the promotion strategy, which performs an essential role in positioning products in the eyes and minds of buyers. Promotion informs, reminds, and persuades buyers and others who influence the purchasing process. Hundreds of billions of dollars are spent annually on promotion ac-tivities. This mandates planning and executing promotion decisions as effectively and ef-ficiently as possible.

IMPLEMENTING AND MANAGING MARKETING STRATEGY

Selecting the customers to target and the positioning strategy for each target moves mar-keting strategy development to the implementation stage (Exhibit 1–3). This stage considers the design of the marketing organization and implementation and control of the strategy.

The Marketing Organization

A good organization design matches people and work responsibilities in a way that is best for accomplishing the firm's marketing strategy. Deciding how to assemble people into organizational units and assigning responsibility to the various mix components that make up marketing strategy are important influences on marketing performance. Organizational structures and processes must be matched to the business and marketing strategies that are developed and implemented. The marketing organization has to be flexible to respond to changing conditions and strategy needs. Organizational design needs to be evaluated on a regular basis to assess its adequacy and to identify necessary changes. Restructuring and reengineering of many organizations in the 1990s led to many changes in the marketing units.

Implementing and Controlling Marketing Strategy

Marketing strategy implementation and control consists of: (1) preparing the marketing plan and budget, (2) implementing the plan, and (3) managing and controlling the strategy on an ongoing basis.

Marketing Plan.   The typical marketing plan includes details concerning targeting, positioning, and marketing mix activities. The plan spells out what is going to happen over the planning period, who is responsible, how much it will cost, and expected results (e.g., sales forecasts). We discuss the preparation of the marketing plan in the next section.

Implementation Strategy.   The marketing plan includes action guidelines for the activities to be implemented, who does what, the dates and location of implementation, and how implementation will be accomplished. Several factors contribute to implementation effectiveness, including the skills of the people involved, organizational design, incentives, and the effectiveness of communication within the organization and externally.

Evaluation and Control of Marketing Performance.   Marketing strategy is an ongoing process of making decisions, implementing them, and gauging their effectiveness over time. In terms of its time requirements, strategic evaluation is far more demanding than planning. Evaluation and control are concerned with tracking performance and, when necessary, altering plans to keep performance on track. Evaluation also includes looking for new opportunities and potential threats in the future. It is the connecting link in the strategic marketing planning process shown in Exhibit 1–3. By serving as both the last stage and the first stage (evaluation before taking action) in the planning process, strategic evaluation assures that strategy is an ongoing activity.

Rubbermaid Inc. offers an interesting insight into evaluation and control. After more than a decade of superior performance, the company experienced problems in 1995.[27] Sales slowed down and profits declined. Increases in the costs of resin used in plastic products triggered price increases to retailers. This irritated retailers, who reduced Rubbermaid's shelf space. The already slow consumer demand for housewares was further impacted by higher retail prices. Rubbermaid's management implemented cost reductions, speeded up new-product introductions, and increased promotions to consumers to move results closer to expectations.

PREPARING THE MARKETING PLAN

Marketing plans vary widely in scope and detail. Nevertheless, all plans need to be based on analyses of the product-market and segments, industry and competitive structure, and the organization's competitive advantage. We will look at several important planning issues that provide a checklist for plan preparation.

Planning Relationships and Frequency

Marketing plans are developed, implemented, evaluated, and adjusted to keep the strategy on target. Since the marketing strategy extends beyond one year, typically, it is useful to develop an annual plan to manage short-term marketing activities. Planning is really a series of annual plans guided by the marketing strategy.

The frequency of planning activities varies by company and marketing activity. Normally, market targeting and positioning strategies are not changed significantly during the year. Tactical changes in product, distribution, price, and promotion strategies may be included in the annual plan. For example, the aggressive response of competitors to Healthy Choice's successful market entry required changes in Con Agra's pricing and promotion tactics.

Planning Considerations

Suppose that you need to develop a plan for a new product to be introduced into the national market next year. The plan for the introduction should include the expected results (objectives), market targets, actions, responsibilities, schedules, and dates. The plan indicates details and deadlines, product plans, a market introduction program, advertising and sales promotion actions, employee training, and other information necessary to launching the product. The plan needs to answer a series of questions—what, when, where, who, how, and why—for each action targeted for completion during the planning period.

Responsibility for Preparing Plans.   Normally, a marketing executive is responsible for preparing the marketing plan. Some companies combine the business plan and the marketing plan into a single document. Regardless of the format used, the marketing plan is developed in close coordination with the strategic plan for the business. There is also much greater emphasis today to involve all business functions in the marketing planning process. Planning teams may be used as illustrated in the Rubbermaid example (Exhibit 1–2). A product or marketing manager may draft the formal plan for his/her area of responsibility, coordinating and receiving inputs from advertising, marketing research, sales, and other marketing specialists. Coordination with other business functions (R&D, finance, operations) is also essential.

Planning Unit.   The choice of the planning unit may vary due to the product-market portfolio of the organization. Some firms plan and manage by individual products or brands. Others work with product lines, markets, or specific customers. The planning unit may reflect how marketing activities and responsibilities are organized. The market target is a useful basis for planning regardless of how the plan is aggregated. Focusing on the target helps to keep the customer in the center of the planning process and keeps the positioning strategy focused on the market target.

Preparing the Marketing Plan

The Conference Board offers several examples of plan formats in its excellent report on marketing planning.[28] Format and content depend on the size of the organization, managerial responsibility for planning, product and market scope, and other situational

---

EXHIBIT 1–6   Outline for Preparing an Annual Marketing Plan

Strategic Situation Summary

A summary of the strategic situation for the planning unit (business unit, market segment, product line, etc.).

Market Target(s) Description

Define and describe each market target, including customer profiles, customer preferences and buying habits, size and growth estimates, distribution channels, analysis of key competitors, and guidelines for positioning strategy.

Objectives for the Market Target(s)

Set objectives for the market target (such as market position, sales, and profits). Also state objectives for each component of the marketing program. Indicate how each objective will be measured.

Marketing Program Positioning Strategy

State how management wants the firm to be positioned relative to competition in the eyes and mind of the buyer.
A. *Product Strategy*
   Set strategy for new products, product improvements, and product deletions.
B. *Distribution Strategy*
   Indicate the strategy to be used for each distribution channel, including role of middlemen, assistance and support provided, and specific activities planned.
C. *Price Strategy*
   Specify the role of price in the marketing strategy and the planned actions regarding price.
D. *Promotion Strategy*
   Indicate the planned strategy and actions for advertising, publicity, personal selling, and sales promotion.
E. *Marketing Research*
   Identify information needs and planned projects, objectives, estimated costs, and timetable.
F. *Coordination with Other Business Functions*
   Specify the responsibilities and activities of other departments that have an important influence upon the planned marketing strategy.

Forecasts and Budgets

Forecast sales and profit for the marketing plan and set the budget for accomplishing the forecast.

Contingency Plans

Indicate planned actions if events differ from those assumed in the plan.

---

factors. An outline for a typical marketing plan is shown in Exhibit 1–6. A discussion of the major parts of the planning outline illustrates the nature and scope of the planning process. In our discussion the market target serves as the planning unit.

The Situation Summary.   This part of the plan describes the market and its important characteristics, size estimates, and growth projections. Market segmentation analysis indicates the segments to be targeted and their relative importance. The competitor analysis indicates the key competitors (actual and potential), their strengths and weaknesses, probable future actions, and the organization's competitive advantage(s) in each segment of interest. The summary should be brief. Supporting information for the summary is sometimes placed in an appendix or in a separate analysis.

Describing the Market Target.   A description of each market target, size and growth rate, end-users' characteristics, positioning strategy guidelines, and other available information useful in planning and implementation are essential parts of the plan. When two or more targets are involved, management should indicate priorities to aid in resource allocation.

Objectives for the Market Target(s).   Here we spell out what the marketing strategy is expected to accomplish during the planning period. Objectives are needed for each market target, and they may be financial, market position, and customer satisfaction targets. Objectives are also usually included for each marketing mix component. Such objectives often indicate intermediate results that move the strategy toward the market target objectives. An example of an advertising objective is increasing market target awareness of a brand by some specified amount.

Marketing Program Positioning Strategy.   The positioning statement indicates how management wants the targeted customers and prospects to perceive the brand. Specific strategies for product, distribution, price, and promotion are explained in this part of the plan. Actions to be taken, responsibilities, time schedules, and other implementation information are included at this point in the plan.

Planning and implementation responsibilities often involve more than one person or department. A planning team may be assigned the responsibility for each market target and each marketing mix component. Product and geographical responsibilities are sometimes allocated to people. The responsibilities and coordination requirements need to be indicated for marketing units and other business functions. Importantly, the planning process should encourage participation from all of the areas responsible for implementing the plan.

Contingency plans may be included in the plan. The contingencies consider possible actions if the anticipated planning environment is different from what actually occurs. The contingency plan considers how the marketing strategy will be changed if the future is different than anticipated. Companies often use planning meetings during the planning period to discuss contingencies that affect the original plans.

Forecasting and Budgeting.   Financial planning includes forecasting revenues and profits and estimating the costs necessary to carry out the marketing plan (see the Appendix to Chapter 1 for details). The people responsible for market target, product, geographical area, or other units may prepare the forecast. Comparative data on sales, profits, and expenses for prior years is a useful link of the plan to previous results.

International Planning Process.   The major phases of planning for a multinational firm operating in several countries is shown in Exhibit 1–7. The first step in the planning process is the market opportunity analysis. This may represent a major activity for a company that is entering a foreign market for the first time. Because of the risks and uncertainties in international markets, the market assessment is very important for both new market entrants and experienced firms.

Phase 1 determines which targets to pursue and establishes relative priorities for resource allocation. Phase 2 fits the positioning strategy to each target market. The

EXHIBIT 1–7   International Planning Process

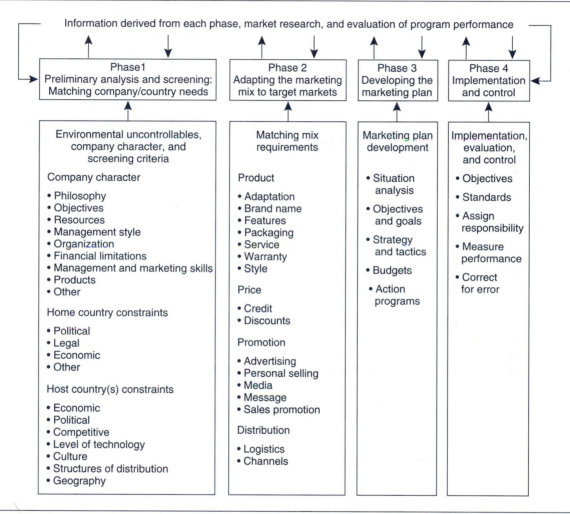

Information derived from each phase, market research, and evaluation of program performance

| Phase 1 Preliminary analysis and screening: Matching company/country needs | Phase 2 Adapting the marketing mix to target markets | Phase 3 Developing the marketing plan | Phase 4 Implementation and control |

Environmental uncontrollables, company character, and screening criteria

Company character

• Philosophy
• Objectives
• Resources
• Management style
• Organization
• Financial limitations
• Management and marketing skills
• Products
• Other

Home country constraints

• Political
• Legal
• Economic
• Other

Host country(s) constraints

• Economic
• Political
• Competitive
• Level of technology
• Culture
• Structures of distribution
• Geography

Matching mix requirements

Product

• Adaptation
• Brand name
• Features
• Packaging
• Service
• Warranty
• Style

Price

• Credit
• Discounts

Promotion

• Advertising
• Personal selling
• Media
• Message
• Sales promotion

Distribution

• Logistics
• Channels

Marketing plan development

• Situation analysis
• Objectives and goals
• Strategy and tactics
• Budgets
• Action programs

Implementation, evaluation, and control

• Objectives
• Standards
• Assign responsibility
• Measure performance
• Correct for error

Source: Philip R. Cateora, *International Marketing,* 9th ed. (Burr Ridge, IL: Richard D. Irwin, 1996), p. 335.

objective is to match the mix requirements to the needs identified and the positioning concept management selects. Phase 3 consists of the preparation of the marketing plan. Included are the situation assessment, objectives, strategy and tactics, budgets and forecasts, and action programs. Finally in Phase 4, the plan is implemented and managed. Results are evaluated and strategies adjusted when necessary to improve results. Although the planning process is similar to planning domestic marketing strategies, the environment is far more complex and uncertain in international markets.

SUMMARY

Management's vision about how the business should compete is guided by deciding where the business has the best competitive advantage. The strategy selected for the business sets important guidelines for marketing strategy. Business strategy decisions call for knowledge of market needs and trends, competition, and the strengths (and weaknesses) of the organization.

Market orientation makes the customer the focus of the entire organization. Market orientation requires a customer focus, competitor intelligence, and coordination among the business functions. Becoming market-oriented involves making major changes in the culture, processes, and structure of the traditional pyramid organization organized into functional units.

Marketing strategy is an analysis, planning, implementation, and control process designed to satisfy customer needs and wants by providing superior customer value. The first part of the process includes product-market analysis, market segmentation, competition analysis, and continuous learning about markets. These analyses guide the choice of marketing strategy. Market definition establishes the overall competitive arena. Market segmentation describes possible customer groups for targeting by businesses. Competitor analysis looks at the strengths, weaknesses, and strategies of key competitors. Continuous learning about markets supplies information for analysis and decision making.

Designing the marketing strategy is the second stage in strategy development. The selection of the people (or organizations) to be targeted is guided by the situation analysis. The market target decision indicates the buyer groups whose needs are to be satisfied by the marketing program positioning strategy. The positioning strategy indicates how the firm will position itself against its key competitors in meeting the needs of the buyers in the market target. The relationship strategy spells out the relationships to be developed with consumers, other organizations, and company personnel. New product strategies are essential to generate a continuing stream of new entries to replace mature products that are eliminated.

The third phase of the strategy process is designing the marketing program. Specific marketing mix strategies for products, distribution, price, and promotion must be developed to implement the positioning strategy management has selected. The objective is to combine the marketing mix components to accomplish market target objectives in a cost-effective manner.

Finally, in the last phase of the process, strategy implementation and management of marketing strategy are examined. These activities focus on the marketing organizational design and marketing strategy implementation and control. This is the action phase of marketing strategy.

The marketing plan spells out the actions to be taken, who is responsible, deadlines to be met, and the sales forecast and budget. The plan describes the marketing decisions and it guides the implementation of the decisions, and the evaluation and management of the marketing strategy.

QUESTIONS FOR REVIEW AND DISCUSSION

1. Discuss some of the reasons why managing in an environment of constant change will be necessary in the future.

2. Explain how a company may achieve a competitive advantage.

3. Discuss the relationship between superior customer-value and marketing strategy.

4. Why is product/service innovation important in achieving customer satisfaction?

5. Explain the use of market orientation as a guiding philosophy for a social service organization, giving particular attention to user needs and wants.

6. Identify and discuss the problems a company may encounter if management does not develop and implement strategic plans for gaining a competitive advantage.

7. Suppose you have been appointed to the top marketing post of a corporation and the president has asked you to explain what marketing strategy is all about to the board of directors. What will you include in your presentation?

8. Discuss the importance of developing a strategic vision about the future for competing in today's business environment.

9. Why is a global perspective important for the top management of any company regardless of where it competes?

10. Discuss the issues that are important in transforming a company into a market-oriented organization.

NOTES

1. Regis McKenna, "Marketing Is Everything," *Harvard Business Review,* January–February 1991, p. 72.
2. John Case, "Customer Service: The Last Word," *Inc.,* April 1991, pp. 89–93. See also Don Clark, "Intuit's Cook Details Ambitious Plans to Change Way People Manage Money," *The Wall Street Journal,* March 7, 1995, p. B9.
3. The illustration is based on Margaret Studer, "SMH Leads a Revival of Swiss Watchmaking Industry," *The Wall Street Journal,* January 20, 1992, p. B4.
4. Michael E. Porter, *Competitive Advantage* (New York: Free Press, 1985), p. 3.
5. This discussion is based on Porter, *Competitive Advantage,* and George S. Day and Robin Wensley, "Assessing Advantage: A Framework for Diagnosing Competitive Superiority," *Journal of Marketing,* April 1988, pp. 1–20.
6. Studer, "SMH Leads a Revival," p. B4.
7. Frederick W. Gluck, "A Fresh Look at Strategic Planning," *Journal of Business Strategy,* Fall 1985, pp. 16–17.
8. Brian Dumaine, "What the Leaders of Tomorrow See," *Fortune,* July 3, 1989, p. 50.
9. Studer, "SMH Leads a Revival," p. B4.
10. Stanley F. Slater and John C. Narver, "Market Orientation, Customer Value, and Superior Performance," *Business Horizons,* March/April 1994, p. 22.
11. George S. Day, *Market-Driven Strategy: Processes for Creating Value* (New York: Free Press, 1990).
12. Philip Kotler, *Marketing Management,* 8th ed. (Englewood Cliffs, NJ: Prentice Hall, 1994), chap. 2.
13. Slater and Narver, "Market Orientation," p. 23.
14. George Day, "Continuous Learning about Markets," *California Management Review,* Summer 1994), pp. 9–31.
15. Benson P. Shapiro, "What the Hell Is Market Oriented," *Harvard Business Review,* November–December 1988, p. 120.
16. Ibid., p. 122.
17. Peter F. Drucker, *Management: Tasks, Responsibilities, Practices* (New York: Harper & Row, 1974), p. 63.
18. Frederick E. Webster, Jr., "The Changing Role of Marketing in the Organization," *Journal of Marketing,* October 1992, p. 11.
19. David W. Cravens, "Developing Marketing Strategies for Competitive Advantage," in *Handbook of Business Strategy 1988/89,* ed. H. E. Glass (New York: Warren, Gorham, and Lamont, 1989), pp. 16–1 through 16–19.
20. George S. Day, *Strategic Market Planning* (St. Paul, MN: West Publishing, 1984), p. 3.
21. Joshua Levine, "Swatch Out," *Forbes,* June 5, 1995, pp. 150, 152.
22. Day, "Continuous Learning about Markets," pp. 9–31.
23. This example is based on D. John Loden, *Megabrands* (Burr Ridge, IL: Irwin Professional Publishing, 1992), pp. 184–85.

24. *Business Week,* "Masters of Innovation," April 10, 1989, pp. 58–63.
25. Webster, "The Changing Role of Marketing," p. 13.
26. Yoram Wind and Henry J. Claycamp, "Planning Product Line Strategy: A Matrix Approach," *Journal of Marketing,* January 1976, p. 2.
27. Paulette Thomas, "Rubbermaid Stock Plunges Over 12% on Projected Weak 2nd-Quarter Profit," *The Wall Street Journal,* June 12, 1995, p. B6.
28. David S. Hopkins, *The Marketing Plan* (New York: The Conference Board, Inc., 1981). See also Howard Sutton, *The Marketing Plan in the 1990s* (New York: The Conference Board, Inc., 1990).

APPENDIX 1A

Financial Analysis for Marketing Planning and Control

Several kinds of financial analyses are needed for marketing analysis, planning, and control activities. Such analyses represent an important part of case preparation activities. In some instances it will be necessary to review and interpret financial information provided in the cases. In other instances, analyses may be prepared to support specific recommendations. The methods covered in this appendix represent a group of tools and techniques for use in marketing financial analysis. Throughout the discussion, it is assumed that accounting and finance fundamentals are understood.

UNIT OF FINANCIAL ANALYSIS

Various units of analysis that can be used in marketing financial analysis are shown in Exhibit 1A–1. Two factors often influence the choice of a unit of analysis: (1) the purpose of the analysis and (2) the costs and availability of the information needed to perform the analysis.

EXHIBIT 1A–1   Alternative Units for Financial Analysis

Market	Product/Service	Organization
Market	Industry	Company
Total market	Product mix	Segment/division/unit
Market niche(s)	Product line	Marketing department
Geographic area(s)	Specific product	Sales unit:
Customer groups	Brand	Region
Individual customers	Model	District branch
		Office/store
		Salesperson

FINANCIAL SITUATION ANALYSIS

Financial measures can be used to help assess the present situation. One of the most common and best ways to quantify the financial situation of a firm is through ratio analysis. These ratios should be analyzed over a period of at least three years to discern trends.

Key Financial Ratios

Financial information will be more useful to management if it is prepared so that comparisons can be made. James Van Horne comments upon this need:

> To evaluate a firm's financial condition and performance, the financial analyst needs certain yardsticks. The yardstick frequently used is a ratio or index, relating two pieces of financial data to each other. Analysis and interpretation of various ratios should give an experienced and skilled analyst a better understanding of the financial condition and performance of the firm than he would obtain from analysis of the financial data alone.[1]

As we examine the financial analysis model in the next section, note how the ratio or index provides a useful frame of reference. Typically, ratios are used to compare historical and/or future trends within the firm, or to compare a firm or business unit with an industry or other firms.

Several financial ratios often used to measure business performance are shown in Exhibit 1A–2. Note that these ratios are primarily useful as a means of comparing:

1. Ratio values for several time periods for a particular business.

2. A firm to its key competitors.

3. A firm to an industry or business standard.

There are several sources of ratio data.[2] These include data services such as Dun & Bradstreet, Robert Morris Associates' *Annual Statement Studies,* industry and trade associations, government agencies, and investment advisory services.

Other ways to gauge productivity of marketing activities include sales per square feet of retail floor space, occupancy rates of hotels and office buildings, and sales per salesperson.

Contribution Analysis

When the performance of products, market segments, and other marketing units is being analyzed, management should examine the unit's profit contribution. Contribution margin is equal to sales (revenue) less variable costs. Thus, contribution margin represents the amount of money available to cover fixed costs, and contribution margin less fixed costs is net income. An illustration of contribution margin analysis is given in Exhibit 1A–3. In this example, product X is generating positive contribution margin. If product X were eliminated, $50,000 of product net income would be lost, and the remaining products would have to cover fixed costs not directly traceable to them. If the product is retained, the $50,000 can be used to contribute to other fixed costs and/or net income.

FINANCIAL ANALYSIS MODEL

The model shown in Exhibit 1A–4 provides a useful guide for examining financial performance and identifying possible problem areas. The model combines several important financial ratios into one equation. Let's examine the model, moving from left to right. Profit margin multiplied by asset turnover yields return on assets. Moreover, assuming that the performance target is return on net

---

[1] James C. Van Horne, *Fundamental of Financial Management,* 4th ed. (Englewood Cliffs, NJ: Prentice Hall, 1980), pp. 103–4.

[2] A useful guide to ratio analysis is provided in Richard Sanzo, *Ratio Analysis for Small Business* (Washington, DC: Small Business Administration, 1977).

EXHIBIT 1A–2 Summary of Key Financial Ratios

Ratio	How Calculated	What It Shows
Profitability ratios:		
1. Gross profit margin	$$\frac{\text{Sales} - \text{Cost of good sold}}{\text{Sales}}$$	An indication of the total margin available to cover operating expenses and yield a profit.
2. Operating profit margin	$$\frac{\text{Profits before taxes and before interest}}{\text{Sales}}$$	An indication of the firm's profitability from current operations without regard to the interest charges accruing from the capital structure.
3. Net profit margin (or return on sales)	$$\frac{\text{Profits after taxes}}{\text{Sales}}$$	Shows after-tax profits per dollar of sales. Subpar profit margins indicate that the firm's sales prices are relatively low or that its costs are relatively high or both.
4. Return on total assets	$$\frac{\text{Profits after taxes}}{\text{Total assets}}$$ or $$\frac{\text{Profits after taxes} + \text{Interest}}{\text{Total assets}}$$	A measure of the return on total investment in the enterprise. It is sometimes desirable to add interest to after-tax profits to form the numerator of the ratio, since total assets are financed by creditors as well as by stockholders; hence it is accurate to measure the productivity of assets by the returns provided to both classes of investors.
5. Return on stockholders' equity (or return on net worth)	$$\frac{\text{Profits after taxes}}{\text{Total stockholders' equity}}$$	A measure of the rate of return on stockholders' investment in the enterprise.
6. Return on common equity	$$\frac{\text{Profits after taxes} - \text{Preferred stock dividends}}{\text{Total stockholders' equity} - \text{Par value of preferred stock}}$$	A measure of the rate of return on the investment which the owners of common stock have made in the enterprise.
7. Earnings per share	$$\frac{\text{Profits after taxes} - \text{Preferred stock dividends}}{\text{Number of shares of common stock outstanding}}$$	Shows the earnings available to the owners of common stock.
Liquidity ratios:		
1. Current ratio	$$\frac{\text{Current assets}}{\text{Current liabilities}}$$	Indicates the extent to which the claims of short-term creditors are covered by assets that are expected to be converted to cash in a period roughly corresponding to the maturity of the liabilities.
2. Quick ratio (or acid-test ratio)	$$\frac{\text{Current assets} - \text{Inventory}}{\text{Current liabilities}}$$	A measure of the firm's ability to pay off short-term obligations without relying upon the sale of its inventories.
3. Cash ratio	$$\frac{\text{Cash \& Marketable securities}}{\text{Current liabilities}}$$	An indicator of how long the company can go without further inflow of funds.
4. Inventory to net working capital	$$\frac{\text{Inventory}}{\text{Current assets} - \text{Current liabilities}}$$	A measure of the extent to which the firm's working capital is tied up in inventory.

Leverage ratios:

Ratio	Formula	How calculated / Indication
1. Debt to assets ratio	$$\frac{\text{Total debt}}{\text{Total assets}}$$	Measures the extent to which borrowed funds have been used to finance the firm's operations.
2. Debt to equity ratio	$$\frac{\text{Total debt}}{\text{Total stockholders' equity}}$$	Provides another measure of the funds provided the creditors versus the funds provided by owners.
3. Long-term debt to equity ratio	$$\frac{\text{Long-term debt}}{\text{Total stockholders' equity}}$$	A widely used measure of the balance between debt and equity in the firm's overall capital structure.
4. Times-interest-earned (or coverage ratios)	$$\frac{\text{Profits before interest and taxes}}{\text{Total interest charges}}$$	Measures the extent to which earnings can decline without the firm's becoming unable to meet its annual interest costs.
5. Fixed-charge coverage	$$\frac{\text{Profits before taxes and interest} + \text{Lease obligations}}{\text{Total interest charges} + \text{Lease obligations}}$$	A more inclusive indication of the firm's ability to meet all of its fixed-charge obligations.

Activity ratios:

Ratio	Formula	How calculated / Indication
1. Inventory turnover	$$\frac{\text{Cost of Goods Sold}}{\text{Inventory}}$$	When compared to industry averages, it provides an indication of whether a company has excessive inventory or perhaps inadequate inventory.
2. Fixed-assets turnover*	$$\frac{\text{Sales}}{\text{Fixed assets}}$$	A measure of the sales productivity and utilization of plant and equipment.
3. Total-assets turnover	$$\frac{\text{Sales}}{\text{Total assets}}$$	A measure of the utilization of all the firm's assets; a ratio below the industry average indicates the company is not generating a sufficient volume of business given the size of its asset investment.
4. Accounts receivable turnover	$$\frac{\text{Annual credit sales}}{\text{Accounts receivable}}$$	A measure of the average length of time it takes the firm to collect the sales made on credit.
5. Average collection period	$$\frac{\text{Accounts receivable}}{\text{Total sales} \div 365}$$ or $$\frac{\text{Accounts receivable}}{\text{Average daily sales}}$$	Indicates the average length of time the firm must wait after making a sale before it receives payment.

*The manager should also keep in mind the fixed charges associated with noncapitalized lease obligations.

Source: Adapted from Arthur A. Thompson, Jr., and A. J. Strickland III, *Strategy and Policy*, 4th ed. (Burr Ridge, IL: Richard D. Irwin, 1987), pp. 270–71.

EXHIBIT 1A–3   Illustrative Contribution Margin Analysis for Product X ($000)

Sales	$300
Less: Variable manufacturing costs	100
Other variable costs traceable to product X	50
Equals: Contribution margin	150
Less: Fixed costs directly traceable to product X	100
Equals: Product net income	$ 50

EXHIBIT 1A–4   Financial Analysis Model

Profit margin ↓		Asset turnover ↓		Return on assets ↓		Financial leverage ↓		Return on net worth ↓
Net profits (after taxes)	×	Net sales	→	Net profits (after taxes)	×	Total assets	=	Net profits (after taxes)
Net sales		Total assets		Total assets		Net worth		Net worth

worth (or return on equity), the product of return on assets and financial leverage determines performance. Increasing either ratio will increase net worth. The values of these ratios will vary considerably from one industry to another. For example, in grocery wholesaling, profit margins are very low, typically, whereas asset turnover is very high. Through efficient management and high turnover, a wholesaler can stack up impressive returns on net worth. Furthermore, space productivity measures are obtained for individual departments in retail stores that offer more than one line, such as department stores. The measures selected depend on the particular characteristics of the business.

EVALUATING ALTERNATIVES

As we move through the discussion of financial analysis, it is important to recognize the type of costs being used in the analysis. Using accounting terminology, costs can be designated as fixed or variable. A cost is *fixed* if it remains constant over the observation period, even though the volume of activity varies. In contrast, a *variable* cost is an expense that varies with sales over the observation period. Costs are designated as mixed or semivariable in instances when they contain both fixed and variable components.

EXHIBIT 1A–5   Illustrative Break-Even Analysis

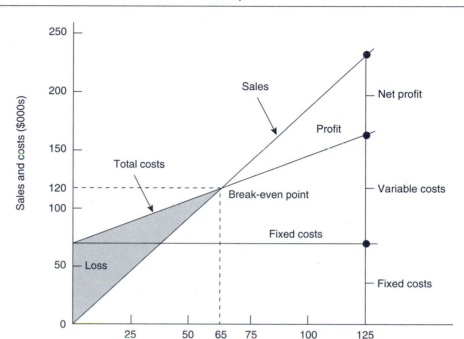

Break-Even Analysis[3]

This technique is used to examine the relationship between sales and costs. An illustration is given in Exhibit 1A–5. Using sales and cost information, it is easy to determine from a break-even analysis how many units of a product must be sold in order to break even, or cover total costs. In this example 65,000 units at sales of $120,000 are equal to total costs of $120,000. Any additional units sold will produce a profit. The break-even point can be calculated in this manner:

$$\text{Break-even units} = \frac{\text{Fixed costs}}{\text{Price per unit} - \text{Variable cost per unit}}$$

Price in the illustration shown in Exhibit 1A–5 is $1.846 per unit, and variable cost is $0.769 per unit. With fixed costs of $70,000, this results in the break-even calculation:

$$\text{BE units} = \frac{\$70,000}{\$1.846 - \$0.769} = 65,000 \text{ units}$$

---

[3] This illustration is drawn from David W. Cravens, Gerald E. Hills, and Robert B. Woodruff, *Marketing Decision Making: Concepts and Strategy,* rev. ed. (Burr Ridge, IL: Richard D. Irwin, 1980), pp. 335–36.

EXHIBIT 1A–6   Cash Flow Comparison ($000s)

	Project X	Project Y
Start-Up Costs	<1,000>	<1,000>
Year 1	500	300
Year 2	500	400
Year 3	200	600

This analysis is not a forecast. Rather, it indicates how many units of a product at a given price and cost must be sold in order to break even. Some important assumptions that underlie the above break-even analysis include the use of constant fixed costs and one price.

In addition to break-even analysis, several other financial tools are used to evaluate alternatives. Net present value of cash flow analysis and return on investment are among the most useful. For example, assume there are two projects with the cash flows shown in Exhibit 1A–6.

Though return on investment is widely used, it is limited in its inability to consider the time value of money. This is pointed out in Exhibit 1A–7. Return on investment for *both* projects X and Y is 10 percent. However, a dollar today is worth more than a dollar given in three years. Therefore, when assessing cash flows of a project or investment, future cash flows must be discounted back to the present at a rate comparable to the risk of the project.

Discounting cash flows is a simple process. Assume the firm is considering projects X and Y, and its cost of capital is 12 percent. Additionally, assume that both projects carry risk comparable to the normal business risk. Under these circumstances, the analyst should discount the cash flows back to the present at the cost of capital, 12 percent. Present value factors can be looked up, or computed using the formula $1/(1 + i)n$, where i equals our discounting rate per time period and n equals the number of compounding periods. In this example, the present value of cash flows would be as shown in Exhibit 1A–7.

Because both projects have a positive net present value, both are good. However, if they are mutually exclusive, the project with the highest net present value should be selected.

FINANCIAL PLANNING

Financial planning involves two major activities: (1) forecasting revenues and (2) budgeting (estimating future expenses). The actual financial analyses and forecasts included in the strategic marketing plan vary considerably from firm to firm. In addition, internal financial reporting and budgeting procedures vary widely among companies. Therefore, consider this approach as one example rather than the norm.

The choice of the financial information to be used for marketing planning and control will depend on its relationship with the corporate or business unit strategic plan. Another important consideration is the selection of performance measures to be used in gauging marketing performance. The objective is to indicate the range of possibilities and to suggest some of the more frequently used financial analyses.

Pro forma income statements can be very useful when projecting performance and budgeting. Usually, this is done on a spreadsheet so that assumptions can be altered rapidly. Usually, only a

---

EXHIBIT 1A–7 Present Value of Cash Flows

	Time	Cash Flow	PV Factor	NPV of Cash Flow
Project X				
	0	<1,000>	$1/(1 + .12)^0 = 1$	<1,000>
	1	500	$1/(1 + .12)^1 = 0.8929$	= 446.45
	2	500	$1/(1 + .12)^2 = 0.7972$	= 398.60
	3	300	$1/(1 + .12)^3 = 0.7118$	= 213.54
			Present value	+ 58.59
Project Y				
	0	<1,000>	$1/(1 + .12)^0 = 1$	<1,000>
	1	300	$1/(1 + .12)^1 = 0.8929$	= 267.87
	2	400	$1/(1 + .12)^2 = 0.7972$	= 318.88
	3	600	$1/(1 + .12)^3 = 0.7118$	= 427.08
			Net present value	+ 13.83

---

few assumptions need be made. For example, sales growth rates can be projected from past trends and adjusted for new information. From this starting point, cost of goods can be determined as a percentage of sales. Operating expenses can also be determined as a percentage of sales based on past relationships, and the effective tax rate as a percentage of earnings before taxes. However, past relationships may not hold in the future. It may be necessary to analyze possible divergence from past relationships.

Business Strategy and Competitive Advantage

Demanding buyers, fast-moving technologies, intense global competition, deregulation, and social change create new challenges and opportunities for a wide range of businesses. Developing strategies in this environment of constant change is a key corporate success requirement.

The business strategy pursued by Benetton Group S.P.A., the Italian casual wear producer, has enabled the company to successfully compete in the very competitive and rapidly changing apparel market.[1] After experiencing explosive growth, in the late 1980s management halted the expansion program because of weak demand in the United States. Benetton's growth priorities in the 1990s shifted to Latin America, eastern Europe, and Asia. Management plans to open 300 new stores in China in the late 1990s. Strategy changes include upgrading the quality and expanding the range of goods in its core markets in Western Europe (70% of sales). Benetton lost market position in the late 1980s in the United States because of strong competition from The Limited and The Gap, conflicts with its retailers, adverse reaction to its controversial socially active "United Colors of Benetton" advertising campaign, and the termination of many licensing agreements with retailers. The number of U.S. stores fell from 800 in 1988 to only 150 in 1994. The Benetton corporate structure is quite flexible, enabling management to quickly adapt its strategies to new competitive challenges. Benetton's product designs and the cutting, dyeing, and packing are handled in-house. All other production is outsourced. This capability is important in the fast-changing world of fashions. Benetton has a 200-person design team and administrative offices in Ponzano Veneto, Italy. The clothing items are produced in raw wool and cotton and dyed at the time of shipment. This enables

Benetton to respond quickly with colors that are in fashion. All of the more than 7,000 retail stores in 110 countries are licensed to independent owners, who agree to purchase apparel from Benetton in return for using its name for the retail shop. The social-issues advertising campaign pushed the brand into a strong global position. One ad showing the bloodstained clothes of a Bosnian war casualty created calls for a boycott in France and widespread attention throughout the world. The company continues to set growth records for both sales and profits, though it faces a continuing tough competitive environment.

Business strategy consists of deciding the scope and purpose of the business, its objectives, and the actions and resources necessary to achieve the objectives. Marketing strategy is guided by the decisions top management makes about how, when, and where to compete. Because of this close relationship, it is important to examine the major aspects of designing and implementing business strategy.

We begin the chapter with a look at the nature and scope of organizational change. A discussion of the sources of competitive advantage and the requirements for achieving advantage follows. Next, several key features of business strategy are considered. Finally, strategic analysis and strategy selection are discussed.

ORGANIZATIONAL CHANGE

The Benetton illustration shows how companies are responding to a demanding market and competitive pressures. To gain a firmer grasp of these issues, we will define business strategy, discuss several issues in organizational competitiveness, examine the process of organizational renewal, and describe some of the new organization forms of the 1990s.

What Is Business Strategy?

Business strategy consists of the decisions made by top management and the resulting actions taken to achieve the objectives set for the business. The major strategy components and several key issues related to each component are shown in Exhibit 2–1. The issues highlight important questions that management must answer in charting the course of the enterprise. Management's skills and vision in addressing these issues are critical to the performance of the corporation. Essential to corporate success is matching the competitive advantage of the organization with opportunities to achieve long-term customer satisfaction.

Global Competitive Challenges

As the world catapults into the 21st century, companies are drastically altering their business and marketing strategies to get closer to their customers, counter competitive threats, and strengthen competitive advantages. While changes confronting managers in the 1980s were unprecedented, the 1990s display even greater diversity and turbulence.[2] Challenges to management include escalating international competition, political and economic upheaval, the dominance of the customer, and increasing market complexity.

EXHIBIT 2–1 Corporate Strategy Components and Issues

Strategy Component	Key Issues
Scope, mission, and intent	• What business(es) should the firm be in?
	• What customer needs, market segments, and/or technologies should be focused on?
	• What is the firm's enduring strategic purpose or intent?
Objectives	• What performance dimensions should the firm's business units and employees focus on?
	• What is the target level of performance to be achieved on each dimension?
	• What is the time frame in which each target should be attained?
Development strategy	• How can the firm achieve a desired level of growth over time?
	• Can the desired growth be attained by expanding the firm's current businesses?
	• Will the company have to diversify into new businesses or product-markets to achieve its future growth objectives?
Resource allocation	• How should the firms' limited financial resources be allocated across its businesses to produce the highest returns?
	• Of the alternative strategies that each business might pursue, which will produce the greatest returns for the dollars invested?
Sources of synergy	• What competencies, knowledge, and customer-based intangibles (e.g., brand recognition, reputation) might be developed and shared across the firm's businesses?
	• What operational resources, facilities, or functions (e.g., plants, R&D, salesforce) might the firm's businesses share to increase their efficiency?

Source: Orville C. Walker, Jr., Harper W. Boyd, Jr., and Jean-Claude Larréché, *Marketing Strategy* (Burr Ridge, IL: Richard D. Irwin, 1992),p. 38.

Successful managers recognize the mandate for adapting to the turbulent and rapidly changing global environment. They seek to reduce costs, create more flexible organizational designs, and build competitive advantage around the core competencies of the organization. Core competencies are what a company does best, as illustrated by Gillette's skills in developing shaving products. Gaining competitive advantage often requires cooperation because a single organization may need to draw from the skills and resources of other organizations.

The global business challenge centers on two important competitive issues. First, companies with the skills and resources for competing beyond their domestic markets have major opportunities for growth. And these opportunities are not restricted to industry giants. Second, maintaining a competitive position in the domestic market requires knowledge of key competitors in the global marketplace. The successful competitor in domestic markets keeps informed of foreign competitors' strategies and strengths.

New market arenas are rapidly developing through the world. The Pacific Rim countries, western Europe, eastern Europe, and other regions offer promising markets and

---

EXHIBIT 2–2   International Labor Cost Comparisons

Dimensions of the Challenge

The Wage Gap
Average 1993 hourly labor costs in manufacturing, in dollars

Western Germany	$24.87	Italy	$14.82	Hungary	$1.82
Switzerland	21.90	Britain	12.37	Poland	1.40
Belgium	21.00	Ireland	11.88	Czech Republic	1.14
Netherlands	19.83	Spain	11.73	Thailand	0.71
Austria	19.26	Taiwan	5.46	Romania	0.68
Denmark	19.21	Singapore	5.12	Philippines	0.68
Sweden	18.30	South Korea	4.93	Bulgaria	0.63
Japan	16.91	Portugal	4.63	China	0.54
U.S.	16.40	Hong Kong	4.21	Russia	0.54
France	16.26	Mexico	2.41	Yugo/Serbia	0.40

Sources: DRI McGraw-Hill; Morgan Stanley Research

Source: Terence Roth, "Gordion Knot," *The Wall Street Journal*, September 30, 1994, p. R4.

new sources of competition as they change and develop. An interesting illustration of the global competitive challenge is shown in Exhibit 2–2. Note the huge differences in wage rates (including benefits). Moreover, several of the countries with very low wages, like China, also have the skills to produce high-quality products. The competitive pressures are particularly acute for the countries at the top of the wage rankings:

> Western Europeans on average work fewer hours, earn more pay, take longer vacations, and enjoy far more social entitlements and job protection than their chief competitors in North America and Asia. An average Western German worker, the best paid in Europe, earned $24.87 an hour in wages and benefits in 1993, compared with between $16 and $17 an hour for the average American and Japanese and $4.93 an hour for a South Korean. It is a lifestyle that few Europeans are willing to abandon.[3]

One consequence of these competitive realities is the movement of manufacturing, distribution, and marketing operations to countries which offer comparable labor skills at lower wage rates. For example, Siemens AG of Germany moved its semiconductor assembly to southeast Asia.[4] Siemens workers at its Singapore plant earn $4.40 per hour for the same work previously performed in Germany at $25 per hour.

Requirements for competing globally are both different and more demanding than competing domestically. Differences in customs, languages, currency, and trade practices create risks and uncertainty for new market entrants. The social and political changes that occurred in eastern Europe in 1989 are illustrative. Almost overnight, access to these countries was possible and major social, political, and economic reforms were initiated.

Organizational Renewal

During the last decade massive changes were made in the size and structure of many business firms. These changes are described as rightsizing, reengineering, and reinventing the organization. Typically, the renewal (reforming) of the traditional organization moves through three phases: vertical disaggregation, internal redesign, and network formation.[5]

Vertical Disaggregation.   Disaggregation reduces the size of the organization by eliminating jobs and layers of middle managers and flattening the hierarchy. The Conference Board reports that 90 percent of its members downsized during the last five years, and about two-thirds of the executives representing a broad cross-section of business say downsizing will continue.[6]

The resulting horizontal corporation may organize its activities into a small number of key processes (e.g., new product planning, sales generation, and customer service).[7] Multifunctional teams are the primary organizational units, and providing superior customer value is a key objective and measure of performance. Employees are encouraged to make regular contact with suppliers and customers.

Internal Redesign.   Organizational renewal is more than just reducing staff, eliminating layers of management, and adopting worker empowerment processes. The second phase alters the internal design of the organization. The new organization forms are lean, flexible, adaptive, and responsive to customer needs and market requirements.[8] Technology is a core advantage, involving innovation in designing products to meet customer needs, arranging supply and distribution networks, and constantly staying in touch with the marketplace. A priority of these organizations is understanding customer needs, offering value to customers, and retaining customers.

Network Formation.   The third phase of renewal involves the formation of relationships with other organizations. Although interorganizational relationships are often present in the traditional organization, companies are expanding these relationships with suppliers, customers, and even competitors. These new organization forms are called networks since they involve several collaborative arrangements. Benetton displays several characteristics of the network organization. Networks are more likely to be launched by entrepreneurs, since the traditional vertically integrated, hierarchically organized company finds difficulty in shifting to the network paradigm. Transformation means fewer people on the corporate payroll, different management challenges, drastic cultural changes, and complex collaborative relationships with other organizations. Nevertheless, traditional companies like General Electric are successfully transforming themselves to more flexible and adaptive network forms.

COMPETITIVE ADVANTAGE

Southwest Airlines illustrates how competitive advantage influences business performance. The regional carrier built a strong advantage over competing U.S. domestic airlines in the 1990s.[9] Its costs per revenue passenger mile are much lower than other

EXHIBIT 2–3   The Elements of Competitive Advantage

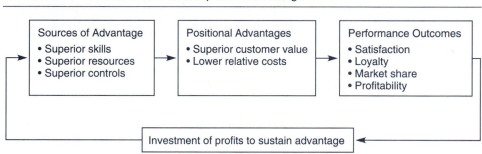

Source: George S. Day and Robin Wensley, "Assessing Advantage: A Framework for Diagnosing Competitive Superiority," *Journal of Marketing,* April 1988, p. 30.

carriers'. Southwest does not serve meals, offers no seat reservations, and flies only Boeing 737 aircraft. A key competitive advantage is high aircraft utilization by minimizing the time between landing and takeoff. Southwest's entire workforce is market-oriented (see Case 1–4).

We will now discuss obtaining competitive advantage, how competitive position is analyzed, how to sustain competitive advantage, and how market-entry barriers create advantage.

Obtaining Competitive Advantage

Day and Wensley emphasize the importance of viewing competitive advantage as a dynamic process rather than an outcome.[10] The process shown in Exhibit 2–3 includes use of sources of advantage to achieve positional advantages, which lead to performance outcomes, and investment of part of profits to sustain advantage. We look at each element of the process, showing its role in the advantage process.

Sources of Advantage.   Competitive advantage analysis looks at the differences among competitors or uniqueness, in the case of a firm holding a monopoly position. The sources of advantage are superior skills, resources, and controls.[11]

Superior skills enable an organization to select and implement strategies that will distinguish the organization from its competition. Skills include technical, managerial, and operational capabilities. For example, knowledge of customers' needs and requirements helps a company use its capabilities to satisfy its customers. Research and development expertise is another skill.

Superior resources are the enabling aspects of advantage. Examples include strong distribution networks, production capability, marketing power (experienced sales force), technology, and natural resources. De Beers' control of over 80 percent of the supply of uncut diamonds is illustrative. This monopoly position enables the company to control the flow and prices of diamonds throughout the world.

Superior controls include capabilities in monitoring and analyzing business processes and results. For example, superior cost controls constrain costs and identify areas where management assessment and action are needed. Control systems also provide performance benchmarks. Monitoring efforts should extend beyond internal operations to include customers, competition, and distribution networks. Companies with powerful computerized information systems like Wal-Mart (discount stores) and Frito-Lay (snack foods) have superior controls.

Positional Advantages.   As discussed in Chapter 1, positional advantage results from cost leadership or differentiation that gives customers superior value.[12] Lower costs enable a firm to offer superior value by pricing an equivalent product at a lower price than its competitors. Differentiated product features that match buyers' preferences offer unique benefits that more than offset a higher price. An important factor in seeking advantage is deciding where and how to compete. For example, the decision of Home Depot's management to target do-it-yourself home improvement needs (rather than professionals) enabled the firm to concentrate its efforts on this market segment, offering buyers low prices and experienced salespeople who assist customers in selecting hardware, plumbing, and electrical items. The company has large warehouse stores, located in areas convenient to homeowners.

Performance Outcomes.   When the company's skills, resources, and controls are used to gain a value and/or cost advantage, the positional advantage leads to favorable performance outcomes (customer satisfaction, brand loyalty, market share and profitability), as shown in Exhibit 2–3. Competitive advantage is a moving target, so management must use a portion of profits to sustain advantage. For example, highly successful Tootsie Roll Industries annually uses a substantial portion of profits to improve production operations and reduce the cost of producing its popular candy products.

Analyzing Competitive Position

Determining the organization's competitive advantage or identifying a new opportunity to gain advantage requires analyzing customers and competition. We discuss several techniques for customer- and competitor-oriented advantage analysis.

Customer-Oriented Analysis.   This activity includes determining who is the customer, identifying the values they are seeking, comparing the organization's performance to its competition, and identifying why customers consider one firm superior to another.[13] Analysis may be necessary at several levels, including the business unit (discussed later in the chapter), the industry, market segment, and product category. Methods of customer analysis are discussed in Chapters 3 and 4.

Customer analysis guided ValuJet Airlines Inc. in targeting budget-conscious leisure travelers to selected locations. The new airline began operations in 1993 and experienced rapid growth in sales and profits. The Competitive Advantage Feature describes ValuJet's strategy for competing in the highly competitive air travel market, and highlights passenger safety issues attributed to the airline's rapid expansion.

COMPETITIVE ADVANTAGE STRATEGY   ValuJet Airline's No Frills Strategy

---

ValueJet bought old but reliable DC-9-30 aircraft because financing newer aircraft was not feasible.

The 39 used planes kept costs low and, in 1995, helped ValueJet gain first place in profitability in the industry.

Revenues for the first six months of 1995 were nearly $150 million with a net income of $26 million.

ValuJet appeals to travelers with low prices and no-frills flights. A city-to-city strategy is used, with the destinations carefully selected by management.

ValuJet's major competitive hurdle is obtaining the aircraft needed to fuel its growth since the supply of DC-9's is very limited.

New aircraft will cost up to $20 million, three times the cost of a used DC-9.

ValuJet is adding 1.5 to 2 planes per month, so in 1996 the new-plane strategy became essential to growth.

Several aircraft operating problems and the May 1996 crash in the Florida Everglades which killed 110 people raised questions about ValuJet's rapid expansion, tight cost controls, use of older planes, and passenger safety.

Source: Martha Brannigan and Eleena DeLisser, "ValuJet May Change Successful Old-Plane Strategy," *The Wall Street Journal*, September 12, 1995, p. B4. Reprinted by permission of *The Wall Street Journal*, © 1995 Dow Jones & Company, Inc. All Rights Reserved Worldwide.

Competitor-Centered Analysis. Two techniques useful in competitor analysis are value-chain analysis and benchmarking. "The value chain desegregates a firm into its strategically relevant activities in order to understand the behavior of costs and the existing and potential sources of differentiation."[14] The activities that an organization performs to design, produce, market, deliver, and support its products or services comprise its value chain. A marketing-driven value chain is shown in Exhibit 2–4. A value system is composed of the chains of organizations such as suppliers, a manufacturer, and distribution network (e.g., distributors, dealers, retailers). Competitive advantage occurs when the organization performs value-chain activities (e.g., product design, marketing, production, distribution) at lower costs, or better, than competing firms. Value-chain analysis examines each key activity to determine where an organization has a competitive edge.

"Benchmarking is the process of continually comparing a company's performance on critical customer requirements against the best in the industry (direct competitors) or the class (companies recognized for superiority in performing certain processes) in order to determine which areas should be targeted for improvement."[15] Benchmarking places attention on the entire value chain rather than only completed products. The tool was developed by Xerox in 1979 to compare the manufacturing cost and features of its copying machines to competitors' products. Today, many companies are using benchmarking.

Sustaining Competitive Advantage

"For a producer to enjoy a competitive advantage in a product/market segment, the difference or differences between him and his competitors must be felt in the market place; that is, they must be reflected in some *product/delivery attribute* that is a *key*

EXHIBIT 2–4 A Marketing-Driven Value Chain

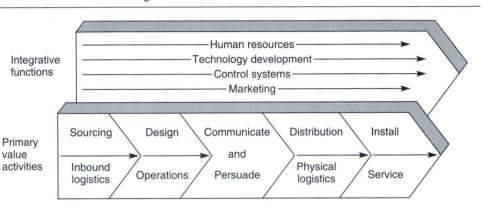

Source: George S. Day, *Market Driven Strategy* (New York: Free Press, 1985), p. 3.

buying criterion for the market."[16] A capability gap is the difference between a firm's position and that of its strongest competitor for a buying criterion. Competitive advantage occurs when an organization's capability exceeds that of the strongest competitor for a factor (e.g., Intuit's user-friendly QUICKEN software) that is important to buyers. Competitive advantage is gained by finding a product/service attribute that the targeted customers will perceive as a superior value and that cannot be easily duplicated by the competition.

Competitors are always trying to reduce (or eliminate) an organization's competitive advantage, so it is essential to be striving for continuous improvement in the value offered to buyers and/or reducing the costs of providing the product or service. New products that meet buyers' needs better than existing products create advantage. Hewlett-Packard's continuous stream of new products is illustrative.

Market Entry Barriers

Companies that compete in the market often have an inherent advantage over others planning to enter the market.[17] This edge results from the market entry barriers that the new entrant will encounter. Understanding the entry barriers present in a product-market is important both to incumbents and to potential competitors. Entry barrier analysis includes (1) identifying the barriers and their relative importance, (2) estimating the effect of the barriers on entry at different stages of product-market maturity, and (3) recognizing how entry barriers vary in different product-markets (e.g., consumer and industrial products).

Entry Barriers. The major barriers are described in Exhibit 2–5 with accompanying definitions.[18] A variety of specific barriers can be identified within the six areas suggested by Exhibit 2–5. For example, cost advantage may be due to volume production, design efficiency, and experience.

EXHIBIT 2–5   Market Entry Barriers

Concept	*Definition*
Cost advantages of incumbents	The advantages include the decline in unit cost of a product as the absolute volume of production per period increases, as well as the reduction in unit cost resulting from product know-how, design characteristics, favorable access to raw materials, favorable locations, government subsidies, and learning or experience curve.
Production differentiation of incumbents	Established firms have brand identification and customer loyalties stemming from past advertising, customer service, product differences, or simply being first into the market.
Capital requirements	The need to invest large financial resources to enter a market and compete in that market.
Customer switching costs	One-time costs to the buyer due to switching from one supplier to another (i.e., employee retraining costs, cost of new ancillary equipment, need for new technical help, product redesign, etc.).
Access to distribution channels	The extent to which logical distribution channels for a product are already served by the established firms in the market.
Government policy	The extent to which government limits or forecloses entry into industries with such controls as licensing requirements and limits access to raw materials (i.e., regulated industries and Environmental Protection Agency laws).

Source: Fahri Karakaya and Michael J. Stahl, "Barriers to Entry and Market Entry Decisions in Consumer and Industrial Goods Markets," *Journal of Marketing,* April 1989, p. 85.

A study of Fortune 500 executives in a simulated business environment found all of the six barriers to be relevant.[19] Cost advantages were viewed as the most important entry barrier, with capital requirements second and product differentiation third. No distinct relative importance pattern was found for the other factors.

Early versus Late Market Entry.   The market pioneer (first to enter) often gains a sustainable competitive edge over firms entering the market later.[20] Being first does not assure the pioneer of a favorable market and profit position. Initial entry offers an opportunity for rewards but is also risky, since later entrants can benefit from the early entrant's mistakes. The successful pioneer must select and implement strategies for sustaining competitive advantage.

Entry Barriers in Different Product-Markets.   The importance of the six entry barriers may vary across consumer and industrial markets. In one study all of the barriers except capital requirements were different for industrial and consumer markets.[21] Product differentiation and access to distribution channels are more influential in early entry for consumer markets. Variation in the importance of entry barriers appears to be influenced by product-market characteristics.

BUSINESS STRATEGY

Developing strategies for sustainable competitive advantage, implementing them, and adjusting the strategies to respond to new environmental requirements are a continuing process. It begins by defining the mission of the business. Managers monitor the market and competitive environment. The corporate mission may, over time, be changed because of problems or opportunities identified by monitoring. An important part of business strategy in a firm made up of more than one business area (e.g., different products and/or markets) is managing the portfolio of business units. These units often have different objectives and strategies. The strategy for each unit indicates how it will fulfill its assigned role in the corporation. Underlying each unit's strategic plan are functional strategies for marketing, finance, research and development, and operations.

Deciding Corporate Mission

The corporate mission defines what the business is and what it does and provides important guidelines for managing and improving the corporation. The founder initially has a vision about the firm's mission, and management may alter the mission over time. Strategic choices about where the firm is going in the future—choices that take into account company capabilities, resources, opportunities, and problems—establish the mission of the enterprise.

Early in the strategy-development process management defines the mission of the corporation. The mission is reviewed and updated as shifts in the strategic direction of the enterprise occur over time. The mission statement sets several important guidelines for business operations.[22]

1. The reason for the company's existence and its responsibilities to stockholders, employees, society, and other stakeholders.

2. The firm's customers and the needs (benefits) that are to be met by the firm's products or services (areas of product and market involvement).

3. The extent of specialization within each product-market area and the geographical scope of operations.

4. The amount and types of product-market diversification desired by management.

5. The stage in the distribution system (level of participation in the sequence of stages in the value-added system from raw materials to the end-user).

6. Management's performance expectations for the company.

7. Other general guidelines for overall business strategy, such as technologies to be used and the role of research and development in the corporation.

Core Competence.   It is important to place a company's strategic focus on its distinct capabilities.[23] These core competencies may offer the organization the potential to compete in different markets, provide significant value to end-user customers, and create barriers to competitor duplication. For example, Hewlett-Packard has an awesome core competence in ink jet printer technology, enabling the company to become the world

---

EXHIBIT 2–6   Illustrative Distinctive Capabilities

- L. L. BEAN

  L. L. Bean's mail order products offer value to its customers but it is widely acknowledged for its *order fulfillment* capabilities.

- RUBBERMAID

  Rubbermaid has been unusually successful in competing in the commodity kitchenware market with a successful *new product development* process that creates many new products each year.

- SINGAPORE AIRLINES

  Singapore Airlines performs many commercial air transportation functions well, but it is widely recognized as the industry leader in *customer service delivery*.

- WAL-MART

  Wal-Mart has value-priced products and convenient retail locations but its efficient and responsive *distribution system* is how it mapped the path to competitiveness.

---

leader in printers. It leveraged this competency to develop the ink jet fax with a Japanese partner, which provided a core competency in fax technology.

Core competency is an important factor in shaping the organization's mission. In contrast to the diversification wave of the 1970s, today many companies are deciding what they do best and concentrating their efforts on these core competencies. Examples of distinctive capabilities for four companies are shown in Exhibit 2–6.

A key influence on the mission is management's decision about what it wants the business to be. Acknowledging the constraining nature of capabilities, resources, opportunities, and problems, management has a lot of flexibility in selecting the mission as well as changing it in the future. Sometimes the priorities and preferences of the CEO or the board of directors may override factual evidence in selecting the business mission. For example, many of the diversifications pursued by companies in the 1970s didn't work very well, and resulted in the restructuring and downsizing of many companies during the last decade.

Corporate Objectives.   Objectives need to be set so that the performance of the enterprise can be gauged. Corporate objectives are often established in the following areas: *marketing, innovation, resources, productivity, social responsibility,* and *finance.*[24] Examples include growth and market-share expectations, improving product quality, employee training and development, new-product targets, return on invested capital, earnings growth rates, debt limits, energy reduction objectives, and pollution standards. Objectives are set at several levels in an organization beginning with those indicating the enterprise's overall objectives.

Corporate Development Alternatives

Several possible directions of growth that may be taken from the core (initial) business of the corporation are shown in Exhibit 2–7. There are, of course, many specific combinations of these corporate development options. Success often leads to expanding into related

---

EXHIBIT 2–7 Corporate Development Options

```
                        ┌──────────────┐
                        │ Core business │
                        └──────────────┘
            ↙                  ↓                  ↘
┌──────────────────┐                      ┌──────────────────┐
│ New products for │                      │  New markets for │
│ existing markets │                      │ existing products│
└──────────────────┘                      └──────────────────┘
                        ┌──────────────┐
                        │Diversification│
                        └──────────────┘
                    ↙                    ↘
        ┌──────────────┐          ┌──────────────┐
        │  Unrelated to │          │  Related to   │
        │ core business │          │ core business │
        └──────────────┘          └──────────────┘
```

---

areas and sometimes entirely new product-market areas. We will take a brief look at each alternative.

Core Business.   The initial venture of an enterprise is the core business, as bakery products are for Sara Lee. Many firms start out competing in one product-market. This strategy offers the advantage of specialization but also the risks of being dependent on one set of customer needs. As the corporation grows and prospers, management often decides to move into other product and market areas, as shown in Exhibit 2–7. For example, Sara Lee expanded into underwear, leisure wear, and Coach leather goods. Reducing dependence on the core business is a major factor in corporate development. Of course, financial resources are necessary to expand into related or new areas. Sara Lee's food business generates the cash needed to expand into other consumer goods lines.

New Markets for Existing Products.   One way to expand away from serving a single product-market is to target other customer groups using the same product or a similar product. For example, Gore-Tex supplies its high-performance fabric to apparel producers and it is used as dental floss. For many companies, expanding into new markets is a natural way to expand operations. This strategy reduces the risks of depending on a single market yet it allows the use of existing technical and production capabilities. When deciding to pursue this strategy, a company must have the resources for expansion and must develop a marketing strategy for the new customer group(s).

New Products for Existing Markets.   Another strategy for shifting away from dependence on one product is to expand the product mix offered to the firm's target market. In the 1980s Maytag, the washer and dryer manufacturer, added to its appliance offering by acquiring lines of ranges, ovens, refrigerators, and freezers. Use of common distribution channels, promotional support, research and development, and production technology are among the possible advantages of this strategy. New products can be developed internally, although acquisition may be faster. Resources are necessary to support either alternative.

Diversification.   Diversification is movement into a new product and new market area by internal development or by acquisition. This option is often the riskiest and costliest of all those shown in Exhibit 2–7. Yet it may be an attractive avenue for growth if the firm's existing product-market areas face slow growth, if the resources for diversification are available, and if good choices are made. Unfortunately the success record for diversification has been dismal.[25] A comprehensive study of the diversifications of 33 large U.S. companies during the 1950–1986 period found that most of the firms: (1) disposed of many of their acquisitions and (2) dissipated instead of created shareholder value. Successful diversification appears to be closely related to industry attractiveness, reasonable cost of entry, preplanning of the acquisition, and the opportunity for improving competitive advantage.[26]

Movement beyond the core business is not unusual as businesses grow and mature. Several factors may influence the rate and direction of corporate development activities, including available resources, management's preferences, pending opportunities and threats, and the desire to reduce total dependence of the corporation on a single product-market area. Responding to slowdowns in growth in its apparel markets Benetton expanded into sporting goods in the late 1980s by acquiring Nordica Spa (ski equipment maker). Benetton also acquired Prince tennis rackets and Rollerblade inline skates. Sporting goods accounts for about one-fifth of Benetton's worldwide sales.

Business Composition

Defining the composition of the business is helpful in both corporate and marketing strategy design. In single-product firms, such as Tootsie Roll Industries (candy products), it is easy to determine the composition of the business. In many other firms it is useful to separate the business into parts to facilitate strategic analyses and planning. When firms are serving multiple markets with different products, grouping similar business areas together aids decision making.

Business Segment, Group, or Division.   These terms are used to identify the major areas of business of a diversified corporation. Each segment, group, or division often contains a mix of related products (or services), though a single product can be assigned such a designation. The term *segment* does not correspond to a market segment (subgroup of end-users in a product-market), which we discuss throughout the book. Most large corporations break out their financial reports into business or industry segments according to the guidelines of the Financial Accounting Standards Board. Some firms may establish subgroups of related products within a business segment that are targeted to different customer groups.

Strategic Business Unit.   A business segment, group, or division is often too large in terms of product and market composition to use in strategic analysis and planning, so it is divided into more specific strategic units. A popular name for these units is the *strategic business unit* (SBU). Typically, SBUs display product and customer group similarities. A

EXHIBIT 2–8   Characteristics of the Ideal Strategic Business Unit

---

Characteristic	*Rationale*
• Serves a homogeneous set of markets with a limited number of related technologies	Minimizing the diversity of a business unit's product-market entries enables the unit's manager to do a better job of formulating and implementing a coherent and internally consistent business strategy.
• Serves a unique set of product-markets	No other SBU within the firm should compete for the same set of customers with similar products. This enables the firm to avoid duplication of effort and helps maximize economies of scale within its SBUs.
• Has control over the factors necessary for successful performance, such as R&D, production, marketing, and distribution	This is not to say that an SBU should never share resources, such as a manufacturing plant or a sale force, with one or more business units, but the SBU should have authority to determine how its share of the joint resource will be used to effectively carry out its strategy.
• Has responsibility for its own profitability	Because top management cannot keep an eye on every decision and action taken by all its SBUs, the success of an SBU and its managers must be judged by monitoring its performance over time. Thus, the SBU's managers should have control over the factors that affect performance, and then be held accountable for the outcomes.

Source: Orville C. Walker, Jr., Harper W. Boyd, Jr., and Jean-Claude Larréché, *Marketing Strategy* (Burr Ridge, IL: Richard D. Irwin, 1992), p. 76.

strategic business unit is a single product or brand, a line of products, or a mix of related products that meets a common market need or a group of related needs, and the unit's management is responsible for all (or most) of the basic business functions. The characteristics of the ideal SBU are described in Exhibit 2–8. Typically, the SBU has its own strategy rather than a shared strategy with another business area. It is a cohesive organizational unit that is separately managed and produces sales and profit results.

An important issue is whether the use of SBUs to guide strategy and organization enhances corporate performance. AMR Corporation, parent of American Airlines, is recognized as a well-managed transportation services company. American's information technology business is an interesting example of the use of strategic business units. SABRE is divided into three business areas: (1) the SABRE Computer Services Division provides support for American Airlines; (2) the SABRE Travel Information Network markets reservations, ticketing, and other services to travel agencies and corporations; and (3) AMR Information Services, Inc., has seven strategic business units that market information services to other airlines, hotel and car rental companies, freight shippers and telemarketers and provide technical training and data-entry services.[27]

Corporate Strategy

Top management sets the guidelines for long-term strategic planning of the corporation. In a business that has two or more strategic business units, decisions must be made at two levels. Corporate management must first decide what business areas to pursue and set priorities for allocating resources to each SBU. The decision makers for each SBU must select the strategies for implementing the corporate strategy and producing the results that corporate management expects. Corporate-level management should assist SBUs in achieving their objectives.

Corporate strategy and resources should help an SBU to compete more effectively than if the unit operates on a completely independent basis. "To remain competitive, corporations must provide their business units with low-cost capital, outstanding executives, corporate R&D, centralized marketing where appropriate and other resources in the corporate arsenal."[28] Corporate resources and synergies help the SBU establish its competitive advantage. The strategic focus and priorities of corporate strategy guide SBU strategies. Finally, top management's expectations for the corporation indicate the results expected from an SBU, including both financial and nonfinancial objectives. When viewed in this context, the SBUs become the action centers of the corporation.

STRATEGY ANALYSIS AND CHOICE

The corporate strategy determines the business portfolio of an organization and how it will compete in each business area.[29] The strategy components include the corporate mission, objectives, development strategy, resource allocation, and sources of synergy (Exhibit 2–1). The strategy also spells out the organization's role in society, its responsibilities to the stakeholders (employees, stockholders, etc.), ethical guidelines, and environmental priorities.

Selecting a strategy for an organization requires deciding on the product-markets in which to compete (corporate-level strategies) and how to compete within those environments (business-level strategies).[30] Performance is the consequence of a combination of the strategy choices and how well the strategy is implemented.

Analyzing Current Strategies

Researchers, consultants, and managers have devoted extensive efforts to develop ways of classifying generic business strategies. The logic of generic strategy is that it can be followed by any organization encountering the same situational factors. Generic strategies offer several advantages in guiding strategy selection:[31]

1. They combine separate, situation-specific strategies, capturing their major commonalities so that they facilitate the understanding of broad strategic patterns.
2. They guide corporate-level decisions concerning business portfolio management and resource allocation.
3. They assist business-level strategy development by suggesting priorities and indicating broad guidelines for action.

Importantly, the generic strategies are not complete strategies. Their value is in indicating the type of strategy (e.g., downsizing) that is appropriate for a particular situation. The generic strategy suggests what should be accomplished (e.g., growth).

Management must decide how to achieve the strategy. Strategic classification models and generic strategy guidelines are useful in setting business-unit priorities and suggesting general strategy guidelines. Combining this information with more specific customer and competitor analysis, strategic plans are developed for each business unit in the corporate portfolio.

One type of generic classification model places business units into strategy categories (e.g., growth, retrenchment) using two or more contingency factors as the basis of classification. These models position a corporation's business units on two-way grids based on market attractiveness and business strength. For example, attractiveness can be measured by the estimated future growth rate of the market. Relative market share compared to the market leader is one gauge of business strength. The objective of the analysis is to determine how to allocate resources to each of the business units in the corporate portfolio. Two examples of these models are the Boston Consulting Group (BCG) growth-share matrix and the General Electric/McKinsey screening grid.

Although the BCG growth-share matrix helped establish the concept of business portfolio analysis, companies have moved beyond using only market growth and market share measures for positioning SBUs or products on grids. The evaluation of multiple factors may be necessary to fully understand a company's strategy situation. The GE screening grid is an example of the multiple factor model (Exhibit 2–9). SBUs can be plotted as circles on the Exhibit 2–9 grid, using areas proportional to the SBU's contribution to total company sales. Those units that fall into the high-high categories are in a desirable zone for investing/growing the business, whereas a low-low positioning indicates harvesting or divesting the unit. The premise is that return on investment will be high in a high-high category, and so on.[32]

Generic Strategies

In an effort to synthesize the different classifications like those discussed above, Herbert and Deresky propose four generic strategies: *develop, stabilize, turnaround,* and *harvest.*[33] The classification scheme has the following features:

1. It is based on common (or overlapping) variables and characteristics of strategic types in other models.

2. It proposes strategies that are independent of other strategies, environmental situations, or organizational or product development stages. Thus, a *harvest* strategy could occur within a rapidly *developing* business.

3. It encompasses/explains major and common types of generic strategies and their characteristics.

4. It has been tested using data from a sample of companies. Consistent and interrelated findings were found in the research results.[34]

The Develop Strategy.   Organizations using the develop strategy are relatively new businesses, firms with rapidly changing technology and product line, or companies entering new product-markets because of unfavorable conditions in the existing business

EXHIBIT 2–9   The Industry Attractiveness–Business Position Matrix

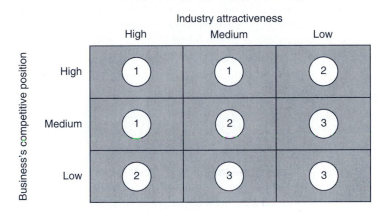

1 Invest / grow
2 Selective investment / maintain position
3 Harvest / divest

Variables that might be used to evaluate:

Business's competitive position		**Industry attractiveness**	
Size	Distribution	Size	Profitability
Growth	Technology	Growth	Technological sophistication
Relative share	Marketing skills	Competitive intensity	Government regulations
Customer loyalty	Patents	Price levels	
Margins			

Source: Orville C. Walker, Jr., Harper W. Boyd, Jr., and Jean-Claude Larréché, *Marketing Strategy* (Burr Ridge, IL: Richard D. Irwin, 1992), p. 57.

arena. The develop strategy seeks long-term growth via new-product and/or market development. Firms in this category pursue market leadership strategies. Intuit's pioneering entry strategy in the personal finance computer software market is an example of the develop strategy.

The Stabilize Strategy.   Companies that want to stabilize are found in mature, stable industries (e.g., textiles, chemicals). In markets where buyers' needs are relatively similar, management's strategies emphasize cost leadership. In differentiated markets, market segmentation (or focus) strategies or some type of product specialization are employed. The strategy typically emphasizes high-quality products and service and close contact with customers. In the tire industry Goodyear follows this strategy.

The Turnaround Strategy.   This strategy is appropriate for survival and rebuilding situations. Emphasis may be on improving cash flow and reducing costs or refocusing the organization. Downsizing and other forms of restructuring may occur. The cost strategy involves actions to increase efficiency, where refocusing may include reorganization,

---

STRATEGY FEATURE   Deciding How to Compete in the Clothing Retail Market

---

Laura Ashley's clothing gained a strong brand image around the world with its English country fashions.

In recent years the Ashley image became blurred due to an extensive array of products, including clothing, home furnishings, wallpaper, and children's clothes, and the use of different positioning approaches in different markets.

The new chief executive officer, Ann Iverson, launched a turnaround strategy in 1995 to increase revenues and profits. During the past five years, the retailer experienced substantial losses.

Turnaround actions include developing a shared vision about the market and Laura Ashley's brand positioning.

Since 83 percent of sales are from only 22 percent of products, nearly one-third of clothing styles and one-fifth of the home furnishing line were dropped.

Distribution practices to retail stores are being improved to lower costs. Greater use of outside manufacturers is also being evaluated.

Source: Tara Parker-Pope, "Laura Ashley's Many Faces Hurt Bottom Line," *The Wall Street Journal Europe,* September 22–23, 1995, p. 3. Reprinted by permission of *The Wall Street Journal Europe,* © 1995 Dow Jones & Company, Inc. All Rights Reserved Worldwide.

---

diversification, and acquisitions (or mergers). The Strategy Feature describes Laura Ashley's turnaround strategy.

The Harvest Strategy.   A business in this category is a candidate for removal from the corporate portfolio. The factors driving the decision to harvest the business include poor financial performance, lack of compatibility with the core business, no competitive advantage, and poor fit with the future direction of the corporation. General Electric's sale of its small appliance business to Black & Decker is an example of a harvest strategy.

Generic strategies do not provide specific guides to action. Instead, they indicate direction or end results (e.g., harvest). They offer broad guides to action. Specific action plans must be developed by management.

Strategy Issues

During the 1990s an array of strategy guidelines was offered by consultants, executives, and academics to guide business strategy formulation. These strategy paradigms propose a range of actions, including reengineering the corporation, implementing total quality management, building core competencies, reinventing the organization, and strategic partnering. It is not feasible to review the various strategy approaches that have been developed into many books, seminars, and consulting projects. Instead, we look at whether choosing the right strategy matters, followed by a discussion of several characteristics that are common to the more popular strategy paradigms.

Strategy Does Matter.   Does the uncontrollable environment largely determine business performance or, instead, does the organization's strategy have a major impact on its performance? While the environment does influence corporate performance, there are successful businesses operating in very demanding market and competitive environments.

EXHIBIT 2–10 Cornerstones of Competitiveness

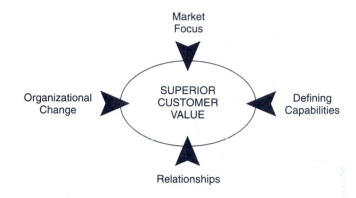

Examples include Southwest Airlines (air travel), Hewlett-Packard (electronics), and Wal-Mart (discount retailing).

The evidence suggests that strategic choices matter.[35] While environmental factors such as market demand, intensity of competition, government, and social change influence corporate performance, the strategic choices made by specific companies also have an important impact on their performance. Importantly, the impact may be positive or negative. For example, Kmart held a lead market position over Wal-Mart in 1980, but Wal-Mart overtook Kmart by investing heavily in information systems and distribution to develop a powerful customer-driven, low-cost retail network.

Cornerstones of Competitiveness. Four main cornerstones of competitiveness are shown in Exhibit 2–10. Strategy authorities agree that an organizational focus on providing superior customer value is essential to achieving superior performance. As we noted in the earlier discussion of competitive advantage, value is gained through product differentiation, low cost, or a combination of the two. We will briefly examine each cornerstone. One or more is included in many of the strategy paradigms.

The importance of a *market focus* is considered in Chapter 1, where we looked at the process of becoming market-oriented and reviewed the evidence that market-oriented firms achieve better performance than those that are not market-oriented. Market focus also highlights the need to recognize diversity in buyers' needs and wants by segmenting markets and targeting specific segments.

Earlier in the chapter we looked at the compelling logic of finding out what a company does best and leveraging this capability in achieving superior customer value. The *capabilities approach to strategy* is widely cited as an important strategy focus. Day proposes classifying capabilities as outside-in, inside-out, and spanning processes, as shown in Exhibit 2–11.[36]

Collaborative *relationships* are increasingly cited as essential components of business strategy. Environmental risk and uncertainty, as well as resource and skill gaps, encourage

EXHIBIT 2–11   Classifying Capabilities

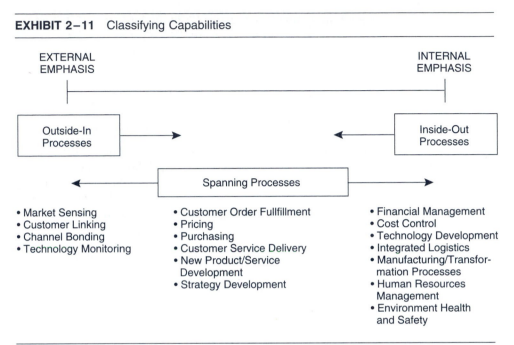

Source: George S. Day, "The Capabilities of Market-Driven Organizations," *Journal of Marketing,* October 1994, p. 41.

companies to partner with others. Included are relationships with customers, suppliers, internal partners, and even competitors. Such relationships are common to many business strategies.

Organizational change is part of the strategies of many companies. Managers are restructuring and redesigning traditional pyramid structures, focusing people on key business processes (e.g., new product planning, customer management) and creating multifunctional teams to manage the processes. The dramatic changes in the structure and processes of IBM in the 1990s are illustrative.

The Capabilities Approach to Strategy[37]

The competing on capabilities framework has the central objective of superior customer value. Moreover, its key dimensions include the cornerstones of competitiveness (Exhibit 2–10). A look at the major dimensions of the approach shows how the cornerstones fit into the framework.

Capabilities Framework.   The following steps seek to define and exploit the organization's unique capabilities.

- Diagnosis of current capabilities, using mapping and benchmarking methodologies.
- Anticipation of future needs for capabilities in light of the strategy for creating customer value.

- Bottom-up redesign, based on the formation of teams responsible for continuous improvement or radical redesign of underlying processes.

- Top-down direction from senior managers, who demonstrate a clear, continuing commitment to putting customers first.

- Use of information technology to enable the organization to do things it could not do before.

- Monitoring of progress toward improvement targets.[38]

The entire process has a strong market focus. The first step defines and evaluates current capabilities. Next, future needs for capabilities are matched to opportunities for creating customer value. The third and fourth steps address needs for organizational change and top management commitment and leadership. The fifth step recognizes the importance of information technology in market sensing and organizational learning. Finally, step six highlights the need to monitor the improvement process.

Comparative Advantage and Performance.[39]   The comparative advantage theory is closely related to the capabilities approach. By finding its comparative advantage an organization uses the resources which provide the greatest opportunity for achieving a positional advantage (value and/or cost). Sustained positional advantage leads to superior financial performance. An important premise is that the performance incentive will drive the search for comparative advantage from existing resources and the creation of new advantage resources:

> Competition, then, consists of the constant struggle among firms for a comparative advantage in resources that will yield a marketplace position of competitive advantage and, thereby, superior financial performance. Once a firm's comparative advantage in resources enables it to achieve superior performance through a position of competitive advantage in some market segment or segments, competitors attempt to neutralize and/or leapfrog the advantaged firm through acquisition, imitation, substitution, or major innovation. The comparative advantage theory of competition is therefore inherently dynamic.[40]

The comparative advantage view of competition incorporates several important realities of the marketplace. It helps to explain why some companies display impressive performance while others are marginal or poor performers. Management is faced with the complex task of targeting the best existing resources and developing the most promising new resources.

Deciding How to Compete

There seems to be general agreement among business strategists that finding and exploiting comparative advantage should be the core focus of business strategy. A more complex issue is deciding how to find the best strategy. The various strategy paradigms that are proposed by management consultants, company executives, and academics stress the importance of *market focus, capabilities, relationships,* and *the organizational change* (Exhibit 2–10).

One interesting analysis of successful companies proposes three possible strategies for successful differentiation from competitors to gain market leadership: operational excellence, product leadership, and customer intimacy.[41] *The Discipline of Market Leaders* proposes that a company should not try to be superior in all three disciplines. Instead, management needs to be superior in the discipline where the company has the greatest comparative advantage while maintaining competitive parity in the two other disciplines. The three disciplines are described:

> Operationally excellent companies deliver a combination of quality, price, and ease of purchase that no one else in their market can match. They are not product or service innovators, nor do they cultivate one-on-one relationships with their customers.[42]

American Airlines, Southwest Airlines, and Wal-Mart are examples of operationally excellent companies. Hewlett-Packard and Nike correspond to the product innovator discipline, while the United States Automobile Association has one-on-one relationships with its military personnel members who purchase automobile insurance.

Developing the Strategic Plan for Each Business

The objective of strategic analysis is twofold: (1) to diagnose the SBU's strengths and limitations, and (2) to select strategies for maintaining or improving performance. Management decides what priority to place on each business unit regarding resource allocation and implements a strategy to meet the objectives for the SBU. The strategic plan indicates the action agenda for the business. An example of a plan outline is shown in Exhibit 2–12. The "major strategies" shown in Part VI of the plan include the major strategic actions planned for business development, marketing, quality, product and technology, human resources, manufacturing/facilities, and finance.

The situation assessment guides establishing the SBU's mission, setting objectives, and determining the strategy to use to meet these objectives. The SBU's strategy indicates market target priorities, available resources, financial constraints, and other strategic guidelines needed to develop functional plans. Depending upon the size and diversity of the SBU, the functional plans may either be included in the SBU plan or developed separately.

SUMMARY

Our discussion of the changing patterns of global competition highlights the importance of coping with change in the dynamic competitive arena. Factors creating market turbulence include changes in customer needs, industry structure, distribution trends, and environmental influences. These factors often require adjustments in business strategy. Gaining and keeping a competitive advantage is essential to achieving high performance. Advantage is a moving target in the turbulent and rapidly changing marketplace. The primary sources of competitive advantage are superior skills, superior resources, and superior controls. These sources of advantage are used to gain value and cost positional

---

EXHIBIT 2–12 Plan Outline—A High-Technology Products Manufacturer

---

  I. Management Summary

 II. Business Definition
   —Mission
   —Purpose
   —Role

III. Progress Report
   —Comparison of key financial and market indicators
   —Progress made on major strategies

IV. Market and Customer Analysis
   —Potential versus served market
   —Market segmentation

 V. Competitive Analysis
   —Description of three major competitors
   —Analysis of competitors' strategies

VI. Objectives, Strategies, and Programs
   —Key objectives
   —Major strategies to accomplish the objectives
   —Action programs to implement strategies
   —Major assumptions and contingency programs
   —Market share matrix

VII. Financial Projections
   —Financial projections statement
   —Personnel projections

Source: Rochelle O'Connor, *Facing Strategic Issues: New Planning Guides and Practices*, Report No. 87 (New York: The Conference Board, Inc., 1985), p. 32.

advantage. Sustaining competitive advantage requires creating capability gaps relative to competitors. Strategic planning guides the business in managing the forces of change and maintaining a competitive edge.

Strategy formulation for the corporation includes: (1) defining the corporate mission and setting objectives, (2) determining strategic business units, and (3) establishing strategy guidelines for long-term strategic planning of the corporation and its business units. Top management must decide what corporate strategies will move the firm toward its objectives. After implementing the strategy, management considers how the strategy is progressing and what adjustments are needed. Successfully executing these steps requires penetrating and insightful analyses.

The corporate mission statement spells out the nature and scope of the business and provides strategic direction for the corporation. The firm's objectives indicate the performance desired by management. If management decides to move away from the core business, several paths of corporate development are possible, including expansion into new products and/or markets as well as diversification.

Strategic analysis begins by assessing the situational advantage of each business in the corporate portfolio. Classification models assist in deciding what generic strategy to select for each business in the corporate portfolio. Four broad generic strategies are described: develop, stabilize, turnaround, and harvest strategies. The generic strategy provides a strategic focus for developing a specific action plan.

The available evidence indicates that well-formulated and executed business strategies lead to superior performance. While there are several approaches to strategy development, they share common features, including the objective of superior customer value and one or more of the key dimensions of market focus, competing on capabilities, relationships, and organizational change. The competing-on-capabilities framework is a promising process for creating superior customer value.

The SBU strategies are guided by corporate strategy guidelines. The process begins by considering each business unit's market opportunity, position against competition, financial situation and projections, and strengths and weaknesses. The situation analysis shows the strategy alternatives for the SBU. Management then selects a strategy and develops a strategic plan. The plan is implemented and managed.

QUESTIONS FOR REVIEW AND DISCUSSION

1. One important part of a corporate/business unit situation assessment is the identification and evaluation of competitors. Finding potential competitors is a key problem in preparing such a situation assessment. Suggest several ways to determine potential competitors of a company.

2. Top management of companies probably devoted more time to reviewing (and sometimes changing) their corporate mission in the early 1980s than in any other period in the past. Discuss the major reasons for this increased concern with the business mission.

3. What advantages do you see in defining a corporate mission in a very specific way? Are there any disadvantages to clearly describing the corporate purpose?

4. Discuss the major issues that top management should consider in deciding whether or not to expand business operations beyond the core business.

5. Discuss the environmental factors that should be assessed on a regular basis by a large retail corporation like the Dayton Hudson Corporation.

6. What are the advantages of combining two or more strategic business units into a division or group, compared to keeping the planning units as separate organizational units?

7. Discuss what you consider to be the major issues in trying to divide a corporation into strategic business units, indicating for each problem suggestions for overcoming it.

8. What do you consider to be the major advantages in using one of the product-market grid methods for strategic analysis of a firm's planning units?

9. Is there any value to a single product-market firm in using one of the strategic analysis methods? Discuss.

10. What considerations may be important in deciding between the use of specific products and lines of products as the unit of analysis in strategic planning?

11. Discuss the role of generic strategies in an organization's strategic planning.

12. Identify some logical reasons why top management might decide *not* to adopt a formal method of strategic analysis, and rely instead upon management's judgment and experience as the basis of deciding how to allocate resource to business units.

13. Discuss the importance of finding a competitive advantage. Indicate how a company of your choice has accomplished this objective.

14. Discuss the role of the cornerstones of competition in helping an organization provide superior customer value.

15. Explain the concept of competing on capabilities, indicating its role in guiding business strategy.

NOTES

1. Guy Collins, "Benetton Weaves Strategy for Growth," *The Wall Street Journal*, February 4, 1992, p. A7A; Teri Agins, "Shrinkage of Stores and Customers in U.S. Causes Italy's Benetton to Alter Its Tactics," *The Wall Street Journal*, June 24, 1992, pp. B1, B10; and "Benetton: The Next Era," *The Economist*, April 23, 1994.
2. Fred Steingraber, "Managing in the 1990s," *Business Horizons*, January–February 1990, pp. 50–61.
3. Terence Roth, "Gordion Knot," *The Wall Street Journal*, September 30, 1994, p. R4.
4. Ibid.
5. Raymond Miles and Charles Snow, "Fit, Failure, and the Hall of Fame," *California Management Review*, Spring 1984, pp. 10–28; and James Brian Quinn, *Intelligent Enterprise* (Free Press: New York, 1992), chap. 5.
6. Observation made by Preston Townley, the chief executive officer of the Conference Board, during an address at Texas Christian University in Fort Worth, Texas, February 15, 1994.
7. David W. Cravens, Shannon H. Shipp, and Karen S. Cravens, "Reforming the Traditional Organization: The Mandate for Developing Networks," *Business Horizons*, July–August 1994, pp. 19–28.
8. *Business Week*, "The Virtual Corporation," February 8, 1993, pp. 98–102.
9. Bridget O'Brian, "Flying on the Cheap: Southwest Airlines Is a Rare Air Carrier: It Still Makes Money," *The Wall Street Journal*, October 26, 1992, pp. A1, 7.
10. The discussion in this section is based on George S. Day and Robin Wensley, "Assessing Advantage: A Framework for Diagnosing Competitive Superiority," *Journal of Marketing*, April 1988, pp. 1–20.
11. George S. Day, *Market Driven Strategy* (New York: Free Press, 1990), pp. 128–31.
12. Michael E. Porter, *Competitive Advantage* (New York: Free Press, 1985), p. 3.
13. Day, *Market Driven Strategy*, pp. 138–47.
14. Porter, *Competitive Advantage*, p. 33.
15. Ernst & Young Quality Improvement Consulting Group, *Total Quality* (Burr Ridge, IL: Irwin Professional Publishing, 1990), p. 50.
16. Kevin P. Coyne, "Sustainable Competitive Advantage— What It Is, What It Isn't," *Business Horizons*, January/February 1986, p. 55.
17. Michael Porter, "Industry Structure and Competitive Strategy: Keys to Profitability," *Financial Analysts Journal*, July–August 1980, pp. 30–41.
18. Ibid.
19. Ibid.
20. See, for example, ibid.; also see William T. Robinson, "Sources of Market Pioneer Advantages: The Case of Industrial Goods Industries," *Journal of Marketing Research*, February 1988, pp. 87–94.
21. Fahri Karakaya and Michael J. Stahl, "Barriers to Entry and Market Entry Decisions in Consumer and Industrial Goods Markets," *Journal of Marketing*, April 1989, pp. 80–91.
22. Based in part on George S. Day, *Strategic Market Planning* (St. Paul, MN: West Publishing, 1984), pp. 18–22.
23. C. K. Prahalad and Gary Hamel, "The Core Competence of the Corporation," *Harvard Business Review*, May–June 1990, pp. 79–91.
24. Peter F. Drucker, *Management* (New York: Harper & Row, 1974), p. 100.
25. Michael E. Porter, "From Competitive Advantage to Corporate Strategy," *Harvard Business Review*, May–June 1987, pp. 43–59.
26. Ibid., p. 46; see also Willard I. Zangwill, "Models for Successful Mergers," *The Wall Street Journal*, December 18, 1995, p. A14.
27. David A. Ludlum, "Is Service Keeping Airline Aloft Despite AMR's New Competition?" *Computer World Premier 100*, September 11, 1989, pp. 20–21.
28. This discussion is based on Boris Yavitz and William H. Newman, "What the Corporation Should Provide Its Business Units," *Journal of Business Strategy* 3, no. 1 (Summer 1982), p. 14.
29. Kenneth R. Andrews, *The Concept of Corporate Strategy* (Burr Ridge, IL: Richard D. Irwin, 1980).
30. Theodore T. Herbert and Helen Deresky, "Generic Strategies: An Empirical Investigation of Typology Validity and Strategy Content," *Strategic Management Journal*, 1987, pp. 135–47.
31. Ibid., p. 135.
32. Derek F. Abell and John S. Hammond, *Strategic Market Planning* (Englewood Cliffs, NJ: Prentice Hall, 1979), pp. 374–75.

33. Herbert and Deresky, "Generic Strategies," pp. 136–38.

34. The following description is drawn from ibid., pp. 141–44. More extensive discussion is provided in the source.

35. Shelby D. Hunt and Robert M. Morgan, "The Comparative Advantage Theory of Competition," *Journal of Marketing*, April 1995, pp. 1–15.

36. George S. Day, "The Capabilities of Market-Driven Organizations," *Journal of Marketing*, October 1994, pp. 37–52.

37. The following discussion is based on ibid.

38. Ibid., p. 49.

39. Hunt and Morgan, "The Comparative Advantage Theory."

40. Ibid., p. 8.

41. Michael Treacy and Fred Wiersema, *The Discipline of Market Leaders* (Reading, MA: Addison-Wesley), 1995.

42. Ibid., p. 3.

Cases for Part I

CASE 1–1 **Hewlett-Packard Co.**

It was such sweet revenge.

Last year, Hewlett-Packard Co. faced a challenge from NEC Corp. The Japanese giant had plans to attack H-P's hegemony in the burgeoning computer-printer market in time-honored Japanese fashion: by undercutting prices with new, better-designed models. Over a decade ago, the tactic helped other Japanese companies grab the lead from H-P in a business it had pioneered, hand-held calculators.

This time it didn't work. Months before NEC could introduce its inexpensive monochrome inkjet printer, H-P launched an improved color version and slashed prices on its bestselling black-and-white model by 40 percent over six months. NEC withdrew its entry, now overpriced and uncompetitive, after about four months on the market.

"We were too late," says John McIntyre, then a marketing director at NEC's U.S. unit. "We just didn't have the economies of scale" to compete with H-P.

A few years ago, U.S. companies were ruing Japan's unbeatable speed to market and economies of scale in many industries, and printers were a prime example: Japan made four out of five personal-computer printers that Americans bought in 1985. But now many American and Japanese companies are trading places, a shift confirmed by an annual global survey that reported Tuesday that the United States has replaced Japan as the world's most competitive economy for the first time since 1985.

H-P is one of the most dramatic of an increasing number of U.S. take-back stories, in technologies including disk drives, cellular phones, pagers, and computer chips. H-P

63

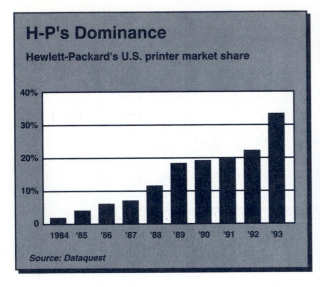

H-P's Dominance

Hewlett-Packard's U.S. printer market share

Source: Dataquest

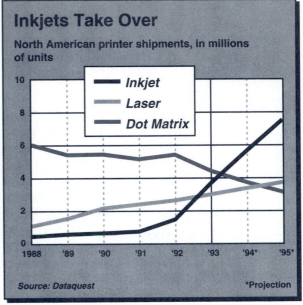

Inkjets Take Over

North American printer shipments, in millions of units

- Inkjet
- Laser
- Dot Matrix

Source: Dataquest   *Projection

didn't even start making PC printers until 1984, but it is expected to have about $8 billion in printer revenue this year (see Exhibits).

Among other things, the H-P story dispels common myths about the relative strengths of the United States and Japan, showing how big U.S. companies, under proper leadership, can exploit American creativity while using their huge resources to deploy "Japanese" tactics. H-P used its financial might to invest heavily in a laboratory breakthrough, then kept market share by enforcing rules that are gospel in Japan: Go for mass markets, cut costs, sustain a rapid fire of product variations and price cuts, and target the enemy.

Richard Hackborn, the H-P executive who led the charge, also succeeded because he could do what his Japanese counterparts couldn't: Buck the system. His printer-business teams were in outposts like Boise, Idaho—far from H-P's increasingly bureaucratic Palo Alto, Calif., headquarters—where they were permitted, though sometimes reluctantly, to go their own way.

H-P's other top executives for the most part preached high-profit, high-cost products for niche markets—which is how H-P lost the calculator business. Mr. Hackborn's troops set profit margins below the corporate norm and went for the mass market themselves. They moved fast and defied corporate rules when it meant winning customers.

"If you're going to leverage American culture but compete globally, you need a balance of entrepreneurship and central leverage," says Mr. Hackborn, who retired last year to become an H-P director. "The rugged individualism of cowboy culture alone doesn't work; but to be centrally directed doesn't either, because you lose the tremendous contribution of local innovation and accountability."

Japanese industrialists have often sermonized about U.S. complacency and myopia, but Japanese success, it turns out, can breed the same. H-P kept its huge lead because Japanese manufacturers, flush with success, spent too long squeezing profits out of old technologies and ignored signs that the American market—the bell-wether—was rapidly changing.

"H-P understood computers better, it understood American customers better, it got good products to market faster," says Takashi Saito, head of Canon Inc.'s inkjet-printer business. Japanese makers' culture hindered the kind of quick decision-making needed in the fast-paced U.S. computer market, he says, and as a result, "The market is H-P's garden."

Hewlett-Packard's journey to the top of the printer market began with a laboratory accident in 1979 and culminated in a rout of the Japanese beginning in 1992.

When H-P started thinking of entering the printer market, it realized it couldn't unseat the dominant Japanese makers, such as Seiko Epson Corp. and Oki Electric Industry Co., without a technological advance. Japan had a lock on the mass market with low-cost, well-engineered "dot matrix" printers, which form relatively rough letters.

The seeds for the H-P breakthrough had been nurtured by engineers in a converted janitor's closet at a Vancouver, Washington plant since 1980. The year before, an H-P scientist noticed drops of liquid splattered over his lab bench. He had been testing a thin metal film by zapping it with electricity; when the metal grew hot, liquid trapped underneath began to boil and spurted out. The discovery evolved into the "thermal" inkjet.

Mr. Hackborn saw that inkjet technology had compelling advantages over laser printers for the mass market: It was cheaper, it was more easily adaptable for color printing and no one else had perfected it. The idea of using a jet to spit ink on paper had been around for years, but no one had found a good way to pump the ink through tiny holes.

H-P's first inkjet printer in 1984 was hardly a knockout. It needed special paper, the ink tended to smear and it could print only 96 dots per inch, compared with today's 600 dots. "H-P's first inkjet was terrible quality," says Norio Niwa, president of Epson's U.S. unit. "Our engineers thought that if they announced such a product, they'd lose face."

H-P saw it differently. It had also introduced a successful line of expensive laser printers for corporate customers, but the company believed that ordinary computer users would soon demand higher-quality printouts of text, graphics and photographs. There was a mass market in the making—the kind that H-P had previously blown. To prevent a repeat, H-P had to invest heavily in its low-cost inkjet technology, Mr. Hackborn says, and "learn from the Japanese" by building it into a family of products.

Meanwhile, the Japanese were making mistakes. Canon, which had edged ahead of H-P in patenting early inkjet designs but had agreed to share the patents, chose a complex implementation that would set it years behind. And Epson, the king of dot-matrix printers, ignored warnings of changing consumer tastes.

Executives from Epson's U.S. unit began traveling to Japan around 1985 to tell headquarters that low-budget PC users would soon demand high-quality printers and that Epson should invest more in technologies such as inkjets, says Peter Bergman, a former Epson marketing executive. "Their approach was, 'Who are these Americans to come over and tell me how to build our products?'" he says.

Epson had an inkjet technology of its own, but it was an expensive variation. Besides, says Mr. Niwa, the Epson executive, "Every engineer was looking at dot matrix because we had a big market, big profits, big business, and the technology itself had a long history."

The same kind of mistake could have happened at H-P. Headquarters became increasingly bureaucratic, with product plans requiring many levels of approval. But business units are set up as fiefs, each having great autonomy. "We had the resources of a big company, but we were off on our own," says Richard Belluzzo, who has taken over from Mr. Hackborn. "There wasn't central planning . . . , so we could make decisions really fast."

SBU's

Based on decisions made in the hinterlands, H-P engineers adopted two Japanese tactics: They filed a blizzard of patents to protect their design and frustrate rivals, and embarked on a process of continual improvement to solve the inkjet's problems. They developed print heads that could spit 300 dots an inch and made inks that would stay liquid in the cartridge but dry instantly on plain paper. One engineer tested all types of paper: bonded, construction, toilet—and, for good measure, added sandpaper, tortillas and socks.

Competitive advantage

In 1988, H-P introduced the Deskjet, the plain-paper printer that would evolve into the model now taking market share away from the Japanese. No rivals loomed, but the line still wasn't meeting sales goals in 1989. It was competing with H-P's own more-costly laser printers. Sales were too low to pay the high costs of research and factories. The inkjet division needed new markets to avert a financial crisis.

That autumn, a group of engineers and managers assembled for a two-day retreat at a lodge on Oregon's Mount Hood. They pored over market-share charts. That, says Richard Snyder, who now heads H-P's PC inkjet business, is "when the lights went on." H-P hadn't targeted the right enemy. Instead of positioning the inkjet as a low-cost alternative to H-P's fancy laser printers, the managers decided, they should go after the Japanese-dominated dot-matrix market.

Dot matrix, the biggest section of the market, had serious flaws—poor print quality and color. Epson, the No. 1 player, had a soft underbelly: No competitive inkjet and the distraction of an expensive and failing effort to sell a PC. "We said, 'Maybe this is a good time to attack,' " Mr. Snyder says.

H-P did so with the obsessive efficiency of a Japanese company. A week later, H-P teams were wearing "Beat Epson" football jerseys. The company began tracking Epson's market share, studying its marketing practices and public financial data, surveying loyal Epson customers, and compiling profiles of Epson's top managers. Engineers tore apart Epson printers for ideas on design and manufacturing, a tactic the Japanese often use.

Among the findings: Epson's marketers got stores to put their printers in the most prominent spots; Epson used price cuts as tactical weapons to fend off challengers; consumers liked Epson machines for their reliability; Epson's printers were built to be manufactured easily. H-P responded, demanding that stores put its inkjet printers alongside Epson's. It tripled its warranty to three years and redesigned printers with manufacturing in mind.

Engineers learned Epson got huge mileage out of a product by creating a broad line consisting of slight variations of the same basic printer. By contrast, "we were taken with the notion at H-P that you had to come up with a whole new platform every time," Mr. Snyder says. Change came hard. In 1990, as H-P was developing a color printer, engineers were set on creating a completely new, full-featured mechanical marvel. Marketers suggested that a simpler, slightly clumsier approach, would be good enough for most consumers.

There was a near mutiny among the engineers until a product manager named Judy Thorpe forced them to do telephone polls of customers. It turned out people were eager for the product the engineers considered a "kludge." H-P learned that "you can tweak your not-so-latest thing and get the latest thing," Ms. Thorpe says. By sticking to the existing platform, H-P was able to get the jump on competitors in the now-booming color-printer market.

By 1992, it became clear to Japanese makers that dot-matrix printers were under assault, with sales falling for the first time as inkjet sales soared.

When the Computer City division of Tandy Corp., the Fort Worth, Texas, company, was preparing to open its first stores in the summer of 1991, it told printer makers that it expected inkjets to be a hot category, says Alan Bush, president of the chain. The Japanese responded that they didn't have anything ready. "We were very astounded," says Mr. Bush. "In the summer of '91, for an inkjet-product line you had your choice: H-P, H-P or H-P."

When Japanese printer makers that had been investing in inkjet research tried to move into the market, they ran into a brick wall: H-P had a lock on many important patents. Citizen Watch Co. found H-P had "covered the bases to make it very difficult for anyone else to get there," says Michael Del Vecchio, senior vice president of Citizen's U.S. unit. Citizen engineers trying to develop print heads learned H-P had some 50 patents covering how ink travels through the head. "It's like being in a maze: You go down this path and suddenly you're into an area that may infringe on their main patents and you have to back up and start over."

This barrier to entry meant competitors lost valuable time. "Every year that went by that we and other people were unsuccessful in reinventing the wheel, [H-P] got a greater and greater lead," says Mr. McIntyre, the former NEC executive.

Then there were H-P's economies of scale, which allowed it to undercut almost anyone else's prices; by the time Canon came out with the first credible competition, H-P had sold millions of printers and had thousands of outlets for its replacement cartridges. And H-P used its experience to make continual improvements in manufacturing. In constant dollars, for example, today's Deskjet costs half as much to make as the 1988 model.

This has allowed H-P to carry out a vital strategy: When a rival attacks, hit back quickly and hard. When Canon was about to introduce a color inkjet printer last year, H-P cut the price of its own version before its rival had even reached the market. The black-and-white printer, priced at $995 in 1988, now lists for $365.

"They've been very good about eating their own young," Mr. McIntyre says.

And consuming the competition as well. H-P now holds 55 percent of the world market for inkjets. The success in printers, including lasers, has propelled enormous overall growth at H-P, making it one of the two fastest-growing major U.S. multinationals (the other is Motorola Inc.). H-P's other divisions have been transformed by the printer people's mass-market approach and now seek to make the lowest-cost personal and hand-held computers on the market.

H-P's lead in printers could bring even more profits because inkjet mechanisms are finding their way into facsimile machines and color copiers. Sales could explode if, as expected, inkjet becomes the technology of choice inside TV-top printers for interactive-TV services. Printers will "be like toilets," says Mr. Hackborn. "They'll play a central role in the home."

Source: Stephen Kreider Yoder, "Shoving Back: How H-P Used Tactics of the Japanese to Beat Them at Their Game," *The Wall Street Journal*, September 8, 1992, pp. A1, A6. Reprinted by permission of *The Wall Street Journal*, © 1994 by Dow Jones & Company, Inc. All Rights Reserved Worldwide.

CASE 1–2   Toyota Motor Corp.

Eiko Shiraishi neither needs nor wants a new car. The Tokyo housewife has never set foot in an auto dealership, kicked a tire, or taken a test drive.

So how does she end up with a $30,000 gleaming silver Toyota in her driveway?

Chalk up another sale for Hiroyuki Saito, a door-to-door salesman who peddles cars the way the Avon Lady sometimes still hawks cosmetics. Mr. Saito is one reason America's trade deficit with Japan is so large, and so intractable.

Japanese cars may be high-tech, but Japanese salesmanship is curiously old-fashioned. As many as half the cars sold in Japan are peddled by door-to-door salesmen, according to the Japan Automobile Dealers Association. Such sales tactics, coupled with high-quality vehicles, stack the odds against the Big Three's U.S.-made cars ever making more than a dent in the Japanese market—even if all the trade barriers they huff and puff about crumble away.

Says the head of General Motors Japan, J. Michael Durrie: "There isn't any silver bullet that would make it easier to sell products in this very competitive, very expensive marketplace."

Cars are again at center stage of the United States–Japan relationship. Roughly two-thirds of the United States $59 billion bilateral trade deficit is auto-related, and the deficit keeps widening. It grew nearly 3 percent last month.

With the clock ticking toward Friday's U.S.-set deadline for imposing trade sanctions, a thorny issue remains unresolved: U.S. negotiators want the Japanese to assure that substantially more auto dealerships in Japan will stock American vehicles. The Japanese say they can't force private dealerships to stock products they don't want to carry. Yesterday, the Japanese offered a compromise "dealership-matchmaking" process to identify dealerships that might be interested in carrying foreign cars.

But even stocking the cars might not change much. Making the rounds with the solicitous Mr. Saito strongly suggests that the imbalance in automotive trade is due less to regulation than to relationships. The Americans undoubtedly face hassles in getting cars into Japan, but, Mr. Durrie of the General Motors Corp. unit says, "If that was all we had to deal with, we could cope with it."

To be sure, Detroit is making some progress in Japan, the world's second-largest car market. In the first eight months of this year, U.S. auto exports to Japan have nearly doubled from a year earlier. But, at just 22,543 vehicles, they still represent fewer than 1 percent of the total sold in Japan. Moreover, Honda Motor Co. alone has done more to lift American exports to Japan than the U.S. Big Three combined; it exported 29,000 made-in-Ohio Accords and Civics during the same period.

Instead of tariffs—there aren't any—the Big Three face armies of car-pushers such as Mr. Saito. Toyota Motor Corp. alone has more than 100,000 door-to-door salespeople in a country the size of California; that's half as many as the entire sales force in the United States for all kinds of cars. It is also what puts Toyota so far ahead of its eight Japanese rivals, who peddle cars the same way. Toyota sells two of every five cars in Japan—and virtually every white-collar Toyota executive begins his career by selling cars.

"Toyota's sales force is so strong they just blow everybody else off the face of the earth," says Keith Donaldson, an auto analyst at Salomon Brothers Asia Ltd., whose Tokyo home gets bombarded by car salesmen.

Toyota's itinerant dealers drum up demand literally by walking the extra mile. "We must go outside and, just like a fighter plane, hit the customers," says Mario Sasakura, a spokesman for the giant Tokyo dealership that employs Mr. Saito and 1,300 other salesmen at 79 outlets.

Many Japanese car buyers never go into a dealership. Though the outlets are about as ubiquitous in Tokyo as delicatessens in Manhattan, they serve primarily as bases for the sales armies pounding the pavement. Pitches are made and contracts are signed in peoples' living rooms—a genuine home-shopping network.

Serious and ever-polite—but with an easy laugh—Mr. Saito has often knocked on each of the 3,000 doors in his turf in southwest Tokyo. His black book contains details on the 370 customers to whom he has sold cars; many are repeat customers circled in red. The son of a Toyota parts designer, Mr. Saito started out knocking on about 100 doors a day after graduating from college, but no longer needs to visit so many now that he has developed a regular clientele. He sells about seven cars a month and earns some $70,000 a year, mostly from salary and only little from commissions.

Looking dapper in a navy blue Italian-cut suit and gold silk tie, Mr. Saito knows precisely how to time his pitches: just before the customer's car turns three years old or every two years thereafter. That's when the owner faces an expensive government inspection system, known as the *shaken,* in which replacement of several parts is mandatory.

Mr. Saito also has a special target: the housewife. He plots his visits around her schedule—and the "small window of opportunity" when she is likely to have a few moments to spare: not too early in the morning when she's getting the kids ready for school or doing household chores, not too late in the afternoon when she's headed to the market or fixing dinner. "Once I'm disliked by the housewife," he confides, "the sales activity will end miserably."

In Mrs. Shiraishi's case, Mr. Saito came by with brochures, then drove back with the dealership's Mark II model. He returned with it on the weekend when her husband was on hand to give the final approval. When her new car came in—complete with the lace seat covers that nearly every buyer in Japan orders—Mr. Saito personally delivered it to her house and drove her trade-in back to the dealership.

"At first, I had no intention of buying a new car," Mrs. Shiraishi says, "but Mr. Saito is very good at proposing reasons why I should change"—namely, the $1,600 shaken she faced.

The long-term relationships between dealer and customer are, in essence, mini-*keiretsu,* the Japanese system of doing business with those they know and trust. Extensive face-to-face meetings first establish trust in virtually all fields, long before business is even broached. Even Japan's huge banks drum up deposits by going door-to-door when corporations dole out semiannual bonuses to employees.

The relationships don't end with a sale. Mr. Saito maintains constant contact with customers. There are calls after a purchase to inquire how the car is running, handwritten greeting cards and special invitations for low-cost oil changes and dealer events. Beginning in the 1950s, Toyota set up driving schools in big cities to help people obtain licenses—and new Toyotas. All this diligence also brings in crucial intelligence and introductions to customers' friends who might be interested in a new car.

Because most new customers are introduced by a previous buyer, buying a Toyota in Japan is like joining a fraternity. Once in the family, many never consider leaving—nor would their personal salesmen give them much opportunity. Just ask Mrs. Shiraishi: "I'm very loyal to Toyota, so there was no choice."

On his rounds on this sweltering day, Mr. Saito knows he is in enemy territory, but he stops anyway at a house with a Toyota sedan parked in front. This is a customer of his former boss, "a good salesman," who now is working for a neighboring Toyota dealership that split off from Mr. Saito's. Bowing half-a-dozen times during a brief conversation, Mr. Saito apologizes for bothering the housewife. He strikes out. "We already have a strong relationship with another Toyota dealer," she explains, referring to his former boss.

Then it's on to pay a few courtesy calls on regular customers who have sent other buyers his way, including the client who just replaced his two-year-old, 12,000-mile car with another Mark II sedan—the third Mark II that he has bought from Mr. Saito in about six years. "They didn't really say they wanted one, but I know they like new cars," he says.

Once, when Mr. Saito arrived at a house and realized that both he and a Nissan salesman had been summoned at the same time, Mr. Saito fled. "I try to avoid conflict," he says. He followed up later, though, and ultimately clinched the sale.

Not surprisingly, some Japanese think the door-to-door car dealer is a relic. Japan's longest-ever recession has cut car sales for four years in a row. Some 40 percent of the dealers are bleeding red ink, their association says. Walk-in sales at dealerships have been edging up as fewer women are home to answer the door and customers seek out the latest new fad, sport-utility vehicles.

Ford Motor Co., the most aggressive of the Big Three in Japan, is trying to pull in customers the American way: mounting a media and advertising blitz aimed at enticing would-be buyers into the showroom.

Ford dealers say they don't knock on doors unsolicited, terming that tactic inefficient and costly. But trying to do things differently in Japan can be frustrating. "We need to come up with some ideas to sell more cars without door-to-door sales, but the reality is that we haven't come up with any," says Nobumasa Ogura, a Ford dealership manager in Tokyo. Several Ford dealers do visit customers who have stopped by the showroom, however.

But even some Ford dealers think that success in Japan means doing things the Japanese way, starting with offering high-enough quality to match Japanese rivals. In Japan, a country rich in public transportation, how a car drives is less important than how it looks. Cars are more like ornaments, to be washed and polished constantly but used only occasionally.

Yasutaka Ohata, manager of a Nissan dealership that now also sells Fords in Tokyo, points to a sporty black Mustang convertible on his showroom floor. He grimaces at a five-millimeter gap at the top of the driver's-side door that tapers to just three millimeters, scratchy plastic edges inside the passenger compartment, and rough surfaces inside the hood top and glove compartment. "You wouldn't find these on a Japanese car," he says. "Americans believe these kinds of things don't affect driving, but Japanese are very picky about small imperfections."

Tetsuhiko Nakamura, managing director of Ford's largest dealership, notes another problem. He says he has difficulty keeping replacement parts in stock. Getting replacement bumpers can take weeks. During this excruciatingly hot summer, Mr. Nakamura says, many customers complained because they couldn't obtain parts for their air-conditioning systems. It is precisely this replacement-parts problem that Japanese dealers cited in a recent survey as a reason for not stocking foreign autos.

Meanwhile, the door-to-door competition is getting even tougher. Japan's manufacturers are shifting factory workers—idled amid weak domestic demand and a shift of production overseas—onto the streets. Some 3,000 Nissan Motor Co. workers, for example, are now making sales calls rather than assembling cars.

"It would be great if we could just wait with an open mouth for customers to come in and feed us," says Mr. Sasakura, the spokesman for Mr. Saito's dealership, where just 20 percent of the sales are to walk-in customers. "But times are tight, and I don't foresee that happening soon."

Source: Valerie Reitman, "Toyota Calling: In Japan's Car Market, Big Three Face Rivals Who Go Door-to-Door," *The Wall Street Journal*, September 29, 1994, pp. A1, A6. Reprinted by permission of *The Wall Street Journal*, © 1994 by Dow Jones & Company, Inc. All Rights Reserved Worldwide.

CASE 1–3   EuroDisney

In April 1992, EuroDisney SCA opened its doors to European visitors. Located by the river Marne some 20 miles east of Paris, it was designed to be the biggest and most lavish theme park that Walt Disney Company (Disney) has built to date—bigger than Disneyland in Anaheim, California, Disneyworld in Orlando, Florida, and Tokyo Disneyland in Japan. In 1989, "EuroDisney" was expected to be a surefire moneymaker for its parent Disney, led by Chairman Michael Eisner and President Frank Wells. Since then, sadly, Wells was killed in an air accident in spring of 1994, and EuroDisney lost nearly $1 billion during the 1992–93 fiscal year.

Much to Disney management's surprise, Europeans failed to "go wacky" over Mickey, unlike their Japanese counterparts. Between 1990 and early 1992, some 14 million people had visited Tokyo Disneyland, with three quarters being repeat visitors. A family of four staying overnight at a nearby hotel would easily spend $600 on a visit to the park. In contrast, at EuroDisney families were reluctant to spend the $280 a day needed to enjoy the attractions of the park, including *les hamburgers* and *les milkshakes*. Staying overnight was out of the question for many because hotel rooms were so high priced. For example, prices ranged from $110 to $380 a night at the Newport Bay Club, the largest of EuroDisney's six new hotels and one of the biggest in Europe. In comparison, a room in a top hotel in Paris costs between $340 and $380 a night.

In 1994, financial losses were becoming so massive at EuroDisney that Michael Eisner had to step in personally in order to structure a rescue package. EuroDisney was put back on firm ground. A two-year window of financial peace was introduced, but not until after some acrimonious dealings with French banks had been settled and an unexpected investment by a Saudi prince had been accepted. Disney management rapidly introduced a range of strategic and tactical changes in the hope of "doing it right" this time. Analysts are presently trying to diagnose what went wrong and what the future might hold for EuroDisney.

Expansion into Europe was supposed to be Disney's major source of growth in the 1990s, bolstering slowing prospects back home in the United States. "Europe is our big project for the rest of this century," boasted Robert J. Fitzpatrick, chairman of Euro-Disney in spring 1990. The Paris location was chosen over 200 other potential sites stretching from Portugal through Spain, France, Italy, and into Greece. Spain thought it had the strongest bid based on its year-long temperate-and-sunny Mediterranean climate, but insufficient acreage of land was available for development around Barcelona.

In the end, the French government's generous incentives, together with impressive data on regional demographics, swayed Eisner to choose the Paris location. It was calculated that some 310 million people in Europe live within two hours' air travel of EuroDisney, and 17 million could reach the park within two hours by car—better demographics than at any other Disney site. Pessimistic talk about the dismal winter weather of northern France was countered with references to the success of Tokyo Disneyland, where resolute visitors brave cold winds and snow to enjoy their piece of Americana. Furthermore, it was argued, Paris is Europe's most-popular city destination among tourists of all nationalities.

According to the master agreement signed by the French government in March 1987, 51 percent of EuroDisney would be offered to European investors, with about half of the new shares being sold to the French. At that time, the project was valued at about FFr 12 billion ($1.8 billion). Disney's initial equity stake in EuroDisney was acquired for FFr 850 million (about $127.5 million). After the public offering, the value of Disney's stake zoomed to $1 billion on the magic of the Disney name.

Inducements by the French government were varied and generous:

- Loans of up to FFr 4.8 billion at a lower-than-market fixed rate of interest.
- Tax advantages for writing off construction costs.
- Construction by the French government, free of charge, of rail and road links from Paris out to the park. The TGV (*très grande vitesse*) fast train was scheduled to serve the park by 1994, along with road traffic coming from Britain through the Channel Tunnel or "Chunnel."
- Land (4,800 acres) sold to Disney at 1971 agricultural prices. Resort and property development going beyond the park itself was projected to bring in about a third of the scheme's total revenues between 1992 and 1995.

As one analyst commented, "EuroDisney could probably make money without Mickey, as a property development alone." These words would come back to haunt Disney in 1994 as real estate development plans were halted and hotel rooms remained empty, some even being closed during the first winter.

Disney had projected that the new theme park would attract 11 million visitors and generate over $100 million in operating earnings during the first year of operation. EuroDisney was expected to make a small pre-tax profit of FFr 227 million ($34 million) in 1994, rising to nearly FFr 3 billion ($450 million) in 2001. By summer 1994, EuroDisney had lost more than $900 million since opening. Attendance reached only 9.2 million in 1992, and visitors spent 12 percent less on purchases than the estimated $33 per head. European tour operators were unable to rally sufficient interest among vacationers to meet earlier commitments to fill the park's hotels, and demanded that EuroDisney renegotiate their deals. In August 1992, Karen Gee, marketing manager of Airtours PLC, a British travel agency, worried about troubles yet to come: "On a foggy February day, how appealing will this park be?" Her winter bookings at that time were dismal.

If tourists were not flocking to taste the thrills of the new EuroDisney, where were they going for their summer vacations in 1992? Ironically enough, an unforeseen combination of transatlantic airfare wars and currency movements resulted in a trip to Disneyworld in Orlando being cheaper than a trip to Paris, with guaranteed good weather and beautiful Floridian beaches within easy reach.

EuroDisney management took steps to rectify immediate problems in 1992 by cutting rates at two hotels up to 25 percent, introducing some cheaper meals at restaurants, and launching a Paris ad blitz that proclaimed "California is only 20 miles from Paris."

One of the most worrying aspects of EuroDisney's first year was that French visitors stayed away. They had been expected to make up 50 percent of the attendance figures. Two years later, Dennis Spiegel, president of the International Theme Park Services consulting firm, based in Cincinnati, framed the problem in these words: "the French see EuroDisney as American imperialism—plastics at its worst." The well-known, sentimental Japanese attachment to Disney characters contrasted starkly with the unexpected and widespread French scorn for American fairy-tale characters. French culture has its own lovable cartoon characters such as Astérix, the helmeted, pint-sized Gallic warrior who has a theme park located near EuroDisney. Parc Astérix went through a major renovation and expansion in anticipation of competition from EuroDisney.

Hostility among the French people to the whole "Disney idea" had surfaced early in the planning of the new project. Paris theater director Ariane Mnouchkine became famous for her description of EuroDisney as "a cultural Chernobyl." A 1988 book, *Mickey: The Sting,* by French journalist Giles Smadja, denounced the $350 million that the government had committed at that time to building park-related infrastructure. In fall 1989, during a visit to Paris, Michael Eisner was pelted with eggs by French communists. Finally, many farmers took to the streets to protest against the preferential sales price of local land.

Early advertising by EuroDisney seemed to aggravate local French sentiment by emphasizing glitz and size, rather than the variety of rides and attractions. Committed to maintaining Disney's reputation for quality in everything, Chairman Eisner insisted that more and more detail be built into EuroDisney.

For example, the centerpiece castle in the Magic Kingdom had to be bigger and fancier than in the other parks. He ordered the removal of two steel staircases in Discoveryland, at a cost of $200,000 to $300,000, because they blocked a view of the Star Tours ride. Expensive trams were built along a lake to take guests from the hotels to the park, but visitors prefered walking. An 18-hole golf course, built to adjoin 600 new vacation homes, was constructed and then enlarged to add another 9 holes. Built before the homes, the course cost $15- to $20 million and remains underused. Total park construction costs were estimated at FFr 14 billion ($2.37 billion) in 1989 but rose by $340 million to FFr 16 billion as a result of all these add-ons. Hotel construction costs rose from an estimated FFr 3.4 billion to FFr 5.7 billion.

EuroDisney and Disney managers unhappily succeeded in alienating many of their counterparts in the government, the banks, the ad agencies, and other concerned organizations. A barnstorming, kick-the-door-down attitude seemed to reign among the U.S. decision makers. Beatrice Descoffre, a French construction industry official, complained that "they were always sure it would work because they were Disney." A top French banker involved in setting up the master agreement felt that Disney executives had tried to steamroller their ideas. "They had a formidable image and convinced everyone that if we let them do it their way, we would all have a marvelous adventure."

Disney executives consistently decline to comment on their handling of management decisions during the early days, but point out that many of the same people complaining about Disney's aggressiveness were only too happy to sign on with Disney before conditions deteriorated. One former Disney executive voiced the opinion, "We were arrogant—it was like 'We're building the Taj Mahal and people will come—on our terms.' "

Disney and its advisors failed to see signs at the end of the 1980s of the approaching European recession. As one former executive said, "We were just trying to keep our heads above water. Between the glamour and the pressure of opening and the intensity of the project itself, we didn't realize a major recession was coming." Other dramatic events included the Gulf War in 1991, which put a heavy brake on vacation travel for the rest of that year. The fall of communism in 1989 after the destruction of the Berlin Wall provoked far-reaching effects on the world economy. National defense industries were drastically reduced among western nations. Foreign aid was requested from the West by newly emerging democracies in Eastern Europe. Other external factors that Disney executives have cited in the past as contributing to their financial difficulties at EuroDisney were high interest rates and the devaluation of several currencies against the franc.

Difficulties were also encountered by EuroDisney with regard to competition. Landmark events took place in Spain in 1992. The World's Fair in Seville and the 1992 Olympics in Barcelona were huge attractions for European tourists. In the future, new theme parks are planned for Spain by Anheuser-Busch with their $300-million Busch Gardens near Barcelona, as well as Six Flags Corporation's Magic Mountain park to be located in Marbella.

Disney management's conviction that it knew best was demonstrated by their much-trumpeted ban on alcohol in the park. This proved insensitive to the local culture because the French are the world's biggest consumers of wine. To them a meal without *un verre de rouge* is unthinkable. Disney relented. It also had to relax its rules on personal grooming of the projected 12,000 cast members, the park employees. Women were allowed to wear redder nail polish than in the U.S., but the taboo on men's facial hair was maintained. "We want the clean-shaven, neat and tidy look," commented David Kannally, director of Disney University's Paris branch. The "university" trains prospective employees in Disney values and culture by means of a one-and-a-half-day seminar. EuroDisney's management did, however, compromise on the question of pets. Special kennels were built to house visitors' animals. The thought of leaving a pet at home during vacation is considered irrational by many French people.

Plans for further development of EuroDisney after 1992 were ambitious. The initial number of hotel rooms was planned to be 5,200, more than in the entire city of Cannes on the Côte d'Azur. This number was supposed to triple in a few years as Disney opened a second theme park to keep visitors at the EuroDisney resort for a longer stay. There would also be a huge amount of office space, 700,000 square meters, just slightly smaller than France's largest office complex, La Défense in Paris. Also planned were shopping malls, apartments, golf courses, and vacation homes. EuroDisney would design and build everything itself, with a view to selling at a profit. As a Disney executive commented with hindsight, "Disney at various points could have had partners to share the risk, or buy the hotels outright. But it didn't want to give up the upside."

Disney management wanted to avoid two costly mistakes it had learned from the past: letting others build the money-making hotels surrounding a park (as happened at Disneyland in Anaheim); and letting another company own a Disney park (as in Tokyo where Disney just collects royalties). This time, along with 49 percent ownership of EuroDisney, Disney would receive both a park management fee and royalties on merchandise sales.

The outstanding success record of Chairman Eisner and President Wells in reviving Disney during the 1980s led people to believe that the duo could do nothing wrong. "From the time they came on, they had never made a single misstep, never a mistake, never a failure," said a former Disney executive. "There was a tendency to believe that everything they touched would be perfect." This belief was fostered by the incredible growth record achieved by Eisner and Wells. In the seven years before EuroDisney opened, they took Disney from being a company with $1 billion in revenues to one with $8.5 billion, mainly through internal growth.

Dozens of banks, led by France's Banque Nationale de Paris, Banque Indosuez, and Caisse des Depôts & Consignations, eagerly signed on to provide construction loans. One banker who saw the figures for the deal expressed concern. "The company was overleveraged. The structure was dangerous." Other critics charged that the proposed financing was risky because it relied on capital gains from future real estate transactions.

The Disney response to this criticism was that those views reflected the cautious, Old World thinking of Europeans who didn't understand U.S.-style free-market financing. Supporters of Disney point out that for more than two years after the initial public offering of shares, the stock price continued to do well, and that initial loans were at a low rate. It was the later cost overruns and the necessity for a bail-out at the end of the first year that undermined the initial forecasts.

Optimistic assumptions that the 1980s boom in real estate in Europe would continue through the 1990s and that interest rates and currencies would remain stable led Disney to rely heavily on debt financing. The real estate developments outside EuroDisney were supposed to draw income to help pay down the $3.4 billion in debt. That in turn was intended to help Disney finance a second park close by—an MGM Studios film tour site—which would draw visitors to help fill existing hotel rooms. None of this happened. As a senior French banker commented later in 1994, EuroDisney is a "good theme park married to a bankrupt real estate company—and the two can't be divorced."

Mistaken assumptions by the Disney management team affected construction design, marketing and pricing policies, and park management, as well as initial financing. For example, parking space for buses proved much too small. Restroom facilities for drivers could accommodate 50 people; on peak days there were 200 drivers. With regard to demand for meal service, Disney executives had been erroneously informed that Europeans don't eat breakfast. Restaurant breakfast service was downsized accordingly, and guess what? "Everybody showed up for breakfast. We were trying to serve 2,500 breakfasts in a 350-seat restaurant (at some of the hotels). The lines were horrendous. And they didn't just want croissants and coffee. They wanted bacon and eggs," lamented one Disney executive. Disney reacted quickly, delivering prepackaged breakfasts to rooms and other satellite locations.

In contrast to Disney's American parks where visitors, typically, stay at least three days, EuroDisney is at most a two-day visit. Energetic visitors need even less time. Jeff Summers, an analyst at debt broker Klesch & Co. in London, claims to have "done" every EuroDisney ride in just five hours. "There aren't enough attractions to get people to spend the night," he commented in summer of 1994. Typically, many guests arrive early in the morning, rush to the park, come back to their hotel late at night, then check out the next morning before heading back to the park. The amount of check-in and check-out traffic was vastly underestimated when the park opened; extra computer terminals were installed rapidly in the hotels.

In promoting the new park to visitors, Disney did not stress the entertainment value of a visit to the new theme park. The emphasis on the size of the park "ruined the magic," said a Paris-based ad agency executive. But in early 1993, ads were changed to feature Zorro, a French favorite; Mary Poppins; and Aladdin, star of the huge money-making movie success. A print ad campaign at that time featured Aladdin, Cinderella's castle, and a little girl being invited to enjoy a "magic vacation." A promotional package was offered—two days, one night, and one breakfast at an unnamed EuroDisney hotel—for $95 per adult and free for kids. The tagline said, "The kingdom where all dreams come true."

Early in 1994 the decision was taken to add six new attractions. In March the Temple of Peril ride opened; Storybook Land followed in May; and the Nautilus attraction was planned for June. Donald Duck's birthday was celebrated on June 9. A secret new thrill ride was promised in 1995. "We are positioning EuroDisney as the No. 1 European destination of short duration, one to three days," said a park spokesperson. Previously no effort had been made to hold visitors for a specific length of stay. Moreover, added the spokesperson, "One of our primary messages is, after all, that EuroDisney is affordable to everyone." Although new package deals and special low-season rates substantially offset costs to visitors, the overall entrance fee has not been changed and is higher than in the U.S.

With regard to park management, seasonal disparities in attendance have caused losses in projected revenues. Even on a day-to-day basis, EuroDisney management has had difficulty forecasting numbers of visitors. Early expectations were that Monday would be a light day for visitors, and Friday a heavy one. Staff allocations were made accordingly. The opposite was true. EuroDisney management still struggles to find the right level of staffing at a park where high-season attendance can be 10 times the number in the low season. The American tradition of "hiring and firing" employees at will is difficult, if not impossible, in France where workers' rights are stringently protected by law.

Disney executives had optimistically expected that the arrival of their new theme park would cause French parents to take their children out of school in midsession for a short break. It did not happen, unless a public holiday occurred over a weekend. Similarly, Disney expected that the American-style short but more frequent family trips would displace the European tradition of a one-month family vacation, usually taken in August. However, French office and factory schedules remain the same, with their emphasis on an August shutdown.

Faced with falling share prices and crisis talk among shareholders, Disney was forced to step forward in late 1993 to rescue the new park. Disney announced that it would fund EuroDisney until a financial restructuring could be worked out with lenders. However, it was made clear by the parent company, Disney, that it "was not writing a blank check."

In November 1993, it was announced that an allocation of $350 million to deal with EuroDisney's problems had resulted in the first quarterly loss for Disney in nine years.

Reporting on fourth-quarter results for 1993, Disney announced its share of EuroDisney losses as $517 million for fiscal 1993. The overall performance of Disney was not, however, affected. It reported a profit of nearly $300 million for the fiscal year ending September 30, 1993, thanks to strong performance by its U.S. theme parks and movies produced by its entertainment division. This compared to a profit of $817 million for the year before.

The rescue plan developed in fall 1993 was rejected by the French banks. Disney fought back by imposing a deadline for agreement of March 31, 1994, and even hinted at possible closure of EuroDisney. By mid-March, Disney's commitment to support EuroDisney had risen to $750 million. A new preliminary deal struck with EuroDisney's lead banks required the banks to contribute some $500 million. The aim was to cut the park's high-cost debt in half and make EuroDisney profitable by 1996, a date considered unrealistic by many analysts.

The plan called for a rights offering of FFr 6 billion (about $1.02 billion at current rates) to existing shareholders at below-market prices. Disney would spend about $508 million to buy 49 percent of the offering. Disney also agreed to buy certain EuroDisney park assets for $240 million and lease them back to EuroDisney on favorable terms. Banks agreed to forgive 18 months of interest payments on outstanding debt and would defer all principal payments for three years. Banks would also underwrite the remaining 51 percent of the rights offering. For its part, Disney agreed to eliminate for five years its lucrative management fees and royalties on the sale of tickets and merchandise. Royalties would gradually be reintroduced at a lower level.

Analysts commented that approval by EuroDisney's 63 creditor banks and its shareholders was not a foregone conclusion. Also, the future was clouded by the need to resume payment of debt interest and royalties after the two-year respite.

In June 1994, EuroDisney received a new lifeline when a member of the Saudi royal family agreed to invest up to $500 million for a 24 percent stake in the park. Prince Al-Walid bin Talal bin Abdul-Aziz Al-Saud is a well-known figure in the world of high finance. Years ago he expressed the desire to be worth $5 billion by 1998. Western-educated, His Royal Highness Prince Al-Walid holds stock in Citicorp worth $1.6 billion and is its biggest shareholder. The prince has an established reputation in world markets as a "bottom-fisher," buying into potentially viable operations during crises when share prices are low. He also holds 11 percent of Saks Fifth Avenue, and owns a chain of hotels and supermarkets, his own United Saudi Commercial Bank in Riyadh, a Saudi construction company, and part of the new Arab Radio and Television Network in the Middle East. The prince plans to build a $100-million convention center at EuroDisney. One of the few pieces of good news about EuroDisney is that its convention business exceeded expectations from the beginning.

The prince's investment could reduce Disney's stake in EuroDisney to as little as 36 percent. The prince has agreed not to increase the size of his holding for 10 years. He also agreed that if his EuroDisney stake ever exceeds 50 percent of Disney's, he must liquidate that portion.

The prince loves Disney culture. He has visited both EuroDisney and Disneyworld. He believes in the EuroDisney management team. Positive factors supporting his investment include the continuing European economic recovery, increased parity between European currencies, the opening of the Chunnel, and what is seen as a certain humbling in the attitude of Disney executives. Jeff Summers, analyst for Klesch & Co. in London, commented on the deal, saying that Disney now has a fresh chance "to show that Europe really needs an amusement park that will have cost $5 billion."

This case was prepared by Professor Lyn S. Amine and graduate student Carolyn A. Tochtrop, Saint Louis University, St. Louis, MO, as a basis for class discussion rather than to illustrate either effective or ineffective handling of a situation.

SOURCES

"An American in Paris." *Business Week,* March 12, 1990, pp. 60–61, 64.

"A Charming Prince to the Rescue?" *Newsweek,* June 13, 1994, p. 43.

"EuroDisney Rescue Package Wins Approval." *The Wall Street Journal,* March 15, 1994, pp. A3, A13.

"EuroDisney Tries to End Evil Spell." *Advertising Age,* February 7, 1994, p. 39.

"EuroDisney's Prince Charming?" *Business Week,* June 13, 1994. p. 42.

"Disney Posts Loss: Troubles in Europe Blamed." *Los Angeles Times,* November 11, 1993, pp. A1, A34.

"How Disney Snared a Princely Sum." *Business Week,* June 20, 1994, pp. 61–62.

"Mickey Goes to the Bank." *The Economist,* September 16, 1989, p. 38.

"The Mouse Isn't Roaring." *Business Week,* August 24, 1992, p. 38.

"Mouse Trap: Fans Like EuroDisney but Its Parent's Goofs Weigh the Park Down." *The Wall Street Journal,* March 10, 1994, p. A12.

"Saudi to Buy as Much as 24% of EuroDisney." *The Wall Street Journal,* June 2, 1994, p. A4.

CASE 1–4   Southwest Airlines

Wally Mills is watching the clock.

At 3:15 P.M., Southwest Airlines Flight 944 from San Diego lands, on time, at Sky Harbor International Airport here. By 3:30, Mr. Mills, a rotund crew leader, and six other Southwest ramp agents must have this plane turned around and on its way to El Paso, Texas. "I think of this as a game," says Mr. Mills. "I like to play against the [gate agents] up there working with the people to see if we can beat them."

With Indy pit-stop precision, workers attach the push-back gear to the Boeing 737, unload the Phoenix bags, load the ones for El Paso, restock the galleys, and pump aboard 4,600 pounds of fuel. A last-minute bag costs the ramp crew the race with the gate agents, who have boarded 49 passengers. Then Mr. Mills puts on a headset and prepares to direct the jet away from the gate. It is 3:29.

Mr. Mills and his team have done in less than 15 minutes what other airlines, on average, need triple the time to do. That kind of hustle isn't a fluke at Southwest: 80 percent of its 1,300 flights a day get into the air as quickly as Flight 944.

"It all boils down to Herb's corporate philosophy," says Southwest pilot Roy Martin, invoking company Chairman Herb Kelleher. "Those airplanes aren't making any money while they're sitting on the ground."

In an industry decimated by nearly three years of steep losses—about $7.5 billion in red ink, in all—Southwest has a singular distinction: It makes money. In fact, the Dallas-based carrier has been profitable for all but the first 2 of its 21 years. Last week other airlines began reporting the extent to which they were ravaged by the recession and the summer's fare war, with Delta Air Lines posting a $106.7 million loss, for instance, and American parent AMR Corp. an $85 million deficit. Only Southwest showed a third-quarter profit—up 71 percent from a year earlier to $26.9 million.

How does Southwest do it? For starters, its managers have always been financially conservative, eschewing the airline acquisitions—and debt—of the past decade. Its costs are the industry's lowest, primarily because of a classic no-frills approach to service. Drawn by bargain fares, many customers are loyal to the carrier, sometimes passing up hometown airlines or even driving hours to fly Southwest. And as competitors falter, especially here in Phoenix, in Chicago, and in California, Southwest swoops in to pick up market share.

On top of this, Southwest has a highly motivated, productive work force—and one of the most fun-loving. Its flight attendants have been known to sing safety regulations to the tune of the *William Tell Overture* and to hide in overhead luggage bins to surprise passengers. The company's top government-affairs lawyers—all men—recently threw a lunchtime luau for the headquarters staff, wearing grass skirts and coconut-shell "bras" for the occasion. Mr. Kelleher, the 61-year-old chairman, is an indefatigable prankster who arm-wrestled another chief executive earlier this year to settle a dispute over an advertising slogan. He likes to impersonate Elvis.

If you've never heard of Southwest, it's probably because you live in one of the 35 states it doesn't serve. The seventh largest U.S. carrier, with annual revenue last year of $1.31 billion, Southwest has just 2.6 percent of the nation's air-travel market. It flies only as far east as Cleveland, and its route map is dominated by a series of short hops. Travel agents won't find Southwest in any of the big reservations computers because it deems booking fees too costly. They have to get in touch with the airline.

Yet within the beleaguered airline industry, tiny Southwest has become the carrier to emulate. And as airlines try to copy various aspects of its service, even some passengers who have never flown Southwest will find their air-travel experiences changing because of the maverick's success.

"We're taking much of what Southwest is doing correctly and applying it to putting [our carrier] together," says John Anderson, who this year helped launch Kiwi Airlines in Newark, N.J. Robert Crandall, chairman of AMR and American Airlines, the nation's largest carrier, has ordered up studies on whether American should convert some flights to Southwest's bare-bones style. "Airlines of that ilk have a big-time future," he predicts.

For the passenger, flying Southwest is an entirely democratic affair. There is no first class. Seats aren't assigned. Gate agents issue reusable numbered plastic cards on a first-come, first-aboard basis. And because meals are expensive and Southwest flights are so short—55 minutes, on average—expect only peanuts and drinks (with vanilla wafers or peanut butter cookies on longer flights). Shunning meal service is the primary way Southwest keeps its ground time to a minimum.

Even with this proletarian approach, Southwest carries more than two-thirds of the passengers flying within Texas, the second largest market outside the West Coast. In California, where Southwest has become a dominant player, some San Jose residents drive an hour north to board Southwest's Oakland flights, skipping the local airport where American has a hub. Similarly, so many Atlantans were forgoing, Delta's huge base there and driving 150 miles to Birmingham, Ala., to fly Southwest that an entrepreneur started a van service between the two airports.

"Sure you get herded on the plane, and sure you only get peanuts and a drink," says Richard Spears, vice president of a Tulsa, Okla., oil research firm. "But Southwest does everything they can to get you to the right place on time, and that's most important." Indeed, Mr. Kelleher boasts of the eight times that Southwest has won the industry's triple crown—a given month's best on-time performance, lowest customer complaints, and fewest lost bags. No other airline, he notes, has won it even once.

Mr. Spears figures it's only because of Southwest that he can keep his office in Tulsa rather than Houston, where most of his clients are. "So long as Herb keeps his prices low and his planes exactly on-time," he says, "I can promise I'll be a regular."

The efficient, low-fare, high-frequency service that Mr. Spears likes would be a lot harder to achieve if Southwest didn't have such low operating costs. Its 140-plane fleet includes just one kind of aircraft—fuel-efficient Boeing 737s—keeping maintenance costs down. (Southwest recently placed a $1.2 billion order for 34 new Boeing 737s for delivery starting in 1995.)

Despite its aggressive growth, Southwest's debt, at 49 percent of equity, is the lowest among U.S. carriers. Southwest also has the industry's highest Standard & Poor's credit rating, A-minus.

The airline spends an average $43,707 a year on salary and benefits for each unionized worker, compared with Delta's $56,816 and the industry average of $45,692, according to Airline Economics Inc. Yet workers have been known to complain when they thought they weren't busy enough. Maintenance supervisors in Kansas City felt so underworked in 1985 that four of them formed the "Boredom Club," petitioning management to increase flights from three a day.

"We had two to three hours between flights, and you can only clean so much," says Kay Porter, a charter member who now works in Southwest's training department. The Boredom Club has disbanded now that Southwest has 37 flights a day into Kansas City.

Employees say they're willing to work hard because they feel appreciated and are encouraged to have fun. An orientation video for new employees is done in rap. Flight attendants have bunny costumes for Easter and wear turkey outfits on Thanksgiving and reindeer antlers at Christmas. As the official carrier to SeaWorld in San Antonio, Southwest has three planes painted to resemble Shamu, the whale.

It was flight attendant Raelene Chilcoat who used to hide in overhead bins and pop out as passengers tried to stow bags. She says she stopped after an elderly passenger grabbed his chest and called for oxygen.

By leading from the front lines, Mr. Kelleher has forged *esprit de corps* among his troops. Ms. Chilcoat recalls one crowded flight with Mr. Kelleher aboard in which the chairman put ice in the glasses while she took drink orders. In explaining the company's placid labor relations, union head Tom Burnett, who represents Southwest mechanics and cleaners, says: "Lemme put it this way. How many CEOs do you know who come into the cleaners' break room at 3 A.M. on a Sunday passing out doughnuts or putting on a pair of overalls to clean a plane?"

Debi Marchovik, a Southwest flight attendant for six years, sums up what motivates a lot of the airline's employees: "You don't want to let Herb down."

Although he is 61, questions about Mr. Kelleher's retirement or a successor are generally shrugged off at Southwest. Senior management has a tradition of longevity; Jack Vidal, vice president of maintenance, is 74. Mr. Kelleher addresses the issue with a quick "I'm immortal" before adding, more seriously, "There's plenty of life after Herb Kelleher for Southwest Airlines."

A bigger concern is that the company's recent growth spurts might change things for the worse for employees and passengers. Currently, even with 11,500 workers, Mr. Kelleher still attaches the right name to the right face most of the time. Judy Haggart, a six-year employee in the marketing department, says Mr. Kelleher asks about her son Andrew by name. But some worry that Mr. Kelleher's personal, laugh-a-minute management style won't work as well if Southwest grows too big. The airline is so concerned that it has formed a team of 44 employees from various locations to devise ways of keeping Southwest intimate.

"You have to take into account that you're getting bigger," Mr. Kelleher says, fidgeting as usual and puffing on an ever-present Barclay. "You modify your tactics, but you don't change your strategy or your basic approach."

Southwest's approach is the byproduct of a monumental legal battle that it lost but turned to its advantage. In 1974 the carrier avoided a forced move from Dallas's Love Field to the new Dallas/Fort Worth International Airport, 30 minutes farther from downtown. But in 1978, competitors sought to have Congress bar flights from Love Field to anywhere outside Texas. The airline finally was able to wangle a compromise, now known as the Wright Amendment, that allowed flights from Love Field to the four states contiguous to Texas. Thus was born the strategy of short flights that's been a key to the carrier's success.

"As long as they stick to the formula they know and the moderate pace of expansion they have planned," says Ed Greenslet, an airline consultant, "I don't think there's any inherent reason why it runs out of room to work."

In a couple of markets, Southwest has found itself growing a lot faster than planned. In Phoenix, America West Airlines cut back service, trying to conserve cash after its Chapter 11 bankruptcy filing last year. Southwest picked up the slack, as it did also in Chicago when Midway Airlines folded last November. In California, several big airlines abandoned the Los Angeles–San Francisco run after Southwest forced ticket prices down with a $59 one-way fare on routes to airports near those cities. Before Southwest arrived, fares had been as high as $186 one way.

Cities outside Southwest's route system beg for service. Sacramento Metropolitan Airport sent two county supervisors, the president of the chamber of commerce, and the airport director to Dallas early last year to beseech Mr. Kelleher to initiate service. A few months later, he did. The airline got 51 such requests in 1991.

On many routes, Southwest's fares are so low they compete with the bus, and can even coax people out of their cars. In June, Southwest started flights between Chicago and Columbus, Ohio, at $49 one way, $39 with restrictions. During last summer's fare wars, Southwest executives joked that they'd have to *raise* fares to match competitors.

Southwest officials don't joke much about a proposed high-speed train in Texas, however. The airline opposes the train, which it says would strike at the heart of its route system with an unfair advantage—government subsidies. "We just don't want to fight with a transportation company that has billions of dollars of government money invested in it, and access to more," Mr. Kelleher says. He has offered to drop his opposition if rail proponents vow to never take public money. "That's a fair fight," he says.

Mr. Kelleher, a New Jersey-born graduate of New York University law school, moved to San Antonio in 1961 with his Texas-born wife. (They met as students at Wesleyan University.) In 1966, Southwest founder Rollin King hired Mr. Kelleher as outside counsel, and he joined the board and bought an early stake in the airline. Southwest flew its first flight in 1971, and Mr. Kelleher was named president in 1978.

He currently owns 1.9 percent of the stock, worth $21.8 million. Nevertheless, several years ago an ad campaign exhorted, "Fly Southwest: Herb needs the money."

Source: Bridget O'Brian, "Flying on the Cheap: Southwest Airlines Is a Rare Air Carrier: It Still Makes Money," *The Wall Street Journal,* October 26, 1992, pp. A1, A7. Reprinted by permission of *The Wall Street Journal,* © 1992 by Dow Jones & Company, Inc. All Rights Reserved Worldwide.

EPILOGUE

Nearly three months after getting dumped, Southwest Airlines is doing just fine.

Since May, when several reservation systems eliminated the low-fare carrier's prices and schedules from most of the networks travel agents use to book tickets, Southwest's traffic has soared. In June, Southwest filled a higher percentage of its seats than during any month since August 1980, when it was one-tenth its current size in terms of revenue, which totaled $2.30 billion last year, and July traffic, to be released next week, is expected to be strong. Second-quarter earnings jumped 37 percent, and the outlook for the rest of the summer is good, the carrier says.

That's not what's expected when a commodity product has access to nearly half its distribution network blocked. Its ability to thrive despite being shut out shows the power low-fare carriers wield and reinforces the notion that in these bargain-seeking times, consumers drive the market. "In most places where Southwest operates, they have, in effect, trained their passengers to buy tickets in a certain way," says Ed Greenslet, editor and publisher of the newsletter *Airline Monitor*.

The airline is about to train its fliers further still. Starting August 22, Southwest will test a "ticketless" system among its corporate travelers and frequent fliers in four of the 41 cities it serves. Passengers flying in or out of Houston, Dallas, Corpus Christi, Texas, and Little Rock, Arkansas, can make reservations, check luggage or board their flights without a ticket; they'll get a confirmation number, as those who rent cars or book hotel rooms do, and exchange the number for a boarding pass once they reach the gate. Travel agents still will be able to book the reservations.

Even before the reservation-system brouhaha, Southwest sold only 55 percent of its tickets through travel agents, compared with the industry average of 85 percent. Indeed, with its Spartan point-to-point service and simple, refundable fares, "Southwest doesn't need travel agents," says Michael Boyd, president of Aviations Systems Research Inc., a consulting firm.

Apollo, System One, and Worldspan all delisted Southwest's fares and schedules, as well as those of about 100 other smaller or foreign carriers, saying they no longer would include airlines that don't pay them booking fees. Southwest has never paid booking fees, which average about $2.50 per round trip, except to American Airlines' Sabre system. (Southwest reluctantly joined Sabre in 1984, as part of a package agreement when it bought software for its internal reservation system from the AMR Corp. unit. Since Sabre is the biggest outside system, Southwest says it sees no reason to pay for the others.)

But the delisting came just as Southwest was attracting more imitators, including major airlines that own two of the reservations systems that dropped Southwest. "If Southwest is allowed to be a freeloader on the system," said Bill Diffenderffer, president of System One, which is owned by Continental Airlines, "then other major carriers who are competing with Southwest and contemplating the development of Southwest-like products . . . will also have to consider operating the same way Southwest does."

Continental Airlines' low-fare product, called Continental Lite, now covers half its route system. USAir Group Inc. and UAL Corp., which are part of a consortium of investors in Galileo International, which owns Apollo, are launching their own low-fare carriers. (Worldspan is owned by Delta Air Lines, Trans World Airlines, and Northwest Airlines.) The reservation systems deny any connection between the delisting and the start-up of Southwest-style service by their owners. But UAL, for one, says it expects to cut the amount it pays in travel-agency commissions on its new low-fare West Coast service by 40 percent.

Still, the timing of the delisting isn't lost on Herbert D. Kelleher, Southwest's chairman and chief executive. "They [the reservations systems] thought there were only two outcomes, in my estimation," he says. "That Southwest is going to have to become a subscriber, in which event our costs go up, and we have to increase our fares and they hurt us that way. Or we don't become a subscriber, and we'll lose an enormous amount of traffic as a consequence." Of a third possibility, that Southwest gets locked out and does just fine, Mr. Kelleher adds, "I don't believe that ever crossed their minds."

Even so, Southwest is taking no chance that its low-fare product might be lumped in with the new crop of emulators. The airline is running ads in national newspapers that spell out who was first.

Joyce Rogge, Southwest's vice president of advertising and promotion, says the company thought there was a lot of confusion in the marketplace. "We don't go on sale, our fares stay low, but people only watch for sale ads," she says.

Southwest never asked to be listed by the reservations systems, Mr. Kelleher says. "They put us in to make the product more saleable" to travel agents, he says.

To be sure, Southwest's lockout hasn't been that easy. Admittedly surprised by the move, Southwest at first scrambled to get its tickets out. Dozens of employees volunteered to stuff envelopes for a new overnight delivery service to agents who booked tickets by 5 p.m. The airline installed computer terminals at agencies that book many Southwest tickets, giving them access to the airline's internal system. The carrier's ticket-by-mail service, fine-tuned to deliver tickets in seven days instead of 10, was fine-tuned again so tickets arrive within three days. Mr. Kelleher promises that a more advanced system, using personal computers, will be tested at travel agencies by the fall.

But those efforts aren't enough to please agents who find themselves working harder for 10 percent commissions on a low-fare carrier. Asked how she's managing, agency owner Maureen Rafoul sighs deeply. "Can you quote that?" she asks. She considers the new computer a cumbersome stopgap measure because it takes extra steps. Recently, she and her partner quietly advised several clients whose accounts involve more than 40 percent of travel on Southwest to take their business elsewhere. Other agents fear taking that step. "You can't tell someone who buys a first-class trip to London that you won't sell them a $79 ticket," said Michelle O'Flynn, owner of Travel Trends, Houston.

Southwest also is benefiting from market changes sweeping travel agencies and computer-reservations systems. Several big agencies have switched systems to Sabre, which still lists Southwest, but "if they're switching now, it's probably quite coincidental," says Tom Woodall, publisher of newsletter CRS Update.

The largest agency in Seattle, a new Southwest market, says its recent conversion to Sabre was part of a national move by its parent, USTravel Inc. of Rockville, Maryland. Murdoch Travel, a large agency in Salt Lake City, will drop Worldspan at year's end in favor of Sabre, a decision made long before the delisting.

Still, such changes haven't gone unnoticed by the reservations systems, some of which have tempered their rhetoric and now are talking of Southwest like a well-liked but difficult house guest. "We'd love to find a way of embracing them, of encouraging them into the system, but at the moment we haven't," said a spokesman for Galileo International. "But we live in hope."

Source: Bridget O'Brian, *The Wall Street Journal,* August 3, 1994, p. B4. Reprinted by permission of *The Wall Street Journal,* © 1994 by Dow Jones & Company, Inc. All Rights Reserved Worldwide.

MARKETING SITUATION ANALYSIS

CHAPTER

3

Analyzing Markets and Competition

Rapid change, global competition, and the diversity of buyers' preferences in many markets require the constant attention of market watchers to see the shifting requirements of buyers, evaluate changes in competitive positioning, and spot opportunities for new products and services. A broad view of the market is important, even when interest centers on one or a few market segments. Mapping the entire market is necessary to understand and anticipate market changes and competitive threats. "Equipped with this map, a company can be in a position to examine all of the players serving the arena and anticipate what changes may occur between and among the segments of the map."[1] Defining markets and evaluating the opportunities they offer for sales and profits assist management in market targeting and positioning decisions. Market and competitor analysis (1) identifies promising business opportunities, (2) evaluates existing and potential competition, (3) guides the choice of which buyers to target, and (4) indicates the customer requirements to be satisfied by the marketing positioning strategy.

The dangers of faulty market sensing are illustrated by the experience of the Schwinn Bicycle Company. During several generations the company's products forged a strong reputation with consumers.[2] Surprisingly, management did not see the new competitive threats that developed in the 1980s. The firm's annual sales of bicycles were constant during the 1980s at 900,000 units, while industry sales nearly doubled from 6.7 million bikes in 1982 to 12.6 million in 1987. The rapid sales growth of the mountain bike was a major contributor. Schwinn's management made several mistakes, including not taking the competition seriously and not responding to changing consumer tastes. The company relied too heavily on the famous Schwinn name and was slow to innovate. Competitive advantage slipped away. Production was moved abroad to control costs, but this led to quality problems. Schwinn's market share fell from 25 percent in the 1960s to 8 percent. Dealers were attracted to competing brands. Monitoring existing and potential competitors would have alerted Schwinn's management to new market needs and competitive threats. Schwinn's loss of market position negatively impacted the firm's sales and profits. The company filed for bankruptcy in late 1992.

The chapter begins with a discussion of how to define product-markets and market boundaries. Next, we look at how buyers are described and analyzed, followed by a discussion of competitor analysis. Finally, we consider market size estimation. Additional forecasting guidelines are available in Appendix 3A.

DEFINING PRODUCT-MARKETS

Markets are defined in many different ways, and they are constantly changing, as illustrated in the Market Feature, which describes trends in food consumption. We will look at how buyer needs, coupled with product benefits, help to define product-markets, and we will discuss several considerations in forming product-markets.

Matching Needs with Product Benefits

The term *product-market* recognizes that markets exist only when there are buyers with needs who have the ability to purchase products, and products available to satisfy the needs. Intuitively, it is easy to grasp the concept of a product-market, although there are differences in how managers define the term. Markets are groups of people who have the *ability* and *willingness* to buy something because they have a need for it.[3] Ability and willingness indicate that there is a demand for a particular product or service. People with needs and wants buy the benefits provided by a good or service. A product-market matches people with needs—needs that lead to a demand for a good or service—to the product benefits that satisfy those needs. Unless the product benefits are available, there is no market—only people with needs. Likewise, there must be people who have a demand for what a given product can do for them. Thus, a product-market combines the benefits of a product with the needs that lead people to express a demand for that product. Markets are defined in terms of needs substitutability among different products and brands and by the different ways in which people choose to satisfy their needs. "A product-market is the set of products judged to be substitutes within those usage situations in which similar patterns of benefits are sought by groups of customers."[4]

By understanding how a firm's specific product is positioned within the more general product-market, management can monitor and evaluate changes to determine whether alternative targeting and positioning strategies and product offerings are needed. In defining a product-market, it is essential to establish boundaries that contain all of the relevant product categories that are competing for the same needs.

The product-market contains an interrelated group of brands (or products) whose relationships concerning need substitution and competition are strong enough so that each brand's sales are influenced by the others in the product-market.[5] The influence becomes

MARKET FEATURE   Trends in Food Consumption in the United States

Food consumption trends affect both consumers and producers. Interestingly, eating establishment expenditures are growing faster than for food consumed at home. The table shows trends since 1970 for per capita consumption of selected foods.

Several factors influence the food consumption trends including (1) age group composition and diversity of the population, (2) information on the relationship between diet and health, (3) production and processing technology, (4) income growth, and (5) the marketing efforts of industry groups and individual firms.

Per capita consumption of selected foods, pounds

	1970–79 Average	1980–89 Average	1990–92 Average	1993	1994
Beef	80.9	71.8	63.3	61.5	63.7
Pork	45.0	47.7	47.6	48.7	49.4
Chicken	28.4	36.2	44.4	48.5	49.4
Turkey	6.8	9.9	14.0	14.1	14.2
Fish and shellfish	12.4	14.2	14.8	14.9	n.a.
Eggs	36.6	33.0	30.1	30.1	30.4
Milk (gal.)	29.8	26.5	25.6	24.8	n.a.
Fats and oils	53.6	60.7	63.9	65.0	n.a.
Fresh fruit	99.4	113.1	117.6	124.3	n.a.
Fresh vegetables	147.0	155.3	165.2	170.7	n.a.
Processed fruit	24.4	22.4	23.1	22.8	n.a.
Processed vegetables	183.9	189.4	215.5	218.6	n.a.
Juice (gal.)	6.4*	7.7	7.3	8.4	n.a.
Flour and cereal products	138.0	157.3	185.3	189.2	n.a.
Caloric sweetners	124.6	129.0	141.3	147.1	n.a.

*1971–79 average.
SOURCE: U.S. Department of Agriculture.

Source: Federal Reserve Bank of Chicago, *AgLetter,* No. 1865, June 1995, pp. 1–3.

stronger the closer the substitutability and the more direct the competition. The Ford Taurus competes directly with the Toyota Camry, whereas apparel purchases compete with entertainment expenditures due to the consumer's budget constraints.

Defining Product-Market Boundaries and Structure

Market definition and analysis provide important information for developing effective business and marketing strategies. The analyses also alert management to new competition. Considering only a company's brands and its direct competitors may not indicate potential competitive threats or opportunities. A company's brands of products compete with other brands in generic, product-type, and product-variant product-markets.

Product-Market Structure.   The *generic product-market* includes a broad group of products that satisfy a general, yet similar, need. For example, several classes or types of products can be combined to form a generic product-market for kitchen appliances. The starting point in product-market definition is to determine the particular customer need or want that a group of products satisfies, such as kitchen functions. Since people with a similar need may not satisfy it in the same manner, generic product-markets are often heterogeneous, that is, they comprise different end-user groups.

The *product-type product-market* includes all brands of a particular product type or class, such as ovens or refrigerators. The product type is a product category or product classification that offers a specific set of benefits intended to satisfy a customer's need or want in a specific way. Differences in products within a product-type (class) product-market may exist, creating *product-variants.*[6] For example, there are electric, gas, and microwave ovens.

Guidelines for Definition.   It is helpful to identify the geographical boundary (or other basis of identifying buyers) of the product-market, the market size and characteristics, and the brand and/or product categories competing for the needs and wants of specific end-user groups. Suppose the management of a kitchen appliance firm wants to expand its mix of products. The present line of laundry and dishwashing products meets a generic need for the kitchen functions of cleaning. Other kitchen use situations include heating and cooling of foods. A logical expansion for the appliance firm would be to move into a closely related product type to gain the advantages of common distribution channels, manufacturing, advertising, and research and development. The Maytag Company illustrates this situation with its line of washers, dryers, and dishwashers. In the 1980s Maytag's management acquired several companies, expanding from a specialty producer into a full line of kitchen appliances, including refrigerators, stoves, and microwave ovens.

The structure of a product-market can be defined by following the steps shown in Exhibit 3–1. Let's see how this process is used in evaluating possible opportunities in the kitchen appliance product-market. In this example the generic need is performing various kitchen functions. The products that perform kitchen functions are ways of satisfying the generic need. The break out of products into specific product-markets (e.g., A, B, C, and D) would include equipment for washing and drying clothing, appliances for cooling food, cooking appliances, and dishwashers. Management can analyze the buyers in various specific product-markets and the different brands competing in these product-markets. The process of defining the product-market structure begins by identifying the generic need (function) satisfied by the product of interest to management. Need identification is the basis for selecting the products than can satisfy the need.

An illustrative product-market structure for analyzing the fast-food market is shown in Exhibit 3–2. A fast-food restaurant chain such as McDonald's should include more than its regular customers and direct competitors in the market opportunity analysis. For example, microwave oven preparation of foods affects fast-food patronage. The consumption need being satisfied is fast and convenient preparation of food. The buyer has several

---

EXHIBIT 3–1   Breaking Out Product-Market Boundaries

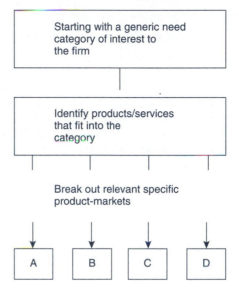

EXHIBIT 3–2   Illustrative Fast-Food Product-Market Structure

---

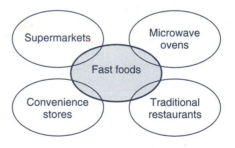

---

ways of meeting the need, including purchasing fast foods, microwave preparation in the home, patronizing supermarket delis, buying prepared foods in convenience stores, or ordering takeouts from traditional restaurants. Thus, it is essential to analyze market behavior and trends in the markets shown in Exhibit 3–2. Competition may come from any of the alternative services.

Considerations in Forming Product-Markets

The considerations that influence defining product-market boundaries include the purpose of the analysis, the changes in market composition over time, and factors affecting market complexity.

COMPETITION FEATURE   How New Competition Expands Markets

In only a few years Chile gained the second position in the world in the production of farmed salmon (165 million pounds in 1994). The growth of farmed salmon has almost doubled the world supply.

Consumers benefit via prices much lower than before (producer prices fell from $2.35 a pound in 1988 to $0.89 in 1994). Alaska's market share of world salmon sales declined from 46 percent to 32 percent over the decade.

The market was also influenced by government action. Commercial fishing interests in

Alaska obtained a state ban on fish farming. The United States placed a 24 percent import duty on Norwegian farmed salmon in response to Maine salmon farmers. These actions gave a great market opportunity to Chile and increased the U.S. trade deficit. Environmentalists have created hurdles against plans to farm salmon in Washington's Puget Sound.

Source: Nina Monk, "Real Fish Don't Eat Pellets," *Forbes,* January 30, 1995, pp. 70–71.

Purpose of Analysis.   If management is deciding whether or not to exit from a business, primary emphasis may be on financial performance and competitive position. Detailed analysis of product-market structure may not be necessary. Alternatively, if the firm is trying to find an attractive market segment to target in a product-market, a much more penetrating analysis is necessary. For example, when different products satisfy the same need, the product-market boundaries should contain all relevant products and brands. Product-market boundaries should be formed in a manner that will be of strategic value, allowing management to capitalize on existing and potential opportunities and to help avoid possible threats.

Changing Composition of Markets.   Product-market composition may change as new technologies become available and new competition emerges. New technologies offer buyers alternative ways of meeting their needs. For example, fax technology gave people in need of overnight letter delivery an alternative way to transmit the information. The entry into the market by new competitors also alters market composition. The Market Feature describes how suppliers' resistance to change and government action helped Chile develop a booming salmon industry, resulting in much lower prices for consumers and an altered competitive structure.

An existing industry classification may not properly define product-market boundaries. Industry-based definitions do not include alternative ways of meeting needs. Industry classifications, typically, have a product supply rather than a demand orientation. Of course, since industry associations, trade publications, and government agencies generate much information about products and markets, these sources should be used in the market analysis.

Factors Affecting Market Complexity.   Three aspects of markets capture a large portion of the variation in the scope of markets: (1) the *functions* or uses of the product performed by the customer, (2) the *technology* contained in the product to provide the desired function, and (3) the *customer segment* using the product to perform a particular function.[7]

Customer function considers what the product or service does. It is the benefit provided to the customer. Thus, the function satisfies the needs of the customers. Functions relate to the types of use situations each user encounters.[8] In the case of athletic shoes, the function is the type of body movement of the person wearing the shoes. Also, multiple functions/benefits may be involved. The teenager living in the large city who buys two or three pairs of sneakers a month is meeting more than a body movement need.

Different *technologies* may satisfy a customer function. Steel and aluminum meet a similar need in various use situations. A technology consists of the materials and designs incorporated into products. In the case of a service, technology relates to how the service is rendered. Fax technology delivers a letter via electronic transmission. Federal Express transports a letter by air. A courier hand carries a letter from the sender's location to the recipient.

Customer segment recognizes the diversity of the needs of customers for a particular product such as automobiles. The same model and color of a brand won't satisfy all buyers' needs and wants. Two broad market segments for automobile use are households and organizations. These classifications can be further divided into more specific customer segments, such as preferences for European-style luxury sedans, four-wheel drive vehicles, and sports cars.

It is helpful to focus on the consumer (or organizational) end-user of the product when defining the market. The end-user drives demand for the product. When the end-users' needs and wants change, the market changes. Thus, even though a manufacturer considers the distributor to which its products are sold to be the customer, the market is really defined by the consumer and organizational end-users who consume the product.

Illustrative Product-Market Structure

Suppose you are a brand manager for a cereal producer. You know that brands like Life, Product 19, and Special K compete for sales to people that want nutritional benefits from cereal. Nonetheless, our earlier discussion highlights the value of looking at a more complete picture of how competing brands like Life, Product 19, and Special K also may experience competition from other ways of meeting needs. For example, a person may decide to eat a Kellogg's Nutri-Grain cereal bar instead of a bowl of cereal, and the consumer may want to vary the type of cereal, eating a natural or regular type of cereal. Because of the different product types and variants competing for the same needs and wants, the cereal brand manager will find it useful to develop a picture of the product-market structure within which her/his brand is positioned. Exhibit 3–3 is an example of the product-market structure for cereals. It can be expanded to portray the structure of other relevant product types (e.g., breakfast bars) in the food and beverages generic product-market.

EXHIBIT 3–3   Illustrative Product-Market Structure

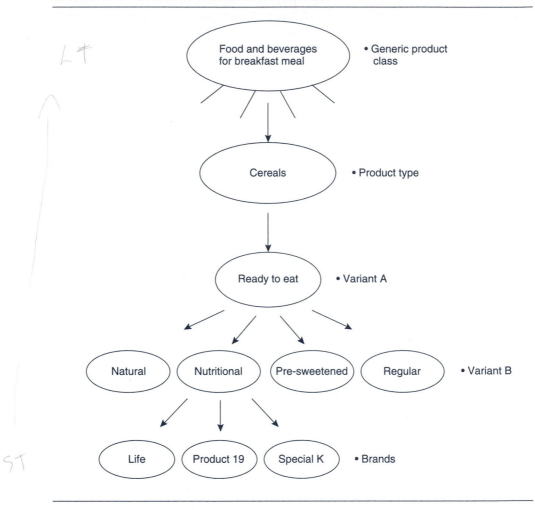

DESCRIBING AND ANALYZING END-USERS

It is useful to develop profiles of end-user buyers for the generic, product-type, and product-variant levels of the product-market. Buyers are identified, described, purchase choice criteria are indicated, and environmental influences (e.g., interest rate trends) on buyers are evaluated. We consider describing the buyers in the market segments within a product-market in Chapter 4.

Identifying and Describing Buyers

Characteristics such as family size, age, income, geographical location, sex, and occupation are often useful in identifying buyers in consumer markets. Illustrative factors used to identify end-users in business markets include type of industry, size, location, and product application. Many published sources of information are available for use in identifying and describing customers. Some examples include U.S. Census data, trade association publications, and studies by advertising media (TV, radio, magazines). When experience and existing information do not clearly identify buyers, research studies may be necessary to locate and describe customers and prospects.

A research study of supermarket customers highlights the differences among buyers in the generic product-market for foods.[9] The study was conducted for the Coca-Cola Retailing Research Council. The findings indicate that changes in cooking and eating habits have created six types of supermarket customers. Each group has different shopping needs and attitudes as described below:

Avid shoppers	Traditional supermarket customers who cook practically all family meals, shop frequently, and look for bargains (slightly more than 25 percent of total).
Kitchen strangers	Childless men and women who find cooking an inconvenience and rely instead on take-out food and restaurants (about 20 percent of total).
Constrained shoppers	Low income families and individuals who buy little but basic food needs (less than 20 percent of total).
Hurried shoppers	Busy people who mostly eat at home but look for shopping and cooking shortcuts (less than 20 percent of total).
Unfettered shoppers	Primarily older working people whose kids have flown the nest, leaving them with more disposable income to spend on food (about 13 percent of total).
Kitchen birds	Mainly very old people who are light eaters (about 6 percent of total).

The information for the study was obtained from focus groups (small group interviews), consumer surveys, trade journal reports, and retailers' experiences.

How Buyers Make Choices

Often, simply describing buyers does not provide enough information for targeting and positioning decisions. We need to try to find out *why* people buy products and brands. When considering how customers decide what to buy, it is useful to analyze how they move through the sequence of steps leading to a decision to purchase a particular brand. Buyers normally follow a decision process. They begin by recognizing a need; next, they seek information; then, they identify and evaluate alternative products; and finally, they choose a brand. Of course, this process varies by product and situation. Decisions that are repetitive and for which a buyer has past experience, tend to be routine. One part of studying buyer decision processes is finding out what criteria people use in making decisions. For example, how important is the brand name of a product in the purchase decision?

Environmental Influences

The final step in building customer profiles is to identify external factors that influence buyers. These influences include the government, social change, economic shifts, technology, and other environmental factors that alter buyers' needs and wants. Typically, these factors are not controlled by the buyer or the firms that market the product. Substantial changes in these influences can have a major impact on customers. Therefore, it is important to identify the relevant external influences on a product-market and to estimate their future impact. During the past decade various changes in market opportunities occurred as a result of uncontrollable environmental factors. Illustrations include the shifts in age-group composition, changes in tax laws affecting investments, and variations in interest rates. Consider, for example, the population trends for the 50 states in the United States from 1990 to 2000. Some states (Exhibit 3–4) have high growth rates while others have declined in size.

Building Customer Profiles

The profiling process starts with the generic product-market. The earlier discussion of the six types of supermarket customers illustrates the information often included in the customer profile. Of course, a complete profile has much more detail. The product-type and variant profiles are similar to the generic profiles, although they are more specific about customer characteristics (needs and wants, use situations, activities and interests, opinions, purchase processes and choice criteria, and uncontrollable influences on buying decisions). Normally, product-type analysis considers the organization's product and closely related product types.

The marketing strategy issue is deciding which buyers to target within generic, product-type, and product-variant markets, and how to position to each target. The profiles help marketing management make these decisions. More comprehensive analyses are often undertaken in market segmentation analysis which we discuss in Chapter 4.

ANALYZING THE COMPETITION

Analyzing the competition follows the five steps shown in Exhibit 3–5. We begin by defining the industry structure in which an organization competes and describing the characteristics of the industry. Steps two and three identify, describe, and evaluate the organization's key competitors. Steps four and five consider competitors' future actions and identify potential competitors that may enter the market.

EXHIBIT 3–4 Projected Percent Change in State Populations: 1990 to 2000

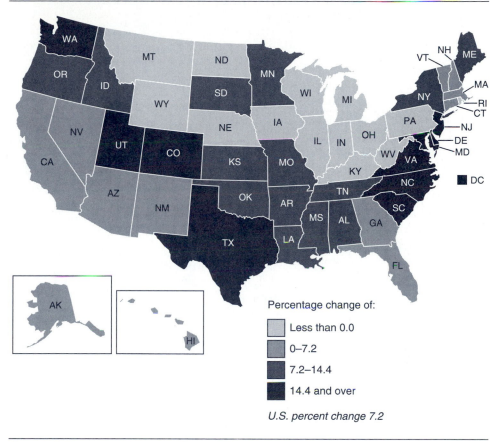

Percentage change of:

- Less than 0.0
- 0–7.2
- 7.2–14.4
- 14.4 and over

U.S. percent change 7.2

Source: U.S. Department of Commerce, Bureau of Census.

Defining the Competitive Arena

Competition often includes more than the firms that are direct competitors, like Coke and Pepsi. Exhibit 3–6 shows the different levels of competition for diet colas. The product form (variant) is the most direct form of competition. Nevertheless, other product category soft drinks also compete for buyers, as do various beverages. A complete understanding of the competitive arena helps to guide strategy design and implementation. Since competition often occurs within specific industries, an examination of industry structure is important in defining the competitive arena.

The competitor analysis is conducted from the point of view of a particular firm. For example, a soft drink producer such as Coca-Cola should include other beverage producers in its industry analysis. This analysis looks at two kinds of information: (1) a description of the industry and (2) an analysis of the distribution channels that link

---

EXHIBIT 3–5   Analyzing Competition

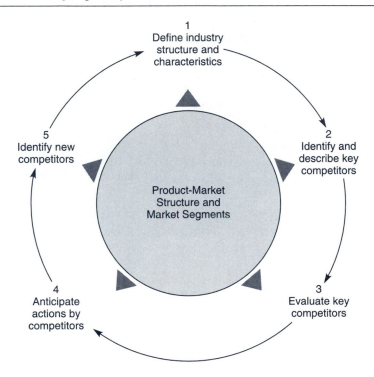

---

together the various organizations in the value-added system serving end-users. The industry study is a horizontal analysis covering similar types of firms (e.g., soft drink producers), whereas the distribution channel analysis focuses on the vertical value-added system of firms that supply materials and/or parts, produce products (and services), and distribute the products to end-users.

The soft drink market in Japan is an interesting competitive arena. As many as 1,000 new products are introduced each year by national and international companies, regional producers, and private label suppliers. Vending machines are popular, offering 20 different brands. Coca-Cola Japan alone operates 700,000 vending machines. Colas comprise about 10 percent of the Japanese beverage market (see Coca-Cola Japan case).

Industry Analysis.   The information needed for an industry analysis includes: (1) industry characteristics and trends, such as sales, number of firms, and growth rates, and (2) operating practices of the firms in the industry, including product mix, service provided, barriers to entry, and geographical scope.

First, we need to identify the companies that comprise the industry and develop descriptive information on the industry and its members. It is useful to examine industry structure beyond domestic market boundaries, since international industry developments

EXHIBIT 3-6 Example of Levels of Competition

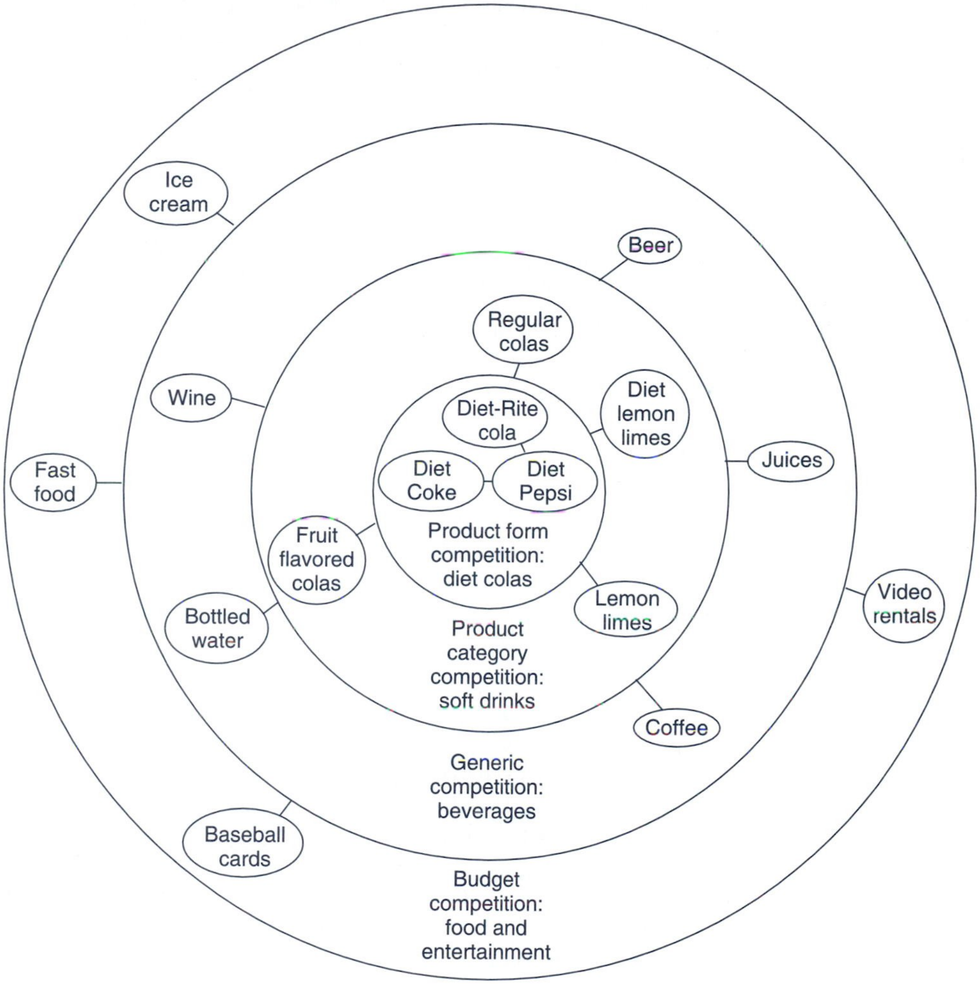

Source: Donald R. Lehmann and Russell S. Winer, *Analysis for Marketing Planning,* 2nd ed. (Burr Ridge, IL: Richard D. Irwin, 1991), p. 22.

may affect regional, national, and international markets. For example, the Free Trade Agreement between Canada and the United States created a wave of cross-border consolidations. The two countries before free-trade were the world's largest trading partners, conducting some $150 billion in trade each year with each other.[10] Further changes in industry structure and composition will continue in the future. Total exports by the United States should reach $1 trillion in 1998, with over half of sales to Europe, Canada, and Japan. General Motors is the top U.S. exporter.

The industry definition is based on the organization conducting the market analysis. Thus, an automobile producer should look at the industry comprised of automobile producers. The industry identification is based on product similarity, location at the same level in the channel of distribution (e.g., manufacturer, distributor, retailer) and geographical scope. The industry analysis includes:

- Industry size, growth, and composition.
- Typical marketing practices.
- Industry changes that are anticipated.
- Industry strengths and weaknesses.
- Strategic alliances among competitors.

Analysis of the Value-Added System.   A study of supplier and distribution channels is important in understanding and serving product-markets. While in some instances producers go directly to their end-users, many work with other organizations through distribution channels. The extent of vertical integration by competitors backward (supply) and forward toward end-users is also useful information. The types of relationships (collaborative or transactional) in the distribution channel should be identified and evaluated. Different channels that access end-user customers should be included in the channel analysis. For example, vending machines comprise an important distribution channel in Japan. By looking at other distribution approaches, we can identify important patterns and trends in serving end-users. Distribution analysis can also uncover new market opportunities that are not served by present channels of distribution. Finally, information from various distribution levels can help in forecasting end-user demand.

Analysis of the value added system considers important trends (e.g., supplier consolidation), relative power of organizations at different levels in the system, and possible changes in the system. It is important to identify different value-added systems used by other firms in the industry to move materials and supplies to producers and producers' products to consumer and organizational end-users. These variations in value-added systems may indicate potential opportunities or threats for the organization conducting the competitor analysis.

Competitive Forces.   Porter offers a useful framework for examining competitive forces in the value-added system. The traditional view of competition is expanded by recognizing five competitive forces that determine industry performance:

1. Rivalry among existing firms.
2. Threat of new entrants.
3. Threat of substitute products.
4. Bargaining power of suppliers.
5. Bargaining power of buyers.[11]

The first force recognizes that active competition among firms helps determine industry performance. This is the most direct and intense form of competition. Rivalry may occur within a market segment or across an entire product-market. The nature and scope of competition may vary according to the type of industry structure. For example, competition in an emerging industry consists of the market pioneer and a few other early entrants.

The second force highlights the possibility of new competitors entering the market. Existing firms may try to discourage new competition by aggressive expansion and other types of entry barriers. IBM's 1995 proposed acquisition of Lotus Development Corp. is an interesting entry strategy in the software market. This move indicates IBM's intent to compete with Microsoft, the software giant.

The third force considers the potential impact of substitutes. New technologies that satisfy the same customer need are important sources of competition. Including alternative technologies in the definition of product-market structure identifies substitute forms of competition. Western Union's failure to recognize the competitive threat posed by fax machines is an example of the dangers of defining competitive boundaries too narrowly.

The fourth force is the power that suppliers may have on the producers of an industry. For example, the high costs of labor and aircraft exert a major impact on the commercial airline industry. Companies may pursue vertical integration strategies to reduce the bargaining power of suppliers. Alternatively, collaborative relationships respond to the needs of both partners. The emphasis on quality improvement by many producers is strengthening cooperation between suppliers and their customers and reducing the number of suppliers servicing manufacturers.

Finally, buyers may use their purchasing power to influence their suppliers. Wal-Mart, for example, has a strong influence on the suppliers of its many products. Understanding which organizations have power and influence in the distribution channel provides important insights into the structure of competition. Power may be centered at any level in the channel, though producers and retailers often display strong buying power.

A major consequence of Porter's view of competition is that the competitive arena may be altered as a result of the impact of the five forces on the industry. The five competitive forces also highlight the existence of vertical and horizontal types of competition. Horizontal competition consists of rivalry among firms in the same industry, such as personal computer producers. Vertical competition involves rivalry among and within distribution channels. The intensity of vertical competition is related, in part, to the bargaining power of suppliers and buyers. The location (level) of an organization in its distribution channel and the extent of its control over the channel may affect the marketing strategy.

The intense competition between Reebok and Nike in the sneaker market offers interesting insights about channel of distribution power.[12] Foot Locker's 2,800 stores account for nearly one-fourth of U.S. sneaker sales. Nike has worked aggressively in building a collaborative relationship with Foot Locker while Reebok has been less responsive to this key sneaker customer. Customers with buying power like Foot Locker want better terms, advance information on new products, exclusive lines, and fast response to orders. Nike's sales in 1995 to Foot Locker were $620 million, compared to less than $200 million for Reebok. Only two years earlier Nike sold $550 million to Foot Locker compared to Reebok's $228 million (see the accompanying Nike advertisement).

1-800-645-6023

Courtesy of Nike, Inc.

Key-Competitor Analysis

Competitor analysis is conducted for directly competing firms (e.g., Nike and Reebok) and other companies that management may consider important in strategy analysis (e.g., potential market entrants). The priority companies place on competitor analysis is apparent from a Conference Board survey of the strategic practices of 214 companies in various size groups covering manufacturing, distribution, and service industries:

> The use of competitive intelligence, competitor analysis, and new techniques for gaining a competitive edge has been a major factor in developing strategies over the past five years, according to the survey results. This is exemplified by a large insurance company's planning director, who remarks: "We now watch with varying degrees of interest about 200 competitors, most of which were never considered competitors four years ago. We used to watch about five companies."[13]

Nearly half of the surveyed firms had revised their competitive intelligence procedures, compared to the prior five years. Much greater emphasis is placed on monitoring, analyzing, and evaluating competitors and specific industry environments.

The process of key competitor analysis begins with: (1) preparing the descriptive profile for each competitor and (2) evaluating the competitor's strengths and weaknesses (steps 2 and 3 of Exhibit 3–5).

EXHIBIT 3–7   Information Needed for Describing Key Competitors

---

- Business scope and objectives
- Management experience, capabilities, and weaknesses
- Market position and trends
- Market target(s) and customer base
- Marketing program positioning strategy
- Financial, technical, and operating capabilities
- Key competitive advantages (e.g., access to resources, patents)

Describing the Competitor.   A *key competitor* is a firm going after the same market target as the firm conducting the analysis. American, Delta, and United Airlines are key competitors on many U.S. routes. Key competitors are often brands that compete in the same product-market or segment(s) within the market. Different product types that satisfy the same need or want may also actively compete against each other. For example, surgical stapling equipment competes with needle and suture closure procedures.

A checklist of information included in the competitor profile is shown in Exhibit 3–7. Sources of information include annual reports, industry studies by government and private organizations, business magazines and newspapers, trade publications, company reports by financial analysts (e.g., *Value Line Investment Survey*), government reports, standardized data services (e.g., Information Resources, Inc., and Nielsen), databases, suppliers, customers, and salespeople.

It is important to gain as much knowledge as possible about the background, experience, and qualifications of key executives of each major competitor. This information includes the executives' performance records, their particular areas of expertise, and the types of firms where they were previously employed. These analyses may suggest future strategies of a key competitor. Business and industry publications and newspapers are useful sources of this information for executives who work in large firms. Other sources include suppliers, customers, and marketing channel organizations.

The descriptive profile of a competitor includes a historical picture of management's marketing decisions. Past decisions show the pattern of changes in marketing strategy and tactics as management responded to changing market conditions. Analysis of these decisions should attempt to match them with specific changes taking place in markets or with competitors. An experienced marketer can then develop a feel for the management style of the key competitor by looking for patterns or consistencies in these decisions.

Evaluating the Competitor.   Although competitor description and evaluation are interrelated, it is useful to separate the two activities. Evaluation shows the strengths and weaknesses of each competitor in the four areas shown in Exhibit 3–8.

Market coverage analysis centers on the market segments targeted by the competitor and the competitor's actual and relative market-share position. Relative market position is measured by comparing the share of the firm against the competitor with the highest

---

EXHIBIT 3–8   Evaluation of the Competition

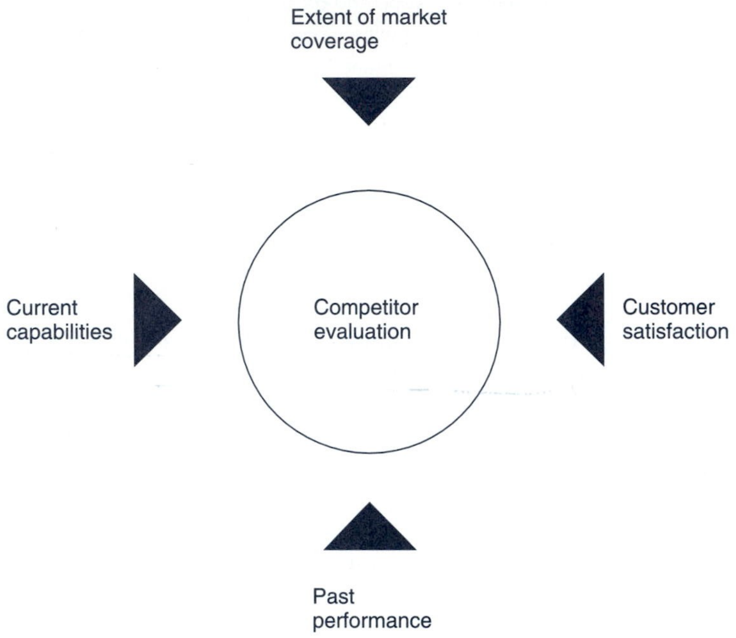

Extent of market
coverage

▼

Current
capabilities   ▶   Competitor
evaluation   ◀   Customer
satisfaction

▲

Past
performance

---

market share in the segment. All segments in the product-market that could be targeted by the firm should be included in the competitor evaluation. Consider, for example, the brand positioning map shown in Exhibit 3–9. The map was used by Chrysler Corporation to evaluate possible positioning opportunities. The upper-right quadrant offers a possible position for Chrysler and other U.S. automobile manufacturers. Honda introduced the Acura Legend in 1986 to compete in this quadrant. A few years later Toyota introduced the successful Lexus 400. This analysis suggests segments where competitors are not providing market coverage and alerts a firm to potential new competition.

The Industry Feature describes competition in the ready-to-eat cereal market. Kellogg and General Mills dominate the market with a combined market share of 66 percent.

The starting point in assessing how well competitors meet customer needs is finding out what criteria buyers use to rate each supplier. Customer-focused measures of customer satisfaction are more useful than relying on management judgments of satisfaction. Measurement methods include customer comparisons of attributes of the firm versus its competitors, customer satisfaction surveys, loyalty measures, and the relative market share of end-use segments.[14] Preference maps like the one shown in Exhibit 3–9 are useful in comparing the competing brands for attributes that are important determinants of customer satisfaction.

An analysis of each competitor's past sales and financial performance indicates how well the competitor has performed on a historical basis. A typical period of analysis is five

---

EXHIBIT 3–9   Analyzing Market Coverage for Automobile Brands

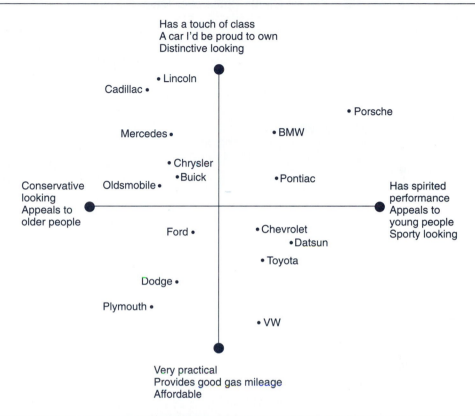

Source: John Koten, "Car Makers Use 'Image' Map as Tool to Position Products," March 22, 1984. Reprinted by permission of *The Wall Street Journal*, © 1984 by Dow Jones & Company, Inc. All rights reserved worldwide.

years or longer depending on the rate of change in the market. Performance information may include sales, market share, net profit, net profit margin, cash flow, and debt. Additionally, for specific types of businesses other performance information may be useful. For example, sales per square foot is often used to compare the performance of retail stores. Operating cost per passenger mile is used in airline comparisons.

Determining market coverage, customer satisfaction, and past performance supplies useful information about competitors. Using this information, we can develop an overall evaluation of the key competitor's current strengths and weaknesses. Additionally, the summary assessment of current capabilities includes information on the competitor's management capabilities and limitations, technical and operating advantages and weaknesses, marketing strategy, and other key strengths and limitations. Since competitors often have different capabilities, it is important to highlight these differences. A checklist for evaluating competitor strengths and weaknesses is shown in Exhibit 3–10.

INDUSTRY FEATURE   Cereal Giants Battle over Market Share

The ready-to-eat cereal market illustrates the intense competitive battles for market share that occur in many consumer markets. Kellogg holds the top position in this $7.5 billion-a-year market (see chart).

- Kellogg and General Mills are using aggressive advertising, sales promotion, and pricing strategies and tactics, making it tough for the small competitors.

- Kellogg spent an estimated $100 million *more* on marketing in the third quarter of 1991 compared to 1990.

- Holding a market share of 1 percent ($75 million in sales) is significant with profit margins at 20 percent or more.

- Cereals are important for supermarkets since cereals are the second-largest-selling branded food item after soft drinks.

- The name-brand cereals also compete against the retailer's private-label products, offered at substantially lower prices (e.g., $1.69 versus $3.26).

- A stream of new products is introduced to target market segments and maintain market momentum.

Source: Richard Gibson, "Cereal Giants Battle over Market Share," *The Wall Street Journal*, December 16, 1991, pp. B1, B4. Reprinted by permission of *The Wall Street Journal*, © 1991 Dow Jones & Company, Inc. All Rights Reserved Worldwide.

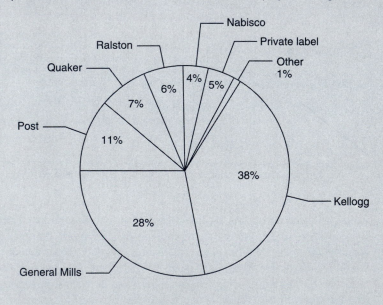

Anticipating Competitors' Actions

Step 4 in competitor analysis (Exhibit 3–5) considers what each key competitor may do in the future, but we also need to identify potential competitors (Step 5). The information obtained in the previous steps of the analysis is helpful in estimating future trends.

EXHIBIT 3–10 Areas of Evaluation of Competitor Strengths and Weaknesses

---

- Sales and market position in segments served
- Level of customer satisfaction
- Business approach (price, quality, service, aggressiveness)
- Financial performance (current and historical)
  —net profit/sales ratio
  —return on investment
  —number of employees
  —facilities
- Financial resources and leverage
- Cost position relative to key competitors
- Relative product quality
- Innovativeness
- Product portfolio
- Management capabilities
- Marketing strategy and effectiveness
- Methods of distribution
- Summary of key strengths and weaknesses

Estimating Competitors' Future Strategies.   Competitors' future strategies may continue the directions that they have established in the past, particularly if no major external influences require changing their strategies. Nevertheless, assuming an existing strategy will continue is not wise. Competitors' current actions may signal probable future actions.

Recall our discussion of SMH's Swatch line of watches in Chapter 1. Swatch's strong market position was threatened by new competitors. By 1995 it was clear that Timex would continue its aggressive new product and promotion strategy aimed at expanding its market position at the expense of Swatch.[15] Timex launched an array of new brands, including licensing the Nautica, Joe Boxer, and Timberland brand names, and offered the new $40 Expedition line. Failure to anticipate Timex's response to Swatch's market success created serious problems for Swatch in the U.S. market. By the early 1990s the number of retailers carrying Swatch had declined while consumer tastes shifted from plastic to metal watches. Swatch's market sensing was faulty. To counter competition Swatch's 1995 advertising budget was over 12 times larger than in previous years, and new watch designs were introduced.

Identifying New Competitors.   New competitors often come from three major sources: (1) companies competing in a related product-market, (2) companies with related technologies, and/or (3) companies already targeting similar customer groups with other products. Market entry by a new competitor is more likely under these conditions:

- High profit margins are being achieved by market incumbents.
- Future growth opportunities in the market are attractive.

- No major market-entry barriers are present.
- Competition is limited to one or a few competitors.
- Gaining an equivalent (or better) competitive advantage over the existing firm(s) serving the market is feasible.

If one or more of these conditions is present in a competitive situation, new competition will probably appear.

During the mid-1970s Tylenol held most of the nonaspirin pain relief market. Tylenol's profits were very large, and its marketing costs were low for a consumer product. No consumer advertising had been used to promote Tylenol. Instead, promotion efforts were concentrated in medical and dental professional publications and sales force contacts with doctors. Because of the large market opportunity, the attractive profit margins, the market dominance by one firm, and the ease of product duplication, the entry of a new competitor was not surprising. Datril entered the market with an aggressive advertising campaign and prices substantially below Tylenol's. Tylenol's management immediately reduced its prices to meet Datril's. Interestingly, a decade later Tylenol dominated the market. Even the cyanide deaths in 1983, which were attributed to tampering with Tylenol packages, failed to topple Tylenol from its strong market position. A responsive effort was made to immediately recall Tylenol from store shelves and implement protective packaging.

MARKET SIZE ESTIMATION

An important part of market opportunity analysis is estimating the present and potential size of the market. Market size is usually measured by dollar sales and/or unit sales for a defined product-market and specified time period. Other size measures include the number of buyers, average purchase quantity, and frequency of purchase. Three key measures of market size are: *market potential, sales forecast,* and *market share.*

Market Potential

Market potential is the maximum amount of product sales that can be obtained from a defined product-market during a specified time period. It includes the total opportunity for sales by all firms serving the product-market. Market potential is the upper limit of sales that can be achieved by all firms for a generic, product-type, or product-variant product-market. Often, actual industry sales fall somewhat below market potential because the production and distribution systems are unable to completely meet the needs of all buyers who are both *willing* and *able* to purchase the product during the period of interest.

Sales Forecast

The sales forecast indicates the expected sales for a defined product-market during a specified time period. The industry sales forecast is the total volume of sales expected by all firms serving the product market. The sales forecast can be no greater than market potential and, typically, falls short of potential, as discussed above. A forecast can be made for total sales at any product-market level (generic, product-type, variant) and for specific subsets of the product-market (e.g., market segments). A sales forecast can also be made for sales expected by a particular firm.

An interesting forecasting situation is estimating the growth in sales for a product in a country where present market penetration is very low. Consider, for example, projecting the number of new telephone lines in India from 1994 to 2000. In 1994 the number of telephone lines as a percentage of the population was only 1 percent in India.[16] The potential for sales is huge as India's consumers increase their ability to buy. It is likely that the number of telephone lines will grow rapidly. One forecast is that the fewer than 10 million new lines in 1994 will increase to 24 million by 2000.

Market Share

Company sales divided by total sales of all firms for a specified product-market determines the market share of a particular firm. Market share is calculated on the basis of actual sales or forecasted sales. Market share can be used to forecast future company sales and to compare actual market position among competing brands of a product. Market share may vary depending on the use of dollar sales or unit sales due to price differences across competitors.

Exhibit 3–11 shows the relationships among the different estimates. Industrial painting units are used to apply paint for industrial applications such as buildings and equipment. The line at the top of the chart shows the market potential from 1990 to 1996 and an estimate of potential for 1997. The next line is industry sales trend and the 1997 forecast. The difference between potential and the industry sales is the amount of unrealized potential. The third line shows the company sales and the forecast. Dividing company sales by the industry sales forecast yields the market share (actual or forecast). Comparison of competitor and industry sales results and forecasts with company sales information should be made with caution. Sales and forecasts may vary due to differences in product-market definition, product type, time period, and channel of distribution level (wholesale versus retail).

Evaluating Market Opportunity

It is essential in preparing forecasts to specify exactly what is being forecasted (defined product-market), the time period involved, and the geographical area. Otherwise, comparisons of sales and market share with those of competing firms will not be meaningful. Several operational problems may occur in forecasting as a result of differences in measures of sales (e.g., dollars versus units), problems in defining the relevant market, leads and lags in product movement through distribution channels, promotional pricing practices, and the handling of intracompany transfers.[17] Additional forecasting guidelines are provided in the Appendix to Chapter 3.

Since a company's sales depend, in part, on its marketing plans, forecasts and marketing strategy are closely interrelated. Forecasting involves what-if analyses. Alter-

EXHIBIT 3–11   Product-Market Forecast Relationships for Industrial Painting Units

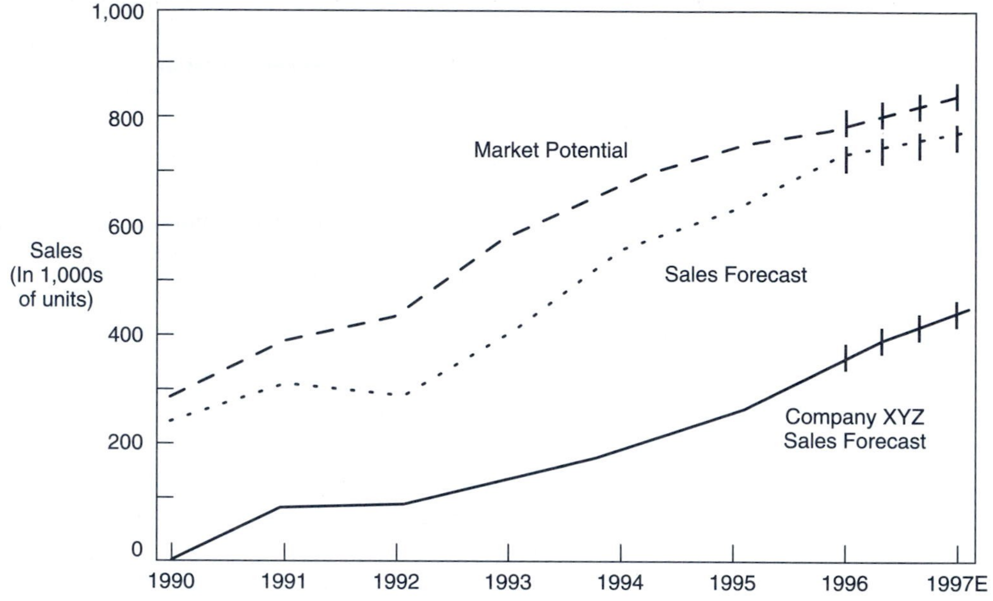

native positioning strategies (product, distribution, price, and promotion) must be evaluated for their estimated effects on sales. Because of the marketing effort/sales relationship, it is important to consider both potential and planned marketing expenditures in determining the forecast. Also important is considering the variation in production and other marketing distribution costs for alternative sales forecasts. The impact of different sales forecasts must be evaluated from a total business perspective. These forecasts affect production planning, human resource needs, and financial requirements.

The global market for personal computers in households is an interesting market potential and forecasting application. Rapidly declining prices and software availability are stimulating sales around the world. Penetration of PCs in households is shown in Exhibit 3–12. Taiwan's Acer Group estimates sales outside the United States to account for 40 percent of its total sales in 1996 compared to 20 percent in 1995.[18] One estimate of total industry sales in 2000 for Asia and Europe is 25 million units, compared to 16 million units in the United States. Other forecasters are more conservative but acknowledge the huge sales opportunities in many countries around the world.

The demise of Grandmother Calendar Company illustrates the critical importance of sales forecasts in the business planning of small companies.[19] While personalized photo calendars are not new, Harvey Harris, who founded the company, offered an array of options in the calendar kits sold by retailers. Priced at $20 ($5 under competitors),

---

EXHIBIT 3–12 Global Household Penetration of Personal Computers

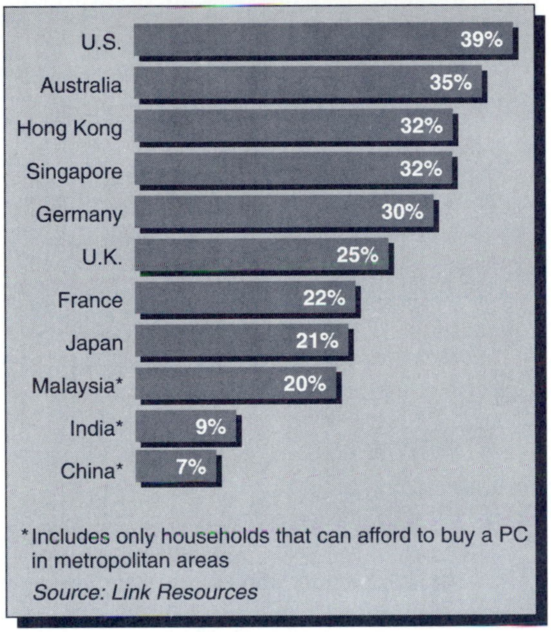

U.S.	39%
Australia	35%
Hong Kong	32%
Singapore	32%
Germany	30%
U.K.	25%
France	22%
Japan	21%
Malaysia*	20%
India*	9%
China*	7%

*Includes only households that can afford to buy a PC in metropolitan areas

Source: Link Resources

Source: Jim Carlton, "Foreign Markets Give PC Makers a Hearty Hello," *The Wall Street Journal,* September 15, 1995, p. B8. Reprinted by permission of *The Wall Street Journal,* © 1995 Dow Jones & Company, Inc. All Rights Reserved Worldwide.

retailers signed on and consumers bought the kits, selected their options, and sent them to Grandmother Calendar for Processing. Without giving much thought to how much business the company could handle, Harris offered the kits to major chains, catalog companies, and thousands of other retailers. One catalog company sold 25,000 kits in six months, compared to a forecast of 8,000. Grandmother Calendar increased its output to 300 calendars a day but was receiving 1,000 orders a day. Success killed the company. Harvey ran out of operating capital and couldn't expand fast enough to meet the demand. Planning and forecasting could have limited initial distribution, allowing management market feedback to better forecast sales.

Sales forecasts of target markets are needed so that management can estimate the financial attractiveness of both new and existing market opportunities. The market potential and growth estimates gauge the overall attractiveness of the market. The sales forecast for the company's brand in combination with cost estimates provides a basis for profit projections. The decision to enter a new market or to exit from an existing market depends heavily on financial analyses and projections. Alternative market targets under consideration can be compared using sales and profit projections. Similar projections of key competitors are also useful in evaluating market opportunities.

SUMMARY

Analyzing markets and competition are essential to making sound business and marketing decisions. The uses of product-market analyses are many and varied. An important aspect of market definition and analysis is moving beyond a product focus by incorporating market needs into the analysts' viewpoint.

This chapter has examined the nature and scope of product-market structure. By using different levels of aggregation (generic, product-type, and product-variant), products and brands are positioned within more aggregate categories, thus helping to better understand customers, product interrelationships, industry structure, distribution approaches, and key competitors. The approach to product-market analysis offers a consistent guide to needed information, regardless of the type of product-market being analyzed. Analyzing market opportunity includes (1) defining product-markets, (2) describing and analyzing end-users, (3) conducting industry and value added system analyses, (4) evaluating key competitors, and (5) estimating market size and growth rates.

After determining the product-market boundaries and structure, information on various aspects of the market is collected and examined. First, it is important to study the people or organizations that are the end-users in the product-market at each level (generic, product type, and variant). These market profiles of customers are useful in evaluating opportunities and guiding market targeting and positioning strategies. Next, is identification and analysis of the firms that market products and services at each product-market level aid strategy development. Industry and key competitor analysis considers the firms that compete with the company performing the market opportunity analysis. Thus, industry analysis for a producer would include the producers that make up the industry. The analysis should also include firms operating at all stages in the value-added system, such as suppliers, manufacturers, distributors, and retailers.

The next step is a comprehensive assessment of the major competitors. The key-competitor analysis should include both actual and potential competitors that management considers important. Competitor analysis includes: (1) describing the company, (2) evaluating the competitor, and (3) anticipating the future actions of competitors. It is also important to identify possible new competitors. Competitor analysis is an ongoing activity and requires coordinated information collection and analysis. Increasingly, corporations and business units are using competitor intelligence systems for this purpose.

An important part of product-market analysis is estimating potential and forecasting sales. The forecasts often used in product-market analysis include estimates of market potential, sales forecasts of total sales by firms competing in the product-market, and sales forecast for the firm of interest. This information is needed for various purposes and is prepared for different units of analysis, such as type of product, brands, and geographical areas. The forecasting approach and techniques should be matched to the organization's needs. Forecasting methods are examined in the Appendix.

QUESTIONS FOR REVIEW AND DISCUSSION

1. Discuss the important issues that should be considered in defining the product-market for a totally new product.

2. Under what product and market conditions is the consumer more likely to make an important contribution to product-market definition?

3. What recommendations can you make to the management of a company competing in a rapid growth market to help it identify new competitive threats early enough so that counterstrategies can be developed?

4. There are some dangers in concentrating product-market analysis only on a firm's specific brand and those brands that compete directly with a firm's brand. Discuss.

5. Using the approach to product-market definition and analysis discussed in the chapter, select a brand and describe the generic, product type, and brand product-markets of which the brand is a part.

6. For the brand selected in Question 5, indicate the kinds of information needed in order to conduct a complete product-market analysis. Suggest sources for obtaining each type of information.

7. Select an industry and describe its characteristics, participants, and structure.

8. A competitive analysis of the 7UP soft drink brand is being conducted. Management plans to position the brand against its key competitors. Should the competitors consist of only other noncola drinks?

9. Outline an approach to competitor evaluation, assuming you are preparing the analysis for a regional bank holding company.

10. Discuss how a small company (less than $1 million in sales) should analyze its competition.

11. Many of the popular forecasting techniques draw from past experience and historical data. Discuss some of the more important problems that may occur in using these methods.

NOTES

1. William E. Rothschild, "Surprise and Competitive Advantage," *Journal of Business Strategy,* Winter 1984, p. 10.

2. This example is based on Timothy L. O'Brien, "Beleaguered Schwinn Seeks Partner to Regain Its Luster," *The Wall Street Journal,* May 20, 1992, p. B2.

3. This discussion is based upon suggestions provided by Professor Robert B. Woodruff of the University of Tennessee, Knoxville.

4. Rajendra K. Srivastava, Mark I. Alpert, and Allan D. Shocker, "A Customer-Oriented Approach for Determining Market Structures," *Journal of Marketing,* Spring 1984, p. 32.

5. Frank M. Bass, Charles W. King, and Edward A. Pessemier, *Applications of the Sciences in Marketing Management* (New York: John Wiley, 1968), p. 252.

6. George S. Day, *Strategic Marketing Planning: The Pursuit of Competitive Advantage* (St. Paul, MN: West Publishing, 1984), p. 72.

7. Derek F. Abell, *Defining the Business: The Starting Point of Strategic Planning* (Englewood Cliffs, NJ: Prentice Hall, 1980).

8. George S. Day, "Strategic Market Analysis: A Contingency Perspective" (Working Paper, University of Toronto, July 1979).

9. Alan L. Otten, "People Patterns," *The Wall Street Journal,* June 13, 1989, p. B1.

10. "The North American Shakeout Arrives Ahead of Schedule," *Business Week,* April 17, 1989, pp. 34–35. See also James Aley, "New Lift for the U.S. Export Boom," *Fortune,* November 13, 1995, pp. 73, 74, 76, and 78.

11. Michael E. Porter, *Competitive Advantage* (New York: Free Press, 1985), p. 5.

12. Joseph Pereira, "Sneaker Attacks," *The Wall Street Journal,* September 22, 1995, pp. A1 and A5.

13. Rochelle O'Connor, *Facing Strategic Issues: New Planning Guides and Practices,* Report No. 867 (New York: The Conference Board, Inc., 1985), p. 9.

14. George S. Day and Robin Wensley, "Assessing Advantage: A Framework for Diagnosing Competitive Superiority," *Journal of Marketing,* April 1988, pp. 12–16.

15. Fara Warner, "Timex, Swatch Get Set for Battle with Expensive Ad Campaigns," *The Wall Street Journal,* May 31, 1995, p. B7.

16. Peter Waldman, "India Seeks to Open Huge Phone Market," *The Wall Street Journal,* July 25, 1995, A7.

17. Bernard Catry and Michel Chevalier, "Market Share Strategy and the Product Life Cycle," *Journal of Marketing,* October 1974, p. 29.

18. Jim Carlton, "Foreign Markets Give PC Makers a Hearty Hello," *The Wall Street Journal,* September 15, 1995, pp. B1 and B8.

19. Louise Lee, "A Company Failing from Too Much Success," *The Wall Street Journal,* March 17, 1995, pp. B1 and B2.

APPENDIX 3A

Forecasting Guidelines

The steps in developing sales forecasts consist of: (1) defining the forecasting problem, (2) identifying appropriate forecasting techniques, (3) evaluating and choosing a technique, and (4) implementing the forecasting system. A brief review of each step indicates important issues and considerations.[1]

Defining the Forecasting Problem

The requirements the forecasting method should satisfy and the output required must be decided. Illustrative requirements include the time horizon, level of accuracy desired, the uses to be made of the forecast results, and the degree of disaggregation (nation, state, local), including product/market detail, units of measurement, and time increments to be covered.

Identify, Evaluate, and Select Forecasting Technique(s)

Since several forecasting methods are available, each with certain features and limitations, the user's needs, resources, and available data should be matched with the appropriate techniques. Companies may incorporate two or more techniques into the forecasting process. Typically, one technique is used as the primary basis of forecasting, whereas the other technique is used to check the validity of the primary forecasting method. Also, techniques offer different outputs. Some are effective in obtaining aggregate forecasts, and others are used to estimate sales for disaggregated units of analysis (e.g., products). An overview of the major forecasting techniques is provided below in "Forecasting Techniques."

Implementation

Many firms begin with very informal forecasting approaches based on projections of past experience coupled with a subjective assessment of the future market environment. As the forecasting needs increase, more formalized methods are developed. Factors that often affect the choice of a forecasting system include the type of corporate planning process used, the volatility and complexity of markets, the number of products and markets, and the organizational units that have forecasting needs.

---

[1] The following discussion is based on Lawrence R. Small, *Sales Forecasting in Canada* (Ottawa: The Conference Board of Canada, 1980), pp. 3–7.

FORECASTING TECHNIQUES

The major approaches used to prepare forecasts are briefly described. Forecasting techniques generally follow two basic avenues. The first involves making direct estimates of brand sales. The second forecasts brand sales as a product of several components (e.g., industry sales and market share).[2] Several methods used for forecasting sales are described below:

Judgmental Forecasting. A common approach relies on a jury of executive opinion to obtain sounder forecasts than might be made by a single estimator. To put the results in better perspective, the jury members are usually given background information on past sales, and their estimates are sometimes weighted in proportion to their convictions about the likelihood of specific sales levels being realized.

Sales Force Estimates. The sales personnel of some firms—field representatives, managers, or distributors—are considered better positioned than anyone else to estimate the short-term outlook for sales in their assigned areas.

Users' Expectations. Although the dispersion of product users in many markets (or the cost of reaching them) would make such an approach impractical, some manufacturers serving industrial markets find it possible to poll product users about their future plans, then use this information in developing their own forecasts.

Traditional Time-Series Analysis. In a familiar approach, the historical sales series may be broken down into its components—trends and cyclical and seasonal variations, including irregular variations—which are then projected. Time-series analysis has the advantage of being easy to understand and apply. But there is a danger in relying on strictly mechanized projections of previously identified patterns.

Advanced Time-Series Analysis. For short-term forecasting purposes, several advanced time-series methods have been generating new interest and acceptance. Most rely on a moving average of the data series as their starting point, and requisite computer software facilitates their use. The methods include variants of exponential smoothing, adaptive filtering, Box Jenkins models, and the state-space technique. All assume that future movements of a sales series can be determined solely from the study of its past movements. However, certain of these methods have the alternative advantage of being able to take into account external variables as well.

Econometric Methods. The econometric approach provides a mathematical simplification, or "model," of measurable relationships between changes in the series being forecast and changes in other related factors. Such models are employed most often in the prediction of overall market demand, thus requiring a separate estimate of a company's own share. Increased interest in this approach reflects a growing concern over macroeconomic events as well as a preference for spelling out assumptions that underlie forecasts.

Input–Output Analysis. When developing forecasts for intermediate or commodity products, some firms are finding it advantageous to employ input–output measures within comprehensive forecasting systems that begin with macroeconomic considerations and end with estimates of industry sales. Still other methodologies must be employed in such systems, and specialists are required for the correct application and interpretation of input–output analysis.

---

[2] Vithala R. Rao and James E. Cox, Jr., *Sales Forecasting Methods: A Survey of Recent Developments* (Cambridge, MA: Marketing Science Institute, 1978), p. 17.

New-Product Forecasting. New products pose special problems that are hard for the forecaster to circumvent. A sales forecast for a new product may rest upon any of several bases, including results of marketing research investigations, assumptions about analogous situations in the past, or assumptions about the rate at which users of such products or services will substitute the new item for ones they are presently buying.[3]

Several advantages and limitations of the various forecasting techniques are highlighted in Exhibit 3A–1. A more comprehensive discussion of forecasting techniques is provided by David M. Georgoff and Robert Murdick, "Managers' Guide to Forecasting," *Harvard Business Review,* January–February 1986, pp. 110–20.

Sales Forecast Illustration

The annual forecast of world market demand and airplane supply requirements prepared by the Boeing Commercial Airplane Group is an interesting example of the use of forecasting methods. Copies of the *Current Market Outlook* report can be obtained from the company. The forecasting approach and how the forecasts are used are described in Exhibit 3A–2.

Portions of Boeing's product delivery forecast are shown in Exhibit 3A–3. It is one of many passenger demand and aircraft supply forecasts included in the Boeing report. The report is a penetrating analysis of the commercial aircraft industry. It highlights the importance of forecasting in this industry, where new aircraft designs require several years.

---

[3] David L. Hurwood, Elliott S. Grossman, and Earl L. Bailey, *Sales Forecasting* (New York: The Conference Board, Inc., 1978), pp. i–ii.

EXHIBIT 3A–1 Summary of Advantages and Disadvantages of Various Forecasting Techniques

---

Sales Forecasting Method	*Advantages*	*Disadvantages*
User expectations	1. Forecast estimates obtained directly from buyers 2. Projected product usage information can be greatly detailed 3. Insightful method aids planning marketing strategy 4. Useful for new product forecasting	1. Potential customers must be few and well defined 2. Does not work well for consumer goods 3. Depends on the accuracy of user's estimates 4. Expensive, time-consuming, labor intensive
Sales force composite	1. Involves the people (sales personnel) who will be held responsible for the results 2. Is fairly accurate 3. Aids in controlling and directing sales effort 4. Forecast is available for individual sales territories	1. Estimators (sales personnel) have a vested interest and therefore may be biased 2. Elaborate schemes sometimes necessary to counteract bias 3. If estimates are biased, process to correct the data can be expensive
Jury of executive opinion	1. Easily done, very quick 2. Does not require elaborate statistics 3. Utilizes "collected wisdom" of the top people 4. Useful for new or innovative products	1. Produces aggregate forecasts 2. Expensive 3. Disperses responsibility for the forecast 4. Group dynamics operate
Delphi technique	1. Minimizes effects of group dynamics	1. Can be expensive and time-consuming
Market test	1. Provides ultimate test of consumers' reactions to the product 2. Allows the assessment of the effectiveness of the total marketing program 3. Useful for new and innovative products	1. Lets competitors know what firm is doing 2. Invites competitive reaction 3. Expensive and time-consuming to set up 4. Often takes a long time to accurately assess level of initial and repeat demand
Time-series analysis	1. Utilizes historical data 2. Objective, inexpensive	1. Not useful for new or innovative products 2. Factors for trend, cyclical, seasonal, or product life-cycle phase must be accurately assessed and included 3. Technical skill and good judgment required
Statistical demand analysis	1. Great intuitive appeal 2. Requires quantification of assumptions underlying the estimates 3. Allows management to check results 4. Uncovers hidden factors affecting sales 5. Method is objective	1. Factors affecting sales must remain constant and be accurately identified to produce an accurate estimate 2. Requires technical skill and expertise 3. Some managers reluctant to use method due to the sophistication

---

Source: Adapted from Gilbert A. Churchill, Jr., Neil M. Ford, and Orville C. Walker, *Sales Force Management,* 4th ed. (Burr Ridge, IL: Richard D. Irwin, 1993), pp. 204–5.

EXHIBIT 3A–2   How Boeing Forecasts Aircraft Demand

A long-range forecast is developed annually at Boeing to determine the outlook for world air travel and cargo growth and the consequent commercial jet airplane requirements to meet this demand plus replacement of retired airplanes. It consists of the following:

- Air travel market forecasts (by econometric model)* based on:
  Changes in the cost of air travel.
  Changes in the income of the travel population.
- Airplane retirement assumptions.
- Forecasts for commercial jet airplanes.
  Airplane deliveries in dollars.
  Airplane deliveries in units.
  Categorization by range and size.

The forecasts are used within the Boeing business planning process to develop:

- Financial and production planning.
- Competitor analyses.
- Workforce and inventory requirements.
- Resource allocations.
- New-product evaluations.

The market forecasts reflect the Boeing goal of producing a reasonable outlook for the future of the commercial jet aviation industry. The "balanced" single-line forecast is provided with the expectation that future results will have an equal chance of being higher or lower and will fluctuate around this forecast. There are no "cycles"† in the forecast. Internal planning is driven by this forecast, tempered by other forecasts involving risk and opportunities (i.e., evaluation of upside and downside potential), and melded with the near-term order base and sales forecasts.
This document provides a summary of the baseline market forecast prepared by Boeing. It is separated into three major sections.

- The world market demand involving growth in air travel and cargo plus replacement of retired airplanes.
- The airplane supply requirement.
- The manufacturer's position in the industry.

---

*Boeing models are based on the interrelationships between variables that represent the forces believed to drive the commercial jet aviation industry. Airplane deliveries predicted by the forecast process are based on judgments about reasonable future values for variables in the models and are constrained to match industry requirements.

†Cycles, by definition, mean regularly sequenced phenomena. The Boeing view is that unique circumstances caused the major adverse changes in the historical market and that such events are random and, therefore, not predictable (e.g., energy crises, wars). Even economic growth is hardly cyclical. Good monetary and fiscal policies can prevent major economic disruptions. Only two major world recessions have occurred in the jet era, and they were begun by energy crises.

Source: *Current Market Outlook,* Boeing Commercial Airplane Group, February 1992, p. 1.1.

EXHIBIT 3A–3   Product Delivery Forecast

World Commercial Jet Airplane Deliveries

- Total commercial jet airplane delivery requirements are forecast to amount to $380 billion through the year 2000 (1992 dollars) and $857 billion through the year 2010.
  This is nearly the same level as forecast in last year's *Current Market Outlook.*
- Non-U.S. airlines' future share of the market is 64%, up from 62%, from 1970 through 1990.
- 65% of demand through the year 2000 will come from growth and 35% from replacement. Through 2010, 73% of the demand is for growth and 27% for replacement because two-thirds of the fleet retirements are assumed to occur through the year 2000.
- Delivery dollars will average $45 billion per year through the year 2010, 150% higher than the 1970-to-1991 average of $18 billion.
- The Asia/Pacific area will show the greatest percentage gain.
- The U.S. market will maintain its position as the largest market.
- The total backlog of orders and firm options is expected to surpass the ASM capacity required in the mid-1990s. This reflects airline and leasing company strategy to protect upside potential requirements.

World Annual Commercial Airplane Deliveries

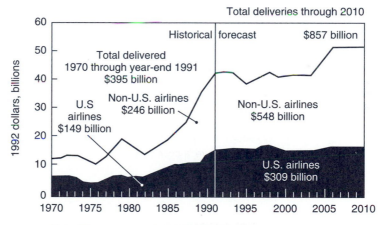

Note: Three-year moving average.

EXHIBIT 3A–3   *(concluded)*

Share for Airlines by Geographic Area (1992 delivery dollars)

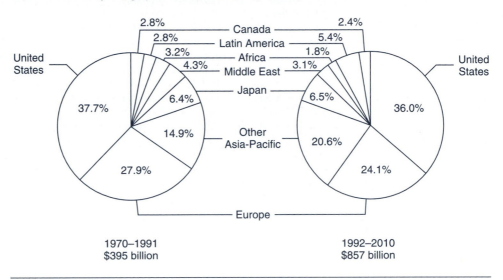

1970–1991 $395 billion	1992–2010 $857 billion

Source: *Current Market Outlook,* Boeing Commercial Airplane Group, February 1992, pp. 304, 305.

CHAPTER

4

Segmenting Markets

Understanding how buyers' needs and wants vary is essential in the design of marketing strategy. Buyers often display different preferences and priorities for products. They want goods and services that satisfy their needs at competitive prices. Buyers vary according to how they use products, the needs and preferences that the products satisfy, and their consumption patterns. Such differences create market segments. Segmenting markets is the process of identifying and analyzing the buyers in a product-market with similar response characteristics (e.g., frequency of purchase).

The most specific form of market segmentation is to consider each buyer a market segment. Such fine-tuned segmentation is possible for many products due to mass customization techniques. It offers an exciting new approach to serving the unique needs and wants of individual buyers. Custom designed products satisfy individual buyer's needs and wants at prices comparable to mass-produced products. By coupling information technology and production efficiencies, products can be designed to meet individual needs at prices that are competitive with mass-produced products. For example, a woman can walk into an Original Levi Store in New York, be measured by a salesperson and try on a few pairs of jeans selected by computer from over 400 pairs to match her specific measurements. If one does not provide a perfect fit, the information is put into the computer to refine the fit specifications. The final match is a perfect fit at a price only $10 more than the mass-produced jeans. Since stocking a supply of each of the 400 jeans in every store would be very costly, the buyer's pair of jeans is shipped to the store or the buyer from the distribution center.

We begin the chapter with a discussion of segmentation, targeting, and positioning, followed by a look at how segmentation can enhance competitive advantage. A discussion of the variables used to identify segments and methods for forming segments follows. Finally, we look at how market segments are analyzed to determine their attractiveness as market targets.

SEGMENTATION, TARGETING, AND POSITIONING

Market segmentation, market targeting, and positioning are closely interrelated. *Market segmentation* is the process of placing the buyers in a product-market into subgroups so that the buyers in a segment display similar responsiveness to a particular marketing positioning strategy. Buyer similarities are indicated by the amount and frequency of purchase, loyalty to a particular brand, and other measures of responsiveness. So, segmentation is an identification process aimed at finding subgroups of buyers within a total market. The opportunity for segmentation occurs when differences in buyers' demand (response) functions allow market demand to be divided into segments, each with a distinct demand function.[1] The term *market niche* is sometimes used to refer to a market segment.

Segmentation identifies customer groups within a product-market, each containing buyers with similar preferences toward specific product attributes. A segment is a possible market target for an organization competing in the market. Segmentation offers a company an opportunity to better match its products to buyers' preferences. Customer satisfaction can be improved by using a marketing program designed for the buyers in a segment. *Market targeting* consists of evaluating and selecting one or more segments that a company decides to serve.

In Chapter 1, *positioning strategy* is described as the combination of marketing actions management takes to meet the needs and wants of each market target. The strategy consists of product(s) and supporting services, distribution, pricing, and promotion components. Management's choices about how to influence target buyers to favorably position the product in their eyes and minds help in designing the positioning strategy.

Market segmentation lays the groundwork for market targeting and positioning strategies. The skills and insights used in segmenting a product-market may give a company important competitive advantages by identifying buyer groups that will respond favorably to the firm's marketing efforts. Faulty segmentation reduces the effectiveness of targeting and positioning decisions.

SEGMENTATION AND COMPETITIVE ADVANTAGE

The reality that makes segmentation analysis so critical is that the buyers in many markets are different. The following excerpt from a Massachusetts Institute of Technology study of global competitiveness highlights how segmentation impacts business performance:

> All of the successful firms that we observed are making a concerted effort to develop closer ties to their customers. These ties enable companies to pick up more differentiated signals from

the market and thus to respond to different segments of demand. They also increase the likelihood of rapid response to shifts in the market.[2]

We will now discuss (1) targeting practices, (2) competitive advantage opportunities through segmentation, and (3) choosing the level of the market to be segmented.

Targeting Practices

Companies appeal to only a portion of the people or organizations in a product-market, typically, regardless of how many segments are targeted. Management may decide to target one specific segment, a few segments, or several segments. Alternatively, although a specific segment strategy is not used, the marketing program selected by management is likely to appeal to a particular subgroup within the market. Segment identification and targeting are obviously preferred. Finding a segment by chance does not give management the opportunity of evaluating different segments in terms of the financial and competitive advantage implications of each segment. When segmentation is employed, it should be by design, and the underlying analyses should lead to the selection of one or more promising target opportunity. Targeting is discussed in Chapter 6.

Segmentation and Competitive Advantage

While broad competitive comparisons can be made for an entire product-market, more penetrating insights about competitive advantage and market opportunity result from market segment analyses. Examining specific market segments helps to identify how a firm can (1) attain a closer match between buyers' preferences and the organization's capabilities and (2) compare the organization's strengths (and weaknesses) to those of the key competitors in each segment.

Matching Preferences with Capabilities.   Customer preferences can often be better satisfied within a segment, compared to the total market. Consider, for example, customers' needs for banking services. The banking needs of business and institutional customers vary considerably. Even within the business sector, users' needs vary by size and type of business, financial strengths, and other banking requirements. For example, using a segment-level strategy to meet customer needs helps First Business Bank perform well. Targeting companies with annual sales between $3 million and $100 million, the Los Angeles bank has a customer-focused array of services, including sending couriers to pick up deposits.[3] The bank's strong performance includes low loan losses and high return on equity, return on assets, and growth.

Competitive Advantage Analysis.   The companies that compete in a market often have different strengths and weaknesses. Segment analysis guides actions to improve targeting and positioning advantages over competitors. Segment information helps management design effective marketing programs. First Business Bank's management recognized that the major banks in the Los Angeles market put their attention on big companies and were

---

EXHIBIT 4–1   Identifying the Health and Beauty Supplies Product-Market to Be Segmented

---

Level of Competition	Product Definition	Illustrative Competitors	Need/Want Satisfied
Generic	Health and beauty aids	Consumer products companies	Enhancement of health and beauty
Product type	Shaving equipment	Gillette, Remington, Bic	Shaving
Product variant	Electric razors	Braun, Norelco, Remington, Panasonic	Electric shaving

---

not adequately meeting the needs and requirements of mid-size companies.[4] The gap in satisfaction between these customers' expectations and the actual service performance of the major banks gave First Business Bank a competitive edge. Actions were implemented to meet these needs. Founded in 1981, the bank has an objective of $1 billion in assets by 1995.

Selecting the Market to Be Segmented

Market segmentation may occur at any of the product-market levels shown in Exhibit 4–1. Generic-level segmentation is illustrated by the supermarket shopper types, discussed in Chapter 3, who purchase health and beauty aids. Product-type segmentation is shown by the differences in price, quality, and features of shaving equipment. Product variant-segmentation considers the segments within a category such as electric razors.

An important consideration in defining the market to be segmented is estimating the variation in buyers' needs and requirements at the different product-market levels and identifying the types of buyers included in the market. In the First Business Bank example, management defined the product-market to be segmented as banking services for business organizations in the Los Angeles metropolitan area. Segmenting the generic product-market for financial services was too broad in scope. The market definition selected by management excluded buyers (e.g., consumers) that were not of primary interest to management while including companies with different financial service needs.

IDENTIFYING MARKET SEGMENTS

After the market to be segmented is defined, one or more variables are selected to identify segments. For example, the United Services Automobile Association (USAA) segments by type of employment. It has built a successful business serving the automobile insurance needs of U.S. military officers located throughout the world. As described in the Technology Feature, USAA keeps close relationships with its 2.6 million members by using powerful information technology. First, we will discuss the purpose of segmentation

TECHNOLOGY FEATURE   United Services Automobile Association's (USAA) One-on-One Customer Relationships

USAA is unknown to many people since its automobile insurance is targeted to military personnel and their families. The customer is a "member" of the Association, encouraging an ongoing relationship. USAA's impressive computerized database enables members to make any changes or additions in coverage, location, and other policy adjustments via a phone call.

The USAA service representative has immediate access to the client's consolidated file, including any recent correspondence with the member. The one-on-one service encounter is personalized because the representative has the complete service file during the conversation. The new or revised insurance policy is sent out the following day to the member. The service representative handles everything, eliminating contacts with other departments. The client has quick and simplified access to USAA from anywhere in the world.

USAA inputs over 30,000 mail items received each day from its members into the electronic data file to provide the 2,500 service representatives with current information in the event the member follows up with a phone call. USAA's 98 percent customer retention rate attests to the effectiveness of its customer relationships.

Source: Leonard L. Berry, "Relationship Marketing of Services—Growing Interest, Emerging Perspectives," *Journal of the Academy of Marketing Science,* Fall 1995, pp. 238–40.

variables; this will be followed by a review of the variables that are used in segmentation analyses.

Purpose of Segmentation Variables

Segmentation variables perform two important functions.[5] The basis variable(s) is used to divide a product-market into segments. The second function is to describe or profile the segments. In practice, the distinction between the two functions is often not apparent since the same variable(s) may be used for both purposes. For example, the basis of segmentation may be company size and financial performance, as in the case of First Business Bank. The same variables also provide descriptive information about each segment.

The categories of variables shown in Exhibit 4–2 include a wide range of segment bases and descriptors. Demographic and psychographic (lifestyle and personality) characteristics of consumers are of interest, since this information is available from the U.S. Census reports and many other sources, including databases. The use situation variables consider how the buyer uses the product, such as purchasing a meal away from home for the purpose of entertainment. Variables measuring buyers' needs and preferences include attitudes, brand awareness, and brand preference. Purchase-behavior variables describe brand use and consumption (e.g., size and frequency of purchase). We examine these variables to highlight their uses, features, and other considerations important in segmenting markets.

EXHIBIT 4–2 Variables for Segmenting Markets

- Characteristics of People and Organizations
- Buyers' Product Use Situation
- Buyers' Needs and Preferences
- Purchase Behavior

Characteristics of People and Organizations

Consumer Markets. The characteristics of people fall into two major categories: (1) geographic and demographic, and (2) psychographic (lifestyle and personality). Demographics are more useful in describing consumer segments than in identifying them. Nevertheless, these variables are popular because available data often relate demographics to the other segmentation variables shown in Exhibit 4–2. Geographic location is useful for segmenting certain kinds of product-markets. For example, there are regional differences in the popularity of transportation vehicles. In several states the most popular vehicle is a pickup truck. The "truck belt" runs from the upper Midwest south through Texas and the Gulf Coast states. The Ford brand is dominant in the northern half of the truck belt, while Chevrolet leads in the southern half.

Demographic variables describe buyers according to their age, income, education, occupation, and many other factors. Demographic information helps to describe groups of buyers such as heavy users of a product or brand. Demographics used in combination with buyer behavior information are useful in segmenting markets, selecting distribution channels, designing advertising strategies, and other decisions on marketing strategy.

Lifestyle variables indicate what people do (activities), their interests, their opinions, and their buying behavior. Lifestyle characteristics extend beyond demographics and offer a more penetrating description of the consumer.[6] Profiles are developed using lifestyle characteristics. This information is used to segment markets, position products, and guide the design of advertising messages.

An array of specialty magazines enables companies to identify and access very specific lifestyle segments. For example, Peterson Publishing Co. publishes 23 monthlies, 9 bimonthlies, and 45 annuals.[7] Its magazine portfolio includes *Motor Trend, MTB* (mountain bikes), *Circle Track,* and *Teen* magazine. Specialty magazines match buyers' lifestyle interests with articles that correspond to the interests. Subscriber profiles help companies to match their market target profiles with the right magazine(s). Many of the specialty magazines conduct subscriber research studies that are useful to companies targeting lifestyle segments.

Organizational Markets. Several characteristics help in segmenting business markets. The type of industry (sometimes called a vertical market) is related to purchase behavior for certain types of products. For example, automobile producers purchase steel, paint, and other raw materials. This form of segmentation enables suppliers to specialize their efforts and satisfy customer needs. Other variables for segmenting organizational markets include size of the company, the stage of industry development, and the stage of the value-added system (e.g., producer, distribution, retailer). Organizational segmentation is aided by first examining (1) the extent of market concentration and (2) the degree of product customization.[8] Concentration considers the number of customers and their relative buying power. Product customization determines the extent to which the supplier must tailor the product to each organizational buyer. If one or both of these factors indicate quite a bit of diversity, segmentation opportunities may exist.

Product Use Situation Segmentation

Markets can be segmented based on how the product is used. As an illustration, Nikon, the Japanese camera company, offers a line of high-performance sunglasses designed for activities and light conditions when skiing, driving, hiking, flying, shooting, and participating in water sports. Nikon competes in the premium portion of the market with prices somewhat higher than Ray-Ban, the market leader. Needs and preferences vary according to the different use situations. Peter R. Dickson identifies several use situations that create market segment opportunities:

> Examples of situation segmentation can be found in the design of furniture, appliances, china, bicycles, motorcycles, automobiles and camping equipment. Some lounge suites are designed for small apartments, others for beachside holiday homes and yet others for executive suites and lounge bars. Color TVs are designed as feature furniture pieces for family rooms and as robust portables for trailers and bedrooms. Special refrigerators are designed for trailers and basement bars. Expensive china is designed for entertaining guests, while cheap, robust Corelle dinnerware is designed for everyday family use. There are commuting motorcycles, dirt motorcycles, farm motorcycles, and highway cruisers. Pick-ups and four-wheel drive station wagons are primarily designed for different usage situations than a VW Rabbit or Rolls Royce. Camping gear is designed to be adaptable, but specialist equipment is designed for use in tropical and/or very cold climates and situations where space and weight are at a premium. The clothing and footwear market has long been person–situation segmented to accommodate not only differing sex and size but also differing weather conditions, physical activities, and social role playing.[9]

As illustrated in the earlier Levi jeans example, mass customization offers a promising means of responding to different use situations at competitive prices. The Segmentation Feature describes how Lutron Electronics gives its buyers customized light dimmer switches by programming desired features using computer chips built into the switches.

Buyers' Needs and Preferences

Needs and preferences that are specific to products and brands can be used as segmentation bases and descriptors. Examples include brand loyalty status, benefits sought, and proneness to make a deal. Buyers may be attracted to different brands because of the benefits offered by a brand. For example, seeking to generate additional

---

SEGMENTATION FEATURE   Lutron Electronics (Light Dimmer Switches)

- Two decades ago the company began a major effort to develop superior-quality, military-specification dimmers at consumer prices.
- As the 1980s commenced, two forces were moving Lutron rapidly into mass customization:

1. Commercial designers, decorators, and retailers wanted customized dimmers.
2. Technology-microprocessors enabled the company to build dimmers in standardized forms and then modified in software. The dimmers could also be taught to react to situations such as creating different lighting environments during the day.

- Lutron's new dimmer requires only one model to do what 40 did in the 1970s.
- Lutron holds 80 percent of all dimmer patents—and holds a 75 percent market share.
- The product catalog includes several thousand product variations in dozens of colors.

Michael Malone, "Pennsylvania Guys Mass Customize," *Forbes ASAP,* April 10, 1995, pp. 82–85.

---

revenues in the mid-1990s, Credit Lyonnaise, France's largest commercial bank, segmented and began targeting customers with annual incomes in excess of 500,000 francs ($100,000 in late 1995) that wanted quality service, financial advice, and upscale facilities.[10] Several new branch offices are designed to appeal to Credit Lyonnaise's wealthy clients. One office in Bordeaux, called Club Tourney, is an elegant townhouse with salons where clients meet with advisors to discuss financial needs. The branch serves 100 wealthy clients.

Consumer Needs.   Needs motivate people to act. Understanding how buyers satisfy their needs provides guidelines for marketing actions. Consumers attempt to match their needs with the products that satisfy their needs. People have a variety of needs, including basic physiological needs (food, rest, and sex), the need for safety, the need for relationships with other people (friendship), and personal satisfaction needs.[11] Understanding the nature and intensity of a need is important in (1) determining how well a particular brand may satisfy the need and/or (2) indicating what change in the brand may be necessary to provide a better solution to the buyer's needs.

An interesting example of segmentation based on needs is the growing desire of consumers for food that is both good-tasting and convenient.[12] Food companies are adding value to products and making them easier to use by tailoring them to the needs of working women, smaller households, and singles. These firms are increasing their profits by helping people solve the problems of food preparation. Studies by the food industry indicate that shoppers from almost every age and income bracket are not as concerned about economizing on food as their counterparts of previous decades were. Many buyers want food that is easy and quick to prepare.

Attitudes.   Buyer's attitudes toward brands are important because experience and research findings indicate that attitudes influence behavior. Attitudes are enduring systems of favorable or unfavorable evaluations about brands.[13] They reflect the buyer's overall liking or preference for a brand. Attitudes may develop from personal experience, interactions with other buyers, or by marketing efforts, such as advertising and personal selling.

Attitude information is useful in a marketing strategy development. A strategy may be designed either to respond to established attitudes or, instead, to attempt to change an attitude. In a given situation, relevant attitudes should be identified and measured to indicate how brands compare. If important attitude influences on buyer behavior are identified and a firm's brand is measured against these attitudes, management may be able to improve the brand's position by using this information. Attitudes are often difficult to change, but firms may be able to do so if buyers' perceptions about the brand are incorrect. For example, if the trade-in value of an automobile is important to buyers in a targeted segment and a company learns through market research that its brand (which actually has a high trade-in value) is perceived as having a low trade-in value, advertising can communicate this information to buyers.

Perceptions.   "Perception is defined as the process by which an individual selects, organizes, and interprets information inputs to create a meaningful picture of the world."[14] Perceptions are how buyers select, organize, and interpret marketing stimuli, such as advertising, personal selling, price, and the product. Perceptions form attitudes. Buyers are selective in the information they process. As an illustration of selective perception, some advertising messages may not be received by viewers because of the large number of messages vying for their attention. Or a salesperson's conversation may be misunderstood or not received fully because the buyer is trying to decide if the purchase is necessary while the salesperson is talking.

People often perceive things differently. Business executives are interested in how their products, salespeople, stores, and companies are perceived. Perception is important strategically in helping management to evaluate the current positioning strategy and in making changes in this positioning strategy. Perception mapping is a useful research technique for showing how brands are perceived by buyers according to various criteria. A set of attributes can be reduced through computer analyses to form two-dimensional maps based on consumer perceptions of brands. We discuss how preference mapping is used to form segments later in the chapter.

Purchase Behavior

Consumption variables such as the size and frequency of a purchase are useful in segmenting consumer and business markets. Marketers of industrial products often classify customers and prospects into categories on the basis of the volume of the purchase. For example, a specialty chemical producer concentrates its marketing efforts on chemical users that purchase at least $100,000 worth of chemicals each year. The firm further segments the market on the basis of how the customer uses the chemical.

Since buying decisions vary in importance and complexity, it is useful to classify them to better understand their characteristics, the products to which they apply, and the marketing strategy implications of each type of purchase behavior. Buyer decisions can

EXHIBIT 4–3   Four Types of Buyer Behavior

	Type of Purchase Decision	
	High-Involvement	*Low-Involvement*
Decision making (information search, consideration of alternatives)	Complex decision making (medical services, autos, financial planning services, diamonds)	Impulse purchasing (cereals, snacks)
Habit (little or no information search, consideration of only one brand)	Brand loyalty (perfume, cigarettes, beverages)	Inertia (light bulbs, soaps, paper towels)

Source: Adapted from Henry Assael, *Marketing Management* (Boston: PWS–Kent Publishing, 1985), p. 127.

be classified according to the extent to which the buyer is involved in the decision and whether it is a decision-making process or an action based on habit.[15] A high-involvement decision may be infrequent, expensive, risky, and important to the consumer's ego and social needs. The decision situation may be simple or complex, depending on whether multiple brands or a single brand are considered. The classification is shown in Exhibit 4–3, based on the amount of involvement and the decision-making situation.

These categories are very broad since the involvement and decision types cover a range of situations. Even so, the four types of buyer behavior provide a useful way to compare and contrast buying situations. Also, a situation may vary from individual to individual. For example, a high-involvement purchase for one person may not be such for another person.

Exhibit 4–4 summarizes the various segmentation variables and shows examples of segmentation bases and descriptors for consumer and organizational markets. As we examine the methods used to form segments, the role of these variables in segment determination and analysis will be illustrated.

FORMING SEGMENTS

American Express (AMEX) identifies market segments based on purchase behavior. One group of cardholders pays the annual fee for the card but rarely (or never) uses it.[16] This group of zero spenders is made up of (1) those who cannot afford much discretionary spending and (2) those who use cash or competitors' cards. AMEX's objective is to identify the second group of potential buyers because they offer sales opportunities and are potential lost cardholders. AMEX uses self-selecting incentive offers (e.g., two free airline tickets

---

EXHIBIT 4–4   Illustrative Segmentation Variables

	Consumer Markets	*Industrial/Organizational Markets*
Characteristics of people/organizations	Age, gender, race Income Family size Life-cycle stage Geographical location Lifestyle	Type of industry Size Geographical location Corporate culture Stage of development Producer/intermediary
Use situation	Occasion Importance of purchase Prior experience with product User status	Application Purchasing procedure New task, modified rebuy, straight rebuy
Buyers' needs/preferences	Brand loyalty status Brand preference Benefits sought Quality Proneness to make a deal	Performance requirements Brand preferences Desired features Service requirements
Purchase behavior	Size of purchase Frequency of purchase	Volume Frequency of purchase

---

for heavy card use over six months) to identify the valuable nonuser cardholders. While the segmentation approach is expensive, it costs less than obtaining a new customer to replace one who leaves AMEX and it avoids using expensive marketing research.

As we shall see shortly, the segmentation variables (Exhibit 4–4) play an essential role in the segmentation process. The requirements for segmentation are discussed first, and then the methods of segment formation are examined.

Requirements for Segmentation

An important question is deciding if it is worthwhile to segment a product-market. While in many instances segmentation makes sense, its feasibility and value need to be evaluated. Five criteria are useful for this purpose.[17]

Response Differences.   Determining differences in the responsiveness of people in the product-market to positioning strategies is central to segment identification. Suppose the customers for a product-market are placed into four groups, each a potential segment, using a basis variable such as income. If each group responds (e.g., amount of purchase) in the same way as all other groups to a marketing mix strategy, then the groups are not market segments. If segments actually exist in this illustration, there must be differences in the responsiveness of the groups to marketing actions, such as pricing, product features, and promotion. The presence of real segments requires actual response differences. Simply finding differences in buyers' characteristics is not enough.

Income is useful in finding response differences in India. A study conducted by a New Delhi think tank identifies a premium segment in the Indian consumer market.[18] Families with annual incomes in excess of 1 million rupees ($29,200 in late 1995) have as much buying power as a U.S. family with three times the same income. Living costs for the Indian family are very low (e.g., two bedroom apartment for $130 a month). The premium segment is a promising target for luxury goods brands like Mercedes-Benz, Cartier, and Christian Dior. There are 600,000 Indian households in the premium segment, including 200,000 in Bombay. BMW has a joint venture with Hero Motors Ltd. to produce luxury cars in India.

Identifiable Segments.   It must be possible to identify the customer groups that exhibit response differences. Finding the correct groups may be difficult because it is not always obvious which variables are appropriate for dividing the market into segments. For example, variations in purchase volume may occur in a market. However, it may not be possible to identify which people correspond to the different response groups in the market. While it is usually feasible to find descriptive differences among the buyers in a product-market, these variations must be matched to response differences. Recall AMEX's approach to identifying cardholders who use the card infrequently. Incentives are used to attract nonuser cardholders with buying power.

Actionable Segments.   A business must be able to aim a marketing program strategy at each segment selected as a market target. Specialty magazines offer one means of selective targeting. Ideally, the marketing effort should focus on the segment of interest and not be wasted on nonsegment buyers. In some situations, promotional efforts for one product or brand may actually attract (cannibalize) customers from another segment targeted by the same organization using a different brand.

Cost/Benefits of Segmentation.   Segmentation must be financially attractive in terms of revenues generated and costs incurred. It is important to evaluate the benefits of segmentation. While segmentation may cost more in terms of research and added marketing expenses, it should also generate more sales. The objective is to use a segmentation approach that offers a favorable revenue and cost combination.

Stability over Time.   Finally, the segments must show adequate stability over time so that the firm's marketing efforts will have enough time to produce favorable results. If buyers' needs change too fast, a group with similar response patterns at one point may display quite different patterns several months later. The time period may be too short to justify using a segmentation strategy.

Sometimes, the distinction between product differentiation and market segmentation is not clear. *Product differentiation* is a product offering perceived by the buyer to differ from the competition on any physical or nonphysical product characteristic, including price.[19] Using a product differentiation strategy, a firm may target an entire market or one (or more) segments. Competing firms may differentiate their product offerings in trying to gain competitive advantage with the same group of targeted buyers.

Approaches to Segment Identification

Segments are formed by: (*a*) grouping customers using descriptive characteristics and then comparing response differences across the groups, or (*b*) forming groups based on response differences (e.g., frequency of purchase) and working backward to see if the

EXHIBIT 4–5 Product-Market Segment Dimensions for Hotel Lodging Services

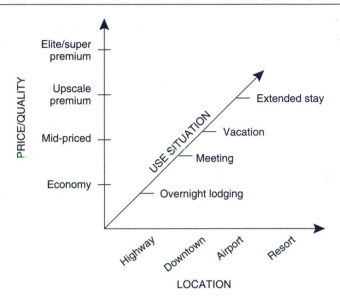

groups can be identified based on differences in their characteristics.[20] Approach (*a*) uses a characteristic such as income on family size believed to be related to buyer response. After the groups are formed, they are examined to see if response varies across groups. Approach (*b*) combines buyers with similar response into groups and then develops buyer profiles using buyer characteristics. We describe each approach to show how it is used to identify segments.

Customer Group Identification

After the product-market of interest is defined, it may be possible to identify promising segments, using management judgment in combination with available information and/or marketing research data. Consider, for example, hotel lodging services. Exhibit 4–5 illustrates ways to segment the hotel lodging product-market. An additional breakdown can be made on the basis of business and household travelers. These categories may be further distinguished by individual customer and group customer segments. Groups may include conventions, corporate meetings, and tour groups. Several possible segment cells can be distinguished. Consider, for example, Marriott's Courtyard hotel chain. These hotels fall into the midpriced category and are targeted primarily to frequent business travelers who fly to destinations, are in the 40-plus age range, and are in a high-income group.

It is necessary to select one or more of the characteristics of people or organizations as the basis of segmentation. Using these variable, firms can designate segments by using (1) management judgment and experience or (2) supporting statistical analyses. The objective is to find differences in responsiveness among the customer groups. We will now look at some of the customer-grouping methods to show how segments are formed.

Experience and Available Information.   Management's knowledge of customer needs is often a useful guide to segmentation. For example, both experience and analysis of published information help segment business markets. Business segment variables include type of industry, size of purchase, and product use application. Recall the use of company size to segment the market for commercial banking services by First Business Bank. Company records often contain information for analyzing the existing customer base. Published data such as industry mailing lists can be used to identify potential market segments. These groups are then analyzed to determine if they respond differently.

Segmenting using management judgment and experience, Prada, an Italian fashion producer and retailer, markets an expensive array of dresses, handbags, hats, shoes, and other women's apparel.[21] The best-selling $450 backpacks are designed to appeal to affluent women that do not want to flaunt their status. Each knapsack has a small triangular logo. Prada's products offer an antistatus appeal to a segment of affluent women. The luxury retailer has 47 stores, including 20 in Japan and only 2 in the United States. Prada's goods are also sold in department stores. The company will introduce menswear and perfume lines in 1996.

Cross-Classification Analyses.   Another method of forming segments is to identify customer groups by using descriptive characteristics and compare response rates (e.g., sales) by placing the information in tabular form. Customer groups form the rows and response categories form the columns. Review of industry publications and other published information may identify ways to break up a product-market into segments. Standardized information services such as Information Resources Inc. and Nielsen collect and publish consumer panel data on a regular basis (see Chapter 5). These data provide a wide range of consumer characteristics, advertising media usage, and other information analyzed by product and brand usage. The panel data are generated from a large sample of households throughout the United States.

A wide array of information is available for use in forming population subgroups within product-markets. The analyst can use many sources, as well as management's insights and hunches regarding the market. The essential concern is whether a segmentation scheme establishes customer groups that display different product and brand responsiveness. The more evidence of meaningful differences, the better chance that useful segments exist. Cross-classification has some real advantages in terms of cost and ease of use. There may be a strong basis for choosing a segmenting scheme that uses this approach. This occurs more often in business and organizational markets where management has a good knowledge of user needs because there are fewer users than there are in consumer product-markets. Alternatively, this approach may be a first step leading to a more comprehensive type of analysis.

Database Segmentation.   The availability of computerized databases offers a wide range of segmentation analysis capabilities. This type of analysis is particularly useful in consumer market segmentation. Databases are organized by geography and buyers' descriptive characteristics. They may also contain customer response information as

EXHIBIT 4–6   Diversity of Gasoline Buyers

Road Warriors:	True Blues:	Generation F3	Homebodies:	Price Shoppers:
Generally higher-income, middle-aged men who drive 25,000 to 50,000 miles a year . . . buy premium with a credit card . . . purchase sandwiches and drinks from the convenience store . . . will sometimes wash their cars at the carwash.	Usually men and women with moderate to high incomes who are loyal to a brand and sometimes to a particular station . . . frequently buy premium gasoline and pay in cash.	(for fuel, food and fast): Upwardly mobile men and women—half under 25 years of age—who are constantly on the go . . . drive a lot and snack heavily from the convenience store.	Usually housewives who shuttle their children around during the day and use whatever gasoline station is based in town or along their route of travel.	Generally aren't loyal to either brand or a particular station, and rarely buy the premium line . . . frequently on tight budgets . . . efforts to woo them have been the basis of marketing strategies for years.
16% of buyers	**16% of buyers**	**27% of buyers**	**21% of buyers**	**20% of buyers**

Source: Alanna Sullivan, "Mobil Bets Drivers Pick Cappuccino over Low Prices," *The Wall Street Journal,* January 30, 1995, p. B1. Reprinted by permission of *The Wall Street Journal*, © 1995 Dow Jones & Company, Inc. All Rights Reserved Worldwide.

shown in the AMEX cardholder illustration. Databases can be used to identify customer groups, design effective marketing programs, and improve the effectiveness of existing programs. The number of available databases is rapidly expanding, the costs are declining, and the information systems are becoming user friendly. Several marketing research firms offer database services.

Segmentation Illustration.   Mobil Corporation studies buyers in the gasoline market to identify segments. The findings, including information obtained from over 2,000 motorists, are summarized in Exhibit 4–6. The research identified five primary purchasing groups.[22] Interestingly, Mobil found that the Price Shopper spends an average of $700 annually, compared to $1,200 for the Road Warriors and True Blues. Mobil's marketing strategy is to offer gasoline buyers a quality buying experience, including upgraded facilities, more lighting for safety, responsive attendants, and quality convenience products. The test results from the new strategy raised revenues by 25 percent over previous sales for the same retail sites.

As illustrated by the profiles described in Exhibit 4–6, needs and preferences vary quite a bit within a market. Trying to satisfy all of the buyers in the market with the same marketing approach is increasingly difficult. There are too many differences across buyers. Analyzing both the customer and the competition is important. Specific competitors may be better (or worse) at meeting the needs of specific customer groups (e.g., Mobil's Road Warriors). Finding gaps between buyers' needs and competitors' offerings provides opportunities for improving customer satisfaction. Also, companies study competitors' products to identify ways to improve their own.

By identifying customer groups using descriptive characteristics and comparing them to a measure of customer responsiveness to a marketing mix such as product usage rate (e.g. number of packages of soap per week), potential segments can be identified. If

EXHIBIT 4–7   Segment Profile of Steel Strapping Customers

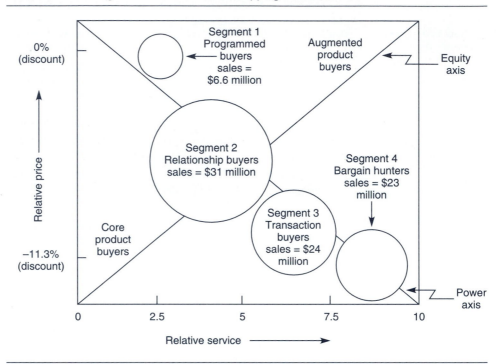

Source: V. Kasturi Rangan, Rowland T. Moriarty, and Gordon S. Swartz, "Segmenting Customers in Mature Industrial Markets," *Journal of Marketing,* October 1992, p. 79.

similar response rates are found within a segment and differences in response exist between segments, then promising segments are identified. Segments do not always emerge from these analyses, because distinct segments for some product-markets may not exist. In others, the segment interrelationships may be so complex that an analysis of these predetermined groupings will not identify useful segments. Product differentiation strategies may be used in these situations.

Forming Groups Based on Response Differences

The alternative to selecting customer groups based on descriptive characteristics is to identify groups of buyers by using one or more bases to form the segments. A look at a segmentation analysis for the packaging division of Signode Corporation illustrates how this method is used.[23] The products consist of steel strappings for various packaging applications. An analysis of the customer base identified the segments shown in Exhibit 4–7. Hierarchical cluster analysis formed the segments using 12 variables concerning price and service trade-offs and buying power. The study included 161 of Signode's national accounts. Measures of the variables were obtained from sales records, sales managers, and sales representatives. Note how the segments vary in responsiveness based on relative price and relative service.

Response difference approaches draw more extensively from buyer behavior information than the customer group identification methods discussed earlier. Note, for example, the information on Signode's customer responsiveness to marketing-mix variables (Exhibit 4–7). We now look at additional applications to more fully explore the potential of the customer response approaches.

Cluster Analysis.   Cluster analysis (a statistical technique) groups people according to the similarity of their answers to questions such as brand preferences on product attributes. This method identified the segments shown in Exhibit 4–7. The objective of cluster analysis is to identify groupings in which the similarity within a group is high and the variation among groups is as great as possible. Each cluster is a potential segment. A lifestyle segmentation study of the snack foods market illustrates how cluster analysis is used in consumer market segmentation.[24] Using a sample of 1,500 snack food users, information on several lifestyle characteristics and benefits sought in snack foods was collected and analyzed. A summary of the results of the study is shown in Exhibit 4–8. Six potential segments are shown. Comparisons of the groups indicate several differences that are useful in market targeting and marketing program development, such as the variation in the type of snacks usually eaten by the members of each segment. Also the demographic characteristics vary substantially across segments.

Perceptual Maps.   Another promising segmentation method uses consumer research data to construct perceptual maps for products and brands. The information helps select market-target strategies and decide how to position a product for a market target.

While the end result of perceptual mapping is simple to understand, its execution is demanding in terms of research skills. Although there are variations in approach, the following steps are illustrative:

1. Select the product-market area to be segmented.
2. Decide which brands compete in the product-market.
3. Collect consumer perceptions about attributes for the available brands (and an ideal brand) obtained from a sample of people.
4. Analyze the data to form one, two, or more composite attribute dimensions, each independent of the other.
5. Prepare a map (two-dimensional X and Y grid) of attributes on which are positioned consumer perceptions of competing brands.
6. Plot consumers with similar ideal preferences to see if subgroups (potential segments) will form.
7. Evaluate how well the solution corresponds to the data that are analyzed.
8. Interpret the results as to market-target and product-positioning strategies.

An example of a perception map is shown in Exhibit 4–9. Each group (I–V) contains people from a survey sample with similar preferences concerning expensiveness and quality

---

EXHIBIT 4–8 Lifestyle Segmentation of the Snack-Food Market

	Nutritional Snackers	Weight Watchers	Guilty Snackers	Party Snackers	Indiscriminate Snackers	Economical Snackers
Percentage of snackers	22%	14%	9%	15%	15%	18%
Lifestyle characteristics	Self-assured Controlled	Outdoor types Influential Venturesome	High anxiety Isolate	Sociable	Hedonistic	Self-assured Price-oriented
Benefits sought	Nutritious No artificial ingredients Natural snack	Low calorie Quick energy	Low calorie Good tasting	Good to serve guests Proud to serve Goes well with beverage	Good tasting Satisfies hunger	Low price Best value
Consumption level of snacks	Light	Light	Heavy	Average	Heavy	Average
Type of snacks usually eaten	Fruits Vegetables Cheese	Yogurt Vegetables	Yogurt Cookies Crackers Candy	Nuts Potato chips Crackers Pretzels	Candy Ice cream Cookies Potato chips Pretzels Popcorn	No specific products
Demographics	Better educated Have younger children	Younger Single	Younger or older Females Lower socio-economic group	Middle-aged Nonurban	Teens	Larger families Better educated

Source: Henry Assael, *Consumer and Marketing Action,* 2nd ed. (Boston: PWS–Kent Publishing, 1984), p. 262.

---

for the product category. The brands (A–E) are positioned using the preference data obtained from the survey participants. If our brand is C, what does the information indicate concerning possible targeting? Group V is a logical market target and III may represent a secondary market target. To appeal most effectively to Group V, we will probably need to change somewhat Group V consumers' price perceptions of Brand C. Offering a second brand less expensive than C to appeal to Group IV is another possible action. Of course, it is necessary to study the research results in much greater depth than this brief examination of Exhibit 4–9. Our intent is to show how the results might be used.

Perceptual mapping, like many of the research methods used for segment identification, is expensive and represents a technical challenge. When used and interpreted properly, these methods are useful tools for analyzing product-market structure to identify possible market targets and positioning concepts. Of course, there are many issues to be considered in specific applications, such as the choice of attributes, identification of relevant products and brands, sampling design, and evaluating the strength of results.

It may be useful for managers to use their market knowledge and experience to create a perception map for their brand and its competitors. While this approach is not a substitute for a map created from a set of data obtained from a sample of buyers, the

EXHIBIT 4–9 An Illustrative Consumer Perception Map

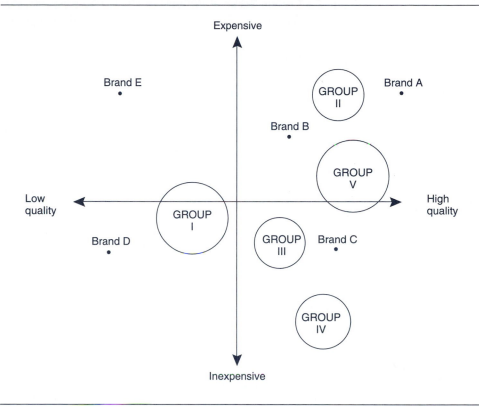

managers' map may help them understand the market. When used in combination with other market and competitor information, the managers' map should help guide targeting and positioning analysis. However, caution should be exercised since managers' perceptions may not be good indicators of buyers' perceptions of brands.

Deciding How to Segment

The choice of a segmentation method depends on such factors as the maturity of market, the competitive structure, and the organization's experience in the market. The more comprehensive the segmentation analysis, the higher the costs of segment identification, reaching the highest level when field research studies are involved. It is important to make maximum use of available knowledge about the product-market. An essential first step in segmentation is analyzing the existing customer base to identify groups of buyers with different response behavior (e.g., frequent purchase versus occasional purchase). It may be helpful to have managers develop a perception map. In some instances this information will provide a sufficient basis for segment formation. If not, experience and existing information are often helpful in guiding the design of customer research studies.

The five segmentation criteria, discussed earlier, help to evaluate potential segments. After examining response differences among the segments, management decides if the criteria are satisfied. The segmentation plan should satisfy the responsiveness criterion plus the other criteria (end-users are identifiable, they are accessible via marketing program, the segment(s) is economically viable, and the segment is stable over time).

It is useful to consider the trade-off between the costs of developing a better segmentation scheme and the benefits gained. For example, instead of using one variable to segment, a combination of two or three variables might be used. The costs of a more insightful segmentation scheme include the analysis time and the complexity of strategy development. The potential benefits include better determination of response differences, which enable the design of more effective marketing mix strategies.

The competitive advantage gained by finding (or developing) a new market segment can be very important. Segment strategies are used by a wide range of small companies with excellent performance records. Consider segmenting the market for paper. One way to segment is according to the use situation. The uses of paper include newspapers, magazines, books, announcements, letters, and other applications. Crane & Company, a firm competing in this market, is the primary supplier of paper for printing money.[25] This segment of the high-quality paper market contains a single customer—the U.S. Treasury. The company's commitment to making quality products has sustained its competitive advantage in this segment since 1879. In 1991 Crane introduced a new currency paper, designed to identify counterfeit bills by placing a polyester thread in the paper. The other three-quarters of Crane's $143 million in sales includes fine writing papers and other high-quality paper products.

STRATEGIC ANALYSIS OF MARKET SEGMENTS

Each market segment of interest needs to be studied to determine its potential attractiveness as a market target. Exhibit 4–10 shows the major areas of analysis. A discussion of each area follows.

Customer Analysis

Customer Profiles. When forming segments, it is useful to find out as much as possible about the customers in each segment. Variables such as those used in dividing product-markets into segments are also helpful in describing the people in the same segments. The discussion of customer profiles in Chapter 3 indicates the information needed to profile a product-market. Similar information is needed for the segment profile, although it is more comprehensive than the product-market profile.

The objective is to find descriptive characteristics that are highly correlated to the variables used to form the segments. Standardized information services are available for some product-markets, including foods, health and beauty aids, and pharmaceuticals. Large markets and many competitors make it profitable for marketing research firms to collect and analyze data that are useful to the firms serving the market.

EXHIBIT 4–10   Analyzing Market Segments

Information Resources, Inc. (IRI), a Chicago-based research supplier, has combined computerized information processing with customer research methods to generate information for market segmentation. Its Behavior Scan system electronically tracks total grocery store sales and individual household purchase behavior through complete universal product code (UPC) scanner coverage. People in the 2,500 household samples in each of several metropolitan markets covered by the service carry special identification cards and are individually tracked via scanner in grocery stores and drugstores. An example of the type of information generated is given in Exhibit 4–11. Note how the information is used to form age-group segments. IRI publishes *The Marketing Fact Book,* which has consumer purchase data on all product categories. The database can be used for follow-up, in-depth analyses to meet the needs of specific companies.

Analyzing Customer Satisfaction.   "Attaining customer satisfaction is the goal of all marketing activities and indicates that these activities have been conducted successfully."[26] Customer satisfaction is measured by comparing customer *expectations* about the product and supporting services with the *performance* of the product and supporting services.[27] Some researches indicate that *prior experience* may be a better basis of comparison than *expectations.*[28]

Customer satisfaction depends on the perceived performance of a product and supporting services and the standards that customers use to evaluate that performance.[29] The customer's standards complicate the relationship between organizational product

EXHIBIT 4–11 Analysis of Age of Soap Purchasers

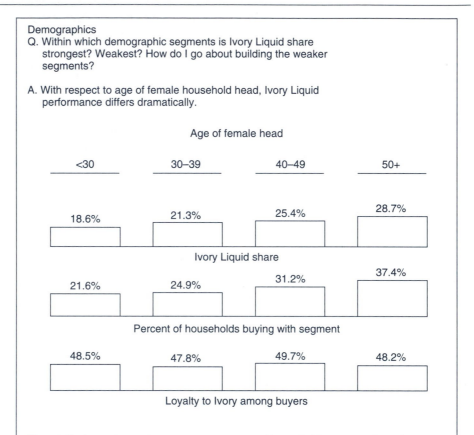

Demographics
Q. Within which demographic segments is Ivory Liquid share strongest? Weakest? How do I go about building the weaker segments?

A. With respect to age of female household head, Ivory Liquid performance differs dramatically.

Age of female head

| <30 | 30–39 | 40–49 | 50+ |

| 18.6% | 21.3% | 25.4% | 28.7% |

Ivory Liquid share

| 21.6% | 24.9% | 31.2% | 37.4% |

Percent of households buying with segment

| 48.5% | 47.8% | 49.7% | 48.2% |

Loyalty to Ivory among buyers

The relatively weaker performance among younger households traces to fewer buyers. Among those who *did* buy, loyalty was similar in all segments.

To build a share, promotions (perhaps high-value coupons) and/or advertising aimed at trial generation among younger female household heads should be considered.

This analysis can, of course, include a fill range of additional demographic variables.

The above data are entirely fictional. Brand names are used only to add an element of reality. Any similarity to actual brand data is entirely coincidental.

Source: *The Marketing Fact Book*® (Chicago: Information Resources, 1986), p. 10.

specifications (e.g., product attribute tolerances) and satisfaction. Standards may involve something other than prepurchase expectations, such as the perceived performance of competing products. Importantly, the standards are likely to vary across market segments.

Defining and monitoring customer satisfaction is a challenging task, involving far more than a simple tracking of satisfaction. Determining segment-specific standards is essential when buyers' needs and wants are differentiated. These standards can and probably do change over time. Additionally, satisfaction is an emotional response to a performance evaluation and therefore may change over time.

Customer satisfaction does not have a simple, one-to-one relationship with other purchase/use processes such as customer complaints. This highlights the importance of monitoring the relevant customer-perceived dimensions of quality. Finally, the performance attributes that lead to customer satisfaction may not correspond exactly to those that influence the initial purchase decision. While there may be substantial overlap, unique attributes of satisfaction may exist. For example, the safety of an automobile may not be an important brand-selection criterion. But later, if the buyer learns that his or her car is unsafe, then dissatisfaction is quite likely to occur.

Competitor Analysis

Market segment analysis considers the set of key competitors currently active in the segment market plus any potential segment entrants. In complex market structures, mapping the competitive arena may require detailed analysis. The competing firms are described and evaluated to highlight their strengths and weaknesses. Information useful in the competitor analysis includes business scope and objectives; market position; market target(s) and customer base; positioning strategy; financial, technical, and operating strengths; management experience and capabilities; and special competitive advantages (e.g., patents). It is also important to anticipate the future strategies of key competitors.

Value chain analysis can be used to examine competitive advantage at the segment level. Chapter 2 has a framework for advantage analysis and discusses the value chain concept. A complete assessment of the nature and intensity of competition in the segment is important in determining whether to enter (or exit from) the segment and how to compete in the segment. As discussed in Chapter 3, examining the five forces suggested by Porter is useful for determining segment attractiveness.[30]

Positioning Analysis

We will consider positioning strategy for each of the firm's market targets in Chapter 6. The issue is briefly considered now since segment analysis involves some preliminary choices about positioning strategy. One objective of segment analysis is to obtain guidelines for developing a positioning strategy.

Flexibility exists in selecting how to position the firm (or brand) with its customers and against its competition in a segment. Positioning analysis shows how to combine product, distribution, pricing, and promotion strategies to favorably position the brand with buyers in the segment. For example, positioning guidelines for different steel strapping market segments are shown in Exhibit 4–7. Similarly, promotion strategy guidelines for younger Ivory Liquid soap potential buyers are suggested by the analysis in Exhibit 4–11. The selected positioning strategy should meet the needs and requirements of the targeted buyers at a cost that yields a profitable margin for the organization.

EXHIBIT 4–12 Segment Financial and Market Attractiveness

Estimated ($ millions)	Segment		
	X	Y	Z
Sales*	10	16	5
Variable costs*	4	9	3
Contribution margin*	6	7	2
Market share†	60%	30%	10%
Total segment sales	17	53	50
Segment position:			
Business strength	High	Medium	Low
Attractiveness‡	Medium	Low	High

*For a two-year period.
†Percent of total sales in the segment.
‡Based upon a five-year projection.

Estimating Segment Attractiveness

The financial and market attractiveness of each segment needs to be evaluated. Included are specific estimates of revenue, cost, and segment profit contribution over the planning horizon. Market attractiveness can be measured by market growth rate projections and attractiveness assessments made by management.

Financial analysis obtains sales, cost, and profit contribution estimates for each segment of interest. Since accurate forecasting is difficult if the projections are too far into the future, detailed projections extend, typically, two to five years ahead. Both the segment's competitive position evaluation and the financial forecasts are used in comparing segments. In all instances the risks and returns associated with serving a particular segment need to be considered. Flows of revenues and costs can be weighted to take into account risks and the time value of revenues and expenditures.

Segment Analysis Illustration

An illustrative segment analysis is shown in Exhibit 4–12. A two-year period is used for estimating sales, costs, contribution margin, and market share. Depending on the forecasting difficulty, estimates for a longer time period can be used. When appropriate, estimates can be expressed as present values of future revenues and costs. "Business strength" in Exhibit 4–12 refers to the present position of the firm relative to the competition in the segment. Alternatively, it can be expressed as the present position and an estimated future position, based upon plans for increasing business strength. Attractiveness is evaluated, typically, for some future time period. In the illustration a five-year projection is used.

The example shows how segment opportunities are ranked according to their overall attractiveness. The analysis can be expanded to include additional information such as profiles of key competitors. The rankings are admittedly subjective since decision makers will vary in their weighting of estimated financial position, business strength, and segment attractiveness. Place yourself in the role of a manager evaluating the segments. Using the information in Exhibit 4–12, rank segments X, Y, and Z as to their overall importance as market targets. Unless management is ready to allocate a major chunk of resources to segment Z to build business strength, it appears to be a candidate for the last-place position. Yet Z has some attractive characteristics. The segment has the most favorable market attractiveness of the three, and its estimated total sales are nearly equal to Y's for the next two years. The big problem with Z is its business strength. The key question is whether Z's market share can be increased. If not, X looks like a good prospect for a top rating, followed by Y, and by Z. Of course, management may decide to go after all three segments.

SUMMARY

Market segmentation is often a requirement for competing in many product-markets because buyers differ in their preferences for products and services. Finding out what these preferences are and grouping buyers with similar needs are an essential part of marketing strategy development. Market segmentation is an opportunity for a small firm to focus on buyers where its competitive advantages are most favorable. Large firms seeking to establish or protect a dominant market position can often do so by targeting multiple segments.

Segmentation of a product-market requires that response differences exist between segments, and that the segments are identifiable and stable over time. Also, the benefits of segmentation should exceed the costs. Segmenting a market involves identifying the basis of segmentation, forming segments, describing each segment, and analyzing and evaluating the segment(s) of interest. The variables useful as bases for forming and describing segments include the characteristics of people and organizations, use situation, buyers' needs and preferences, and purchase behavior.

Segments can be formed by identifying customer groups using the characteristics of people or organizations. The groups are analyzed to determine if the response profiles are different across the candidate segments. Alternatively, customer response information can be used to form customer groupings and then the descriptive characteristics of the groups can be analyzed to find out if segments can be identified. Several examples of segment formation were discussed to illustrate the methods that are available for this purpose.

Segment analysis and evaluation should identify the segments in a product-market and show the strengths and limitations of each segment as a potential market target for the organization. Segment analysis includes customer descriptions and satisfaction analysis, evaluating existing and potential competitors and competitive advantage, marketing program positioning analysis, and financial and market attractiveness. Segment analysis is important in evaluating customer satisfaction, finding new-product opportunities, selecting market targets, and designing positioning strategies. A good segmentation strategy creates an important competitive edge for an organization.

QUESTIONS FOR REVIEW AND DISCUSSION

1. Competing in the unified European market raises some interesting market segment questions. Discuss the segmentation issues regarding this multiple-country market.

2. Why are there marketing strategy advantages in using demographic characteristics to break out product-markets into segments?

3. The real test of a segment formation scheme occurs after it has been tried and the results evaluated. Are there ways to evaluate alternative segmenting schemes without actually trying them?

4. Suggest ways of obtaining the information needed to conduct a market segment analysis.

5. Why may it become necessary for companies to change their market segmentation identification over time?

6. "Market segmentation is a strategy that is primarily suitable for use in U.S. markets." Discuss.

7. Is it necessary to use a unique positioning strategy for each market segment targeted by an organization?

8. Under what circumstances may it not be possible to break up a product-market into segments? What are the dangers of using an incorrect segment formation scheme?

9. What are some of the advantages in using mass customization technology to satisfy the needs of buyers?

NOTES

1. Peter R. Dickson and James L. Ginter, "Market Segmentation, Product Differentiation, and Marketing Strategy," *Journal of Marketing,* April 1987, pp. 1–10.
2. Michael Dertouzos, Richard Lester, and Robert Solow, *Made in America* (Cambridge, MA: MIT Commission on Industrial Productivity, 1989).
3. John H. Taylor, "Niche Player," *Forbes,* April 1, 1991, p. 70.
4. Ibid.
5. Gary L. Lilien and Philip Kotler, *Marketing Decision Making* (New York: Harper & Row, 1983), p. 291.
6. Henry Assael, *Consumer Behavior and Marketing Action,* 2nd ed. (Boston: PWS–Kent Publishing, 1984), p. 225.
7. Jerry Flint, "The Magazine Factory," *Forbes,* May 22, 1995, pp. 160–62.
8. Jay L. Laughlin and Charles R. Taylor, "An Approach to Industrial Market Segmentation," *Industrial Marketing Management* 20 (1991), pp. 127–36.
9. Peter R. Dickson, "Person-Situation: Segmentation's Missing Link," *Journal of Marketing,* Fall 1982, p. 57.
10. Nicholas Bray, "Credit Lyonnaise Targets Wealthy Clients," *The Wall Street Journal,* July 24, 1994.
11. A. H. Maslow, "Theory of Human Motivation," *Psychology Review,* July 1943, pp. 43–45.
12. Betsy Morris, "How Much Will People Pay to Save a Few Minutes of Cooking? Plenty," *The Wall Street Journal,* July 25, 1985, p. 23.
13. Assael, *Consumer Behavior and Marketing Action,* p. 650.
14. Bernard Berelson and Gary A. Steiner, *Human Behavior: An Inventory of Scientific Findings* (New York: Harcourt Brace Jovanovich, 1964), p. 88.
15. Henry Assael, *Marketing Management* (Boston: PWS–Kent Publishing, 1985), pp. 126–27.
16. Louise O'Brien and Charles Jones, "Do Rewards Really Create Loyalty?" *Harvard Business Review,* May–June 1995, p. 78.
17. David W. Cravens, Gerald E. Hills, and Robert B. Woodruff, *Marketing Management* (Burr Ridge, IL: Richard D. Irwin, 1987, pp. 297–300.
18. Miriam Jordan, "In India, Luxury Is Within Reach of Many," *The Wall Street Journal,* October 17, 1995, p. A15.
19. Dickson and Ginter, "Market Segmentation," p. 4.
20. George S. Day, *Market Driven Strategy* (New York: Free Press, 1990), pp. 101–4.
21. Nancy Rotenier, "Antistatus Backpacks, $450 a Copy," *Forbes,* June 19, 1995, pp. 118–20.
22. Allanna Sullivan, "Mobil Bets Drivers Pick Cappuccino over Low Prices," *The Wall Street Journal,* January 30, 1995, pp. B1 and B4.
23. V. Kasturi Ranga, Rowland T. Moriarity, and Gordon S. Swartz, "Segmenting Customers in Mature Industrial Markets," *Journal of Marketing,* October 1992, pp. 72–82.
24. Assael, *Consumer Behavior and Marketing Action,* p. 262.
25. Linda Killian, "Crane's Progress," *Forbes,* August 19, 1991, p. 44.

26. C. W. Park and Gerald Zaltman, *Marketing Management* (Hinsdale, IL: Dryden Press, 1987), p. 196.

27. A. Parasuraman, Valarie A. Zeithaml, and Leonard L. Berry, "A Conceptual Model of Service Quality and Its Implications for Future Research," *Journal of Marketing,* Fall 1985, pp. 41–50.

28. Robert B. Woodruff, Ernest R. Cadotte, and Roger L. Jenkins, "Modeling Consumer Satisfaction Processes Using Experienced-Based Norms," *Journal of Marketing Research,* August 1983, pp. 296–304.

29. The following discussion of customer satisfaction is based on discussions with Robert B. Woodruff, the University of Tennessee, Knoxville.

30. Michael E. Porter, *Competitive Advantage* (New York: Free Press, 1985), pp. 4–8.

Continuous Learning about Markets

We looked at the strong relationship between market orientation and organizational performance in Chapter 1. Understanding markets and competition is critical to achieving market orientation. "Every discussion of market orientation emphasizes the ability of the firm to learn about customers, competitors, and channel members in order to continually sense and act on events and trends in present and prospective markets."[1] Market-driven companies display superior skills in gathering, interpreting, and using information to guide their business and marketing strategies.

The market sensing of Hewlett-Packard Company's (H-P) management in the early 1980s about computer printer technology guided H-P's strategy to become the global market leader.[2] Management's interpretation of market sensing information resulted in a shared vision about the printer market. H-P correctly anticipated that dot matrix technology would eventually be replaced by a superior printing method that was not as expensive as laser printers. H-P's management was convinced its inkjet technology would replace dot matrix printers and offer a cost-effective alternative to laser printers in the mass market. Sales of printers in North America are shown in Exhibit 5–1. In developing the printer, H-P's new product team studied information from customers, competitors, and distributors to guide design, production, and marketing decisions.

In this chapter we examine how continuous learning about markets improves competitive advantage. First, we look at the relationship between market orientation and organizational learning. Next, we discuss several sources of information. The chapter then

This chapter was prepared by Professor Karen S. Cravens, University of Tulsa.

EXHIBIT 5–1 Sales of Printers in North America

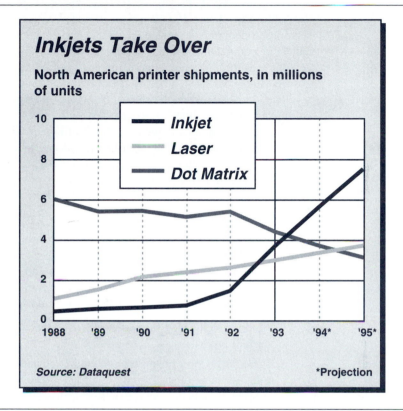

Inkjets Take Over

North American printer shipments, in millions of units

Source: Dataquest   **Projection*

Source: Stephen Kreider Yoder, "Shoving Back: How H-P Used Tactics of the Japanese to Beat Them at Their Game," *The Wall Street Journal,* September 8, 1994, p. A6.

looks at information methods and capabilities, which include marketing research, standardized information services, management information systems, database systems, and decision support systems. Throughout the chapter we consider several important issues concerning continuous learning about markets.

MARKET ORIENTATION AND ORGANIZATIONAL LEARNING

Information plays a vital role in management's decision making at Frito-Lay, a subsidiary of PepsiCo Inc.[3] Responding to the diversity of buyers' preferences, the leading chip maker sells 85 varieties of potato chips. Frito-Lay relentlessly studies what consumers like (and don't like) about snack foods, conducting nearly 500,000 interviews a year. Quality control closely monitors chip thickness, since marketing research indicates that consumers complain if their chips are 8/1,000ths of an inch too thick or thin. Over 6,000 taste tests are conducted each year to gain feedback from consumers on new flavors that are being evaluated. Package colors are tested to make sure consumer reactions are favorable. Frito-Lay's 10,000-person sales force is part of the market sensing process, sending headquarters inventory data and competitors' new product information with their handheld computers. Frito-Lay's commitment to customer satisfaction has helped the company gain an awesome market share position of 47 percent, compared to second position Eagle Snacks (Anheuser-Busch) with a 7 percent share in 1994.

The Frito-Lay example shows the close relationship between a market-oriented culture and organizational learning. We will review the characteristics of a market-oriented culture and look at the importance of organizational learning in creating superior customer value. Next we will describe the process of learning about markets and discuss the role of learning in creating competitive advantage. Finally, we overview the available ways of obtaining information.

Market Orientation

Market orientation is both a culture and a process committed to achieving superior customer value (Chapter 1). The process consists of information acquisition, broad information dissemination, and shared diagnosis and coordinated action.[4] Market orientation provides the foundation for organizational learning, although some cautions need to be considered in achieving the potential of learning.[5]

1. Market intelligence may be so focused that opportunities or threats outside the current product-market are ignored.
2. Prevailing views of market orientation consider current customers and competitors, whereas other learning sources, including suppliers, noncompeting businesses, consultants, and government, may provide important information.

Thus, the market orientation view needs to extend beyond traditional market boundaries to include all of the relevant sources of knowledge and ideas. A key issue is deciding how broad this orientation should be.

Characteristics of the Learning Organization.   Our understanding of the learning organization continues to unfold as the processes used by successful organizations are studied and evaluated. These organizations share several common characteristics:

> Learning organizations are guided by a shared vision that focuses the energies of organizational members on creating superior value for customers. These organizations continuously acquire, process, and disseminate throughout the organization knowledge about markets, products, technologies, and business processes. They do not hesitate to question long-held assumptions and beliefs regarding their business. Their knowledge is based on experience, experimentation, and information from customers, suppliers, competitors, and other sources. Through complex communication, coordination, and conflict resolution processes, these organizations reach a shared interpretation of the information, which enables them to act swiftly and decisively to exploit opportunities and defuse problems. Learning organizations are exceptional in their ability to anticipate and act on opportunities in turbulent and fragmenting markets.[6]

Additional research promises to further expand our knowledge about these complex organizational processes.

Learning and Competitive Advantage.   The advantage gained from learning is that the organization is able to quickly and effectively respond to opportunities and threats, and to satisfy customers' needs with new products and improved services.[7] Learning reduces the time necessary to accomplish projects such as new product development. H-P's success with the inkjet printer is illustrative.

Learning about Markets

Learning about markets requires developing a process throughout the organization for obtaining, interpreting, and acting on information from sensing activities. The learning processes of market-oriented companies follow these steps.[8]

Open-Minded Inquiry.   The danger to be avoided is not being open to exploring new views about markets and competition. Search for information is of little value if management already has a view on which new information will have no influence.

The members of the market-oriented organization recognize the importance of market sensing and coordinated interpretation of market intelligence to guide strategies. Not all companies see the value in continuous learning about markets. Managers who are not part of market-driven cultures may be unwilling to invest in information for decision making. Unfortunately, these same companies often encounter problems because of faulty or incomplete market sensing.

Continuous learning allows firms to capture more information about their customers, suppliers, and competitors. This capability provides the potential for growth based on informed decisions and a more complete representation of the competitive environment. Also, firms can respond much more quickly to competitors' actions and take advantage of situations in the marketplace.

Synergistic Information Distribution.   This step encourages the widespread distribution of information in the organization. The objective is to leverage the value of the information by cutting across business functions to share information on customers, channels of distribution, suppliers, and competitors. Traditional information processing in organizations allocates relevant information to each business function. Synergistic distribution works to remove functional hurdles and practices. Multifunctional teams are useful to encourage transfer of information across functions.

Mutually Informed Interpretations.   The mental model of the market guides managers' interpretation of information. The intent is to reach a shared vision about the market and about the impact that new information has on this vision. The market-oriented culture encourages market sensing. But the process requires more than gathering and studying information. "This interpretation is facilitated by the mental models of managers, which contain decision rules for deciding how to act on the information in light of anticipated outcomes."[9] The model reflects the executives' vision about the forces influencing the market and likely future directors of change. Learning occurs as members of the organization evaluate the results of their decisions based on their vision at the time the decisions were made.

MARKET SENSING FEATURE   Learning about the Foreign Tourist Market in Mexico

---

The $4 billion international tourist market didn't expand as fast as tourist officials expected after the peso was devalued in 1994.

Industry and government officials' shared vision about what drives the market did not correspond with reality. Revenues for 1995 were lower than expected.

Several explanations for the slow foreign growth are offered, including failure to recognize customer diversity (market segments), lack of contact with authentic Mexican culture, limited tour offerings (primarily beaches), political unrest, and relatively high prices for air travel and international hotels.

Mexican officials have a critical need to expand learning about the foreign tourist market. The industry employs some 630,000 people, many located in economically distressed areas.

Development of a shared vision about the market is needed to guide information acquisition and analysis. Successful market sensing will help guide marketing strategies for rebuilding foreign currency reserves, repay the $50 billion in bailout loans, and create jobs.

Source: Craig Torres, "Mexican Officials Find Projections on Tourism Growth Troubling," *The Wall Street Journal*, June 7, 1995, p. A10. Reprinted by permission of *The Wall Street Journal*, © 1995 Dow Jones & Company, Inc. All Rights Reserved Worldwide.

Members of the Mexican tourist industry are concerned about the slow growth of international tourists in Mexico during the mid-1990s. The drop of the peso was expected to attract a new wave of tourists. The Market Sensing Feature describes how tourist officials are trying to learn what influences the foreign tourist market.

Accessible Memory.   This step in the learning process emphasizes the importance of keeping and gaining access to prior learning. The objective is not to lose valuable information that can continue to be used. Hewlett-Packard's inkjet product team continued to learn how to improve the product and develop strategies based on monitoring competitors' actions. For example, prices were lowered when the team sensed that Japanese competitors were about to enter the market.

Urban Outfitters, Inc., is a successful specialty retailer that is guided by management's shared vision about the market. The company has an effective learning process. The company's fiscal 1995 sales were $110 million from 16 stores. The retailer's products include fashion apparel, accessories, household items, and gifts. Urban Outfitters' unique strategy is the shopping environment it provides to the 18–30 targeted age group. To stay ahead of its unpredictable buyers with whimsical tastes, management employs over 75 fashion spies who sense what is happening in fashion in neighborhoods in New York, California, London, and Paris.[10] Salaries and expenses of this market sensing team total $4 million annually. Market feedback guides new product decisions and signals when buyer interest is slowing down. Management is testing new retail concepts to appeal to its buyers when they move into an older age group.

Information, Analysis, and Action

Deciding about the information that is needed is the starting point in planning for and acquiring information. Because of the costs of acquiring, processing, and analyzing information, the potential benefits of needed information need to be compared to costs.

Normally, information falls into two categories: (1) information regularly supplied from internal and external sources and (2) information obtained for a particular problem or situation. Examples of the former are sales costs analyses, market share measurements, and customer satisfaction surveys. Information from the latter category includes new-product concept tests, brand preference studies, and studies of advertising effectiveness.

Several types of marketing information are available. A description of each type of information follows:

Marketing Research Studies. These studies consist of customized information collected and analyzed for a particular research problem. The information may be obtained through surveys and/or published sources.

Standardized Information Services. This information is available from outside vendors on a subscription or single-purchase basis. The services collect and analyze information that is sold to several customers such as prescription sales for drugs marketed to pharmaceutical firms.

Management Information Systems (MIS). Computerized systems supply information for a variety of purposes such as order processing, invoicing, customer analysis, and product performance. The information in these systems may include both internal and external data.

Database Systems. This special form of MIS includes information from internal and external sources that is computerized and used for customer and product analyses, mailing lists, identifying sales prospects, and other marketing applications.

Decision Support Systems. These computerized systems provide decision-making assistance to managers and staff. Their capabilities are more advanced than an MIS.

Competitor Intelligence Systems. Companies are using competitor intelligence systems to help monitor competitors and to identify firms that may become competitors. Intelligence activities include searching databases, conducting customer surveys, interviewing suppliers and other channel members, forming strategic alliances with competitors, hiring competitors' employees, and evaluating competitors' products.

The firm's complete information needs should be considered before committing to major marketing information systems. Most firms benefit from a routine and complete evaluation of their information situation. Cooperation among departments can save the firm countless employee-hours and dollars. Far too often a department launches an expensive information-gathering project only to discover later that another department already had the type of information sought. Synergistic information distribution encourages sharing.

In the remainder of the chapter, we will examine the methods of acquiring and processing information for use in marketing decision making. The objective is to show how the various information capabilities assist decision makers in strategic and operating decisions. A good marketing information management strategy takes into account the interrelationship of these capabilities.

EXHIBIT 5–2   Off-Air Test Marketing Research Project Proposal

---

Brand:	Colgate.
Project:	Copy Test: "Midnight Delight."
Background and Purpose:	A new commercial has been developed—"Midnight Delight." Brand Group is interested in determining its effectiveness. The objectives of this study will be to determine

- Brand recall.
- Copy recall.
- Purchase intent shifts.
- Comparison with previous copy testing results.

Research Method: This research will be conducted using central location mall facilities in Boston, Atlanta, Milwaukee, and San Francisco. Each commercial will be viewed by 200 past-30-week toothpaste users as follows:

		Age Group	Number of Respondents
Males	50%	8–11	30
Females	50%	12–17	50
		18–24	25
		25–34	25
		34–49	10
		50+	10
			150

Information to Be Obtained:

- Brand recall.
- Copy recall.
- Pre- and postpurchase intentions.

Action Standard: This study, which is being done for information purposes, will be used in conjunction with previous copy testing results.

Cost and Timing: The cost for one commercial will be $6,500 ± 10%. The following schedule will be established:

Field work	3 weeks
Top-line reports	1 week
Final report	3 weeks
Total	7 weeks

Supplier: Legget Lustig Firtle, Inc.

Source: William R. Dillon, Thomas J. Madden, and Neil H. Firtle, *Marketing Research in a Marketing Environment*, 3rd ed. (Burr Ridge, IL: Richard D. Irwin, 1994), p. 611.

MARKETING RESEARCH INFORMATION

Marketing research information is obtained from internal records, trade contacts, published information, surveys, and many other sources. An example of a research study is shown in Exhibit 5–2. It is a proposed test of the effectiveness of an advertising commercial. Marketing research studies range in cost from less than $10,000 to over $100,000.

Marketing research is "the systematic gathering, recording, processing, and analyzing of marketing data, which—when interpreted—will help the marketing executive to uncover opportunities and to reduce risks in decision making."[11] Strategies for obtaining marketing research information include collecting existing information, using standardized research services, and conducting special research studies.

Collecting Existing Information

The internal information system of the firm affects the extent and ease of collection of existing information. The nature and scope of the information and the information system network will vary greatly from firm to firm and among industries. Many firms have extensive internal information systems, or at least the capability to implement such systems.

There is considerable value and potential in using the information in the organization's current system. This is essential for the strategic mission of the firm, as well as for efficient utilization of assets. Information is a resource that must be consciously managed.[12] Management should structure the information system to capture this resource and control its use. Information is not a by-product of activities of the firm. It is a scarce, valuable resource that affects the future success or failure of the firm. Management may not have control over the actions of competitors or consumers, but an effective information system provides a way to react.

The product mix and the nature of business operations influence what type of internal marketing information system is appropriate in a particular firm. High-volume sales transactions such as those for banks, groceries, drugs, and other low-unit-price consumer products require computerized tracking-and-analysis capabilities. In contrast, a producer of low-volume, high-cost products such as ships, steam turbines, aircraft, or other large industrial equipment may have less need for this type of system. Instead, such firms may need information on scheduling and on tracking and allocation of costs and materials. Manufacturers have different information requirements than retailers or wholesalers. The size and complexity of the firm also influence the composition of the information system.

The costs and benefits of the information must be evaluated for both short-term and long-term planning. Incremental efforts and expenditures in the early stages of creating an internal information system may avoid future costly modifications. Achieving long-term performance may require temporary losses to finance a system. It is critical to consider a long-term perspective in evaluating information system decisions.

AT&T's competitor-monitoring system draws from a variety of sources. The company has an electronic directory that is a collection of databases designed to assist with competitive intelligence.[13] Employees at all levels in the organization input information into the system. Newspaper and periodical items are also collected from print and electronic sources. A competitive digest is issued to top management daily, and the system is always available for inquiry or special requests. This is an integrated system combining knowledge from a multitude of sources in an organized and standardized manner. It provides a complete analysis of the competitors for AT&T's 70 product lines. Competitors can be analyzed, highlighting growth opportunities or strategies for maintaining market position.

Standardized Information Services

A wide variety of marketing information is available for purchase in special publications and on a subscription basis. In some instances, the information may be free. Suppliers include government agencies, universities, private research firms, industry and trade organizations, and consultants. A key advantage to standardized information is that the costs of collection and analysis are shared by many users. The major limitation is that the information may not correspond well with the user's needs. Such services offer substantial cost advantages, and many are quite inexpensive (e.g., data distributed from the U.S. Census of Population). Many services allow online access to data, enabling subscribers to automatically input external information into their own information systems.

Dun & Bradstreet's portfolio of standardized information services meets a wide range of decision-making needs. Some examples follow:[14]

The A. C. Nielsen subsidiary collects information on audience ratings of TV shows. Decisions to continue or drop shows often depend on these ratings.

The Petroleum Information Corporation unit supplies information on drilling and production for firms interested in oil and gas exploration activities around the world.

Moody's Investors Service supplies over 15 million different pieces of information on more than 22,000 companies worldwide and 28,000 local and state governments.

Nielsen's food and drug data are vital to marketing decisions in these markets. A company can use the large data banks collected and organized by D&B to make many different analyses, depending on its strategic marketing information needs. The cost of the information for use by one company would be prohibitive, but by sharing the database, a wide range of company information needs can be met. An example from one of A. C. Nielsen's food and drug information reports is shown in Exhibit 5–3.

The research firm Information Resources, Inc. (IRI), uses electronic retail store scanning systems to record purchases by people participating on consumer panels.[15] Previously, these purchases were recorded by the consumer in diaries that yielded many discrepancies. In one situation, only one-third of the diaries that listed a purchase of Kellogg's Frosted Flakes were correct. Scanning systems in stores automatically record consumers' purchases, eliminating the need for diaries and providing accurate data. IRI installs a complete electronic monitoring system in each city where it has a consumer panel. IRI can also monitor the television programs watched by participants and insert test commercials into programming. Commercials can be targeted to households with specific demographic characteristics since these data are recorded for all participants. Subsequent purchases measure the effect of the commercial. Additionally, IRI can monitor the use of coupons to test products and the strength of competitors. With this network, IRI can respond to various queries from clients such as Campbell Soup Company, Procter & Gamble, Johnson & Johnson, and General Foods Corporation. IRI monitors consumer reactions and preferences without revealing to them which products are being tested. Firms can introduce advertising campaigns and determine optimal marketing strategies.

EXHIBIT 5–3 Nielsen Food and Drug Retail Index System

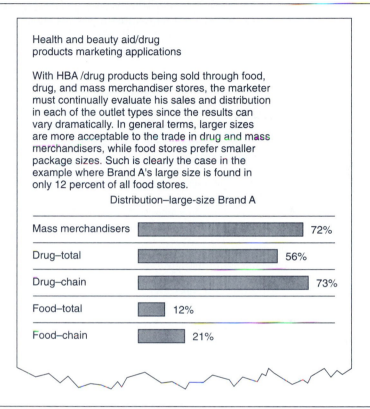

Health and beauty aid/drug
products marketing applications

With HBA /drug products being sold through food, drug, and mass merchandiser stores, the marketer must continually evaluate his sales and distribution in each of the outlet types since the results can vary dramatically. In general terms, larger sizes are more acceptable to the trade in drug and mass merchandisers, while food stores prefer smaller package sizes. Such is clearly the case in the example where Brand A's large size is found in only 12 percent of all food stores.

Distribution–large-size Brand A

Mass merchandisers	72%
Drug–total	56%
Drug–chain	73%
Food–total	12%
Food–chain	21%

Source: A. C. Nielsen Company.

Special Research Studies

Research studies are initiated in response to problems or special information needs. Examples include market segmentation, new-product concept tests, product use tests, brand-name research, and advertising recall tests. Studies may range in scope from exploratory research based primarily on evaluating published information to field surveys involving personal, phone, or mail interviews with respondents who represent target populations.

In deciding whether to employ marketing research and when interpreting the results, several considerations are important.

Defining the Problem.   Care must be exercised in formulating the research problem. It is essential to spell out exactly what information is needed to solve the problem. If this cannot be done, exploratory research should be conducted to help define the research problem and determine the objectives. Caution should be exercised to avoid defining a symptom rather than the underlying problem.

Understanding the Limitations of the Research. Most studies are unable to do everything that the user wishes to accomplish and also stay within the available budget. Priorities for the information that is needed should be indicated. Also, obtaining certain information may not be feasible. For example, measuring the impact of advertising on profits may not be possible due to the influence of many other factors on profits.

Quality of the Research. There are many challenges to obtaining sound research results. The available evidence indicates that some studies are not well designed and implemented and may contain biased results. Factors that affect the quality of study results include the experience of the research personnel, the size of the sample, the wording of questions, and how the data are analyzed. This example highlights the difficulties in achieving reliable results:[16]

> A Gallup poll sponsored by the disposable diaper industry asked: "It is estimated that disposable diapers account for less than 2 percent of the trash in today's landfills. In contrast, beverage containers, third-class mail, and yard waste are estimated to account for about 21 percent of trash in landfills. Given this, in your opinion, would it be fair to ban disposable diapers?"

Not surprisingly, because of the wording of the question, 84 percent of the respondents answered no to the question.

Evaluating and Selecting Suppliers. Typically, research studies are not conducted by the user. When selecting a supplier, it is important to talk with two or three prior clients to determine their satisfaction with the research firm. It is also important to identify consultants who are experienced in conducting the particular type of research needed by the user. Familiarity with the industry may also be important.

Costs. Research studies are expensive. As an example, a proposal for a major market-tracking study is described in Exhibit 5–4. Although telephone interviews are much less expensive than personal interviews, the tracking study is nevertheless very expensive. The factors that affect study costs include sample size, the length of the questionnaire, and how the information will be obtained. The complexity of the study objectives also increases the required professional capabilities of research personnel.

COMPUTERIZED INFORMATION SYSTEMS

There are many types of information systems within the organization. Manual systems are also used and may provide crucial information. Yet, for purposes of this chapter, attention is focused on computerized information systems. "Strategic systems are those that change the goals, products, services, or environmental relationships of organizations."[17] These information systems alter how a firm does business with competitors, suppliers, and customers. Since the scope of strategic planning is so broad, information generated by the system is invaluable in strategic marketing planning. The system may provide information to assist decision makers with strategic planning or may actually prepare a plan and formulate decisions. We describe management information systems, database systems, and decision-support systems.

EXHIBIT 5–4 Market Tracking Proposal

Brand:	Skweeky Kleen Bar Soap.
Project:	Bar Soap National Tracking Study.
Background and Purpose:	The Bar Soap Brand Group has requested that a continuous tracking study be conducted in 1990. This study will be a continuation of the 1989 tracking study. The objectives of this study will be

1. To determine track changes in brand awareness and use since the introduction of new products.
2. To determine changes in volume contribution within the market.
3. To analyze consumer perceptions and to measure changes in those perceptions among various market segments.

Research Method:	The 1990 study will be conducted during the course of the year, and monthly waves of interviewing will begin in January. This monthly tracking system was also used in 1989. As in previous studies, interviewing will be conducted by WATS telephone from a central location. Telephone numbers will be selected via strict probability methods from all working exchanges and numbers in the continental United States. Respondents will be randomly selected within households. A total of 2,400 past-30-day bar soap users will be interviewed (200 per month for the 12 months of January through December 1989). The basic questionnaire will follow the format used in the 1989 study and will include the following question areas:

- Brand awareness (unaided and aided).
- Brand use (ever, past 30 days, most often).
- Number of bars used past 30 days.
- Brand ratings for brands ever used, but not past 30 days.
- Importance of product attributes.
- Other diagnostic question areas (to vary).

Cost and Timing:	Fieldwork will be conducted monthly, beginning in January. Top line reports on brand awareness and use will be provided monthly, whereas more complete reports will be reported quarterly and when all the interviews are completed. The specific timing will be (continued)

Management Information Systems

Management information systems (MIS) provide raw data to decision makers within a firm. The system collects data on the transactions of the firm and may include competitor and environmental information. The decision makers (and systems analysts) are responsible for extracting the data relevant for a decision and in the appropriate format to facilitate the process. The system can provide information for decisions at all levels of the organization. Yet, lower- and middle-level managers use the system most often for operating decisions. The system may generate routine reports for frequent operating decisions, such as weekly sales by product, or may be queried for nonroutine decisions on an as-needed basis. Nonroutine decisions may consist of tracking the sales performance of a sales district over several months, determining the number of customer returns for a particular good, or listing all customers or suppliers within a given geographic area. The basic MIS collects data and allows for retrieval and manipulation of format in an organized manner. Typically, the MIS does not interact in the decision-making process. More advanced MIS capabilities provide important decision analysis capabilities.

EXHIBIT 5–4 (concluded)

Interview Date	Number of Interviews	Timing of Monthly Top-Lines	Timing of Quarterly Top-Lines	Final Report
January	200	2/13	—	—
February	200	3/13	—	—
March	200	4/10	—	—
1st quarter	600	—	5/15	—
April	200	5/8	—	—
May	200	6/12	—	—
June	200	7/15	—	—
2nd quarter	600	—	8/14	—
July	200	8/11	—	—
August	200	9/11	—	—
September	200	10/12	—	—
3rd quarter	600	—	11/13	—
October	200	11/9	—	—
November	200	12/11	—	—
December	200	1/13	—	—
4th quarter	600	—	1/23	—
Total	2,400			

The cost of this study will be $100,000 ± 10%.

Supplier: Burke Marketing Research.

Source: William R. Dillon, Thomas J. Madden, and Neil H. Firtle, *Marketing Research in a Marketing Environment*, 3rd ed. (Burr Ridge, IL: Richard D. Irwin, 1994), p. 625.

Consider this MIS application. A sophisticated marketing information system enables a major airline to focus on the needs of specific market segments.[18] The system determines mileage awards for frequent flyers and provides a reservation support database, organized by market segments. The company's top 3 percent of customers accounts for 50 percent of sales. These key accounts are highlighted on all service screens and reports. Reservations agents are alerted that a person is an important customer. The frequent flyers receive a variety of special services, including boarding priority and first class upgrades.

Database Systems

Target uses an effective database system to respond to customer diversity in its stores. Management's model of the market takes into account differences in product needs and preferences by store location. The Database Feature describes how Target uses micromarketing to satisfy customers. It also indicates how internal personnel initially resisted the learning process.

DATABASE FEATURE   Micromarketing in Action

The purpose of micromarketing is to tailor retail store offerings to customers' needs and preferences.

Rather than offer the same merchandise at all of Target's 600+ retail stores, the discount chain uses computer technology to offer specialized merchandise.

The objective is to have the right merchandise in the location where and when buyers want it.

Target's internal buyers resisted micromarketing because they were accustomed to using buyer power to get the best prices.

Individual stores can add merchandise without headquarter's approval.

Target's sophisticated computerized buying, planning, and store operations systems help create merchandise mixes that cater to racial, ethnic, and age characteristics of different customer segments.

Store managers further refine the merchandise offering based on local tastes and practices.

Interestingly, the merchandise variation that responds to the customer is only 15 to 20 percent. The plan is to raise this to 30 percent.

Source: Gregory A. Patterson, "Different Strokes: Target 'Micromarkets' Its Way to Success; No Two Stores Are Alike," *The Wall Street Journal,* May 31, 1995, pp. A1 and A9. Reprinted by permission of *The Wall Street Journal,* © 1995 Dow Jones & Company, Inc. All Rights Reserved Worldwide.

Databases are a form of MIS. Some database systems offer capabilities similar to those of decision-support systems. Computerized databases are indispensable for companies pursuing direct marketing strategies. Chapter 13 includes discussion of database marketing as a form of promotional strategy.

The components of database systems include relational databases, personal computers, electronic publishing media, and voice systems.[19] The intent of database marketing is effectively using a computerized customer database to facilitate a significant and profitable communication with customers.

Decision-Support Systems

A decision-support system (DSS) assists in the decision making process using the information captured by the MIS. A marketing decision-support system (MDSS) integrates data that are not easily found, assimilated, formatted, or readily manipulated with software and hardware into a decision-making process that provides the marketing decision maker with assistance when needed.[20] The MDSS allows the user flexibility in applications and in format. A MDSS can be used for various levels of decision making, ranging from determining reorder points for inventory to launching a new product.

The components of the MDSS consist of the database, the display, the models, and the analysis capabilities.[21]

Database.   Various kinds of information are included in the database, such as standardized marketing information produced by Nielsen and other research suppliers, sales and cost data, and internal information such as product sales, advertising data, and price information. The design and updating of the database are vital to the effectiveness of

MDSS. The information should be relevant and organized to correspond to the units of analysis used in the system.

Display.   This component of the MDSS enables the user to communicate with the database. Marketing managers and their staff need to interact with the database:

> They must be able to extract, manipulate, and display data easily and quickly. Required capabilities range from simple ad hoc retrieval to more formal reports that track market status and product performance. Also needed are exception reports that flag problem areas. Many presentations should have graphics integrated with other materials.[22]

Models.   This component of the MDSS provides mathematical and computational representations of variables and their interrelationships. For example, a sales force deployment model would include an effort-to-sales response function model and a deployment algorithm for use in analyzing selling effort allocation alternatives. The decision-support models are useful in analysis, planning, and control.

Analysis.   This capability consists of a portfolio of analysis methods such as regression analysis, factor analysis, time series, and preference mapping. Various software capabilities may be included in the system. Analysis may be performed on a data set to study relationships, identify trends, prepare forecasts, and examine the impact of alternative decision rules.

MDSS may operate autonomously or instead may require interaction with the decision maker during the process. There may be several points before a recommendation is formed where the decision maker responds to queries to refine the scenario. Thus, an interactive MDSS requires more assistance from the decision maker and has more room for variation than an autonomous MDSS. The system is dependent on the quality and accuracy of the information and assumptions that are used in the system. The process should be viewed as a tool to assist in decision making, and not as a final product in itself.

Ideally, the experience and shared vision of management are built into the model. But often information is missing, and the decision maker has the best grasp of the entire situation. The most complete decisions incorporate the recommendation of the MDSS, but do not rely upon them solely. However, a DSS often serves to create or support a consensus, and evidence exists that a DSS does yield favorable decision-making performance when it is properly designed and applied to appropriate decision situations. Evaluations of DSS effectiveness show mixed results.[23] In a controlled laboratory test using senior undergraduate students enrolled in a business policy course, researchers found that groups using the DSS made significantly better decisions than their non-DSS counterparts. Thus, there is supporting evidence of the value of DSS. Nevertheless, further evaluation is needed to better define the conditions and applications where success is likely to occur.

The concept of the MDSS as a tool is most apparent when considering strategic decisions rather than operating decisions. Clear, concise answers may not always be possible, yet the system is a very valuable tool in the process. Consider the following:

> A DSS developed by William Luther analyzes key success factors in the marketplace and makes comparisons with competitors. This system is called a Strategic Planning Model, and is most useful for smaller companies. Managers input their definition of key success factors by means of a standardized questionnaire format. Comparisons are made between the firm and

competitors for these factors. The factors can be weighted for importance, and multiple situations can be considered. The model makes projections and recommendations of strategies.[24]

In using this system it is important that managers identify key success factors; otherwise the model will lose a great deal of credibility. When properly applied it offers a useful framework for decision makers, recognizing that it is not a complete replica of the decision-making situation.

SUMMARY

Information performs a vital strategic role in an organization. Information capability creates a sustainable competitive advantage by improving the speed of decision making, reducing the costs of repetitive operations, and improving decision-making results. Market sensing is vital to the effectiveness of the market-oriented company. Managers' models of their markets guide the interpretation of information and the resulting strategies designed to keep the firm ahead of its competition. Learning about markets necessitates open-minded inquiry, widespread distribution of information with the organization, mutually informed interpretation, and development of memory to provide access to prior learning.

Marketing information capabilities include marketing research, marketing information systems, database systems, decision-support systems, and expert systems. Research information supports marketing analysis and decision making. This information may be obtained from internal sources, standardized information services, and special research studies. The information may be used to solve existing problems, evaluate potential actions such as new-product introductions, and as inputs to computerized data banks.

Computerized information systems include management information systems, database systems, and decision-support systems. These systems have capabilities for information processing, analysis of routine decision making, and decision recommendations for complex decision situations. The vast array of information processing and telecommunications technology that is available offers many opportunities to enhance the competitive advantage of companies.

The development of useful computerized information systems is a key success requirement for competing in the rapidly changing and shrinking global business environment. Marketing decision-making results are improved by the use of effective information systems. Importantly, gaining information advantage requires more than technology. The systems demand creative (and cost-effective) design that focuses on decision-making-information needs.

QUESTIONS FOR REVIEW AND DISCUSSION

1. Discuss how an organization's marketing information skills and resources contribute to its competitive advantage.

2. What is the relationship between market orientation and continuous learning about markets?

3. Outline an approach to developing an effective market-sensing capability.

4. Compare and contrast the use of standardized information services as an alternative to special research studies for tracking the performance of a new packaged-food product.

5. Discuss how cable television facilitates marketing research.

6. Comment on the usefulness and limitations of test-market data as a source of marketing information.

7. Suppose the management of a retail wallpaper chain is considering a research study to measure household awareness of the retail chain, reactions to various aspects of wallpaper purchase and use, and identification of competing firms. How could management estimate the benefits of such a study in order to determine if the study should be conducted?

8. Are there similarities between marketing strategic intelligence and the operations of the U.S. Central Intelligence Agency? Do companies ever employ business spies?

9. Discuss how manufacturers of U.S. and Swiss watches could have used market sensing to help avoid the problems that several firms in the industry encountered in the 1970s.

10. Discuss the strategic implications for small independents and regional chains of the expanding strategic use of information technology by large retailers.

NOTES

1. George S. Day, "The Capabilities of Market-Driven Organizations," *Journal of Marketing,* October 1994, p. 43.
2. Stephen Kreider Yoder, "Shoving Back: How H-P Used Tactics of the Japanese to Beat Them at Their Game," *The Wall Street Journal,* September 8, 1994, pp. A1 and A6.
3. Robert Johnson, "In the Chips," *The Wall Street Journal,* March 22, 1992, pp. B1 and B2.
4. Stanley F. Slater and John C. Narver, "Market Orientation, Customer Value, and Superior Performance," *Business Horizons,* March/April 1994, pp. 22–27.
5. Stanley F. Slater and John C. Narver, "Market Orientation and the Learning Organization," *Journal of Marketing,* July 1995, pp. 63–74.
6. Ibid., p. 71.
7. Ibid.
8. The following discussion is based on Day, "The Capabilities of Market-Driven Organizations." See also Stanley F. Slater and John C. Narver, "Market-Oriented Isn't Enough: Build a Learning Organization," Report No. 94–103 (Cambridge, MA: Marketing Science Institute, 1994).
9. Day, "The Capabilities of Market-Driven Organizations," p. 43.
10. Robert La Franco, "It's All about Visuals," *Forbes,* May 22, 1995, pp. 108, 110, and 112.
11. William R. Dillon, Thomas J. Madden, and Neil H. Firtle, *Marketing Research in a Marketing Environment,* 2nd ed. (Burr Ridge, IL: Richard D. Irwin, 1990), p. 828.
12. Kenneth C. Laudon and Jane Price Laudon, *Management Information Systems* (New York: Macmillan, 1988), p. 235.
13. Blaine E. Davis and Martin Stark, "American Telephone & Telegraph Co.: A Network of Experts," in Howard Sutton, *Competitive Intelligence,* Report No. 913 (New York: The Conference Board, Inc., 1988), pp. 22–24.
14. Johnnie L. Roberts, "Credibility Gap," *The Wall Street Journal,* October 5, 1989, pp. A1 and A16.
15. This illustration is based on Michael Days, "Wired Consumers," *The Wall Street Journal,* January 23, 1986, p. 3.
16. Cynthia Crossen, "Margin of Error," *The Wall Street Journal,* November 11, 1991, p. A1.
17. Laudon and Laudon, *Management Information Systems,* p. 62.
18. Michael Miron, John Cecil, Kevin Bradicich, and Gene Hall, "The Myths and Realities of Competitive Advantage," *DATAMATION,* October 1, 1988, p. 76.
19. Bob Shaw and Merlin Stone, "Competitive Superiority through Database Marketing," *Long Range Planning,* October 1988, pp. 24–40.
20. John D. C. Little and Michael Cassettari, *Decision Support Systems for Marketing Managers* (New York: AMA, 1984), p. 7.
21. Ibid., pp. 12–15.
22. Ibid., p. 14.
23. A discussion of DSS effectiveness is provided in Ramesh Sharda, Steve H. Barr, and James C. McDonnell, "Decision Support System Effectiveness: A Review and an Empirical Test," *Management Science* 34, no. 2 (February 1988), pp. 139–59.
24. Illustration from Robert J. Mockler, "Computer Information Systems and Strategic Corporate Planning," *Business Horizons,* May/June, 1987, p. 35.

Cases for Part II

CASE 2–1   Reebok International Ltd.

At Foot Locker stores, salespeople wear black-and-white stripes to look like referees. In the big leagues of sneaker sales, their calls are going against Reebok International Ltd.—to damaging effect.

Unable to rekindle the earnings growth that made it a 1980s highflier, Reebok faces a group of institutional shareholders in open revolt. The institutions own about 15 percent of Reebok's stock and include Government Employees Insurance Co., a major Warren Buffett investment, and Chieftain Capital Management, a New York money-management firm. They say they are fed up with management missteps, rising costs, earnings disappointments, and a sagging stock. Some of them are pressing for the resignation of Paul Fireman as Reebok's chief executive, even though he built up the company from a small operation with $1.5 million of revenue in 1980.

Apparently contradicting statements made as recently as last week, Mr. Fireman says he "isn't opposed to" bringing in a new chief operating officer or even chief executive officer, adding, "Titles don't mean anything." For the past six months, he says, Reebok has needed "a consolidation of leadership and a focus."

He also says Reebok, which is based in the Boston suburb of Canton, Massachusetts, is moving to fix its problems by, among other things, cutting costs and overhauling its order and information-tracking system. And he is devising a strategic plan to appease shareholders calling for his ouster or a takeover bid.

Reebok lost its No. 1 position in sneakers in 1990 to Nike Inc., which has savvy advertising and winning spokesmen such as Michael Jordan and Pete Sampras. Lately, Nike has begun pulling away in the footwear race. It rang up sales of $4.7 billion in the four quarters ended August 31; Reebok lagged behind, with $3.37 billion through June 30. Critics pan Reebok for a lackluster team of endorsers and a creaky distribution system.

Current and former Reebok insiders say the toughest fight with Nike is being waged at Woolworth Corp.'s Foot Locker unit—and Reebok is losing. With little fanfare, the shoe retailer has grown into a behemoth: Its 2,800 outlets chalk up about 23 percent of U.S. sneaker sales. Foot Locker and related Woolworth units account for $1.5 billion of the $6.5 billion in U.S. athletic-shoe sales.

When a retailer achieves such dominance in a product category, it expects to get preferred terms from manufacturers, early looks at new models, and speedy shipments. Nike, of Beaverton, Oregon, has been playing the game. Reebok has not—and seems to be paying the price.

This year, according to several estimates in the industry, Foot Locker's Nike sales are expected to rise to $750 million, while the chain's Reebok sales will drop for their second year running, to $172 million. Foot Locker accounts for a whopping 58 percent of the expected $1 billion domestic sales gap between Nike and Reebok this year. In 1993, by contrast, Nike's $300 million in Foot Locker sales wasn't far ahead of Reebok's $228 million.

William DeVries, who heads Woolworth's footwear units, dismisses talk of bad relations with Reebok and attributes the lagging sales to changing consumer tastes. "We're only selling what the customer wants," he says.

But it goes beyond that, securities analysts and Reebok officials say. Early on, Mr. Fireman expressed disdain for Foot Locker and its demands, people close to him say. They add that Reebok has often been sloppy in getting samples on time to Foot Locker, which, because of its size, must make decisions early in the buying season. "Sometimes the samples would come in late and sometimes not at all—which got Foot Locker mad," a former Reebok official says. Explains another Reebok official: "Sometimes, fashions last less than six weeks; if you don't get it in right then, there goes a major sale."

Tension between Reebok and Foot Locker goes back to the late 1980s. Reebok's aerobics shoes were "flying off the shelves," says Josie Esquivel, an analyst at Morgan Stanley Group Inc. And when Foot Locker asked shoemakers to turn out special lines solely for itself, Ms. Esquivel adds, "Reebok basically has thumbed its nose" at the retailer. Reebok "was selling to whomever it wanted, including the discounter down the street from Foot Locker." Reebok's attitude was like a blister at Foot Locker, which values exclusive lines as one of its few weapons against discounters and was getting special treatment from other sneaker makers.

Several years ago, Nike began making exclusive lines for Foot Locker and now has a dozen products sold only at the chain. Recently, Nike introduced Flight 65 and Flight 67, high-priced basketball shoes that sell only at Foot Locker and come in the chain's trademark black and white.

Earlier this year, Reebok agreed to make some shoes exclusively for Foot Locker, but so far none have reached the stores.

Mr. Fireman is penitential about Reebok's rocky relations with Foot Locker. He says, "Reebok wasn't as good a listener to [Foot Locker], which happens to have a good ear as to what's happening on the street and with consumers." But Mr. Fireman says he is trying to fix that. He has spent the past few days with buyers of Woolworth's footwear units "trying to discern their needs." Relations have improved dramatically as a result of conciliatory efforts, he adds.

In the past few years, Reebok has hired an army of testers to shop at Woolworth's shoe chains—Foot Locker, Lady Foot Locker, and Champs—to find out whether Reebok is getting equal treatment with other brands, especially Nike. Reebok has been disappointed with its findings, insiders say.

Random visits to Foot Locker stores find that next to Nikes, Reeboks are the most plentiful shoes on the shelves. But they seem to get little help from salespeople. One evening in a Foot Locker in Boston, two teenagers wonder out loud which shoe to buy. A salesman suggests a pair of bright-colored Nike running shoes on the new-arrivals shelf. Nikes are in, he says; just look at "people's feet on the street." Soon, he rings up a Nike sale.

Are the customers happy with their selection? "Well, Foot Locker tells me that Nikes are hip," says Cecily Jackson, 17.

One hurdle Reebok faces in cracking Foot Locker's market is that the retailer's customers aren't Reebok core clientele. Foot Locker mainly attracts teens and Generation-X customers, who are often willing to pay $80 to $90 for shoes.

"There's no question Nike owns that market," Mr. Fireman concedes. "There's no one really in that market to compete against them in the high-end niche." Reeboks appeal to older consumers and to pre-teens unwilling or unable to pay those prices.

Reebok heavy-handedness on pricing also has caused problems. In 1992, according to the Federal Trade Commission, the company created a sales policy, the Centennial Plan, under which it told retailers their supplies would be cut off if they discounted Reebok shoes too much. Under the plan, the FTC said, retailers weren't allowed to sell Reebok's high-end shoes below a suggested price or to discount less-expensive lines more than 10 percent.

In May, Reebok agreed to pay $9.5 million to settle price-fixing charges brought by the government over Centennial. Among the government's witnesses were buyers for Foot Locker. Reebok said at the time that the investigations had "failed to establish any evidence of wrongdoing" and that it agreed to settle to avoid expensive litigation.

Among Reebok's other problems, the piqued shareholders have been alarmed by a surge in operating costs, which ran 32.7 percent of sales in the second quarter of this year, compared with 24.4 percent in 1991. They also exceeded the industry average of 27 percent.

Without providing an exact breakdown, Reebok says the added spending stems partly from an aggressive pursuit of endorsement agreements with athletes and teams and from sporting-event sponsorships. About 3,000 athletes will wear Reebok shoes and apparel at next year's summer Olympics in Atlanta, up from about 400 four years earlier. Reebok has also inked agreements for the San Francisco 49ers and other NFL teams to wear its shoes and sideline apparel, and it recently signed up basketball star Rebecca Lobo.

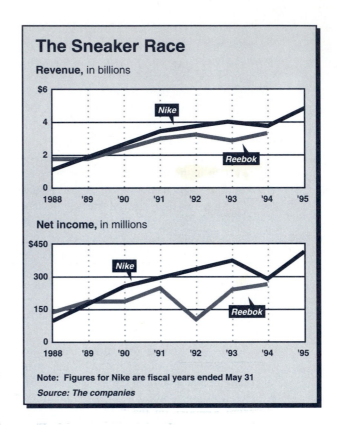

The Sneaker Race

Revenue, in billions

Nike

Reebok

1988 '89 '90 '91 '92 '93 '94 '95

Net income, in millions

Nike

Reebok

1988 '89 '90 '91 '92 '93 '94 '95

Note: Figures for Nike are fiscal years ended May 31
Source: The companies

Shareholders are dubious because some of Reebok's other alliances haven't worked out as planned. It signed tennis pro Michael Chang for a reported $15-million-a-year endorsement contract. But Mr. Sampras and Andre Agassi, both Nike endorsers, have eclipsed Mr. Chang in competition—and revved up their sponsor's sales.

Another marquee player, Orlando Magic star Shaquille O'Neal, is unhappy with his $3-million-a-year Reebok contract and has been shopping himself around for bigger money. Reebok's early line of Shaq Attaq shoes, hampered by design problems, has been only moderately successful, Mr. Fireman concedes. But he adds that a new line holds great promise.

Reebok's costs also have been increased by its investments in the information systems aimed at fixing the distribution snags and by the opening of a new apparel distribution facility in Memphis.

In addition, Reebok has weathered some management turmoil, much of it related to Mr. Fireman's changing views of how involved he should be in operations; on two occasions over the years, for example, he has been distracted by building a golf course. Since April, the co-presidents of the Reebok division, John H. Duerden and Roberto Muller, have both resigned. Mr. Duerden, who was trying to improve rapport with retailers, had sought to be president of the entire company, but Mr. Fireman rebuffed his aspirations, say people familiar with the situation.

Those departures and other resignations have left some shareholders wondering whether Mr. Fireman is too difficult a boss. "How do you attract first-rate talent when there's been a history of turnover at the top?" asks John Shapiro of Chieftain Capital, one of the critical institutions—and one that has taken management scalps before. Its criticism of alleged insider dealings at Boston Bancorp led to the chief executive's resignation earlier this year.

Yet Reebok still finds new ways to get customers to buy sneakers. Its Step Aerobics shoes, designed for an exercise routine with a Reebok step-cushion, were top sellers that Nike has copied. And Reebok's sponsorship of amateur pick-up basketball games, broadcast by CBS, has fueled sales of Reebok Black Top shoes.

Another bright spot is Reebok's international sales, which grew to $1.25 billion in 1994 from $1.08 billion in 1993. In Latin America and Asia, Reebok's sales top Nike's; in Europe, the two companies are in a close race.

And Reebok is pushing ahead with cost-cutting. In April, it announced plans to save $75 million a year by eliminating 579 jobs, about 9 percent of its workforce, and by consolidating European operations. Mr. Fireman also has told shareholders that his staff is working on projects related to inventory control and other matters to improve financial performance.

But many Reebok watchers say that getting back on good footing with Foot Locker is critical. For teenagers who buy lots of shoes, Foot Locker "is such a hot spot," says Faye Landis of Smith Barney, that many of them "carry Foot Locker shoeboxes around to give the impression that they bought sneakers there."

More Reeboks on the feet of the cognoscente would certainly help the company regain momentum. It might also save Mr. Fireman's job.

Source: Joseph Pereira, "Sneaker Attacks," *The Wall Street Journal,* September 22, 1995, pp. A1 and A5.

CASE 2–2   AT&T PersonaLink

Paul Saffo, director of the Institute for the Future in Menlo Park, California, has spent the past decade vainly trying to keep up with a daily flood of electronic mail. Tomorrow, he will get an assistant who will sort through his E-mail and alert him to important messages by pager, save others, fax some to colleagues, or simply dump a bunch of them in the trash.

The assistant isn't human, but something called an electronic agent, a breed of autonomous software that can go off to a computer network and work while the user is doing something else, somewhere else. Agents have been studied for years at research centers and actually used for, among other things, monitoring computer networks. But they haven't achieved widespread commercial use.

Until now. Tomorrow, AT&T Corp. will begin operating a kind of turbo-charged online service, a nationwide network called PersonaLink that will provide a relatively simple way for ordinary people to launch their own electronic servants into the ether. Those agents will communicate with agents of other people or of merchants and information publishers, performing work such as alerting their owners to a nose-diving stock or buying concert tickets. At the same time, Sony Corp. will begin shipping the first device—a hand-held communicator—that can deploy agents on PersonaLink.

AT&T's marketers make some startling claims for PersonaLink, saying it will eventually change the way commerce is conducted and people socialize. Skeptics say AT&T has taken leave of its normally acute marketing senses, detouring into the never-never land of science fiction. Salespeople and teachers deploying remote programmable agents and navigating cyberspace? It's all too complex.

But the idea behind PersonaLink is that just the opposite is true, that it will make life simpler by harnessing a new kind of agent. AT&T stands a good chance of pulling its strategy off because of a technology known as Telescript, developed by the software consortium General Magic Inc. of Mountain View, California.

Telescript, a computer-programming language, allows PersonaLink agents to do something no other agents have been able to do: move around a computer network until they can complete the transactions they were assigned. The bigger the network and the more services on it, the greater the potential power of agents. General Magic has also developed another critical piece: Magic Cap, software that makes programming an agent as easy as filling out a short to-do list.

Two of the great ills of the information age are that there is too much useless information, and valuable information is too hard to find. Managers are inundated with E-mail messages; consumers are inundated with catalogs. Telescript agents are capable right now of autonomously performing much of the scut work of daily living, such as sifting through junk mail or scheduling appointments, and in a year or two will be capable of doing some things that now consume hours or days, such as finding the cheapest camcorder or the best vacation package to Hawaii.

Agents traveling over networks can, like the telephone and the automobile, compress time and space, in this case by letting people do many things at once in many places. People who have seen or used PersonaLink devices already remark on the phenomenon. "It's probably akin to taking the first trans-Atlantic flight," says Mary Furlong, president of SeniorNet, a community of 14,000 older people on America On-Line. "You know life won't be the same."

Mr. Saffo, though a self-styled "technology skeptic," is convinced something big is afoot. He has tested the Sony communicator and says the experience is "like seeing a thread hanging down from the future, pointing the way."

AT&T's immediate customers for PersonaLink will be some of the estimated 20 million people who send electronic messages and want a better way of doing so. Its next customers will be merchants who hope to sell electronically, with the help of Telescript agents that will watch how shoppers behave in their virtual stores, anticipate their needs, and keep in touch with them. Gradually, agent-based networks may spread and become accepted by at least the most educated and affluent 20 percent of the population.

But that future is going to unfold at a slow pace, perhaps painfully slow for AT&T, which faces a monumental chicken-and-egg problem. Subscribers won't flock to PersonaLink until there are many merchants and services on-line; the service providers won't rush to sign up until there are many subscribers. AT&T has essentially built a $100 million chicken in PersonaLink, to provide a place for the process to begin. And it will be at least a half year before users can tap PersonaLink from their personal computers rather than expensive hand-held devices.

Meanwhile, competitors loom. Powerful Oracle Corp., the king of software for managing complex databases, has started shipping programs that allow people with wireless devices to send agents to a single computer. Oracle says that although its agents are limited to communication between one computer and a host, creating them isn't as complex as on Telescript and they do almost as much.

Other companies, such as Legent Corp. of Herndon, Virginia, are already selling software to companies for making customized agents. Mighty Microsoft Corp. and International Business Machines Corp. are developing their own non-mobile-agent software.

But AT&T's rivals "just don't get it," contends Stewart Alsop, editor of the trade weekly *Infoworld*. Rivals' agents, he says, don't tap the power of an open network, in which agents can move around. Pattie Maes, an assistant professor at Massachusetts Institute of Technology's Media Laboratory, says, "The novel thing about Telescript is that it is a language that makes it possible for agents to move from one machine to another. It means a user doesn't have to be connected to those other machines."

As of tomorrow, users of Sony's device can choose from a short list of things to do with messages, such as discarding them or sending them to certain people or companies via fax, pager, or electronic mail. One of the lines on the list, for example, says: "Forward a copy of all messages from [blank] about [blank] to [blank]." Users who seek someone but don't know the electronic address can send an agent to scan PersonaLink's directory and come back with any information the intended recipient left in the directory.

While messaging agents are ready now, General Magic is working on making it easier to let agents do much more. One program, for example, allows a user to connect to a brokerage firm. The user taps an icon, then fills in blanks on a list to identify a stock, designate a price range and trigger an alert, which can be sent via pager if the range is exceeded. The agent is left inside the brokerage firm's database to wait and search for the event as long as the user is willing to pay for the privilege.

Such watching-and-notifying agents will be available in 6 to 12 months, General Magic says, along with the most powerful agents, which search across many databases. James White, a lanky General Magic vice president who invented Telescript and was a key developer of the software that created E-mail to begin with, explains how such searches will work to shop for a VCR:

A user will tap a list, probably supplied by a shopping service, and fill in blanks identifying the kind of stores to be searched, the VCR model, the price range and the number of bids desired. The digital list will be sent via phone line to a PersonaLink directory, on which stores have identified themselves as sellers of VCRs. Then—and this is the heart of the matter—the agent will "travel" to each virtual store and compare its data to the list of VCR models and prices in the store's own computer, until it exhausts all the lists or has the right number of matches. Then it will go home, either paging the user or putting itself in an electronic in-box. If the user has provided a credit-card number, the agent can even buy the VCR.

Mr. White says the idea for Telescript came to him when he was fooling around with Adobe Postscript, a computer language that allows a printer to recognize a document as a program and execute its instructions. Suddenly, he thought of agents as programs recognized by the network. "I said, 'Oh my God, what if we thought of a network as a programmable computing environment rather than just plumbing,' " Mr. White recalls. On top of that concept, he built the program to be "a computation that moves after it starts to run," to a second, third, or more machines.

"That's the critical operation," Mr. White says. "I remember the day I thought of it, thinking this is really crazy, that if I pursued it, people would likely consider me on the lunatic fringe."

Not AT&T. In meetings with Mr. White three years ago, AT&T engineers realized such a network could act as a host to a horde of unruly developers who would put on their own Telescript applications, to provide goods and services to millions of people. As with the telephone network, AT&T wouldn't determine who would send or receive the messages, as long as the traffic was legal.

William Fallon, PersonaLink's marketing director, says AT&T quickly understood the implications—that it could create an electronic marketplace with Telescript because most of the buying and selling could be both automated and spontaneous, with agents talking to agents.

Starting 2½ years ago, several hundred engineers built the network and helped Mr. White's crew develop a more powerful programming language and help Telescript agents handle transactions faster. But, Mr. Fallon notes, "It all began as a brilliant idea in Jim White's head."

Mr. Fallon says the service will initially be marketed to an affluent target group—heavy long-distance users, people who are "technologically optimistic mobile professionals," or TOMPs for short. For the next six months, TOMPs will be offered a deal: all the messages they want to send for $9.95 a month.

Mr. Fallon won't say where the price will go after that, but vows the service will be affordable. AT&T's goal is to make most of its money by charging merchants a fee for each transaction, and perhaps for such things as billing and security.

"We want to get a piece of the action," says Mr. Fallon's boss, Gordon Bridge, president of AT&T's consumer interactive services.

Software developers have the same dream. eShop Inc., a software firm in San Mateo, California, acting as the general contractor for AT&T's virtual mall, will ship programs before year's end that will allow companies to build their own stores on PersonaLink with agents that keep track of shoppers' agents—what they buy and what they just look at. The store's agents will eventually be able to identify shoppers' agents, remember their past preferences, and alert them to sales or special items. eShop will split fees with AT&T based on the volume of transactions conducted through its software.

It remains to be seen how readily merchants will accept fee arrangements with AT&T and software developers. While publishers of financial and other information can charge consumers, traditional merchants probably won't be able to charge customers for a

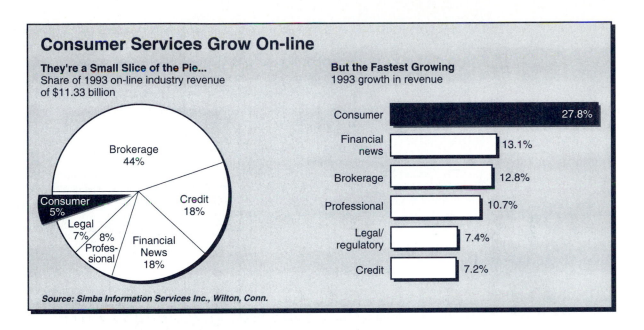

Consumer Services Grow On-line

They're a Small Slice of the Pie...
Share of 1993 on-line industry revenue
of $11.33 billion

- Brokerage 44%
- Credit 18%
- Financial News 18%
- Professional 8%
- Legal 7%
- Consumer 5%

But the Fastest Growing
1993 growth in revenue

Consumer	27.8%
Financial news	13.1%
Brokerage	12.8%
Professional	10.7%
Legal/regulatory	7.4%
Credit	7.2%

Source: Simba Information Services Inc., Wilton, Conn.

transaction, any more than people would be charged for entering a bricks-and-mortar store.

The growth of electronic agentry will also depend in part on the success of General Magic's efforts to get Telescript accepted as a world standard. Marc Porat, the consortium's chairman and a man known for his persuasive powers, says he wants to license the technology to all comers, even AT&T archrival MCI Communications Corp. He has already talked the world's three largest consumer-electronics companies and the largest telecommunications companies in the United States, Japan, and France into joining his group. Although he won't comment on future partners, he is believed to be negotiating with IBM and the communications giants of Britain and Germany.

Mr. Bridge says PersonaLink has been "inundated" with inquiries from retailers interested in getting on the network. About 30 have been picked to work with eShop, industry executives say. Mr. Bridge predicts PersonaLink will grow slowly, having little significant activity in 1995 but achieving critical mass of about a million subscribers in several more years.

Mr. Fallon says even Domino's Pizza Inc. has expressed interest in providing a PersonaLink directory so hungry travelers could send an agent to find the nearest Domino's and execute an order for, say, pepperoni with anchovies. He suggests calling them POMPs—pizza-optimistic mobile professionals.

The implications of autonomous software 10 to 20 years down the road are profound, if not weird. Some mathematicians fear agents will run amok or consume all of the capacity of computer networks, based on chaos theory and the idea that human beings will overuse agents. "Too many agents spoil the network," says Jeffrey Kephart, an IBM research scientist.

The metabolism of some human endeavors will certainly be speeded up, as numerous agents perform tasks for an individual simultaneously in many parts of the world. This trend could lead to the ultimate virtual rat race, or, as Ms. Furlong, SeniorNet's president, suggests, a chance for more leisure as servant agents perform mundane, time-consuming tasks.

Mr. Saffo, the futurist, goes even further. Along with other experts, he says he sees people eventually launching their alter egos into cyberspace: "There are going to be ghosts in our machines doing things for us."

Source: G. Christian Hill, "Cyber Servants: Electronic 'Agents' Bring Virtual Shopping a Bit Closer to Reality," *The Wall Street Journal,* September 27, 1994, pp. A1, 6. Reprinted by permission of *The Wall Street Journal*, © 1994 by Dow Jones & Company, Inc. All Rights Reserved Worldwide.

CASE 2–3   Gillette Co.

Several mornings a week, Alfred M. Zeien performs an odd ritual. After lathering his face, he shaves with two razors—one for each side of his face.

Then he runs his fingers over his cheeks to check the closeness of the shave. "That's the only way to really compare shaves," declares Mr. Zeien, chairman and chief executive officer of Gillette Co., who tests both his company's razors and competitors'.

Gillette is a company obsessed with shaving. How many whiskers on the average man's face? Thirty thousand, by Gillette's count. How fast do men's whiskers grow? By 15/1,000ths of an inch a day, or 5½ inches a year. Dry beard hair, Gillette has determined, is about as tough as copper wire of the same thickness.

"We spend more time than you can imagine studying facial hair growth—which is quite different from the growth of other hair on your head—because that's the way to improve your product," explains the very clean-shaven Mr. Zeien, who keeps a drawerful of experimental Gillette blades in his office for trying out.

In the annals of American business, few companies have dominated an industry so much and for so long as this one. "Gillette was the lead brand in 1923 and is the lead brand in 1992," says Jack Trout, a marketing consultant. And not by a little: Its 64 percent share of the U.S. wet-shaving market (in dollars) compares with 13 percent at No. 2 Schick, a unit of Warner-Lambert Co.

But Gillette is one of America's noteworthy corporate successes not just because it has done so well, but also because it once blundered so remarkably—and came back.

In 1962, a small foreign company, Wilkinson Sword Ltd., introduced the first coated stainless steel blade, cutting sharply into Gillette's market share. Swallowing its pride, Gillette came out with its own stainless steel blade.

Humbled, Gillette used the experience to learn lessons many companies don't learn until too late: Never take a rival for granted, no matter how small. Don't concede market niches to competitors, because niches have a way of growing. And don't dally in bringing out new products for fear of cannibalizing old ones; if you don't bring them out, a competitor may.

"Every American corporation of any great size or importance was founded on a core business. Why didn't certain of those companies survive, or [survive] only in a diminished way? They took their eye off the core business," contends Milton Glass, Gillette's vice president of finance. "Gillette has never done that. Each morning Gillette executives face south, to south Boston"—home of its biggest plant, which churns out nearly 2 billion blades a year—"and bow to our razor-blade business. Everything else is secondary."

Gillette so dominates shaving worldwide that its name has come to mean a razor blade in some countries. It is the leader in Europe with a 70 percent market share and in Latin America with 80 percent. Indeed, for every blade it sells at home, it sells five abroad, a figure likely to grow as joint ventures expand sales in China, Russia, and India.

Retaining its dominance in razors also has meant spending hundreds of millions of dollars to develop the innovative twin-blade Trac II razor in 1972, the pivoting-head Atra in 1977, and the hugely successful Sensor, with independently suspended blades, in 1989. It also meant rushing out—albeit reluctantly—a disposable razor in 1976 to fend off French rival Societé Bic SA, even though the cheap throwaways cut into sales of higher-profit Gillette products.

While shaving will account for only a bit more than one-third of Gillette's $5 billion in sales this year, razors will ring up nearly two-thirds of profits of $500 million—attesting to the manufacturing efficiencies and profit margins that go with its dominance [Exhibit 1].

Gillette's performance in other businesses—deodorants, pens, cosmetics—is decidedly mixed. Braun electric shavers and small electric appliances and Oral-B toothbrushes, bought when they were small companies, have grown rapidly under Gillette. While Braun isn't dominant in electric razors, it is a major player, enabling Gillette to hedge its bet by being in a business that holds a steady 30 percent share of the shaving market.

But Right Guard deodorant, once the leading brand, has been surpassed by rivals. Bic clobbered Gillette in disposable lighters, prompting Gillette to sell its Cricket business. And in writing instruments, Gillette's Paper Mate and other brands produce only so-so profits and growth. Efforts to diversify into everything from hearing aids to eyewear have flopped.

Those problems, combined with the growing market share of low-margin disposable razors, slowed Gillette's sales and earnings growth in the 1980s. Corporate raiders launched hostile takeover bids, criticizing management as lethargic, while some dissident shareholders waged a proxy battle to oust some directors.

Although ultimately unsuccessful, those attacks moved Gillette management to act. The company slashed its bloated staff by 8 percent. And to stem the growth of throwaway razors, Gillette tried a risky strategy—positioning its new Sensor as an alternative to lower-priced disposables. It worked.

Mustaches and beards are rare among Gillette managers, and not only because of a corporate fondness for clean-shaven cheeks. Gillette is a conservative company that expects slavish devotion from its managers, many of whom are 30- and 40-year veterans. Indeed, the only time Gillette ever reached outside for a top executive was in the early 1970s, when it hired marketing whiz Edward Gelsthorpe as president. Known as "Cranapple

EXHIBIT 1   Gillette: On the Cutting Edge

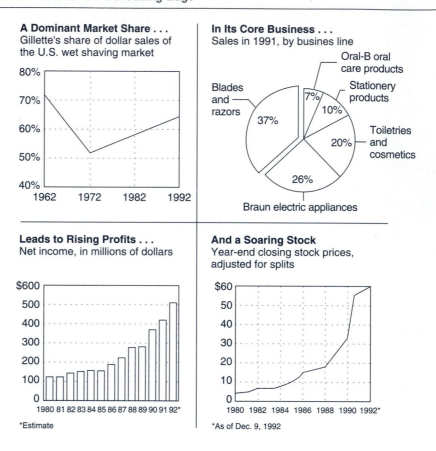

A Dominant Market Share . . .
Gillette's share of dollar sales of
the U.S. wet shaving market

In Its Core Business . . .
Sales in 1991, by busines line

Blades and razors 37%
Oral-B oral care products 7%
Stationery products 10%
Toiletries and cosmetics 20%
Braun electric appliances 26%

Leads to Rising Profits . . .
Net income, in millions of dollars

*Estimate

And a Soaring Stock
Year-end closing stock prices,
adjusted for splits

*As of Dec. 9, 1992

Ed"—for introducing the Ocean Spray cranberry and apple juice drink—he lasted just 15 months at Gillette. He won't comment, but insiders say he simply didn't fit in.

Those who aren't passionate about Gillette need not apply. A business-school graduate, assured of a position with Gillette after several interviews, was asked in a final meeting whether she had any qualms. Half in jest, she said, "Well, I'm not sure I want to spend the rest of my life worrying about underarms." She didn't get the job.

Nowhere is the obsession more evident than at the South Boston manufacturing and research plant. Here, some 200 volunteers from various departments come to work unshaven each day. They troop to the second floor and enter small booths with a sink and mirror, where they take instructions from technicians on the other side of a small window: try this blade or that shaving cream or this aftershave, then answer questionnaires. Besides men's faces, the research includes the legs of women volunteers; women account for 29 percent of razor sales in the United States.

"We bleed so you'll get a good shave at home. This is my 27th year. I came here my first week. Haven't missed a day of shaving," says George Turchinetz, manager of the prototype model shop, proudly noting that he is a "preferred" tester because he is "real fussy."

For a close look at the mechanics of shaving, Gillette uses a boroscope—a video camera attached to a blade cartridge using fiber optics. Magnifying the film hundreds of times, researchers can precisely determine how twin blades catch the whiskers, pull them out of the follicles and cut them. Sometimes they collect debris after test shaves and measure the angle of the cut whiskers; the flatter the angle, the less force it took to cut the hair.

"We test the blade edge, the blade guard, the angle of the blades, the balance of the razor, the length, the heft, the width," explains Donald Chaulk, vice president of the shaving technology laboratory. "What happens to the chemistry of the skin? What happens to the hair when you pull it? What happens to the follicle? We own the face. We know more about shaving than anybody. I don't think *obsession* is too strong a word."

He pauses. "I've got to be careful. I don't want to sound crazy."

Despite the conservatism of Gillette, its research and development effort is a testament to risk taking. At any given time, Gillette has up to 20 experimental razors in development. One promising prototype has been in the works for four years—and won't be ready for eight more. "We're spending more than $1 million a year on that project, knowing we can't launch till 2000 or 2001," says Mr. Zeien, the chairman. "That's assuming we'll overcome the technical barriers, and we're not sure we can."

To understand the Gillette of 1992, it's important to understand the Gillette of 1962. Gillette's market share had just reached its highest point ever—72 percent. The company had long been a power overseas as well, having gone abroad in 1905, only a decade after King C. Gillette invented the first safety razor.

"We have," an executive boasted to *Forbes* magazine in 1962, "no complaints on how things are going."

They soon would. Wilkinson Sword—which forged the famous swords for British cavalry at the height of the Empire, but by the 1960s made mostly garden tools—decided to get into blades. Its Super Sword-Edge stainless steel blade, coated with a thin chemical film to protect the edge, lasted up to 12 shaves, or two or three times as many as Gillette's own coated Super Blue Blade, made of softer carbon steel.

Gillette was stunned. "They were the talk of the town," recalls shaving-division vice president Scott Roberts, then a salesman in New York. "Our leadership was threatened."

Gillette knew stainless steel was harder than carbon steel. It also knew about stainless blade coatings—in fact, Wilkinson later had to license technology for making its coated blade from Gillette, which had a patent. But making a stainless blade would have made much of Gillette's manufacturing equipment obsolete.

It was tempted to do what many big companies do: Ignore its rival, hoping the market niche would remain small, or improve its existing carbon-blade technology. Eventually, Gillette decided it had no choice and introduced a stainless blade in late 1963. By then, two other small players had introduced stainless blades, and Gillette's U.S. market share had begun a precipitous drop that would bottom out at around 50 percent.

In retrospect, Gillette was lucky Wilkinson didn't have the firepower to exploit its weakness. "I had nightmares thinking that someone at Procter & Gamble would shave with [a stainless blade] and decide to get in the business or buy out Wilkinson," confesses William G. Salatich, a retired Gillette executive. (Unable to duplicate the breakthrough it made with stainless blades, Wilkinson has become a minor player in most countries; Gillette, in fact, bought Wilkinson's blade business outside Europe and the United States several years ago.)

Though short-lived, the debacle galvanized Gillette in a way a lesser threat wouldn't have. Russell B. Adams, Jr., author of a corporate biography for the company, says, "It has become part of the myth and folklore: 'This is what happens to you if you're not up there keeping ahead of the market.' "

Indeed, the ordeal prepared Gillette for the next major challenge to its razor and blade business.

Only a few years after Gillette had reasserted itself with the twin-blade Trac II, Bic sold its first inexpensive disposables in Greece in 1974. Again there was skepticism about the product because it offered a worse shave, not a better one. "We'd get samples and I would try them and wonder why anybody would compromise their shave to save a little money," remembers Mr. Scott, the Gillette vice president.

Moreover, why come out with a new razor that cost more to make (because disposables had a handle and blade, as opposed to a cartridge that fit on an existing razor) but sold for less? Especially when it might take sales from more profitable brands. It was similar to the issue Detroit would face when the Japanese invaded the United States with small cars.

"There was sizable debate whether we should or shouldn't make a disposable," says Robert E. Ray, a former overseas manager who now is a management consultant. "If you sit down with pencil and paper, you conclude, 'This ain't such a hot idea, we're going to make less money.' But after a while you didn't have to be rocket scientist to figure out that consumers wanted disposables."

A short while. Bic took a 10 percent market share in Greece almost overnight, then moved into Austria and Italy. With the 1960s disaster in mind, Gillette began a crash program to develop a disposable. Gillette rolled out its Good News disposable—using the Trac II twin-blade technology, compared with Bic's single blade—nationwide in April 1976, months before Bic introduced its razor regionally.

Says former president Stephen Griffin: "We were giving up profitability, but we had to do that to maintain our customers."

"Gillette did exactly the right thing," says Mr. Trout, the marketing guru. "Guys who say they don't like the world to change, guess what—it changes underneath them. That's what kills companies."

Nonetheless, Bic has proven to be a formidable competitor. By forcing Gillette into disposables, Bic contributed to Gillette's problems in the 1980s. Gillette initially thought disposables might get 10 percent of the market. In fact, by the late 1980s disposables had a share of nearly 50 percent in dollars and some 60 percent in units.

While it held a narrow lead over Bic in units and a wide lead in dollars in disposables (Gillette's are priced higher), its profit margins were being squeezed.

The answer came from Gillette's R&D labs. One of the savvy developments of Gillette researchers over the past 20 years has been to design razors that are hard for competitors to make. In the days of the double-edge blade, it was easy for others to make blades that fit Gillette's razors; Trac II and other twin-blade razors changed that. Rivals generally come out with cartridges compatible with new Gillette razors, but only after a lag.

The idea for a razor with twin blades that move independently—the Sensor—originated in Gillette's British labs in the late 1970s. Perfecting it, and figuring out how to make it by the billions, would take a decade and more than $200 million.

Some Gillette managers wanted to use the technology on disposables. But John W. Symons, a now-retired Gillette executive, argued that it offered such a superior shave that it could command a premium price, thus reversing the growth of disposables and increasing profit margins at the same time. Otherwise, he contends, "Our great brand would become a commodity business." Gillette stopped advertising disposables, and—in a huge bet—put nearly all its marketing money on Sensor.

To the astonishment of many, both inside and outside Gillette, the strategy worked. Since Sensor was introduced in 1989, the market share of disposables in dollars has declined to 45 percent from a peak of 49 percent. Though Schick has followed with a variation of the flexible-blade idea, called the Tracer, no rival has yet reproduced the Sensor design—in part because the manufacturing equipment needed to make it is so expensive and complicated.

What's next? Gillette has a Sensor II in development that company officials vow will "supersede" Sensor. "That's one of the successes of the Japanese: They always have their next play in hand when making their current play," says Scott Roberts, the Gillette vice president.

And in another move from the Japanese playbook, the next generation razor isn't likely to be introduced first in the United States, says Mr. Zeien, the chairman. "This is what the auto companies learned from the Japanese," he says. "If you want to be a leader on a global basis, you can't just be a leader in your home market."

Source: Lawrence Ingrassia, "Keeping Sharp: Gillette Holds Its Edge by Endlessly Searching for a Better Shave," *The Wall Street Journal,* December 10, 1992, pp. A1 and A5. Reprinted by permission of *The Wall Street Journal,* © 1992 by Dow Jones & Company, Inc. All Rights Reserved Worldwide.

CASE 2–4 Radio Shack

Sitting in a morning meeting early last week, Radio Shack Executive Vice President Dave Christopher is slipped a note that would stop some executives dead in their tracks.

His boss, Radio Shack President Leonard Roberts, is on the phone and wants to talk to Christopher "immediately."

In some organizations, such impromptu calls can mean only one thing: Something has gone wrong, and the boss is calling to chew you out.

"Hi, Len," Christopher says, picking up the line.

After a silent pause in which you might expect him to start shuffling the papers on his desk or begin spitting out excuses, Christopher instead laughs heartily at something Roberts has said, gives his boss a quick piece of information and returns to the meeting.

Roberts, formerly a top executive at the Arby's and Shoney's restaurant chains, is prompting a lot of smiles at Radio Shack these days.

Since arriving to head the 6,600-store operation in July 1993, Roberts has helped engineer a turnaround at Tandy Corp.'s once-moribund flagship consumer electronics chain. It can be argued that Radio Shack has seen more changes in the past 20 months than it had in the previous 20 years.

Radio Shack no longer harbors illusions of slugging it out toe to toe with such consumer electronics superstores as Circuit City or Best Buy. Nor does it fancy itself any longer as a leading distributor of personal computers.

Seeking shelter in more profitable businesses, Radio Shack has returned to its roots. Now focusing on selling small-ticket electronics gadgets and providing customer services, Radio Shack posted its largest sales gains of the 1990s last year.

Now, Roberts is talking enthusiastically about taking Radio Shack from its estimated $2.86 billion in 1994 sales to the $4 billion level within five years. (Exhibit 1.)

"All of the assets were already here," Roberts says of Radio Shack's revamping. "What we have done is identified the strengths of Radio Shack and become good at capitalizing on them." (Exhibit 2.)

However you describe the changes, the Radio Shack of 1995 looks radically different from the Radio Shack that entered the decade.

Under Roberts, the company has revamped its marketing program, streamlined its merchandising strategy, and changed the way it manages inventory. It has launched potentially lucrative new services, such as gift delivery and gadget repair, and has set up a separate unit to look at other potential business expansions.

Along the way, Roberts' team, made up mostly of Tandy veterans shifted into new roles, has officially abandoned some long-held Radio Shack traditions.

The Shack, which built its highly profitable business selling only its own brand of merchandise, now openly embraces name-brand manufacturers. And after spending the 1980s staking its growth on its success in selling personal computers, Radio Shack is working to diversify its product mix.

The changes appear to be working.

In November, Radio Shack posted its first month of double-digit percentage sales gains in more than six years. For the year, the chain logged a sales gain of nearly 5 percent. Not bad for a company that saw sales drop for three consecutive years from 1990 to 1992 before posting a modest 2.4 percent sales gain in 1993.

Wall Street may be more interested in Radio Shack's rising profit margins as it shifts from selling low-margin personal computers in favor of smaller-ticket items that deliver higher returns, such as cables and wires, batteries and telephones.

"The improving gross margins at Radio Shack may be the single most important thing happening at Tandy right now," Tandy Chairman John Roach says.

With its improving margins, the Radio Shack of today is looking more and more like the Radio Shack of the late 1970s, before the company lunged into the personal computer business in a big way, says Christopher, who joined Radio Shack 28 years ago.

EXHIBIT 1   Radio Shack Sales

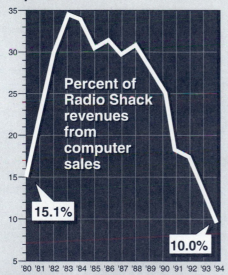

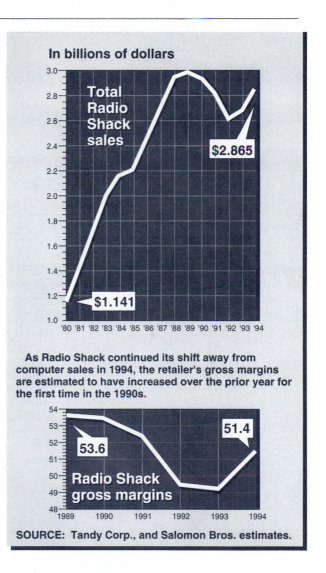

Radio Shack®
A DIVISION OF TANDY CORPORATION

The impact of personal computers on Radio Shack sales has taken the consumer electronic retailer on a trip back to the future.

At the beginning of the Pc boom in 1980, computers accounted for about 15 percent of Radio Shack sales. The PC then mushroomed to one-third of Radio Shack's sales, driving the chain's fast-paced growth in the 1980s. As the retailer seeks to rebuild its traditionally high profit margins, the emphasis on selling PCs has decreased and the profit percentage has rebounded.

In percent

Percent of Radio Shack revenues from computer sales

15.1%

10.0%

As Radio Shack wrestled with a declining percentage of PC sales in the early 1990s, overall revenues declined for three consecutive years. As PCs play a smaller role in Radio Shack's sales, expansion in other product categories has put the retailer back on a growth track.

In billions of dollars

Total Radio Shack sales

$2.865

$1.141

As Radio Shack continued its shift away from computer sales in 1994, the retailer's gross margins are estimated to have increased over the prior year for the first time in the 1990s.

53.6

51.4

Radio Shack gross margins

SOURCE: Tandy Corp., and Salomon Bros. estimates.

During the PC boom of the 1980s, computer sales fueled fast-paced expansion for Radio Shack and eventually grew to more than one-third of the chain's overall revenues. But the same computer category that drove Radio Shack's growth in the '80s also proved to be its undoing in the '90s. Competition drove profit margins lower, and Radio

EXHIBIT 2   Advertising Polishes a Shopworn Image

FORT WORTH—After touting itself for most of the past decade as "America's Technology Store," Radio Shack spent most of 1994 trying to revamp its image.

Trying to cast itself as a consumer-electronics service provider, it began using its advertising last year to tell consumers, "You've got questions, we've got answers."

This year, consumers will see that Radio Shack not only has answers, but it also has sophisticated databases.

Following up on its television campaign, which was designed to polish its general image, the Fort Worth-based retailer plans to use targeted marketing techniques this year that are most commonly associated with direct-mail advertisers.

Previously, Radio Shack has simply mailed advertising fliers to customers on its database. This year, it will develop specific advertising packages for carefully targeted customer groups, company President Leonard Roberts says.

"I can assure you that this time next year, every person that moves into a new apartment or new home will get a nice specialized mailing from Radio Shack within a week of when they move in," he says.

People settling into new homes are highly likely to be in the market for wires, cables, and other accessories carried by Radio Shack, Roberts says.

Radio Shack can also develop advertising targeted at other groups. For example, it may pitch electronic security products in a flier to be mailed to women living alone or to senior citizens, he says.

Having tracked customer purchases for decades, Radio Shack has a rich database that also tracks buying patterns, Executive Vice President Dave Christopher says.

"We've had some of this information for a long time," he says. "We just have not tried to use it until now."

By targeting specific groups likely to be interested in identifiable product categories, Radio Shack may better reach customers willing to pay a premium for service and convenience, Roberts says.

"We've become more relevant to people's lives," he says. "We're not out there just touting prices."

Indeed, Radio Shack revamped its entire marketing program last year in an effort to deliver its new message to the general market.

For the first time, the company hired an outside advertising agency—New York's Young & Rubicam—to help steer its marketing campaign.

Working with Radio Shack's marketing department, the outside agency developed the "You've got questions, we've got answers" theme.

Although Radio Shack's estimated annual advertising budget of $185 million did not change much, the way it spent its money did.

The company previously spent about 20 percent of its advertising money for television and radio commercials; now it spends about 30 percent.

Historically a buyer of air time mostly during sports events, Radio Shack also switched most of its television spending to prime-time shows to reach a broader audience.

The rest of the marketing budget continues to be spent on print advertising.

The marketing changes were necessary and effective, says Mark Seavy, associate editor of *Television Digest,* a New York newsletter that tracks the consumer electronics industry.

"The last year and a half, they've picked up their marketing considerably," Seavy says. "Up until then, Radio Shack had suffered from a pretty dowdy image."

—Steven Vonder Haar

Shack's relatively small 2,300-square-foot stores were ill-suited for selling the growing range of PC products the maturing computer industry offers.

This is more us," Christopher says of Radio Shack's resumed focus on selling lower-priced electronics gadgets. "We understand this stuff. We can explain it. Our stores are just more physically suited to selling these items."

Last year, Radio Shack computer sales dropped by 20 percent to just more than 10 percent of overall revenues. The drop in the sales of high-ticket computers meant that the chain had to sell a lot more batteries and cables just to stay even, much less post sales growth.

With Radio Shack expecting its computer sales to stabilize in the 10 percent range, the chain is poised for growth, says Mark Mandel, analyst with the Salomon Bros. investment banking firm in New York.

"The shift out of computers has really masked the strong performance of their core business in recent years," Mandel says.

The restructuring of Radio Shack has involved much more, however, than simply returning to the retail roots company patriarch Charles Tandy planted. The company is also employing more sophisticated operating techniques necessary for a retailer trying to compete in the 1990s.

Radio Shack, for example, has officially shed its disdain for name-brand merchandise. For decades, the company believed that selling only merchandise carrying its own brand name, such as Realistic, was the way to protect its profit margins.

After Tandy's move to sell the bulk of its manufacturing operations in 1993, Radio Shack is aggressively pursuing partnerships with outside companies, such as Motorola.

Motorola is making ham radio products that Radio Shack will sell exclusively but that will carry the Motorola name.

"If there's any weakness that Radio Shack had, according to our research, there's some types of product lines that folks were only interested in high-profile brand names," Roberts says. "Radio Shack will quickly overcome that barrier."

Last year, Radio Shack experimented with selling Sony products in a trial in San Antonio, and Roberts says the chain is continuing efforts to strike deals with other name-brand manufacturers.

Radio Shack executives are also working for better management of the merchandise already in its retail system.

For the first time ever, Radio Shack executives have in the past 18 months assembled a detailed merchandise plan that projects monthly sales for each individual product along with the marketing efforts that will be used to achieve those monthly sales goals.

"Nothing happens until you have a plan," Roberts says.

New ways for managing inventory will even affect what kinds of products Radio Shack shoppers see in stores.

Last year, the chain launched what it calls its "custom replenishment system," in which the inventory of individual Radio Shack stores is tailored to match its strengths.

Under the system, a Radio Shack outlet with a history of selling lots of cellular telephones will carry more models and a deeper inventory of merchandise in that category.

Over time, each store will offer a unique combination of merchandise suited for its customer base and the talent of the sales team in that store, Christopher says.

"One of the hits that we've taken in market research is that our stores have too much clutter," he says. "This system helps the individual stores to better merchandise the stuff they're good at selling."

Such a system, however, is not without risk. Shopping at a national chain, some shoppers may expect a standard set of merchandise that can be found at any of its stores nationwide.

"You also run the risk of missing the opportunity to grow in an expanding market because you're focusing on selling primarily the things that used to sell well," says David Goldstein, president of Channel Marketing Corp., a Dallas-based consulting firm.

Even so, Radio Shack's willingness to implement the new inventory system and other new programs is a healthy sign of a company looking for growth opportunities, Goldstein says.

"A lot of people like to look at Radio Shack and remind them of the failures they've had," he says. "But if you don't take the risks, you can't hit the big rewards."

Two of Radio Shack's most promising new programs focus on its goal to establish itself as a source for consumer electronics services. Last year, the company launched the Repair Shop at Radio Shack and its Gift Express program.

With its Repair Shop, Radio Shack will take a name-brand consumer electronics item in need of repair, give the customer an estimate, and send it to one of its more than 100 repair centers nationwide. After a regional rollout last year, Radio Shack plans to begin aggressive national marketing of its repair services February 17.

With Gift Express, Radio Shack is trying do for electronics what flower shops have done for bouquets. The company promises to wrap and deliver items purchased at Radio Shack via Federal Express.

The new services are not expected to have a substantial effect on revenues immediately, but they represent strong long-range growth potential, says Otis Bradley, an analyst with the Gilford Securities investment banking firm in New York.

"Any service by definition requires time to build up," he says. "But once you get it, it's a more stable and consistent revenue stream."

Radio Shack executives view the service programs as another way to bring new customers into their stores. They also help the company take advantage of existing infrastructure and build new systems that make other services possible.

For Gift Express, for example, Radio Shack established a centralized order fulfillment distribution center in Fort Worth.

With the distribution center up and running, Radio Shack started offering free home delivery two months ago of products that in-store shoppers could not find in stock, Christopher says.

The system allows store clerks to complete a sale before the customer walks out the door, and it makes the buying experience more convenient for consumers, Christopher says. And it's a program that would not have been possible without the distribution center that Radio Shack established to support the Gift Express program, he says.

For now, however, Radio Shack's challenge is to deliver strong 1995 results following up on the signs of life the chain showed last year. Even Roberts says he will be disappointed if Radio Shack does not beat the 5 percent growth rate this year that caught Wall Street's attention in 1994.

Source: Steven Vonder Haar, "Radio Shack Back on Track," *Tarrant Business, Fort Worth Star-Telegram* February 6–12, 1995, pp. 1, 14, 15, 23.

III

DESIGNING MARKETING STRATEGY

CHAPTER
6

Market Targeting and Positioning Strategies

Deciding which buyers to target and how to position the firm's products for each target are the foundations of marketing strategy. These decisions set the framework within which the marketing program is developed and implemented. Good targeting and positioning strategies offer the company an opportunity for superior performance. Faulty decisions negatively impact performance.

Insightful market target and positioning decisions enabled Waterford Wedgwood PLC to make a comeback in the U.S. premium crystal market segment (over $25 for a stemware item).[1] More than 100 companies compete for a piece of this market segment. After experiencing sales declines, the Irish company conducted marketing research in three countries, which led to the introduction in 1990 of Marquis Crystal by Waterford. The brand was Waterford's first new product in 200 years, priced over 20 percent below the traditional Waterford line. The Marquis decision involved the possible risks of stealing sales (cannibalism) from the traditional line and weakening its brand equity (perceived value) in the marketplace. The plan was to target price-conscious buyers willing to pay for sensible consumption by positioning Marquis differently enough in price and design, while gaining from the association with Waterford. The marketing strategy is working. Waterford's U.S. market share was up 7 percent in 1994 to 34 percent compared to 1990. Marshall Field's Waterford sales increased 30 percent in 1994.

In analyzing the strategies of successful companies, like Waterford Wedgwood PLC, one feature stands out. Each has a market target and positioning strategy that is a major factor in gaining a strong market position for the firm, although the strategies of companies are often quite different. Examples of effective targeting and positioning strategies are found in all kinds and sizes of businesses, including those marketing industrial and consumer goods and services. We will begin this chapter by examining market-targeting strategies, and we will discuss how market targets are selected. We will then consider the choice of a positioning concept and describe the available methods for use in positioning analysis. We will conclude with a discussion of the selection and management of the positioning strategy.

MARKET-TARGETING STRATEGY

The market-targeting decision identifies the people or organizations in a product-market toward which an organization directs its positioning strategy. Selecting a good market target is one of management's most demanding challenges. For example, should the organization attempt to serve all people who are willing and able to buy a particular product or service or instead selectively focus on one or more subgroups? Study of the product-market, its buyers, the organization's competitive advantages, and the structure of competition is necessary in order to make this decision. The situation analysis chapters in Part II provide important supporting analyses for the targeting decision.

Targeting Strategies

Targeting and positioning strategies consist of: (1) identifying and analyzing the segments in a product-market, (2) deciding which segment(s) to target, and (3) designing and implementing a positioning strategy for each target.

Many companies use some form of market segmentation. We know that buyers have become increasingly differentiated as to their needs and wants. Microsegmentation is becoming popular, aided by effective segmentation and targeting methods such as database marketing. We shall assume that the product-market is segmented on some basis. Emerging markets may require rather broad macrosegmentation, resulting in a few segments, whereas more mature markets can be divided into several microsegments. A new market may need to advance to the growth stage before meaningful segmentation is feasible.

Targeting Alternatives

The targeting decision indicates how many segments will be served. Management may select a few segments or go after intensive coverage of the product-market by targeting all or most of the segments. A specific marketing effort (positioning strategy) is directed toward each segment that management decides to serve. Anheuser-Busch Companies, Inc., the leading U.S. brewer, with its multiple offering of beer brands, targets several major population groups within the total product-market. Some of the targets are quite large, and some people buy more than one of the Anheuser-Busch brands. The firm's market target strategy is a segmentation approach since different brands, prices, distribution, and promotional programs are involved.

EXHIBIT 6–1 Marketing Targeting Approaches

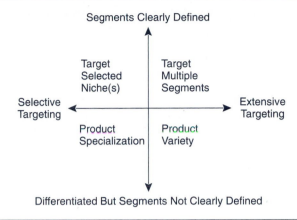

In certain product-markets organizations may select market target strategies that offer buyers a variety of products. While there is diversity in needs and wants, preferences are diffused, making it difficult to define segments.[2] Sometimes we may be unable to distinguish whether a firm is using a segmentation or a variety strategy, and there may be some elements of both strategies present. For example, the firm may offer variety to buyers in a particular market segment, such as providing customers with different flavors or varieties of food products. The variety strategy is especially popular in food and beverage product markets.

Market targeting approaches tend to fall into two major categories: segment targeting and targeting through product differentiation. As shown in Exhibit 6–1, segment targeting ranges from a single segment to targeting all or most of the segments in the market. When segments are difficult to identify, even though diversity in preferences exists, companies may appeal to buyers through product specialization or product variety. Specialization involves offering buyers a product differentiated from competitor's products and designed to appeal to customer needs and wants not satisfied by competitors. Several targeting examples are shown in Exhibit 6–2.

Factors Influencing Targeting Decisions

Market segment analysis, discussed in Chapter 4, helps to rank the overall attractiveness of the segments under consideration as market targets. These evaluations include analysis of customers, competitor positioning, and the financial and market attractiveness of the segments under consideration. We can use information to evaluate both existing and potential market targets.

Two questions need to be answered in deciding the targeting strategy to be used: (1) Are there opportunities for multiple targeting? (2) Should the organization target a

---

EXHIBIT 6–2   Market Targeting Examples

Market-Targeting Approach	*Targeting Examples*
• Selective targeting	Mercedes (automobiles), Autodesk (computer aided design software)
• Extensive targeting	American Airlines (air travel), General Motors (automobiles)
• Product specialization	Earth's Best (organic baby food), Church & Dwight (baking soda products)
• Product variety	Kellogg (breakfast cereals), Coca-Cola (beverages)

---

single segment, selectively target a few segments, or target all or most of the segments in the product-market? The factors that influence the choice of the targeting strategy include:

- Stage of product-market maturity.
- Extent of diversity in preferences.
- Industry structure.
- Competitive advantage.

We will look at each factor to assess its influence on the market target decision. The relative importance of each factor often varies by company situation. The objective is to consider how each factor affects the market target strategy. Since several of the factors often vary according to the stage of product-market maturity, it serves as the basis for describing different targeting situations.

TARGETING IN DIFFERENT MARKET ENVIRONMENTS

Michael E. Porter suggests that the industry environment is influenced by the extent of concentration of its firms, the stage of its maturity, and its exposure to international competition. Five generic environments describe the range of industry structures:[3]

Emerging. These industries are newly formed or reformed, created by factors such as a new technology, the changing needs of buyers, and the identification of unmet needs by suppliers.

Fragmented. In this type of industry, no company has a strong position regarding market share or influence. Typically, a large number of relatively small firms make up the industry. Services like lawn care are examples of fragmented industries.

Transitional. These industries are shifting from rapid growth to maturity, as represented by the product life cycles of the products in the industry. Having grown rapidly a decade ago, microwave ovens are now in the maturity stage.

EXHIBIT 6–3 Life Cycle of a Typical Product

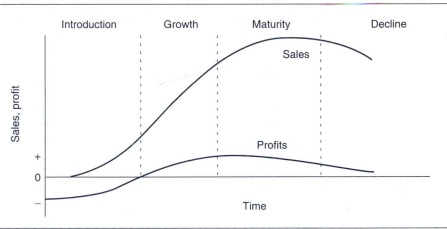

Declining. In this type of industry, sales are declining. This industry category is not cyclical, where sales rise and fall over time. Rather, a declining industry is actually fading away instead of experiencing a temporary decline. Traditional typewriter producers are a declining industry.

Global. Firms in this category compete on a global basis. Examples include automobiles, consumer electronics, steel, and telecommunications.

The five industry categories are neither exhaustive nor mutually exclusive. Moreover, changing environmental and industry conditions may alter an industry classification.

The stages of the life cycles of the products in the industry offer useful insights about the industry environment. Porter's generic environments are closely related to the product life cycle (PLC) stages. Looking at competition during the product life cycle and at different product-market levels provides insights into different types and intensities of competition. Products, like people, move through life cycles.

The life cycle of a typical product is shown in Exhibit 6–3. Sales begin at the time of introduction and increase over the pattern shown. Profits initially lag sales since expenses often exceed sales during the initial stage of the product life cycle as a result of heavy introductory expenses. Industry sales and profits decline after the product reaches the maturity stage. Often profits fall off before sales.

Since an industry may contain more than one product-market and different industries may compete in a given market, we will use the market as the basis of discussion. We will describe emerging, growth, mature, declining, and global markets to illustrate different targeting situations.

Emerging Market

"The most pervasive feature of emerging markets is uncertainty about customer acceptance and the eventual size of the market, which process and product technology will be dominant, whether cost declines will be realized, and the identity, structure, and actions of competitors."[4] Market definition and analysis are rather general in the early stages of product-market development. Buyers' needs and wants are not highly differentiated because buyers lack experience with the product. Determining the future scope and direction of growth of product-market development may be difficult, as will forecasting the size of market growth.

Buyer Diversity.   The similarity of buyers' preferences in the new product-market often limits segmentation efforts. But it may be possible to identify a few broad segments. For example, heavy, medium, and low product usage can be used to segment a new product-market where usage varies across buyers. If segmentation is not feasible, an alternative is to define and describe an average or typical user, directing marketing efforts toward these potential users.

Industry Structure.   Study of the characteristics of market pioneers indicates that new enterprises are more likely to enter a new product-market than are large, well-established companies. The exception is a major innovation in a large company coupled with strong entry barriers. The pioneers developing a new product-market "are typically small new organizations set up specifically to exploit first-mover advantages in the new resource space."[5] These entrepreneurs often have limited access to resources and must pursue product-market opportunities that require low levels of investment.

Industry development is influenced by various factors, including the rate of acceptance of the product by buyers, entry barriers, the performance of firms serving the market, and future expectations. The pioneer's proprietary technology may make entry by others impossible until they can gain access to the technology. For instance, Xerox, with its copying process, and Polaroid, with its instant film, held monopoly positions for several years. The initial period of development may include many changes in industry structure, creating both high risks and high rewards for the firms that enter. Major change during the initial years is a common feature of emerging industries.

Strategy for Competitive Advantage.   A firm entering a new product-market is more likely to achieve competitive advantage by offering buyers unique benefits rather than lower prices for equivalent benefits. Nonetheless, cost may be the basis of superior value when the new product is a lower-cost alternate technology to an existing product. For example, fax transmission of letters and brief reports is both faster and less expensive than overnight delivery services.

Research concerning the order of market entry indicates that the pioneer has a distinct advantage over subsequent firms entering the market. These studies estimate that the second firm entering the market will obtain 60 to 70 percent of the share of the pioneer.[6] The pioneer can develop entry barriers, making it more difficult and costly for others to enter. The advantage of an early follower is the opportunity to evaluate the pioneer's performance and thus reduce the risk of entry failure. Entry timing may also depend on the firm's resources and skills.

Targeting Strategy.   Despite the uncertainties in an emerging industry, some evidence indicates "that more successful or longer-living firms engage in less change than firms which fail."[7] Instead, these firms select and follow a consistent strategy on a continuing basis. If this behavior is characteristic of a broad range of successful new ventures, then choosing the entry strategy is very important.

EXHIBIT 6–4 Illustrative Market-Entry Situations for New Products

Targeting Strategy	New Market	Existing Market
Single target	A. Targeting a new product-market (new drug for incurable disease)	B. Targeting existing product-market (surgical staplers for surgery closure)
Multiple targets	D. Targeting a few broad segments	C. Targeting several substitute markets (fax machines for overnight delivery and other substitutes)

New product-market entry situations are shown in Exhibit 6–4. In situation A, the customer target is the potential user of a product that meets a need not previously satisfied. A cure for the AIDS virus is an example. The targeting strategy for this type of entry should include a substantial portion of potential buyers that are willing and able to buy the product. The price of the product, how well it satisfies buyers' needs and wants, and other factors may restrict the size of the potential market.

Entry situation B requires a more focused strategy than A. U.S. Surgical, in its market entry strategy, identified potential users in the surgery closure product-market, where surgical stapling offers an advantage over conventional closure methods. U.S. Surgical's market-targeting strategy has successfully expanded its sales. The company is the world market leader for surgical stapling equipment.

Situation C involves targeting two or more segments in the product-markets where a new product offers a promising substitute solution to buyers' needs and wants. As mentioned earlier, fax communication technology is a substitute for other communications alternatives. For example, one segment for fax machines is made up of large- and medium-size businesses that have been using overnight delivery services for letters and short reports.

Situation D may occur when there is some opportunity for buyer need differentiation and the entering firm wants to establish a dominant position in the new market. If the initial targeting is too narrow, the firm may fail to develop its capabilities in meeting customer needs for more than one group of users.

Growth Market

If not already present in the emerging market, segments should be identifiable in the growth stage. Finding customer groups with similar needs improves targeting, and "experience with the product, process, and materials technologies leads to greater efficiency and increased standardization."[8] The market environment moves from highly uncertain to moderately uncertain. Further change is likely, but information is available about the forces that influence the size and composition of the product-market.

Patterns of use can be identified and the characteristics of buyers and their use patterns can be determined. Segmentation by type of industry may be feasible in industrial markets. Characteristics such as age, income, and family size may identify broad macrosegments for consumer products such as food and drugs. Analysis of the characteristics and preferences of existing buyers yields useful guidelines for estimating market potential.

Industry Structure.   We often assume that high-growth markets are very attractive, and that early entry offers important competitive advantages. Nevertheless, there are some warnings for industry participants:

> First, a visible growth market can attract too many competitors—the market and its distribution channel cannot support them. The intensity of competition is accentuated when growth fails to match expectations or eventually slows. Second, the early entrant is unable to cope when key success factors or technologies change, in part because it lacks the financial skills or organizational skills.[9]

Industry structure generalizations in growth markets are difficult. There is some evidence that large, established firms are more likely to enter growth markets rather than emerging markets. This is because they may not be able to move as quickly as small specialist firms in exploiting the opportunities in the emerging product-market.[10] The established companies have skills and resource advantages for achieving market leadership. These powerful firms can overcome the timing advantage of the market pioneers. Later entrants also have the advantage of evaluating the attractiveness of the product-market during its initial development.

Strategy for Competitive Advantage.   Survival analysis of firms in the minicomputer industry highlights two performance characteristics in the rapid growth stage of the product-market: (1) survival rates are much higher for aggressive firms competing on a broad market scope compared to conservative firms competing on the same basis and (2) survival rates are high (about three-quarters) for both aggressive and conservative specialists.[11] This research suggests that survival requires aggressive action by firms that seek large market positions in the total market. Other competitors are likely to be more successful by targeting one or a few market segments.

Targeting Strategy.   Targeting decisions in a growth market are influenced by several factors: (1) the capabilities and resources of the organization, (2) the competitive environment, (3) the extent to which the product-market can be segmented, (4) the future potential of the market, and (5) the market-entry barriers confronting potential competitors. There are at least three possible targeting strategies: extensive market coverage by firms with established businesses in related markets, selective targeting by firms with diversified product portfolios, and market niche strategies by small organizations serving one or a few market segments.[12]

Narrow Market Scope.   This targeting strategy is feasible when buyers needs are differentiated or when products are differentiated. The segments that are not served by large competitors provide an opportunity for the small firm to gain competitive advantage. The market leader(s) may not find small segments attractive enough to seek a position in the segment. If the buyers in the market have similar needs, a small organization may gain advantage through product specialization. This strategy would concentrate on a specific product or component.

Dell Computer is an interesting example of a company that competed successfully in the growth stage of the personal computer market. The company used standard components to assemble computers that it marketed through mail-order channels. Dell's computers still offer speed and price advantages over competing units; the company's phone contact with customers provides direct feedback from the market place.

Broad Market Scope.   The objective of this targeting strategy is to cover a large portion of the buyers in the product-market. The number of specific targets depends on the segments that exist in the market. During the growth stage of the business market for personal computers, the three major segments were small, medium, and large companies. Segments in the growth stage are likely to be few and identified by one or a few general characteristics (e.g., size of business). When segments are not apparent, extensive targeting is guided by a general profile of buyers. This profile becomes the target.

Strategies for Mature and Declining Markets

Not all firms that enter the emerging and growth stages of the market survive during the maturity stage. The needs and characteristics of buyers also change over time. Market entry at the maturity stage is less likely than in previous life cycle stages.

Buyer Diversity.   Segmentation is often essential at the maturity stage of the life cycle. At this stage, the product-market is clearly defined, indicating buyers' preferences and the competitive structure. The factors that drive market growth are often apparent. The market is not likely to expand or decline rapidly. Nonetheless, eventual decline may occur unless actions are taken to extend the product life cycle through product innovation and development of new-product applications.

Identification and evaluation of market segments are necessary to select targets that offer each firm a competitive advantage. Since the mature market has a history, experience should be available concerning how buyers respond to the marketing efforts of the firms competing in the product-market. Knowledge of the competitive and environmental influences on the segments in the market helps to obtain accurate forecasts.

The maturity of the product-market may reduce its attractiveness to the companies serving the market, so the market-driven organization may benefit from (1) scanning the external environment for new opportunities that are consistent with the organization's skills and resources (core competencies), (2) identifying potential competitor threats to the current technologies for meeting customer needs, and (3) identifying opportunities within specific segments for new and improved products.

Buyers in mature markets are experienced and often demanding. They are familiar with competing brands and often display preferences for particular brands. The key marketing issue is developing and sustaining brand preference, since buyers are aware of the product type and its features. Many of the top brands like Coca-Cola, Gillette, and Wrigley's have kept their leading positions for more than half a century. This highlights the importance of obtaining and protecting a lead position at an early stage in the development of a market.

Industry Structure.   The characteristics of mature industries include intense competition for market share, emphasis on cost and service, slowdown in new-product flows, global competition, pressures on profits, and increases in the power of channel organizations that link manufacturers with end-users.[13] Deciding how to compete successfully in the mature product-market is a demanding challenge.

The typical industry structure consists of a few companies that dominate the industry and several other firms that pursue market selectivity strategies. The larger firms may include a market leader and two or three competitors with relatively large market positions. Entry into the mature product-market is often difficult because of major barriers and intense competition for sales and profits. Those that enter follow market or product selectivity strategies. Acquisition is often the best way of market entry, rather than trying to develop products and marketing capabilities. Mature industries are increasingly experiencing pressures for global consolidation. Examples include automobile tires, foods, household appliances, prescription drugs, and consumer electronics.

Strategy for Competitive Advantage. The strategies of companies competing in mature product-markets may be to *stabilize, turn around,* or *harvest* the business (Chapter 2). The stabilize objective is pursued through cost reduction, selective targeting, or product differentiation. Turning around the corporation is undertaken to try to improve financial performance. Harvesting is the decision not to compete.

Audi AG implemented a major turnaround strategy in the mid-1990s designed to appeal to automobile buyers with an exciting image. The midrange Audi A4, introduced in 1995, attracted new buyers and was part of a major new product strategy to increase sales and profits. The A4's initial entry was very successful. Supported by a major advertising campaign, the new model attracted younger buyers. Appealing to this target was a major objective of the new marketing strategy.

Targeting. Both targeting and positioning strategies may change in moving from the growth to maturity stages of the product-market. Targeting may be altered to reflect changes in priorities among market targets. Positioning within a targeted market may be adjusted to improve customer satisfaction and operating performance. When the product-market reaches maturity, management is likely to place heavy emphasis on efficiency.

Targeting segments is appropriate for all firms competing in the mature product-market. The strategic issue is deciding which segments to serve. Market maturity may create new opportunities and threats in the firm's market target(s). Firms pursuing extensive targeting strategies may decide to exit from certain segments. Those targets retained in the portfolio are prioritized to help guide product research and development, channel management, pricing strategy, advertising expenditures, and selling effort allocations. Exits from some targets and shifts in targeting priorities by large competitors may create new opportunities for smaller competitors that use selective targeting strategies.

Global Market

Understanding global markets is important regardless of where an organization decides to compete, since domestic markets often include international competitors. The increasingly smaller world linked by instant communications, global supply networks, and international finance markets mandates evaluating global opportunities and threats. In

GLOBAL FEATURE   Hermés' Strategy for Competitive Advantage

Competing in Asia, Europe, and on a limited scale in the United States, Hermés offers an array of luxury goods, including $175 leather chewing gum holders, $2,000 men's shoes, and $225 silk scarves. Asia is targeted for half of Hermés' sales by 2000 (30% in 1993).

Hermés has a powerful brand image attracting consumers who are willing to buy its expensive products throughout the world. During the last several years new product lines have been added. Hermés produces textiles, leather, and perfume products sold in its shops and establishes alliances with suppliers of its other products.

The expanded lines, including tableware, furniture, and stationery, are targeted to affluent career women. The objective is to expand Hermés' traditional customer base by offering glamour and status through symbolic positioning.

Hermés' performance is impressive, with $1,300 sales per square foot in its over 60 stores worldwide. Sales and profits increased during the early 1990s. During this same period, other luxury goods companies' performance declined. The Christmas season accounts for one-quarter of Hermés' sales.

Sources: Nancy Rotenier, "Tie Man Meets Queen of England," *Forbes,* September 13, 1993, pp. 46–48; "Hermés' Net Income Jumped 19% in 1993 to $36.8 Million Total," *The Wall Street Journal,* April 5, 1994, p. B4.

selecting strategies for global markets, there are two primary options for consideration: (1) the advantages of global reach and standardization and (2) the advantages of local adaptation.[14]

Global Reach and Standardization.   This strategy considers the extent to which standardized products and other strategy elements can be designed to compete on a global basis. The world is the market arena; buyers are targeted without regard to national boundaries and regional preferences. Global strategy products are not commodities. Instead they are differentiated but standardized across nations. The objective is to identify market segments that span global markets and to serve these needs with global positioning strategies.

Hermés SA, the French luxury-goods company, is an example of targeting upscale buyers across national boundaries. Attracting affluent buyers with expensive leather, silk, and clothing items, Hermés sales and profits held up well during the global economic slowdown in the early 1990s. The Global Feature describes Hermés strategy for competitive advantage.

Local Adaption Requirements.   In some markets domestic customers are targeted, and positioning strategies designed, to consider the requirements of domestic buyers. A wide variety of social, political, cultural, economic, and language differences among countries affect buyers' needs and preferences. These variations need to be accounted for in targeting and positioning strategies. Consider, for example, the comparisons of food markets and habits shown in Exhibit 6–5. Note the differences in cereal consumption, frozen-food consumption, and microwave availability in homes. Such differences offer possible market

---

EXHIBIT 6–5 Food Markets and Habits

The Major Players
1988 European food companies, ranked by sales, in billions of dollars*

Company	Nationality	1988 sales, *in billions of dollars
Nestlé	Swiss	$8.76
Unilever	Britain/Neth.	5.98
BSN	French	3.46
Eridania	Italy	3.33
Hillstown Holdings	Britain	2.56
General Foods-Europe**	Britain	2.52
Jacobs Suchard	Swiss	2.48
Daigety	Britain	2.01
Associated British Food	Britain	1.88
United Biscuits	Britain	1.88

*Based on exchange rate of December 30, 1988
**Excludes acquisition of Kraft at end of 1988

Source: UBS Phillips and Drew Ltd.

Breakfast of Choice
1988 per-capita cereal consumption, in pounds

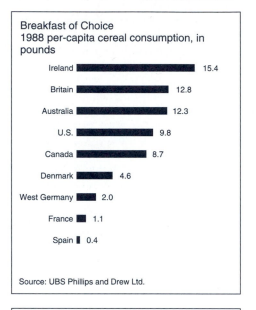

Ireland	15.4
Britain	12.8
Australia	12.3
U.S.	9.8
Canada	8.7
Denmark	4.6
West Germany	2.0
France	1.1
Spain	0.4

Source: UBS Phillips and Drew Ltd.

Where Convenience Rules
1988 per-capita frozen-food consumption, in pounds

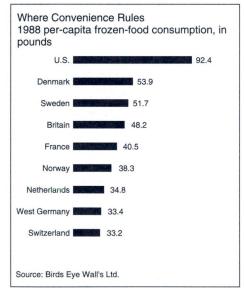

U.S.	92.4
Denmark	53.9
Sweden	51.7
Britain	48.2
France	40.5
Norway	38.3
Netherlands	34.8
West Germany	33.4
Switzerland	33.2

Source: Birds Eye Wall's Ltd.

Fast cooking
Percentage of homes with microwave ovens

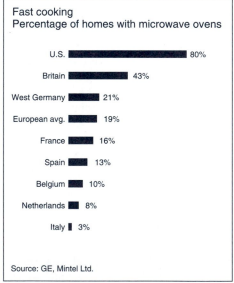

U.S.	80%
Britain	43%
West Germany	21%
European avg.	19%
France	16%
Spain	13%
Belgium	10%
Netherlands	8%
Italy	3%

Source: GE, Mintel Ltd.

Source: Joann S. Lublin, "Slim Pickings: U.S. Food Firms Find Europe's Huge Market Hardly a Piece of Cake," *The Wall Street Journal*, May 15, 1990, p. A18. Reprinted by permission of *The Wall Street Journal*, © 1990 Dow Jones & Company, Inc. All Rights Reserved Worldwide.

opportunities. Low consumption rates may also indicate the purchasing resistance of buyers. For example, instant coffee is popular in Britain but not in France.

Industry Structure.   Industry structure and competition are changing throughout the world as companies seek to improve their competitive advantage in the rapidly shrinking global marketplace. Industry scope needs to be examined using a global perspective since many competitive boundaries extend beyond national borders. Corporate actions include restructuring, acquisition, merger, and strategic alliances. For example, General Mills has a strategic alliance with Nestlé to market General Mills products in Europe, offering a major opportunity for General Mills to increase sales of cereal products. Nestlé has the experience and distribution network needed to tap the cereal market. Kellogg, a key competitor, is already serving European markets.

Targeting.   Strategies for competing in international markets range from targeting a single country, regional (multinational) targeting, or targeting on a global basis. The strategic issue is deciding whether to compete internationally and, if so, how to compete. Also, the choice of a domestic focus requires an understanding of relevant global influences on the domestic strategy.

Global and domestic strategies require examining the trade-offs between global reach/standardization and local adaptation.[15] If neither standardization nor local adaptation provides an advantage, strengths may be found elsewhere—for instance, in applying a successful domestic strategy from one country to other countries with similar needs and market conditions. When both standardization and local adaptation are important, a composite strategy can be followed using decentralized marketing and a standard product with selected options.

Buzzell and Quelch suggest three strategic options for a multinational threatened by global competition.[16] One possibility is to convert to a global strategy. The strategies used by Boeing for commercial aircraft and by IBM for computers are examples of global strategies. A second option is establishing a strategic alliance with one or more companies that provide market access and other global benefits (see Chapter 7). A third option is to target a market segment that the organization can dominate and build entry barriers against global competitors. The segment strategy may be domestic or international in scope. Producers of expensive Swiss watches follow this strategy. Millipore in water treatment equipment also follows this strategy.

THE POSITIONING PROCESS

The close relationship between market targeting and positioning is illustrated by Johnson & Johnson's marketing strategy for Tylenol, the leading brand in the pain relief market. Johnson & Johnson's strategy for positioning its successful Tylenol brand is described in the accompanying Strategy Feature.

In the rest of the chapter we will examine positioning strategy. First, we will overview the positioning process and discuss the selection of the positioning concept. We

---

STRATEGY FEATURE   Positioning Tylenol with Doctors and Consumers

---

Tylenol's success in gaining and keeping its dominant brand position in the pain relief market is due to a brilliantly executed marketing strategy that simultaneously targets doctors, hospitals, and consumers with effective, complementary positioning programs. Tylenol's sustained competitive advantage is particularly impressive in view of the devastating product tampering problems in the early 1980s and strong competitive challenges by several competitors going after Tylenol's $600 million in sales.

- A core element in Tylenol's strategy is its strong association with doctors and hospitals.
- Using a micromarketing strategy for the Tylenol line, Johnson & Johnson targets its professional and consumer segments using different product mixes, separate sales

organizations, and specific communications programs.

- Tylenol with codeine is a prescription product that is available from physicians, enabling the brand to sustain a strong loyalty with physicians.
- Consumer advertising positions the Tylenol brand featuring its doctor and hospital heritage.
- All of the Tylenol advertising is focused on Extra-Strength Tylenol which supports the regular-strength product and creates name awareness for other advertised line extensions in related categories.
- Competitors describe Tylenol's powerful brand image as being "in a class by itself."

Source: D. John Loden, *Megabrands* (Burr Ridge, IL: Irwin Professional Publishing, 1992), pp. 141–42.

---

will then examine the choice of the positioning strategy and how the positioning components are combined. Finally, we will consider how positioning effectiveness is assessed.

The Positioning Process

Positioning may focus on an entire company, a mix of products, a specific line of products, or a particular brand, although positioning is often centered on the brand. Exhibit 6–6 describes the major steps in the positioning process. The buyers in the market target are the focus of the positioning strategy. The *positioning concept* is the product (brand) meaning derived from the needs of the buyers in the market target.[17] For example, the positioning concept used by Hermés is intended to position its products as status symbols. Selecting the positioning concept requires an understanding of buyers' needs, wants, and perceptions of competing brands. The *positioning strategy* is the combination of marketing mix strategies used to portray the positioning concept to targeted buyers. It includes the product, supporting services, distribution channels, price, and promotion. The positioning objective is to have each targeted customer perceive the brand as distinct from other competing brands and favorably compared to the other brands. The position of the brand is determined by the buyer's perceptions of the firm's positioning strategy (and their perceptions of competitors' strategies). Positioning is in the eyes and mind of the buyer. Companies' marketing strategies try to persuade buyers to

---

EXHIBIT 6–6   The Positioning Process

Positioning concept
The product (brand) meaning
derived from the needs of
the buyers comprising
the market target.

Positioning effectiveness
The extent to which
management's positioning
objectives are achieved
in the market target.

Market
target

Positioning strategy
The combination of marketing
actions used to portray
the positioning concept
to targeted buyers.

---

favorably position companies' brands. *Positioning effectiveness* considers how well management's positioning objectives are achieved in the market target.

Selecting the Positioning Concept

The positioning concept indicates the perception or association that management wants target market buyers to have concerning the company's brand. Aaker and Shansby comment on the importance of this decision:

> The position can be central to customers' perception and choice decisions. Further, since all elements of the marketing program can potentially affect the position, it is usually necessary to use a positioning strategy as a focus for the development of the marketing program. A clear positioning strategy can ensure that the elements of the marketing program are consistent and supportive.[18]

Choosing the positioning concept is an important first step in developing the positioning strategy. The positioning concept is "the general meaning that is understood by customers in terms of its relevance to their needs and preferences."[19] The positioning strategy is the combination of marketing mix actions that implement the product (brand) concept into a specific position with targeted buyers.

Positioning Concepts.[20]   The positioning concept should be linked to buyers' needs and wants. The concept may be *functional, symbolic,* or *experiential.* The *functional* concept applies to products that solve consumption-related problems for externally generated consumption needs. Examples of brands using this basis of positioning include Crest toothpaste (cavity prevention), Clorox liquid cleaner (effective cleaning), and a checking account with ABC Bank (convenient services). The *symbolic* concept relates to the buyer's internally generated needs for self-enhancement, role position, group membership, or ego identification. Examples of symbolic positioning are Rolex watches and Hermés luxury goods. Finally, the *experiential* concept is used to position products that provide sensory pleasure, variety, and/or cognitive stimulation. Several automobile brands are positioned using an experiential concept that emphasizes the driving experience.

Three aspects of positioning concept selection are important.[21] First, the concept applies to a specific brand rather than to all of the competing brands that compose a product classification such as toothpaste. Second, marketing management uses the concept to guide positioning decisions over the life of the brand, while recognizing that the brand's specific position may change. Third, if two or more concepts, for example, functional and experiential, are used to guide positioning strategy, the multiple concepts are likely to confuse buyers and perhaps weaken the effectiveness of positioning actions. Of course, the specific concept selected may not fall clearly into one of the three classifications.

Selecting the Positioning Concept.   The positioning concept indicates how management wants to position the brand relative to the competition. It may be necessary to study the positioning of competing brands using attributes that are important to existing and potential buyers of the competing brands. The objective is to find the preferred (or ideal) position of the buyers in each market segment of interest and to compare this preferred position with the actual positions of competing brands.

Later in the chapter we will consider factors such as determining the existing positioning of a brand relative to targeted buyers and deciding whether it satisfies management's positioning objectives. But first we discuss the choice of the positioning strategy and look at several resource allocation guidelines for combining the positioning components.

CHOOSING THE POSITIONING STRATEGY

The positioning strategy places the marketing mix components into a coordinated set of actions designed to achieve the positioning objective(s). The decisions include selecting the activities and results for which each marketing program component (product, distribution, price, promotion) will be responsible, determining the amount to spend on each program component, and deciding how much to spend on the entire program.

Determining the positioning strategy may involve a combination of management judgment and experience, trial and error, some experimentation (e.g., test marketing), and, sometimes field research. First, we will look at several considerations that affect targeting and supporting activities. Then we will consider factors used in deciding how much to spend for the positioning strategy. Finally, we will discuss allocating resources to the marketing program components.

Considerations about Targeting/Supporting Activities

A positioning strategy is usually centered on a single brand (microwave ovens) or a line of related products (kitchen appliances) for a specific market target. Whether the strategy is brand-specific or broader in scope depends on such factors as the size of the product-market, characteristics of the product or service, the number of products involved, and product interrelationships in the consumer's use situation. For example, the marketing programs of Procter & Gamble, Johnson & Johnson, and Cheesebrough-Pond's position their various brands, whereas firms such as General Electric Company, Caterpillar, and IBM use the corporate name to position the product-line or product-portfolio. When serving several market targets, an umbrella strategy covering multiple targets may be used for some of the marketing program components. For example, advertising can be designed to appeal to more than a single target, or the same product targeted to different buyers through different distribution channels.

Marketing Program Decisions

A look at the positioning strategy of Pier 1 Imports shows how the retailer combines marketing mix components into a coordinated strategy.[22] This specialty retailer competes in the United States, Canada, England, and Mexico. Pier 1's estimated 1995 sales approached $800 million. Its positioning strategy includes unique merchandise, strategically located stores, outstanding customer service, and modern retail systems.

Product Strategy.   Pier 1's array of merchandise includes decorative home furnishings, gifts, and related items. The assortment is unique and ever-changing, imported from 44 countries around the world. The objective is to create a casual, sensory store environment. The merchandise offers customers an opportunity to satisfy their desire for diversity.

Distribution Strategy.   The retailer has developed a vertical marketing system (management of the distribution process from supplier to end-user), integrating its global supply network with its retail stores. Management has an objective of increasing its nearly 800 stores in 42 states to 1,000 before the year 2000. Pier 1 uses freestanding and strip retail sites that are more quickly and conveniently accessed by customers. Store layouts and exteriors are attractively designed. Information systems are installed throughout company operations to provide real-time information to manage the business. Seven regional distribution centers supply merchandise to the retail store networks.

Pricing Strategy.   Pier 1's global supply network and purchasing know-how result in merchandise costs that enable the company to sell quality merchandise at attractive prices. China, Taiwan, and India account for the majority of Pier 1's products. Information systems target slow-moving merchandise for possible pricing actions. The pricing strategy emphasizes the value and uniqueness of the merchandise.

Promotion Strategy.   The retailer uses an effective combination of advertising, sales promotion, personal selling, and public relations to communicate with customers (see the accompanying Pier 1 advertisment). Its aggressive advertising strategy positions Pier 1 as "The Place to Discover." Attractive color ads encourage people to visit the stores. Experienced store managers and sales associates share the corporate culture of a customer-driven company. The customer service policy states, "The customer is always right." Pier 1 began using television advertising in 1995, which generated favorable sales response.

Courtesy of Pier 1 Imports.

Competitive Advantage.   Pier 1's advantage is a combination of value and uniqueness of merchandise that is competitively priced. The slowdown in household relocation during the 1990s will encourage spending on accent pieces and decorative home furnishings. Furniture sales declined during the early 1990s because of the recession. These pressures forced many small retailers to close, strengthening Pier 1's market position. Management's continual investment in market research studies keeps the retailer's strategy focused on customers' needs and wants.

An overview of the various decisions that are made in developing a positioning strategy is shown in Exhibit 6–7. Several of these actions are included in the Pier 1 illustration. Each positioning strategy component is examined in detail in Chapters 9–13. The present objective is to show how they fit into the positioning strategy. The positioning concept is the core focus for designing the integrated strategy. The positioning strategy indicates how (and why) the product mix, line, or brand is to be positioned in the target market. This strategy indicates:

- The product strategy, including how the product(s) will be positioned against the competition in the product-market.

EXHIBIT 6–7 Positioning Strategy Overview

Product positioning strategy		Product/service strategy
Product objectives	Channel of distribution objectives	Distribution strategy
Branding strategy	Type of channel	Price position relative to competition
Product management strategy	Distribution intensity	How active will price be
	Channel configuration	Pricing objectives
Advertising/sales promotion role and objectives	Channel management strategy	Price management strategy
Creative strategy		Advertising and sales promotion strategy
Media and programming strategy	Role and objectives of sales force	
Advertising management strategy	Size and deployment strategy	Sales force strategy
	Sales force management strategy	

Marketing program positioning strategy

- The distribution strategy to be used.
- The pricing strategy, including the role and positioning of price relative to competition.
- The advertising and sales promotion strategy and the objectives these promotion components are expected to achieve.
- The sales force strategy and direct marketing strategy, indicating how they are used in the positioning strategy.

Designing the Positioning Strategy.   First, it is necessary to establish the major strategy guidelines for every marketing program component. For example, what type of channel of distribution should be developed? Recall Pier 1's use of a vertical marketing system for the distribution of its products. Second, management strategies for each of the program components are implemented. For example, the distribution management strategy in Pier 1's case involves informing store managers about new merchandise, providing logistical support to the stores, and making necessary changes in the strategy over time.

Functional Relationships.   Responsibilities for the positioning strategy components (product, distribution, price, and promotion) are often assigned to various functional units within a company or business unit. These functions, typically, are not combined into an integrated marketing strategy budget. This separation of responsibilities (and budgets) highlights the importance of coordinating the positioning strategy. Someone should be responsible for managing all aspects of the positioning strategy. Some companies use strategy teams for this purpose. For example, Rubbermaid assigns responsibility for managing new product planning to teams of people from different business functions.

Effort-to-Response Relationship

A key factor in selecting a positioning strategy is estimating how the market target will respond to a proposed marketing program. Response is often measured by sales. Other response measures include profit contribution, brand awareness, market share, and size of purchase. Effort is measured by the expenditures for the program. The intent is to determine the combination of marketing effort and sales response which provides the greatest response less expenditures.

An example shows how effort and response are analyzed. The sales-to-marketing effort relationships for marketing program strategies in two target markets are shown in Exhibit 6–8. The solid circles are the present allocations of expenditures in markets A and B. The company wants to compete in markets A and B and the margins over direct costs are the same in both markets. By shifting expenditures in A and B as shown, sales are increased at no total increase in marketing expenditures. This type of analysis of revenues and costs is central to making marketing resource allocation decisions. While Exhibit 6–8 is simplified, it demonstrates the nature of the marketing programming task.

In the next section we will discuss and illustrate several methods used to analyze the relationship between effort and response.

DETERMINING POSITIONING EFFECTIVENESS

Finding out how a company or brand is positioned by buyers helps decide what future actions regarding positioning strategy should be. Positioning analysis is concerned with identifying the competitors serving a target market; determining how they are perceived, evaluated, and positioned by buyers; and analyzing customer needs and preferences.[23] "Positioning helps customers know the real differences among competing products so that they can choose the one that is of most value to them."[24] Positioning shows how a company or brand is distinguished from its competitors. Buyers position companies or brands using specific attributes or dimensions about products or corporate values. The objective is to gain (or sustain) a preferred position for the company or brand.

EXHIBIT 6–8   Effort-to-Response Example

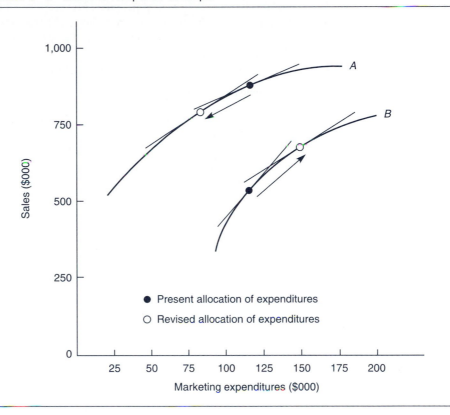

Several methods are available for determining positioning effectiveness, including customer and competitor research, market testing of proposed strategies, and the use of analytical models.

Customer/Competitor Research

Research studies provide useful buyer and competitor information for designing positioning strategies. Several of the research methods discussed in Part II help to determine the position of a brand. For example, preference maps about the product and brand positioning can be helpful in formulating marketing program strategy by mapping customer preferences for various competing brands.

Methods are available for considering the effects of several marketing program components on sales response. For example, a screening experiment can be used to identify important causal factors affecting market response.[25] A medical equipment firm identified seven factors as possible influences on the sales of a new product for use by surgeons in the operating room. The factors include: (1) special training for salespeople, (2) monetary incentives for salespeople, (3) vacation incentives for salespeople, (4) mailing of product information to physicians, (5) mailing of product information to operating room supervisors, (6) letter from the president of the firm describing the product, and (7) a customized surgical product (in contrast to a standardized product). The effect of each factor was measured by using field tests to vary the amount of the factor exposed to targeted buyers. For example, the high level of factor 1 consisted of training whereas the low-level treatment was no training. A fractional factorial experimental design was used to evaluate the effects of the seven factors. Different factor combinations were tested. One factor combination included no training, a monetary incentive, no vacation incentive, no mailing to physicians, mailing to operating room supervisors, letter from the president, and the standard product. Sixty-four salespeople were randomly selected for the sample, and groups of eight were randomly assigned to each of the eight treatment combinations. The eight treatment combinations were designed to enable testing the effects of each factor plus the influence of various combinations of factors.

One useful finding was that several of the factors had no impact on sales. For example, the customized product did not sell as well as the standard product. This information saved the firm an estimated $1 million in expenses by eliminating the need to offer customized product designs. Before conducting the experiment, management had planned to customize the product for surgeons' use. The other results of the screening experiment were useful in designing the marketing strategy for the product. Interestingly, of all of the factors, the vacation incentive had the largest effect on sales of all of the factors, surpassing even the money incentive.

Test Marketing

Test marketing supplies information about the commercial feasibility of a promising new product or about new positioning strategies for new products. The research method can also be used to test possible changes in the marketing program components (e.g., different amounts of advertising expenditures). The decision to test market depends on the following factors:

1. How much risk and investment are associated with the venture? When both are low, launching the product without a test market may be appropriate.
2. How much of a difference is there between the manufacturing investment required for the test versus the national launch? A large difference would favor a test market.
3. What are the likelihood and speed of the competitive response to the product offering?
4. How do the marketing costs and risks vary with the scale of the launch?[26]

While usually costing less than a national introduction, test marketing is nevertheless expensive. Market tests of packaged consumer products often cost $2 million or more depending on the scope of the tests and locations involved.[27] Also, the competitive risks of revealing one's plans must be weighed against the value of having the test market information. The major benefits of testing are risk reduction through better demand forecasts and the opportunity to fine-tune a marketing program strategy.

Test marketing provides market (sales) forecasts and information on the effectiveness of alternative marketing program strategies. Both are highly dependent on how well results from one or a few test markets provide accurate projections of the national market or regional market. Model-based analysis is an approach designed to help overcome problems associated with idiosyncrasies of test cities. It uses a detailed behavioral model of the consumer to analyze test market measurements and to develop forecasts that take account of the effects of modified marketing strategies.[28] We will discuss test marketing of new products in Chapter 8.

Positioning Models

Obtaining information about customers and prospects, analyzing it, and then developing strategies based on the information coupled with management judgment is the crux of positioning analysis. Some promising results have been achieved by incorporating research data into formal models of decision analysis. For example, ADVISOR is a comprehensive marketing mix budgeting model developed for industrial products.[29] It sets a marketing budget, then splits it into budgets for personal and impersonal (e.g., advertising) communications. ADVISOR is a multiple-regression type of model that has several predictor variables, including the number of users, customer concentration, fraction of sales made to order, attitude differences, proportion of direct sales, life-cycle stage, product plans, and product complexity. ADVISOR concentrates on the marketing budget and its components rather than on offering complete strategies for business units or products. Comprehensive discussion of marketing modeling is available from other sources.[30]

Positioning Effectiveness

How do we know if we have a good positioning strategy? The objective is that the company's marketing offer and image be both distinct and valued in the minds of the customers in the market target.[31] Does it yield the results expected concerning sales, market share, profit contribution, growth rates, customer satisfaction, and other competitive advantage outcomes? Gauging the effectiveness of a marketing program strategy using specific criteria such as market share and profitability is more straightforward than evaluating competitive advantage. Yet developing a marketing program strategy that cannot be easily copied is an essential consideration. For example, a competitor would need considerable resources—not to mention a long time period—to duplicate the powerful SABRE information system developed by American Airlines. In contrast, an airline can respond immediately with a price cut to meet the price offered by a competitor. The strong information systems advantage is more difficult for a competitor to copy than a price cut.

Companies do not alter their positioning strategies on a frequent basis, although adjustments are made at different stages of product-market maturity and in response to environmental, market, and competitive forces. For example, Pier 1 changed its promotion mix in 1995. Even though frequent changes are not made, a successful positioning strategy should be evaluated on a regular basis to identify shifting buyer preferences and changes in competitor strategies.

Positioning and Targeting Strategies

Recognizing the interrelationship between market target and positioning strategies is important:

> Positioning usually means that an overt decision is being made to concentrate only on certain segments. Such an approach requires commitment and discipline because it's not easy to turn your back on potential buyers. Yet, the effect of generating a distinct, meaningful position is to focus on the target segments and not be constrained by the reaction of other segments.[32]

Positioning becomes particularly challenging when management decides to target several segments. The objective is to develop an effective positioning strategy for each segment. The use of a different brand for each targeted segment is one way of focusing a positioning strategy.

Determining Positioning Feasibility

"It is tempting but naive—and usually fatal—to decide on a positioning strategy that exploits a market need or opportunity but assumes that your product is something it is not."[33] In selecting a positioning strategy, management must realistically evaluate the feasibility of the strategy, taking into consideration the product's strengths, the positions of competing brands, and the probable reactions of buyers to the strategy.

Cherry Coke, which was introduced nationally in 1985, surprised many industry observers with its strong sales performance at the same time that New Coke and Classic Coke were in the limelight.[34] Network TV and radio spots positioned Cherry Coke as an "out and outrageous" alternative to the other cokes. The new brand was launched with a $50 million budget, which generated a surprisingly strong and fast payback. Positioning was in terms of the flavor of the soft drink, thus using an experiential positioning concept.

SUMMARY

Choosing the right market target strategy can affect the performance of the enterprise. This decision is critical to properly positioning a brand or company in the marketplace. Sometimes a single target cannot be selected because the business competes in several markets. Moreover, locating the firm's best competitive advantage may first require a detailed analysis of several segments. Market target decisions integrate strategic planning and marketing strategy. Targeting decisions establish key guidelines for strategic planning and decisions about the positioning strategy used to design the marketing program.

The targeting options include a single segment, selective segments, or extensive segments. Choosing among these options involves consideration of the stage of product-market maturity, buyer diversity, industry structure, and the organization's competitive advantage.

Market targeting decisions vary depending on the product-market life cycle stage. Risk and uncertainty are high in the emerging market stage because of the lack of experience in the new market. Targeting in the growth stage benefits from prior experience, although competition is likely to be more intense than in the emerging market stage. Targeting approaches may be narrow or broad in scope based on the firm's resources and competitive advantage. Targeting in mature and declining markets often involves multiple targeting (or product variety) strategies by a few major competitors and single/selective (or product specialization) strategies by firms with small market shares. Global targeting ranges from local adaptation to global reach.

The positioning concept describes how management wants to have the brand positioned by the buyers in the market target. The concept used to position the brand may be based on the functions provided by the product, the experience it offers, or the symbol it conveys. Buyers position brands whereas companies seek to influence how buyers position brands.

Developing the positioning strategy requires the blending of the product, distribution, price, and promotion strategies to focus them on a market target. The result is an integrated strategy designed to achieve management's positioning objectives while gaining the largest possible competitive advantage. Shaping this bundle of strategies is a major challenge to marketing decision makers. Since the strategies span different functional areas and responsibilities, close coordination is essential.

Building on an understanding of the market target and the objectives to be accomplished by the marketing program, positioning strategy matches the firm's capabilities to buyers' needs. These programming decisions include selecting the amount of expenditure, deciding how to allocate these resources to the marketing program components, and making the most effective use of resources within each mix component. The factors that affect program strategy include the market target, the competition, resource constraints, management's priorities, and the product life cycle. The positioning statement describes the desired positioning relative to the competition.

Central to the positioning decision is examining the relationship between the marketing effort and the market response. Positioning analysis is useful in estimating the market response as well as in evaluating competition and buyer preferences. The analysis methods include customer/competitor research, market testing, and positioning models. Analysis information, combined with management judgment and experience, is the basis for selecting a positioning strategy. The close tie between positioning and segmentation strategies requires the coordination of these strategies.

QUESTIONS FOR REVIEW AND DISCUSSION

1. Discuss why it may be necessary for an organization to alter its targeting strategy over time.

2. What factors are important in selecting a market target?

3. Discuss the considerations that should be evaluated in targeting a macromarket segment whose buyers' needs vary versus targeting three microsegments within the macro segment.

4. How might a medium-sized bank determine the major market targets served by the bank?

5. Select a product and discuss how the size and composition of the marketing program might require adjustment as the product moves through its life cycle.

6. Suggest an approach that can be used by a regional family restaurant chain to determine the firm's strengths over its competitors.

7. Select and discuss a strategy that corresponds to each of these positioning approaches: attribute, price/quality, competition, application, product users, and product class.

8. Discuss some of the more important reasons why test market results may *not* be a good gauge of how well a new product will perform when it is launched in the national market.

9. "Evaluating marketing performance by using return-on-investment (ROI) measures is not appropriate because marketing is only one of several influences upon ROI." Develop an argument against this statement.

10. Two factors complicate the problem of making future projections as to the financial performance of marketing programs. First, the flow of revenues and costs is likely to be uneven over the planning horizon. Second, sales may not develop as forecasted. How should we handle these factors in financial projections?

11. Discuss the relationship between the positioning concept and positioning strategy.

12. Select a product type product-market (e.g., ice cream). Discuss the use of functional, symbolic, and experiential positioning concepts in this product category.

13. Discuss the conditions that might enable a new competitor to enter a mature product-market.

14. Competing in the mature market for air travel promises to be a demanding challenge in the 21st century. Discuss the marketing strategy issues facing Delta Air Lines during the next decade.

NOTES

1. Based on Judith Valente, "A New Brand Restores Sparkle to Waterford," *The Wall Street Journal,* November 10, 1994, pp. B1 and B4.

2. Ravi S. Achrol, "Evolution of the Marketing Organization: New Forms for Turbulent Environments," *Journal of Marketing,* October 1991, pp. 82–83.

3. Michael E. Porter, *Competitive Strategy* (New York: Free Press, 1980), chap. 9.

4. Mary Lambkin and George S. Day, "Evolutionary Processes in Competitive Markets: Beyond the Product Life Cycle," *Journal of Marketing,* July 1989, p. 4.

5. Ibid., p. 13.

6. See, for example, William T. Robinson and Claes Fornell, "Sources of Market Pioneer Advantages in Consumer Goods Industries," *Journal of Marketing Research,* August 1985, pp. 305–15; and Glen L. Urban, Theresa Carter, Steven Gaskin, and Zofia Mucha, "Market Share Rewards to Pioneering Brands: An Empirical Analysis and Strategic Implications," *Management Science,* June 1986, pp. 645–59.

7. Elaine Romanelli, "New Venture Strategies in the Minicomputer Industry," *California Management Review,* Fall 1987, p. 161.

8. Lambkin and Day, "Evolutionary Processes in Competitive Markets," p. 14.

9. David A. Aaker and George S. Day, "The Perils of High-Growth Markets," *Strategic Management Journal* 7 (1986), p. 419.

10. Lambkin and Day, "Evolutionary Processes in Competitive Markets," p. 11.

11. Romanelli, "New Venture Strategies," pp. 170–72.

12. Lambkin and Day, "Evolutionary Processes in Competitive Markets," p. 12.

13. Porter, *Competitive Strategy,* pp. 238–40.

14. George S. Day, *Market-Driven Strategy* (New York: Free Press, 1990), pp. 266–70.

15. Ibid.

16. Robert D. Buzzell and John A. Quelch, *Multinational Marketing Management* (Reading, MA: Addison-Wesley Publishing, 1988), pp. 7–8.

17. C. Whan Park, Bernard J. Jaworski, and Deborah J. Macinnis, "Strategic Brand Concept-Image Management," *Journal of Marketing,* October 1986, pp. 135–45.

18. David A. Aaker and J. Gary Shansby, "Positioning Your Product," *Business Horizons,* May–June 1982, pp. 56–62.

19. C. W. Park and Gerald Zaltman, *Marketing Management* (Chicago: Dryden Press, 1987), p. 248.

20. This discussion is based on Park, Jaworski, and Macinnis, "Strategic Brand Concept," pp. 136–37.

21. Ibid., pp. 135–45.

22. This illustration is drawn from *Pier 1 Imports 1992 Annual Report* and discussions with management.

23. Aaker and Shansby, "Positioning Your Product," p. 60.

24. Edward D. Mingo, "The Fine Art of Positioning," *The Journal of Business Strategy,* March/April 1988, p. 34.

25. David W. Cravens, Charles H. Holland, Charles W. Lamb, Jr., and William C. Moncrief III, "Marketing's Role in Product and Service Quality," *Industrial Marketing Management,* November 1988, p. 301.

26. N. D. Cadbury, "When, Where, and How to Test Market," *Harvard Business Review,* May–June 1975, pp. 97–98.

27. Glen L. Urban and John R. Hauser, *Design and Marketing of New Products,* 2nd ed. (Englewood Cliffs, NJ: Prentice Hall, 1993), p. 495.

28. Ibid.; see Chapter 17 for a discussion of alternative methods for analyzing test markets.

29. Gary L. Lilien, "Advisor Z: Modeling the Marketing Mix Decision for Industrial Products," *Management Science,* February 1979, pp. 191–204.

30. See, for example, Gary L. Lilien, Philip Kotler, and K. Sridhar Moorthy, *Marketing Models* (Englewood Cliffs, NJ: Prentice Hall, 1992).

31. Philip Kotler, *Marketing Management,* 8th Ed. (Englewood Cliffs, NJ: Prentice Hall, 1994), p. 307.

32. Aaker and Shansby, "Positioning Your Products," p. 61.

33. Ibid., p. 62.

34. Julie Franz, "Cherry Coke Takes the Fizz out of Sister Brands," *Advertising Age,* October 28, 1985, p. 4.

Relationship Strategies

Strategic relationships among suppliers, producers, distribution channel organizations, and customers occur for several reasons. The objective may be to gain access to markets, reduce the risks generated by rapid environmental change, share complementary skills, or obtain resources beyond those available to a single enterprise. These relationships are not recent innovations, but they are escalating in importance because of the environmental complexity and risks of a global economy, and the skill and resource limitations of a single organization.[1] Strategic alliances, joint ventures, and supplier–producer collaborations are examples of cooperative relationships between independent firms. Gaining competitive advantage increasingly demands cooperative relationships to access technology, expand resources, improve productivity and quality, and penetrate new markets.

American Family Life Assurance Company (AFLAC) is the world's largest marketer of cancer insurance.[2] The U.S. company has a very successful strategy for selling its insurance policies in Japan, which accounted for 75 percent of AFLAC's over $6 billion revenues in 1995. The company sells its cancer insurance to consumers through partnerships with over 90 percent of Japanese companies. They encourage their employees to buy the insurance and the premiums are deducted from employees' paychecks. AFLAC insures 28 million people in Japan. The relationship strategy eliminates the high costs of selling direct to consumers and the cooperative relationship with employers helps build AFLAC's brand image with consumers. If the employer cooperates with the insurance provider, this endorsement should have a positive effect on employees' perceptions about AFLAC.

Marketing relationships are important avenues to building strong bonds with customers. The AFLAC illustration indicates how essential it is to consider all of the participating organizations involved in linking buyers with sellers in the relationship strategy. The objective

EXHIBIT 7–1   Strategic Relationships among Various Partners

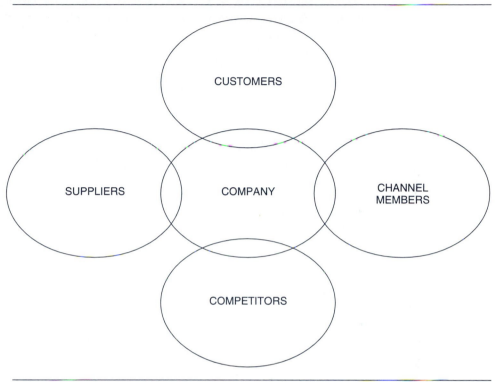

is to offer end-user customers superior value through collaboration of the organizations involved in the process.

Often, business and marketing strategies involve more than a single organization. In this chapter we examine the nature and scope of the strategic relationships among various partners (Exhibit 7–1). First, we consider what drives interorganizational relationships and discuss the logic underlying collaborative relationships. Next, we look at different kinds of relationships among organizations, followed by a discussion of several considerations that are important in developing effective interorganizational relationships. Finally, we consider several issues concerning global relationships.

WHAT DRIVES INTERORGANIZATIONAL RELATIONSHIPS?

In the past, companies established relationships to achieve tactical objectives, such as selling in minor overseas markets.[3] Today strategic relationships among organizations consider the elements of overall competitive strength—technology, costs, and marketing. Unlike the tactical relationships, the effectiveness of these strategic agreements among companies can affect the long-term performance of the business.

Several factors create a need to establish cooperative strategic relationships with other organizations. These influences include the diversity, turbulence, and riskiness of the global business environment; the escalating complexity of technology; the existence of large resource requirements; the need to gain access to global markets; and the availability of an impressive array of information technology for coordinating intercompany operations. The various drivers of relationships fall into two broad categories: (1) environmental turbulence and diversity and (2) skill and resource gaps.[4]

Environmental Turbulence and Diversity

Since the global business environment is examined in several chapters, the present discussion is brief. Diversity refers to differences between the elements in the environment, including people, organizations, and social forces affecting resources.[5] Interlinked global markets create important challenges for companies.

Coping with diversity involves both the internal organization and its relationships with other organizations. Environmental diversity reduces the capacity of an organization to respond quickly to customer needs and new-product development.[6] Organizations meet this challenge by: (1) altering their internal organization structures and (2) establishing strategic relationships with other organizations.

Environmental diversity makes it difficult to link buyers and the goods and services that meet buyers' needs and wants of the marketplace. Because of this, companies are teaming up to meet the requirements of fragmented markets and complex technologies. These strategies may involve supplier and producer collaboration, strategic alliances between competitors, joint ventures between industry members, and network organizations that coordinate partnerships and alliances with many other organizations.[7] Examples of these organization forms are discussed later in the chapter.

The business environment creates risks for organizations that are unable to make rapid changes. Turbulence is caused by technological innovation/obsolescence stimulated by the pace of growth in knowledge and its proliferation.[8] One response to turbulence and risk is to establish flexible relationships with other organizations, thus avoiding ownership investments in sources of supply, production, and distribution. Ownership of the entire value-added system may be less effective and more risky in a turbulent environment. The Strategy Feature describes growth trends in strategic relationships by companies in several countries.

Companies may coordinate an independent network of suppliers, producers, and distributors. For example, as we saw in Chapter 2, Benetton, the global casual wear company, contracts much of its production to producers throughout the world. All of Benetton's retailers are independent dealers. The Benetton core organization coordinates and directs the global production and distribution system, using its powerful information capabilities. The computer network monitors sales and sends incoming orders to the factories. Similar strategies involving networks of participating organizations are employed by Casio in electronics, Nike in athletic shoes, and the Bombay Company in furniture and fixtures.

STRATEGY FEATURE   Growth in Strategic Relationships among Companies

The chart shows the results of a 1993 Conference Board survey of 350 chief executive officers from the United States, Europe, Canada, and Mexico. Growth in all forms of strategic relationships is indicated by the executives surveyed.

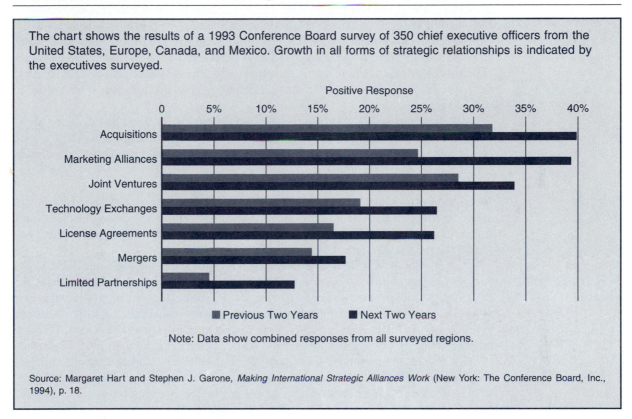

Note: Data show combined responses from all surveyed regions.

Source: Margaret Hart and Stephen J. Garone, *Making International Strategic Alliances Work* (New York: The Conference Board, Inc., 1994), p. 18.

Skill and Resource Gaps

During the last two decades, expenditures for research and development have grown three times faster than spending on capital assets.[9] The skills and resource requirements of technologies in many industries often surpass the capabilities of a single organization. Thus, the sharing of complementary technologies and risks are important drivers for strategic partnerships. In addition to technology, financial constraints, access to markets, and availability of information systems encourage establishing relationships among independent organizations.

Increasing Complexity of Technology.   Technology constraints impact industry giants as well as smaller firms. Small companies with specialized competitive strengths are able to achieve impressive bargaining power with larger firms because of their high levels of competence in specialized technology areas, and their ability to substantially compress development time. The partnerships between large and small pharmaceutical companies are illustrative. The small firm gains financial support, while the large firm gets access to specialized technology. For example, Glaxo Holdings, PLC, the large British company, has collaborative agreements with a small U.S. company developing a novel treatment for diabetes and with a biotechnology company involved in genetics research.[10] These cooperative relationships allow large pharmaceutical companies to access smaller partners that have expertise in emerging research areas, thus accelerating the process of moving new drugs to the marketplace.

Access to technology and other skills, specialization advantages, and the opportunity to enhance product value are important motivations for establishing relationships among organizations. These relationships may be vertical between suppliers and producers or horizontal across industry members.

Financial Constraints.   The financial needs for competing in global markets are often greater than the capacity of a single organization. As a result, many companies must seek partners in order to obtain the resources essential for competing in many industries, or to spread the risks of financial loss with another firm.

The development of large commercial aircraft illustrates the limitations of a single company trying to compete in this global market. In 1995 Boeing and Airbus Industrie, the industry leaders, were examining strategies for competing in the 21st century. One option is a supersonic long-range aircraft and the other is a substantially larger successor to the Boeing 747. Development costs are estimated to be as high as $15 billion. This size of expenditure is not feasible for Boeing. Airbus could cost share with its consortium members (four companies from England, France, Germany, and Spain form Airbus). Another alternative is a joint development effort between competing Airbus and Boeing. Boeing announced in early 1996 that it would develop two new versions of the 747 aircraft at an estimated cost of $4 billion. One version would have more seats while the other would have an extended flying range.

Access to Markets.   Organizational relationships are also important in gaining access to markets. Products have been distributed, traditionally, through marketing intermediaries such as wholesalers and retailers in order to access end-user markets. These vertical channels of distribution are important in linking supply and demand. During the 1990s several horizontal relationships were established between competing firms to access global markets and domestic market segments not served by the cooperating firms. These cooperative marketing agreements expand the traditional channel of distribution coverage and gain the advantage of market knowledge in international markets.

International strategic alliances are used by many companies competing throughout the world.[11] For example, it is typical for Fanuc, the leading Japanese computer numerical controls and robot producer, to work with a local partner to market its high-technology products. Many other cooperative arrangements provide companies access to markets. Some are between competing firms, such as the research and marketing alliance between IBM and Apple computers.

Information Technology.   Information technology makes establishing organizational relationships feasible in terms of time, cost, and effectiveness. Advances in information technology provide an important resource for improving the effectiveness of both internal and interorganizational communications:

> Advances in information technology and telecommunications have removed many of the communications barriers that prevented companies from drawing on overseas technical resources. Indeed, the ability to transmit documents and even complex design drawings instantaneously from one part of the globe to another by electronic mail means that it is often more efficient to collaborate globally in product development.[12]

Information systems enable organizations to effectively communicate even though the collaborating firms are widely dispersed geographically.

The Logic of Collaborative Relationships

Collaborative relations include shared activities such as product and process design, applications assistance, long-term supply contracts, and just-in-time inventory programs.[13] The amount of collaboration may vary substantially among industries. Moreover, in a given competitive situation a firm may pursue different degrees of collaboration across its customer base. Some supplier–customer relationships are transactional, but the same supplier may seek collaborative relationships with other customers.

Collaborative relationships between suppliers and their customers are widely advocated by business authorities. These partnerships are important aspects of total quality management (TQM) programs. Nevertheless, the decision of a supplier to develop a strong collaborative partnership should include assessment of these factors:[14]

1. **Philosophy of Doing Business.** The partners' approach to business should be compatible. For example, if one firm has adopted a TQM philosophy and the other partner does not place a high priority on TQM, conflicts are likely to develop in the working relationship.

2. **Relative Dependence of the Partners.** The collaborative relations are more likely to be successful if the dependence is important and equivalent between the two organizations.

3. **Technological Edge Contributions.** The buyer may represent an opportunity for a supplier to improve its product or process because of the customer's leading-edge application of the supplier's product or service. For example, collaborative codesign of industrial equipment can contribute to the supplier's competitive advantage.

These same criteria can be evaluated from the customer's perspective to assess the value and limitations of establishing a strong cooperative relationship. If such a tie is not advisable, the firms can still operate in a transactional buyer/seller relationship.[15] The transactional working relationship is the simple exchange of basic products at competitive prices. In contrast, collaborative association is much more interactive and adaptive in nature. The partners build strong social, economic, service, and technical relationships over a long time horizon.

EXHIBIT 7–2 Diminishing Suppliers

Many companies are cutting back the number of suppliers they use and demanding higher quality from those they keep.

	Number of Suppliers*		
	Current	Previous†	% Change
Xerox	500	5,000	–90%
Motorola	3,000	10,000	–70
Digital Equipment	3,000	9,000	–67
General Motors	5,500	10,000	–45
Ford Motor	1,000	1,800	–44
Texas Instruments	14,000	22,000	–36
Rainbird	380	520	–27
Allied-Signal Aerospace	6,000	7,500	–20

*Companies have different ways of counting their supplier base. For example, some count only direct manufacturing suppliers, while others count service and support suppliers.
† Number of suppliers firm had prior to starting reduction programs.
Source: John R. Emshwiller, "Suppliers Struggle to Improve Quality as Big Firms Slash Their Vendor Roles," *The Wall Street Journal,* August 16, 1991, p. B1. Reprinted by permission of *The Wall Street Journal,* © 1991 Dow Jones & Company, Inc. All Rights Reserved Worldwide.

In the United States, producers are drastically reducing the number of suppliers, as shown in Exhibit 7–2. TQM philosophy advocates working with one supplier rather than several suppliers of the same materials or parts. The objective is to build a strong collaborative relationship between the supplier and producer.

Adaptation between two organizations is an essential part of a collaborative relationship. Understanding the adaptation process is important for several reasons:[16]

1. Considerable investments may be required by one or both firms.

2. The adaptation may be essential to conducting business with a specific customer or for the customer in securing needed products from the supplier.

3. These interfirm investments often cannot be transferred to other business relationships.

4. The relationship may have important consequences for the long-term competitiveness of both firms.

Thus, evaluating the extent to which a company should enter into a collaborative relationship is an important issue for both partners.

TYPES OF ORGANIZATIONAL RELATIONSHIPS

A useful way to examine organizational relationships is to consider whether the tie between firms is vertical or horizontal, as shown in Exhibit 7–3. The symbols used in the diagram refer to manufacturer (M), wholesaler (W), retailer (R), and end-user (EU). An organization may participate in both vertical and horizontal relationships. We will first

---

EXHIBIT 7–3 Illustrative Interorganizational Relationships

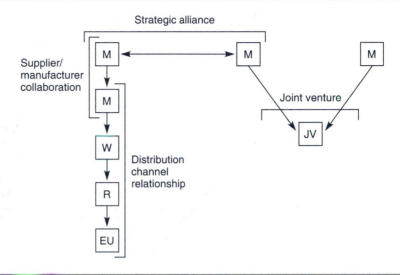

Source: This diagram is adapted from an example suggested by David Wilson, Penn State University.

---

look at vertical relationships among organizations, and then strategic alliances and joint ventures. Evolving global relationships among organizations are examined in a subsequent section.

Customer–Supplier Relationships

A typical method for moving products through various stages in the value-added process is the linking of suppliers, manufacturers, distributors, and consumer and business end-users of goods and services into vertical channels. Functional specialization and efficiency create the need for different types of organizations. For example, wholesalers stock products in inventory and deploy them when needed to retailers, thus reducing the delays of ordering direct from manufacturers.

The suppliers and buyers of a vast array of raw materials, parts and components, equipment, and services (e.g., consulting, maintenance) are linked together in vertical channels of distribution. As noted earlier, the relationships between the supplier and customer range from transactional to collaborative. Exhibit 7–4 describes Eastman Chemical Company's collaborative relationships with its industrial chemical customers.

Distribution Channel Relationships

Vertical relationships also occur between producers and marketing intermediaries (e.g., wholesalers and retailers) as shown in Exhibit 7–3. These channels provide the producer access to consumer and organizational end-users. Channel relationships vary from highly collaborative to transactional ties. A strong collaborative relationship exists in a vertical

---

EXHIBIT 7–4 Eastman Chemical Company

In 1982 Eastman Chemical started the quality management program (QMP) called Customers and Us. These are the major QMP activities:

- Review and assessment of customer relationships (including suppliers).
- Identify opportunities for improvements.
- Initiate projects to make those improvements.
- Report these improvements back to the customer.

Eastman has a flattened structure comprising 10 major business units (e.g., packaging plastics, coatings, fine chemicals).

- $4 billion in worldwide sales.
- 7,000 customers served by a 500 person sales organization.
- Some 250 quality improvement teams following a problem-solving approach called Make Eastman the Preferred Supplier (MEPS).

MEPS projects focus on process improvement (e.g., delivery, product improvement, order processing).

Cross-functional teams are assembled depending on the nature and scope of the MEPS project:

- A team may include representatives from supply and distribution, manufacturing, product support services, sales, and the customer.
- The project may be ongoing or targeted to solve a particular problem.

The two most valuable inputs to Eastman's market sensing are the:

- Complaint process.
- Customer satisfaction survey.

Complaint Process

Salespeople are encouraged to ask customers about problems:

- A 24-hour 800 number is available for reporting problems and complaints.
- Customer service advocates are assigned by the complaint hotline (they must call the customer back within 24 hours).

Customer Satisfaction Survey

Managed by the sales organization:

- There are eight variations for major customer groups (printed in nine languages).
- The survey comprises about 25 performance factors (order processing/delivery, product quality, pricing practice, introduction of new products, management contacts, and sharing market information).

Customers rate Eastman on each performance factor—this is also done for the customer's "best" other supplier (18-month cycle).

Internal responsibility is assigned for the different factors reported in the survey (factor stewardship program).

- On-time and correct delivery is the responsibility of supply and distribution.
- Pricing policy is the responsibility of the individual business unit.
- Follow-up is the responsibility of the sales organization.

Survey results show composite rankings of all Eastman customers in that product group.

The salesperson focuses discussion on the customer ratings that differ significantly from the composite.

The salesperson highlights improvements efforts completed or underway that may affect the customer's satisfaction rating.

Source: William Keenan, Jr., "What's Sales Got to Do with It?" *Sales and Marketing Management,* March 1994, pp. 66–73.

marketing system (VMS).[17] These systems are managed by one of the channel members such as a retailer, distributor, or producer. The VMS may be owned by a channel firm, linked together contractually (e.g., a franchise system), or the relationship held together by the power and influence of the firm administering the channel relationships.

The theory related to power and dependence suggests that "in working relationships, a firm adapts to a counterpart to the degree that it is dependent on that counterpart."[18] This may result in supplier dependence or customer dependence. Illustrative aspects of dependence include the importance of the customer, buyer concentration, supplier importance, supplier market share, and product complexity.

A conventional (non-VMS) distribution channel has no center of power, and has a transactional rather than collaborative linkage. The participants function on an independent basis, completing the necessary buying and selling transactions between each other. Distribution channel strategy is discussed in Chapter 10.

End-User Customer Relationships

The driving force underlying marketing relationships is that a company may enhance its ability to satisfy customers and cope with a rapidly changing business environment through partnering. Although building collaborative relationships may not always be the best course of action, this avenue for gaining a competitive edge is increasing in popularity.

Customer Focus.   Relationship marketing starts with the customer—understanding needs and wants and how to satisfy requirements and preferences:

> Customers think about products and companies in relation to other products and companies. What really matters is how existing and potential customers think about a company in relation to its competitors. Customers set up a hierarchy of values, wants, and needs based on empirical data, opinions, word-of-mouth references, and previous experiences with products and services. They use that information to make purchasing decisions.[19]

The importance of understanding customers' needs and wants encourages developing long-term collaborative relationships. Driving the necessity of staying in close contact with buyers is the reality that customers often have several suppliers of the products they wish to purchase. Customer diversity compounds the competitive challenge. Developing a customer-oriented organization includes:

- Instilling customer-oriented values and beliefs supported by top management.
- Integrating market and customer focus into the strategic planning process.
- Developing strong marketing managers and programs.
- Creating market-based measures of performance.
- Developing customer commitment throughout the organization.[20]

Assessing Customer Value.   An important issue is selecting the customers with which to develop relationships since some may not want to partner and others may not offer enough potential to justify partnering with them. A look at Marriott's partnering strategy is illustrative.

Building customer relationships is the core sales strategy of Marriott International, Inc.'s Business Travel Sales Organization. The travel manager is the target for the selling activities of the 2,500-person sales organization. The key features of the major account sales strategy are: (1) choose customers wisely (Marriott follows a comprehensive customer evaluation process); (2) build customer research into the value proposition (understanding what drives customer value and satisfaction); (3) lead with learning by following a step-by-step sales process; (4) invest in the customer's goal setting process, rather than Marriott's; and (5) develop a relationship strategy with a sense of purpose, trust, open access, shared leadership, and continuous learning. Marriott's management recognizes that customers who regularly purchase the company's services are valuable assets who demand continuous attention by high-performance teams. Rapidly changing markets and customer diversity add to the importance of developing strong ties with valuable customers to stay in touch with their changing requirements.[21]

Relationship strategies need to recognize differences in the value of customers to the seller as well as the specific requirements of customers.[22] Marriott's emphasis on carefully selecting customers with whom to partner illustrates the importance of prioritizing sales strategies by segmenting accounts for corporate influence and profit. Relationship building is appropriate when large differences exist in the value of customers. Valuable customers may want close collaboration from suppliers in product design, inventory planning, and order processing, and they proactively pursue collaboration. The objective is to develop buyer and seller relationships so that both partners benefit from the relationship.

Strategic Alliances

A strategic alliance between two organizations is an agreement to cooperate to achieve one or more common strategic objectives. The relationship is horizontal in scope (Exhibit 7–3). While the term *alliance* is sometimes used to designate supplier–producer partnerships, it is used here to identify collaborative relationships between companies at the same level in the distribution channel. The alliance relationship is intended to be long-term and strategically important to both parties. The following discussion assumes an alliance between two parties recognizing that a company may have several alliances.

Each organization's contribution to the alliance is intended to complement the partner's contribution. The alliance requires each participant to yield some of its independence. "Alliances mean sharing control."[23] The rationale for the relationship may be to gain access to markets, utilize existing distribution channels, share technology development costs, or obtain specific skills or resources.

The alliance is not a merger between two independent organizations, although the termination of an alliance may lead to an acquisition of one partner by the other partner. It is different from a joint venture launched by two firms or a formal contractual relationship between organizations. Moreover, the alliance extends beyond purchasing stock in another company. Instead, it is a commitment to actively participate on a common project or program that is strategic in scope.

General Electric's jet engine partnership with Snecma, a French-government-controlled aerospace company, is an example of a successful long-term strategic alliance.[24]

Formed in 1974 to help GE sell aircraft engines in Europe, the alliance was successful for both partners. The relationship illustrates several of the challenges and success requirements of strategic partnerships:

- GE's personnel must resolve cultural, linguistic, logistical, and foreign-exchange problems.
- Investment and revenue are shared on equal basis by GE and Snecma.
- The two partners delegate broad responsibilities to their senior engine executives.
- GE is responsible for system design and most of the complex engine technology.
- Snecma concentrates on fans, boosters, low-pressure turbines, and related work.
- Snecma's marketing role is expanding, although, until the early 1990s, GE was responsible for most of the marketing activities.

The GE–Snecma partnership is a model of a well-structured alliance. First, we will discuss the success record of alliances. Next, we will describe several uses of alliances. Finally, we will examine several alliance success requirements.

Success of Alliances.   The competitive realities of surviving and prospering in the complex and rapidly changing business environment encourage companies to form strategic alliances in many different industries. The record of success of alliances is not particularly favorable, although there are some notable successes such as the GE–Snecma jet engine alliance. While the alliance is a promising strategy for enhancing the competitive advantage of the partners, several failures have occurred due to the complexity of managing these relationships.

The Conference Board in 1993 surveyed the chief executive officers (CEOs) of 350 companies in the United States, Europe, Canada, and Mexico concerning their experiences with strategic alliances. The CEOs considered about half of their recent alliances to be successful. Several reasons are cited for those that were not successful. Exhibit 7–5 summarizes their experiences in alliances failures, which are divided into logic failures and process failures.

Kinds of Alliances.   The alliance, typically, involves one or more marketing, research-and-development, operations (manufacturing), and financial relationships between the partners. Capabilities may be exchanged or shared. In addition to functions performed by the partners, other aspects of alliances may include market coverage and effectively matching the specific characteristics of the partners.

The alliance helps each partner to obtain business and technical skills and experience that are not available internally. One partner contributes unique capabilities to the other organization in return for needed skills and experience. The rationale of the alliance is that both parties benefit from sharing complementary functional responsibilities rather than independently performing them.

Alliance Success Requirements.   The success of the alliance may depend heavily on effectively matching the capabilities of the participating organizations and on achieving the full commitment of each partner to the alliance. The benefits and the trade-offs in the alliance must be favorable for each of the partners. The contribution of one partner should

---

EXHIBIT 7–5 Why Strategic Alliances Fail

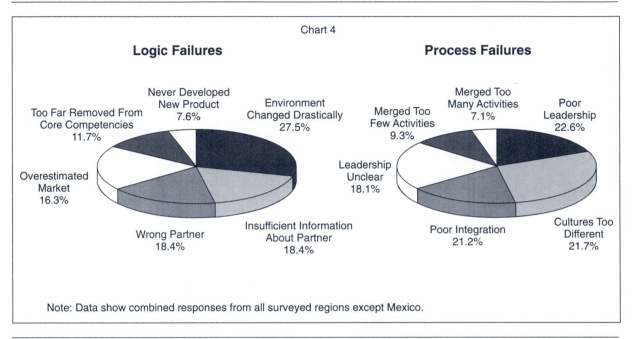

Chart 4

Logic Failures

Too Far Removed From Core Competencies 11.7%
Never Developed New Product 7.6%
Environment Changed Drastically 27.5%
Overestimated Market 16.3%
Wrong Partner 18.4%
Insufficient Information About Partner 18.4%

Process Failures

Merged Too Few Activities 9.3%
Merged Too Many Activities 7.1%
Poor Leadership 22.6%
Leadership Unclear 18.1%
Poor Integration 21.2%
Cultures Too Different 21.7%

Note: Data show combined responses from all surveyed regions except Mexico.

Source: Margaret Hart and Stephen J. Garone, *Making International Strategic Alliances Work,* R-1086 (New York: The Conference Board, Inc., 1994), p. 19.

fill a gap in the other partner's capabilities. In the GE–Snecma alliance, GE gained market access and knowledge of Airbus operations while Snecma obtained technical skills and experience in engine design and production. Both benefitted from the financial success of the venture.

One important concern in the alliance relationship is that the partner may gain access to confidential technology and other competitive advantages. While this issue is important, the essential consideration is assessing the relationship's risks and rewards and the integrity of the alliance partner. A strong bond of trust between the partners exists in most successful relationships. The purpose of the alliance is for each partner to contribute something distinctive rather than to transfer core skills to the other partner.[25] It is important for management in each organization to evaluate the advisability and risks concerning the transfer of skills and technologies to the partner. The Relationship Feature indicates several factors to consider in the legal assessment of collaborative relationships.

Joint Ventures

Joint ventures are agreements between two or more firms to establish a separate entity. These relationships may be used to develop a new market opportunity, access an international market, share costs and financial risks, gain a share of local manufacturing profits, or acquire knowledge or technology for the core business.[26] While joint ventures are similar to strategic alliances, the ventures differ in several ways. They result in the creation of a new

RELATIONSHIP FEATURE   Factors to Consider in a Legal Assessment of Collaborative Relationships

Likelihood of legal suspicion:

More suspect							**Less suspect**
Illegal ◄–––► Legal							

Factors:

Evidence of collaboration
Formal
Informal

Structure of the alliance
Horizontal
Vertical
Hybrid

Functional area/purpose
**Product development/
standardization**

Price

Distribution—
Divide markets
Allocate customers

Promotion

Exclude competitors

Exchange of information

Nature of collaboration
Closeness—
broad scope
deep scope

Spillover effects

**Collateral terms
(not ancillary to collaborate)**

Competitive market structure
Increased market concentration

Source: Jakki J. Mohr, Gregory T. Gundlach, and Robert Spekman, "Legal Ramifications of Strategic Alliances," *Marketing Management* 3, no. 2 (1994), p. 42.

organization. Environmental turbulence and risk set the rationale for the venture more so than a major skill/resource gap, although both pressures may be present.

Honeywell, Inc., has several joint ventures worldwide. The manufacturer and marketer of control systems and components for homes and businesses has been operating outside the United States for nearly 60 years. The company's chief executive officer, Michael R. Bonsignore, describes one venture:

> *Sinopec-Honeywell* involves one of Honeywell's customers, the Chinese National Petroleum Company—Sinopec. In January 1993, Honeywell entered into a joint equity company with Sinopec for a number of reasons: geographic expansion, market share, and risk diversification. Orders from Sinopec doubled in the first year and Honeywell has since attained the central government's acceptance. However, says Bonsignore, "we do have a number of concerns that we monitor constantly, such as MFN, the potential for Sinopec to become a competitor, and ongoing decentralization of the decision authority in the Chinese government."[27]

A study of cooperative research joint ventures among competitors in Japan provides some interesting findings concerning power and dependence in organizational relationships:[28]

1. Cooperative research is likely to be more successful for projects involving applied rather than basic research.

2. Research-and-development (R&D) costs are reduced and the chances of project success increased when the partners provide complementary skills and resources.

3. Large firms have a greater incentive to cooperate, although they favor small partners (thus limiting the loss of revenues from the venture's results).

4. Small firms, if they possess the necessary skills and resources, prefer to conduct their own R&D efforts. (Thus, power and dependence may be an important driver of establishing the relationship.)

5. Because of the hesitancy of small firms to cooperate with large companies, relationships may be more likely to occur among large competitors.

Not surprisingly, this research indicates that competitive relationships offer potential for conflict among the participants.

Internal Relationships

The success of external marketing relationship strategies requires developing strong internal relationships that cut across functional boundaries. As discussed in earlier chapters, many companies are using teams of people from various functions to manage processes such as new-product development, order processing, and delivery of products. As described in Exhibit 7–4, Eastman Chemical includes customer representatives on some of its teams.

As we discuss in Chapter 1, the market-driven company is committed to delivering superior customer value through market sensing and interfunctional cooperation. Several guidelines for developing effective internal relationships follow:[29]

1. Demonstrate management support.

2. Start with a pilot team.

3. Keep the teams small—and together.

4. Link the teams to the strategy.

5. Seek complementary skills for the team—and look for potential.

6. Educate and train.

7. Address the issue of team leadership.

8. Motivate and reward team performance, not just individual performance.

The relationship strategy requires attention to the internal structure. The starting point is building a collaborative customer-driven internal culture.

DEVELOPING EFFECTIVE RELATIONSHIPS BETWEEN ORGANIZATIONS

It is apparent from the prior discussion that developing effective collaborative partnerships between independent organizations is complex. The purpose of the present discussion is to look further into the process of developing effective relationships between independent organizations. The objective of the cooperative relationship is considered, followed by a discussion of several relationship guidelines.

Objective of the Relationship

Several major strategic objectives are considered to illustrate how strategic relationships are used to achieve the objectives.[30] In some situations both an internal (single organization) strategy and collaborative action may be used for the same purpose.

Identifying and Obtaining New Technologies and Competencies.   This objective is a continuing challenge for many companies because of the increasing complexity of technology and the short time span between identifying and commercializing new technologies. Failure to identify and monitor important telecommunications technologies was a key factor in the serious competitive problems of Western Union Corporation during the 1980s.

There are several ways to locate and exploit external sources of research and development:

- Collaboration with university departments and other research institutions.
- Precompetitive collaborative R&D to spread research resources more widely.
- Corporate venturing—making systematic investments in emerging companies to gain a window on the technologies and market applications of the future.
- Joint ventures and other forms of strategic partnership that enable a company to acquire new competencies by "borrowing" from a company with a leadership position.[31]

Japanese companies aggressively pursue all of these strategies, whereas U.S. companies rely more heavily on internal R&D. However, the future trend is toward expanded use of external research-and-development collaboration by U.S. and other companies throughout the world.

Developing New Markets and Building Market Position.   Alliances and other collaborative relationships may be effective alternatives for a single company interested in developing a market. This strategy requires finding potential partners that have strong marketing capabilities and/or market position. Collaboration may be used to enter a new product market or to expand a position in a market already served.

Increasingly, major corporations are pursuing collaborative strategies in research and development and in gaining market access. General Electric has a corporate objective of globalization, which requires participation in each major market in the world: "This requires several different forms of participation: trading technology for market access; trading market access for technology; and trading market access for market access. This 'share to gain' becomes a way of life."[32]

GE's globalization objective has led to forming over 100 collaborative relationships.[33]

Market Selectivity Strategies.   Competing in mature markets often involves either market domination or market selectivity strategies. Competition in these markets is characterized by a small core of major firms and several smaller competitors that concentrate their efforts in market segments. Firms with small market position need to adopt strategies that enable them to compete in market segments where they have unique strengths and/or where the segments are not of interest to large competitors. Cooperative relationships may be appropriate for these firms. The possible avenues for relationships include purchasing components to be processed and marketed to one or a few market segments, subcontracting to industry leaders, and providing distribution services to industry leaders.

The high entry barriers in producing semiconductors encourage the formation of strategic alliances.[34] Partnerships are essential in developing niche markets in this industry. Alliances are being formed between small U.S. firms that have specialized design expertise and Japanese, Korean, Taiwanese, and European companies with large-scale electronics manufacturing capabilities. The alliances make possible market entry for the design specialists. The cost of moving a complex new chip design to commercialization is an estimated $1 billion.

Restructuring and Cost-Reduction Strategies.   The realities of competing in international markets often require companies to restructure and/or reduce product costs. Restructuring may result in forming cooperative relationships with other organizations. Cost reduction requirements may encourage the firm to locate low-cost sources of supply. Many producers in Europe, Japan, and the United States establish relationships with companies in newly industrialized countries such as Korea, Taiwan, and Singapore. These collaborative relationships enable companies to reduce plant investment and product costs.

Relationship Management Guidelines

While collaborative relationships are increasingly necessary, the available concepts and methods for managing these partnerships are limited. Contemporary business management skills and experience apply primarily to a single organization, rather than offering guidelines for managing interorganizational relationships. However, the experience that

---

EXHIBIT 7–6   Success Guidelines for Strategic Partnership Management

---

1. The critical importance of planning.
2. Balance trust with self-interest.
3. Anticipate conflicts.
4. Establish strategic leadership.
5. Provide flexibility.
6. Accommodate cultural differences.
7. Orchestrate technology transfer.
8. Learn from partner's strengths.

Source: Timothy M. Collins and Thomas L. Doorley, *Teaming Up for the 90s* (Burr Ridge, IL: Irwin Professional Publishing, 1991), pp. 101–2.

companies have gained in managing distribution-channel relationships provides a useful, although incomplete, set of guidelines. To expand the existing base of management knowledge, Collins and Doorley conducted a major global study of strategic partnerships.[35] Companies in North America, Europe, Japan, and Korea participated in the study. The research identified the eight key guidelines for strategic-partnership management, shown in Exhibit 7–6. A brief discussion of each guideline follows.

Planning.   Comprehensive planning is critical when combining the skills and resources of two independent organizations to achieve one or more strategic objectives. The objectives must be specified, alternative strategies for achieving the objectives evaluated, and decisions made concerning how the relationship will be structured and managed. To determine the feasibility and attractiveness of the proposed relationship, the initiating partner may want to evaluate several potential partners before selecting one.

Trust and Self-Interest.   Authorities generally agree that successful partnerships involve trust and respect between the partners and a willingness to share with each other on various self-interest issues. Confrontational relationships are unlikely to be successful. Prior informal experience may be useful in showing whether participants can cooperate on a more formalized strategic project.

Trust is enhanced by meaningful communication between the partners.[36] The process of building trust leads to better communication. Thus, building and sustaining partnership relationships require both communication and the accumulation of trust between the organizations. Trust, in turn, leads to better cooperation among the partners.

Conflicts.   Realizing that conflicts will occur is an important aspect of the relationship. The partners must respond when conflicts occur and work proactively to resolve the issues:

> Even firms in successful partnerships would readily acknowledge that disagreements are inevitable. Rather than allowing these conflicts to run their course capriciously, however, adroit partner firms develop mediating mechanisms to diffuse and settle their differences rapidly.[37]

Mechanisms for conflict resolution include training the personnel who are involved in relationships, establishing a council or interorganizational committee, and appointing a mutually acceptable ombudsman to resolve problems.

Leadership Structure.   "Failure to create an effective leadership structure can be fatal; it makes coordination difficult and expensive, slows down development, and can seriously erode the decision-making process."[38] Strategic leadership of the partnership can be achieved by (1) developing an independent leadership structure or (2) assigning the responsibility to one of the partners. The former may involve recruiting a project director from outside. The latter option is probably the more feasible of the two in many instances.

Flexibility.   Recognizing the interdependence of the partners is essential in building successful relationships. Each organization has different objectives and priorities. "Management must be predominantly by persuasion and influence, with a willingness to adapt as circumstances change."[39] Relationships change over time. The partnership must be flexible in order to adjust to changing conditions and partnership requirements.

Cultural Differences.   Strategic relationships among companies from different nations are influenced by cultural differences. Both partners must accept these realities. If partners fail to respond to the cultural variations, the relationship may be adversely affected. These differences may be related to stage of industrial development, political system, religion, economic issues, and corporate culture.

Technology Transfer.   When the partnership involves both developing technology and transferring the technology into commercial applications, special attention must be given to implementation. Important issues include dealing with organizational problems, identifying a commercial sponsor, appointing a team to achieve the transfer, and building transfer mechanisms into the plan. Planners, marketers, and production people are important participants in the transfer process.

Learning from Partner's Strengths.   Finally, the opportunity for an organization to expand its skills and experience should be exploited. Japanese companies are particularly effective in taking advantage of this opportunity. One objective of the partnership should be to learn the skills of the cooperating firm, as well as completing a specific project or program.[40] Surprisingly, U.S. companies often fail to capitalize on this opportunity in their interorganizational relationships. Japanese companies view cooperative ventures as another form of competition where they can transfer acquired skills to other parts of the business.

GLOBAL RELATIONSHIPS AMONG ORGANIZATIONS

Several traditional organizational forms are used to compete in global markets. One is the multinational corporation that may compete in several countries, often using a separate organization in each country. We will focus the present discussion on organizational forms that involve relationships with other organizations.

EXHIBIT 7–7   Cooperative Agreements, 1978–1989

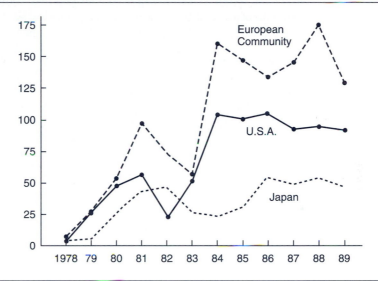

Source: INSEAD (Fontainbleu, France). Reproduced in Timothy M. Collins and Thomas L. Doorley, *Teaming Up for the 90s* (Burr Ridge, IL: Irwin Professional Publishing, 1991), p. 4.

Several examples of the use of joint ventures and strategic alliances to compete in international markets were discussed earlier in the chapter. Exhibit 7–7 shows the expanded use of cooperative agreements by companies in the United States, Japan, and the European Community. The growth of such agreements increased more than five times during the decade covered in the chart.

The need to develop more flexible organizational concepts for competing in rapidly changing global markets is illustrated by two types of organizations: (1) the network corporation and (2) the Japanese form of trading company.[41] We also discuss the strategic role of government in global relationships among organizations.

The Network Corporation.   This kind of organization consists of a core corporation that coordinates activities and functions between sources of supply and end-users of the product. The network, or hollow corporation, has a relatively small workforce, relying instead on independent suppliers often located at several places throughout the world. The organizations are linked by a sophisticated information system. The core company may be vertically integrated at the retail level or, instead, may utilize an independent distribution system. A successful example of the network organization form is Benetton.

One organization of the network manages the various partnerships and alliances. This network organization coordinates R&D, finance, global strategy, manufacturing, information systems, marketing, and the management of relationships.[42] The primary organizing concept is a small network control center that uses independent specialists to perform various functions. Thus, the priority is placed on "buying" rather than "producing" and on "partnership" rather than "ownership." The network organization must define the skills and resources that it will use to develop new knowledge and skills. For example, a core competency of the network organization may be designing, managing, and controlling partnerships with customers, suppliers, distributors, and other specialists.

Trading Companies. The use of trading companies dates far back into history in Asia. Since they share certain of the characteristics of network organizations, a look at this organization form provides additional insights into interorganizational relationships. The Japanese have been very successful in developing and coordinating extensive global operations and information management.[43] These *sogo shosha* concentrated primarily on commodity products, worked most directly with suppliers, and maintained a strong national (rather than global) perspective. Exhibit 7–8 shows an example of a trading company's network of relationships. This trading company functions as an intermediary organization for the steel industry by developing sources of supply and demand.

The skills and experience developed by Japanese companies through the *sogo shosha* provide these companies with an important competitive advantage in developing other forms of flexible organizations, like the network company discussed above. Japan's needs for natural resources were important influences on the development of trading companies. Today, these giant organizations are active in helping emerging countries, such as China and Vietnam, develop their markets.

The Strategic Role of Government

While the role of the government in the United States is largely one of facilitating and regulating free enterprise, the governments in several other countries play a more active role with business organizations. For example, the Japanese government encouraged the development of the *sogo shosha*. In considering the role of government, we will look at three types of relationships between government and private industry: (1) the single-nation partnership, (2) the multiple-nation partnership, and (3) the government corporation.

Single-Nation Partnership. A country's government may form a partnership with one or a group of companies to develop an industry or achieve some other national objective. Japan has successfully used this method of creating a national competitive advantage in a targeted industry in several instances.[44] For example, the Japanese Ministry of International Trade and Industry (MITI) performs a coordinating role in industry development. MITI resources and personnel establish alliances among companies, provide planning and technical assistance, and sponsor research. Government policy helped Japan build its competitive advantage by encouraging demand in new industries, fostering intraindustry competition, and identifying and encouraging the development of emerging technologies.

Multiple-Nation Partnerships. Regional cooperation among nations may lead companies to form consortium relationships in selected industries. The Airbus Industrie consortium is an example. Airbus Industrie members have received more than $12 billion in loans from the governments of the participating companies.[45] Airbus Industrie reported profits in only one of the first 20 years of operation. Boeing and McDonnell

EXHIBIT 7-8 How Japanese Trading Companies Contribute to Trade Development

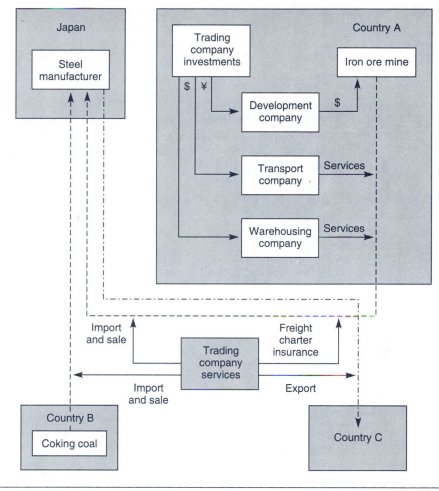

Source: "The Role of Trading Companies in International Commerce" (Tokyo: Japan External Trade Organization, 1983), pp. 15–16. Courtesy of JETRO (Japan External Trade Organization).

Douglas dominated the industry until government subsidies and multination sharing of skills and resources enabled Airbus to gain second place in the worldwide market for large commercial aircraft in the early 1990s.

Government Corporations.   Several nations operate government-owned corporations. In recent years a trend toward privatization of these corporations has occurred in the United Kingdom, Australia, Mexico, and other countries. Nevertheless, government-supported corporations continue to compete in various global industries, including air transportation, chemicals, computers, and consumer electronics. Not surprisingly, competitors often are critical of government organizations because of their unfair advantage resulting from government financial support. Interestingly, in the European airline industry, the privatized carriers show substantially stronger profit performance compared to state-owned carriers.[46] For example, in 1994 British Airways (private) had a net profit of $514 million whereas Air France (state-owned) had a loss of $254 million. Other profitable carriers included Lufthansa (36% state-owned), KLM (38% state-owned), SAS (50% state-owned), and Swissair (21% state-owned). Olympic Airways (100% owned by Greece) lost $500 million.

Government Legislation.   Antitrust laws in the United States prohibit certain kinds of cooperation among direct competitors in an industry. The intense global competition and loss of competitiveness in many industries seem to be changing the traditional view of lone-wolf competition among companies. While the antitrust laws are in place, there may be more flexibility by government agencies in interpreting whether collaboration among firms in an industry is an antitrust issue.

SUMMARY

The competitive realities of surviving and prospering in the complex and rapidly changing business environment encourage teaming up with other companies. Cooperative strategic relationships among independent companies are escalating in importance. The major drivers of interorganizational relationships are environmental turbulence and diversity, and skill and resource gaps. The increasing complexity of technology, financial constraints, the need to access markets, and the availability of information technology all contribute to skill and resource gaps.

Relationships between organizations range from transactional exchange to collaborative partnerships. These relationships may be vertical or horizontal in scope. Vertical relationships may involve collaboration between suppliers and producers and distribution channel linkages among firms. Horizontal partnerships may involve competitors and other industry members. These horizontal forms include strategic alliances and joint ventures.

Collaborative relationships are complex and may generate conflicts. Many horizontal relationships have not been particularly successful, even though the number of these partnerships is growing throughout the world. Trust between the partners is critical to building a positive relationship.

Several objectives may be achieved by strategic relationships, including accessing new technologies, developing new markets, building market position, implementing market selectivity strategies, and pursuing restructuring and cost-reduction strategies. The requirements for successfully managing interorganizational relationships include planning, balancing trust and self-interest, recognizing conflicts, defining leadership structure, achieving flexibility, adjusting to cultural differences, facilitating technology transfers, and learning from partners' strengths.

Global relationships among organizations may include conventional organizational forms, alliances, joint ventures, network corporations, and trading companies. Governments in several countries play a proactive role in organizational relationships through coordination, financial support, and government corporations.

QUESTIONS FOR REVIEW AND DISCUSSION

1. Discuss the major factors that encourage the formation of strategic partnerships between companies.

2. Compare and contrast vertical and horizontal strategic relationships between independent companies.

3. Discuss the similarities and differences between strategic alliances and joint ventures.

4. A German electronics company and a Japanese electronics company are discussing the formation of a strategic alliance to market the other firm's products in their respective countries. What are the important issues in making this relationship successful for both partners?

5. Establishing successful interorganizational relationships is difficult, according to authorities. Will the success record improve in the future as more companies pursue this strategy?

6. Are vertical relationships more likely to be successful than horizontal relationships? Discuss.

7. Suppose you are seeking a Japanese strategic alliance partner to market your French pharmaceutical products in Asia. What characteristics are important in selecting a good partner?

8. Discuss how alliances may enable foreign companies to reduce the negative reaction that is anticipated if they tried to purchase companies in other countries.

9. Discuss how government may participate in helping domestic companies develop their competitive advantages in an industry such as aerospace products.

NOTES

1. David W. Cravens, Shannon H. Shipp, and Karen S. Cravens, "Analysis of Cooperative Interorganizational Relationships, Strategic Alliance Formation, and Strategic Alliance Effectiveness," *Journal of Strategic Marketing,* March 1993, pp. 55–70.

2. Peter Lynch, "A Company after My Own Heart," *Worth,* March 1994, pp. 31, 32, and 34.

3. Timothy M. Collins and Thomas L. Doorley, *Teaming Up for the 90s* (Burr Ridge, IL: Irwin Professional Publishing, 1991), p. 5.

4. Cravens, Shipp, and Cravens, "Analysis of Cooperative Interorganizational Relationships."

5. Ravi S. Achrol, "Evolution of the Marketing Organization: New Forms for the Turbulent Environments," *Journal of Marketing,* October 1991, pp. 78–79.

6. Ibid.

7. Frederick E. Webster, Jr., "The Changing Role of Marketing in the Organization," *Journal of Marketing,* October 1992, pp. 1–17.

8. Achrol, "Evolution of the Marketing Organization," p. 81.

9. Timothy M. Collins and Thomas L. Doorley, *Teaming up for the 90s,* p. 5.

10. Udayan Gupta and Jeffrey A. Tannenbaum, "Small Drug Firms Break Through with Research Deals," *The Wall Street Journal,* December 2, 1991, p. 32.

11. Collins and Doorley, *Teaming Up for the 90s,* p. 8.

12. Ibid.

13. The following discussion is based on James C. Anderson and James A. Narus, "Partnering as a Focused Market Strategy," *California Management Review,* Spring 1991, pp. 96–97.

14. Ibid., pp. 100–103.

15. Ibid., pp. 96–97.

16. Lars Hallen, Jan Johanson, and Nazeem Seyed-Mohamed, "Interfirm Adaptation in Business Relationships," *Journal of Marketing,* April 1991, p. 30.

17. Bert C. McCammon, Jr., "Perspectives for Distribution Programming," in *Vertical Marketing Systems,* ed. Louis P. Bucklin (Glenview, IL: Scott, Foresman, 1970), p. 43.

18. Lars Hallen, Jan Johanson, and Nazeem Sayed-Mohamed, "Interfirm Adaptation in Business Relationships," pp. 31–32.

19. Regis McKenna, *Relationship Marketing* (Reading, MA: Addison-Wesley Publishing, 1991), p. 43.

20. Frederick E. Webster, Jr., "The Rediscovery of the Marketing Concept," *Business Horizons,* May–June 1988, p. 37.

21. David W. Cravens, "The Changing Role of the Sales Force in the Corporation," *Marketing Management,* Fall 1995, p. 50.

22. Ibid.

23. Kenichi Ohmae, *The Borderless World* (New York: Harper Business, 1990), p. 114.

24. This illustration is based on Bernard Wysocki, Jr., "Global Reach: Cross-Border Alliances Become Favorite Way to Crack New Markets," *The Wall Street Journal,* March 26, 1990, pp. A1 and A5.

25. Gary Hamel, Yves L. Doz, and C. K. Prahalad, "Collaborate with Your Competitor—and Win," *Harvard Business Review,* January–February 1989, pp. 135–36.

26. Timothy M. Collins and Thomas L. Doorley, *Teaming Up for the 90s,* pp. 205–9.

27. Margaret Hart and Stephen J. Garone, *Making International Strategic Alliances Work,* R-1086 (New York: The Conference Board, 1994), p. 19.

28. Deepak K. Sinha and Michael A. Cusumano, "Complementary Resources and Cooperative Research: A Model of Research Joint Ventures among Competitors," *Management Science,* September 1991, pp. 1091–1106.

29. Leonard L. Berry, *On Great Service* (New York: Free Press, 1995), pp. 139–42.

30. The following discussion is based on Collins and Doorley, *Teaming Up for the 90s,* chap. 3.

31. Ibid., p. 30.

32. General Electric Company, *Operating Objectives to Meet the Challenges of the 90s* (Fairfield, CT: General Electric Company), March 14, 1988.

33. George S. Day, *Market-Driven Strategy* (New York: Free Press, 1990), pp. 275–76.

34. William B. Scott, "Global Alliances Spur Development of Niche Market Semiconductors," *Aviation Week and Space Technology,* September 9, 1991, pp. 70–71.

35. The following discussion is drawn from Collins and Doorley, *Teaming Up for the 90s,* chap. 5.

36. James C. Anderson and James A. Narus, "A Model of Distributor Firm and Manufacturer Firm Working Partnerships," *Journal of Marketing,* January 1990, p. 45.

37. Ibid., p. 56.

38. Timothy M. Collins and Thomas L. Doorley, *Teaming Up for the 90s,* p. 108.

39. Ibid., p. 110.

40. Bernard Wysocki, "Global Reach," pp. A1 and A5.

41. Achrol, "Evolution of the Marketing Organization," pp. 84–85, and Webster, "The Changing Role of Marketing," pp. 8–9.

42. Webster, "The Changing Role of Marketing," pp. 8–9.

43. Achrol, "Evolution of the Marketing Organization," p. 84.

44. Michael E. Porter, *The Competitive Advantage of Nations* (New York: Free Press, 1990), pp. 414–16.

45. David W. Cravens, H. Kirk Downey, and Paul Lauritano, "Global Competition in the Commercial Aircraft Industry: Positioning for Advantage by the Triad Nations," *Columbia Journal of World Business,* Winter 1992, pp. 46–58.

46. Brian Coleman, "Among European Airlines, the Privatized Soar to the Top," *The Wall Street Journal,* July 19, 1995, p. B4.

CHAPTER
8

Planning for New Products

New products are the center of attention in most companies because of the obvious contribution of products to the survival and prosperity of the enterprise. Planning for new products is an essential and demanding core process of all organizations. New products, when matched to customer needs, help an organization to strengthen its position in existing product-markets and to move into new product-markets.

New products may launch new companies and sometimes new industries.[1] For example, the snowboard breathed new life into the ski industry and created over 300 companies. Snow skier visits to ski resorts had displayed no growth during the 1980s. Jake Burton, CEO of Burton Snowboards, Inc., saw the potential of this sport over two decades ago when he received a gift of a snow skateboard made by the Brunswick Corporation. Jake's relentless commitment to creating a serious recreational sport eventually resulted in $1 million sales in 1984. He improved designs and created awareness in the marketplace. He also had to overpower resistance by ski resorts to allow snowboarding. The resorts became more favorable toward snowboards by the mid-1990s due to the flat market for skiing and the popularity of snowboarding. Burton's 1995 sales comprised an estimated 30 percent of the $750 million (at retail) snowboard industry. The size of the market will double by the turn of the century. Most of the snowboarders are between 13 and 25, while the traditional skier population is aging. There were 2 million snowboarders compared to 10.6 million alpine skiers in the United States in 1995.

In this chapter we will consider the planning of new products, beginning with a discussion of customer needs analysis. Next, we will discuss the steps in new-product planning, including generating ideas, screening and evaluating the ideas, business analysis, development and testing, designing the marketing strategy, market testing, and new-product introduction.

PRODUCT PLANNING AS A CUSTOMER SATISFACTION PROCESS

New-product introductions can be classified according to (1) newness to the market and (2) newness to the company, resulting in the following six categories of new products:

1. *New-to-the-world products:* new products that create an entirely new market (10 percent of total new introductions).

2. *New product lines:* new products that, for the first time, allow a company to enter an established market (20 percent of the total).

3. *Additions to existing product lines:* new products that supplement a company's established product lines (26 percent of the total).

4. *Improvements in and/or revisions to existing products:* new products that provide improved performance or greater perceived value and that replace existing products (26 percent of the total).

5. *Repositioning:* existing products that are targeted to new markets or market segments (7 percent of the total).

6. *Cost reductions:* new products that provide similar performance at lower cost (11 percent of the total).[2]

Typically, a company's new-product program includes items in several of the six categories. Totally new products account for only 10 percent of all new-product introductions. The planning process discussed in this chapter applies to any of the six categories and is used in planning for new services as well as tangible products.

New-product planning is guided by customer needs analysis. Even new-to-the-world product ideas should have some relationship to needs that are not being met by existing products. For example, the snowboard offered an alternative to traditional skiing.

Corporate and Business Strategies

The business mission, objectives, and strategies identify the product-market areas that are of interest to management. Business purpose and scope set important guidelines for new-product planning. The entire management team considers product-market opportunities and establishes priorities to guide product planning. Customer needs yield important information for determining where competitive advantage can be gained by developing new products.

Market segment identification and evaluation help determine which segments offer new-product opportunities to the organization. Extensive analysis of existing and potential customers and competition are vital to effective new-product planning.

EXHIBIT 8–1   Finding Customer Satisfaction Opportunities

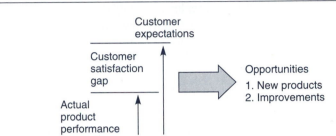

Finding Customer Satisfaction Opportunities

Customer satisfaction monitoring seeks to identify gaps in satisfaction that may offer opportunities for product innovation. The gaps are determined by comparing the customer's expectations about the product and supporting services with the actual performance of the product and supporting services.

Customer satisfaction analysis finds opportunities for: (1) new products, (2) improvements in existing products, (3) improvements in production processes, and (4) improvements in supporting services. The entire organization is involved in customer satisfaction analysis. This market-driven approach to product planning helps to avoid a mismatch between technologies and customer needs.

Market segment analyses are often necessary to identify specific customer needs and competitive opportunities. The objective is to find gaps between buyers' expectations and the extent to which they are being satisfied. As Exhibit 8–1 shows, a large gap may offer a new-product opportunity. For example, U.S. Surgical Corporation (USS) produces and markets staplers for use in skin closure and other surgical applications. An alert USS salesperson saw an opportunity to satisfy a customer need that was not being met with existing products. The close working relationship of USS sales representatives with surgeons in operating rooms gives USS a critical competitive advantage.[3] The salesperson identified a new-product opportunity by observing early experiments in laparoscopy. Using this procedure, the surgeon inserts a tiny TV camera into the body with very thin surgical instruments. USS responded quickly to this need by designing and introducing a laparoscopic stapler in early 1990. The product is used in gall bladder removal and other internal surgical applications. These instruments contributed $315 million to USS's 1991 sales.

Buyers' satisfaction with existing products and brands is evaluated by considering various product/service attributes that express buyers' preferences and by comparing competing brands. These comparisons may include preference mapping and the other analyses we discussed in earlier chapters. The objective of these techniques is to identify important preferences of buyers in specific market segments. Opportunities for new and improved products are highlighted by the existence of major preference gaps for attributes that are important to buyers in the product category (e.g., internal surgery equipment) of interest to the organization.

Quality Function Deployment

Quality function deployment (QFD) is used to find customer satisfaction opportunities. It is a management system for new-product planning that assures that customer needs drive product design and production processes.[4] Developed in Japan in the early 1970s, QFD offers several potential benefits in guiding new-product planning:

- Product objectives based on customer requirements are not misinterpreted at subsequent stages.

- Particular marketing strategies, or "sales points," do not become lost or blurred during the translation process from marketing through planning and on to execution.

- Important production control points are not overlooked—everything necessary to achieve the desired outcome is understood and in place.

- Tremendous efficiency is achieved because misinterpretation of program objectives, marketing strategy, and critical control points—and need for change—are minimized.[5]

QFD is a comprehensive analysis-and-planning process centered on customer needs. The objective is to translate customer requirements into important final-product control characteristics that guide the organization's design, production, and marketing process.[6] QFD involves the use of a two-way matrix that relates customer requirements and product characteristics. One of the matrices used in planning a new automobile design is shown in Exhibit 8–2. Several matrices are used in the overall process:

> The number of phases (or translations) needed to move from general customer requirements to highly specific production process controls varies with the product's complexity. As with much of QFD, these are no absolute rules—use as much or as little as necessary to ensure that key customer requirements will be met every time.[7]

Success Criteria

Exhibit 8–3 highlights several factors that contribute to the success of new products, based on responses obtained from more than 700 U.S. manufacturers of over 13,000 new products introduced during a five-year period. The study found some differences between industrial and consumer products firms, as well as across different industries. Technological superiority is considered more important by industrial products firms, while top management support is a greater concern for consumer durable and nondurable companies. The study also found that the importance of these factors varies by the type of new product being developed.

Case studies of successful innovators point to several common characteristics even though the companies are from various industries. The characteristics include:[8]

- A corporate obsession about the products produced by the company.

- A long-term vision about how the market will look in the future.

- Extensive use of "project-based teams" to institutionalize cooperation across functional (and national) boundaries.

EXHIBIT 8–2 Illustrative QFD Planning Matrix

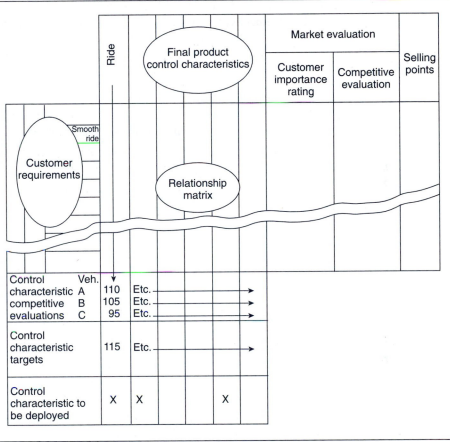

Source: L. P. Sullivan, "Quality Function Deployment," *Quality Progress,* June 1986, p. 46.

- Successful innovators listen to their customers.
- Strong leadership and rigorous measurement provide overall direction for team projects.
- Most successful innovators "benchmark" their product-generation skills against their rivals.
- Getting every aspect of the product development process right—from design to production.
- Innovators keep score in different ways:
    Rubbermaid—"Bury competitors in such a way that they can't copy us."
    Toyota and Ikea—Offering value for money.
- Leaders recognize that the product generation race is never won.

EXHIBIT 8–3   Factors Contributing to the Success of New Products

Percentage of responses

	0	10	20	30	40	50	60	70	80	90	100

Product fit with market needs

Product fit with internal functional strengths

Technological superiority of product

Top management support

Use of new product process

Favorable competitive environment

Structure of new product organization

Source: *New Products Management for the 1980s* (New York: Booz Allen & Hamilton, 1982), p. 16.

STEPS IN NEW-PRODUCT PLANNING

A new product does not have to be a high-technology breakthrough to be successful but it must provide customer satisfaction. Post-it Notes proved to be a big winner for Minnesota Mining & Manufacturing Co. (3M)[9] The notepaper pads come in various sizes. Each page has a thin strip of adhesive on the back and can be attached to reports, telephones, walls, and other places. The idea came from a 3M employee (he had used slips of paper to mark songs in his hymn book, but the paper kept falling out). Interestingly, office-supply vendors saw no market for the sticky-back note paper. The 3M company used extensive sampling to show users the value of the product. Using the name of the 3M chairman's secretary, samples were sent to executive secretaries at all Fortune 500 companies. After using the supply of samples, they wanted more. Today, the product is indispensable in both offices and homes.

Deciding Which Customer Needs to Target

To define the scope of new products to consider, businesses often define the product-market arena for new-product planning. Management decides the product-markets and market segments in which to compete. These decisions become important guidelines for the new-product planning process. Customer satisfaction analyses determine opportunities for new products and processes.

Consider, for example, the new-product planning activities of companies competing in unified Europe. Meeting the needs of consumers in the different nations of the

European Union (EU) is a complex product-planning challenge. Trade restrictions have been reduced, banking regulations altered, and other actions taken to create a unified market. However, the EU is divided by important differences in consumer tastes and national preferences as shown in this illustration:

> Pillsbury did extensive research in preparation for a new-product rollout in the United Kingdom last fall. Taste tests in London revealed that the English like their baked goods flaky and dry rather than moist and chewy, and they abhor strong flavors. Pillsbury changed recipes and, because U.K. consumers associate plastic tubes with cheap sausage, repacked its cookie-dough products in plastic tubs.[10]

In certain product categories companies must adapt to local attitudes and buying habits when developing new products and positioning existing products.

New-Product Planning Process

Developing successful new products like 3M Post-it Notes requires systematic planning to coordinate the many decisions, activities, and functions necessary to move a new-product idea to commercial success. The major stages in the planning process are shown in Exhibit 8–4. We will examine each stage to see what is involved, how the stages depend on each other, and the importance of interfunctional coordination of new-product planning. There are two key considerations in new-product planning: (1) generating a stream of new-product ideas that will satisfy management's requirements for new products and (2) establishing procedures and methods for evaluating new-product ideas as they move through the planning stages.[11] Customer needs analysis drives the planning process.

Four aspects of the planning process are important in effectively developing and introducing new products. First, the process involves various business functions, so it is essential to develop ways of coordinating the activities involved in the planning process. Second, compressing the time span of product development creates an important competitive advantage. U.S. Surgical's quick response to laparoscopy equipment needs is illustrative. Third, the planning process is expensive and must be managed so that the results deliver high levels of customer satisfaction at acceptable costs. Finally, the planning process is used for new-service development as well as for physical products. Certain differences in new-service planning will be highlighted as we discuss the planning stages.

Exhibit 8–5 describes the guidelines 3M follows to accelerate the innovation process. A strong commitment to innovation exists throughout the organization. It is part of the 3M culture.

Responsibility for New-Product Planning

Since new-product development involves business functions such as marketing, finance, production, and research and development (R&D), ways of cross-functional interaction and coordination must be developed. Various mechanisms are employed to coordinate

---

EXHIBIT 8–4   New-Product Planning Process

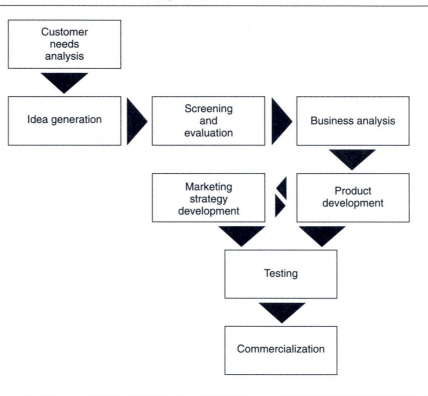

---

interfunctional interactions that are essential in developing successful new products, including:[12]

- Coordination by a high-level general manager.
- Interfunctional coordination by new-product planning representatives.
- Forming a temporary task force responsible for new-product planning.
- Appointing a new-products manager to coordinate planning among departments.
- Adopting a matrix organizational structure for integrating new-product planning with business functions.
- Forming a design center similar in concept to a design team, except the center is a permanent part of the organization.

The design team and design center are recent new-product coordination mechanisms. Though cross-functional teams are widely cited as promising new-product planning mechanisms, research findings suggest that they may be more appropriate for planning truly new and innovative products.[13] The more traditional bureaucratic structures may be

---

EXHIBIT 8–5   How 3M Accelerates the Innovation Process

- 3M has over 60,000 products, from stationery and reflecting road signs to image processing systems and stethoscopes.
- $1 billion of 1994's revenues were from new products launched during the year.
- 3M registered 543 patents in 1994.
- 6% to 7% of revenues are spent on R&D
- The 8,000 person R&D staff spend 15% of their time on projects of their own choosing.
- 3M measures results—for example, 30% of sales must come from products less than four years old.
- Selects a relatively small number of big technologies and products that offer the potential of competitive breakthroughs.
- Market sensing is an important input to product planning.
- Customer preferences are constantly reevaluated at each stage of a new product's development.
- Cross-functional teams manage the planning processes—3M has developed a culture of cooperation.

Source: *The Economist,* March 18, 1995, p. 72.

better in planning line extensions and product improvements. We will discuss organizational concepts for managing marketing processes in Chapter 14.

IDEA GENERATION

Finding promising new ideas is the starting point in the new-product development process. Idea generation ranges from incremental improvements of existing products to new-to-the-world products. An example of an incremental improvement is a glaucoma drug for eye treatment that is comparable to an existing glaucoma drug, but has fewer side effects. An example of a totally new product is a drug that will cure AIDS.

Idea Generation

New-product ideas come from many sources. Limiting the search for new-product ideas to those generated by internal R&D activities is far too narrow an approach for most firms. Sources of new-product ideas include company personnel, customers, competitors, outside inventors, acquisition, and channel members. Both solicited and spontaneous ideas may emerge from these sources, and some even occur by accident. Procter & Gamble's Ivory soap, for example, was the result of an accident; overmixing in the manufacturing process created air bubbles in the soap, causing it to float.

The objective is to establish an idea-generation and -evaluation program that meets the needs of the enterprise. Answering these questions is helpful in developing the idea-generation program:

- Should idea search activities be targeted or open-ended? Should the search for new-product ideas be restricted to ideas that correspond to corporate mission, business segment, and SBU strategies?

- How extensive and aggressive should new-product idea search activities be? Should the search be an active or passive function within the firm?

- What specific sources are best for generating a regular flow of new-product ideas?

- How can new ideas be obtained from customers?

- Where will responsibility for new-product idea search be placed? How will new-product planning activities be directed and coordinated?

Research findings indicate that financial performance in high-technology companies is greater for those firms that develop distinctive competence in a core technology.[14] Companies that focus their product strategy performed much better over a long time span than those that did not focus their new-product strategies. These findings came from a study of 236 products across 26 small- and medium-sized companies.

For most firms, the idea search program should probably be targeted within a range of product and market involvement that is consistent with corporate mission and objectives and business unit strategy. While some far-out new-product idea may occasionally change the future of a company, more often an open-ended idea search dissipates resources and misdirects efforts.

The favorable performance of several companies argues strongly for pursuing an aggressive and continuing effort of finding and developing new-product ideas. Companies like 3M, Johnson & Johnson, Hewlett-Packard, Rubbermaid, and U.S. Surgical develop a continuing flow of new products.

It is difficult to generalize about the best idea sources and how to manage new-product planning since these issues depend on many factors such as the size and type of firm, technologies involved, new-product needs, resources, management's preferences, and corporate capabilities. Management needs to consider these issues and develop a plan for idea generation that will satisfy the firm's requirements.

Many new-product ideas originate with the users of products and services. Lead-user analyses offer promising potential for the development of new industrial products.[15] Lead users are companies whose existing needs and requirements identify broad marketplace trends that will develop in the future. The approach is to try to identify these market leaders and to study their needs to improve the productivity of new-product development in product-markets that change rapidly. The objective is to satisfy the lead users' needs, thus accelerating new product adoption by other companies.

Methods of Generating Ideas

We will now look at several ways of obtaining ideas for new products. Typically, a company uses more than one of these options.

Search.   Tapping several information sources may be helpful in identifying new-product ideas. New-product idea publications are available from companies that wish to sell or license ideas they do not wish to commercialize. New technology information is available through commercial and government computerized search services. News

---

EXHIBIT 8–6   Uses of Focus Groups

Generating New Creative Ideas

Listening to consumers talk about how they use a product or what they like or dislike about a product can provide input for creative teams in developing advertising copy. Advertising agencies often use focus group interviews for this reason.

Uncovering Basic Consumer Needs and Attitudes

In talking about a product or product category, consumers often express basic needs and attitudes that can be useful in generating hypotheses about what may or may not be accepted and about the factors responsible for the perceived similarity or dissimilarity among a set of brands.

Establishing New-Product Concepts

Focus group interviews are particularly useful in providing information on the major strengths and weaknesses of a new-product idea. In addition, the focus group interview can be effective in judging whether strategy-supporting promises of end-benefits have been communicated clearly.

Generating New Ideas about Established Markets

Listening to consumers talk about how they discovered ways to put a product to alternative use can stimulate marketing executives to recognize new uses for old products.

Interpreting Previously Obtained Quantitative Data

In some instances focus group interviews are used as the last step in the research process to probe for detailed reasons behind quantitative test results obtained in earlier marketing research studies.

Source: William R. Dillon, Thomas J. Madden, and Neil H. Firtle, *Marketing Research in a Marketing Environment*, 2nd ed. (Burr Ridge, IL: Richard D. Irwin, 1990), p. 160.

---

sources may also yield information about the new-product activities of competitors. Many trade publications contain new-product announcements. Companies need to identify the relevant search areas and assign responsibility for searching to an individual or group.

Marketing Research.   Surveys of product users help to identify needs that can be satisfied by new products. One particularly useful technique for identifying and evaluating new-product concepts is the focus group, which can be used for both consumer and industrial products. A group of 8 to 12 people is invited to meet with an experienced moderator to discuss new-product ideas. Idea generation may start with a discussion of the product requirements for a particular product-use situation. Group members are then asked to suggest new-product ideas. Later, focus group sessions are used to evaluate product concepts intended to satisfy the needs identified in the initial session. More than one focus group can be used at each stage in the process. Focus groups can be conducted using channel members and company personnel as well as customers. Exhibit 8–6 describes several uses of focus groups.

Another consumer research technique that is used to generate new-product ideas is the advisory panel. These groups are selected to represent the firm's target market. For example, a producer of mechanics' hand tools would include mechanics on the panel. Customer advisory groups are used by companies in various industries, including telecommunications and pharmaceuticals. These groups provide insights and evaluations for new and existing products.

Internal and External Development.   Companies' research and development laboratories generate many new-product ideas. For example, AT&T's Bell Laboratories has a world-renowned reputation for state-of-the-art technology.[16] As a result of deregulation, AT&T is placing more emphasis on identifying new-product ideas with commercial potential. A vice president who heads a management group at Bell Laboratories called Venture Technologies is responsible for identifying and evaluating ideas. When the group was first formed, letters were sent to 150 laboratory directors asking for promising ideas outside of AT&T's traditional telephone markets. The directors responded with 800 proposals for new products.

New-product ideas may also originate from development efforts outside the firm. Sources include inventors, private laboratories, and small high-technology firms. Also, strategic alliances between companies may result in identifying new-product ideas, as well as sharing responsibility for other activities in new-product planning.

Other Idea-Generation Methods.   Incentives may be useful for getting new-product ideas from employees, marketing middlemen, and customers. The amount of the incentive should be high enough to encourage submission. Management should also prevent employees from leaving the company and developing a promising idea elsewhere. For this reason many firms require employees to sign secrecy agreements.

Finally, acquiring another firm offers a way to obtain new-product ideas. This strategy may be more cost-effective than internal development and can substantially reduce the lead time required for new-product planning. IBM's 1995 acquisition of Lotus Development is an example.

Idea generation identifies one or more product concepts, which are then screened and evaluated. An idea for a new product must be transformed into a defined product concept. The concept states what the product will do (anticipated attributes) and the benefits that are superior to available products.[17] For example, the pump toothpaste dispenser (attribute) offers a simple and quick alternative (benefit) to the traditional tube.

Introducing companies' products in other countries offers opportunities for sales growth. The Global Feature describes an instance of this practice: introducing ready-to-eat cereal in India.

SCREENING, EVALUATING, AND BUSINESS ANALYSIS

Moving too many ideas too far into development and testing is expensive. Management needs a screening and evaluation procedure that will kill unpromising ideas as soon as possible while keeping the risks of rejecting good ideas at acceptable levels. Expenditures build up from the idea stage to the commercialization stage, whereas the risks of developing a bad new product fall as more and more information is obtained about the product and the market. The objective is to eliminate the least promising ideas before too

---

GLOBAL FEATURE   Introducing Ready-to-Eat Cereal in India

- Kellogg India Ltd.'s management estimates the potential cereal market to be four to five billion rupees ($130 to 160 million) per year.

- Targeting India's middle class (100- to 200 million people), Kellogg introduced cereals in 1994.

- Only an estimated 3%+ of Indian households eat breakfast cereal (produced by Indian companies).

- Kellogg's marketing challenge is to expand this small base of the cereal users.

- Management believes that increased concerns about health consciousness will encourage consumption of cereals among middle-class Indians.

- The company recognizes that penetrating the Indian breakfast market may take a decade or longer.

- Management is counting on India's high milk consumption (about 10% of the world's total) to encourage people to try cereals.

Source: Sudman Dubey, "Kellogg Invites India's Middle Class to Breakfast of Ready-to-Eat Cereal," *The Wall Street Journal*, August 29, 1994, p. B3.

much time and money are invested in them. The tighter the screening procedure, the higher the risk of rejecting a good idea. Based on the specific factors involved, a company needs to establish a level of risk that is acceptable.

Evaluation occurs regularly as an idea moves through the new-product planning stages. Ideas may be rejected at any stage, even though the objective is to eliminate the poor risks as early as possible in the planning process. The evaluation techniques used at each stage in the planning process are matched to the evaluation task. We illustrate them as the stages in new-product planning are discussed.

Screening

A new-product idea receives an initial screening to determine its strategic fit in the company or business unit. Two questions need to be answered: (1) Is the idea compatible with the organization's mission and objectives? (2) Is the venture commercially feasible? The compatibility of the idea considers factors such as internal capabilities (e.g., development, production, marketing), financial needs, and competitive factors. Commercial feasibility considers market attractiveness, technical feasibility, and social and environmental concerns.

Screening eliminates ideas that are not compatible or feasible for the business. These assessments are often subjective, since management must establish how narrow or wide the screening boundaries should be. For example, managers from two otherwise similar firms may have very different missions and objectives as well as different propensities toward risk. An idea may be strategically compatible in one firm and not in another: "The dimensions on which management evaluates ideas/concepts/products encompass all key management areas and in particular should reflect the corporate idiosyncrasies and unique situational factors."[18]

Some firms use various scoring and importance weighting techniques for the factors considered in the screening process. Summing the weighted scores gives a score for each idea being screened. Management can set ranges for passing and rejecting. The effectiveness of these methods is highly dependent on gaining agreement on the relative importance of the screening factors from the managers involved.

Evaluation

The boundaries between idea screening, evaluation, and business analysis are not clearly drawn. Some firms combine these evaluation stages. After completing initial screening, each idea that survives receives a more comprehensive evaluation. Several of the same factors used in screening may be evaluated in greater depth, including buyers' reactions to the proposed concept.

Concept tests are useful in evaluating and refining new-product ideas. The purpose of concept testing is to obtain a reaction to the new-product concept from a sample of potential buyers before the product is developed. Concept tests can be used at various stages in the new-product planning process. The technique supplies important information for reshaping, redefining, and coalescing new-product ideas.[19] Concept tests help to evaluate the relative appeal of ideas or alternative product positionings, supply information for developing the product and marketing strategy, and identify potential market segments. Exhibit 8–7 describes a proposal to conduct a concept test for evaluating alternative investment products. The estimated cost of the test is $15,000.

The concept test is a useful way to evaluate a product idea very early in the development process. The costs of these tests are reasonable, given the information that can be obtained. Nonetheless, there are some important cautions. The test is a very rough gauge of commercial success. Since an actual product and a commercial setting are not present, the test is somewhat artificial.

The concept test is probably most useful in signaling very favorable or unfavorable product concepts. It also offers a basis for comparing two or more concepts. An important requirement of concept testing is that the product can be expressed as a concept and that the participant has the experience and capability to evaluate the concept. The respondent must be able to visualize the proposed product and its features based on a verbal or written description and/or picture.

Business Analysis

Business analysis gauges the commercial performance of the new-product concept. Obtaining an accurate financial projection depends on the quality of the revenue-and-cost forecasts. Business analysis is normally accomplished at several stages in the new-product planning process, beginning before the product concept moves into the development stage. Financial projections are refined at later stages.

EXHIBIT 8–7   Project Proposal: New-Product Concept Screening Test

---

Brand:	New products.
Project:	Concept screening.
Background and Objectives:	The New York banking group has developed 12 new-product ideas for investment products (services). The objectives of this research are to assess consumer interest in the concepts and to establish priorities for further development.
Research Method:	Concept testing will be conducted in four geographically dispersed, central location facilities within the New York metropolitan area.
	Each of the 12 concepts plus 1 retest control concept will be evaluated by a total of 100 men and 100 women with household incomes of $25,000. The following age quotas will be used for both male and female groups within the sample:
	18–34 = 50 percent 35–49 = 25 percent 50 & over = 25 percent
	Each respondent will evaluate a maximum of eight concepts. Order of presentation will be rotated throughout to avoid position bias.
	Because some of the concepts are in low-incidence product categories, user groups will be defined both broadly and narrowly in an attempt to assess potential among target audiences.
Information to Be Obtained:	This study will provide the following information to assist in concept evaluation: Investment ownership.
	Purchase interest (likelihood of subscription). Uniqueness of new service. Believability. Importance of main point. Demographics.
Action Standard:	In order to identify concepts warranting further development, top-box purchase intent scores will be compared to the top-box purchase intent scores achieved by the top 10 percent of the concepts tested in earlier concept screening studies. Rank order of purchase intent scores on the *uniqueness, believability,* and *importance* ratings will also be considered in the evaluation and prioritization of concepts for further development.
Material Requirements:	Fifty copies of each concept.
Cost and Timing:	The cost of this research will be $15,000 ± 10%
	This research will adhere to the following schedule:
	Field work 1 week Top-line 2 weeks Final report 3 weeks
Supplier:	Burke Marketing Research.

Source: Adapted from William R. Dillon, Thomas J. Madden, and Neil H. Firtle, *Marketing Research in a Marketing Environment*, 3rd ed. (Burr Ridge, IL: Richard D. Irwin, 1994), p. 562.

Revenue Forecasting.   The newness of the product, the size of the market, and the competing products all influence the accuracy of revenue projections. In the case of an established market such as breakfast cereals, estimates of total market size can usually be obtained from industry information. Several industry associations publish industry forecasts. The more difficult task is estimating the market share that is feasible for a new-product entry. For example, the size of the ready-to-eat (RTE) cereal market can be projected accurately, but estimating the market share of a new cereal brand is far more difficult. A range of feasible share positions can be indicated at the concept stage and used as a basis for preliminary financial projections. Established markets also may have success norms. For example, a 1 percent market share is considered a successful entry for a new RTE cereal. A norm provides a basis for estimating the possibility of reaching a successful level of sales. Accurate forecasts of market acceptance require some type of acceptance test, such as a market test, after the product has been developed.

Preliminary Marketing Plan.   An initial marketing strategy is often developed as a part of the business analysis. Included are market targets, positioning concepts, and marketing mix plans. While this plan is preliminary, it encourages strategy development and coordination with marketing, production, and other business functions early in the planning process. The choice of the marketing strategy is necessary in developing the revenue forecast.

Cost Estimation.   Several different costs occur in the planning and commercialization of new products. One way to categorize the costs is to estimate them for each stage in the new-product planning process (Exhibit 8–4). The costs increase rapidly as the product concept moves through the process. The costs for each planning stage can be further divided into functional categories (e.g., marketing, R&D, and manufacturing).

Profit Projections.   Several types of profit projections can be used to gauge a new product's financial performance. Illustrative financial analysis techniques are examined in the Appendix to Chapter 1. Those appropriate for new-product business analysis include break-even computation, cash flow, return on investment, and profit contribution. Break-even analysis is particularly useful to show how many units of the new product must be sold before it begins to make a profit. Management can use the break-even level to examine the feasibility of the project.

Management needs to determine the appropriate length of time for projecting sales, costs, and profits. For example, the product may be required to recoup all costs within a certain time period. Business analysis estimates should take into consideration the estimated flow of revenues and costs over the time span used in the analysis. Typically, new products incur heavy costs before they start to generate revenues.

Other Considerations.   Several other issues are considered in the business analysis of a new-product concept. First, management often has guidelines for the financial performance of new products. These can be used to accept, reject, or further analyze the product concept. Another issue is assessing the amount of risk. This factor should be included either in the financial projections or as an additional consideration beyond the financial estimates. Finally, the possible cannibalization of sales by the new product from existing products needs to be considered. New products that are substitutes for existing products often cannibalize sales. For example, a major premise in Gillette's business analysis of the Sensor razor was that its superior shaving effectiveness would attract substantial sales from disposable razors rather than resulting in a major cannibalization of Atra and Trac II sales. Sensor's sales in the first year of introduction (1990) were 25 million razors compared to a forecast of 10 million.[20] The new razor obtained a higher-than-was-forecast portion of total sales from users of disposable shavers who shifted to Sensor. The new product was profitable in the first year of introduction, even with R&D, engineering, and marketing costs totaling $300 million.

DEVELOPMENT AND TESTING

After successfully completing the business analysis stage, the new-product concept is developed and tested. During the development stage the concept is transformed into one or more prototypes. The prototype is the actual product, but it is produced by R&D rather than by an established manufacturing process. The development-and-testing stage includes manufacturing development as well as product design.

Our earlier discussion of customer-guided new-product design and manufacturing emphasizes the importance of transferring customer preferences into internal guidelines for new-product planning. The methods of QFD are illustrative. Technical people recognize that product design decisions need to be guided by customer preferences and analysis of competitor advantages and weaknesses. Product development should involve the entire new-product planning team.

Product Development

Exhibit 8–8 is a description of product, package, and service design, including the constraints and guidelines that affect product design. Since product development is largely a technical activity, our discussion considers the input information to R&D and the output of development and testing.

Product Specifications. Research and development needs guidelines in order to develop the product. These specifications describe what the product will do rather than how it should be designed. Product specifications indicate product planners' expectations regarding benefits based on customer analysis, including essential physical and operating characteristics.[21] This allows R&D to determine the best physical structure for delivering the benefits.

Recall the earlier discussion of U.S. Surgical's development of laparoscopy equipment. Illustrative specifications for developing this type of product include equipment size, features (e.g. ease of operation), functions to performed (visual view of inside the patient's body via TV camera), types of material, and cleaning requirements. The more complete the specifications for the product, the better the designers can incorporate the requirements into the design.

Prototype.   Research and development uses the product specifications to create one or more physical products. At this stage the product is called a prototype since it is not ready for commercial production and marketing. It is a custom version. Many of the parts may be custom-built, and materials, packaging, and other details may differ from the commercial version. Nevertheless, the prototype needs to be capable of delivering the

EXHIBIT 8–8 Product, Package, and Service Design and Its Determinants

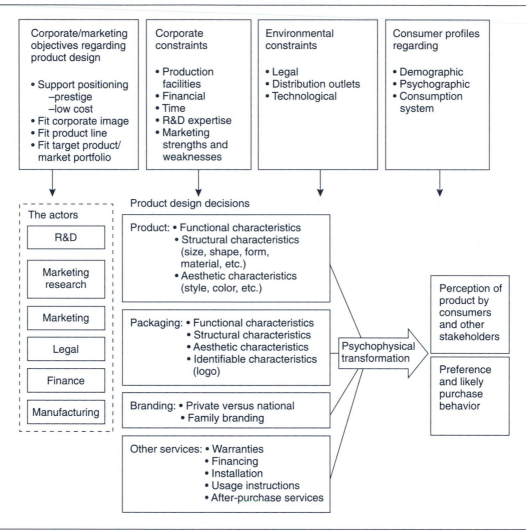

Source: Yoram J. Wind, *Product Policy: Concepts, Methods, and Strategy* (Reading, MA: Addison-Wesley Publishing, 1982), p. 340.

benefits spelled out in the specifications. Scale models are used in some kinds of products, such as commercial aircraft. Models can be tested in wind tunnels to evaluate their performance characteristics.

Use Tests.   The prototype may be tested in a use situation. If use testing is feasible, designers can obtain important feedback from users concerning how well the product meets the needs included in the product specifications. A standard approach to use testing

---

EXHIBIT 8–9   Project Proposal: Product Test

Brand:	New product: Hardy Soup.
Project:	Campbell's versus new Hardy Soup blind product test.
Background and Objectives:	R&D has developed a new Hardy Soup in two different flavors (chicken noodle and mushroom). Additionally, each flavor has been developed at two different flavor strengths. The brand groups have requested that research be conducted to determine (1) whether this product should be considered for introduction, (2) if so, if one or both flavors should be introduced, and (3) which flavor variation(s) would be preferred most by the consumer.
	The objective of this research will be to determine consumers' preferences for each flavor variation of the new product relative to Campbell's Chunky products.
Method:	There will be four cells. In each cell, a blind paired-product test will be conducted between a different flavor variation of the new product and the currently marketed Campbell's product, as follows:
	• Campbell's Chunky Chicken Noodle versus Hardy's Chicken Noodle 1.
	• Campbell's Chunky Chicken Noodle versus Hardy's Chicken Noodle 2.
	• Campbell's Chunky Mushroom versus Hardy's Mushroom 1.
	• Campbell's Chunky Mushroom versus Hardy's Mushroom 2.
	In each cell, there will be 200 past-30-day ready-to-serve soup user/purchasers.
	Respondents will be interviewed in a shopping mall and given both products to take home and try. Additionally, respondents must be positively disposed toward chicken noodle or mushroom flavors in order to be used in the test. Order of product trial will be rotated to minimize position bias. Telephone callbacks will be made after one-week period.
Action Standard:	Each new soup flavor will be considered for introduction if one or more of its flavor variations achieves at least absolute parity with its Campbell's Chunky control.
	If for either flavor alternative more than one flavor level variation meets the action standard, the one that is preferred over Campbell's at the highest level of confidence will be recommended to be considered for introduction.
	A single-sample *t*-test for paired comparison data (two-tail) will be used to test for significance.
Cost and Timing:	The cost of this study will be $32,000 ± 10%.
	The following schedule will be established:
	Field work 2 weeks Top-line 2 weeks Final report 4 weeks
Research Firm:	Burke Marketing Research.

Source: William R. Dillon, Thomas J. Madden, and Neil H. Firtle, *Marketing Research in a Marketing Environment,* 3rd ed. (Burr Ridge, IL: Richard D. Irwin, 1994), p. 583.

is to distribute the product to a sample of users, asking them to try the product. Follow-up occurs after the test participant has had sufficient time to evaluate the product. The design of new industrial products may include the active involvement of users in testing and evaluating the product at various stages in the process. The relatively small number of users in industrial markets, compared to consumer markets, makes use testing very feasible. Use tests are also popular for gaining user reactions to new consumer products such as foods, drinks, and health and beauty aids.

Exhibit 8–9 describes an example of a proposed use test for a new soup flavor. Unlike a market test, the use test does not identify the brand name of the product or the company name. While the use test is not as indicative of market success as the market test, it yields important information such as preferences, ratings, likes/dislikes, advantages/limitations, unique features, usage and users, and comparisons with competing products.[22]

Manufacturing Development.   A company must next develop a process for producing the product in commercial quantities. Manufacturing the product at an acceptable cost is a critical determinant of profitability. The new product may be feasible to produce in the laboratory but not in a manufacturing plant, because of costs, production rates, and other considerations. Initial production delays can also jeopardize the success of a new product.

The success of the Japanese in penetrating U.S. and European markets with high-quality, value-priced products mandates quality improvement as a top priority throughout U.S. industry. One consequence of improved product quality is that production costs are reduced.[23] By considering quality improvement throughout the design process, the high costs of scrapping and reworking products are avoided. A close working relationship between all business functions is essential to producing high-quality products and services.

Japanese new-product designers have modified the planning process (Exhibit 8–4) by determining a target cost based on the price the market is likely to accept for a new product *before* design is initiated.[24] The target cost is an integral part of the planning process. Cost engineers, with experience in purchasing, design, and other functions such as sales, participate in the planning process to assure that the product meets the desired target cost. This eliminates the need to redesign products whose costs are too high. This planning approach also helps to compress product development time.

Collaborative Design and Manufacturing.   Collaborative research and development partnerships are used to increase the competitive advantage of a single company and reduce the time required to develop and market new products. These relationships may be strategic alliances or supplier-producer collaborations (Chapter 7). The development of Hewlett-Packard's (H-P) H-P FAX-300 was the result of an alliance between H-P and Matsushita, a leading Japanese producer of fax machines.[25] H-P applied the technology from its very successful DeskJet printer, and Matsushita contributed the fax technology. H-P gained important copier cost savings by producing the fax in the same plant as the DeskJet. The result was a plain-paper fax at a price competitive with thermal fax machines and far below that of laser machines.

DEVELOPING MARKETING STRATEGY AND TEST MARKETING

Regardless of how new the product actually is, reviewing the proposed marketing strategy helps to avoid problems and identify opportunities. Guidelines for marketing strategy depend largely on the new product being developed. A totally new product requires complete targeting and positioning strategies. A product improvement may need only a revised promotion strategy to convey to target buyers information on the benefits the improved product offers. It is also important to consider how the new product will affect the sales of existing products.

Marketing Decisions

Product evaluation efforts (e.g., use tests) conducted during product development supply information for designing the marketing strategy. Examples of useful planning guidelines include user characteristics, product features, advantages over competing products, use situations, feasible price range, and buyer information.

The design of the marketing strategy begins as soon as possible in new-product planning, since several activities need to be completed, and shortening the time to market introduction is an important competitive advantage. Marketing strategy planning can be initiated during product development. Activities such as packaging, environmental considerations, product information, colors, materials, and product safety must also be decided among engineering, manufacturing, and marketing.

Market Targeting. Selection of the market target(s) for the new product can range from offering a new product to an existing target to identifying an entirely new group of potential users. A totally new product requires a new targeting strategy. Examining the prior marketing research for the new product may yield useful insights as to targeting opportunities. It may also be necessary to conduct additional research before finalizing the market targeting strategy.

Positioning Strategy. Several positioning decisions are resolved during the marketing strategy development stage. Product strategy regarding packaging, name selection, sizes, and other aspects of the product must be decided. A channel strategy is needed to access new channels of distribution. It is also necessary to formulate a price strategy and to develop an advertising and sales promotion strategy. Testing of advertisements may occur at this stage. Finally, sales management must design a personal selling strategy, including deciding about sales force training and allocation of selling effort to the new product.

Market-Testing Options

Market testing can be considered after the product is fully developed, assuming the product is suitable for market testing. Market tests are used to gauge buyer response to the new product and evaluate one or more positioning strategies. Test marketing is used for many consumer products, such as foods, beverages and health and beauty aids. In addition to conventional test marketing, less-expensive alternatives are available.

Simulated Test Marketing. One way of implementing this test method is recruiting potential buyers while they are shopping.

> [It] involves intercepting shoppers at a high-traffic location, sometimes prescreening them for category use, exposing the selected individuals to a commercial (or concept) for a proposed new product, giving them an opportunity to buy the new product in a real life or laboratory setting, and interviewing those who purchased the new product at a later date to ascertain their reaction and repeat-purchase intentions.[26]

Simulated tests offer several advantages, including speed (12 to 16 weeks), low cost (less than $100,000 compared to an excess of $2 million for full-scale market tests), and

---

MARKET SENSING FEATURE   Forecasting New-Product Sales Using Simulated Test Marketing (STM)

- STM consists of analyzing detailed marketing plan information, estimated costs, and responses from a sample of target market prospects.
- Potential buyers of the good or service are exposed to the new product and the competitors' products in a simulated store environment.
- Participants are asked questions about possible purchase of the product and reactions to variations in features (e.g., different prices).
- As prospects move through different scenarios about features and price, estimates can be made about how the

alternative offerings will perform during market introduction.
- The marketing plan details, costs, and participant response information are analyzed using a STM computer model developed to fit the specific market environment.
- STM generates sales and profit forecasts and valuable insights about improving the effectiveness of marketing mix components.
- STM helps answer important questions such as describing the target market, positioning preferences, and responsiveness to pricing.

Source: Kevin J. Clancy and Robert S. Shulman, "Test for Success," *Sales and Marketing Management*, Oct. 1995, pp. 111–14.

---

relatively accurate forecasts of market response.[27] The tests also eliminate the risk in conventional testing that competitors will jam the test. The use of simulated test marketing is described in the Market Sensing Feature.

Scanner-Based Test Marketing.   This method is less artificial than simulated testing and is less expensive than the conventional market test. Information Resources Inc.'s BehaviorScan system pioneered the use of cable television and a computerized database to track new food and drug products. The system uses information and responses from 2,500 panel members in each test city. Each member has an identification card to show to participating store cashiers. Purchases are electronically recorded and transmitted to a central data bank. Cable television enables this system to use controlled advertisement testing. Some viewers can be exposed to ads while the ads are being withheld from other viewers.

Conventional Test Marketing.   Market testing puts the product under actual market conditions in one or more test cities. It is used for frequently purchased consumer products. Test marketing uses a complete marketing program including advertising and personal selling. Product sampling is often an important factor in launching the new product in the test market. The product is marketed on a commercial basis in each city, and test results are then projected to the national or regional target market. Because of its high cost, conventional test marketing represents the final evaluation before full-scale market introduction. Firms sometimes decide not to test market in order to avoid competitor awareness and high testing costs and to accelerate introduction.

Several decisions are necessary when conducting market tests.[28] The number of markets to use must be determined. The more the better, but high costs of testing usually limit the number of locations to two or three. The size of the markets to be tested is another issue. Also important is finding cities with representative demographics. Finally, geographic selection of the test cities is desirable so that buyers in other nearby cities do not affect the test results.

Testing Industrial Products. Market testing can be used for various industrial products. Selection of test sites may need to extend beyond one or two cities to include sufficient market coverage. The test firm has substantial control of an industrial products test since it can use direct mail and personal selling. The relatively small number of customers also aids targeting of marketing efforts. The product should have the characteristics necessary for testing: It should be producible in test quantities, relatively inexpensive, and not subject to extensive buying center influences throughout the organization.

Factors in Test Marketing. Many factors are important in testing, such as selecting good test sites, determining the length of the test, controlling for external influences on the test (such as competition), and interpreting results. A. C. Nielsen's experience indicates that about 75 percent of products that are test-marketed are successful, compared to an 80 percent failure rate for new products that are not fully tested.[29]

Selecting Test Sites. Test sites should exhibit the buyer and environmental characteristics of the commercial market target. Since no site is perfect, the objective is to find a reasonable match between the test and commercial market. These criteria are often used to evaluate potential test sites:

1. Representation as to population size.
2. Typical per capita income.
3. Typical purchasing habits.
4. Stability of year-round sales.
5. Relative isolation from other cities.
6. Not easily jammed by competitors.
7. Typical of planned distribution outlets.
8. Availability of retailers that will cooperate.
9. Availability of media that will cooperate.
10. Availability of research and audit service companies.[30]

America's best metropolitan test markets are profiled in Exhibit 8–10. These areas are ranked according to an "index of dissimilarity."[31] The index takes into account age, race, and housing value (proxy for income). Detroit has the lowest cumulative index value of the 20 best metropolitan areas. An index of zero is a perfect match to overall U.S. demographics. Detroit's 23 is a very good score.

Length of the Test. The length of the test affects the test results. A. C. Nielsen's analyses of more than 100 market tests of new-brand introductions indicate that the predictability of national results from test market data increases significantly with time.[32] After 4 months of testing, 37 percent of the predictions were correct; after 18 months the

EXHIBIT 8–10   America's Best Test Markets

Rank	Metropolitan Area	1990 Population	Cumulative Index	Housing-Value Index	Age Index	Race Index
1	Detroit, MI	4,382,000	22.8	11.8	1.5	9.5
2	St. Louis, MO-IL	2,444,000	22.8	15.1	1.6	6.2
3	Charlotte-Gastonia-Rock Hill, NC-SC	1,162,000	24.1	13.5	2.7	7.9
4	Fort Worth-Arlington, TX	1,332,000	25.0	17.0	5.9	2.2
5	Kansas City, MO-KS	1,566,000	25.4	17.9	2.7	4.8
6	Indianapolis, IN	1,250,000	25.5	16.7	2.4	6.3
7	Philadelphia, PA-NJ	4,857,000	26.7	18.0	1.7	7.1
8	Wilmington, NC	120,000	27.2	15.1	4.1	8.0
9	Cincinnati, OH-KY-IN	1,453,000	27.2	19.1	1.6	6.6
10	Nashville, TN	985,000	27.6	18.5	2.9	6.2
11	Dayton-Springfield, OH	951,000	27.6	19.5	1.9	6.2
12	Jacksonville, FL	907,000	27.6	17.2	2.5	7.9
13	Toledo, OH	614,000	27.8	20.0	2.4	5.5
14	Greensboro-Winston-Salem-High Point, NC	942,000	27.8	17.6	2.9	7.3
15	Columbus, OH	1,377,000	28.4	19.0	3.8	5.7
16	Charlottesville, VA	131,000	28.5	16.9	6.3	5.2
17	Panama City, FL	127,000	28.6	20.1	2.6	6.0
18	Pensacola, FL	344,000	28.7	21.8	2.2	4.7
19	Milwaukee, WI	1,432,000	28.8	23.4	1.4	4.1
20	Cleveland, OH	1,831,000	28.9	18.2	3.4	7.4

Note: An index of zero indicates that the area's demographics match the United States perfectly.
Source: Judith Waldrop, "All-American Markets," *American Demographics,* January 1992, p. 26.

figure was 100 percent. Manufacturers need 10 months to be reasonably sure that market share data are representative. Market tests of more than a year are common.

External Influences.   Probably the most troublesome external factor that may affect test market results is competition that does not operate on a normal basis. Competitors may attempt to drive test market results awry by increasing or decreasing their marketing efforts and making other changes in their marketing actions. It is also important to monitor the test market environment to identify other unusual influences during the test period. For example, unusual economic conditions may affect test results for some products.

New-Product Models

New-product models are useful in analyzing test market data and predicting commercial market success. Some models also consider the effects of marketing mix components. Product newness and repurchasability are useful for classifying the models.[33] They fall into two categories: (1) first-purchase models designed to predict the cumulative number of new-product tries over time and (2) models designed to predict the repeat purchase rate of those buyers who have tried the product. The latter type combines a first-purchase model with a repeat-purchase model. A brief overview of the consumer adoption process for new products sets the stage for our look at the two types of models.

Consumer Adoption Process.   Research concerning the adoption of innovations indicates that (1) new-product adopters follow a sequence of stages in their adoption process, (2) their characteristics vary according to how soon they adopt the product after introduction, and (3) adoption findings may be of value in new-product planning. The adoption stages are awareness, interest, evaluation, trial, and adoption.[34] By finding and targeting such "early adopters," firms may be able to accelerate a new product's adoption. Early adopters tend to be younger, of generally higher socioeconomic status, and more in contact with impersonal and cosmopolitan sources of information than later adopters.[35] The early adopter also uses a variety of information sources and is more cosmopolitan than the later adopters.

First-Purchase Models.   These models are based on the diffusion of the new product into the market. The models generate a life cycle sales curve using a mathematical model that contains a small number of parameters.[36] The parameters are estimated based on the experiences of similar products, consumer pretests, or early sales results. The models range from simple exponential curve-fitting using market potential and rate of penetration as parameters, to more complex, multistage models. Mahajan and Peterson have developed a comprehensive critique and comparative assessment of first-purchase diffusion models of new-product acceptance.[37]

Repeat-Purchase Models.   Many consumer and industrial new products are nondurables that are repurchased on a regular basis. Models are available for projecting sales of these products and for evaluating marketing program positioning strategy. The ASSESSOR model illustrates this group of models.[38] It evaluates the new product before test marketing but after decisions have been made regarding positioning strategy. Management can use this information, in combination with direct behavior and attitude data obtained from laboratory and usage tests, to make market share predictions and diagnostic information. Trial/repeat and attitude models are built into the structure of ASSESSOR. The model uses two parallel approaches (trial/repeat and preference models) to estimate the brand's market share. This is a key feature. The use of a laboratory facility and a simulated shopping experiment is also innovative. Applications, typically, use samples of 300 people.

New-product models such as ASSESSOR are very data-dependent and complex. Their validity has not been fully tested, although for certain kinds of applications the results have been promising. Strengths of such models include their capacity to analyze interrelationships among several variables and to generate outputs based on input data. Applications appear most appropriate for frequently purchased nondurable products that are not totally new, so that purchasers have some experience with the product category. Model applications like ASSESSOR are expensive, but they cost a small fraction of a market test or full-scale commercialization.[39] Considering the stakes involved in the introduction of new products, the use of modeling to reduce risks is likely to expand in the future.

NEW PRODUCT FEATURE   Benetton and Motorola Create a Fashion Beeper

---

A U.S. phone pager manufacturer, Motorola, teamed up with a fashion apparel company, Benetton, to design, produce, and market a new line of beepers targeted to the young and fashion-conscious.

Priced at £99 ($137) in Britain and DM269 in Germany, the owner pays no monthly fee since the new billing method in Europe charges the caller for the message.

The colorful pagers carry the "United Colors of Benetton" logo, are packaged to appeal to young people from 16 to 25 throughout the world, and include several codes that trigger special messages (e.g., "Want a beer?"). The corporate partners forecast sales of $160 million by 2000.

Source: Richard L. Hudson, "United Beepers of Benetton to Send Fashion Message with Motorola's Aid," *The Wall Street Journal*, June 2, 1995, p. A6.

COMMERCIALIZATION

Introducing new products into the market includes finalizing the marketing plan, coordinating introduction activities with business functions, implementing the marketing strategy, and monitoring and control of the product launch. Benetton and Motorola moved a new product into the commercialization stage in 1995, which they jointly developed as a fashion accessory. The alliance involves an interesting marketing challenge to position the new phone pager to appeal to millions of young people around the world. The New Product Feature describes the venture.

The Marketing Plan

Market introduction at the commercialization stage requires a complete marketing strategy. It should be coordinated with the various people responsible for the introduction, including salespeople, sales managers, and managers in other functional areas such as production, distribution, finance, and human resources. Responsibility for the new-product launch is normally assigned to the marketing manager or product manager. Companies may form product-planning and market introduction teams.

The timing and geographical scope of the launch are important decisions. The options range from a national market introduction to an area-by-area rollout. In some instances the scope of the introduction may extend to international markets. The national introduction is a major endeavor, requiring a comprehensive implementation effort. Some firms prefer to introduce the product on a stage-by-stage basis. This reduces the scope of the introduction and enables management to adjust marketing strategy based on experience gained in the early stages of the launch. One limitation of the rollout approach is that, like market testing, rollout gives competition more time to react.

Faulty planning often leads to problems. The Walt Disney Company saw the potential of extending the image of one of its popular movies, *The Lion King*. Disney introduced a CD-ROM version for the 1994 holiday season.[40] A $3 million advertising program helped to generate sales of over 200,000 units by mid-January 1995. With nearly 8 million home computers that can read CD-ROM packages, the market potential is very promising. Unfortunately, several of the disks were not compatible with buyers' computers. The user information provided on the disks was not prominently displayed. Also, the program was marketed with known errors and Disney's customer service staff were not prepared for the unhappy parents whose kids could not view *The Lion King* on their home computers. The idea was sound but the execution was faulty.

Monitoring and Control

Real-time tracking of new-product performance at the commercialization stage is extremely important. Standardized information services are available for monitoring sales of products such as foods, health and beauty aids, and prescription drugs. Information is collected through store audits, consumer diary panels, and scanner services. Special studies may be necessary for products that are not included in standardized information services.

It is important to include product performance standards in the new-product plan to evaluate how well the product is performing. Performance targets often include profit contribution, sales, market share, and return-on-investment objectives—including the time horizon for reaching objectives. It is also important to establish values for objectives that indicate unacceptable performance. For example, market share threshold levels are sometimes used to gauge new-product performance. Regular measures of customer satisfaction are also important measures of market performance. Management can designate zones for new-product performance, such as very good, acceptable, poor, and unacceptable. Management needs to be prepared to drop a new product if it is apparent that poor performance will continue.

SUMMARY

New-product planning is a vital activity in every company. It applies to services as well as physical products. Companies that are successful in new-product planning follow a formal process of new-product planning combined with effective organization structures for managing new products. Experience helps these firms to improve product planning over time. The corporate cultures of companies like 3M are responsive to the demands of new-product planning.

The steps in new-product planning include customer needs analysis, idea generation, screening and evaluation, business analysis, product development, marketing strategy development, market testing, and commercialization (Exhibit 8–4).

Idea generation starts the process of planning for a new product. The idea is evaluated as it moves through the process and the costs of new-product planning accumulate. There are various internal and external sources of new-product ideas. Ideas are generated by information search, marketing research, research and development, incentives, and acquisition. Screening, evaluation, and business analysis help determine if the new-product concept is sufficiently attractive to justify proceeding with development.

Development and testing transform the concept to a product prototype. Product development creates one or more prototypes. Use testing gains user reaction to the prototype. Manufacturing development determines how to produce the product in commercial quantities at costs that will enable the firm to price the product at a level attractive to buyers. Marketing strategy development begins early in the product-planning process. A complete marketing strategy is needed for a totally new product. Product line additions, modifications, and other changes require a less-extensive development of marketing strategy.

Completion of the product design and marketing strategy moves the process to the market-testing stage. At this point management often wants some form of user reaction to the new product. Testing options include simulated test marketing, scanner-based test marketing, and conventional test marketing. Industrial products are not tested as much as consumer products, although frequently purchased nondurables can be tested. Instead, use tests of product prototypes are more typical for industrial products. Commercialization completes the planning process, moving the product toward sales and profit performance objectives.

QUESTIONS FOR REVIEW AND DISCUSSION

1. Discuss the relationship between customer satisfaction and quality function deployment.

2. In many consumer products companies, marketing executives seem to play the lead role in new-product planning, whereas research and development executives occupy this position in firms with very complex products such as electronics. Why do these differences exist? Do you agree that such differences should occur?

3. Discuss the features and limitations of focus group interviews for use in new-product planning.

4. Identify and discuss the important issues in selecting an organizational approach for new-product planning.

5. Discuss the issues and trade-offs of using tight evaluation versus loose evaluation procedures as a product concept moves through the planning process to the commercialization stage.

6. What factors affect the length of the new-product planning process?

7. Compare and contrast the use of scanner tests and conventional market tests.

8. Is the use of a single city test market appropriate? Discuss.

NOTES

1. Randall Lane, "The Culture That Jake Built," *Forbes,* March 27, 1995, pp. 45–46; Echo Montgomery Garrett, "Bored with Skiing? Why Not Try 'Boarding,' " *Investor's Business Daily,* January 8, 1996, pp. 1–2.

2. *New Products Management for the 1980s* (New York: Booz Allen & Hamilton, 1982), p. 8.

3. "Getting Hot Ideas from Customers," *Fortune,* May 18, 1992, pp. 86–87.

4. L. P. Sullivan, "Quality Function Deployment," *Quality Progress,* June 1986, pp. 39–50.

5. Ibid., p. 40.

6. Ibid., pp. 39–50.

7. Ronald M. Fortuna, "Quality of Design," in *Total Quality: An Executive's Guide for the 1990s* (Burr Ridge, IL: Irwin Professional Publishing, 1990), p. 119.

8. "Producer Power," *The Economist,* March 4, 1995, p. 70.

9. Lawrence Ingrassia, "By Improving Scratch Paper, 3M Gets New-Product Winner," *The Wall Street Journal,* March 31, 1983, p. 272.

10. Phil Davies, "Europe Unbound," *Express,* Spring 1992, p. 19.

11. *New Products Management for the 1980s,* p. 11.

12. Eric M. Olsen, Orville C. Walker, Jr., and Robert W. Ruekert, "Organizing for Effective New-Product Development: The Moderating Role of Product Innovativeness," *Journal of Marketing,* January 1995, pp. 48–62.

13. Ibid.

14. Marc H. Meyer and Edward B. Roberts, "Focusing Product Technology for Corporate Growth," *Sloan Management Review,* Summer 1988, pp. 8–16.

15. Glen L. Urban and Eric von Hippel, "Lead User Analyses for the Development of New Industrial Products," *Management Science,* May 1988, pp. 569–82.

16. Janet Guyon and Charles W. Stevens, "AT&T's Bell Labs Adjusts to Competitive Era," *The Wall Street Journal,* August 13, 1985, p. 6.

17. C. Merle Crawford, *New Products Management,* 4th ed. (Burr Ridge, IL: Richard D. Irwin, 1994), chap. 4.

18. Yoram J. Wind, *Product Policy: Concepts, Methods, and Strategy* (Reading, MA: Addison-Wesley Publishing, 1982), pp. 303–4.

19. William R. Dillon, Thomas J. Madden, and Neil H. Firtle, *Market Research in a Marketing Environment,* 3rd ed. (Burr Ridge, IL: Richard D. Irwin, 1994), pp. 558–60.

20. Subrata N. Chakravarty, "We Had to Change the Playing Field," *Forbes,* February 4, 1991, p. 83.

21. Crawford, *New Products Management,* chap. 10.

22. Dillon, Madden, and Firtle, *Marketing Research,* pp. 582–84.

23. W. Edwards Deming, *Out of the Crisis* (Cambridge, MA: Massachusetts Institute of Technology, Center for Advanced Engineering Study, 1986).

24. Ford S. Worthy, "Japan's Smart Secret Weapon," *Fortune,* August 12, 1991, pp. 72–75.

25. "Hewlett-Packard's Generation Gap," *Ad Week's Marketing Week,* November 4, 1991, pp. 34–35.

26. Dillon, Madden, and Firtle, *Marketing Research,* p. 639.

27. Ibid.

28. Ibid., p. 536.

29. Lee Adler, "Test Marketing—and Its Pitfalls," *Sales and Marketing Management,* March 15, 1982, p. 78.

30. Dillon, Madden, and Firtle, *Marketing Research,* p. 638.

31. Judith Waldrop, "All-American Markets," *American Demographics,* January 1992, pp. 24–28.

32. "The True Test of Test Marketing Is Time," *Sales and Marketing Management,* March 15, 1982, p. 76.

33. Gary L. Lilien and Philip Kotler, *Marketing Decision Making* (New York: Harper & Row, 1983), chap. 19.

34. Everett M. Rogers, *Diffusion of Innovations* (New York: Free Press, 1962).

35. Ibid.

36. Lilien and Kotler, *Marketing Decision Making,* p. 706.

37. Vijay Mahajan and Robert A. Peterson, "First-Purchase Diffusion Models of New-Product Acceptance," *Technological Forecasting and Social Change* 15 (1979), pp. 127–46.

38. Glen L. Urban and John R. Hauser, *Decision and Marketing of New Products,* 2nd ed. (Englewood Cliffs, NJ: Prentice Hall, 1993), pp. 463–67.

39. Ibid.

40. Frederick Rose and Richard Turner, "A Jungle Out There," *The Wall Street Journal,* January 23, 1995, pp. A1 and A6.

Cases for Part III

CASE 3–1   Wal-Mart

Was Sam simply smarter?

The forced resignation Tuesday of Joseph Antonini represents an official verdict. For seven years, he led a discount store to battle against what appeared to be its twin. The two chains looked alike, sold the same products, sought each other's customers. They even dated back to the same year—1962—and bore similar names: Kmart and Wal-Mart.

The competition, however, is over: Sam Walton's Wal-Mart Stores Inc. won.

So bleak are the prospects for Kmart Corp. that in February an advertising agency bidding for its business, N. W. Ayer & Partners, recommended that it stop competing against Wal-Mart and transform itself into a big convenience chain where customers could go for milk and cigarettes. "It seems that the only way for [Kmart] to survive is to find a different niche," says one person familiar with the presentation. Kmart rejected the idea.

Though a savvy new leader could spark high hopes for ringing cash registers, Kmart still has "major operational and managerial issues to deal with," says Marilyn Weinstein of the College Retirement Equities Fund, a Kmart shareholder.

While an air of inevitable defeat had recently settled over Kmart, a short look back finds many observers believing deeply in Kmart and Mr. Antonini. In fact, many of the investors who demanded his ouster as president and chief executive officer this week gambled on him to outfox his counterparts at Wal-Mart not so long ago. They questioned some of the strategies of Mr. Walton, Wal-Mart's founder. They also thought Mr. Antonini had more pizazz, better locations, and a solid turnaround plan.

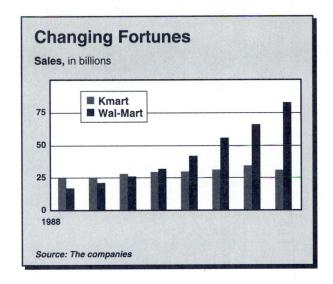

Changing Fortunes

Sales, in billions

- ■ Kmart
- ■ Wal-Mart

Source: The companies

"He's taken a tired, dispirited company and revived it," declared a prominent retail analyst in a 1991 *Forbes* magazine article that described Wal-Mart's stock as overpriced and Kmart as a good bet.

Considering the similarity of their stores and missions, analysts attribute the different fates of Kmart and Wal-Mart primarily to management. Sam Walton, they say, was smarter than Mr. Antonini. That is easy to say this week. But it wasn't always a simple call.

When Mr. Antonini took the reins of Kmart in 1987, he had his hands full. He inherited some stores that were as old as 17 years, with water-warped floors, broken light fixtures, shelves placed too close together and cheap displays set in the middle of aisles. Also, his predecessors had neglected to implement the sophisticated computer systems that were helping Wal-Mart track and replenish its merchandise swiftly and efficiently.

But considering that the two chains had begun the same year, Kmart was way ahead. It had nearly twice as many discount stores, 2,223 to 1,198. The Troy, Michigan, chain also had sales of $25.63 billion, compared with $15.96 billion for Wal-Mart. Thanks to advertising and its large urban presence, Kmart and its red "K" logo also had greater visibility.

Although Wal-Mart had a more consistent record of earnings and revenue growth, in the eyes of many experts it had never played in the major leagues. Unlike Kmart, whose stores sat on expensive urban real estate and competed against other big discounters, Wal-Mart sat in pastures outside small towns and picked off the customers of aging mom-and-pop shops.

Like a minor leaguer admiring a star in the bigs, Mr. Walton regarded Kmart with awe. "So much about their stores was superior to ours," Mr. Walton said in his autobiography, "that sometimes I felt like we couldn't compete."

For his part, the 53-year-old Mr. Antonini was heard by company insiders to dismiss Wal-Mart executives as "snake-oil salesman"—something he denies.

So rapidly was Wal-Mart multiplying across the rural landscape that an invasion of urban America—and a confrontation with Kmart—became inevitable. To prepare for the encounter, Mr. Antonini focused on his own strength: marketing and merchandising. A self-promoter with a boisterous voice and wide smile, Mr. Antonini invested heavily in national television campaigns and glamorous representatives such as Jaclyn Smith, a former "Charlie's Angels" television star who has her own line of clothes for Kmart.

That effort only widened a public-awareness gap between the two retailers. Even before the successful campaign with Ms. Smith, Kmart's "blue-light special" was famous around the country. Meanwhile, as recently as the late 1980s, most Americans had never seen a Wal-Mart advertisement, not to mention a store.

Mr. Walton did little to change that. He avoided publicity. And instead of marketing, he became obsessed with operations. He invested tens of millions of dollars in a company-wide computer system linking cash registers to headquarters, enabling him to quickly restock goods selling off the shelves. He also invested heavily in trucks and distribution centers, around which he located his stores. Besides enhancing his control, these moves sharply reduced costs.

That was a gamble. While Kmart tried to improve its image and cultivated store loyalty, Mr. Walton kept lowering costs, betting that price would prove more important than any other factor.

As discounting fever deepened across America, analysts and shareholders came to expect huge growth from these retailers. In trying to meet these expectations, Messrs. Antonini and Walton once again trod different paths.

Mr. Antonini tried bolstering growth by overseeing the purchase of other types of retailers: the Sports Authority sporting-goods chain, OfficeMax office-supply stores, Borders bookstores, and Pace Membership Warehouse clubs. Besides additional revenue, these chains would decrease dependence on profits from discounting. "It's the way of the future," Mr. Antonini declared of such diversification.

In Bentonville, Arkansas, meanwhile, Mr. Walton was taking precisely the opposite tact—betting everything on discount retailing. He started Sam's Club, a deep-discount, members-only retailer that was modeled after California-based Price Club, which devised the concept. Then Mr. Walton tried a brand of discounting that Kmart had already tried and abandoned in the 1960s—groceries. His first experiment, a massive Hypermart more than 230,000 square feet in size, suffered. Customers complained that produce that wasn't fresh or well-presented—and that they were having trouble finding things in stores so big that stockers wore roller skates. The Hypermart, Mr. Walton conceded, didn't work.

Undaunted, he launched a revised concept: the Supercenter, a combination discount store and grocery that was smaller than the Hypermart.

By 1990, three years after Mr. Antonini took charge of Kmart, Wal-Mart surpassed it. For the retail year that ended in January 1991, Wal-Mart had sales of $32.6 billion, compared with Kmart's $29.7 billion. For Kmart, the scary part was that Wal-Mart still had fewer stores—1,721 to Kmart's 2,330.

But Mr. Antonini and other Kmart supporters took comfort in knowing that Wal-Mart was running out of small towns to conquer. To continue growing, it would have to invade Kmart's turf: the more-expensive and competitive big city.

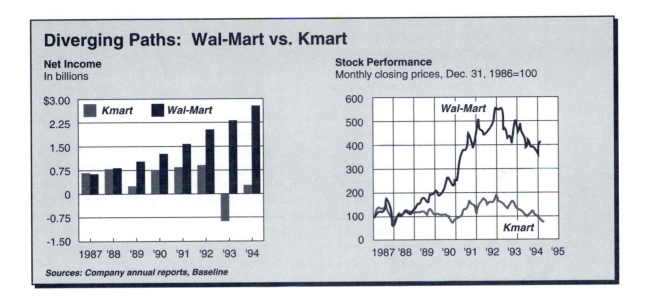

Diverging Paths: Wal-Mart vs. Kmart

Net Income
In billions

Stock Performance
Monthly closing prices, Dec. 31, 1986=100

Sources: Company annual reports, Baseline

To prepare for that invasion, Mr. Antonini launched a $3.5 billion, five-year plan to renovate, enlarge, or replace Kmart's oldest and shabbiest stores. Analysts called him a "visionary," and often joined him on tours of prototype stores.

But the least visible difference between Wal-Mart and Kmart was beginning to matter a lot. Wal-Mart's incredibly sophisticated distribution, inventory, and scanner systems meant that customers almost never encountered depleted shelves or price-check delays at the cash register.

The halls of Kmart, meanwhile, were filled with distribution horror stories. Joseph R. Thomas, who oversaw distribution, said that in retrospect, he should have smelled trouble when he found warehouses stuffed full of merchandise on December 15, the height of the Christmas season.

Although Mr. Antonini poured a fortune into a frantic attempt to catch up, Kmart was so behind that a November 1993 internal company report found that Kmart employees woefully lacked the training and skill to plan and control inventory. Kmart's cash registers often didn't have up-to-date information and would enter wrong prices. That led to a lawsuit by the Riverside County district attorney's office, claiming that 72 California Kmart stores had overcharged customers. In May 1994, Kmart settled for $985,000.

Take the case of Anita Joy Winter. She went to a Naperville, Illinois, Kmart with three items on her list: underwear for her husband, contact-lens cleaner, and dish towels. The store was out of everything but the towels, and even then didn't have the beige color she wanted. After that, the register rang up a price more than 70 cents above what the shelf advertised, which took 10 minutes to straighten out.

The consequence? "It's been 'Thank God for Wal-Mart' ever since," says Ms. Winter, who shops at a suburban Chicago Wal-Mart at least twice a week.

To the surprise of many, the higher cost and greater competitiveness of big cities hardly registered at Wal-Mart, now under the leadership of David Glass, the successor to Mr. Walton, who died in 1992 at age 74. The company had pared costs so aggressively in so many areas that it was passing on the high cost of, say, Long Island, New York, real estate and still easily underpricing Kmart. Moreover, its stores were often twice as large as older Kmarts. "The effect, when Wal-Mart put in a 125,000 square foot, slick new store across from an old 60,000-square-foot competitor, was just devastating," says William W. Whyte, retail analyst with Stephens Inc. in Little Rock.

Of the two retailers' diversification efforts, Kmart again proved the least successful. Mr. Antonini's plan to make Kmart a combination discount and specialty-retailing empire began to unravel at the end of 1993. While the specialty stores—those offering books, office supplies, or sporting goods—had contributed 30% of sales the year before, they only made up 15% of operating profit. And Kmart's discount stores were quickly losing market share to Wal-Mart. Shareholders demanded Mr. Antonini get rid of his prize jewels and focus on the discount stores. At the insistence of shareholders and against Mr. Antonini's wishes, Kmart announced at the end of last year a plan to sell majority stakes in three of its specialty retail chains.

Wal-Mart, meanwhile, couldn't roll out its new Supercenters fast enough. The concept of buying general merchandise and groceries in one store—at a discount—was proving successful around the country, prompting Kmart to start a similar chain.

But the cost of opening Super Kmarts only detracted from the continuing, and largely disappointing, effort to renovate general-merchandise Kmarts. Though the stores were all supposed to have a new look by 1996—with wider aisles, gleaming floors and expanded departments—a third of them remain untouched. And those that have been renovated aren't producing the sales gains that had been anticipated.

As a result, even after $1.8 billion in asset sales last year, Kmart's operating profit was so disappointing that the company could barely cover its 96-cents-a-share annual dividend and had to scale back capital spending to about $800 million from at least $1 billion.

The most telling statistic: Since Mr. Antonini took over as chairman, president, and chief executive officer in 1987, Kmart's market share of total discount sales has dropped to 22.7% from 34.5%, according to Tactical Retail Solutions Inc. in New York. Wal-Mart's soared to 41.6% from 20.1%.

In the end, attitude may have made a bigger difference than strategy. In Bentonville, Mr. Walton and Mr. Glass asked subordinates what wasn't working, and chided them for failing to deliver any bad news. Executives, expected to spend much of their week visiting stores, actively solicit proposals from subordinates. And Mr. Walton always acted as if a fierce competitor was just behind him and gaining. Even publicly, he and Mr. Glass were likelier to discuss Wal-Mart's weaknesses than its strengths.

In Troy, by contrast, Mr. Antonini didn't think others could tell him much about the business. A Kmart employee since 1964, when he started as an assistant manager, he bristled at criticism and was known as a "Teflon-coated" boss because suggestions for change slid right off. Insiders say he didn't do much hiring of managers from outside the company who might challenge him, and he flayed or fired consultants who recommended everything from management changes to targeting a narrower consumer market.

In the fall of 1993, munching a sandwich in a shiny new Super Kmart store, Mr. Antonini expressed the possibility of following the lead of Mr. Walton and writing a book detailing a retail success.

"We've got a few things to get done first," he said. "But we're on our way."

Source: Christina Duff and Bob Ortega, "Loss Leader: How Wal-Mart Outdid a Once-Touted Kmart in Discount-Store Race," *The Wall Street Journal,* March 24, 1995, pp. A1, A4. Reprinted by permission of *The Wall Street Journal,* © 1995 by Dow Jones & Company, Inc. All Rights Reserved Worldwide.

CASE 3-2   Yoplait USA

In 1990, Chap Colucci, vice president of marketing and sales at Yoplait USA, was concerned about Yoplait's performance. Yoplait had failed, for two consecutive years, to meet targets set by top management at General Mills. Yoplait's share of market was declining, and its profitability was unacceptable by any standards. Yoplait USA was part of the Consumer Foods Group subsidiary of General Mills, Inc.

Colucci felt certain that a new marketing strategy was needed for Yoplait USA. Colucci's situation analysis had identified some very serious concerns surrounding Yoplait's marketing-mix components and had pinpointed the fact that Yoplait's current strategy was a hold-over from the product's introductory days.

The Company

Incorporated in 1928, General Mills, Inc., became the world's largest grain processor when James Ford Bell, president of Washburn Crosby Company, brought together several flour millers. General Mills' original product, Gold Medal Flour, was still popular in the 1990s.

Two very successful food-type groups were owned by General Mills. The **Consumer Foods Group** was comprised of products such as *Big G* cereals (e.g., Cheerios, Lucky Charms, Wheaties, Kix, Basic 4); *Betty Crocker* desserts, main meals, popcorn, and snacks (e.g., SuperMoist cake mixes, Creamy Deluxe frosting, Supreme brownie mixes, Hamburger Helper, Recipe Sauces, Pop Secret, FundaMiddles, Fruit Roll-Ups, Squeez-its); flour and baking mixes (e.g., Gold Medal, Bisquick, Robin Hood); *Gorton's* (seafood); and *Yoplait* yogurt. Also included in the Consumer Foods Group were the foodservice division[1] and the international foods operations (in Canada and Latin America, and in joint ventures with Nestlé and PepsiCo Foods International).

This case was prepared by Victoria L. Crittenden, Associate Professor of Marketing at Boston College, as the basis for class discussion rather than to illustrate either effective or ineffective handling of a managerial situation. Research assistance was provided by Jennifer Fraser and Stephanie Hillstrom, Boston College. All material from secondary sources.

[1]In addition to the grocery store channel, which sold to individual end consumers, many food manufacturers sold their products through foodservice channels to commercial (e.g., restaurants, cafeterias) and noncommercial (e.g., airlines, schools, hospitals) operations.

The **Restaurants Group** managed three casual-dining operations. The *Red Lobster* was a full-service seafood restaurant with 581 units operating in 47 states in the United States, 57 units operated in Canada, and 50 restaurants operated in the Tokyo market in a partnership venture with JUSCO, a leading Japanese retailer. *The Olive Garden* offered more than 110 different versions of its menu across the United States in 379 restaurants in 42 states and 21 units in Canada. The *China Coast* restaurant, a new business venture for General Mills, provided Mandarin, Cantonese, and Szechuan dishes. Plans were to open around 30 China Coast units in the United States by the mid-1990s.

Consumer Foods Group was the larger of the two groups.[2] It accounted for approximately two-thirds of the company's total sales revenue from the food and restaurant groups. The consumer foods business contributed slightly over $640 million in operating income (on sales of almost $5 billion) in 1990. This was more than twice the level in 1985.

In the 1980s and 1990s, the U.S. food industry grew about 1 percent yearly. General Mills sales volume in the U.S. increased 6 percent in 1990. Net earnings at General Mills increased 20 percent annually from 1985 to 1990.

Dairy Products

There were a number of socioeconomic and demographic factors that contributed to consumers' tastes and preferences for dairy products.[3] These factors included:

- Size and composition of the household consuming unit.
- Age distribution of the population.
- Degree of urbanization and regionality.
- Employment status of household members.
- Degree of nutritional education and lifestyle.

Just as important, however, was that by the late 1980s American consumers had become very concerned with their dietary intake. Emphasis was on the need to reduce total fat while increasing complex carbohydrates. Americans wanted the nourishment of dairy products, without the potential hazards of cholesterol, calories, fat, and sodium. Additionally, convenience, variety, and premium choices had begun to dominate the American consumer's buying habits.

The dairy product that benefited the most from the beginning of the health craze was yogurt. Yogurt was produced by adding bacteria to milk. The bacteria then multiplied in the milk, consuming the milk's sugar lactose and replacing it with acids. These acids then

---

[2]The Consumer Foods Group and the Restaurants Group comprised General Mills business. A third group, New Business Ventures, covered General Mills' development of new businesses. However, each of the new businesses in this third group fit nicely within one of the two food groups. For example, China Coast was technically still a new business venture.

[3]These were reported in published research by Osama A. Al-Zand and Eric Andriamanjay. "Consumer Demand for Dairy Products in Canada," *Agribusiness,* May 1988, pp. 233–44.

curdled the milk and gave the yogurt its tart flavor and thick consistency. For years, yogurt had been popular in France. Yet only 55 percent of Americans had tried yogurt by the beginning of the 1980s, which amounted to around 90 million cases.[4]

Yogurt was touted as the fat-free alternative to cream cheese and salad dressings, as well as a convenient breakfast and snack food. In addition to complying with the needs of the health food craze of the late 1980s, research had shown that yogurt had biological benefits as well. It was thought that yogurt could strengthen the immune system and help prevent recurring yeast infections.

By 1986, retail sales had jumped to almost $840 million. It was reported that there were 45 brands of cup yogurt in the market, with more than 30 producers. Yogurt was considered the fastest-growing product in the dairy case through the end of the 1980s. By 1990, however, growth had plateaued, with retail sales of $946 million which was a decline of 4.5 percent from the previous year.[5] While health consciousness was still important to American consumers, manufacturers had begun providing alternatives to yogurt both in the dairy case and outside. Refrigerated pastas and sauces, juice blends, puddings, ice creams, and soups had successfully stalled gains posted in the yogurt market during the decade of the 1980s. As well, lighter, fat-reduced products (including low-fat and no-fat yogurts) began joining or replacing traditional selections in the dairy case. Because of the increase in the number of dairy items, dairy products were the fastest growing part of the supermarket by 1990.

By 1990, the three major competitors in the yogurt market were Dannon (owned by a French company, BSN-Gervais Danone), Light n' Lively and Breyers (owned by Kraft, Inc.), and Yoplait. The market share leader was Dannon with almost 33 percent of the market. Yoplait, with 16 percent of the market, was No. 2 in market share. The No. 3 player in the market was Kraft with about 14 percent market share.

Beatrice Foods was one of the leading food corporations in the United States. In 1982, Beatrice Foods sold Dannon yogurt to BSN-Gervais Danone, a French company, for $84 million. A Beatrice spokesperson said that the company, believing yogurt to be a mature product, unfortunately sold a money machine.

Dannon yogurt was positioned as a nutritional product that offered value. Dannon attempted to transform yogurt's image from a health food to a healthy snack. Advertising portrayed nontraditional yogurt eaters and placed yogurt as a competitive item against fast foods. Unlike other yogurt producers which shipped to chain warehouses, Dannon distributed its products via store door delivery.[6]

Kraft, Inc., was a multibillion-dollar franchise owned by Philip Morris Companies, Inc. In addition to Breyers and Light n' Lively yogurt products, Kraft produced cheese products, spoonable dressings, dry dinners, ketchup, and peanut butter. Kraft focused on value for consumers, high quality and visibility, efficient manufacturing, and focused marketing. They had won worldwide consumer loyalty across different food categories and markets.

---

[4]There were 12 cups per case, with an average retail price per 8-ounce cup of 40 cents.

[5]By 1990, yogurt's penetration level in the U.S. consumer market was less than 40 percent. This compared to a 70 percent market penetration in Europe.

[6]With store door delivery, the yogurt was delivered direct to the supermarket where delivery truck drivers actually stocked the shelves.

The strategy for Breyers was to focus on its superior taste as a natural yogurt. Light n' Lively was targeted toward light users and nonusers of yogurt. Emphasis was upon its superior, natural taste. Media expenditures were almost equally divided between the two yogurt products. Combined spending on media was greater than Yoplait's expenditures, but not as large as Dannon's media expenditures.

Yoplait USA

Yoplait was the leading yogurt in the French market in the 1970s. Sodima, a French dairy cooperative, sold the rights to market Yoplait products in the United States to General Mills in October 1977.[7] Yogurt was not a standard product for General Mills. Products such as flour, breakfast cereals, and cake mixes had long shelf lives, while yogurt had to be refrigerated and had a 30-day shelf life. The nontraditional status of yogurt prompted General Mills to integrate the Yoplait acquisition into the company by forming the Yoplait USA subsidiary of the Consumer Foods Group and recruiting the marketing director of General Mills' New Business Division, Steven M. Rothschild, as president of Yoplait USA.

Rothschild (age 33) formed an entrepreneurial management team to lead Yoplait USA and General Mills into the yogurt market. Early market research conducted by the team found that around 95 percent of yogurt consumed by Americans was flavored and/or mixed with fruit. Yogurt came in one of four styles: sundae (fruit on the bottom), swiss (fruit blended into the yogurt), western (fruit on the bottom with flavored syrup on top), and frozen.[8] The typical container for this yogurt was an eight-ounce cup.

The early yogurt market was a regional, fragmented market. This regional focus led Yoplait USA to a geographic marketing organization, with three regions: Eastern, Central, and Western. By 1988, the most established markets were in the Northeast, the West, and in Florida. The best opportunities for yogurt growth existed in the Southwest and Midwest.

Yoplait was introduced in Southern California in April 1978. Amid bicycle races, hot-air balloons, and prime-time TV advertising, Yoplait outsold Cheerios in terms of unit sales. Yoplait's advertising campaign focused on the idea that Yoplait was the yogurt of France. Ads featured Loretta Swit and Tommy Lasorda[9] speaking French while devouring and adoring Yoplait yogurt. Yoplait was offered in six-ounce cups rather than the traditional eight-ounce cups. It was thought that a six-ounce serving was the serving size consumers wanted and that an eight-ounce serving was a little more than consumers really wanted to eat at one time.

Current Situation.   While Yoplait had quickly become a national brand preferred by many Americans and had gained the No. 2 market position, Yoplait's performance, at the beginning of the 1990s, was not at the level hoped for by General Mills management.

---

[7]Sodima had been licensing the rights to sell Yoplait yogurt in the United States to Michigan Brand Cottage Cheese. Bill Bennett, owner of this regional dairy company, had not been as successful as General Mills thought possible. A major problem was that the package Bennett used was faulty and leaked on the store shelf.

[8]By 1987, frozen yogurt sales were around $26 million.

[9]Swit was a well-known actress from the television series, *M*A*S*H*. Lasorda was manager for the Los Angeles Dodgers baseball club.

Chap Colucci had conducted a situation analysis as a starting point in revamping the product's marketing strategy. Colucci found:

- Yoplait's pricing was not in tune with the market. Its retail price for a six-ounce cup was, at times, higher than competitors' prices for eight-ounce cups. For example, Yoplait's 4-pack cups were priced 20 percent higher per cup than Dannon's and Kraft's 6-pack cups.

- Yoplait's communication strategy was out of line with the market. Yoplait was still using the advertising campaign of its introductory days. No follow-up campaign had been developed. Competitors were focusing heavily on couponing. Yoplait was not. Yoplait was spending a disproportionate amount relative to the competition on trade promotions, with very little directed toward the end consumer.

- Yoplait's product strategy was not keeping up with changes in consumers' tastes and demands nor with offerings by direct competitors. The only product line extension was Yoplait's Lite products. Competitors had begun to target product extensions to new markets (e.g., yogurt targeted toward children,[10] yogurt drinks).

- Yoplait USA's geographic marketing organization had caused management to focus on geographic issues such as increased sales to a particular account in a particular region rather than focusing upon increasing sales of Yoplait as a whole.

- The product was bringing in below standard gross margins. Production and overhead costs were escalating causing the product to experience margin problems.

Colucci needed to use these findings, along with his understanding of the dairy and yogurt markets and the company's competitors, to formulate a new marketing strategy for Yoplait yogurt. What did all of this suggest for Yoplait? Colucci wondered if he needed more information. He did not have a lot of time, but a hurried mistake could mean serious problems for his subsidiary. General Mills' top management wanted to see a strategy that would move Yoplait out of the doldrums it was in.

SOURCES

Al-Zand, Osama A., and Andriamanjay, Eric. "Consumer Demand for Dairy Products in Canada." *Agribusiness,* May 1988, pp. 233–44.

Cohn, Fred. "Consumer Expenditures Study: Dairy." *Supermarket Business,* September 1988, pp. 139, 210.

Dagnoli, Judann, and Julie Liesse Erickson. "Yogurt Breaks Out of Chilled Section." *Advertising Age,* October 3, 1988, p. S6.

Edwards, Brian. "Consumer Expenditures Study: Dairy." *Supermarket Business,* September 1990, pp. 149–50.

Gershman, Michael. "Packaging's Role in Remarketing." *Management Review,* May 1987, pp. 41–45.

Hammel, Frank. "Dairy." *Supermarket Business,* September 1992, pp. 111–12.

[10]Children, ages 6–14, spent an estimated $7 million annually. They were thought to influence another $120 million annually in family spending.

Liesse, Julie. "Brand Extensions Take Center Stage." *Advertising Age,* March 8, 1993, p. 12.

_____. "Fat-Free: Fad or Food of the Future?" *Advertising Age,* September 10, 1990, p. 6.

_____. "Yogurt Drinks Have Juicy Future." *Advertising Age,* May 3, 1993, p. 17.

_____. "Yogurt Grows as Staple of U.S. Culture." *Advertising Age,* January 18, 1993, p. 18.

_____. "Yogurts Sprinkle in Fun to Stir Kids." *Advertising Age,* February 8, 1993, pp. 27–28.

McMath, Robert. " 'Hot' Ice Cream, Frozen Yogurt Market Is More than Seasonal." *Brandweek,* September 20, 1993, pp. 66–67.

Miller, Alan B., Jr. "SAMI Charts Slight Food-Store Gains in '86." *Advertising Age,* December 29, 1986, pp. 4, 6.

Perlis, Paula. "Dairy." *Supermarket Business,* September 1989, pp. 173–74, 210.

Sellers, Patricia. "A Boring Brand Can Be Beautiful." *Fortune,* November 18, 1991, pp. 169–79.

Smith, Katherine. "It's Much Easier to Cheat a Lot of Customers Out of 10 Cents than to Cheat One Person Out of a Million Dollars." *Supermarket Business,* September 1993, pp. 43–44.

"Sports Drink, Yogurt Marketers Try to Mine Gold in Kids' Market." *Marketing News,* April 26, 1993, p. 2.

CASE 3–3   White Dove Philippines Company

According to industry sources, shampoo was first introduced in the Philippine market by a multinational company after World War II. Since then the product has grown in popularity and usage largely due to massive advertising and extensive distribution. While specific figures on shampoo production and consumption were unavailable from national or local government agencies, a survey of Filipino family expenditures in 1988 was available from the National Census and Statistics Office (NSCO). It showed that a family spent 3.3 percent of its annual income for personal care products, which included shampoo. Based on this percentage of expenditures, the value of the personal care products industry would be close to 11 billion pesos. Knowledgeable persons involved in the shampoo business put its value at about 10 percent of that, or 1.1 billion pesos.

Shampoo is distributed nationwide by several companies, with more than a dozen brands of shampoo in the market. Shampoo is sold in sari-sari (sari-sari is a Filipino word meaning variety store) stores, drugstores, department stores, supermarkets, superettes or minimarts, beauty specialty shops, salons or beauty parlors, and megamalls. Its users, both male and female, young and old, come from all income levels.

In the subcategory of hair care products (from the class of personal care products), a companion item to shampoo was developed which was called hair conditioner or simply conditioner. Celia Torres, production manager of White Dove Philippines Company (WDPC), explained the distinction between the two: "Shampoo is a chemical preparation for cleaning scalp and hair, while a conditioner is a chemical preparation applied to hair to help restore the strength of, and give body to, hair."

This case was written by Professor Renato S. Esquerra, De La Salle University, Manila, Philippines.

The Company

The beginning of White Dove Philippines Company can be traced back to 1973. Koji Izumi, president of White Dove Company of Japan, was a visitor to the Philippines looking for a company that could be a distributor of his company's products. While he was having his hair cut in the barbershop of a five-star hotel in Manila, the brand of the barber's chair caught his eye. It was a very familiar brand: Nikko-Montand. He thought then that if the barber's chair could be sold here, then his White Dove shampoo also would find a good market here. In Japan, White Dove products had been extensively marketed through beauty salons. He sought the barber's help to locate the distributor of the Nikko-Montand barber's chair. The distributor was Leonardo Paras's Commercial Company, a firm engaged in the importation and distribution of barbershop and beauty shop equipment like steamers, hair dryers, shampoo bowls, chairs, and other accessories from Japan. Paras was an architect-businessman.

When they met, Izumi explained the purpose of his visit and quickly offered the distributorship of White Dove products in the Philippines to Paras. Izumi believed that, as a distributor of barbershop and beauty salon equipment and accessories, Paras's company would be the right organization to distribute White Dove products in the Philippines. Paras's immediate reaction to Izumi's offer was, "But I don't know anything about shampoo."

Izumi assured Paras of all technical assistance, as well as assistance in marketing and research. He invited Paras to Japan.

As an importer of Japanese products, Paras went to Japan every quarter. During one of those trips, he called on Izumi and was given a tour of the White Dove plant. Before leaving for Manila, Paras was given samples of White Dove products. Back home, he distributed the samples to beauty salons. Happily for him, the feedback from the beauty salon's owners and their customers was positive.

Research and Development

It took three years before White Dove Philippines Company became a licensee of White Dove Japan. WDPC was as interested and concerned as its Japanese licensor was in the production of hair care products of high quality and standards. Before the formulations were developed for the products to be marketed in the Philippines, samples of various types of water from many areas in the country were sent to Japan for testing and analysis. Specimens of Filipinos' hair strands were also collected for study. Since White Dove products' formulations were made for Asians, it was not necessary to test for sensitivity of the Filipinos' skin. However, in the matter of essence or scent, it was found that the Filipinos had a preference for stronger scent while the Japanese preferred a milder scent.

Thus, it was 1976 before White Dove Philippines Company officially started. Its first factory was a 60-square-meter backyard space at the Manila residence of Paras. It was there that its initial products—shampoo, rinse, and hair treatment—were packed. Packaging was done in plastic bottles made in the Philippines from molds lent by White Dove Japan.

After four years in Manila, the factory had to move to a suburban town to streamline its operation with modern machinery from Japan. That modernization increased WDPC's production tenfold. The installation of the machinery and the training of manufacturing

EXHIBIT 1   White Dove Philippines Company Print Media Advertising Expenditures[*] (in percent)

Publication	1989	1990	1991	1992[†]
Newspapers:				
Manila Bulletin	40%	35%	40%	40%
Philippine Daily Inquirer	15	20	15	15
The Philippine Star	5	5	5	5
Magazines:				
Mod	10	10	15	15
Woman Today	15	15	10	10
Miscellaneous	10	10	10	10
Women's Quarterly	5	5	5	5
Total	100%	100%	100%	100%

[*] In selected media only.
[†] Projected.

personnel was supervised by a Japanese technician. To assure that product quality standards set by the licenser were adhered to, White Dove Japan sent a chemist to WDPC every quarter to check on the formulations and the finished products.

Advertising and Promotion

The promotion of White Dove products started with free sampling in beauty salons. This was done in keeping with the system used by White Dove Japan. In Japan, White Dove products were classified as institutional products and sold to and at beauty salons, not directly to the consumer.

Sampling was followed by other promotional activities. A hairstyling show and seminar featuring a foreign hairdresser was held in a five-star hotel in Manila. It was attended by more than 1,000 amateur and professional hairdressers. The success of that promotional activity made White Dove Philippines Company a byword among hairdressers and beauty salon patrons.

Eventually, White Dove became a regular sponsor or cosponsor of hairstyling shows and competitions, and national and international beauty contests, and a regular exhibitor in cosmetics and beauty products' fairs. The Hair and Cosmetologists Association of the Philippines (HACAP) had become a regular beneficiary of White Dove's sponsorship of tie-in advertising and promotional shows.

Advertising of WDPC products had been limited to cinema advertising, radio, and print media. A larger bulk of its annual advertising budget, roughly four percent of its national annual sales, went to print media, specifically daily newspapers and weekly and monthly magazines, especially those read by women and young girls. (See Exhibit 1.)

White Dove had used more testimonial advertising than any other type. In its ads, professional hairdressers' photos, the names of shops, and their testimonials on White

---

EXHIBIT 2   White Dove Philippines Company's Other Hair Care Products (1992)

1. Avocado Cream Rinse
2. Lemon Cream Rinse
3. Hair Treatment Liquid
4. Hot Oil Treatment
5. Hair and Scalp Rejuvenator Tonic
6. Hair and Scalp Rejuvenator Tonic (with pump spray)
7. Fashionable Gel
8. Hair Styling Gel
9. Hair Spray
10. Styling Mousse

Dove's products were featured. The hairdressers were very happy about these testimonial ads, which they often posted in their shops for their customers to see. The success of White Dove's testimonial advertising eventually induced other shampoo manufacturers to do similar types of advertising.

To tap the retail market, WDPC set up display counters in selected department stores and supermarkets, especially in Metro Manila.

Distribution

The initial promotional sampling of WDPC products in beauty salons, hotels, and motels set the pace of the company's distribution. For several years, more than half of WDPC sales were made through these institutions. According to the WDPC marketing department, there were about 10,000 beauty shops in the Philippines in 1991. Twenty-five percent of them and their customers had been using WDPC products. One of the WDPC products contributed about 60 percent of the beauty salons' annual income, according to WDPC research department.

Beauty salons were classified into A, B, and Upper C as markets for WDPC products. Class A and B salons were usually bigger, had more personnel, were air-conditioned, offered more services than just hair trimming and styling, and carried inventory of WDPS products. Class A beauty salons carried an inventory of White Dove products worth P30,000 and up; Class B, P10,000 to P30,000; and Upper C, P3,000 to P10,000. (See Exhibit 2.)

The average annual sales of White Dove shampoo and conditioner during the period of 1989–1992 was P27,000,000. These figures represented about 40 percent of its national annual sales. (See Exhibit 3.) The remaining 60 percent represented sales of other WDPC products. According to the sales department of WDPC, its annual sales of shampoo and conditioner were roughly equal to about 5 and 4 percent, respectively, of the Philippine market.

EXHIBIT 3   White Dove Philippines Company Annual National Sales, 1989–1992 (in percent)

Area	1989	1990	1991	1992*
Greater Manila area	76.58%	76.31%	75.74%	67.58%
North Luzon	8.74	9.47	10.82	12.25
South Luzon	6.20	4.39	5.90	9.31
Visayas	7.63	8.20	5.16	7.03
Mindanao	.85	1.63	2.38	3.83
Total	100.00%	100.00%	100.00%	100.00%

* The 1992 figures were based on projections by the company.

EXHIBIT 4   White Dove Philippines Company's Suggested Retail Prices of Shampoo and Conditioner (1992)

	Bottle Size		
Product	100 ml	200 ml	600 ml
Avocado Oil Shampoo	P34.00	P59.50	P165.00
Lemon Shampoo*	31.00	54.00	148.00
Oil Shampoo	31.00	54.00	148.00
Treatment Shampoo	30.00	52.00	†
Treatment Conditioner	30.00	55.00	†
Balance Shampoo	†	52.00	†
All Over Bath Shampoo	(Sold in 175 ml size only for P29.00)		

* Also available in 1,000 ml. bottle for P195.00.
† Not available in this size bottle.

WDPC distributes its products nationwide through retail outlets which include supermarkets, department stores, drugstores, grocery stores, minimarts, superettes, beauty salons, and barbershops. These outlets are serviced by 11 sales representative and 16 distributors covering the retailers; seven sales representatives, six territorial representatives, and 18 subdistributors servicing the salons; and one corporate distribution outfit which serves as its marketing arm in the Metro Manila area.

Pricing

The pricing policy of White Dove had been governed by its Mission Statement. Each WDPC product was priced primarily for the A- and B-class market. However, according to Ruben Panlilio, White Dove's marketing director, the prices of WDPC products were set at a competitive level, allowing the company a fairly reasonable return on investment and a margin of profit. (See Exhibit 4.)

EXHIBIT 5   White Dove Philippines Company Mission Statement

White Dove Philippines Company will strive for leadership in the personal care products market by providing the best quality products, with particular emphasis on the products for the care of hair, to Philippine consumers, ensuring that any addition to the product line or mix offering will contribute desirably to the company's volume and market position and, ultimately, its profit standing.

New Products for White Dove Philippines Company

In early 1993, Ruben Panlilio, a retired Philippine marketing executive, accepted the invitation of Leonardo Paras, president and general manager of WDPC, to be its full-time marketing director.

Eighteen months earlier, WDPC had retained the personal services of Panlilio as marketing consultant on a part-time basis. During that period, Panlilio worked with Paras on the company's marketing operations. The latter had to oversee his company's marketing operations for lack of a senior marketing executive.

During Panlilio's part-time involvement, Paras had asked Panlilio to make a thorough study of the company's operations and submit his recommendations. It was after Paras had read Panlilio's report that he invited Panlilio to assume the post of marketing director.

One of Panlilio's recommendations was for WDPC to introduce new products to increase sales volume and improve its market position and profitability in pursuit of its corporate mission. (See Exhibit 5.) Two products were recommended by Panlilio. One was a hair cream that would serve as a quick setter and, at the same time, would work as a hair darkener whose effectiveness would be reached after repeated usage. The other was a combination shampoo and conditioner.

Paras and Panlilio both agreed that the two products would be launched in late 1994. Sometime in the middle of 1993, however, a multinational company launched a product described as "2-in-1," which was a combination of shampoo and conditioner. The introduction of the new product was heavily supported by mass-media advertising. Toward the end of the year, about six months after the launch of this new product, Paras called Panlilio to remind him about their meeting to finalize the plans for the two WDPC products' launch.

After receiving the call, Panlilio went over his files of the latest sales figures. The figures showed that the introduction of the 2-in-1 shampoo-conditioner of one of WDPC's competitors had not had any adverse effect on WDPC sales to its institutional customers, beauty salons. At the same time, the shampoo-conditioner's sales at the retail outlets had been increasing, and were, in Panlilio's view, threatening WDPC's sales to beauty salons. To him, it seemed that sales through retail outlets would far exceed sales to beauty salons, thus reversing the trend established over the past many years.

As Panlilio mulled over the market situation revealed by WDPC sales figures, the memory of his conversation with a White Dove Japan chemist, on his quarterly quality inspection trip to the Marikina plant, came to mind. The chemist had said, "Shampoo is shampoo, Panlilio-san, and conditioner is conditioner. We do not believe they should be mixed."

Panlilio was a liberal arts graduate of the University of Santo Tomas and had majored in literature. He thought that what the chemist said was something like a line from a poet's words, "East is East, and West is West, and never the twain shall meet." He stood up, gathered his files, walked out of the room, closed the door, and went down the passageway toward Paras's office, where they would review the WDPC planned launch of a 2-in-1 shampoo and a 2-in-1 hair cream.

CASE 3–4   Apex Chemical Company

The Executive Committee of Apex Chemical Company—a medium-sized chemical manufacturer with annual sales of $60 million—is trying to determine which of two new compounds the company should market. The two products were expected to have the same gross margin percentage. The following conversation takes place among the vice president for research, Ralph Rogovin, the vice president for marketing, Miles Mumford, and the president, Paul Prendigast.

VP-Research: Compound A-115, a new electrolysis agent, is the one; there just isn't any doubt about it. Why, for precipitating a synergistic reaction in silver electrolysis, it has a distinct advantage over anything now on the market.

President: That makes sense, Ralph. Apex has always tried to avoid "me too" products, and if this one is that much better . . . what do you think, Miles?

VP-Marketing: Well, I favor the idea of Compound B-227, the plastic oxidizer. We have some reputation in that field; we're already known for our plastic oxidizers.

VP-Research: Yes, Miles, but this one isn't really better than the ones we already have. It belongs to the beta-prednigone group, and they just aren't as good as the stigones are. We *do* have the best stigone in the field.

President: Just the same, Ralph, the beta-prednigones are cutting into our stigone sales. The board of directors has been giving me a going-over on that one.

VP-Marketing: Yes, Ralph, maybe they're not as good scientists as we are—or think we are—but the buyers in the market seem to insist on buying beta-prednigones. How do you explain that? The betas have 60 percent of the market now.

VP-Research: That's your job, not mine, Miles. If we can't sell the best product— and I can prove it *is* the best, as you've seen from my data and computations—then there's something wrong with Apex's marketing effort.

President: What do you say to that, Miles? What *is* the explanation?

VP-Marketing: Well, it's a very tricky field—the process in which these compounds are used is always touch-and-go; everyone is always trying something new.

VP-Research: All the more reason to put our effort behind Compound A-115, in the electrolysis field. Here we know that we have a real technical breakthrough. I agree with Paul that that's our strength.

President: What about that, Miles? Why not stay out of the dogfight represented by Compound B-227, if the plastic oxidizer market is as tricky as you say?

VP-Marketing: I don't feel just right about it, Paul. I understand that the electrolysis market is pretty satisfied with the present products. We did a survey and 95 percent said they were satisfied with the Hamfield Company's product.

President: It's a big market, too, isn't it, Miles?

VP-Marketing: Yes, about $10 million a year total.

President: And only one strongly entrenched company—Hamfield?

VP-Marketing: Yes, I must admit it's not like the plastic oxidizer situation—where there are three strong competitors and about a half-dozen who are selling off-brands. On the other hand, oxidizers are a $40 million market—four times as big.

President: That's true, Ralph. Furthermore our oxidizer sales represent 25 percent of our total sales.

VP-Research: But we've been losing ground the past year. Our oxidizer sales dropped 10 percent, didn't they, Ralph? While the total oxidizer market was growing, didn't you say?

VP-Marketing: Well, the electrolysis field is certainly more stable. Total sales are holding level, and as I said before, Hamfield's share is pretty constant, too.

President: What about the technical requirements in the electrolysis field? With a really improved product we ought to be able . . .

VP-Marketing: Well, to tell you the truth, I don't know very much about the kind of people who use it and how they . . . you see, it's really a different industry.

President: What about it, Ralph?

VP-Research: It's almost a different branch of chemistry, too. But I have plenty of confidence in our laboratory men. I can't see any reason why we should run into trouble . . . It really does have a plus-three-point superiority on a scale of 100—here, the chart shows it crystal clear, Miles.

VP-Marketing: But aren't we spreading ourselves pretty thin—instead of concentrating where our greatest know-how . . . You've always said, Paul, that . . .

President: Yes, I know, but maybe we ought to diversify, too. You know, all our eggs in one basket.

VP-Marketing: But if it's a good basket . . .

VP-Research: Nonsense, Miles, it's the kind of eggs you've got in the basket that counts—and Compound A-115, the electrolysis agent, is scientifically the better one.

VP-Marketing: Yes, but what about taking eggs to the market? Maybe people don't want to buy that particular egg from us, but they would buy Compound B-227—the plastic oxidizer.

President: Eggs, eggs, eggs—I'm saying to both of you, let's just be sure we don't lay any!

Source: Edward C. Bursk and Stephen A. Greyser, *Cases in Marketing Management,* 2nd ed. (Englewood Cliffs, NJ: Prentice Hall, 1975), pp. 204–7, 208–10. Reprinted by permission of Prentice Hall, Englewood Cliffs, NJ.

MARKETING PROGRAM DEVELOPMENT

Product, Branding, and Customer-Service Strategies

Few business decisions have such widespread influence on performance as do choices about new products and product improvements. These decisions cut across every functional area and affect all levels of an organization.

A look at Church & Dwight's product strategy is illustrative. Church & Dwight (C&D) is not a well-known household name but its popular baking soda (bicarbonate of soda) in the little yellow box can be found in the kitchen of most homes. Baking soda is used in several ways other than as a baking ingredient. Examples include cleaning teeth and as a freshener in refrigerators. In the 1980s C&D's management decided to launch a broad product strategy for bicarbonate of soda, intended to take advantage of the sales potential for industrial cleaners, baking soda toothpaste, laundry detergent, cat litter, carpet deodorizer, air freshener, and antiperspirant.[1] During the decade ending in 1992, the company's sales and profits more than tripled, and it had 60 percent of the world market, successfully competing against the French giant Rhône Poulenc and the U.S. FMC Corporation. By 1994 Arm & Hammer toothpaste held over a 40 percent share in the $300 million baking soda toothpaste market. C&D's 1994 sales totaled $491 million. The company's problems started in 1995. C&D's earnings fell 77 percent and its market shares of toothpaste and laundry detergent had major declines. Management tried to enter too many markets too fast. Faulty marketing decisions such as pricing toothpaste too high created problems competing against aggressive and experienced companies like Procter & Gamble, Colgate, and Unilever.

Developing and implementing product strategies require a variety of decisions like those confronting C&D. First we will examine product quality and competitive advantage, then we will discuss product portfolio analysis and strategy selection. Next, we will consider branding strategy. We will conclude the chapter with a discussion of customer service strategy.

PRODUCT QUALITY AND COMPETITIVE ADVANTAGE

"A product is anything that is potentially valued by a target market for the benefits or satisfactions it provides, including objects, services, organizations, places, people, and ideas."[2] This view of the product covers a wide range of situations, including both tangible goods and intangible services. Thus, political candidates are products, as are travel services, medical services, refrigerators, gas turbines, and computers.

Services differ from physical products in several ways. A service is intangible.[3] It cannot be placed in inventory; the service is consumed at the time it is produced. There is often variability in the consistency of services rendered. Services are often linked to the people who produce the service. Establishing a brand image for a service requires association with the tangible components that produce the service or are somehow related to the service. The use of well-known personalities in the advertisements of the American Express Card is illustrative.

First, we will look at the relationship between product quality and cost, then describe the elements that make up a quality improvement strategy. Next, we will discuss how influences other than the product affect product success. Finally, we will examine marketing's role in product strategy.

Product Quality and Cost Relationship

Improving product and service quality is a critical competitive challenge facing companies competing in the global marketplace.[4] Product quality improvement reduces cost and increases competitive advantage. The successful adoption of a customer-driven organizational strategy is essential for improving product quality.

The experience of the Japanese shows that high product quality creates a sustainable competitive advantage, providing there is a continuing organizational commitment to quality improvement. Improving all processes of the business increases the uniformity of the products produced, reduces rework and mistakes, and reduces waste of manpower, machine-time, and materials usage.[5] These improvements lead to productivity gains, lower costs, better competitive position, and job satisfaction. The benefits of improving product quality contradict the view widely held in the United States during the 1970s and 1980s that high quality requires higher costs. The traditional and contemporary total quality management (TQM) views of quality are compared in Exhibit 9–1.

Executives generally agree that quality improvement is essential to competing in global markets. The success of the Japanese in penetrating world markets has created a need to reduce major quality gaps in the products produced by U.S. and European manufacturers. Increasingly, companies are implementing total business strategies to increase quality, productivity, and customer-perceived value.

EXHIBIT 9–1   Two Views of Quality

Traditional View
- Productivity and quality are conflicting goals.
- Quality is defined as conformance to specifications or standards.
- Quality is measured by degree of nonconformance.
- Quality is achieved through inspection.
- Some defects are allowed if the product meets minimum quality standards.
- Quality is a separate function and focused on evaluating production.
- Workers are blamed for poor quality.
- Supplier relationships are short-term and cost-oriented.

Total Quality Management View
- Productivity gains are achieved through quality improvements.
- Quality is conformance to correctly defined requirements satisfying user needs.
- Quality is measured by continuous process/product improvement and user satisfaction.
- Quality is determined by product design and is achieved by effective process controls.
- Defects are prevented through process-control techniques.
- Quality is part of every function in all phases of the product life cycle.
- Management is responsible for quality.
- Supplier relationships are long-term and quality-oriented.

Source: V. Daniel Hunt, *Quality in America* (Burr Ridge, IL: Irwin Professional Publishing, 1992), p. 76.

Quality Improvement Strategy

Successfully implementing TQM requires developing a quality culture, focusing on managing business processes (rather than functions), and applying statistical methods to monitor and improve product and supporting service quality.

Quality Culture.   Analysis of successful business strategies for improving product and service quality indicates that a corporate culture committed to product quality and a participative management philosophy involving everyone in the organization are essential success factors. Quality improvement is the responsibility of everyone in the organization. Essential managerial style and leadership characteristics in developing a quality-oriented culture include attention to detail, complete planning, problem monitoring, high personal standards, ongoing commitment to quality improvement, responsive and participative management style, and trustworthiness.[6]

Process View of the Business.   In addition to a favorable corporate culture, the various processes of the organization (e.g., new-product planning, customer service) are managed by the people that participate in each process. The quality improvement approach to business operations centers on defining and analyzing the various processes that create business results. For example, processes manufacture products, create new product designs, market products, and provide customer service and other results essential to the functioning of the business. Importantly, the focus of the organization shifts from specialized functions to team-oriented multifunctional processes.

As an illustration, consider the process that produces a small kitchen appliance. Several factors contribute to the quality of the final product, including the production equipment, workers, product design, materials, and supervision. The objective is to define the overall process and various subprocesses that produce, distribute, and service products. Once it is clear how the process works, attention is directed to improving it.

Statistical Methods.   The last part of the product quality improvement strategy is using statistical quality control concepts and methods to analyze, control, and improve the business's processes. Process control charts and other methods help to analyze the processes of the business, identifying process changes that will improve product quality. Quality improvement professionals indicate that much of the potential for improvement comes from changing the processes of the business rather than trying to improve the outputs of a given process.

Product Success Depends on Other Influences

Products are essential to execute a business strategy, but they alone do not guarantee successful performance. It is necessary to match the firm's products with market needs. Consider, for example, the difference in the sales performance of the Plymouth Laser and the Mitsubishi Eclipse sports coupes. These cars are identical in design. Both are produced by Diamondstar Motors (equal partnership between Chrysler and Mitsubishi).[7] In 1990 Laser sales averaged 13 cars per dealer compared to 100 cars per Eclipse dealer. The Japanese quality image may help explain Eclipse's high sales, but Mitsubishi also used a more effective marketing strategy. Both brands targeted women but different positioning strategies were employed. Mitsubishi launched an earlier and more focused advertising program. The Eclipse was positioned as a woman's car, using a symbolic positioning concept—the "in" car to own. Contests encouraged aerobics students to take test drives. This experience suggests that a high-quality product alone cannot achieve management's performance goals and must be matched with other key business and marketing strategies.

Competitive pressures and the changing needs and wants of buyers help to explain why many companies devote a lot of attention to planning the product portfolio. Product strategies are often a key component in top management's plans for improving the performance of a business. Actions may include modifying products, introducing new products, and eliminating products. Some examples of product decisions are shown in Exhibit 9–2.

Marketing's Role in Product Strategy

Marketing management has three major responsibilities in the organization's product strategy. First, market sensing is needed at all stages of product planning, providing information for matching new-product ideas with consumer needs and wants. The knowledge, experience, and marketing research methods of marketing professionals are

---

EXHIBIT 9–2   Illustrative Product Decisions and the Strategy Implications

Decision	Strategic Implications of the Decision
Coca-Cola's withdrawal of Classic (old) Coke from the market.	Coca-Cola's market share was threatened by Pepsi. On the basis of extensive favorable taste tests of a new, sweeter formula, old Coke was replaced by new Coke. Loyal old Coke consumers revolted and management reintroduced old Coke as Classic Coke. By later 1985 the old formulation was outselling new Coke by a substantial margin.
Hewlett-Packard's introduction of the DeskJet printer in the early 1990s.	HP relentlessly pursues a product strategy that offers both value and cost advantages to customers.
Gillette's introduction of the Sensor razor in 1988.	The new razor was an awesome market success and was followed by the Sensor for Women.
The Beef Industry Council's marketing strategy to promote beef consumption.	Responding to declining per capita consumption of beef, advertising, public relations, and product development activities were launched during the 1980s to increase the demand for beef.

---

essential in product strategy development. Customer and competition information is needed in finding and describing unmet needs, in evaluating products as they are developed and introduced, and in monitoring the performance of existing products.

The Global Feature describes the differences in customer preferences for various products in Europe and highlights the need for market sensing. Several methods of product evaluation and testing are available in the marketing professional's portfolio of techniques. They are discussed in this and the previous chapter.

Marketing's second responsibility in product strategy concerns product specifications. Increasingly, top management is looking to marketing executives in identifying the characteristics and performance features of products. Information about customers' needs and wants is translated into specifications for the product. The customer is the cornerstone of TQM. Matching customer needs with product capabilities is essential in designing and implementing successful product strategies. Quality function development, discussed in Chapter 8, offers one approach for translating customer requirements into product design guidelines.

The third responsibility of marketing in product strategy is guiding target-market and program-positioning strategies. These decisions are often critical to the success of both new and existing products. Since the choice of product specifications and positioning are very much interrelated, product positioning needs to be considered at an early stage in the product planning process. Positioning decisions may include a single product or brand, a line of products, or a mix of product lines within a strategic business unit.

Product decisions affect all businesses, including suppliers, producers, wholesalers, distributors, and retailers. While many of these decisions involve the evaluation, selection, and dropping of products that are developed by manufacturers, intermediaries may also develop new products and services. For example, Boston Chicken, the popular fast-food chain, became Boston Market in 1995, offering an expanded menu. The new

---

GLOBAL FEATURE   Where "European" Customers Fit

It is useful to determine the geographical market in which a company competes. The diagram below shows five different positions ranging from local (e.g., Parisian bakery shop) to globalization (e.g., Airbus Industrie large commercial aircraft).

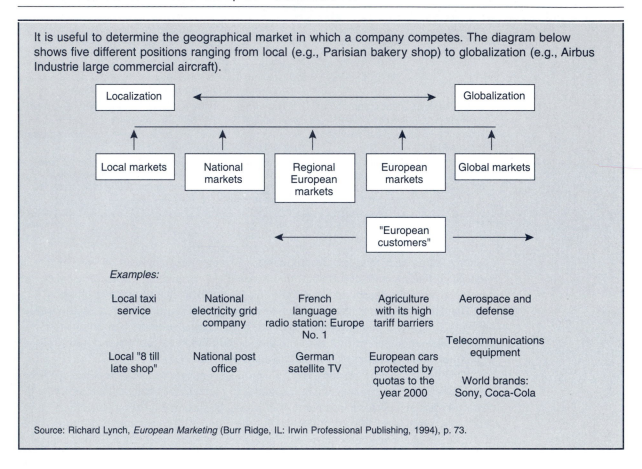

Source: Richard Lynch, *European Marketing* (Burr Ridge, IL: Irwin Professional Publishing, 1994), p. 73.

---

logo also included "Home Style Meals" instead of "Rotisserie." The purpose of the new product strategy is to offer customers a more extensive range of entrée choices.

MANAGING EXISTING PRODUCTS

The products that make up the product portfolio of a company may consist of a single product, a product line, or a mix of product lines. In the discussion of managing existing products, we assume that product strategy decisions are being made for a strategic business unit (SBU). The product composition of the SBU is determined by one or more product lines and by the specific product(s) that make up each line. The SBU may have a single product or single line or various lines and specific products within each line.

EXHIBIT 9–3   Tracking Product Performance

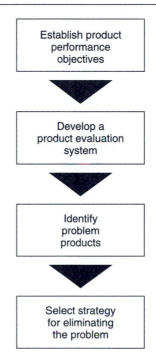

Evaluating the performance of the product portfolio helps guide strategies for new products, product modification, and product elimination. Consider, for example, the competitive battle for the leading position in the $1 billion U.S. toothpaste market. Procter & Gamble's Crest brand, the market leader, was attacked in 1980 with sweet-tasting gels and pump dispensers.[8] Crest's share declined from double Colgate's market share to only 3 percent above Colgate's 28 percent by 1985. Colgate's strategy was to overtake Crest with Dentagard, launched in 1985 with a $30 million marketing budget. Colgate's introduction of a gel form of toothpaste, ahead of P&G, also helped narrow the share gap between the two brands. P&G should have reacted earlier to competitive threats from gels and pumps. P&G countered with an aggressive product and advertising strategy. Crest's market share in 1992 was about 31 percent compared to Colgate's 22 percent. Colgate lost market share to the new market entrant, the Arm & Hammer brand, which held the third largest share position.

Analysis Objectives

Evaluating existing products requires tracking the performance of the various products in the portfolio, as shown in Exhibit 9–3. We first need to establish the criteria and acceptable levels of performance for gauging product performance. Criteria may include both financial and nonfinancial factors. Because of the demand and cost interrelationships among products, it is important to sort out the sales and costs attributable to each product to show how well it is doing. The purpose of the tracking system is to maintain a product review process that will spot problem products. The information from the analysis also helps management decide how to eliminate the problem.

An interesting application of portfolio analysis is the pricing and yield management system used by American Airlines to evaluate route performance and service strategies. Each route (e.g., Los Angeles–D/FW) is a unit in the route portfolio. Using data based on performance, forecasts of demand, competition, and other strategic and tactical considerations, the airline makes decisions to expand, reduce, or terminate service throughout the route network.

We will look at product life cycle analysis, product portfolio analysis, and positioning analysis to illustrate how to diagnose product performance and how to identify product strategy alternatives.

Product Life Cycle Analysis

In Chapter 6 we described the major stages of the product life cycle (PLC): introduction, growth, maturity, and decline. Relevant issues in PLC analysis include:

- Determining the length and rate of change of the product life cycle.
- Identifying the current PLC stage and selecting the product strategy that corresponds to that stage.
- Anticipating threats and finding opportunities for altering and extending the PLC.

Rate of Change.   Product life cycles are becoming shorter for many products due to new technology, rapidly changing preferences of buyers, and intense competition. A clothing style may last only one season, whereas a new commercial aircraft may be produced for several years. Determining the rate of change of the PLC is important because management needs to adjust its marketing strategy to correspond to the changing conditions.

Failure to respond to life cycle changes eventually led to bankruptcy for Smith Corona Corporation in the mid-1990s. It was one of the last American typewriter makers.[9] The threat of personal computers might have been anticipated, considering the rapid growth of the computer market since the early 1980s. Perceptive market sensing would have alerted Smith Corona's management about the need to develop a product strategy to counter the threat.

Stage and Strategy Identification.   The PLC stage of the product has important implications regarding all aspects of targeting and positioning (see Chapter 6). Four strategy phases are encountered in moving through the PLC, as shown in Exhibit 9–4. These guidelines illustrate the changing focus of marketing strategy over the PLC. In the first stage the objective is to establish the brand in the market through brand development activities such as advertising. In the growth stage the brand is reinforced through

---

EXHIBIT 9–4   Illustrative Product Strategy at Each PLC Stage

---

Marketing strategy considerations	Types of brand strategies			
Type	Brand development	Brand reinforcement	Brand repositioning	Brand modification
Objectives	Establish market position	Expand target market	Seek new market segments	Prepare for reentry
Product strategy	Assure high quality	Identify weaknesses	Adjust size, color, package	Modify features
Advertising objectives	Build brand awareness	Provide information	Use imagery to differentiate from competitors	Educate on changes
Distribution	Build distribution network	Solidify distribution relationships	Maintain distribution	Reestablish and deliver new version
Price	Skimming or penetration strategy	Meet competition	Use price deals	Maintain price
Phase in life cycle	**Introduction**	**Growth**	**Maturity**	**Decline**

Source: Adapted from Ben M. Enis, Raymond La Grace, and Arthur E. Press, "Extending the Product Life Cycle," *Business Horizons* 20 (June 1977), p. 53. Copyright 1977 by the Foundation for the School of Business at Indiana University. Reprinted by permission.

---

marketing efforts. During the maturity stage, product repositioning efforts may occur by adjusting size, color, and packaging to appeal to different market segments. Finally, during the decline stage the features of the product may be modified.

Analysis of the growth rate, sales trends, time since introduction, intensity of competition, pricing practices, and competitor entry/exit information are useful in PLC position analysis. Identifying when the product has moved from growth to maturity is more difficult than determining other stage positions. Analysis of industry structure and competition helps in estimating when the product has reached maturity.

PLC Planning Model.   Some progress has been made in predicting the sales volume of a product class and identifying the factors that influence the shape and amplitude of the volume projections.[10] A PLC model has been developed for short- and long-range planning for housewares and consumer electronics goods. While the model is intended for use in evaluating new-product development projects, the approach can also predict the PLC of an existing product. Estimating the timing and magnitude of turning points of a successful product introduction is one application of the model.

The planning model forecasts sales volume by combining estimates of original purchases and replacements.[11] Original purchases are estimated using three predictor variables: (1) consumer needs and wants, (2) number of competitors, and (3) amount of advertising and promotional effort (industry total). Replacement estimates are a function of the product's useful life, the percentage of owners who will replace it, the trade-off of repair versus replacement, and the level of the initial purchases. The validity tests of model predictions against actual PLCs indicate a close correspondence between PLC shapes.

Product Portfolio Analysis

Product portfolio analysis considers whether each product is measuring up to management's minimum performance criteria, and assesses the strengths and weaknesses of the product relative to other products in the portfolio. The comparative analysis of products can be performed by using the grid methods for SBU evaluation (Chapter 2). These grids highlight differences among products. After identifying the relative attractiveness and business strength of the products in the portfolio, analysis of specific performance factors may also be useful, including: profit contribution; barriers to entry; sales fluctuations; extent of capacity utilization; responsiveness of sales to prices, promotional activities, and service levels; technology (maturity, volatility, and complexity); alternative production and process opportunities; and environmental considerations.[12]

Positioning Brands

Perceptual maps are useful in comparing brands. Recall our discussion of these methods in earlier chapters. The map is developed by obtaining preference information on a set of competing brands or firms from a sample of buyers. Various product attributes are used, and the results are summarized by the preference map.

Competitive mapping analysis offers useful guidelines for strategic product positioning. The analyses can relate buyer preferences to different brands and indicate possible brand repositioning options. New-product opportunities may also be identified through the analysis of preference maps. These are shown by preferences that are not satisfied by the existing brands. Positioning studies over time can measure the impact of repositioning strategies.

Other Product Analysis Methods

The financial analysis tools in the Appendix to Chapter 1 are used to evaluate product financial performance. Other product analysis methods include research studies that show the relative importance of product attributes to buyers and rate brands against these attributes. This information indicates brand strengths and weaknesses. Many of the standardized information services provided by marketing research firms, such as Information Resources, Inc. and A. C. Nielsen Company, are useful in monitoring the market performance of competing brands of food and drug products. Industry trade publications also publish market share and other brand performance data.

A major consideration when introducing new products that meet needs similar to those met by a firm's existing brands is estimating how much sales volume the new product will attract from one or more existing brands. Such cannibalization may reduce the contribution of the new product to the overall performance of the product portfolio. For example, Gillette's Sensor razor offered a possible cannibalization threat to Atra and Trac II sales.[13] Gillette's plan was to target disposable users, recognizing that some cannibalization would occur. Also, the Sensor blades were priced about 25 percent higher than Atra. Since both Atra and Trac II were in the mature stages of their life cycles, the new brand was needed to hold Gillette's position in the market. The Sensor performed even better than the sales and profit forecasts made by Gillette's management. The Sensor for Women, introduced in 1992, gained the leading market position in women's razors.

DEVELOPING PRODUCT STRATEGIES

The portfolio analysis determines how well existing product strategies are performing. This information helps management to identify new product needs, and it points to where existing product strategies should be altered.

Brands that have been successful over a long time period offer useful insights about product strategies. Established brands like Coca-Cola, Levi's, Budweiser, and Hershey continue to build strong market positions. These good performance records are the result of: (1) marketing skills, (2) product quality, and (3) strong brand preference developed through years of successful advertising.[14] The financial value (brand equity) of the well-respected brand names of RJR Nabisco, Kraft, and Pillsbury made these firms very attractive takeover candidates in the 1980s. Kohlberg Kravis Roberts & Co. paid $25 billion in 1989 to acquire RJR Nabisco, Inc. The brand equity that has been developed for the company's many famous brands is a valuable asset. A common characteristic of many enduring brands is that the targeting and positioning strategy initially selected has generally been followed during the life of each brand. "These brands haven't strayed much from the basic marketing strategies that made them stars."[15] We will discuss brand equity in the next section.

The evidence suggests that selecting and implementing good product strategies pays off. Research findings indicate that the leading brands are 50 percent more profitable than their nearest competitors.[16] Developing product strategies includes decisions for each product, product line, and the product mix, as shown in Exhibit 9–5. Product-line actions may consist of adding a new product, reducing cost, improving the product, altering marketing strategy, and dropping a product. Product mix strategy may involve adding a product line, deleting a line, or changing the priority of a line (e.g., increasing the marketing budget for one line and cutting the budget for another line). We will now look at the nature and scope of these decisions.

Strategies for Existing Products

Eastman Kodak Company has tried for many years to take market share from Fuji Photo Film Company.[17] Compared to Fuji's 75 percent share, Kodak has an 8 percent share of the Japanese film market. In 1995 Kodak changed its product strategy by offering a

---

EXHIBIT 9–5 Product Strategies

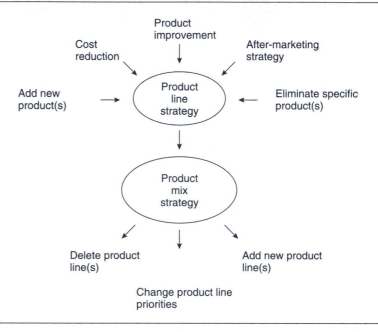

---

private-label film, "COOP," sold in 2,500 stores of the Japanese Consumer Cooperative Union. Pricing was an estimated 38 percent below the comparable Fuji and Kodak brands. The danger in the new strategy is the possible cannibalization of Kodak film sales. Since private-label brands are relatively new in Japan, Kodak's management apparently believes the rewards of the product strategy exceed the risks. Interestingly, Kodak also released a 300-page report alleging that Fuji was blocking Kodak's access to distribution channels in Japan. Fuji's management countered with claims that the charges were untrue and self-serving. Observers indicate that Fuji's share in Japan is similar to Kodak's in the U.S. and indicate that Kodak was slow to cut prices, did not adopt Japanese distribution methods, and was slow in new-product introduction.

Once the need to change the strategy of an existing product is identified, there are several options for responding to the situation (Exhibit 9–5). We will discuss each strategy to indicate the issues and scope of the action.

Cost Reduction. We know that low costs give a company a major advantage over the competition. Recall our discussion in Chapter 2 of gaining competitive advantage through lower costs than the competition. As an illustration, Nabisco's Ritz cracker was introduced in 1934 and is today the best-selling cracker in the world.[18] Nearly 16 billion crackers are sold each year, generating $150 million in sales. The original ingredients are essentially the same today as they were 60 years ago. In addition to a flavor that has wide appeal, Ritz's low price compared to other types of crackers gives it a major competitive advantage. Ritz's high-volume production helps to keep costs low. A product's cost may be reduced by changes in its design, manufacturing improvements, reduction of the costs of supplies, and increases in marketing productivity.

Product Improvement.   Products are often improved by changing their features, quality, and styling. Automobile features and styles are modified on a continuing basis. Many companies allocate substantial resources to the regular improvement of their products. Compared to a decade ago, today's products, such as disposable diapers, cameras, computers, and consumer electronics, show vast improvements in their performance and features.

One way to differentiate a brand against competition is with unique *features*. Another option is to let the buyer select the features desired in a product. Optional features offer the buyer more flexibility in selecting a brand. This strategy is used by manufacturers employing mass customization strategies. The capability to produce products with varied features that appeal to market diversity is an important competitive advantage. Japanese automobile manufacturers have plants that can economically produce smaller unit volumes than U.S. producers. This advantage can be used to meet the specific needs of the different market segments targeted by the firm.

An important strategy for increasing competitive advantage is *quality* improvement. As discussed earlier in the chapter, companies are adopting total quality management as a basic business strategy. For example, an international study of quality management practices conducted by Ernst & Young and the American Quality Foundation found that "virtually every organization in the sample believes that quality is a critical factor in its strategic performance."[19] The sample included more than 500 businesses in Canada, Germany, Japan, and the United States.

Despite the probably greater importance of product quality, *style* may offer an important competitive edge for certain products. Moreover, style may serve as a proxy for quality in some product categories. Seiko has very effectively used style (and other features) to make its watches attractive to buyers. The many different styles offered by Seiko allow consumers a wide range of choice. Other examples of product style strategies include Ethan Allen in furniture, Lexus in automobiles, and Escada in women's clothing. Ethan Allen concentrates on one style, traditional American furniture. Lexus has created a strong customer preference for its European style luxury autos. Escada A. G. offers a variety of high priced women's apparel using its different labels. The Global Feature looks at competitive challenges in fashion design.

Marketing Strategy Alteration.   Some changes in market targeting and positioning are often necessary as a product moves through its life cycle. Problems or opportunities may point to adjusting marketing strategy during a PLC stage. For example, Grand Metropolitan PLC faced a major challenge in turning around the Green Giant Company, acquired in the late 1990s with the purchase of Pillsbury Company.[20] Management moved out of food processing using strategic alliances to reduce inventories and fixed manufacturing expenses. These changes provided money for product development and marketing. The results have been favorable. Green Giant's 1994 sales were an estimated $900 million worldwide. By 1995 Green Giant had a 21 percent market share for frozen

---

GLOBAL FEATURE   Competitive Challenges in the Fashion Design Industry

---

France, the center of fashion design for a century, is loosing its leadership position.

Industry observers say French design has become outdated and is being challenged by German, Italian, and United States designers.

One authority predicts that half of the remaining 18 French couture houses will be closed in a few years.

French designers were complacent and did not respond to changing preferences and lifestyles, weakened their brand names through extensive licensing, and encountered innovative competitors like Armani, Escada, Prada, and Donna Karan.

Savvy competitors market to both affluent and middle-class consumers, allocating large promotion budgets to building brand image.

The new designers target professional women who want comfortable, understated clothing and accessories.

French designers continue to dominate markets in Asia (40% of their revenues).

Source: Teri Agins, "Not So Haute," *The Wall Street Journal,* August 29, 1995, pp. A1 and A8.

---

vegetables compared to Birds Eye's 14 percent. In 1988 both brands held nearly equal 16 percent shares. Research and development is being directed to value-added frozen items such as Rice Accents—a mixture of rice, vegetables, and seasonings.

Product Elimination.   Dropping a problem product may be necessary when cost reduction, product improvement, or marketing mix alteration strategies are not feasible. In deciding to drop a product, management may consider a variety of performance criteria in addition to the product's sales and profit contribution. Elimination may occur at any PLC stage, although it is more likely to be considered in either the introduction or decline stages. Management may decide to halt production and sell off its existing inventory or to try to sell the product(s) to another company. Sales of entire lines to other companies occurred during the 1980s and 1990s: Black & Decker purchased General Electric's small household appliance lines, and a French computer firm purchased Zenith's computer business.

Environmental Effects of Products.   Environmental issues about product labeling, packaging, use, and disposal need to be considered in the marketing strategies of most companies. Protection of the environment involves a complex set of trade-offs among social, economic, political, and technology factors. Companies like McDonalds, Procter & Gamble, Rubbermaid, and many others incorporate environmental considerations into their product strategies. Moreover, these environmental issues are global in scope.

Many of the environmental issues and concerns are very complex and may require consumers to change their use and disposal behavior. Even the technical authorities do not always agree on the extent to which environmental problems exist or how to solve the problems. Nevertheless, many companies, governments, and special-interest groups are proactively working toward reducing environmental contamination.

Product Mix Modifications

Adding a new line of products to the product mix is a major product strategy change. The motivation for changing the product mix may be:

- Increasing the growth rate of the business.
- Offering a complete range of products to wholesalers and retailers.
- Gaining marketing strength and economies in distribution, advertising, and personal selling.
- Capitalizing on an existing brand position.
- Diversifying to avoid dependence on one product area.

The product mix may be expanded through internal development or by purchase of an entire company or a line of products. Purchase was a popular option in the 1990s because, in effect, stock market prices were lower than the costs of internal development. Acquisition also offers a faster means of expanding the product mix. Strategic alliances among competitors are used for gaining access to new markets and expanding product lines. These collaborative relationships have escalated in importance during the 1990s (see Chapter 7).

Product mix changes are not always successful. In the early 1990s the Quaker Oats Company made several changes in its product portfolio that were costly, failed to meet the expectations of management, and raised questions as to whether the product strategy was in the interests of the company. The product changes are described in the Product Feature.

Who Manages Products?

Responsibility for product strategy extends to several organizational levels. We will look at three product management levels that often exist in companies that have strategic business units, different product lines, and specific brands within lines.

Product/Brand Management.   This activity consists of planning, managing, and coordinating strategy for a specific product or brand. These responsibilities include market analysis, targeting, positioning strategy, product analysis and strategy, identification of new product needs, and management and coordination of product/brand marketing activities. Marketing plans for specific products or brands are often prepared at this level. Product or brand managers, typically, do not have authority over all product management activities. Nevertheless, they do have product responsibility. These managers are sponsors or advocates of their products, negotiating on behalf of their products with the sales force, R&D, operations, marketing research, and advertising support managers.

Product Group/Marketing Management.   A business with several products or brands may assign responsibility for managing its product or brand managers to a product director, group manager, or marketing manager. This person coordinates the activities and approves the recommendations of a group of product or brand managers. The nature and scope of the group responsibilities are similar to those of product/brand managers. Additionally, the product group manager coordinates product management activities and decisions with the SBU management.

PRODUCT FEATURE   Quaker Oats' Product Mix Challenges

Quaker acquired Snapple Beverage Corporation in 1994 for $1.7 billion. To help pay for the purchase Quaker sold U.S. and European pet food lines and some other small-volume lines.

The intent was to strengthen the Gatorade beverage line. Coca-Cola and PepsiCo, Inc., are aggressively competing against both lines, cutting Quaker's sales and profits.

Initial plans to integrate the distribution of Gatorade into the Snapple system did not work out. The margins for Gatorade were too low for the 300 distributors who deliver to retail stores (Gatorade goes to warehouses).

Some observers question Quaker's sale of pet food product lines with annualized earnings of $110 million while the acquired Snapple lines are expected to contribute only $12 million in 1995.

Quaker has reduced delivery time to Snapple distributors from three weeks to three days and has the top 50 linked by computer. Quaker spent 26% of total sales on advertising and merchandising in 1995.

Retail distribution of Snapple is being expanded, taste improvements have been made, and the number of flavors reduced.

Snapple and Gatorade account for 40 percent of Quaker's sales. Distributors appear positive about the actions underway to build Snapple's market position.

Sources: Richard Gibson, "At Quaker Oats, Snapple Is Having a Bad Aftertaste," *The Wall Street Journal*, August 7, 1995, p. B4; and Zina Moukheiber, "He Who Laughs Last," *Forbes*, January 1, 1996, pp. 42–43.

Product Mix Management.   Normally, this responsibility is assigned to the chief executive at the SBU or corporate level of an organization or to a team of top executives (see the Quaker Oats Product Feature). Illustrative decisions include product acquisitions, R&D priorities, new-product decisions, and resource allocation. Evaluation of product portfolio performance is also centered at this level. In a corporation with two or more SBUs, top management may coordinate and establish product management guidelines for the SBU management. We will look at the organization of marketing activities in Chapter 14.

By the mid-1990s many companies were reevaluating the traditional approaches to managing products. The changes were particularly apparent in fast-moving consumer goods as described below:[21]

- Unilever's British soap unit and Elida Gibbs' personal products division eliminated their marketing director positions.

- Marketing and sales groups were combined and focused on consumer research and product development.

- Customer development teams were formed to work with retailers across all of the companies' brands.

Similar changes are being made by other companies to integrate sales, marketing, and other business functions into multidisciplinary teams. A study by the Boston Consulting Group indicated that 90 percent of the responding companies have restructured their marketing departments.

EXHIBIT 9–6   Alternative Branding Strategies

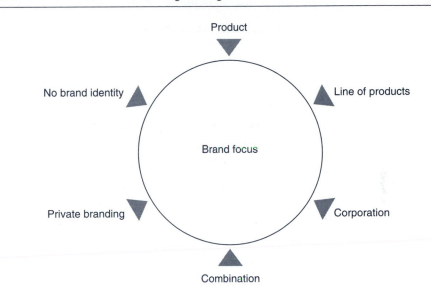

BRANDING STRATEGY

A strong brand image offers an organization several important advantages. The brand name distinguishes the product from competitors' products. A powerful brand identity creates a major competitive advantage. A brand that is recognized by buyers encourages repeat purchases. Because of these advantages for more than a decade the Korean consumer electronics company LG Electronics, Inc. (formerly Gold Star Company), has worked to increase its brand image and awareness with American consumers.[22] In 1995 it acquired Zenith Electronics Corp., the U.S. television maker. While Zenith had been losing money since 1984, the brand offers LG Electronics a quality image and strong brand loyalty by consumers.

One of several brand strategy options may be appropriate for a company. We will look at the features of each strategy, followed by a section highlighting the strategic advantages of brand identity.

Branding Strategies

The major branding strategy alternatives are shown in Exhibit 9–6. Branding applies to services as well as physical products. There are many examples of strong brand images for services, including American Express, American Airlines, Citibank, Marriott, and United Parcel Service (UPS).

No Brand Identity.   Many small- and medium-sized manufacturers do not have an established brand identity even though the company name is printed on the package or item. The lack of financial resources and marketing capabilities make it difficult for a small firm with an unknown brand to build buyer awareness in the marketplace. Major expenditures are required to introduce and promote the brand. A firm in this situation often relies on wholesalers or retailers to encourage buyers to purchase its brand. Buyers associate the unknown brand to the intermediaries that carry the brand. Typically, the producer of an unknown brand concentrates its marketing efforts on wholesalers and retailers rather than end-users. These products may develop consumer loyalty over time if the users' experiences with the product are favorable and if it is purchased frequently. Even if a firm does not have the resources to aggressively promote a brand, it should use a brand name for the product, particularly if the item is repurchased on a continuing basis. Favorable use experience and word-of-mouth promotion with friends will help to build the brand's reputation with buyers.

Private Branding.   Retailers with established brand names, such as The Limited, Target, and Wal-Mart Stores, Inc., contract with producers to place the retailers' brands on the products manufactured. Called private branding, the major advantage to the producer is eliminating the costs of marketing to end-users, although a private-label arrangement makes the manufacturer dependent on the firm using the private brand. Producing private-label merchandise for a single company is risky since the arrangement may be terminated by the buyer. Nevertheless, the arrangement can yield benefits to both the producer and middleman. The sales volume of the producer is expanded rapidly. The retailer uses its private brand to build store loyalty, since the private brand is associated with the retailer's stores. Private brands are often profitable for retailers. For example, the profit margins of the private brands carried by supermarkets typically run 10 percent to 15 percent higher than other brands.[23] Private brands account for about 13 percent of total sales in supermarkets.

Corporate Branding.   This strategy builds brand identity using the corporate name to identify the entire product offering. Examples include IBM in computers, AT&T in communications, and Detroit Diesel in truck engines. Corporate branding has the advantage of using one advertising and sales promotion program to support all of the firm's products. It also simplifies the promotion of new products. The shortcomings of corporate branding include a lack of focus on specific products and the adverse effects on the product portfolio if the company encounters negative publicity for one of its products. Using corporate branding as a primary approach to branding is appropriate when it is not feasible to establish specific brand identity and when the product offering is relatively narrow.

Product-Line Branding.   This strategy places a brand name on a line of related products. Hartmarx, a mens' apparel producer, has several brands of men's suits, such as Austin Reed. Product-line branding provides more focus than corporate branding, and offers cost advantages by promoting the entire line rather than each product. This strategy is effective when a firm has one or more lines, each of which represents an interrelated

---

EXHIBIT 9–7   Annual Advertising Expenditures for Various Brands ($ millions)

American Express	$107
CitiBank	89
Healthy Choice	24
Huggies	30
Pert Plus	21
Plax	21
Tylenol	134

Source: "Superbrands 1991," *AdWeek Marketing Week.*

offering of product items. Timberland, for example, is marketed as a line of apparel rather than establishing a brand identity for each item in the line.

Specific Product Branding.   The strategy of assigning a brand name to a specific product is used by various producers of frequently purchased items, such as Procter & Gamble's Crest toothpaste, Pampers diapers, and Ivory soap. The brand name on a product gives it a unique identification in the marketplace. A successful brand develops a strong customer loyalty over time. Products that are low-involvement purchases benefit from a popular brand name. The major limitation of using brand names on individual products is the expense of building and supporting each brand through advertising and sales promotion. One danger is that the brand name may be so popular that it becomes a generic term for the product type. When this happens the company may loose its brand name. Companies work aggressively to avoid this and other misuses of their popular brand names. The annual advertising expenditures for several specific brands are shown in Exhibit 9–7. Building a new brand name through advertising initially can cost over $50 million, plus the expense of maintaining the brand identity in the market place.

Combination Branding.   A company may use a combination of the branding strategies shown in Exhibit 9–6. Sears, for example, employs both product-line and corporate branding (e.g., the Kenmore appliance and Craftsman tool lines). The Rolex brand name identifies the line of watches while each item in the line also has a name (e.g., the Rolex Daytona). Combination branding benefits from the buyer's association of the corporate name with the product or line brand name. However, corporate advertising may not be cost-effective for inexpensive, frequently purchased consumer brands. For example, companies like Procter & Gamble and Cheesebrough-Ponds (Vaseline, Q-Tips) do not actively promote the corporate identity.

Brand Equity

Recognizing the value (equity) of a brand name and managing the name to gain maximum competitive advantage for the owner of the name are very important. "Brand equity is a set of brand assets and liabilities linked to a brand, its name, and symbol that add to or subtract from the value provided by a product or service to a firm and/or to that firm's customers.''[24] The assets and liabilities that impact brand equity include brand loyalty, name awareness, perceived quality and other brand associations, and proprietary brand assets (e.g., patents).

The possible inclusion of brand equity values on balance sheets is the subject of considerable debate. The intent is to show a brand's financial worth. Several methods for valuation have been proposed. One method is momentum accounting, which considers how the earning power of the brand changes over its life cycle because of the revenues and expenses associated with the brand:

> Momentum accounting uses functions similar to depreciation curves in conventional accounting to monitor the sources of change in brand value over time. Momentum accounting tries to capture managers' intuition about the reasons for momentum change in terms of "impulses"— the marketing, competitive, and environmental events that affect a brand's value.[25]

Young & Rubicam (Y&R) has developed a brand evaluation tool, Brand Asset Valuator (BAV).[26] The technique uses the brand's vitality (relevance and differentiation) and brand stature (esteem and familiarity) to gauge the health of the brand. Y&R conducted studies with 30,000 consumers and 6,000 brands in 19 countries in 1993–94. Brands with high differentiation include Disney, Jaguar, and Victoria's Secret. AT&T and Kodak fall into the high-relevance category. Brands with high esteem include Band-Aid and Rubbermaid, while Coca-Cola and Kellogg's fall into the high-familiarity category.

How to measure equity and whether or not to include its value on the balance sheet continue to be discussed. Nevertheless, the attention given to brand equity has increased executives' recognition of the power and value of brand names and the importance of managing brand equity over the life cycle of the brand.

Leveraging Brand Identity

Established brand names may be useful in introducing other products by linking the new product to an existing brand name. A brand name that is familiar to many buyers can be used to identify other products in a company's portfolio. The primary advantage is immediate name recognition for the new product. Two methods of capitalizing on an existing brand name are brand extension and licensing.

Brand Extension. This approach uses consumers' familiarity with an existing brand name in a product class to launch a new product line in another product class.[27] The new line may or may not be closely related to the brand from which it is being extended. Examples of related extensions include Ivory shampoo and conditioner, Hershey chocolate milk, and Swiss Army watches (see accompanying advertisement).

Critics of brand and line extensions indicate that extensions often do not succeed and may damage the mother product.[28] They argue that a brand name is weakened when it stands for two things. For example, some observers have questioned Procter & Gamble's use of the Duncan Hines brand image to launch its bagged cookies because certain ads encourage using baking mixes while others promote purchase of ready-made cookies.

Regardless of the possible dangers of brand extension, it continues to be used. Two considerations are important. First, there should be a logical tie between the core brand

Courtesy of The Forschner Group; photography by John Manno.

and the extension. It may be a different product type while having some relationship to the core brand. For example, the Swiss Army knife brand was used to introduce Swiss Army watches. Second, the extension needs to be carefully evaluated as to any negative impact on the brand equity of the core brand.

Licensing.   Another popular method of using the core brand name is licensing. The sale of a firm's brand name to another company for use on a noncompeting product is a major business activity. Total retail sales of licensed products were estimated at $75 billion in 1990.[29] Apparel and accessories account for 38 percent of licensed products followed by 19 percent of toys and games, 12 percent of publishing and stationery, and 11 percent of gifts and novelties. The firm granting the license obtains additional revenue with only limited costs. It also gains free publicity for the core brand name. The main limitation is that the licensee may create an unfavorable image for the brand. Licensing may be used for corporate, product-line, or specific brands. Anheuser-Busch Companies, Inc. (Budweiser beer), is one of the largest corporate licensors.

Variations in Brand Loyalty. Brand loyalty varies across consumer products, as Exhibit 9–8 shows. Loyalty to brands is stronger for products that have distinctive flavors.[30] Some erosion of brand loyalty may have occurred during the 1980s. Heavy promotional programs, bargain prices, and nutritional and environmental concerns caused consumers to shift brands. A *Wall Street Journal* survey of 2,000 consumers in 1989 found that over 12 percent of those responding are not brand-loyal for *any* of the products shown in Exhibit 9–8. Nearly half of them are loyal for one to five of the categories. Brand loyalty also varies by age. Apparently older buyers display stronger preference toward specific brands.

CUSTOMER-SERVICE STRATEGY

Customer service is an important and sometimes neglected part of product strategy. We define customer service and discuss the responsibility for this product function in the organization.

Defining Customer Service

The activities included in customer service are requests for product specifications such as performance data, requests for quotation, purchase order processing, order status inquiries, and warranty service.[31] As shown in Exhibit 9–9, customer service involves many functions in the organization. A major problem in providing effective services is coordinating the activities of the various functions. This array of product and supporting services must be managed to achieve high levels of customer satisfaction. Various attributes of customer service may be important depending on the type of product and requirements of specific customers. Customer services enhance the value of products to the customer.

Responsibility for Customer Service

An important factor in effectively managing customer service is viewing it as a major part of marketing strategy. It is necessary to define the internal processes that impact customer service, establish service objectives, develop and manage strategies for providing services, and assign responsibilities for customer service. The fragmentation of service activities in many companies is described:

> The different activities required to develop and process an order, typically, have no one function or manager responsible for overseeing all the required activities. The closest thing to an order overseer in many companies is the formal customer-service staff, which usually plays a reactive role to customer complaints and has little actual authority to expedite or alter the flow of an order.[32]

EXHIBIT 9–8 Brand Loyalty by Product Category

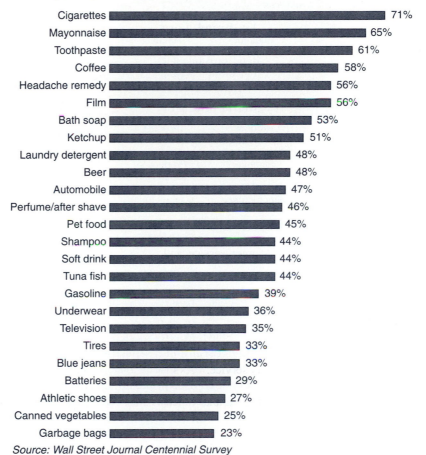

Percentage of users of these products who are loyal to one brand

Product	Percentage
Cigarettes	71%
Mayonnaise	65%
Toothpaste	61%
Coffee	58%
Headache remedy	56%
Film	56%
Bath soap	53%
Ketchup	51%
Laundry detergent	48%
Beer	48%
Automobile	47%
Perfume/after shave	46%
Pet food	45%
Shampoo	44%
Soft drink	44%
Tuna fish	44%
Gasoline	39%
Underwear	36%
Television	35%
Tires	33%
Blue jeans	33%
Batteries	29%
Athletic shoes	27%
Canned vegetables	25%
Garbage bags	23%

Source: Wall Street Journal Centennial Survey

Source: Ronald Alsop, "Brand Loyalty Is Rarely Blind Loyalty," *The Wall Street Journal,* October 19, 1989, p. B1. Reprinted by permission of *The Wall Street Journal,* © 1989 Dow Jones & Company, Inc. All Rights Reserved Worldwide.

Creating an integrated and coordinated customer service strategy requires developing plans and budgets, measuring performance, and assigning responsibility for service. Customer service needs to be part of the marketing strategy of the organization and to involve the various business functions whose activities impact customers.

Customer service responsibility is often assigned to the salesforce or to a marketing staff unit which processes customer inquires and complaints. A better approach is to develop strategies (and priorities) for service, assigning responsibility to the various functions involved in providing service. Customer service is a process of activities that add value to the buyer–seller relationship. The process must be defined, analyzed, and managed with the objective of improving customer satisfaction.

EXHIBIT 9–9   Customer Service Involves Most Functions in an Organization

---

Customer

Activities:

Request for specs	Request for quotation	Purchase order	Order status inquiry	Warranty service

Functions involved:

Sales	Sales	Sales	Sales	Sales
Product management	Product management	Order entry	Order entry	Customer service
Finance	Production scheduling	Production scheduling	Production scheduling	Field engineering
Manufacturing	Manufacturing	Warehousing/ billing	Warehousing/ shipping	
Engineering	Warehousing/ billing			
	Finance/ billing			

Source: Frank V. Cespedes, "Once More: How Do You Improve Customer Service?" *Business Horizons,* March–April 1992, p. 61.

A major benefit of customer service is the opportunity to develop a database to aid product design and marketing.[33] One estimate indicates that companies will spend over $1 billion on customer service computers and information processing technology in 1995. These systems can alert companies to product defects and other customer problems. For example, Whirlpool has information on 15 million customers and over 20 million installed appliances.

SUMMARY

Product strategy, which sets the stage for selecting strategies for each of the remaining components of the positioning strategy, forms the leading edge of the strategy. Product strategy is matched to the right distribution, pricing, and promotion strategies. Product decisions shape both corporate and marketing strategies, and are made within the guidelines of the corporate mission and objectives. The major product decisions for a strategic business unit include selecting the mix of products to be offered, deciding how to position an SBU's product offering, developing and implementing strategies for the products in the portfolio, selecting the branding strategy for each product, and planning and implementing customer service strategies.

The importance of product quality to competing in global markets requires the development of an organizational philosophy and management process for improving quality.

Quality is the responsibility of everyone in the organization. Competitive advantage in the 1990s depends on the success of the company's product quality improvement and cost reduction. Quality improvement involves developing a philosophy toward product quality, implementing quality improvement programs, and applying statistical methods to improve business processes.

Evaluating a company's existing products helps to establish priorities and guidelines for managing the product portfolio. These methods include the analysis of the product life cycle, portfolio screening, positioning analysis, and financial analysis. It is necessary to decide for each product (1) whether a new product should be developed to replace or complement the product; (2) whether the product should be improved (and, if so, how); or (3) whether the product should be eliminated. Product strategy alternatives for the existing products include cost reduction, product alteration, marketing strategy changes, and product elimination. Product mix modification may also occur.

Most successful corporations have found that an individual or organizational unit should be assigned responsibility for product planning. The approaches that are used range from a committee to a product-planning department. Product managers for planning and coordinating product activities are used by many companies.

Branding strategy involves deciding among private branding, corporate branding, product-line branding, specific-product branding, and combination branding. Brand equity is an important asset which needs to be protected and developed over time. Brand identification in the marketplace offers a firm an opportunity to gain a strategic advantage through brand extension and licensing.

Finally, the influence of customer service on the buyer–seller relationship must be recognized. It is often neglected or treated in a fragmented manner in many organizations. Customer service is a process; it involves most of the functions in an organization. Competitive advantage can be gained by developing an integrated and coordinated customer service strategy, assigning responsibility for the activities, and involving the various functions in providing services.

QUESTIONS FOR REVIEW AND DISCUSSION

1. Eli Lilly & Company manufactures a broad line of pharmaceuticals with strong brand positions in the marketplace. Lilly is also a manufacturer of generic drug products. Is this combination branding strategy a logical one? If so, why?

2. Discuss the advantages and limitations of following a branding strategy of using brand names for specific products.

3. In 1985 Philip Morris Incorporated acquired General Foods Company. Discuss the advantages and limitations of acquiring a company in order to obtain its established brand names.

4. To what extent are the SBU strategy and the product strategy interrelated?

5. Suppose that a top administrator of a university wants to establish a product-management function covering both new and existing services. Develop a plan for establishing a product-planning program.

6. Many products like Jell-O reach maturity. Discuss several ways to give mature products new vigor. How can management determine whether it is worthwhile to attempt to salvage products that are performing poorly?

7. How does improving product quality lower the cost of producing a product?

8. Why do some products experience long successful lives while others have very short life cycles?

9. Discuss why it is important to coordinate the organization's customer service functions.

NOTES

1. This illustration is based on Meera Somasundaram, "Missteps Mar Church & Dwights' Plans," *The Wall Street Journal,* April 28, 1995, p. B5A; Gabriella Stern, "Baking-Soda Toothpaste Gains Popularity," *The Wall Street Journal,* December 28, 1993, p. B6; and Peter Nulty, "No Product Is Too Dull to Shine," *Fortune,* July 27, 1992, pp. 95–96.

2. David W. Cravens, Gerald E. Hills, and Robert B. Woodruff, *Marketing Management* (Burr Ridge, IL: Richard D Irwin, 1987), p. 375.

3. Leonard Berry, "Services Marketing Is Different," *Business,* May–June 1980, pp. 24–30.

4. The following discussion is based on David W. Cravens, Charles W. Holland, Charles W. Lamb, Jr., and William C. Moncrief III, "Marketing's Role in Product Service/Quality," *Industrial Marketing Management,* November 1988, pp. 285–303.

5. W. Edwards Deming, *Quality, Productivity, and Competitive Position* (Cambridge, MA: Massachusetts Institute of Technology, Center for Advanced Engineering Study, 1982).

6. Frank S. Leonard and W. Earl Sasser, "The Incline of Quality," *Harvard Business Review,* September–October 1982, pp. 163–71.

7. John Harris, "Advantage Mitsubishi," *Forbes,* March 18, 1991, pp. 100, 104.

8. Kathleen Deveny, "Colgate Puts the Squeeze on Crest," *Business Week,* August 19, 1985, pp. 40 and 41; and "Toothpaste Makers Tout New Packaging," *The Wall Street Journal,* November 10, 1992, pp. B1, B10.

9. Jonathan Auerbach, "Smith Corona Files under Chapter 11; Typewriter Maker Loses Ground to PCs," *The Wall Street Journal,* July 6, 1995, p. C11.

10. Steven G. Harrell and Elmer D. Taylor, "Modeling the Product Life Cycle for Consumer Durables," *Journal of Marketing,* Fall 1981, pp. 68–75.

11. Ibid., pp. 70–71.

12. George S. Day, "Diagnosing the Product Portfolio," *Journal of Marketing,* April 1977, p. 37.

13. Lawrence Ingrassia, "Face-Off: A Recovering Gillette Hopes for Vindication in a High-Tech Razor," *The Wall Street Journal,* September 29, 1989, pp. A1, A4.

14. Ronald Alsop, "Enduring Brands Hold Their Allure by Sticking Close to Their Roots," *The Wall Street Journal,* Centennial Edition, pp. B4 and B5.

15. Ibid.

16. Ibid.

17. Wendy Bounds, "Kodak Pursues a Greater Market Share in Japan with New Private Label Film," *The Wall Street Journal,* March 7, 1995, p. B11; *"Shuttered," The Economist,* August 5, 1995, pp. 59–60.

18. "If It's Not Broken, Don't Fix It," *Forbes,* May 7, 1984, p. 132.

19. American Quality Foundation and Ernst & Young, *International Quality Study,* 1991, p. 4.

20. Richard Gibson, "How Grand Met Made Ailing Green Giant Jolly Again," *The Wall Street Journal,* June 6, 1995, p. B4.

21. "Death of the Brand Manager," *The Economist,* April 9, 1994, pp. 67–68.

22. Steven P. Galante, "Korea's Gold Star Is Banking on Quality to Build an Image in the U.S. TV Market," *The Asian Wall Street Journal,* November 26, 1984, p. 12; Steve Glain, "New Look LG Tunes in to Faster Times," *The Wall Street Journal,* August 8, 1995, p. A6.

23. Alix M. Freedman, "Supermarkets Push Private-Label Lines," *The Wall Street Journal,* November 15, 1988, p. B1.

24. David A. Aaker, *Managing Brand Equity* (New York: Free Press, 1991), p. 15.

25. Peter H. Farquhar, Julie Y. Han, and Yuji Iiri, "Brands on the Balance Sheet," *Marketing Management,* Winter 1992, p. 19.

26. Chip Walker, "How Strong Is Your Brand," *Marketing Tools,* January/February 1995, pp. 46–53.

27. Aaker, *Managing Brand Equity,* p. 208.

28. Ronald Alsop, "Firms Unveil More Products Associated with Brand Names," *The Wall Street Journal,* December 13, 1984, p. 31.

29. Joanne Y. Cleaver, "Licensing: Starring on Marketing Team," *Advertising Age,* June 6, 1985, pp. 15–16.

30. Ronald Alsop, "Brand Loyalty Is Rarely Blind Loyalty," *The Wall Street Journal,* October 19, 1989, p. B1.

31. Frank Cespedes, "Once More: How Do You Improve Customer Service?" *Business Horizons,* March–April 1992, pp. 61–62.

32. Ibid., p. 62.

33. John W. Verity, "The Gold Mine of Data in Customer Service," *Business Week,* March 21, 1994, pp. 113–14.

CHAPTER

10

Distribution Strategy

The channel of distribution connects suppliers and producers with the end-users of goods or services. An effective and efficient distribution channel provides the member organizations with an important strategic edge over competing channels. Distribution strategy concerns how a firm reaches its market targets. While some producers market their products directly to the end-users of goods and services, many others move their products through one or more channels of distribution. Various independent channel intermediaries (e.g., wholesalers, retailers) perform the necessary distribution functions.

Escada A.G. is a leading producer of high-fashion women's apparel.[1] The German company experienced rapid growth during the last decade. Escada's success in the marketplace is based on aggressive distribution combined with stylish designs. It is vertically integrated from manufacturing to retailing. Escada's designs offer far more variety than its competitors', many colors remain constant so that customers can add to their wardrobes each year. Escada's 40 automated factories in Bavaria produce 6 million items of clothing each year at very short lead times. Satisfied customers cite high-quality workmanship and attention to detail as key features of Escada garments. Escada distributed its products initially in the United States through department stores and boutique retailers. The company's current retail strategy of distribution in its own stores, department stores and boutiques, and Escada factory outlets is a major concern with its independent retailers. For example, in New York an Escada boutique is located in the same block with Bergdorf Goodman and Saks Fifth Avenue, which have Escada departments. These and other retailers helped to build the Escada brand name and are now competing with the apparel producer. Management has major plans to open

Courtesy of Escada.

company-owned stores in the United States and around the world. Twelve Escada boutiques were opened in the United States during the early 1990s (see accompanying Escada apparel advertisement).

While some manufacturers distribute direct to consumer or organizational end-users using a company sales force, many producers use marketing intermediaries to perform all or part of the distribution functions. A good distribution strategy requires a penetrating analysis of the available alternatives in order to select the most appropriate channel network. Channel-of-distribution decisions are important to organizations in a wide range of industries. A company's channel strategy may involve: (1) developing and managing the channel or (2) gaining entry into a particular channel by a producer, wholesaler, or retailer.

We will first look at the role of distribution channels in marketing strategy and discuss several channel strategy issues. Next, we will examine the process of selecting the type of channel, determining the intensity of distribution, and choosing the channel configuration of organizations. This will be followed by a discussion of managing the distribution channel. Finally, we will look at distributing through international channels.

STRATEGIC ROLE OF DISTRIBUTION

A good distribution network creates a strong competitive advantage for an organization. For example, international airlines are adopting collaborative distribution strategies by forming strategic partnerships to gain market access, share reservation codes, coordinate

---

EXHIBIT 10−1 Basic Channels of Distribution

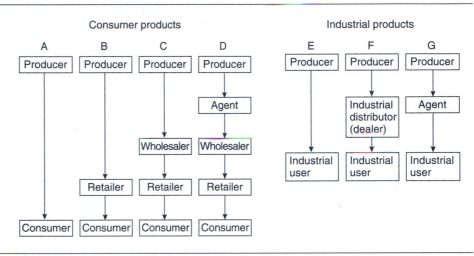

Source: Paul S. Busch and Michael J. Houston, *Marketing* (Burr Ridge, IL: Richard D. Irwin, 1985), pp. 458−59.

---

marketing activities, and utilize partners' travel routes. A strategic alliance between KLM Royal Dutch Airlines and Northwest Airlines has been very successful. The distribution relationship resulted in 1995 estimated profits of $150 million.[2] The alliance enabled the two airlines to gain an additional 350,000 passengers a year. It is one of over 400 in the international airline industry, an increase of 200 since 1990. The benefits include offering seamless routing between international locations, better equipment utilization, airport access, reduced capital expenditures, and expanded market coverage.

The airline alliance illustration highlights the importance of distribution strategy in business performance and also shows that distribution strategy is relevant to companies distributing services as well as goods. First, we will describe the distribution functions in the channel and then discuss distribution for services. Finally, we will examine several factors affecting the choice of whether to use distribution channels.

Distribution Functions

The *channel of distribution* is a network of organizations performing functions that connect the producer to the end-users. The distribution channel consists of *interdependent* and *interrelated* institutions and agencies, functioning as a system or network, who cooperate in their efforts to produce and distribute a product to end-users. Thus, hospitals, ambulance services, physicians, test laboratories, insurance companies, and drugstores make up a channel of distribution for health care services.[3] Examples of channels of distribution for consumer and industrial products are shown in Exhibit 10−1. In addition to the intermediaries that are shown, many facilitating organizations perform services. These specialists include financial institutions, transportation firms, advertising agencies, and insurance firms.

Several functions are necessary in moving products from producers to end-users. *Buying and selling* activities by marketing intermediaries reduce the number of transactions for producers and end-users. *Assembly* of products into inventory helps to meet buyers' time-of-purchase and variety preferences. *Transportation* eliminates the locational gap between buyers and sellers, thus accomplishing the physical distribution function. *Financing* facilitates the exchange function. *Processing and storage* of goods involves breaking large quantities into individual orders, maintaining inventory, and assembling orders for shipment. *Advertising and sales promotion* communicate product availability, location, and features. *Pricing* sets the basis of exchange between buyer and seller. *Reduction of risk* is accomplished through mechanisms such as insurance, return policies, and futures trading. *Communications* between buyers and sellers include personal selling contacts, written orders and confirmations, and other information flows. Finally, *servicing and repairs* are essential for many types of products.

Major factors in channel strategy are deciding the functions that are needed and which organizations will be responsible for each function. Middlemen offer important cost and time advantages in the distribution of a wide range of products. Steel service centers illustrate functional specialization.[4] These firms buy steel coil or bar in bulk from steel producers. They cut and shape the steel at lower costs than the producers, and the centers can react more quickly than steel mills to customer needs. This responsiveness helps reduce the buyer's inventory. These cost-effective middlemen are expected to continue to take over more processing of bulk steel from producers.

When first selecting a channel of distribution for a new product, the pricing strategy and desired positioning of the product may influence the choice of the channel. For example, a decision to use a premium price and a symbolic positioning concept calls for retail stores that buyers will associate with this image. Escada's entry into the U.S. high-fashion women's apparel market was enhanced by selecting department stores and specialty retailers with prestigious images.

Once the channel-of-distribution design is complete and responsibilities for performing the various marketing functions are assigned, these decisions establish guidelines for pricing, advertising, and personal selling strategies. For example, the manufacturers' prices must take into account the requirements and functions of middlemen as well as pricing practices in the channel. Likewise, promotional efforts must be matched to the various channel participants' requirements and capabilities. Consumer-products manufacturers often direct advertising to consumers to help *pull* products through distribution channels. Alternatively, promotion may be concentrated on middlemen to help *push* the product through the channel. Intermediaries may also need help in planning their marketing efforts and other supporting activities.

Channels for Services

Services such as air travel, banking, entertainment, health care, and insurance often involve distribution channels. The service purveyor renders the service to the end-users rather than it being produced like a good and moved through marketing intermediaries to the end-user. Because of this the distribution networks for services differ somewhat from those used for goods. While channels for services may not require as many levels (e.g., producer, distributor, retailer), the network may actually be more complex.

A look at the distribution channels for commercial air travel services highlights several of the characteristics of channels for services. While the airline produces the services, it works with several distribution partners. Tickets may be obtained from independent travel agencies, from airline ticket offices, by telephone, and special group arrangements. Airlines have cooperative arrangements with hotel chains, car rental companies, and tour groups. Airline sales forces may call on large corporate customers and other partners. Credit card companies offer charge services and may participate with the airlines' frequent flier programs. Alliances with other airlines may extend a carrier's geographical coverage, as illustrated by the KLM and Northwest Airlines strategic alliance.

The objectives of channels for services are similar to those for goods. Nonetheless, the functions performed in channels differ somewhat from those for goods. Services are normally rendered when needed rather than placed into inventory. Similarly, services may not be transported, although the service provider may go to the user's location to render the service. Processing and storage, normally, are not involved with services. Servicing and repair functions may not apply to many services. The other functions previously discussed apply to both goods and services, such as buying and selling, financing, advertising and sales promotion, pricing, reduction of risk (e.g., lost baggage insurance), and communications.

Several previous independent service providers are becoming part of coordinated distribution networks. Moving into previously fragmented industries, corporate and contractual chains have emerged in medical and dental services, lawn care (ChemLawn), travel services (American Express), real estate brokerage, and office supplies (Office Depot). These efficient marketing systems are affecting the performance of small independent retailers. Similar consolidations have occurred in public accounting and marketing research services.

Direct Distribution by Manufacturers

We will consider channel of distribution strategy from a manufacturer's point of view, although many of the strategic issues apply to firms at any level in the distribution channel—wholesale or retail. Manufacturers are unique because they have the option of going directly to end-users through a company salesforce or serving-end users through marketing intermediaries. Manufacturers have three distribution alternatives: (1) direct distribution, (2) use of intermediaries, or (3) situations in which both (1) and (2) are feasible. The factors that influence the distribution decision include buyer considerations, product characteristics, and financial and control factors.

Buyer Considerations.   Manufacturers look at the amount and frequency of purchases by buyers, as well as the margins over manufacturing costs that are available to pay for direct selling costs. Customers' needs for product information and applications assistance may determine whether a company salesforce or independent marketing intermediaries can best satisfy buyers' needs. Substantial differences in the size and the requirements of the end-user buyers may suggest using two or more distribution channels.

The personal computer (PC) industry is an interesting illustration of the role of distribution in gaining access to end-users. Tandy's Radio Shack retail distribution network gave the firm an early competitive edge when the PC market was first developing. Selling to consumers and small business users required retail outlets. IBM had to create a distribution network for its successful PC line, introduced in 1981. An industry shakeout began in early 1984, when IBM's production of PCs caught up with demand and the company started broadening its distribution channels.[5] IBM also uses its salespeople to push the computers through channels and to make direct contact with large corporate buyers. Several retail chains developed to meet the distribution needs of PC producers. By the mid-1990s competition was intense at both the manufacturing and retail levels of PC channels. Retailers were going after business buyers to survive. This required developing salesforces to make calls on large- and medium-sized business firms. Both businesses and individuals had many options for the purchase of PCs.

Product Characteristics.   Manufacturers often consider product characteristics in deciding whether to use a direct or distribution-channel strategy. Complex products and services often require close contact between customers and the producer, who may have to provide application assistance, service, and other supporting activities. For example, chemical-processing equipment, mainframe computer systems, pollution-control equipment, and engineering-design services are often marketed directly to end-users via company salesforces. Another factor is the range of products offered by the manufacturer. A complete line may make company distribution economically feasible, whereas the cost of direct sales for a single product may be prohibitive. High-volume purchases may make direct distribution feasible for a single product. Companies whose product designs change because of rapidly changing technology often adopt direct-sales approaches. And qualified marketing intermediaries may not be available, given the complexity of the product and the requirements of the customer. Direct contact with the end-user provides feedback to the manufacturer about new-product needs, problem areas, and other concerns.

Financial and Control Considerations.   Some producers do not have the financial resources to market direct to their end-users. Others are unwilling to make large investments in field salesforces and service facilities. It is necessary to decide if resources are available and, if they are, whether selling direct to end-users is the best use of the resources. Both the costs and benefits need to be evaluated. Direct distribution gives the manufacturer control over distribution, since independent organizations cannot be managed in the same manner as company employees. This may be an important factor to the manufacturer.

An example shows how problems may develop with channel members when the producer changes its marketing strategy. Procter & Gamble launched a new strategy in 1991 intended to "reshape the supermarket pricing system and wean Americans off bargain bonanzas and rich coupons."[6] Rather than discounting a product at different times during the year, P&G offers constant list prices that are 8 to 25 percent lower than in the past. Wholesalers and retailers did not like the change. Apparently, P&G implemented the new strategy without holding discussions with its major channel customers. The former trade discounts were significant. Industrywide, the discounts totaled more than $36 billion in 1991, exceeding advertising spending. Two years after

---

EXHIBIT 10–2 Factors Favoring Distribution by the Manufacturer

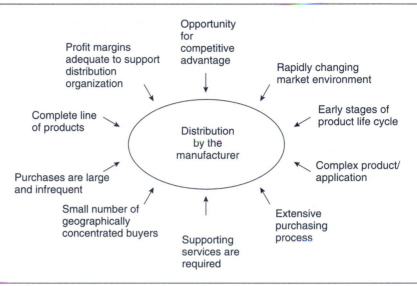

---

implementing the new strategy, it was apparent that the change was successful in improving P&G's market performance.

Exhibit 10–2 highlights several factors favoring distribution by the manufacturer. A firm's financial resources and capabilities may also be important considerations. The producers of business and industrial products are more likely than producers of consumer products to utilize company distribution to end-users. This is achieved by a network of company sales offices and a field salesforce or by a vertically integrated distribution system (distribution centers and retail outlets) owned by the manufacturer. The producer may utilize independent middlemen to avoid consuming extensive financial resources and to gain the benefits of the experience and skills of the channel organizations.

CHANNEL OF DISTRIBUTION STRATEGY

The steps in the channel of distribution strategy include (1) determining the type of channel arrangement, (2) deciding the intensity of distribution, and (3) selecting the channel configuration (Exhibit 10–3). First we will consider various objectives that may underlie the decision to form or join a channel network. We will then look at each step, indicating decisions to be made, important issues, and examples.

Channel Objectives

Management may seek to achieve one or more objectives using the channel of distribution strategy. While the primary objective is gaining access to end-user buyers, other objectives may also be important, as shown in Exhibit 10–4. These include gaining promotional support,

EXHIBIT 10-3   Steps in Channel Strategy Selection

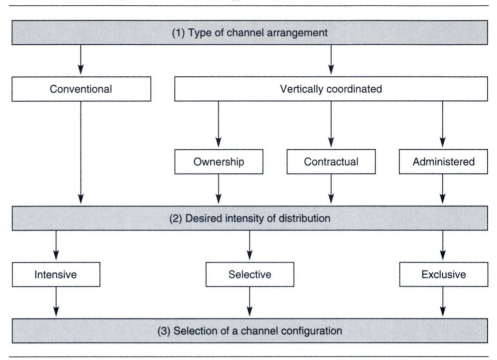

providing customer service, obtaining market information, and gaining favorable revenue/ cost performance.

Type of Channel

The major types of channels are conventional channels and vertical marketing systems (VMS). The conventional channel of distribution is a group of vertically linked independent organizations, each trying to look out for itself, with little concern for the total performance of the channel. The relationships between the channel participants are rather informal, and the members are not closely aligned with each other. The focus of the channel organizations is on buyer–seller transactions rather than collaboration.

The second type of distribution channel is the vertical marketing system. Marketing executives in an increasing number of firms realize the advantages to be gained by managing the channel as a coordinated or programmed system of participating organizations. These vertical marketing systems dominate the retailing sector and are significant factors in the business and industrial products and services sectors. Vertical marketing systems are

> professionally managed and centrally programmed networks preengineered to achieve operating economies and maximum market impact. Stated alternatively . . . vertical marketing

---

EXHIBIT 10–4   Distribution Channel Objectives and Measurement Criteria

Performance Objective	*Possible Measures*	*Applicable Product and Channel Level*
Product Availability		
• Coverage of relevant retailers	• Percent of effective distribution	• Consumer products (particularly convenience goods) at retail level
• In-store positioning	• Percent of shelf-facings or display space gained by product, weighted by importance of store	• Consumer products at retail level
• Coverage of geographic markets	• Frequency of sales calls by customer type; average delivery time	• Industrial products; consumer goods at wholesale level
Promotional Effort		
• Effective point-of-purchase (P-O-P) promotion	Percent of stores using special displays and P-O-P materials, weighted by importance of store	• Consumer products at retail level
• Effective personal selling support	• Percent of salespeoples' time devoted to product; number of salespeople receiving training on product's characteristics and applications	• Industrial products; consumer durables at all channel levels; consumer convenience goods at wholesale level
Customer Service		
• Installation, training, repair	• Number of service technicians receiving technical training; monitoring of customer complaints	• Industrial products, particularly those involving high technology; consumer durables at retail level
Market Information		
• Monitoring sales trends, inventory levels, competitors' actions	• Quality and timeliness of information obtained	• All levels of distribution
Cost-Effectiveness		
• Cost of channel functions relative to sales volume	• Middlemen margins and marketing costs as percent of sales	• All levels of distribution

Source: Harper W. Boyd, Jr., Orville C. Walker, Jr., and Jean-Claude Larréché, *Marketing Management,* 2nd ed. (Burr Ridge, IL: Richard D. Irwin, 1995), p. 332.

EXHIBIT 10–5 Illustrative Vertical Marketing Systems*

	Product/Service	
	Consumer	*Industrial*
Ownership	The Bombay Company (furniture)	Vallen Corporation (industrial safety equipment)
	The Gap (retail)	
Contractual	Ethan Allen, Inc. (furniture)	Snap-On Tools, Inc. (mechanics' tools)
	Wendy's International, Inc. (fast foods)	Deere & Company (farm equipment)
Administered	Procter & Gamble (health and beauty aids)	Johnson & Johnson (health care products)
	Wal-Mart (discount goods)	Loctite Corp. (industrial adhesives)

*Several of the companies fall into more than one of the categories.

systems are rationalized and capital-intensive networks designed to achieve technological, managerial, and promotional economies through the integration, coordination, and synchronization of marketing flows from points of production to points of ultimate use.[7]

A key characteristic of a VMS is the management (or coordination) of the distribution channel by one organization. Programming and coordination of channel activities and functions are directed by the firm that is the channel manager. Operating rules and guidelines indicate the functions and responsibilities of each participant. Management assistance and services are supplied to the participating organizations by the firm that is the channel leader.

There are three types of vertical marketing systems: *ownership, contractual,* and *administered.* A single firm in the channel may own all of the participating organizations in the channel. Alternatively, the contractual VMS establishes formal operating arrangements between channel participants. Finally, in an administered channel, one firm manages the channel by exerting power and influence rather than by ownership or contractual ties. The administrator may be a producer, and its product line(s) comprise only a portion of the products moving through one or more channels. For example, Procter & Gamble is the channel administrator for many of its brands. A marketing intermediary like Wal-Mart may be the channel administrator, coordinating channel activities with various suppliers and performing its own distribution and retailing functions.

Examples of companies using vertical marketing systems are shown in Exhibit 10–5. The firm managing the channel is not always the manufacturer. Through its buying power Wal-Mart exerts considerable influence on its suppliers. A company may also use a combination arrangement (e.g., ownership and contractual). The administered channel is difficult to identify because there is often no formal relationship among the participants. The difference between it and a conventional channel is more one of degree than of kind. One distinction is that the administered channel relationship involves more collaboration than is typical in conventional channels.

Ownership of distribution channels from source of supply to end-user involves a substantial capital investment by the channel coordinator. This kind of VMS is also less

GLOBAL FEATURE   Managing the Worldwide Distribution of Diamonds

DeBeers Consolidated Mines Ltd. controls about 75 percent of the supply of rough diamonds. Its production amounts to about 50 percent of the supply. For over a century DeBeers has maintained strong control over diamond distribution. Its London-based Central Selling Organization (CSO) coordinates the sales of uncut diamonds.

- DeBeers' objective is to achieve market stability and steady price appreciation of polished diamonds.
- Huge investments in rough diamond inventory may be necessary to keep supply and demand in balance so that prices will not experience large decreases or increases.
- Each year some 150 dealers attend 10 "sightings" where each has the opportunity to purchase a box of assorted rough stones.

- DeBeers advertises to consumers to encourage diamond purchases for various occasions.
- Efforts to control distribution have not been entirely successful; retail prices skyrocketed in the early 1980s due to channel members' hoarding of diamond supplies.
- In the mid-1990s the CSO had problems in controlling the unauthorized sales of Russian diamonds, and potential output from new Canadian mines was not included in the CSO.
- Nonetheless, DeBeers continues to exert powerful influence on the worldwide distribution of diamonds.

Sources: Matthew Curtin, "DeBeers Faces Challenge to Its Power," *The Wall Street Journal,* August 22, 1994, p. A58; Diana Henriques, "An Investor's Best Friend? Diamonds' Sparkle Is No Flash in the Pan," *Barron's,* June 13, 1988, p. 16.

adaptable to change compared to the other VMS forms. For these reasons a more popular alternative may be to develop collaborative relationships with channel members (e.g., supplier/manufacturer alliances). Such arrangements tend to reduce the coordinator's control over the channel but overcome the disadvantages of control through ownership.

The contractual form of the VMS may include various formal arrangements between channel participants, including franchising and voluntary chains of independent retailers. Franchising is popular in fast foods, lodging, and many other retail lines. Automobile dealerships are another example of a contractual VMS. Wholesaler-sponsored retail chains are used by wholesalers in food and drug to establish networks of independent retailers. Contractual programs may be initiated by manufacturers, wholesalers, and retailers.

The administered VMS exists because one of the channel members has the capacity to influence channel members. This influence may be the result of financial strengths, brand image, specialized skills (e.g., marketing, product innovation), and assistance and support to channel members. The Global Feature describes how DeBeers manages the worldwide distribution of rough diamonds through its marketing cartel.

The economic performance of vertical marketing systems should be higher than that in conventional channels if the channel network is properly designed and managed. However, the participating firms in the channel must make certain concessions and be willing to work toward overall channel performance. There are rules to be followed, control is exercised in various ways, and, generally, there is less flexibility for the channel members. Also, some of the requirements of the total VMS may not be in the best interests of a particular participant. Recall our earlier discussion of P&G's new pricing strategy and the potential loss of promotion pricing benefits by wholesalers and retailers. Nonetheless, competing in a conventional distribution channel against a VMS is a major competitive challenge, so a channel member may find membership in a VMS to be beneficial.

Distribution Intensity

Step 2 in channel strategy is selecting distribution intensity (Exhibit 10–3). Industrie Natuzzi SpA's management made an important distribution-intensity decision in 1982 when it rejected the R. H. Macy & Company proposal to serve as the leather furniture producer's exclusive retailer in the United States.[8] Instead, the Italian company decided to distribute its products in a wide range of retail outlets. Natuzzi has 10,000 stores carrying its products and holds an estimated 20 percent of the U.S. market compared to 4 percent in Europe and 10 percent worldwide. Sales and profits increased rapidly in the 1990s. Using a form of mass customization, Natuzzi offers many different leather furniture combinations at competitive prices. Production is provided by 20 efficient plants in Italy.

Distribution intensity is best examined in reference to how many retail stores (or industrial product dealers) carry a particular brand in a geographical area. If a company like Natuzzi decides to distribute its products in many of the retail outlets in a trading area that might normally carry such a product, it is using an *intensive* distribution approach. For example, Kodak film is widely available throughout the world. A trading area may be a portion of a city, the entire metropolitan area, or a larger geographical area. If one retailer or dealer in the trading area distributes the product, then management is following an *exclusive* distribution strategy. Examples include Lexus automobiles and Caterpillar industrial equipment. Different degrees of distribution intensity can be implemented. *Selective* distribution falls between the two extremes. Rolex watches and Coach leather goods are distributed on a selective basis.

Choosing the right distribution intensity depends on management's targeting and positioning strategies and product and market characteristics. The major issues in deciding distribution intensity are:

- Identifying which distribution intensities are feasible, taking into account the size and characteristics of the market target, the product, and the requirements likely to be imposed by prospective intermediaries (e.g., they may want exclusive sales territories).

- Selecting the alternatives that are compatible with the proposed market target and marketing program positioning strategy. For example, exclusive distribution was not consistent with Natuzzi's U.S. targeting strategy.

- Choosing the alternative that (1) offers the best strategic fit, (2) meets management's financial performance expectations, and (3) is attractive enough to intermediaries so that they will be motivated to perform their assigned functions.

The characteristics of the product and the market target to be served often suggest a particular distribution intensity. For example, an expensive product, such as a Toyota

Lexus luxury automobile, does not require intensive distribution to make contact with potential buyers. Moreover, several dealers in a trading area could not generate enough sales and profits due to the car's limited sales potential. Similarly, Escada's management, in choosing to serve the middle to upper price-quality segment of the apparel market, essentially preempted consideration of an intensive distribution strategy. In contrast, Kodak film needs to be widely available in the marketplace.

The distribution intensity should fit the marketing strategy management selects. For example, Estée Lauder distributes cosmetics through selected department stores that carry quality products. Management decided not to meet Revlon head-on in the marketplace, and instead concentrates its efforts on a small number of retail outlets. In doing this, Estée Lauder avoids huge national advertising expenditures and instead uses promotional pricing to help attract its customers to retail outlets. Buyers are offered free items when purchasing other specified items.

Strategic requirements, management's preferences, and other constraints help determine the distribution intensity that offers the best strategic fit and performance potential. The requirements of intermediaries are considered, along with management's desire to control and motivate them. For example, exclusive distribution is a powerful incentive to intermediaries and also simplifies management and control for the channel leader. But if the company granted exclusive distribution rights is unable (or unwilling) to fully serve the needs of target customers, the manufacturer will not take advantage of the sales and profit opportunities that could be obtained by using more intermediaries.

Channel Configuration

The third step in selecting the distribution strategy is deciding how many levels of organizations to include in the vertical channel and the specific kinds of intermediaries to be selected at each level (Exhibit 10–3). The type (conventional or VMS) of channel and the distribution intensity selected help in deciding how many channel levels to use and what types of intermediaries to select. Exhibit 10–1 shows different channel levels. As an example, an industrial products producer might choose between distributors and sales agents (kinds of intermediaries) to contact industrial buyers. We will now discuss several factors that may influence the choice of one of the channel configurations shown in Exhibit 10–1.

End-User Considerations.   It is important to know *where* the targeted end-users might expect to purchase the products of interest. The intermediaries that are selected should be contacting the market segment(s) targeted by the producer. Analysis of buyer characteristics and preferences provides important information for selecting firms patronized by end-users. This, in turn, guides decisions concerning additional channel levels, such as the middlemen selling to the retailers that contact the market target customers.

Product Characteristics.   The complexity of the product, special application requirements, and servicing needs are useful in guiding the choice of intermediaries. Looking at how competing products are distributed may suggest possible types of intermediaries. The breadth and depth of the products to be distributed are also important considerations since intermediaries may want full lines of products.

Manufacturer's Capabilities and Resources.   Large producers with extensive capabilities and resources have a lot of flexibility in choosing intermediaries. These producers also have a great deal of bargaining power with the middlemen. Also, the producer may be able (and willing) to perform certain of the distribution functions. Such options are more limited for small producers with capability and resource constraints.

Required Functions.   The functions that need to be performed in moving products from producer to end-user include various channel activities such as storage, servicing, and transportation. Studying these functions is useful in choosing the types of intermediaries that are appropriate for a particular product or service. For example, if the producer is primarily concerned with the direct-selling function, then independent manufacturers' agents may be the right middlemen to use. Alternatively, if inventory stocking and after-sales service are needed, then a full-service wholesaler may be needed.

Availability and Skills of Intermediaries.   Evaluation of the experience, capabilities, and motivation of the intermediaries under consideration is also important. The firms within the same industry often vary in skills and experience. Also, qualified channel members may not be available. For example, some types of middlemen will not distribute competing products.

A channel with only one level between producer and end-user simplifies the channel's coordination and management. The more complex the channel network, the more challenging it is to complete various distribution functions. Nevertheless, using specialists at two (or more) levels (e.g., brokers, wholesalers, dealers) may offer substantial economies of scale through the specialization of functions. The channel configuration that is selected, typically, takes into account several important trade-offs. As an example, manufacturer's agents (independent sales representatives) may provide the producer greater channel control than will full-service wholesalers. However, the agents make it necessary for the manufacturer to perform several functions, such as inventory stocking, invoicing, and service.

Selecting the Channel Strategy

Channel-strategy selection is summarized in Exhibit 10–3. As discussed, management: (1) chooses the type of channel to be used, (2) determines the desired intensity of distribution, and (3) selects the channel configuration. One of the first issues to be resolved is deciding whether to manage the channel or instead to be a participant. This choice often rests on the bargaining power a company can exert in negotiating with other organizations in the channel system and the value (and costs) of performing the channel management role. The options include deciding to manage or coordinate operations in the channel of distribution, becoming a member of a vertically coordinated channel, or becoming a member of a conventional channel system. The following factors often affect the choice of the channel strategy.

Market Access.   The choice of a market target needs to be closely coordinated with channel strategy, since the channel connects products and end-users. The market target decision is not finalized until the channel strategy is selected. Information about the customers in the market target can help eliminate unsuitable channel-strategy alternatives.

EXHIBIT 10–6   Illustrative Channel Strategy Evaluation

Evaluation Criteria	Manufacturer's Representatives	Company Sales Force
Market access	Rapid	One- to three-year development
Sales forecast (two years)	$10 million	$20 million
Forecast accuracy	High	Medium to low
Estimated costs	$1 million*	$2.4 million**
Selling expense (costs/sales)	10%	12%
Flexibility	Good	Fair
Control	Limited	Good

*Includes 8% commission plus management time for recruiting and training representatives.
**Includes $100,000 for 10 salespeople, plus management time.

Multiple market targets may require more than a single channel of distribution. One advantage of the use of middlemen by the manufacturer is that the intermediaries have an established customer base. When this customer base matches the producer's market target(s), market access is achieved very rapidly.

Financial Considerations.   Two financial issues affect the channel strategy. First, are the resources available for launching the proposed strategy? For example, a small producer may not have the money to build a distribution network. Second, the revenue-cost impact of alternative channel strategies needs to be evaluated. These analyses include cash flow, income, return on investment, and operating capital requirements (see Appendix to Chapter 1).

Flexibility and Control Considerations.   Management should decide how much flexibility it wants in the channel network and how much control it would like to have over other channel participants. An example of flexibility is how easily channel members can be added (or eliminated). A conventional channel offers little opportunity for control by a member firm, yet there is a lot of flexibility in entering and exiting from the channel. The VMS offers more control than the conventional channel. Legal and regulatory constraints also affect channel strategies in such areas as pricing, exclusive dealing, and allocation of market coverage.

Channel Strategy Illustration.   Suppose a producer of industrial controls for fluid processing (e.g., valves, regulators) is considering two channel-strategy alternatives: using independent manufacturer's representatives (agents) versus recruiting a company salesforce to sell its products to industrial customers. The representatives receive a commission of 8 percent on their dollar sales volume. Salespeople will be paid an estimated $100,000 in annual salary and expenses. Management time will be required to recruit and train the representatives. Salespeople must be recruited, trained, and supervised.

An illustrative channel strategy evaluation is shown in Exhibit 10–6. The company salesforce alternative is more expensive than the use of independent sales agents. Assuming both options generate contributions to profit, the trade-off of higher expenses needs to be evaluated against flexibility and control considerations. One possibility that is often used by manufacturers seeking access to a new market is to initially utilize manufacturer's representatives, with a longer-term strategy of converting to a company salesforce. This offers an opportunity to gain market knowledge while keeping selling expenses in line with actual sales.

Adequacy of Existing Distribution Systems

The restructuring of many companies during the 1990s called for reviewing channel strategies. Changes in distribution may improve both customer satisfaction and productivity. Companies with direct-salesforces may consider using indirect channels (wholesalers, distributors, dealers, and retailers) to serve part of the customer base. Manufacturers are also using other customer contact methods such as telephone sales, computer ordering, and catalog sales.

An important trend in distribution is the use of multiple channels to gain greater access to end-user customers. For example, Dayton-Hudson markets through its traditional department stores, through its discount retailers (Target and Mervyn's), and through specialty stores. The unifying component of Dayton-Hudson's strategy is merchandising and the merchant orientation of top management.[9] In the mid-1960s, Dayton-Hudson recognized the mass-merchandising trend and moved into discount retailing through Target and more recently Mervyn's to promote the latest fashion and the best deal.

The explosive growth of direct marketing during the last decade represents an important trend in distribution. Customer contact is made by mail or phone. These channels include catalog retailers such as Lands' End and L. L. Bean, phone and media retailers, and electronic shopping. Direct-marketing companies take business away from conventional retailers. Convenience buying is stimulated by today's lifestyles (two-income families, limited leisure time, high incomes), the ease of shopping via catalogs, toll-free phone numbers, and effective marketing by the firms involved.

Using an existing customer list facilitates entry into direct marketing. American Express has been very successful in using its credit card membership list. Database marketing provides access to buyers for direct-marketing programs. An existing customer base must be willing to purchase by mail. We will discuss direct marketing in Chapter 13.

Strategies at Different Channel Levels

We have looked at distribution largely from the producer's viewpoint. Wholesalers and retailers are also concerned with channel strategies, and in some instances they may exercise primary control over channel operations. The Limited is a powerful force in its channels, as is Wal-Mart. Large food wholesalers and retailers are major factors in their channels of distribution. Moreover, decisions by wholesalers, distributors, brokers, and retailers about which manufacturers' products to carry often affect the performance of all channel participants.

Channel strategy can be examined from any level in the distribution network. The major distinction lies in the point of view (retailer, wholesaler, producer) used to develop the strategy. Intermediaries may have fewer alternatives to consider than producers and thus less flexibility in channel strategy. Nevertheless, their approach to channel strategy is often active rather than passive.

MANAGING THE CHANNEL

After deciding on the channel design, the actual channel participants are identified, evaluated, and recruited. Finding competent and motivated intermediaries is critical to successfully implementing the channel strategy. Channel management activities include choosing how to assist and support intermediaries, developing operating policies, providing incentives, selecting promotional programs, and evaluating channel results. These activities consume much of management's time, since the channel design is not modified frequently. Importantly, changes in channel design may have serious consequences for the members. Consider, for example, Goodyear Tire & Rubber Company's decision in 1992 to include Sears, Roebuck & Company in its distribution network. The decision was very unpopular with Goodyear's 2,500 independent dealers.[10] Hundreds of the dealers have taken on competing tire brands. Goodyear's motivation for the change was the rapid growth in tire sales in the previous five years by less-expensive chain stores, department stores, and warehouse clubs, compared to a 4 percent share decline by tire dealerships. Not surprisingly, the dealers are concerned that Goodyear will make further additions to its distribution network by adding Kmart and possibly the warehouse clubs.

To gain a better insight into channel management, we will discuss channel leadership, management structure and systems, physical distribution management, channel relationships, conflict resolution, channel performance, and legal and ethical considerations.

Channel Leadership

Some form of interorganization management is needed to assure that the channel has satisfactory performance as a competitive entity.[11] One firm may gain power over other channel organizations because of its specific characteristics (e.g., size), experience, and environmental factors, and its ability to capitalize on such factors. Thus, the channel leader's power depends on its competitive advantages and its environment.[12] Gaining this advantage is more feasible in a VMS than in a conventional channel.

Performing the leadership role may also lead to conflicts arising from differences in the objectives and priorities of channel members. The conflicts with retailers created by the channel strategy changes of Goodyear and Procter & Gamble, discussed earlier, are illustrative. The organization with the most power may make decisions that are not considered favorable by other channel members.

Management Structure and Systems

Channel coordination and management are often the responsibility of the sales organization (Chapter 13). For example, a manufacturer's salespeople develop buyer–seller relationships with wholesalers and/or retailers. The management structure and systems may vary from informal arrangements to highly structured operating systems. Conventional channel management is more informal, whereas the management of VMS is more structured and programmed. The VMS management systems may include operating policies and procedures, information system linkages, various supporting services to channel participants, and performance targets.

Physical Distribution Management

Physical distribution management has received considerable attention from logistics, marketing, manufacturing, and transportation professionals. The objective is improving the distribution of supplies, goods in process, and finished products. The decision whether to integrate physical distribution with other channel functions or to manage it separately is a question that must be resolved by a particular organization. There are instances when either approach may be appropriate. Physical distribution is a key channel function and thus an important part of channel strategy and management. Management needs to first select the appropriate channel strategy, considering the physical distribution function and other essential channel activities. Once the strategy is selected, physical distribution management alternatives can be examined for the channel network.

Exhibit 10–7 outlines one approach for integrating marketing and logistics activities. The basis of integrating the two groups of activities is customer service. Recall our discussion of integrating business functions to improve customer service, discussed in Chapter 9. Exhibit 10–7 shows the cost trade-offs and indicates illustrative objectives of marketing and logistics. The integration task is to give customers the services that meet their needs while satisfying the organization's performance objectives.

Channel Relationships

In Chapter 7 we considered various forms of relationships between organizations, examining the degree of collaboration between companies, the extent of commitment of the participating organizations, and the power and dependence ties between the organizations. We will now look at how these issues relate to channel relationships.

Degree of Collaboration. Channel relationships are often transactional in conventional channels but become more collaborative in VMSs. The extent of collaboration is influenced by the complexity of the product, the potential benefits of collaboration, and the willingness of channel members to work together as partners. Just-in-time inventory programs and other total quality management activities encourage collaboration between suppliers and producers.

Commitment and Trust Among the Channel Members. The commitment and trust of channel organizations is likely to be higher in VMSs compared to conventional channels. For example, a contractual arrangement (e.g., franchise agreement) is a commitment to work together. Yet, the strength of the commitment may vary depending on the contract terms. For example, contracts between manufacturers and their independent representatives or agents, typically, allow either party to terminate the relationship with a 30-day notification.

EXHIBIT 10–7   Cost Trade-Offs Required in Marketing and Logistics

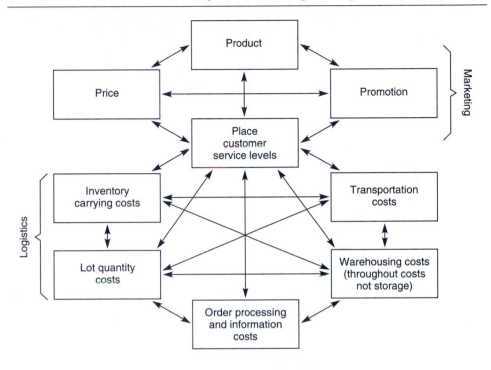

Marketing objective: Allocate resources to the marketing mix to maximize the long-run profitability of the firm.

Logistics objective: Minimize total costs given the customer service objective. (Total costs = Transportation costs + Warehousing costs + Order processing and information costs + Lot quantity costs + Inventory carrying costs)

Source: James R. Stock and Douglas M. Lambert, *Strategic Logistics Management,* 2nd ed. (Burr Ridge, IL: Richard D. Irwin, 1987), p. 42.

Highly collaborative relationships among channel members call for a considerable degree of trust between the partners. The cooperating organizations provide access to confidential product plans, market data, and other trade secrets. Trust normally develops as the partners learn to work with each other and find the relationship to be favorable to each partner's objectives.

Power and Dependence.   In VMSs power is concentrated with one organization and the other channel members are dependent on the channel manager. Power in conventional channels is less concentrated than in VMSs, and channel members are less dependent on each other. Conventional channel relationships may, nevertheless, result in some channel members' possessing more bargaining power than others.

Hallmark Cards is the market leader in the greeting card industry. Changing patterns of distribution present Hallmark with a difficult power and dependence situation. For decades Hallmark relied on independent specialty shops to sell its cards. Yet, mass merchandisers like Target stores now account for a rapidly growing share of the market. If Hallmark expands into this distribution channel, its shop owners will be very unhappy. If Hallmark does not make this change, it is likely to continue to lose market share. Hallmark will likely expand its distribution even at the risk of creating conflicts with its retailers.

Conflict Resolution

Conflicts are certain to occur between the channel members because of differences in objectives, priorities, and corporate cultures. Looking at a proposed channel relationship by each participating organization may identify areas (e.g., incompatible objectives) that may lead to major conflicts. In such situations, management may decide to seek another channel partner. Effective communications before and after establishing the channel relationships can also help to eliminate or reduce conflicts.

Several methods are used to resolve actual and potential conflicts.[13] One useful approach is to involve channel members in the decisions that will affect the members. Another helpful method of resolving or reducing conflict is developing effective communications channels between channel members. Pursuing objectives that are important to all channel members is also a useful approach for reducing conflict. Finally, it may be necessary to establish methods for mediation and arbitration.

Channel Performance

The performance of the channel is important from two points of view. First, each member is interested in how well the channel is meeting the member's objectives. Second, the organization that is managing or coordinating the channel is concerned with its performance and the overall performance of the channel. Tracking performance for the individual channel members includes various financial and market measures such as profit contribution, revenues, costs, market share, customer satisfaction, and rate of growth. Exhibit 10–4 shows several criteria for evaluating the overall performance of the channel.

Companies gain a strategic advantage by improving distribution productivity. Reducing distribution costs and the time in moving products to end-users are high-priority action areas in many companies. The opportunity to lower costs may be substantial. These costs may account for one-third or more of total product costs. Consider these examples:[14]

- Helene Curtis reduced distribution costs 40 percent by replacing six older warehouses with a new distribution center that uses computer-controlled forklifts and automated order processing and shipment.
- Mervyn's has reduced the average time merchandise is in the pipeline from vendor to retail store from 14 days to fewer than 9.
- Sun MicroSystems' distribution is handled by Federal Express Business Logistics Services Unit, which moves Sun's machines from the factory floor to customers.

Monitoring the changes that are taking place in distribution and incorporating distribution-strategy considerations into the strategic-planning process are essential strategic-marketing activities. Market turbulence, global competition, and information technology create a rapidly changing distribution environment.

Legal and Ethical Considerations

Various legal and ethical considerations may impact channel relationships. Legal concerns by the federal government include arrangements between channel members that substantially lessen competition, restrictive contracts concerning products and/or geographical coverage, promotional allowances and incentives, and pricing practices.[15] State and local laws and regulations may also impact channel members.

The importance of ethics is shown by a research survey of Fortune 1000 companies indicating that 40 percent of the responding companies hold ethics workshops and seminars and one-third have ethics committees.[16] Ethical issues are heavily influenced by corporate policies and practices. Corporate pressures on performance may create ethical situations. Deciding whether a practice is ethical is sometimes complex. Channel decisions that impact other channel members may create ethical situations. Many companies have established internal standards on how business should be conducted. Written statements of working relationships among channel members may also include such statements.

INTERNATIONAL CHANNELS

The distribution channels that are available in international markets are not totally different from the channels in a particular country such as the United States. Uniqueness is less a function of structural alternatives and is more related to the vast range of operational and market variables that influence channel strategy.[17] Exhibit 10–8 shows several channel of distribution alternatives. The arrows show many possible channel networks linking producers, middlemen, and end-users.

Examining International Distribution Patterns

While the basic channel structure (e.g., agents, wholesalers, retailer) is similar across countries, there are many important differences in distribution patterns among countries. Several of the factors that create variations in world distribution practices include:[18]

- Target markets within and across countries.
- Objectives for sales, market share, and profits.
- Required financial and personnel resources.
- Amount of control and other channel management requirements.

Generalization about distribution practices throughout the world is obviously not possible. Studying the distribution patterns in the nation(s) of interest is important in

EXHIBIT 10-8 International Channel-of-Distribution Alternatives

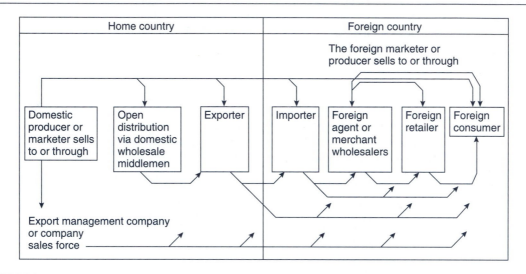

Source: Philip R. Cateora, *International Marketing,* 7th ed. (Burr Ridge, IL: Richard D. Irwin, 1990), p. 572.

obtaining guidelines for distribution strategy. Various global trends such as satellite communications, regional cooperative arrangements (e.g., European Union), and transportation networks (e.g., intermodal services) impact distribution systems in various ways. Global market turbulence and corporate restructuring create additional influences on distribution strategies and practices. The Distribution Feature describes how Coca-Cola is expanding its global distribution.

An interesting example of differences in distribution patterns between countries are the laws influencing retailing in Japan.[19] About 83 percent of Japan's 1.6 million retailers employ fewer than five people. Japan's so-called Large Store Retail Law requires retail organizations building or operating large new stores to apply to the government for permission to: (1) build a store, (2) expand an existing store, (3) stay open later in the evening, or (4) change the days of the month the store is closed. One large Japanese retailer, Ito Yokado, waited for seven years for permission to build a new shopping center in a Tokyo suburb, only to find out that a decision was impossible until more information was provided. Japan's small businesses have extensive collective power over retail decisions. Consumers are often penalized by the retailing laws by being forced to patronize high-markup stores in Japan. To eliminate the problems Japan's tight retail laws are being changed to benefit consumers, to make the distribution structure more flexible, and to make it less difficult for new entrants to gain access.

Factors Affecting Channel Selection

The channel-strategy analysis and selection process presented in the chapter can be used for developing or evaluating international channel strategy, recognizing that many

DISTRIBUTION FEATURE   Distributing Coca-Cola Around the World

Reacting to international challenges and opportunities, the soft drink giant is aggressively introducing new products and expanding international distribution.

- In 1995 bottling plants were opened in Romania, Norway, Fiji, and India, and 10 more are scheduled in China, Hungary, Lithuania, Russia, and Thailand.
- Coke gets four-fifths of its earnings from international markets.
- The fast-changing industry scope includes teas, juices, sports drinks, bottled waters, and other products.

- Companies in Japan launch 700 to 800 new drink products each year, many lasting only a month.
- Entering new international markets calls for fast response, high risk tolerance, and understanding buyers' drink preferences.
- Over 40 new marketing executives have been hired from other industries, including sports and entertainment.

Source: Robert Frank, "Adding Some Fizz: Coca-Cola is Shedding Its Once Stodgy Image with Swift Expansion," *The Wall Street Journal,* August 22, 1995, pp. A1, A6.

situational factors affect channel decisions in specific countries. Several of the factors influencing channel decisions are also similar between nations. The factors affecting the choice of international channels include cost, capital requirements, control, coverage, strategic product-market fit, and the likelihood that the middlemen will remain in business over a reasonable time horizon.[20] The political and economic stability of the country is, of course, very important. Stability needs to be evaluated early in the decision to enter the country.

Strategic Alliances

A strategic alliance between an organization that wants to enter an international market and a firm already serving the market may offer the advantage of existing distribution channels for the foreign firm and a new product for the domestic firm. For example, several American companies are seeking cooperative arrangements with firms serving the European common market. The agreement between General Mills, Inc. and Nestlé S. A. provides entry into Nestlé's vast sales and distribution network and its factories in Europe.[21] General Mills contributes the cereals to stock the shelves of food stores. Implementation of the alliance will require several years. Many cereal eaters around the world are located in English-speaking countries. The development of cereal preference in other countries could provide a huge growth market. Europe has the potential by the year 2000 of being equal in size to the current U.S. cereal market.

A comparison of different ways to gain distribution in Europe is shown in Exhibit 10–9. Each offers certain advantages and disadvantages. As the exporter makes greater commitment in terms of resources to market entry, the risks are higher should the venture not prove to be successful. Of course, greater commitment may enable the exporter to have more influence on performance.

EXHIBIT 10–9 Advantages and Disadvantages of Routes into Europe

---

Advantages	*Disadvantages*
Exporting	
Cheaper	Slow
Lower risk; less commitment	May miss opportunities through lack of knowledge
Good route for unique product	
Allows slow buildup and learning about market conditions	Allows home competitors to assess and build response
More control	Building scale economies may be high-risk and expensive
Keeps economies of scale at home base	
No need to share technology	
Strategic Alliance	
More permanent than mere exporting	Slow and plodding approach
Close contact	Needs constant work to keep relationship sound
Uses joint expertise and commitment perhaps not available to exporter	
Allows potential partners to learn about each other	Partners have only limited joint commitment to success
Locks out other competitors	Unlikely to build economies of scale
Joint Venture	
Build scale quickly	Control lost to some extent
Obtain local knowledge and distribution	Works best where both parties contribute something to the mix
Cheaper than takeover	
Local entry where takeover not possible	Difficult to manage
Can be used where outright takeover not feasible	Share profits with partner
Can be used where similar product available	
Takeover	
Can be relatively fast	Premium paid: expensive
Useful for national expertise acquired	High risk if wrong
Buys presence	Best targets may have already gone in some markets
Buys size and market share	Not always easy to dispose of unwanted parts of company

---

Source: Richard Lynch, *European Marketing* (Burr Ridge, IL: Irwin Professional Publishing, 1994), p. 155.

SUMMARY

The channel of distribution connects the producer with the end-users of goods and services. One or more levels of organizations may operate between the user and producer. A strong channel network is an important way to gain competitive advantage. Distribution channels provide access to market targets. The choice between company distribution to end-users and the use of intermediaries is guided by end-user needs and characteristics, product characteristics, and financial and control considerations.

Manufacturers select the type of channel to be used, determine distribution intensity, design the channel configuration, and manage various aspects of channel operations.

These channels are either conventional or VMS. The VMS, the dominant channel for consumer products, is increasing in importance for business and industrial products. In a VMS, one firm owns all organizations in the channel, a contractual arrangement exists between organizations, or one channel member is in charge of channel administration. Channel decisions also include deciding on intensity of distribution and the channel configuration. Channel management includes implementing the channel strategy, coordinating channel operations, and tracking the performance of the channel.

The choice of a channel strategy begins when management decides whether to manage the channel or to assume a participant role. Strategic analysis identifies and evaluates the channel alternatives. Several factors are evaluated, including access to the market target, channel functions to be performed, financial considerations, and legal and control constraints. The channel strategy adopted establishes several guidelines for price and promotion strategies.

International channels of distribution are similar in structure to those found in the United States and other developed countries. Nevertheless, important variations exist in the channels of different countries because of the stage of economic development, government influence, and industry practices. Strategic alliances offer one means of gaining market access to the existing channels of a company operating in a country of interest to the firm.

QUESTIONS FOR REVIEW AND DISCUSSION

1. In the mid-1990s Southwest Airlines and some other carriers started selling tickets using airport ticket dispensers. Discuss the implications of this method of distribution for travel agencies.

2. Distribution analysts indicate that costs for supermarkets equal about 98 percent of sales. What influence does this high break-even level have on supermarkets' diversification into delis, cheese shops, seafood shops, and nonfood areas?

3. Why do some large, financially strong manufacturers choose not to own their dealers but instead establish contractual relationships with them?

4. What are the advantages and limitations of the use of multiple channels of distribution by a manufacturer?

5. Discuss some likely trends in the distribution of automobiles during the 1990s, including the shift away from exclusive distribution arrangements.

6. During the 1980s, Radio Shack began opening retail computer stores rather than depending on its existing electronics stores to serve the small-computer market. Discuss the logic of this strategy, pointing out its strengths and shortcomings.

7. Identify and discuss some of the factors that should increase the trend toward vertical marketing systems.

8. Why might a manufacturer choose to enter a conventional channel of distribution?

9. Suppose the management of a raw material supplier is interested in performing a financial analysis of a distribution channel consisting of manufacturers, distributors, and retailers. Outline an approach for doing the analysis.

10. Discuss some of the important strategic issues facing a drug manufacturer in deciding whether to distribute veterinary prescriptions and over-the-counter products through veterinarians or distributors.

NOTES

1. Teri Agins, "Bright and Bold: Despite the Recession High-Fashion Escada Expands Worldwide," *The Wall Street Journal,* April 15, 1992, pp. A1, A6.

2. Kathleen M. Berry, "Airline Alliances: Benefits Outweigh the Costs," *Investor's Business Daily,* August 21, 1995, p. A4.

3. Louis W. Stern, Adel I. El-Ansary, and James R. Brown, *Management in Marketing Channels* (Englewood Cliffs, NJ: Prentice Hall, 1989), p. 4.

4. Elizabeth Sangler, "Proving Their Mettle," *Barrons,* July 9, 1984, pp. 13 and 20.

5. John Marcom, Jr., "Consumers Are Taking a Back Seat as Computer Stores Court Business," *The Wall Street Journal,* July 26, 1985, p. 21.

6. Valerie Reitman, "Retail Resistance: Eliminated Discounts on P&G Goods Annoy Many Who Sell Them," *The Wall Street Journal,* August 11, 1992, p. A1.

7. Bert C. McCammon, Jr., "Perspectives for Distribution Programming," in *Vertical Marketing Systems,* ed. Louis P. Bucklin (Glenview, IL: Scott, Foresman, 1970), p. 43.

8. Lisa Bannon, "Natuzzi's Huge Selection of Leather Furniture Pays Off," *The Wall Street Journal,* November 17, 1994, p. B4.

9. M. Howard Gelfand, "Dayton-Hudson Keeps Its Vision," *Advertising Age,* July 9, 1984, pp. 4, 46–47.

10. Dana Milbank, "Independent Goodyear Dealers Rebel," *The Wall Street Journal,* July 8, 1992, p. B2.

11. For a complete discussion of channel management see Louis W. Stern and Adel I. El-Ansary, *Marketing Channels,* 4th ed. (Englewood Cliffs, NJ: Prentice Hall, 1992).

12. Michael Etgar, "Channel Environment and Channel Leadership," *Journal of Marketing Research,* February 1977, p. 70.

13. James A. Narus and James C. Anderson, "Turn Your Industrial Distributors into Partners," *Harvard Business Review,* March–April 1986, pp. 66–71.

14. Rita Koselka, "Distribution Revolution," *Forbes,* May 25, 1992, pp. 54, 58, 60, 62.

15. An expanded discussion of these issues is available in Stern and El-Ansary, *Marketing Channels,* chap. 8.

16. Kenneth Labich, "The New Crisis in Business Ethics," *Fortune,* April 20, 1992, p. 168.

17. Philip R. Cateora, *International Marketing,* 8th ed. (Burr Ridge, IL: Richard D. Irwin, 1993), chap. 14.

18. Ibid., p. 459.

19. This example is based on Robert E. Weigand, "So You Think Our Retailing Laws Are Tough," *The Wall Street Journal,* November 13, 1989, p. A10.

20. Cateora, *International Marketing,* chap. 14.

21. Richard Gibson, "General Mills Would Like to Be Champion of Breakfasts in Europe," *The Wall Street Journal,* December 1, 1989, p. B5.

Pricing Strategy

The pricing of goods and services performs a key strategic role in many firms because of deregulation, intense global competition, slow growth in many markets, and the opportunity for firms to strengthen market position. Price impacts financial performance and is an important influence on buyers' perceptions and positioning of brands. Price becomes a proxy measure for product quality when buyers have difficulty evaluating complex products.

The 1990s marked widespread use of price-promotional merchandising in retailing.[1] The drivers of the new era in pricing strategies throughout the retail sector include the escalated value and price sensitivity of consumers, major demographic changes (e.g., changing age composition, diversity), and explosive growth of off-price retailing (e.g., T. J. Maxx, Office Depot). Retailers reacted to these pressures by adopting price-centered merchandising. Some may have overreacted. Successfully coping with the new reality in retail pricing requires deciding whether to compete on price, or instead selecting the features to use in differentiating the retailer from competition. Competing on price requires that the retailer be a low-cost operator, have the critical mass to attract buyers, offer services that meet and exceed customer expectations, and project an image of market dominance. Wal-Mart has been very successful with its low price strategy, whereas Hermès has effectively differentiated its unique merchandise to attract affluent buyers.

Pricing decisions may have explosive and far-reaching consequences. Once implemented, it may be difficult to alter a price strategy—particularly if the change calls for a significant increase. Pricing actions that violate laws can land executives in jail. Price has

343

many possible uses as a strategic instrument in corporate and marketing strategy. Changes in pricing practices have led to more flexible strategies and tactics by both producers and retailers. The realities of the pricing environment are apparent.[2] Price wars occur frequently in a wide range of markets for both goods and services. The motivation for these wars includes attempts to use production capacity, survival actions by companies operating under Chapter 11 bankruptcy provisions, and competitive pressures on market-share position. Producers have money invested in fixed assets that management is unable or unwilling to liquidate. The companies and products affected by price wars range from potato chips to computers. One of the dangers of these price wars is losing brand equity.

First, we will examine the strategic role of price in marketing program positioning strategy and discuss several pricing situations. Following a step-by-step approach to pricing strategy, we will describe and illustrate the steps. We will then present an approach to situation analysis for pricing decisions, using several applications to highlight the nature and scope of analysis activities. Next, we will consider the choice of a pricing strategy. Finally, we will discuss determining specific policies and examine some special pricing issues.

STRATEGIC ROLE OF PRICE

Several factors influence management's decisions about how price will be used in marketing strategy. An important concern is estimating how buyers will respond to alternative prices for a product or service. The cost of producing and distributing a product sets lower boundaries on the pricing decision. Costs affect an organization's ability to compete. The existing and potential competition in the market segments targeted by management constrains the flexibility in selecting prices. Finally, legal and ethical constraints also create pressures on decision makers.

Pricing plays a key role in the marketing strategy of White Castle System, Inc. It started out in 1921 in Wichita, Kansas, selling five-cent hamburgers.[3] Today, those hamburgers have not changed very much and they sell for only 38 cents. The company was the first fast-food chain, today operating about 300 restaurants. Management has expanded slowly but steadily over the years, keeping operating costs and prices low and avoiding head-on competition with McDonald's and other chains by using low prices, a differentiated product (square hamburger with onions), and locations that are convenient to its customers. White Castle offers a limited menu in efficient, but not fancy, company-owned stores. Plans are to open 150 new outlets over the next decade.

Price in the Marketing Mix

Strategic choices about market targets, products, and distribution set guidelines for both price and promotion strategies. Product quality and features, type of distribution channel, end-users served, and intermediaries' functions all help establish a price range. When an organization forms a new distribution network, selection of the channel and intermediaries may be driven by price strategy. Thus, the influence of one mix component on another may vary in different strategy situations.

Responsibility for pricing decisions varies among organizations. Marketing executives are responsible for price strategy in many companies. Pricing decisions may be made by the chief executive officer in some firms such as aircraft producers and construction firms. Manufacturing and engineering executives may be assigned price responsibility in companies that produce customer-designed industrial equipment. In general, marketing executives are likely to have pricing responsibility for consumer products and services. Price determination for very large purchases may involve the chief executive officer and other members of the top management group. Industrial product companies are more likely to assign pricing responsibility to nonmarketing executives.

Pricing decisions must be coordinated with other decisions in the marketing program. Operations, engineering, and finance executives should, of course, participate in strategic pricing decisions, regardless of where responsibility is assigned. Coordination of strategic and tactical pricing decisions with other aspects of marketing strategy is critical because of the interrelationships involved.

Product Strategy.   When only one product is involved, the price decision is simplified. Yet, in many instances, a line or mix of products must be priced. Consider a situation involving a product and consumable supplies for the product. One popular strategy is to price the product at competitive levels and set higher margins for supplies. Examples include parts for automobiles and cartridge refills for computer printers. Also, the prices for products in a line do not necessarily correspond to the cost of each item. For example, prices in supermarkets are based on a total mix strategy rather than individual item pricing. Understanding the composition of the mix and the interrelationships among products is important in determining pricing strategy, particularly when the branding strategy is built around a line or mix of products rather than on a brand-by-brand basis. Product quality and features affect price strategy. A high-quality product may require a high price to help establish a prestige position in the marketplace and to satisfy management's profit performance requirements. Alternatively, a manufacturer supplying private-branded products to a retailer like Wal-Mart or Kmart must price competitively in order to obtain sales. Pricing executives analyze the product mix, branding strategy, and product quality and features to determine the effects of these factors on price strategy.

Distribution Strategy.   Type of channel, distribution intensity, and channel configuration also influence price strategy. The needs and motivation of intermediaries should be considered in setting prices. Middleman need price margins to pay for their functions and to give them incentives to obtain their cooperation. Pricing is equally important when distribution is performed by the manufacturer. Pricing in vertically coordinated channels reflects total channel considerations more so than in conventional channels. Intensive distribution is likely to call for more competitive pricing than does selective or exclusive distribution.

An important consideration in pricing strategy is the role and influence of various channel members. A particular firm may be very active or passive, depending on its role and power in the channel network. A firm that manages the channel usually plays a key role in pricing for the entire channel, subject to legal constraints and restrictions.

Pricing Situations

Pricing strategy requires continuous attention because of changing external conditions, the actions of competitors, and the opportunities to gain a competitive edge through pricing actions. Pricing situations include:

- Deciding how to price a new product.
- Evaluating the need to adjust price as the product moves through the product life cycle.
- Changing a positioning strategy that requires modifying the current price strategy.
- Responding to the pressures of a price war and other competitive threats.

Decisions for existing products may include increasing or decreasing prices or holding them at current levels. The competitive situation is an important factor in deciding if and when to alter prices. Demand and cost estimates are strong influences on new-product pricing. Deciding how to price a new product also requires considering competing substitutes since few new products occupy a unique position.

American Telephone and Telegraph Co. (AT&T) illustrates the effects on pricing decisions when the business environment changes. Deregulation of the telecommunications industry created a new competitive situation for AT&T. The former monopolist experienced aggressive competition in the late 1980s, forcing AT&T to become more customer-oriented and to offer lower prices on long-distance services.[4] AT&T lost major customers to MCI Communications Corporation and U.S. Sprint Communications Company. A major reason for deregulating the telecommunications industry was achieving lower prices, and this has occurred. The giant holds a very strong market position. AT&T's salesforce is much more responsive to customers than it was in the past. Large numbers of staff personnel have been moved to the field to have direct contact with customers. Promotional pricing discounts are being used. Some industry experts suggest that AT&T's new marketing strengths are helping the company regain its monopoly power.

Uses of Price in Positioning Strategy

Price is used in various ways in the marketing program positioning strategy—as a signal to the buyer, an instrument of competition, a means to improve financial performance, and a way to perform other marketing-mix functions (e.g., promotional pricing).

Signal to the Buyer. Price offers an immediate means of communicating with the buyer. The price is visible to the buyer and provides a basis of comparison between brands. Price may be used to position the brand as a high-quality product or instead to pursue head-on competition with another brand. When the product cannot be evaluated, price is a proxy for value.

Instrument of Competition. Price offers a way to quickly attack competitors or, alternatively, to position a firm away from direct competition. Off-price retailers use a low-price strategy against department stores and other retailers. Price strategy is always related to competition whether firms use a higher, lower, or equal price.

EXHIBIT 11-1   Pricing Strategy for New and Existing Products

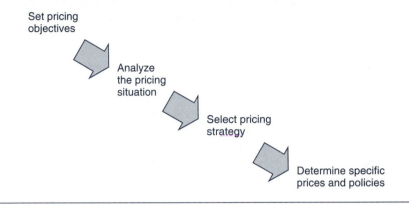

Set pricing
objectives

Analyze
the pricing
situation

Select pricing
strategy

Determine specific
prices and policies

Improving Financial Performance.   Price and costs determine financial performance. Price strategies need to be assessed as to their estimated impact on the firm's financial statements, both in the short and long run. Historically, financial considerations have been major factors in the pricing strategies of large firms in mature industries such as oil, steel, rubber, automobiles, and chemicals. These industries have used target-return methods for pricing; that is, they set a desired profit return and then compute the price necessary to achieve this return. Global competition has forced many firms to adopt pricing approaches that are more demand-oriented. AT&Ts market-driven strategy for long-distance services is illustrative. The issue is the nature and extent to which management uses financial considerations to establish the role of price.

Marketing-Mix Considerations.   Price may serve as a substitute for selling effort, advertising, and product quality. Alternatively, price may be used to reinforce these activities in the marketing program. The role of price often depends on how other variables in the marketing mix are used. For example, price can be used as an incentive to channel members and company salespeople, as the focus of promotional strategy, and as a signal of value. In deciding the role of price in marketing strategy, management evaluates the importance of price to competitive positioning, the buyer, financial requirements, and interrelationships in the marketing mix.

Pricing Strategy

Exhibit 11-1 shows the major steps used to select a pricing strategy for a new product or altering an existing strategy. Pricing objectives provide a frame of reference for strategy development. Next, we need to analyze the pricing situation, taking into account demand, cost, competition, and legal and ethical forces. The analysis shows how much flexibility there is in setting the price for a new product or changing a price. Based on the analysis and the price objectives, the pricing strategy is selected. Finally, specific prices and policies are determined to implement the strategy.

Pricing Objectives

Companies use their price strategies to achieve one or more of several objectives. They may price for results (sales, market share, profit), for market penetration or position, for achieving certain functions (e.g., promotional pricing), or to avoid government intervention. More than one objective is usually involved, and sometimes the objectives may conflict with each other. If so, adjustments may be needed on one of the conflicting objectives. For example, if the pricing objective is to increase market share by 20 percent while another is to price to break even on sales, management should decide if both objectives are feasible. If not, one must be adjusted. Objectives establish essential guidelines for price strategy.

Pricing objectives vary according to the situational factors present and management's preferences. A high price may be set to recover investment in a new product. A low price may be intended to gain market position, discourage new competition, or attract new buyers. Several examples of pricing objectives follow:

Gain market position. The use of low prices to gain sales and market share is illustrative. Limitations include encouraging price wars and reduction (or elimination) of profit contributions.

Achieve financial performance. Prices are selected to contribute to financial objectives such as profit contribution and cash flow. Prices that are too high may not be acceptable to buyers.

Product positioning. Prices may be used to enhance product image, promote the use of the product, create awareness, and other positioning objectives. The visibility of price (high or low) may reduce the effectiveness of other positioning components such as advertising.

Stimulate demand. Price is used to encourage buyers to try a new product or to purchase existing brands during periods when sales slow down (e.g., recessions). A potential problem is that buyers may balk at purchasing when prices return to normal levels.

Influence competition. The objective of pricing actions may be to influence existing or potential competitors. Management may want to discourage market entry or price cutting by current competitors. A price leader may want to encourage industry members to raise prices. One problem is that competitors may not respond as predicted.

Eastman Kodak Company's efforts to gain market share for its film sales in Japan accelerated in late 1995 through a co-branding arrangement with retailers.[5] The new film is sold by 800 sales outlets at about half the price charged by Fuji. Co-branding indicates both a Japanese name and the Kodak name. Kodak was already producing a private label film for the 2,500-store Japanese Consumer Cooperative Union with 70 percent of the market. Fuji was not expected to substantially reduce its film prices. Nonetheless, competitors do not always react as predicted to price changes. Also, the co-branding strategy could attract sales from other Kodak brands.

ANALYZING THE PRICING SITUATION

Pricing analysis is used in evaluating new-product ideas, in developing test marketing strategy, and in selecting a national introduction strategy. Analysis also is necessary for existing products because of changes in the market and competitive environment, unsatisfactory performance of products, and modifications in marketing strategy over the product's life cycle. Analyzing the pricing situation includes: (1) estimating the product-market's responsiveness to price, (2) estimating product costs, (3) analyzing competition, and (4) assessing legal and ethical constraints.

Product-Market Responsiveness to Price

One of the challenges of pricing is estimating how buyers will respond to alternative prices. The pricing of Procter & Gamble Company's new analgesic brand, Aleve, illustrates this situation. The product was introduced in the highly-competitive $2.38 billion market in 1994.[6] Aleve is an over-the-counter version of Naprosyn (developed by Syntex Corporation). P&G estimated first year sales of $200 million. A $100 million marketing effort spearheaded Aleve's market entry. Pricing was the same as Advil even though Aleve lasts 8 to 12 hours instead of Advil's 8 hours. Aggressive promotional pricing (coupons) was expected from market leaders Tylenol ($700 million sales) and Advil ($330 million). Some industry authorities believe Aleve poses a greater threat to the weaker brands (Bayer, Bufferin, and Nuprin).

Product-market responsiveness to price should answer the following questions:

1. How large is the product-market in terms of buying potential?
2. What are the market segments and what market target strategy is to be used?
3. How sensitive is demand in the segment(s) to changes in price?
4. How important are nonprice factors, such as features and performance?
5. What are the estimated sales at different price levels?

Let's examine these questions for Aleve. The analgesic market was growing at about a 3 percent annual rate. Aleve offers extended relief benefits to arthritis sufferers and people with sore muscles. P&G apparently wanted to stress the brand's performance rather than encourage price competition. The $200 million sales estimate would position Aleve in third place behind Tylenol and private label brands. Since forecasting product-market size, segmentation, and targeting are discussed in Chapters 5, 6, and 9, the last three questions are now considered.

The core issue in pricing is finding out what value the buyer places on the product or brand.[7] Pricing decision makers need this information in order to determine price. Basing price only on cost may lead to pricing too high or too low compared to the value perceived by the buyer. Buyers see different values depending on their use situation, so segment analysis is essential. For example, people who want an analgesic that lasts longer will place a high value on Aleve.

EXHIBIT 11–2 Demand Curves with Differing Price Elasticity

| A. Bus service | B. Microwave oven | C. Cigarettes | D. Cancer drug |

Source: David W. Cravens and Robert B. Woodruff, *Marketing* (Reading, MA: Addison-Wesley, 1986), p. 443.

Price Elasticity. Price elasticity is the percentage change in the quantity of a product sold when the price changes divided by the percentage change in price. Elasticity is measured for changes in price from some specific price level and is not necessarily constant over the range of prices under consideration. Surprisingly, research indicates that people will buy more of certain products at *higher* prices, thus establishing a price–quantity relationship that slopes upward to the right. In these instances, people seem to be using price as a measure of quality because they are unable to evaluate the product. Estimating the exact shape of the demand curve (price–quantity relationship) is probably impossible in most instances. Even so, there are ways to estimate the sensitivity of customers to alternative prices. Test marketing can be used for this purpose. Study of historical price and quantity data may be helpful. End-user research studies, such as consumer evaluations of price, are also used. These approaches, coupled with management judgment, help indicate the sensitivity of sales to price in the range of prices that is under consideration.

Demand curves for several products are shown in Exhibit 11–2. Elasticity varies for different products because buyers' responsiveness to price differs from one product to another.

Nonprice Factors. Factors other than price need to be considered when analyzing buying situations. Buyers may be willing to pay a premium price to gain other advantages or instead be willing to forgo certain advantages for lower prices. Factors other than price may be important, such as quality, uniqueness, availability, service, and warranty. In an attempt to recover from intense price competition, fast-food chains are marketing value menus of higher-priced items. These value strategies include the quality of the food, user-friendly service, and attractive dining facilities. For example, McDonald's advertising message, "What you want is what you get," emphasizes the concept of value.

Certain buying situations may reduce the importance of price in the buyer's choice process. The price of the product may be a minor factor when the amount is small compared to the importance of the use situation. Examples include infrequently purchased electric parts for home entertainment equipment, batteries for appliances, and health and beauty aids during a vacation. The need for important but relatively inexpensive parts for industrial equipment is another situation that reduces the role of price in the buyer's purchase decision. Quick Metal, an adhesive produced by Loctite Corporation, is used by maintenance personnel to repair production equipment. At less than $20 a tube, the price is not a major concern since one tube will keep an expensive production line operating until a new part is installed.

Other examples of nonprice factors that affect the buying situation include: (1) purchases of products essential to physical health, such as pain relief; (2) choice between brands of complex products that are difficult to evaluate, such as stereo equipment (a high price may be used as a gauge of quality); and (3) image-enhancement situations such as serving prestige brands of drinks to socially important guests.

Forecasts.   Forecasts of sales are needed for the range of prices that management is considering. In planning the introduction of Aleve, P&G's management could look at alternative sales forecasts based on different prices and other marketing program variations. These forecasts, when combined with cost estimates, indicate the financial impact of different price strategies. The objective is to estimate sales in units for each product (or brand) at the prices under consideration.

Elasticity estimates can be used to develop sales projections, assuming all other marketing-program influences remain constant. This method of forecasting is illustrated in Exhibit 11–3. The parity price (Step 1) corresponds to an index value of 100. This indicates that the firm's price is equal to the average for the product category in which it competes. In Steps 2 and 3, the effects of price changes are estimated. Using these relative measures of elasticity, forecasts can be made from test-market data or from historical sales data in the case of existing products.

There are many forecasting situations when all other marketing-program influences are not constant. In these instances, the effects of other factors must be included in the analysis. Controlled tests are used for this purpose. For example, a fast-food chain can evaluate the effects of different prices on demand through tests in a sample of stores. Experimental designs measure or control the effects of factors other than price. We discussed methods for analyzing the effects of positioning strategy components and positioning results in Chapter 6.

Cost Analysis

Cost information is also needed in making pricing decisions. Exhibit 11–4 is a guide to cost analysis. First, we analyze the composition of the cost of producing and distributing the product. This involves determining fixed and variable components of cost. Also, it is necessary to find the portion of product cost accounted for by purchases from suppliers. For example, a large portion of the cost of a personal computer is the components produced by suppliers. It is useful to separate the cost into labor, materials, and capital categories when studying cost structure.

Volume Effect on Cost.   The next step of cost analysis examines cost and volume relationships. How do costs vary at different levels of production or quantities purchased? Can economies of scale be gained over the volume range that is under consideration, given the target market and program-positioning strategy? At what volumes are significant

EXHIBIT 11–3 Demand Elasticity to Price Change

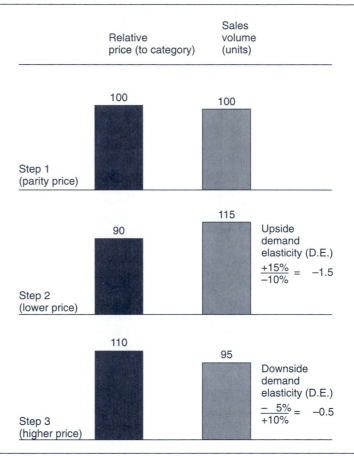

Source: Earl L. Bailey, ed., *Pricing Practices and Strategies* (New York: The Conference Board, Inc., 1978), p. 8.

cost reductions possible? The main task in this part of the analysis is to determine the extent to which the volume produced or distributed should be taken into account in selecting the pricing strategy.

Competitive Advantage.   In analyzing competitive advantage, comparing key competitors' costs is often valuable. Are their costs higher, lower, or about the same? Although such information is sometimes difficult to obtain, experienced managers can often make accurate estimates. We need to place key competitors into relative product cost categories (e.g., higher, lower, same). In some situations analysts can estimate competitive cost information from a knowledge of wage rates, material costs, production facilities, and related information.

Exhibit 11–5 is an illustration of competitive advantage analysis. The basis of comparison is the power output of a commercial equipment product. Notice how price

---

EXHIBIT 11–4 Cost Analysis for Pricing Decisions

- Determine the composition of product cost.
- Estimate how volume of sales affects cost.
- Analyze the competitive advantage of the product.
- Decide how experience in producing the product affects costs.
- Estimate how much control the organization has over costs.

EXHIBIT 11–5 Zones of Competitive Advantage for Competing Products

---

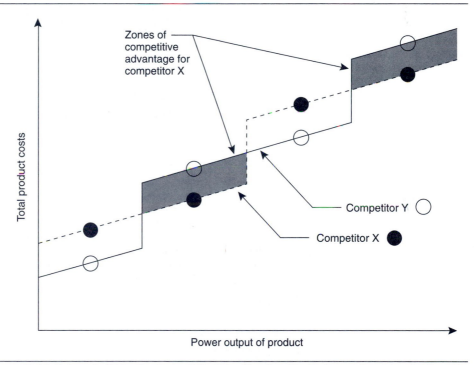

Source: Earl L. Bailey, ed., *Pricing Practices and Strategies* (New York: The Conference Board, Inc., 1978), p. 52.

---

advantage changes at different power outputs for companies X and Y. Company X (which is smaller than Y, the industry leader) has important cost advantages over Y in two zones of power output because of the technical differences in their products. Thus, cost advantages depend on the power output required by buyers. Company X has an advantage for some applications, Y in others.

Experience Effect.   It is important to consider the effect of experience on costs. Experience or learning-curve analysis (using historical data) indicates that costs and prices for various products decline by a given amount each time the number of units produced doubles. Price declines may be uneven because of competitive influences. When unit costs (vertical axis) are plotted against total accumulated volume (horizontal axis), costs decline with volume. This effect occurs when experience increases the efficiency of production operations. The experience-curve effect needs to be examined on an industry and company basis since the effect is not the same across all product categories.

There are several issues to be evaluated in experience-curve estimation, including the effect of aggregation of product data, errors in variables, functional form of the relationship, and measurement.[8] The experience curve can be estimated using the total direct costs required to produce the first unit (or a later unit) and the improvement rate due to experience.[9] The cumulative total direct cost at any point will be equal to cost of the first unit times the number of units raised to the power equal to 1 minus the improvement rate. The improvement rate ranges from 0 to 1, and the equation for cumulative cost is:

$$(\text{Unit 1 cost}) \times (\text{Number of units})^{1-\text{Improvement rate}}$$

Control over Costs. Finally, it is useful to consider how much influence the firm may have over costs in the future. To what extent can research and development, bargaining power with suppliers, process innovation, and other factors, be expected to reduce costs over the planning horizon? These considerations are interrelated with experience-curve analysis, yet may operate over a shorter time range. The bargaining power of an organization in its channels of distribution, for example, can have a major effect on costs, and the effects can be immediate. An example of bargaining power with suppliers in the fast growing retail market in Latin America is described in the Global Feature.

Competitor Analysis

Each competitor's price strategy is evaluated to determine: (1) which firms represent the most direct competition (actual and potential) for the market targets under consideration, (2) how competing firms are positioned on a relative price basis and the extent to which price is used as an active part of their marketing strategies, (3) how successful each firm's price strategy has been, and (4) what key competitors' probable responses to alternative price strategies will be.

The discussion in Chapter 3 considered methods for competitor identification. It is important to determine both potential and current competitors. Sears adopted a new "everyday-low" pricing strategy in 1989, which changed both buyers' perceptions and the retailers with which Sears competes most directly. The new strategy placed Sears in direct competition with retailers actively promoting low prices. Some retailing authorities questioned Sears' choice of the new price strategy.[10] Regardless of its impact on Sears, the low price strategy forced many competing retailers to adopt defensive strategies.

The success of a competitor's price strategy is usually gauged by financial performance, as illustrated by the poor short-term results of Sears' retail operations after implementing the new price strategy. The problem with this measure is accounting for other influences on profits. Interestingly, by 1995 Sears' performance had improved substantially.

The most difficult of the four questions about competition is predicting what they will do in response to alternative price actions. No changes are likely unless one firm's

---

GLOBAL FEATURE   French Retailer Carrefour and Wal-Mart Compete in Argentina

---

Power retailers like Carrefour and Wal-Mart are targeting Latin America to help sustain growth and profits. Carrefour had 11 discount centers in Argentina and over 30 in Brazil when Wal-Mart entered the Argentina market in 1995.

Wal-Mart alleges that the French competitor is pressuring its local suppliers to stop supplying Wal-Mart with personal care, paper products, and other goods. Carrefour denies the charge. Wal-Mart's concern is that without strong support from local manufacturers, the retailer will be unable to purchase 85 percent of its goods in Argentina. Importing will substantially increase Wal-Mart's costs.

The battle for market position by the two giant discounters promises to be interesting. Carrefour has a head start with sales of $1.5 billion in Argentina. Both are matching prices. Wal-Mart is stressing customer service and trying to build collaborative relationships with suppliers. Carrefour does not have a strong reputation for service. The number of supermarkets, hypermarkets, and self-service outlets in Argentina nearly doubled from 1984 to 1994.

Source: Jonathan Friedland, "Big Discounters Duel over Hot Market," *The Wall Street Journal,* August 23, 1995, p. A6. Reprinted by permission of *The Wall Street Journal,* © 1995 Dow Jones & Company, Inc. All Rights Reserved Worldwide.

---

price is viewed as threatening (low) or greedy (high). Competitive pressures, actual and potential, often narrow the range of feasible prices and rule out the use of extremely high or low prices relative to competition. In new-product markets, competitive factors may be insignificant, except for the fact that very high prices may attract potential competitors.

Game theory is a useful method for analyzing competitors' pricing strategies. It can be used to analyze competitive pricing situations. The technique became very popular in the 1990s. Three game theorists won the 1994 Nobel Prize in economics. Exhibit 11–6 describes the basics of this competitor analysis method.

Legal and Ethical Considerations

The last step in analyzing the pricing situation is identifying possible legal and ethical factors that may affect the choice of a price strategy. A wide variety of laws and regulations affect pricing actions. Legal constraints are important influences on the pricing of goods and services in many different national and cooperative regional trade environments. Pricing practices in the United States that have received the most attention from government include:

Horizontal price fixing. Price collusion between competitors. Products with narrow profit margins are more likely to lead to price fixing. The Sherman Act and the Federal Trade Commission Act prohibit price fixing between companies at the same level in the channel.

Price discrimination. Charging different customers different prices without an underlying cost basis for discrimination. The Clayton Act and the Robinson-Patman Act prohibit price discrimination if it lessens or injures competition.

EXHIBIT 11–6 Using Game Theory to Analyze Competitors' Pricing Strategies

---

Game theory is hot. Its champions won the 1994 Nobel Prize in economics and it's been used to analyze everything from the baseball strike to auctions at the Federal Communication Commission. Why? More specifically, why are 50-year-old ideas now being used by companies to answer basic questions about pricing, investments in capacity, purchasing, and other matters? . . .

The theory itself is reasonably straightforward to use. Say you have two competitors, Ace and Smith. Ace expects Smith to enter the market and is trying to understand Smith's likely pricing strategy. To do so, Ace uses something called a "payoff matrix" (see chart). Each quadrant in the matrix contains the "payoffs"—or financial impact—to each player for each possible strategy. If both players maintain prices at current levels, they will both be better off: Ace will earn $100 million and Smith will earn $60 million (Quadrant A). Unfortunately for both Ace and Smith, however, they have perverse incentives to cut prices.

Ace calculates that if he maintains prices, Smith will cut prices to increase earnings to $70 million from $60 million. (See the arrow moving from Quadrant A to Quadrant B.) Smith makes a similar calculation that if she maintains prices, Ace will cut. The logic eventually drives them both to Quadrant D, with both cutting prices and both earning lower returns than they would with current prices in place. This "equilibrium" is unattractive for both parties. If each party perceives this, then there is some prospect that each will separately determine to try to compete largely on other

factors, such as product features, service levels, sales force deployment, or advertising.

But you have to know your industry inside-out before game theory is truly valuable. Whether your goal is to implement game theory by fully quantifying the outcomes of a payoff matrix or by more qualitatively assessing the outcome of the matrix, you will need to understand entry costs, exit costs, demand functions, revenue structures, cost curves, etc. Without that understanding, the answer you get may be wrong.

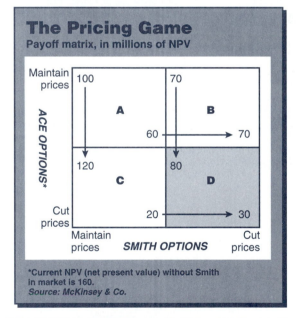

The Pricing Game
Payoff matrix, in millions of NPV

*Current NPV (net present value) without Smith in market is 160.
Source: McKinsey & Co.

Price fixing in channels of distribution. Specifying the prices of distributors. The Consumer Goods Pricing Act places vertical price fixing under the jurisdiction of the antitrust laws.

Price information. Violating requirements concerning the form and the availability of price information for consumers. Unit pricing and consumer credit requirements are examples. For example, the Consumer Credit Protection Act requires full disclosure of annual interest rates and other financial charges.[11]

Ethical issues in pricing are more subjective and difficult to evaluate than legal factors. Some companies include ethical guidelines in their pricing policies. Deciding what is or is not ethical is often difficult. The important consideration is to include evaluation of possible ethical issues when developing a pricing strategy.

Let's consider the pricing ethics of the Franklin Mint, Inc., a coin and collectables-manufacturing and marketing company.[12] Critics argue that the company charges unreasonably high prices for coins (it reentered the coin business in 1994). One collection of 20 ancient Roman coins had an average price per coin of $110. A group of 21 dealers estimated two of nine coins shown in the sales literature to be all but worthless, six ranged from $5 to $20, while the ninth was valued at $20 to $55. If these comparisons reflect the general pricing of Franklin Mint's coin offerings, there may be support for the criticisms. Though people do not have to buy the coins, critics question the ethics of the marketing communications by Franklin Mint.

SELECTING THE PRICING STRATEGY

Analysis of the pricing situation provides essential information for selecting a pricing strategy. Additional considerations include: (1) determining pricing flexibility and (2) deciding how to position price relative to costs and deciding how visible to make the price of the product.

The pricing strategy needs to be developed in the context of the entire marketing program since in most, if not all, instances there are other important influences on buyers' purchasing behavior. The Strategy Feature describes the problems in going after market share rather than pricing for competitive advantage.

How Much Flexibility Exists?

Demand and cost factors determine the extent of pricing flexibility. Within these upper and lower boundaries, competition and legal and ethical considerations also influence the choice of a specific price strategy. Exhibit 11–7 illustrates how these factors determine flexibility. The price gap between demand and cost may be narrow or wide. A narrow gap simplifies the decision; a wide gap suggests a greater range of feasible strategies. Choice of the price strategy within the gap is influenced by competition strategies, present and future, and by legal and ethical considerations. Management must determine where to price within the gap shown in Exhibit 11–7. In competitive markets the feasibility range may be very narrow. Recall, for example, P&G's pricing of Aleve. It was priced the same as a key competitor's brand. New markets or emerging market segments in established markets may allow a firm more flexibility in strategy selection.

Bristol-Myers Squibb's entry into the AIDS drug market is an interesting case study of price-flexibility analysis and strategy design and implementation.[13] The strategy that was selected benefited from management's analysis of the mistakes made by Burroughs-Wellcome in marketing AZT. The company received widespread criticism from patients and their advocates about AZT's high prices (initially $8,000 for a one-year supply). Burroughs responded by lowering the price. The Bristol-Myers drug Videx was given to

---

STRATEGY FEATURE   Market Share and Profitability: Is Bigger Better?

A common myth among marketers is that market share is the key to profitability. If that were true, recent history would have shown General Motors to be the world's most profitable automobile company, Sears Roebuck the most profitable retailer, and Philips the most profitable manufacturer of electrical products ranging from light bulbs to color televisions. In fact, all of these companies, though sales leaders, are financial also-rans.

The source of this myth is a demonstrable correlation between market share and profitability. However, a correlation does not necessarily imply a causal relationship. A far more plausible explanation for the correlation is that both profitability and market share are caused by the same underlying source of business success: a sustainable competitive advantage in meeting customer needs more effectively or efficiently. When a company has a competitive advantage, it can earn higher margins because of either a price premium or a lower cost of production. That advantage, if sustainable, also discourages competitors from targeting the company's customers or from resisting its attempts to expand.

Consequently, whereas a less fortunate company would face equally efficient competitors who could take market shares with margin-destroying price competition, a company with a competitive advantage can sustain higher market share even as it earns higher profits. Rather than being the key to profitability, market share—like profitability—is simply another symptom of a fundamentally well-run company.

Unfortunately, when management misperceives the symptom (market share) as a cause and seeks to increase it by some inappropriate means, such as price cutting, the expected profitability doesn't materialize. On the contrary, a grab for market share unjustified by a competitive advantage can often reduce the company's own and its industry's profitability. The ultimate objective of a strategic plan should not be to achieve or even sustain sales volume, but to build and sustain competitive advantage. Profitability, and in many cases market share, will follow.

In fact, contrary to the myth that a higher market share causes higher profitability, changes in profitability frequently precede changes in market share, not the other way around. For example, Wal-Mart's competitive advantages made it America's most profitable retailer long before it became the largest, whereas Sears' poor profitability preceded by many years its loss of the dominant market share. This same pattern of profitability leading, not following, market share is currently visible in the automobile, steel, and banking industries.

A strategic plan based on building volume, rather than competitive advantage, is essentially a beggar-thy-neighbor strategy—a negative-sum game that ultimately can only undermine industry profitability. Every point of market share won by reducing margins (either by offering a lower price or by incurring higher costs) invariably reduces the value of the sales gained. The only sustainable way to increase relative profitability is by achieving a competitive advantage that will enable you to increase sales and margins. In short, the goal of a strategic plan should not be to become bigger than the competition (although that may happen), but to become better. Such positive-sum competition, rather than undermining the profitability of an industry, constantly renews it.

Source: Thomas T. Nagle, "Managing Price Competition," *Marketing Management* 2, no. 1 (1993), p. 44.

EXHIBIT 11–7 How Much Flexibility in Price Strategy?

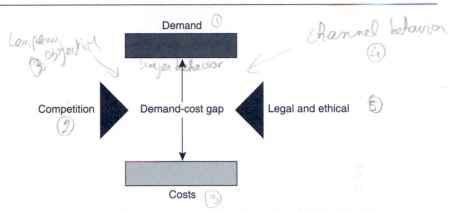

30,000 AIDS patients at no charge before it was approved for sale by the U.S. Food and Drug Administration. Deciding where to position the price in price gap (Exhibit 11–7) was complex. Negative reaction was likely if the price was perceived to be too high. If too low, the millions of dollars spent in developing the drug would not be recovered. The price selected was $1,745 for a year's supply of Videx. Industry analysts considered this price about one-third lower than their estimates using conventional pharmaceutical pricing strategy.

Potential adverse reaction from AIDS groups and U.S. government pressures about reasonable pricing of new drugs apparently influenced the pricing of Videx. Competitive pricing was not a critical influence on the decision since Videx can be taken by patients intolerant of AZT. Interestingly, some doctors and patients consider $1,745 too high. This price should generate annual sales of $50 million for Bristol-Myers.

Price Positioning and Visibility

A key decision is how far above cost to price a new product within the flexibility gap. We assume that management wishes to price somewhere above the cost of the product. Firms can charge a relatively low entry price, with the objective of building volume and market position, or instead set a high price to generate large margins. The former is a "penetration" strategy whereas the latter is a "skimming" strategy. Lack of knowledge about previous market response to the new product complicates the pricing decision. Several factors may affect the choice of a pricing approach for a new product, including the cost and life span of the product, the estimated responsiveness of buyers to alternative prices, and assessment of competitive reaction.

A decision should also be made about how visible price will be in the promotion of the new product. The use of a low entry price requires active promotion of the price to gain market position. When firms use a high price relative to cost, price often assumes a passive role in the marketing mix. Instead, the performance and other attributes of the product are stressed in the marketing program positioning strategy.

EXHIBIT 11–8   Illustrative Pricing Strategies

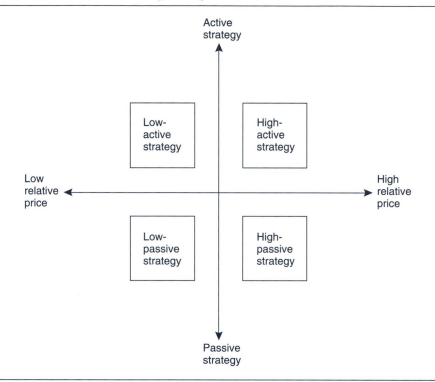

Illustrative Pricing Strategies

The choice of a pricing strategy depends on how management decides to price the product relative to competition, and whether price performs an active or passive role in the marketing program. The use of price as an active or passive factor refers to whether price is discussed in advertising, personal selling, and other promotional efforts. The strategies shown in Exhibit 11–8 illustrate the range of price strategies companies can use. Many firms choose to price at or near the prices of key competitors, emphasizing nonpricing factors in their marketing strategies. We will examine each of the strategies shown in Exhibit 11–8, highlighting their characteristics and features.

High-Active Strategy.   This strategy is sometimes used for prestige brands seeking an affluence image. When the buyer cannot easily evaluate the quality of a product, price can serve as a signal of value. Also, high prices may be essential to gain the margins necessary to serve small target markets, produce high-quality products, or pay for the development of new products. Making price visible and active can appeal to the buyer's perceptions of quality, image, and dependability of products and services. A firm using a high-price strategy is also less subject to retaliation by competitors, particularly if its product are differentiated from other brands.

The underlying logic of emphasizing the high price in promotional activities is to convey to the buyer that because the brand is expensive, it offers superior value. While not widely used, this pricing strategy has been used to symbolically position products such as high-end alcoholic beverages.

High-Passive Strategy.   Relatively high-priced brands are often marketed by featuring nonprice factors rather than using high-active strategies. Product features and performance can be stressed when the people in the target market are concerned with product quality and performance. BMW and Mercedes have successfully followed this strategy for many years. Rubbermaid in kitchen aids (e.g., plastic containers) competes effectively against commodity-type competition using a high-passive strategy through innovation and product differentiation.

Low-Active Strategy.   Several retailers use this strategy, including Home Depot (home improvement), Dollar General Stores (apparel), Office Depot (office supplies), Toys "R" Us (toys), and Pic 'N Pay Shoe Stores (family shoes). The strategy is also popular with discount stockbrokers. When price is an important factor in the buyer's decision, a low-active price strategy is very effective, as indicated by the rapid growth of these retailers. However, this strategy may start a price war. It is a more attractive option when the competition for the market target is not heavy or when a company has cost advantages and a strong position in the product-market.

Low-Passive Strategy.   This strategy may be used by small manufacturers whose products have lower-cost features than other suppliers. By not emphasizing a low price, the firm runs less danger that potential buyers will assume the product quality is inferior to other brands. Some firms participating in conventional channels may not spend much on marketing their products and thus may offer low prices because of lower costs. Other firms that have actual cost advantages for comparable competing products may decide to stress value rather than price even though they are offering prices lower than competing brands.

DETERMINING SPECIFIC PRICES AND POLICIES

The last step in pricing strategy (Exhibit 11–1) is selecting specific prices and formulating policies to help manage the pricing strategy. We will examine pricing methods and discuss pricing policy. The chapter will conclude by examining several special pricing considerations.

Determining Specific Prices

It is necessary either to assign a specific price to each product item or to provide a method for computing price for a particular buyer–seller transaction. Many methods and techniques are available for calculating price.

Price determination is normally based on cost, demand, competition, or a combination of these factors. Cost-oriented methods use the cost of producing and marketing the product as the basis for determining price. Demand-oriented pricing methods consider estimated market response to alternative prices; the most profitable price and market response level is selected. Competition-oriented methods use competitors' prices as a reference point in setting prices. The price selected may be above, below, or equal to competitors' prices. Typically, one method (cost, demand, or competition) provides the basis for pricing, although the other factors have some influence.

Cost-Oriented Approaches.   Break-even pricing is a cost-oriented approach to determine prices. The initial computation is as follows:

$$\text{Break-even (units)} = \frac{\text{Total fixed costs}}{\text{Unit price} - \text{Unit variable cost}}$$

When using this method, we select a price and calculate the number of units that must be sold at that price to cover all fixed and variable costs. Next, we assess the feasibility of exceeding the break-even value and thus generating a profit. One or more possible prices may be evaluated in the analysis. This form of analysis was no doubt included in the Bristol-Myers pricing strategy formulation for the AIDS drug, Videx. Break-even analysis is not a complete basis for determining price, since both demand and competition are important considerations in the pricing decision. With break-even price as a frame of reference, demand and competition can be evaluated. The price selected is typically at some level higher than the break-even price.

Another popular pricing method is cost-plus pricing. This technique uses cost as the basis of calculating the selling price. A percentage amount of the cost is added to cost to determine price. A similar method, markup pricing, calculates markups as a percentage of the selling price. When using markup pricing, this formula determines the selling price:

$$\text{Price} = \frac{\text{Average unit cost}}{1 - \text{Markup percent*}}$$

*Percent expressed in decimal form.

Competition-Oriented Approaches.   Pricing decisions are always affected by the actions of competitors. Pricing methods that use competitors' prices in calculating actual prices include setting prices equal to or at some specified percentage above or below the competition's. In industries such as air travel, one of the firms may be viewed by others as the price leader. When the leader changes its prices, other firms follow with similar prices. American Airlines has attempted to perform such a leadership role in the United States, although its pricing changes are not always adopted by competing airlines. Another form of competition-oriented pricing is competitive bidding, where firms submit sealed bids to the purchaser. This method is used in the purchase of various industrial products and suppliers. Game theory is also a form of competitor-oriented pricing (see Exhibit 11–6).

Demand-Oriented Approaches.   The buyer is the frame of reference for these methods. One popular method is estimating the value of the product to the buyer. The objective is to determine how much the buyer is willing to pay for the product based on its contribution to the buyer's needs or wants. This approach is used for both consumer and business products. Information on demand and price relationships is needed in guiding demand-oriented pricing decisions.

Many pricing methods are in use, so it is important to select specific prices within the guidelines provided by price strategy and to incorporate demand, cost, and competition considerations.[14]

Establishing Pricing Policy and Structure

Determining price flexibility, positioning price against competition, and deciding how active a component it will be in the marketing program do not establish the operating guidelines necessary for implementing a pricing strategy. It is helpful to also determine policy to guide pricing decisions and pricing structure.

Pricing Policy.   An illustration shows how pricing decisions are guided by policies. Mervyn's, the 276-store retail chain, experienced poor performance in the early 1990s due to faulty merchandise selection and pricing policy.[15] Half of its sales are from 125 stores in California, which was experiencing a recession. The pricing policy was to offer large price reductions on many items when they were advertised one week each month. For example, a blanket was sale-priced at $17.99, compared to the regular $25 price. Since buyers were aware of Mervyn's pricing policy, they waited until the week the item of interest was sale-priced. The faulty policy reduced sales and profits.

A pricing policy may include consideration of discounts, allowances, returns, and other operating guidelines. The policy serves as the basis for implementing and managing the pricing strategy. The policy may be in written form, although many companies operate without formal pricing policies.

Pricing Structure.   Anytime more than one product is involved, a firm must determine product mix and line-pricing interrelationships in order to establish price structure. For example, a strategy of low prices does not automatically provide management of Toys "R" Us with specific prices for each item the firm offers. And when more than one market target is involved, what relationship exists between the products offered in each? Assuming differences in products, should price be based on cost, demand, or competition?

Price structure concerns how individual items in the line are priced in relation to one another: The items may be aimed at the same market target or different end-user groups. For example, department stores often offer economy and premium product categories. In the case of a single product-market, typically, price differences among products reflect more than variations in costs. Large supermarket chains price for total profitability of the product offering rather than for performance of individual items. These retailers have developed computer analysis and pricing procedures to achieve sales, market-share, and profit objectives. Similarly, commercial airlines must work with an array of fares in the pricing structure.

The pricing of the Toyota Camry and the Lexus ES 300 is an interesting example of pricing products in relation to each other. The ES 300 is targeted to the semi-luxury market.[16] The ES 300 has essentially the same body as the Camry, but the Lexus sells for substantially more than the Camry. The Lexus has several unique features (e.g., leather seats), but some of the price difference has to be image rather than substance. Both cars display good sales records.

Once product relationships are established, some basis for determining price structure must be selected. Many firms base price structure on market and competitive factors as well as differences in the costs of producing each item. Some use multiple criteria for determining price structure and have sophisticated computer models to examine alternate pricing schemes. Others use rules of thumb developed from experience. The following guidelines are useful in pricing a line of products.

1. Price each product in relation to all others; noticeable differences in products should be equivalent to perceived value differences.

2. The top and bottom prices in the line should be priced so as to facilitate desired buyer perceptions.

3. Price differences between products should become larger as price increases over the line.[17]

Most approaches include, not only cost considerations, but also demand and competitive concerns. For example, industrial-equipment manufacturers sometimes price new products at or close to cost and depend on sales of high-margin items such as supplies, parts, and replacement items to generate profits. The important consideration is to price the entire mix and line of products to achieve pricing objectives.

Special Pricing Considerations

Several special pricing situations may occur in particular industries, markets, and competitive environments.

Price Segmentation.   Price is used in several markets to appeal to different market segments. For example, airline prices vary depending on the conditions of purchase. Different versions of the same basic product may be offered at different prices to reflect differences in materials and product features. Industrial-products firms may use quantity discounts to respond to differences in the quantities purchased by customers. Price elasticity differences make it feasible to appeal to different segments.

Distribution Channel Pricing.   The pricing strategies of manufacturers using marketing middlemen include consideration of the pricing needs of channel members. The strategy adopted by the producer should allow the flexibility and incentives necessary to achieve sales objectives. These decisions require analysis of cost and pricing at all channel levels. If producer prices to intermediaries are too high, inadequate margins may discourage intermediaries from actively promoting the producer's brand. Margins vary based on the nature and importance of the functions that intermediaries in the channel are expected to perform. For example, margins between costs and selling prices must be large enough to compensate a wholesaler for carrying a complete stock of replacement parts.

Price Flexibility.   Another special consideration is deciding how flexible prices will be. Will prices be firm, or will they be negotiated between buyer and seller? Perhaps most important, firms should make price flexibility a policy decision rather than a tactical response. Some companies' price lists are very rigid, while others have list prices that give no indication of actual selling prices. It is also important to recognize the legal issues in pricing products when using flexible pricing policies.

Product Life Cycle Pricing.   Some firms have policies to guide pricing decisions over the life cycle of the product. Depending on its stage in the product life cycle, the price of a particular product or an entire line may be based on market share, profitability, cash flow, or other objectives. In many product-markets, price declines (in constant dollars) as the product moves through its life cycle. Because of life-cycle considerations, different objectives and policies may apply to particular products within a mix or line. Price becomes a more active element of strategy as products move through the life cycle and competitive pressures build, costs decline, and volume increases. Life-cycle pricing strategy should correspond to the overall marketing program positioning strategy used.

SUMMARY

Pricing strategy gains considerable direction from the decisions management makes about the product mix, branding strategy, and product quality. Distribution strategy also influences the choice of how price will work in combination with advertising and sales force strategies. Pricing strategy may also influence other marketing mix decisions. Price, like other marketing program components, is a means of generating market response.

Two important trends are apparent in the use of price as a strategic variable. First, companies are designing far more flexibility into their strategies in order to cope with the rapid changes and uncertainties in the turbulent business environment. Second, price is more often used as an active, rather than passive, element of corporate and marketing strategies. This trend is particularly apparent in the retail sector where aggressive low-price strategies are used by firms such as Wal-Mart, Office Depot, and Home Depot. However, assigning an active role to price does not necessarily lead to low prices relative to competition—companies may use relatively high prices.

Product, distribution, price, and promotion strategies must fit together into an integrated strategy of program positioning. Pricing strategy for new and existing products includes (1) setting pricing objectives, (2) analyzing the pricing situation, (3) selecting (or revising) the pricing strategy, and (4) determining specific prices and policies. Companies use their pricing strategies to achieve one or more of several possible objectives. These include gaining market position, achieving financial performance, positioning the product, stimulating demand, and influencing competition.

Analyzing the pricing situation is necessary to develop a pricing strategy for a mix or line of products, or to select a pricing strategy for a new product or brand. Underlying strategy formulation are several important activities, including analyses of the product market, cost, competition, and legal and ethical considerations. These analyses indicate the extent of pricing flexibility.

The choice of a pricing strategy includes consideration of price positioning and visibility. Price strategies are classified according to the firm's price relative to the competition and how active the promotion of price will be in the marketing program.

Pricing approaches for products include high-active, high-passive, low-active, and low-passive strategies. Variations within the four categories occur. In many industries market leaders establish prices that are followed by other firms in the industry.

The determination of specific prices may be based on costs, competition, and/or demand influences. Implementing and managing the pricing strategy also includes establishing pricing policy and structure. Finally, several special pricing considerations include price segmentation, distribution channel pricing, product life cycle pricing, and price and quality relationships.

QUESTIONS FOR REVIEW AND DISCUSSION

1. Discuss the role of price in the marketing strategy for Rolex watches. Contrast Timex's price strategy with Rolex's strategy.

2. In 1992, Toyota introduced two new automobiles. The redesigned Camry and the Lexus ES 300 were very similar but the ES 300 was priced substantially higher than the Camry. Discuss the features and limitations of this pricing strategy.

3. Indicate how a fast-food chain can estimate the price elasticity of a proposed new product such as a chicken sandwich.

4. Real estate brokers, typically, charge a fixed percentage of a home's sales price. Advertising agencies follow a similar price strategy. Discuss why this may be sound price strategy. What are the arguments against it from the buyer's point of view?

5. Cite examples of businesses to which the experience-curve effect is not applicable. What influence may this have on price determination?

6. In some industries prices are set low, subsidies are provided, and other price-reducing mechanisms are used to establish a long-term relationship with the buyer. Utilities, for example, sometimes use incentives to encourage contractors to install electric- or gas-powered appliances. Manufacturers may price equipment low, then depend on service and parts for profit contribution. What are the advantages and limitations of this pricing strategy?

7. Some private clubs exclude prices from their menus. Analyze and evaluate this price strategy.

8. Discuss some of the ways that estimates of the costs of competitors' products can be determined.

9. Discuss how a pricing strategy should be developed by a new firm to price its business-analysis software line.

10. Suppose a firm is considering changing from a low-active price strategy to a high-active strategy. Discuss the implications of this proposed change.

11. Describe and evaluate the price strategy used for the Toyota Lexus 400 European-style luxury sedan.

NOTES

1. This illustration is based on Walter Kikevy, "Beware, the Pricing Genie Is Out of the Bottle," *Retailing Issues Letter,* Arthur Andersen & Company, November 1994, pp. 1–3.

2. Bill Saporito, "Why the Price Wars Never End," *Fortune,* March 23, 1992, pp. 68–71, 74, 78.

3. This illustration is based on Stephanie Mehta, "White Castle's Successful Recipe: Burger, Burger, Burger, Fries," *The Wall Street Journal,* July 25, 1995, pp. B1 and B2.

4. Janet Guyon, "Stung by Rivals, AT&T Is Fighting Back," *The Wall Street Journal,* June 30, 1989, p. B1.

5. Erle Norton, "Kodak to Slash Prices for Film It Sells in Japan," *The Wall Street Journal,* August 24, 1995, p. A2.

6. Laura Bird, "MARKETSCAN," *The Wall Street Journal,* June 16, 1994, p. B9.

7. Robert J. Dolan, "How Do You Know When the Price Is Right," *Harvard Business Review,* September–October 1995, pp. 174–83.

8. David B. Montgomery and George S. Day, "Experience Curves: Evidence, Empirical Issues, and Applications," in *Strategic Marketing and Management,* ed. H. Thomas

and D. Gardner (Chichester, U.K.: John Wiley & Sons, 1985), pp. 213–38.

9. A guide to determining experience curves is provided in Kent B. Monroe, *Pricing: Making Profitable Decisions* (New York: McGraw-Hill, 1979), pp. 115–19.

10. Francine Schwadel, "Troubles Deepen at Sears as the Christmas Season Nears," *The Wall Street Journal,* October 25, 1989, p. B1.

11. These and other aspects of marketing and the law are discussed in David W. Cravens, Gerald E. Hills, and Robert B. Woodruff, *Marketing Management,* (Burr Ridge, IL: Richard D. Irwin, 1987), chap. 24.

12. Alexandra Peers, "Value of Franklin Mint Collections May Be a Coin Toss," *The Wall Street Journal,* August 3, 1994, pp. C1, C13.

13. This illustration is based on Marilyn Chase, "Deft Distribution: Bristol Myers Guides AIDS Drug through a Marketing Minefield," *The Wall Street Journal,* October 10, 1991, pp. A1, A6.

14. See, for example, Thomas T. Nagle, *The Strategy and Tactics of Pricing* (Englewood Cliffs, NJ: Prentice Hall, 1987).

15. Gregory A. Patterson, "Mervyn's Efforts to Revamp Result in Disappointment," *The Wall Street Journal,* March 29, 1994, p. B4.

16. Jerry Flint, "Alfred Sloan Spoken Here," *Forbes,* November 1991, pp. 96, 101.

17. For a discussion of product-line pricing, see Monroe, *Pricing,* chap. 10.

Promotion, Advertising, and Sales Promotion Strategies

Promotion strategy combines advertising, personal selling, sales promotion, direct marketing, and publicity into a coordinated program for communicating with buyers and others who affect purchasing decisions. Promotion activities are important influences on the sales achieved by companies. Billions are spent every week in the United States and other nations around the world on promotion. Effective management of these expensive resources is essential to gain the optimum return from the promotion expenditures.

Proctor & Gamble spent seven years in building a market position in China, and promotion strategy played a key role in P&G's market entry strategy.[1] The company's shampoo and detergent sales totaled $450 million in 1995, making it the largest daily-use consumer products company in China. P&G used advertising to encourage people to try the Head & Shoulders antidandruff product. It became the leading shampoo in China. Salespeople follow up advertising campaigns, contacting retail establishments and passing out samples to consumers. P&G prepares maps of 228 cities with over 200,000 people, showing the location of retail outlets to guide salespeople in calling on the stores. The company spent $0.5 million persuading washing-machine companies to give buyers free packages of Ariel and Tide. P&G outspends all of its competitors on advertising. Its effective distribution network makes P&G brands available throughout China.

Promotion informs people about products and persuades the company's buyers, channel organizations, and the public at large to purchase brands. Increasingly, marketing management is finding it profitable to combine the promotion components into an integrated strategy for communicating with buyers and others who influence purchasing decisions. Since each form of promotion has certain strengths and shortcomings,

368

the integrated strategy incorporates the advantages of each component into a cost-effective promotion mix.

We will begin the chapter with an overview of promotion strategy and examine several considerations in selecting the strategy. Next, we will discuss the major decisions that comprise an advertising strategy and identify the factors affecting advertising decisions. Finally we will consider the design and implementation of sales promotion strategies.

PROMOTION STRATEGY

Promotion strategy is the planning, implementing, and controlling of the communications from an organization to its customers and other target audiences. The function of promotion in the marketing mix is to achieve various communications objectives with each audience. The components of the promotion mix include advertising, personal selling, sales promotion, direct marketing, and public relations. An important marketing responsibility is planning and coordinating an integrated promotion strategy and selecting strategies for the promotion components. The marketing manager has little or no control over word-of-mouth communications or the communications of other organizations. Nevertheless these communications also influence the firm's target audience(s).

The Components of Promotion Strategy

Advertising.   "Advertising is any paid form of nonpersonal presentation and promotion of ideas, goods, or services by an identified sponsor."[2] Advertising expenditures in the United States were an estimated $187 billion in 1997, up about 7.6 percent from 1996.[3] Global spending on advertising for 1997 totaled about $300 billion. Large advertising expenditures are often necessary to introduce new consumer products and to build the market position of existing products. For example, during the first year Proctor & Gamble spent an estimated $100 million in advertising to introduce the Aleve pain relief over-the-counter drug.[4] The Tagamet HB heartburn drug advertising campaign cost SmithKline Beecham $100 million, while Johnson & Johnson spent an equal amount on the Pepcid AC heartburn drug. In addition to over-the-counter drug advertising, pharmaceutical producers spent $300 million for prescription drug advertising in 1995.

Among the advantages of using advertising to communicate with buyers are the low cost per exposure, the variety of media (newspapers, magazines, television, radio, direct mail, and outdoor advertising), control of exposure, consistent message content, and the opportunity for creative message design. In addition, appeal and message can be adjusted when communications objectives change. Advertising also has some disadvantages. It cannot interact with the buyer and may not be able to hold viewers' attention. Moreover, the message is fixed for the duration of an exposure.

Personal Selling.   "Personal selling is the oral presentation in a conversation with one or more prospective purchasers for the purpose of making a sale."[5] Annual expenditures on personal selling are substantially larger than advertising, perhaps twice as much.

However, both promotion components share some common features, including creating awareness of the product, transmitting information, and persuading people to buy. Personal selling is expensive. For industrial products the cost per field sales call is more than $250 compared to less than $10 per 1,000 exposures for national television advertising. Personal selling has several unique strengths: Salespeople can interact with buyers to answer questions and overcome objections, they can target buyers, and they have the capacity to accumulate market knowledge and provide feedback. Top management often participates in selling by making calls on key customers.

Sales Promotion.   Sales promotion consists of various promotional activities, including trade shows, contests, samples, point-of-purchase displays, trade incentives, and coupons. Sales promotion expenditures are substantially greater than the amount spent on advertising. This array of special communications techniques and incentives offers several advantages: Promotion can be used to target buyers, respond to special occasions, and create an incentive for purchase. One of the more successful sales promotion concepts is the frequent flyer incentive program. American Airlines launched the innovative AAdvantage program in 1981. It was initially developed with a core customer group of 250,000 frequent flyers.[6] AAdvantage has over 15 million members and 200,000 join each month. American's SABRE reservation system enables the company to track mileage and efficiently manage the program. American's costs per member per year for communications and administration are less than $5.

Direct Marketing.   Direct marketing consists of the various communications channels that enable companies to make direct contact with individual buyers. Included are catalogs, direct mail, telemarketing, television selling, radio/magazine/newspaper selling, electronic shopping, and kiosk shopping (e.g., purchase of flight insurance in airports). The distinguishing feature of direct marketing is the opportunity for the marketer to achieve direct access to the buyer. Direct marketing expenditures account for a large portion of promotion expenditures. Electronic shopping is one of the newer forms of direct marketing. While accounting for a small portion of total shopping expenditures today, virtual shopping via computer is expected to total $7 billion by 2000.

Publicity.   "Publicity is nonpersonal stimulation of demand for a product, service, or idea by means of commercially significant news planted in the mass media and not paid for directly by a sponsor."[7] Public relations activities can make an important contribution to promotion strategy if the activity is planned and implemented to achieve specific promotion objectives. (Public relations is also used for other organizational purposes such as communicating with financial analysts.) Publicity can be negative as well as positive, and cannot be controlled to the same extent as other promotion components. Since the organization does not purchase the media coverage, publicity is a cost-effective method of communication. The media are usually willing to cover topics of public interest.

Developing Promotion Strategy

Market targets and positioning strategy guide promotion decisions. Promotion strategy includes deciding: (1) communications objectives, (2) the role of the components that make up the promotion mix, (3) the promotion budget, and (4) a strategy for each mix

---

EXHIBIT 12–1   Developing a Promotion Strategy

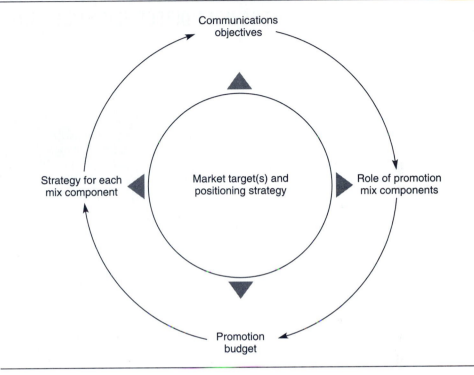

---

component (Exhibit 12–1). Strategies are selected for advertising, personal selling, sales promotion, direct marketing, and public relations.

Market targets and product, distribution, and price decisions guide: (1) deciding the role of promotion strategy in the total marketing program and (2) identifying the specific communications tasks of the promotion activities. One important question is deciding the role promotion will play in marketing strategy. Advertising or personal selling, or a combination of the two, is often a major part of a firm's marketing strategy. In consumer package goods firms, sales promotion and advertising comprise the major part of the promotional mix. In industrial firms, personal selling often dominates the promotion mix, with advertising and sales promotion playing a supporting role. The use of sales promotion and public relations varies considerably among companies. When promotion is not an important part of an organization's marketing program, the function is usually handled by other firms in the distribution channel. For example, producers of private-label brands of clothing rely on retailers to promote the brands to end-users.

Singapore Airlines plays an important promotion role in marketing the nation. It is consistently the most profitable global airline, although ranking 15th in size among carriers.[8] The airline's favorable image helps to position the country to executives, government officials, and tourists who are familiar with Singapore Airline's renowned

Courtesy of Singapore Airlines.

services. The tiny city-state with a population under 3 million has a strong brand image, the result in no small part of the airline's reputation with customers and competitors throughout the world. The "Singapore Girl" is featured in the air carrier's ad campaigns (see accompanying advertisement). Global air travel is expected to double in 2010 compared to 1990 and much of the growth is in Asia.

Communications Objectives

The objectives of the promotion-mix components are interrelated. An illustration will show how these objectives are closely linked together. Suppose that health care Brand A is perceived by buyers in a target segment as being gentle to use but less effective than competing Brand B. In fact, A is equivalent to B regarding effectiveness. Therefore, an important positioning objective is to convince buyers in the target segment that Brand A is both effective and gentle. The communications objective is to communicate to the target segment that A is gentle yet effective. The advertising objective is to communicate this message to the target segment via appropriate media. The salesforce must convey a similar message in direct sales contacts.

Communications objectives help determine how advertising, personal selling, and sales promotion are used in the marketing program. A look at the stages of a buyer's decision process suggest the range of communications objectives possible.

Need Recognition.   One communications objective, typical for new-product introductions, is to trigger a need. Need recognition may also be important for existing products and services, particularly when the buyer can postpone purchasing or choose not to purchase (life insurance is a good example). For example, recall in the China illustration how P&G emphasized the need to control dandruff in its advertising of Head & Shoulders shampoo. The ads focused attention on how dandruff is very visible on people with black hair.

Gathering Information.   Promotion can aid a buyer's search for information. One of the objectives of new-product promotional activities is to help buyers learn about the product. Prescription drug companies advertise to the public to make people aware of diseases and brand names.[9] In the past, they targeted only doctors through ads in medical journals and contacts by salespeople. A U.S. Food and Drug Administration market research study found that consumers want more information on prescription drugs, and drug companies are finding that advertising is an effective way to provide it. Advertising is often a more cost-effective way to disseminate information than personal selling, particularly when the information can be supplied by electronic or printed media.

Evaluation of Alternatives.   Promotion helps buyers evaluate alternative products or brands. Both comparative advertising and personal selling are effective in demonstrating a brand's strengths over competing brands. An example of this form of advertising is to analyze competing brands of a product, showing a favorable comparison for the brand of the firm placing the ad. Specific product attributes (e.g., effectiveness) may be used for the comparison. Salespeople seek to identify buyers' needs and present the features of their brand that correspond to the needs.

Decision to Purchase.   Personal selling is often used to obtain a purchase commitment from the buyers of consumer durable goods and industrial products. Door-to-door selling organizations such as Avon use highly programmed selling approaches to encourage buyers to purchase their products. Communications objectives in these firms include making a target number of contacts each day. Point-of-purchase sales promotions, such as displays in retail stores, are intended to influence the purchase decision, as are samples and coupons. One of the advantages of personal selling over advertising is its flexibility in responding to the buyer's objectives and questions at the time the decision to purchase is being made.

Product Use.   Communicating with buyers after they purchase a product is an important promotional activity. Follow-up by salespeople, advertisements stressing a firm's service capabilities, and toll-free numbers placed on packages to encourage users to seek information or report problems are illustrations of postpurchase communications. Hotels leave questionnaires in rooms for occupants to use in evaluating hotel services.

Various communications objectives may be assigned to promotion strategy. The uses of promotion vary according to the type of purchase, the stage of the buyer's decision process, the maturity of the product-market, and the role of promotion in the marketing program. Communications models are available to guide management in analyzing and selecting promotion objectives and strategies. Two examples are the AIDA model (attention, interest, desire, action) and the hierarchy-of-effects model. The steps in both models move from the awareness to action stages of the purchasing process.[10]

Objectives need to be selected for the entire promotional program and for each promotion component. Certain objectives, such as sales and market share targets, are shared with other marketing program components. Illustrative promotion objectives include:

- Creating or increasing buyers' awareness of a product or brand.
- Influencing buyers' attitudes toward a company, product, or brand.
- Increasing the level of brand preference of the buyers in a targeted segment.
- Achieving sales and market share increases for specific customer or prospect targets.
- Generating repeat purchases of a brand.
- Encouraging trial of a new product.
- Attracting new customers.

The following sections discuss and provide examples of objectives for each promotion component.

Deciding the Role of the Promotion-Mix Components

Promotion objectives can be linked to the specific role of each component in the promotion mix. For example, the role of the sales force may be to obtain sales or instead to inform the channel of distribution organizations about product features and applications. Advertising may play a major or minor role in the promotion strategy. Sales promotion (e.g., trade shows) may be used to achieve various objectives in the promotion mix.

Early in developing the promotion strategy, it is useful to set some guidelines for the promotion-mix components. These guidelines help determine the strategy for each promotion component. It is necessary to decide which communications objective(s) will be the responsibility of each component. For example, advertising may be responsible for creating awareness of a new product. Sales promotion (e.g., coupons and samples) may encourage trial of the new product. Personal selling may be assigned responsibility for getting retailers to stock the new product. It is also important to decide how large the contribution of each promotion component will be. Indicating the relative contribution of each component will help to determine the promotion budget.

Budgeting Approaches

Not surprisingly, achieving an optimal balance between revenues and promotion expenditures is difficult because factors other than promotion also influence sales. Isolating the effects of promotion may require complex analysis. Because of this, more practical budgeting techniques are normally used. These methods include: (1) objective and task, (2) percentage of sales, (3) competitive parity, (4) all you can afford, and (5) budgeting models. Similar approaches are also used to determine advertising and sales promotion budgets. The personal-selling budget is set by the number of people in the sales force and their qualifications.

The promotion budget may be based only on the planned expenditures for advertising and sales promotion. Typically, companies develop separate budgets for the sales organization. Public relations budgeting also may be separate from promotion budgeting. Even so, it is important to consider the size and allocation of total promotion expenses when formulating the promotion strategy. Unless this is done, the integration of the components is likely to be fragmented.

Exhibit 12–2 an example of a promotion budget (excluding sales force and public relations) for a pharmaceutical product. Note the relative size of advertising and sales promotion expenditures. Advertising accounts for only 28 percent of the total budget. The sampling of drugs to doctors by salespeople is often a sizable amount of the promotion budget.

Objective and Task.   This logical and cost-effective method is probably the most widely used budgeting approach. Management sets communications objectives, determines the tasks necessary to achieve the objectives, and adds up costs. This method also establishes the mix of promotion components by selecting the component(s) appropriate for attaining each objective. Marketing management must carefully evaluate how the promotion objectives are to be achieved and choose the most cost-effective promotion components. The effectiveness of the objective and task method depends on the judgment and experience of the chief marketing executive and staff. The budget shown in Exhibit 12–2 was determined using the objective and task method.

Percentage of Sales.   Using this method, the budget is calculated as a percentage of sales and is therefore quite arbitrary. The percentage figure is often based on past expenditure patterns. The fundamental problem with the method is that it fails to recognize that promotion efforts and results are related. For example, a budget that is 10 percent of sales may be too much or not enough promotion expenditure to achieve forecasted sales. This procedure can also lead to too much spending on promotion when sales are high and too little when sales are low. In a cyclical industry where sales follow up-and-down trends, a strategy of increasing promotion expenditures during low sales periods may be more appropriate.

EXHIBIT 12–2   Illustrative Promotion Budget for a Pharmaceutical Product

---

Promotional Activity	1997 Budget
Promotional material	$100,000
Samples	200,000
Direct mail	150,000
Journal advertising	175,000
Total budget	$625,000

Competitive Parity.   Promotion expenditures for this budgeting method are guided by how much competitors spend. A major shortcoming of the method is that differences in marketing strategy between competing firms may require different promotion strategies. For example, Revlon uses an intensive distribution strategy, while Estée Lauder targets buyers by distributing through selected department stores. A comparison of promotional strategies of these firms is not very meaningful, since their market targets and promotion objectives are different.

All You Can Afford.   Since budget limits are a reality in many companies, this method is used in these instances. Top management may specify how much can be spent on promotion. For example, the guideline may be to reduce the budget to 75 percent of last year's actual promotion expenditures. The objective and task method can be combined with the "all you can afford" method by setting task priorities and allocating the budget to the higher priority tasks.

Budgeting Models.   This method sets the budget using a mathematical model, often developed from analysis of historical data. The basic concern in using the model for budget determination is establishing the validity of the model and its stability over time. Advisor 2, a comprehensive model for budgeting the marketing mix for industrial products, determines a marketing budget and allocates expenditures for personal and impersonal (e.g., advertising) communications.[11] Advisor 2 is a multiple-regression type of model that utilizes several predictor variables, including number of users, customer concentration, fraction of sales made to order, attitude difference, proportion of direct sales, life cycle stage, product plans, and product complexity.

Integrating Promotion Strategies

Several factors may affect a firm's promotion mix, as shown by Exhibit 12–3. Advertising, publicity, personal selling, and sales promotion strategies are often fragmented because they are assigned to different organizational units. There are differences in priorities, and evaluating the productivity of the components is complex. The lack of coordination between selling and advertising often occurs in firms marketing to industrial buyers. These firms

---

EXHIBIT 12–3 Illustrative Factors Affecting Promotion Strategy

Advertising/sales promotion driven	Balanced	Personal selling driven
Large	Number and dispersion of buyers	Small
Low	Buyers' information needs	High
Small	Size and importance of purchase	Large
Channel	Distribution	Direct
Low	Product complexity	High
No	Postpurchase contact required	Yes

---

tend to follow personal-selling-driven promotion strategies. The same separation of selling and advertising strategies prevails in a variety of consumer products firms.

Integrated marketing communications (IMC) strategies are replacing fragmented advertising, publicity, and sales programs. These approaches differ from traditional promotion strategies in several ways:

1. IMC programs are comprehensive. Advertising, personal selling, retail atmospherics, behavioral-modification programs, public relations, investor-relations programs, employee communications, and other forms are all considered in the planning of an IMC.

2. IMC programs are unified. The messages delivered by all media, including such diverse influences as employee recruiting and the atmospherics of retailers upon which the marketer primarily relies, are the same or supportive of a unified theme.

3. IMC programs are targeted. The public relations program, advertising programs, and dealer/distributor programs all have the same or related target markets.

4. IMC programs have coordinated execution of all the communications components of the organization.

5. IMC programs emphasize productivity in reaching the designated targets when selecting communication channels and allocating resources to marketing media.[12]

The Limited, the women's apparel retailer, has been unusually successful in implementing an integrated marketing-communications program; Byerly's in Minneapolis uses atmospherics to communicate that the supermarket is the place to be seen by trendy people.[13] The upscale Nordstrom department store chain is another example of a firm using a coordinated promotion program. The retail sales force is the focus of Nordstrom's promotion strategy.

Advertising and sales promotion strategies are examined in the remainder of the chapter to illustrate how these strategies are developed. Public relations is also a very important promotion component. Since these activities vary widely in scope and are similar in certain ways to advertising, they are not included in the discussion.

ADVERTISING STRATEGY

Estimating advertising's impact on buyers helps management to decide advertising's role and scope in the marketing program and to choose specific objectives. Management's perception of what advertising can contribute to promotion objectives has an important influence in deciding advertising's role. The Strategy Feature describes how Gillette positions its new line of toiletries using advertising to link the line with the successful Sensor razor. Advertising plays a key role in this marketing strategy. Recall our discussion of brand extension in Chapter 9.

Advertising strategy begins by identifying and describing the target audience. Next, it is important to set specific objectives and decide on the advertising budget. The selection of the creative strategy follows. It determines how the objectives will be accomplished. Advertising media and programming schedules are used to implement the creative strategy. The final step is implementing the advertising strategy and evaluating its effectiveness. We examine each of these activities, highlighting important features and strategy issues.

Setting Advertising Objectives and Budgeting

Advertising Objectives.   Exhibit 12–4 shows alternative levels for setting advertising objectives. In moving from the most general level (exposure) toward the most specific level (profit contribution), we see that the objectives are increasingly closer to the purchase decision. For example, knowing that advertising causes a measurable increase in sales is much more useful to the decision maker than saying that advertising exposed a specific number of people to an advertising message. The key issue is whether the objectives at the general levels in Exhibit 12–4 are linked to purchase behavior. For example, how much will awareness increase the chances that people will purchase a product? Achievement of very general and mid-level objectives often can be measured whereas the sales and profit impact of advertising is very difficult to measure.

Research indicates that brand awareness leads to increased market share and in turn to greater profits. A study conducted by the Strategic Planning Institute, involving 73 industrial-products businesses, supports the relationship between brand awareness, sales, and profits.[14] Exposure measures of advertising effectiveness are subject to much more

STRATEGY FEATURE   Using Sensor's Success to Launch the Gillette Series Line of Toiletries

The positioning concept for Gillette's new line of toiletries is "The Best a Man Can Get." This theme helped launch the highly successful Sensor razor. The chart shows the market position of the major competitors before the new line was introduced. Gillette's joint advertising budget for Sensor and the Gillette series totaled $60 million for the first year. The objective is to create a mega-brand under the Gillette name. The toiletries line is priced 10 to 20 percent higher than existing-products. A new fragrance, Cool Wave, spans the line. The key challenge is convincing buyers that

the toiletries are better than competing brands. Unlike in razors, Gillette is not the leader in the medicine chest (see chart). Gillette's product tests for the new line were very favorable. One-minute TV commercials will feature the new line of shaving cream and after-shave with Sensor. Gillette chose not to place the Sensor name on the new line.

Source: Laurence Ingrassia, "Gillette Ties New Toiletries to Hot Razor," *The Wall Street Journal,* September 18, 1992, pp. B1, B6.

Competition for the Medicine Chest

U.S. market-share leaders in three big toiletries categories

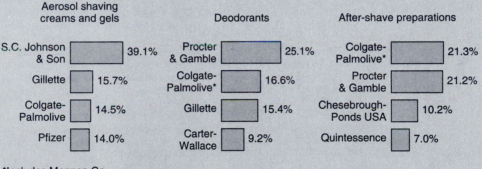

Aerosol shaving creams and gels		Deodorants		After-shave preparations	
S.C. Johnson & Son	39.1%	Procter & Gamble	25.1%	Colgate-Palmolive*	21.3%
Gillette	15.7%	Colgate-Palmolive*	16.6%	Procter & Gamble	21.2%
Colgate-Palmolive	14.5%	Gillette	15.4%	Chesebrough-Ponds USA	10.2%
Pfizer	14.0%	Carter-Wallace	9.2%	Quintessence	7.0%

*Includes Mennen Co.
Source: Towne-Otter & Associates, a unit of Information Resources Inc.

debate. These measures are more useful in guiding media-allocation decisions than in gauging the value of advertising to a firm.

Wendy's International Inc. uses a value-based strategy that emphasizes quality food at competitive prices.[15] The objective of Wendy's advertising is to offer buyers value and product choices. Ads often feature the founder, Dave Thomas, discussing how Wendy's provides value to customers, including a money-back guarantee to any customer who is not satisfied. By following the value strategy Wendy's has avoided the burger industry price wars.

EXHIBIT 12–4   Alternative Levels for Setting Advertising Objectives

Budget Determination.   The budgeting methods for promotion discussed earlier in the chapter are also used in advertising budgeting. Research points to several characteristics of firms whose advertising and promotion expenditures as a percentage of sales are higher than other firms. Additionally, budgeting guidelines indicate the following factors are related to advertising and sales promotion expenditures for the firms in the sample:[16]

Market share.

New products.

Market growth.

Utilization of plant capacity.

Unit price of product.

Product purchases as a percentage of total purchases.

Product pricing.

Product quality.

Breadth of product line.

Standard versus custom (made-to-order) products.

Exhibit 12–5 illustrates four of these factors. The Cahners Publishing Company and the Strategic Planning Institute have developed a guide for estimating the budget.[17] For example, the media advertising budget based on a firm's market share of 12 percent (between 10 percent and 17 percent on chart A of Exhibit 12–5) and annual sales of $100 million is:

$$0.7 \times \frac{\$100,000,000}{1,000} = \$70,000$$

If this computation is repeated for each factor, the results can be averaged to calculate the budget. Weighting can be used to take into account the differences in importance of each factor to a particular firm.

EXHIBIT 12–5 Guidelines for Advertising and Sales-Promotion Expenditure

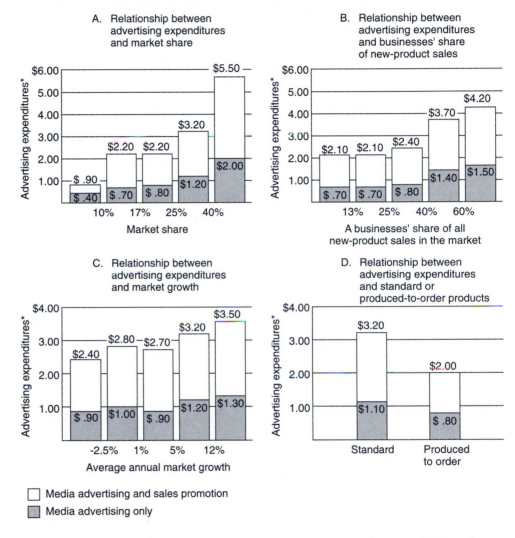

A. Relationship between advertising expenditures and market share

B. Relationship between advertising expenditures and businesses' share of new-product sales

C. Relationship between advertising expenditures and market growth

D. Relationship between advertising expenditures and standard or produced-to-order products

☐ Media advertising and sales promotion
▨ Media advertising only

*Advertising expenditures: media advertising and sales promotion expenditures per $1000 market sales.

Source: Valerie Kijewski, "Advertising and Promotion: How Much Should You Spend?" pamphlet prepared by the Strategic Planning Institute, June 1983, pp. 4, 5, 6, and 11.

This budgeting approach is a useful diagnostic tool for comparing a firm's current advertising and sales promotion budget with the guidelines. When used in conjunction with management's experience, the guide can indicate that a budget may be too high or too low compared to the norms developed from the research.

Creative Strategy

The creative strategy guides the advertising campaign. Two considerations affect the strategy selection: (1) whether the campaign is intended to maintain or to change market conditions and (2) whether the campaign will communicate information or imagery and symbolism.[18] Maintenance and reinforcement strategies are used to support an established brand. A strategy to change market conditions may reposition a brand, expand the market for a brand, or launch a new product. Information messages communicate product benefits, whereas image messages seek to either reinforce or create change using symbolism and imagery.

The creative strategy is guided by the positioning concept selected for the product or brand. Chapter 6 discusses positioning according to the *functions* performed by the brand, the *symbol* to be conveyed by the brand, or the *experience* provided by the brand. The creative theme seeks to effectively communicate the positioning concept to buyers and others influencing the purchase of the brand.

The Wall Street Journal asked several of the advertising industry's top executives their opinions on the best and the worst advertisements of the 1980s.[19] Included in the best categories were the American Express "portrait" series of celebrity "card members," and Nike's "Just Do It" campaign. Among the poor ad campaigns cited were Burger King's disastrous "Herb the Nerd" series and the 1989 Infinity automobile series of Zen-inspired nature scenes featuring pussy willows and rocks. Interestingly, some of the highest-rated and lowest-rated ads were created by the same agency. Television dominated the high ratings, but a print and a billboard campaign also received top ratings.

Creative advertising designs enhance the effectiveness of advertising by providing a unifying concept that binds together the various parts of an advertising campaign. Advertising agencies, which receive 15 percent of gross billings, typically are experts in designing creative strategies. The agency professionals may design unique themes to position a product or firm in some particular way or use comparisons with competition to enhance the firms' brands. Choosing the right creative theme for the marketing situation can make a major contribution to the success of a program. While tests are used to evaluate creative approaches, the task is more of an art than a science. Perhaps the best guide to creativity is an agency's track record.

The creative strategy used for Murphy's Oil Soap shows the importance of a segment focus and brand positioning through creative advertising. For nearly 100 years the soap was marketed in a single region of the country.[20] Fourteen years after a national rollout program starting in 1976, the brand gained sixth position in its product category. Sales in 1990 increased to over $30 million, eight times more than in 1980. The brand is positioned as an effective wood cleaner. Its "Great Houses" advertising campaign portrays impressive old homes that highlight the beauty of wood and the special requirements of a wood-cleaning product. More recently, advertising and sales promotion are positioning the soap as effective in "cleaning wood surfaces . . . and more."

Media/Programming Strategy

A company's advertising agency normally guides media and programming decisions. The agency has the experience and technical ability to match media and programming to the target audience specified by the firm. The media, timing, and programming decisions are influenced largely by two factors: (1) access to the target audience(s) and (2) the costs of reaching the target group(s). Suppose a product-manager is interested in advertising to business executives through printed media. Possible publications and approximate costs for one page, four-color advertisements are:

Magazine	Rate
Business Week (weekly)	$68,300
Fortune (monthly)	$56,260
Forbes (biweekly)	$54,360
Harvard Business Review (6 per year)	$19,000
Inc. (monthly)	$62,155
Money (monthly)	$89,985

Source: *Standard Rates and Data Services,* December 1995, color, full-page ads, one insertion.

Standard Rates and Data Services publishes advertising costs for various media. The costs are determined by circulation levels and the type of publication. It is important for a firm, in deciding which medium to use, to evaluate the cost per exposure and the characteristics of the subscribers.

Media models are available to analyze allocations and decide which media mix best achieves one or more objectives.[21] These models use an exposure measure (Exhibit 12–4), typically, as the basis for media allocation. For example, cost per thousand of exposure can be used to consider alternative media. The models also consider audience characteristics (e.g., age group composition) and other factors. The models are useful in selecting media when many advertising programs and a wide range of media are used.

Role of the Advertising Agency

Advertising agencies perform various functions for clients, including creative designs and media selection. Full-service agencies offer a range of advertising services, including marketing research, sales promotion, and marketing planning. A typical basis of compensation is a 15 percent fee on media expenditures. For example, $1 million of advertising provides a commission of $150,000, which is paid by the media direct to the agency.

Agency Relationship.   The normal basis of operation between a corporate client and the agency is a cooperative effort. The client briefs the agency on the marketing strategy and the role of advertising in the marketing program. In some instances agency executives may be involved in the development of the marketing strategy. The better the agency understands the company's marketing program, the more effective the agency can be in providing advertising services. The agency may assign one or more personnel full-time to an account with a large advertising budget.

Agency Compensation.   The traditional method of compensation of the agency has been the 15 percent commission on media expenditures. Most agencies today operate on some type of commission arrangement, though the arrangement may involve a commission for media placement and a separate arrangement for other services. For example, media placement would receive a 5 percent commission, whereas other services associated with the advertising would yield an additional 10 percent. These changes in the original 15 percent commission are the consequence of advertising specialists (e.g., media buying) offering reduced fees.

Some companies have worked out flexible payment arrangements with their agency. The agency may keep a record of its costs and the client pays for the services it requires. Payment may be greater or less than the traditional 15 percent commission. In some arrangements agencies may share cost savings with the client.

Industry Composition.   Large, full-service agencies like Dentsu in Tokyo and Young and Rubicam in New York account for the dominant portion of billings. Nonetheless, the small agencies have created pressures for change throughout the industry. Concerns of clients about arbitrary commission rates and lack of flexibility in client services have led to placing business with small specialty agencies providing media buying, creative design, and other services. There are many local and regional agencies that serve small- and medium-sized clients.

Problem Areas.   A company does not like for an agency to serve clients competing in the same industry. The agency needs access to sensitive information (e.g., sales by product line or by geographical area) in order to effectively serve the client. The customer is hesitant to share confidential information when the agency has clients who are viewed as competitors. In the case of large accounts, normally, agencies do not work with competing clients. Achieving this objective is more difficult in working with companies that have smaller advertising budgets. It is important when selecting an agency to determine who its clients are and what sort of policies the agency follows concerning serving clients that compete.

Implementing the Advertising Strategy and Measuring Its Effectiveness

Before the advertising strategy is implemented, it is important to establish criteria for measuring its effectiveness. Advertising expenditures are wasted if firms spend too much or allocate expenditures improperly. Measuring effectiveness provides useful feedback for future advertising decisions. Importantly, the quality of advertising can be as critical to getting results as the amount of advertising.

Tracking Advertising Performance.   Advertising's impact on sales is difficult to measure because other factors also influence sales and profits. Most efforts to measure effectiveness consider objectives such as attitude change, awareness, or exposure (Exhibit 12–4). Comparing objectives and results helps firms decide when to stop or alter advertising campaigns. Services such as TV's Nielsen ratings are available for the major media. In recent years Nielsen's long-standing domination of TV ratings has been questioned by rivals.[22] These ratings have a critical impact on the allocation of advertising dollars. Recent research findings question the accuracy of the ratings. One major concern is the possible biased representation of the public's viewing. These issues have resulted in several changes in the rating process.

Methods of Measuring Effectiveness.   Several methods are used to evaluate advertising results. Analysis of historical data identifies relationships between advertising expenditures and sales using statistical techniques such as regression analysis. Recall tests measure consumers' awareness of specific ads and campaigns by asking questions to determine if members of a sample of people remember an ad. Longitudinal studies track advertising expenditures and sales results before, during, and after an advertising campaign. Controlled tests are a form of longitudinal study in which extraneous effects are measured and/or controlled during the test. Test marketing is used to evaluate advertising effectiveness. Effort/results models use empirical data to build a mathematical relationship between sales and advertising effort.

A particularly promising method for measuring advertising effectiveness is the use of consumer panels in cities with cable TV. The panel is a group of consumers that agrees to provide information about their purchases on a continuing basis. Cash register scanning of the purchases of panel members provides data on brands purchased, prices, and other information. Samples of consumers can be split into groups that are exposed or not exposed to advertising on cable television. Using equivalent samples, the influence on sales of factors other than advertising can be controlled. The difference in sales between the control and the experimental (exposed) groups over the test period measures the effect of advertising. This technique is appropriate for certain types of frequently purchased consumer products such as food items and health and beauty aids.

Advertising research is used for more than just measuring the effectiveness of advertising. Research can be used for various activities in advertising strategy development, including generating and evaluating creative ideas and concepts, and pretesting concepts, ideas, and specific ads.

An example of a popular test used to evaluate TV commercials is shown in Exhibit 12–6. The test commercial is shown in several test cities. After the commercial is shown, members of a sample of people who viewed the program are asked several questions to determine their reaction to the commercial. The focus of the evaluation is the respondent's recall about the commercial.

SALES PROMOTION STRATEGY

Sales promotion expenditures are increasing more rapidly than advertising in many companies.[23] Both promotion components are receiving major attention by companies in their attempts to boost productivity and reduce costs. When marketing expenditures account for one-third or more of total sales, the bottom-line impact of improving the effectiveness of promotion expenditures and/or lowering costs is substantial.

We will look at the nature and scope of sales promotion, the types of sales promotion activities, the advantages and limitations of sales promotion, and the decisions that make up sales promotion strategy.

EXHIBIT 12–6 How TV Commercials Are Tested

Brand:	Juicy Fruit.
Project:	"False Start" Burke on-air test.
Background and Objectives:	The William Wrigley Co. has requested a Burke on-air test for the new copy execution "False Start." The objective of this research is to measure the communication effectiveness of the "False Start" execution.
Research Method:	A sample of 150 past-30 day chewing gum users in the commercial audience will be interviewed. The air date is scheduled for the first Tuesday of the month in December, on "NYPD Blue." Interviewing will be conducted within five metro areas: Boston, Atlanta, Indianapolis, Dallas, and Phoenix.
Information to Be Obtained:	—Total commercial recall. —Copy recall. —Visual recall.
Action Standard:	The commercial will be considered acceptable in the areas of memorability and sales message communication if: a. It generates 25 or better related recall score. b. At least 25 of the commercial audience remembers at least one sales message.
Timing and Cost:	Fieldwork First Tuesday in December Top line week Final report weeks The cost for this research will be $15,000 ± 10%.
Research Supplier:	Burke Marketing Research.

Source: William R. Dillon, Thomas J. Madden, and Neil H. Firtle, *Marketing Research in a Marketing Environment*, 3rd ed. (Burr Ridge, IL: Richard D. Irwin, 1994), p. 612.

Nature and Scope of Sales Promotion

Japanese companies employ an interesting form of promotion—showrooms that have hands-on new-product displays.[24] The intent is to show people new products placed in attractive surroundings. The items are not for sale in the showrooms—rather the sponsors want you to see the products, try them out, and become familiar with their features. For example, the Matsushita Electric Works showroom has a state-of-the-art home displaying the newest Japanese furnishings and appliances, as well as many gadgets.

The responsibility for sales promotion strategy is often fragmented among marketing functions, such as advertising, merchandising, product planning, and sales. For example, a sales contest for salespeople, typically, is designed and administered by sales managers and the costs of the contest are included in the sales department budget. Similarly, planning and coordinating a coupon refund program may be assigned to a brand manager. Point-of-purchase promotion displays in retail stores may be handled by the advertising department.

Total expenditures for sales promotion by business and industry are much larger than the total spent on advertising. The complete scope of sales promotion is often difficult to identify because the activities are included in various departments and budgets. There are several similarities between sales promotion and advertising, but there are some important differences as well.

An important issue is how to manage the various sales promotion functions. While these activities are often used to support advertising, pricing, channel-of-distribution, and personal selling strategies, the size and scope of sales promotion suggest that the responsibility for managing the program should be assigned to one executive. Some proponents argue for the establishment of a department of sales promotion. At minimum, the chief marketing executive should coordinate and evaluate sales promotion activities.

Sales Promotion Activities

A variety of activities may fit into the total promotion program, including trade shows, specialty advertising (e.g., imprinted calendars), contests, point-of-purchase displays, coupons, recognition programs (e.g., awards to middlemen), and free samples. Expenditures for sales promotion may be very substantial. For example, Gaines Foods Inc. distributed more than 50 million 50-cent coupons as part of a $20 million advertising, trade, and consumer promotion campaign for its Gaines Burgers, Top Choice, and Puppy Choice brands.[25] At the average coupon redemption rate of 1 in 25, about 2.2 million of the 50-cent coupons were redeemed.

Companies may aim their sales-promotion activities at consumer buyers, industrial buyers, middlemen, and salespeople, as shown in Exhibit 12–7.

Promotion to Consumer Targets.   This form of promotion includes a wide variety of activities, as shown in Exhibit 12–7. Sales promotion is often used in the marketing of many consumer products and services. A key management concern is evaluating the effectiveness of promotions such as coupons, rebates, contests, and other awards. The large expenditures necessary to support these programs require that the results and costs be objectively assessed.

Information technology offers penetrating insights into the productivity of promotion programs.[26] For example, sophisticated checkout scanner data analyses indicate trade and consumer promotions that lose money. This information helps in shifting promotion spending to more productive programs, customer groups, and product categories. Promotion programs can be evaluated on a financial basis by combining customer response data with cost information.

Promotion to Industrial Targets.   Many of the sales promotion methods that are used for consumer products also apply to industrial products, although the role and scope of the methods may vary. For example, trade shows perform a key role in small- and medium-sized companies' marketing strategies. The advantage of the trade show is the heavy concentration of potential buyers at one location during a very short time. The cost per contact is much less than calling on prospects at their offices. While people attending trade shows also spend their time viewing competitors' products, salespeople, product managers, and other company personnel have a unique opportunity to hold the prospects' attention.

EXHIBIT 12–7   Sales Promotion Activities Targeted to Various Groups

Sales Promotion Activity	Targeted To:			
	Consumer Buyers	Industrial Buyers	Middlemen	Salespeople
Incentives				
Contests	X	X	X	X
Trips	X	X	X	X
Bonuses			X	X
Prizes	X	X	X	X
Advertising support			X	
Free items	X	X		
Recognition			X	X
Promotional Pricing				
Coupons	X			
Allowances		X	X	
Rebates	X	X	X	
Cash	X			
Informational Activities				
Displays	X			
Demonstrations	X	X	X	
Selling aids			X	X
Specialty advertising (e.g., pens)	X	X	X	
Trade shows	X	X	X	

Sales promotion to industrial buyers may consume a greater portion of the marketing budget than advertising. Promotional activities support direct-selling strategies. They include catalogs, brochures, product information reports, samples, trade shows, application guides, and promotional items such as calendars, pens, and calculators.

Promotion to Middlemen.   Sales promotion is an important part of manufacturers' marketing efforts to wholesalers and retailers for such products as foods, beverages, and appliances. Catalogs and other product information are essential promotional components for many lines. Promotional pricing is often used to push new products through channels of distribution. Various incentives are popular in marketing to middlemen. Specialty advertising items such as calendars and memo pads are used in maintaining buyer awareness of brands and company names.

Promotion to the Sales Force.   Incentives and informational activities are the primary forms of promotion used to assist and motivate company sales forces. Sales contests and prizes are popular. Companies also make wide use of recognition programs like the "salesperson of the year." Promotional information is vital to salespeople. Presentation kits help salespeople describe new products and the features of existing products.

A high-tech promotion tool with exciting potential is the automated sales presentation created with integrated use of sound, graphics, and video briefcase computers. These multimedia or interactive techniques give salespeople powerful presentation capabilities, allowing them access to a complete product information system available in the notebook computer.

Suppose an Acme Bicycle sales representative is trying to close a sale with a major sporting goods dealership.[27] Acme produces high-quality bicycles and accessories. The salesperson's multimedia package contains videos of bikes in action, photographs of the product line, information on competing models, and text describing key product features. The salesperson makes a presentation to three executives of the firm, as described below.[28]

- A short sound video shows riders, who match the profile of the dealership's target customers, and discusses the features of a high-performance bicycle.
- The salesperson describes Acme's products in words, pictures, and animated graphics.
- The dealer's chief mechanic has reservations about the pedals on the bike shown in the presentation.
- The salesperson counters this objection with a display of several pedal designs available on Acme Bicycles.
- The owner asks for a comparison of Acme's prices and features with those of competitors.
- At the close of the meeting, the salesperson promises a proposal for later that day.
- The salesperson uses the notebook's proposal generator to prepare a customized proposal.
- The proposal is sent to Acme headquarters for approval and returned to the dealer by fax.

Interactive multimedia promotion is becoming an essential selling tool for many products.

Advantages and Limitations of Sales Promotion

Because of its wide array of incentive, pricing, and communication capabilities, sales promotion has the flexibility to contribute to various marketing objectives. A product manager can target buyers, intermediaries, and salespeople and can measure the sales response of the sales promotion activities to determine their effectiveness. For example, a company can track its coupon redemption or rebate success. Many of the incentive and price promotion techniques trigger the purchase of other products.

Sales promotion is not without its disadvantages, however. In most instances, rather than substituting for advertising and personal selling, sales promotion supports other promotional efforts. Control is essential to prevent some people from taking advantage of free offers, coupons, and other incentives. Incentives and price-promotional activities need to be monitored. An effective advertisement can be run thousands of times, but promotional campaigns are usually not reusable. Thus, the costs of development must be evaluated in advance.

Sales Promotion Strategy

The steps in developing the sales promotion strategy are similar to the design of advertising strategy. It is necessary to first define the communications task(s) that the sales promotion program is expected to accomplish. Next, specific promotion objectives are set regarding awareness levels and purchase intentions. It is important to evaluate the relative cost-effectiveness of feasible sales promotion methods and to select those that offer the best results/cost combination. Both the content of the sales promotion and its timing should be coordinated with other promotion activities. Finally, the program is implemented and evaluated on a continuing basis. Evaluation measures the extent to which objectives are achieved. For example, trade show results can be evaluated to determine how many show contacts are converted to purchases.

SUMMARY

Promotion strategy is a vital part of the positioning strategy. The components—advertising, sales promotion, publicity, personal selling, and direct marketing—offer an impressive array of capabilities for communicating with market targets and other relevant audiences. However, promotion activities are expensive. Management must decide on the size of the promotion budget and allocate it to the communications components. Each promotion activity offers certain unique advantages and also shares several characteristics with the other components. The major budgeting methods are objective and task, percentage of sales, competitive parity, all-you-can-afford, and budgeting models. Several product and market factors affect whether the promotion strategy will emphasize advertising, sales promotion, personal selling, or a balance between the forms of promotion. The integration of communications mixes is a major challenge for many firms today.

The steps in developing advertising strategy include identifying the target audience, deciding the role of advertising in the promotion mix, indicating advertising objectives and budget size, selecting the creative strategy, determining the media and programming schedule, and implementing the program and measuring its effectiveness. Advertising objectives may range from audience exposure to profit contribution targets. Advertising agencies offer specialized services for developing creative strategies, designing messages, and selecting media and programming strategies.

The discussion of sales promotion highlights several methods available for use in a total communications program. Typically, firms use sales promotion activities in conjunction with advertising and personal selling rather than as a primary component of promotion strategy. Sales promotion strategy should be based on the correct selection of methods to provide the best results/cost combinations for achieving the communications objectives desired.

QUESTIONS FOR REVIEW AND DISCUSSION

1. Compare and contrast the role of promotion in an international public accounting firm with promotion by American Airlines.

2. Identify and discuss the factors that are important in determining the promotion mix for the following products:
   a. Video tape recorder/player.
   b. Personal computer.
   c. Boeing 757 commercial aircraft.
   d. Residential homes.

3. What are the important considerations in determining a promotion budget?

4. Under what conditions is a firm's promotion strategy more likely to be driven by advertising/sales promotion?

5. Discuss the advantages and limitations of using awareness as an advertising objective. When might this objective be appropriate?

6. Identify and discuss the important differences between advertising and public relations strategies in the marketing/promotion strategy.

7. Coordination of advertising and selling strategies is a major challenge in large companies. Suggest a plan for integrating these strategies.

8. Discuss the role of sales promotion methods in the promotion strategy of a major airline.

NOTES

1. This illustration is based on Joseph Kahn, "Cleaning Up: P&G Viewed China As a National Market and Is Conquering It," *The Wall Street Journal,* September 12, 1995, pp. A1 and A6.

2. Committee on Definitions, *Marketing Definitions: A Glossary of Marketing Terms* (Chicago: American Marketing Association, 1960).

3. Sally Goll Beatty, "Agencies See Record Ad Spending in '96, Slowing Growth Thereafter," *The Wall Street Journal,* December 5, 1995, p. B3.

4. Jim Fuquay, "Drugmakers Prescribe Higher Doses of Advertising to Avoid Revenue Decline," *Fort Worth Star-Telegram,* September 3, 1995, p. B1.

5. Committee on Definitions, *Marketing Definitions.*

6. "Exclusive Interview: Mike Gunn of American Airlines," *Colloquy* 3, no. 2 (1992), pp. 8–10.

7. Committee on Definitions, *Marketing Definitions.*

8. "Singapore Airlines: Flying Beauty," *The Economist,* December 14, 1991, p. 74.

9. "Going to the Public with Ads for Prescription Drugs," *Business Week,* May 21, 1984, pp. 77, 81.

10. For an in-depth discussion of these models, see David A. Aaker and John G. Myers, *Advertising Management,* 2nd ed. (Englewood Cliffs, NJ: Prentice Hall, 1982), chap. 4; and James F. Engel, Martin R. Warshaw, and Thomas C. Kinnear, *Promotional Strategy,* 5th ed. (Burr Ridge, IL: Richard D. Irwin, 1983), chap. 10.

11. Gary L. Lilien, "Advisor 2: Modeling the Marketing Mix Decision for Industrial Products," *Management Science,* February 1979, pp. 191–204.

12. Roger D. Blackwell, "Integrated Marketing Communications," paper presented at the Stellner Symposium, University of Illinois, 1985, pp. 2–3.

13. Ibid., p. 9.

14. "Brand Awareness Increases Market Share, Profits: Study," *Marketing News,* November 28, 1980, p. 5.

15. Marilyn Much, "How Wendy's Avoids Burger Industry Price Wars," *Investor's Business Dailey,* April 11, 1994, p. 4.

16. Valerie Kijewski, "Advertising and Promotion: How Much Should You Spend?" (Cambridge, MA: Strategic Planning Institute, June 1983).

17. *Work Book for Estimating Your Advertising Budget* (Boston: Cahners Publishing).

18. Henry Assael, *Marketing Management: Strategy and Action* (Boston: PWS–Kent Publishing, 1985), p. 392.

19. Joanne Lipman, "Ads of the '80s: The Loved and the Losers," *The Wall Street Journal,* December 28, 1989, pp. B1 and B4.

20. D. John Loden, *Megabrands* (Burr Ridge, IL: Irwin Professional Publishing, 1992), pp. 188–90.

21. Roland T. Rust, *Advertising Media Models* (Lexington, MA: D. C. Heath, 1986).

22. See, for example, Dennis Kneale, "Fuzzy Picture: TX's Nielsen Ratings, Long Questioned, Face Tough Challenges," *The Wall Street Journal,* July 19, 1990, pp. A1, A12.

23. Andrew J. Parsons, "Focus and Squeeze: Consumer Marketing in the '90s," *Marketing Management,* Winter 1992, pp. 51–55.

24. Mary Roach, "Attack of the Killer Showroom,"*American Way,"* November 15, 1995, pp. 108, 110, and 112.

25. Kevin Higgins, "Couponing's Growth Is Easy to Understand: It Works," *Marketing News,* September 28, 1985, p. 12.

26. Parsons, "Focus and Squeeze."

27. Jeff Anderson, "Mastering Multimedia," *Sales and Marketing Management,* January 1993, pp. 55–58.

28. Ibid.

Sales Force and Direct Marketing Strategies

Salespeople make face-to-face contact with buyers, whereas direct marketing reaches customers by phone, mail, television, and computer. Each of these methods of contact enables the marketing firm to communicate one-on-one with buyers. Companies may use a combination of these methods of customer contact.

Sullivan Dental Products, Inc., uses its sales force and catalogs for fast growth.[1] Sullivan makes effective use of over 200 salespeople and a catalog of more than 10,000 dental supply products. Targeting 27,000 dentists, the wholesaler has achieved strong sales and profit performance by combining the industry's two major marketing methods: catalogs and sales representatives. Typically, Sullivan's competitors use only one of these promotional methods because of the high cost of using both methods. Sullivan keeps its costs low using a computerized inventory management system. Salespeople demonstrate products, discuss dentists' future needs, and leave the catalog to simplify placing orders. Commanding less than 5 percent of the market for dental supplies, Sullivan has a lot of room for growth. Sales in 1994 were $204 million, over four times 1990 sales. Sullivan Dental Products performs a distribution channel function of linking producers and end-users. Its management has combined effective selling, distribution channel, and promotion strategies into a successful marketing program. Two key sources of growth are the company's commission-compensated sales force and its acquisition of small suppliers with good customer relationships enhanced by Sullivan's efficient distribution system.

In this chapter we will begin by discussing the role of the sales force in promotion strategy, followed by a look at how the selling process is defined. Next, we will examine alternative sales channels to the customer and different ways of designing the sales organization. Then we will discuss managing the sales force and evaluating its effectiveness. Finally, we will describe and illustrate the various methods of direct marketing.

DEVELOPING AND IMPLEMENTING SALES FORCE STRATEGY

The design of the sales force strategy includes six major steps. First, the role of the sales force in the promotion mix is determined. This requires deciding what personal selling is expected to do in the marketing program. Second, the selling process is defined, indicating how selling will be accomplished with targeted customers. Third, in selecting sales channels, management decides how field selling, major account management, telemarketing, and electronic channels will contribute to the selling process. Fourth, the design of the sales organization is determined, or its adequacy evaluated, in an existing organization. Fifth, salespeople are recruited, trained, and managed. Finally, the results of the selling strategy are evaluated and adjustments are made to narrow the gap between actual and desired results.

The Role of Selling in Promotion Strategy

The role of personal selling varies in different companies. Salespeople may serve primarily as order takers or instead fulfill major responsibilities as consultants to customers. While management has some flexibility in choosing the role and objectives of the sales force in the marketing mix, several factors often shape the role of selling in a firm's marketing strategy (see Exhibit 13–1). The selling effort needs to be integrated into the overall communications program. It is also useful to indicate how the other promotion-mix components such as advertising, support the sales force. Sales management needs to be aware of the plans and activities of other promotion components.

Personal selling plays a central role for direct sales organizations like Avon Products. Avon, Amway, Tupperware and other direct sales companies are experiencing major growth in international markets. Brazil is Avon's largest international market with 1995 estimated sales of $1 billion, over double 1993 sales.[2] The country's Avon sales force totals nearly half a million salespeople. Annual sales of Avon skin cream in Brazil total seven tons. Avon representatives outside cities may travel by foot and by canoe.

The objectives assigned to salespeople frequently involve management's expected sales results. Sales quotas are used to state these expectations. Companies may give incentives to salespeople who achieve their quotas. Team selling incentives may also be used. Objectives other than sales are important in many organizations. These include increasing the number of new accounts, providing services to customers and channel organizations, retaining customers, selecting and evaluating middlemen, and obtaining market information. The objectives selected need to be consistent with marketing strategy and promotion objectives, and measurable so that sales performance can be evaluated.

Illustrative Roles for the Sales Force

The possible roles for the sales force include new business, trade selling, missionary selling, and consultative/technical selling.[3]

EXHIBIT 13–1 Factors Influencing the Role of Personal Selling in a Firm's Marketing Strategy

---

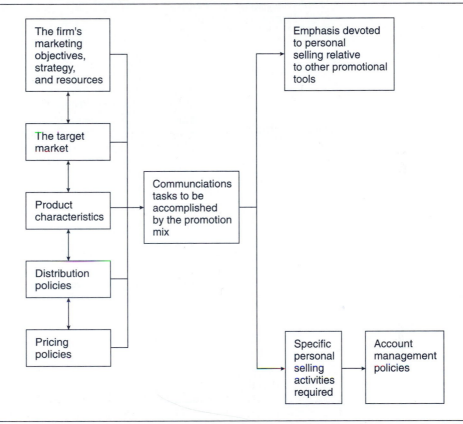

Source: Gilbert A. Churchill, Jr., Neil M. Ford, and Orville C. Walker, Jr., *Sales Force Management*, 4th ed. (Burr Ridge, IL: Richard D. Irwin, 1993), p. 121.

New Business Strategy. This selling role involves obtaining sales from new buyers. The buyers may be one-time purchasers or repeat buyers. For example, the first-time sale of sheet steel by a steel producer to a container manufacturer may lead to further purchases. Alternatively, the selling strategy may be concerned with obtaining new buyers on a continuing basis. Insurance and real estate sales firms use this strategy.

Trade Selling Strategy. This form of selling provides assistance and support to middlemen, rather than obtaining sales. A manufacturer marketing through wholesalers, retailers, or other intermediaries may provide merchandising, logistical, promotional, and product information assistance. Grocery wholesalers' salespeople assist retailers in merchandising and provide other support activities. Exhibit 13–2 describes distribution channel selling activities in Wal-Mart and Deere & Co. channels.

EXHIBIT 13–2   Examples of Distribution Channel Selling Activities

---

*Wal-Mart
Channel*

Suppliers
  ↓   Suppliers sell goods and services to producers.
Manufacturers

                       4,000 manufacturers' major account teams
  ↓   sell and provide supporting service to Wal-Mart.

                       Wal-Mart replaces inventory by computer ordering.
Wal-Mart   Greeters at Wal-Mart stores welcome customers
  ↓   as they enter stores.

Consumers

*Deere & Co.
Channel*

Suppliers   Materials and parts suppliers sell to Deere using
                       field sales forces, major account teams, and
  ↓   manufacturers' representatives.

Deere & Co.   Deere salespeople provide product information and
                       sales support to independent dealers.
  ↓

Dealers   Dealer salespeople sell equipment to farmers and
                       agricultural companies.
  ↓   Dealer also provides service to equipment users.

Farmers and
other end-users

Missionary Selling Strategy.   A similar strategy to trade selling is missionary selling. A manufacturer's salespeople work with the customers of a channel member to encourage them to purchase the manufacturer's product from the channel member. For example, pharmaceutical sales representatives contact physicians, providing them with product information and samples and encouraging them to prescribe the producer's drugs.

Consultative/Technical Selling Strategy.   Firms that use this strategy sell to an existing customer base and provide technical and application assistance. American Express Financial Advisors (AEFA), an American Express Company selling financial products like mutual funds and insurance, employs this strategy. Formerly, AEFA followed a strategy of concentrating on selling to new customers. Management's long-term vision about the financial services market is guiding major changes in the sales strategy.[4] AEFA's 8,000 advisors are forming long-term relationships with clients. The commission basis of pay has been changed; bonuses are used to reward planners and managers for scoring well on customer satisfaction. Sales teams manage processes like client satisfaction and account relations.

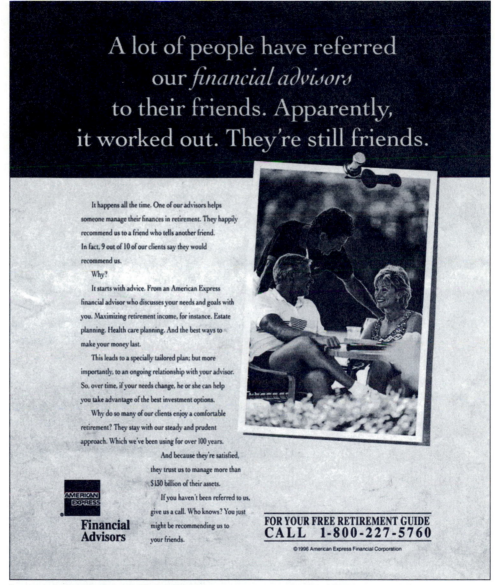

Courtesy of American Express Financial Advisors.

Performance objectives include 95 percent client retention, 80 percent advisor retention after four years, and annual sales growth of 18 percent. Advisor retention under the former commission plan was only 30 percent. The company offers advisors special training to help them shift into relationship building and provides software technology to increase productivity and reduce response time (see accompanying advertisement).

AEFA's experience previews several changes that are underway in many sales organizations.[5] The reforming process requires redesigning the traditional sales organization, leveraging information technology to lower costs and provide quick response, designing the sales strategy to meet different customer needs, and building long-term relationships with customers and business partners. The sales force continues to be a key contributor in organizations like AEFA, but salespeople are being asked to assume new responsibilities and the methods for keeping score are changing.

An organization may use more than one of the above selling strategies. For example, a transportation services company might use a new business strategy for expanding its customer base and a missionary selling strategy for servicing existing customers. The skills needed by the salesperson vary according to the selling strategy used.

Defining the Selling Process

Several activities are involved in moving from identifying a buyer's need to completing the sale and managing the post-sale relationship between buyer and seller. This selling process includes: (1) prospecting for customers, (2) opening the relationship, (3) qualifying the prospect, (4) presenting the sales message, (5) closing the sale, and (6) servicing the account.[6] The process may be very simple, consisting of a routine set of actions designed to close the sale. Alternatively, the process may extend over a long time period, with many contacts and interactions between the buyer, other people influencing the purchase, the salesperson assigned to the account, and technical specialists in the seller's organization.

Sales management defines the selling process by indicating the customers and prospects the firm is targeting and the guidelines for developing customer relationships and obtaining sales results. This process is management's strategy for achieving the sales force objectives in the organization's selling environment. Salespeople implement the process following the guidelines set by management, such as the product strategy (relative emphasis on different products), customer targeting and priorities, and the desired selling activities and outcomes.

Normally, the selling process is managed by the salesperson that has responsibility for a customer account, although some companies are assigning this responsibility to customer teams. Account management includes planning and execution of the selling activities between the salesperson and the customer or prospect. Some organizations analyze this process and set guidelines for use by salespeople to plan their selling activities. Process analysis may result in programmed selling steps or instead may lead to highly customized selling approaches where the salesperson develops specific strategies for each account. A company may also use team selling (e.g., product specialists and salesperson), major account management, telemarketing, and electronic support systems (e.g., computer ordering).

Corporate restructuring in the 1990s has created the need to reengineer sales processes in many companies.[7] Indications of a possible need for a change in the sales process include disappointing sales of a new product, sales declines, lost customers, drops in profit margins, and price wars. The changes underway at Kraft Foods are illustrative.[8]

This division of the Philip Morris company includes Kraft, General Foods, Oscar Mayer Foods, and Maxwell House products. The 3,500 people from the four specialized sales forces now form one unit, organized into 300 marketing support teams, each responsible for a chain of stores. The salesperson, formerly a product specialist, is now responsible for Kraft's entire portfolio of grocery products. Kraft has account-service teams and other support personnel to help manage the various food categories.

The selling process guides sales force recruiting, training, allocation of effort, organizational design, and the use of selling support activities such as telemarketing. Understanding the process is essential in coordinating all elements of the marketing mix.

Sales Channels

Studies conducted by The Conference Board, Inc., show that companies are responding to the pressures of costs and competition in three major directions: (1) field sales forces are being restructured to provide greater specialization by types of users or products (product specialists, major account management); (2) companies are shifting toward greater use of indirect reseller channels; and (3) companies are adopting supplemental sales support channels such as telemarketing and computer-to-computer ordering.[9]

The choice of a particular sales channel is influenced by the buying power of customers, the size of customer groups, and the complexity of buyer-seller relationships.[10] We discuss customer contact requirements to illustrate the strengths and limitations of alternative sales channels.

Customer Buying Power. The purchasing potential of customers and prospects often places them into different importance categories. The "major" or "national" account represents the most important customer category. The major account: (1) purchases a significant volume on an absolute dollar basis and as a percentage of a supplier's total sales and (2) purchases (or influences the purchase) from a central or headquarters location for several geographically dispersed organizational units.[11] The buying power of a supplier's total customer base may range from several major accounts to a large number of very low volume purchasers. Customers and prospects can be classified into major accounts, other customers requiring face-to-face contact, and accounts whose purchases (or potential) do not justify regular contact by field salespeople.

Customer Groups. The number of customers in each buying-power group influences the selection of selling channels. The value of a multiple selling channel strategy should be determined. For example, the amount of telemarketing effort that is needed determines if establishing a telemarketing support unit should be considered. Similarly, enough major accounts should exist in order to develop and implement a major-account program. If the customer base does not display substantial differences in purchasing power and servicing requirements, then the use of a single selling channel may be appropriate.

Complexity of the Customer Relationship. The account management relationship is also a key factor as to the type of sales channel that is appropriate. For example, a customer that: (1) has several people involved in the buying process; (2) seeks a long-term, cooperative relationship with the supplier; and (3) requires specialized attention and service, creates a relatively complex buyer–seller relationship.[12] Such a relationship coupled with sufficient buying power suggests the use of a major account management channel. In contrast, a simple, routinized buying situation suggests telemarketing or electronic buyer–seller linkages. The field selling channel corresponds best to customer relationships that fall between very complex and highly routinized.

Designing the Sales Organization

Designing a sales organization includes selecting an organizational structure and deciding the size and deployment of the sales force.

Organizational Structure.   The organizational approach adopted should support the firm's sales force strategy. As companies adjust their selling strategies, organizational structure may also require changes. Kraft's shift to a single sales force for various product lines is illustrative.

Important influences on organizational design are the customer base, the product, and the geographic location of buyers. The answers to several questions are helpful in the choice of an organizational design.

1. What is the selling job? What functions are to be performed by salespeople?
2. Is specialization of selling effort necessary according to type of customer, different products, or salesperson activities (e.g., sales and service)?
3. Are channel-of-distribution relationships important in the organizational design?
4. How many and what kinds of sales management levels are needed to provide the proper amount of supervision, assistance, and control?
5. How and to what extent will sales channels other than the field salesforce be used?

The sales force organizational design should be compatible with the selling strategy and other marketing-mix strategies. Exhibit 13–3 shows the major types of organization designs. These designs take into account the extent of product diversity and differences in customer needs. When the customer base is widely dispersed, geography is likely to be in the organizational design. The assigned area and accounts that are the responsibility of the salesperson comprise the sales territory.

Sales Force Deployment.   The sales manager must decide how many salespeople are needed and how to deploy them to customers and prospects. Several factors outside the salesperson's control often affect his/her sales results. These influences include market potential, number and location of customers, intensity of competition, and market position of the company. Deployment analysis considers both salesperson factors and the uncontrollable factors.

Several methods are available for analyzing sales force size and the allocation of selling effort including: (1) revenue/cost analysis, (2) single-factor models, (3) sales-and-effort-response models, and (4) portfolio deployment models. Normally, sales and/or costs are the basis for determining sales force size and allocation.

EXHIBIT 13–3   Sales Organization Designs

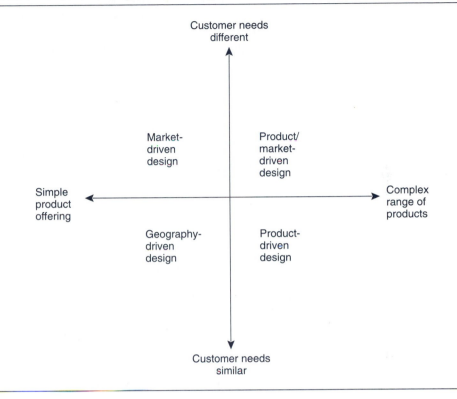

Revenue/cost analysis techniques require information on each salesperson's sales and/or costs. One approach compares each salesperson to an average break-even sales level, thus helping management to spot unprofitable territories. Another approach analyzes the profit performance of accounts or trading areas to estimate the profit impact of adding more salespeople or to determine how many people a new sales organization needs. These techniques are very useful in locating high- and low-performance territories.

Single-factor models assume that size and/or deployment are determined by one factor, such as market potential or workload (e.g., number of calls required), whose values can be used to determine required selling effort. Suppose there are two territories, X and Y. Territory X has double the market potential (opportunity for business) of territory Y. If selling effort is deployed according to market potential, X should get double the selling effort of Y.

Consideration of multiple influences (e.g., market potential, intensity of competition, and workload) on market response can improve deployment decisions. Several promising *sales-and-effort-response models* aid size and deployment decisions.[13] Exhibit 13–4 shows the output provided by these models. The analysis indicates that Jones's territory requires only about 36 percent of a person, whereas Smith's territory can support about 2.36 people. The allocations are determined by increasing selling effort in high-response

---

EXHIBIT 13–4   Sales Force Decision Model Output for Jones's and Smith's Territories

Trading Area†	Present Effort (percent)	Recommended Effort (percent)	Estimated Sales*	
			Present Effort	Recommended Effort
Jones:				
1	10%	4%	$ 19	$ 13
2	60	20	153	120
3	15	7	57	50
4	5	2	10	7
5	10	3	21	16
Total	100%	36%	$ 260	$ 206
Smith:				
1	18%	81%	$ 370	$ 520
2	7	21	100	130
3	5	11	55	65
4	35	35	225	225
5	5	11	60	70
6	30	77	400	500
Total	100%	236%	$1,210	$1,510

*In $000.
†Each territory is made up of several trading areas.

---

areas and reducing effort where sales response is low. Note that Exhibit 13–4 includes only two territories of a large sales organization. Sales response is determined from an empirically derived effort-to-sales relationship.

A *portfolio deployment strategy model* uses a version of the market attractiveness–business strength grid for business unit and product strategic analysis. Promising accounts receive effort allocation based on their position on the grid.[14] An account which has a high market opportunity and where the firm has a strong competitive position receives more effort than an account with less opportunity where the firm's market position is not strong. One major advantage of this technique is that it is easily understood by management and salespeople.

Managing the Sales Force

Salespeople differ in ability, motivation, and performance. Managing them involves the activities of supervising, selecting, training, motivating, and evaluating. A brief look at each activity shows the responsibilities and functions of a sales manager.

Finding and Selecting Salespeople.   A major study of the chief sales executives in over 100 firms asked them to indicate on a 1-to-10 scale how important 29 salesperson characteristics are to the success of their salespeople.[15] The executives indicated that the three most significant success characteristics are (1) being customer-driven and highly

---

EXHIBIT 13–5 Characteristics Related to Sales Performance in Different Types of Sales Jobs

---

Type Sales Job	*Characteristics That Are Relatively Important*	*Characteristics That Are Relatively Less Important*
Trade selling	Age, maturity, empathy, knowledge of customer needs and business methods	Aggressiveness, technical ability, product knowledge, persuasiveness
Missionary selling	Youth, high energy and stamina, verbal skill, persuasiveness	Empathy, knowledge of customers, maturity, previous sales experience
Technical selling	Education, product and customer knowledge—usually gained through training, intelligence	Empathy, persuasiveness, aggressiveness, age
New business selling	Experience, age and maturity, aggressiveness, persuasiveness, persistence	Customer knowledge, product knowledge, education, empathy

---

Source: Gilbert A. Churchill, Jr., Neil M. Ford, and Orville C. Walker, Jr., *Sales Force Management,* 3rd ed. (Burr Ridge, IL: Richard D. Irwin, 1990), p. 404.

committed to the job, (2) accepting direction and cooperating as a team player, and (3) and being motivated by one's peers, financial incentives, and oneself.

Exhibit 13–5 shows several characteristics that are often important for different types of selling situations. The characteristics vary based on the type of selling strategy, so we must first define the job that is to be performed. Managers use application forms, personal interviews, rating forms, reference checks, physical examinations, and various kinds of tests to assist them in making hiring decisions. The personal interview is widely cited as the most important part of the selection process for salespeople.

Training. Some firms use formal programs to train their salespeople; others use informal on-the-job training. Factors that affect the type and duration of training include size of firm, type of sales job, product complexity, experience of new salespeople, and management's satisfaction with past training efforts. Training topics may include selling concepts and techniques, product knowledge, territory management, and company policies and operating procedures.

In training salespeople, companies may seek (1) to increase productivity, (2) to improve morale, (3) to lower turnover, (4) to improve customer relations, and (5) to produce better management of time and territory.[16] These objectives are concerned with increasing results from the salesperson's effort and/or reducing selling costs. Sales training should be evaluated concerning its benefits and costs. Evaluations may include before-and-after training results, participant critiques, and a comparison of salespeople receiving training to those that have not been trained. Product knowledge training is probably more widespread than any other type of training.

Supervising and Motivating Salespeople. The manager that supervises salespeople has a key role in implementing a firm's selling strategy. He or she faces several important management issues. Coordinating the activities of a field sales force is difficult due to lack of regular contact. Compensation incentives are often used to encourage salespeople to sell. Also, as discussed earlier, sales executives want salespeople who are customer-driven and committed to the company and to team relationships.

The most widely used compensation plan is a combination of salary and incentive (80 percent salary and 20 percent incentive pay is a typical arrangement). The compensation plan should be fair to all participants and create an appropriate incentive. Salespeople also respond favorably to recognition programs and special promotions such as vacation travel awards.

Managers assist and encourage salespeople, and incentives highlight the importance of results, but the salesperson is the driving force in selling situations. Sales management must match promising selling opportunities with competent and self-motivated professional salespeople while providing the proper company environment and leadership. Although sales management professionals consider financial compensation the most important motivating force, recent research indicates that personal characteristics, environmental conditions, and company policies and procedures are also important motivating factors.[17]

Sales Force Evaluation and Control

Sales management is continually working to improve the productivity of selling efforts. During the 1990s personal selling costs increased much faster than advertising costs. The evaluation of sales force performance considers sales results, costs, and salesperson behavior and outcome performance. Several issues are important in evaluation, including the unit(s) of analysis, measures of performance, performance standards, and factors that the sales organization and individual salespeople cannot control.

Unit of Analysis.   Evaluation extends beyond the salesperson to include other organizational units, such as districts and branches. Selling teams are used in some types of selling. These companies focus evaluations on team results. Product performance evaluation by geographical area and across organization units is relevant in the firms that produce more than one product. Individual account sales and cost analyses are useful for customers such as national accounts and accounts assigned to salespeople.

Performance Measures.   Management needs yardsticks for measuring salesperson performance. For example, the sales force of a regional food processor that distributes through grocery wholesalers and large retail chains devotes most of its selling effort to calling on retailers. Since the firm does not have information on sales of its products by individual retail outlet, evaluations are based on the activities of salespeople rather than sales outcomes. This type of control system focuses on "behavior" rather than "outcomes."

Sales managers may use both activity (behavior) and outcome measures of salesperson performance. Research indicates that multiple-item measures of several activities and outcomes are used in performance evaluation.[18] The areas include sales planning, expense control, sales presentation, technical knowledge, information feedback, and sales results. Achievement of the sales quota is a widely used outcome measure of sales performance. Other outcome measures include new business generated, market share gains, new-product sales, and profit contributions.

Performance evaluation is influenced by the sales management control system used by the organization. Emphasis may be placed on salesperson activities, outcomes, or a combination of activities and outcomes. The objective is to use the type of control that is most effective for the selling situation. Direct selling organizations like Avon focus more on outcome control. Companies like American Airlines and Eli Lilly include both activity and outcome control in performance evaluation.

Setting Performance Standards.   Although internal comparisons of performance are frequently used, they are not very helpful if the performance of the entire sales force is unacceptable. A major problem in setting sales performance standards is determining how to adjust them for factors beyond the salesperson's control (i.e., market potential, intensity of competition, differences in customer needs, and quality of supervision). A competent salesperson may not appear to be performing well if assigned to a poor sales territory. These differences need to be included in the evaluation process since territories often are not equal in terms of opportunity and other uncontrollable factors.

Evaluating performance is one of sales management's more difficult tasks. Typically, performance tracking involves assessing a combination of outcome and behavioral factors. In compensation plans other than straight commission, performance evaluation affects the salesperson's pay, so obtaining a fair evaluation is important.

By evaluating the organization's personal selling strategy, management may identify various problems requiring corrective action. Problems may be linked to individual salespeople or to decisions that impact the entire organization (e.g., need to change the selling process). A well-designed information system helps in the diagnosis of performance and guides corrective actions when necessary.

DIRECT MARKETING STRATEGIES

An array of direct marketing methods is available, each offering certain advantages and limitations. The rapid growth of direct marketing during the last decade indicates the importance placed by many companies on these direct avenues to customers. For example, Williams-Sonoma, the kitchenware retailer, gets 40 percent of its $255 million annual revenues from catalog sales.[19] Using a two-stage strategy, the company builds a catalog customer base in a metropolitan area and then opens a retail store targeting catalog buyers with store promotion mailings.

First, we will look at several considerations in the use of direct marketing. Next, we will discuss various direct marketing methods. Finally, we will look at how direct marketing strategies are developed and implemented.

Considerations in the Use of Direct Marketing

The rapidly expanding use of direct marketing methods in the 1990s is driven by a combination of factors such as socioeconomic trends, low costs, databases, and buyers' demands for value. We will examine how these influences are affecting companies' use of mail, phone, media, and computers to access individual buyers.

Socioeconomic Trends. Several trends make the use of direct marketing attractive to many buyers. Having two working spouses imposes major time constraints on households, making direct purchases by phone and mail a convenient way of meeting buyers' needs and wants. Many single-person households also favor direct marketing purchases. Buyers can shop at home, save time, and avoid shopping congestion. Rapid response to order processing and shipping enables buyers to obtain their purchases in a few days. Liberal exchange policies reduce the risks of direct purchases.

Low Access Costs. While the cost per contact varies according to the method of direct contact, costs are much lower than face-to-face sales contact. Direct sales calls are $100 and more and telephone contact ranges from $10 to $20, compared to much lower costs per contact by mail and advertising media. The availability of databases that can target specific customer groups enables companies to target buyers selectively. Companies like American Express can market products to their credit-card users. Similarly, airline frequent flyer mailing lists provide cost-effective access to buyers.

Databases. The use of computerized databases escalated during the last decade, motivated by hardware and software technology. The information in the systems includes internal data on customers and purchased data on customers and prospects. The customer and prospect information contained in databases can be used to generate mailing lists and prospect lists and to identify market segments. These segments offer a direct communications channel with customers and prospects.

These systems offer powerful capabilities for identifying and communicating with customers. The database information enables companies to target individuals or small microsegments of people. The systems are very useful in sales and sales management support and for direct marketing programs. Database marketing has three main benefits: (1) strategic advantage through the more effective use of marketing information internally, (2) improvement in the use of customer and market information, and (3) a basis for developing long-term customer relationships.[20] The systems can be applied to mail-order marketing, telemarketing, and support of personal selling activities. A major objective of database marketing is to find and develop strong relationships with the customer base that accounts for a large portion of a firm's annual sales.

The components of database systems include relational databases, personal computers, electronic publishing media, and voice systems.[21] The intent of database marketing is effectively using a computerized customer database to facilitate a significant and profitable communication with customers. The system includes a database, analytical capabilities, a strategy and structure for using the system, procedures for deploying system capabilities, and controls for managing the database.

Value. The shopping information provided via direct marketing, convenience, reduced shopping time, rapid response, and competitive prices gives buyers an attractive bundle of value in many buying situations. Effective database management enables direct marketing to identify buyers who purchase on a continuing basis, becoming valuable assets to the direct marketer.

EXHIBIT 13-6   Direct Marketing

Direct Marketing Methods

Various direct marketing methods are shown in Exhibit 13–6. We will briefly examine each method to highlight its features and limitations.

Catalogs and Direct Mail.   Contact by mail with potential buyers may be intended to generate orders by phone or mail, or instead to encourage buyers to visit retail outlets to view goods and make purchases. Our focus here is on the use of mail contact as a primary basis of generating sales. Examples of companies using catalogs and other printed matter to encourage direct response include Lands' End (clothing), L. L. Bean (outdoor apparel and equipment), Calyx & Corolla (flowers), and The Conference Board, Inc. (management conferences).

Telemarketing.   This form of direct marketing consists of the use of telephone contact between the buyer and seller to achieve all or some of the selling function. Telemarketing offers two key advantages—low contact cost and quick access by both buyer and seller. It may be used as the primary method of customer contact or as a way to support the field sales force. Telemarketing has escalated in importance during the last decade, and today it is a vital part of the selling activities of many companies. The Selling in Action Feature describes how Minnesota Mining & Manufacturing (3M) uses telemarketing in its Medical-Surgical Division.

Direct Response Using the Media.   Many companies use television, radio, magazines, and newspapers to obtain sales from buyers. Direct response from the advertising is obtained by mail and telephone. People see the ads, decide to buy, and order the item from the organization promoting the product.

The TV Home Shopping Network markets a wide range of products for many companies. The products are displayed and their features described. Prices are discounted below list prices. The buyer places an order using a toll-free number. Individual

SELLING IN ACTION FEATURE   Telemarketing in 3M's Surgical Division

Reducing the costs of customer contact is a strong motivation for employing telemarketing. Nevertheless, there are some major obstacles in using telephone sales to support field sales-people. Face-to-face salespeople often feel threatened because they may lose sales, and they consider telephone contact not adequate for maintaining strong customer relationships. These issues must be considered when deciding whether to use telemarketing sales.

Minnesota Mining & Manufacturing Co. implemented a telephone sales program in the medical and surgical products division of its customer base of over 6,000 hospitals in the United States, in which customers were placed in sales-potential categories A, B, and C. The low-volume C category accounts, nearly half of the total customer base, were assigned to telephone sales-people after fully explaining the sales channel strategy to the field sales force. These sales-people were given sales credit for all telemarketing sales in their territories. Using time spared from account coverage, the field salespeople concentrated on the A and B hospitals. Sales costs of $200 per call, with about four calls to make a sale, were reduced to a small fraction of the face-to-face costs. Customer contact via telemarketing was more frequent than before, thus providing better response to the customers in the group.

Source: Adapted from Howard Sutton, *Rethinking the Company's Selling and Distribution Channels* (New York: The Conference Board, Inc., 1986), pp. 23–24.

companies may also market their products using commercials for specific products such as housewares, magazines, and music recordings.

Magazines, newspapers, and radio offer a wide range of direct marketing advertisements. The intent of the direct response communications is to persuade the person reading or hearing the ad to order the product. The advantage of using these media is the very low cost of exposure. While the percentage of response is also low, the returns can be substantial for products that buyers normally purchase through these media.

Electronic Shopping.   The computer age has created two major methods of direct marketing: computer ordering by companies from their supplier, and consumer and business shopping via the Internet. Electronic shopping by business buyers is appropriate when the customer's requirements involve routine repurchase of standard items, and direct access to the buyer is not necessary. Electronic methods may be used to support a field sales force rather than as the sole method of customer contact. Computer ordering helps the seller establish a close link to customers, and reduces order cycles (time from order placement to receipt) and inventory stocks. Computer ordering enables the buyer to reduce inventory levels, cut costs, and monitor customer preferences. For example, Wal-Mart's computerized scanning equipment in its stores enables the retailer to know what (and where) customers are buying, which guides the computerized ordering system. While some customers may resist becoming dependent on suppliers through electronic linkages, there is a strong trend toward closer ties between suppliers and organizational buyers.

Virtual shopping on the Internet has received much publicity during the last few years. Many companies are considering the potential opportunities of direct marketing to computer users. Retail sales via cybershopping were $0.24 billion in 1994 and expected to reach $7 billion by 2000.[22] In many instances buyers phone their orders because of retailers' and consumers' concerns about credit card security. For example, the Bombay Company advertises on the website Catalog 1. Its products include desks and other home decorating items. Buyers can order from an 800 phone number or request a catalog by E-mail.

Kiosk Shopping. Similar in concept to vending machines, kiosks offer buyers the capability to purchase from a stand facility located in a retail complex or other public facility. Airline tickets and flight insurance are examples of products sold using kiosks. In some instances the order may be placed at the kiosk but delivered to the customer's address. The advantage to the seller is exposure to many people, and the buyer benefits from the shopping convenience. Kiosks are best suited for selling products that buyers can easily evaluate due to prior experience.

Direct Marketing Strategy

As highlighted in our discussion direct marketing promotion has a primary objective of obtaining a purchase response from individual buyers. While the methods differ in nature and scope, all require the development of a strategy. The market target(s) must be identified, the objectives set, the communications strategy formulated, the program implemented and managed, and the results evaluated against performance expectations.

In many situations the direct marketing strategy is guided by the organization's marketing strategy. Direct marketing provides the way of reaching the customer. Additionally, product strategy must be determined, prices set, and distribution arranged. Direct marketing may be the only avenue to the customer, as in the case of L. L. Bean's targeting of the outdoor niche using catalog marketing. Other companies may use direct marketing as one of several ways of communicating with their market targets.

SUMMARY

Management analyzes the firm's marketing strategy, the target market, product characteristics, distribution strategy, and pricing strategy to identify the role of personal selling in the promotion mix. New business, trade selling, missionary selling, and consultative/technical selling strategies illustrate the possible roles that may be assigned to selling in various firms. The selling process indicates the selling activities necessary to move the buyer from need awareness to a purchase decision. Various sales channels are used in conjunction with the field sales force to accomplish the selling process activities.

Sales force organizational design decisions include the type of organizational structure to be used, the size of the sales force, and the allocation of selling effort. Deployment involves decisions regarding sales force size and effort allocation. Managing the sales force includes recruiting, training, supervising, and motivating salespeople. Evaluation and control determine the extent to which objectives are achieved and determine where adjustments are needed in selling strategy and tactics.

The purpose of direct marketing is to obtain a sales response from buyers. The rapidly expanding adoption of direct marketing methods in the 1990s is the consequence of several influences including socioeconomic trends, low costs of exposure, computer technology, and buyers' demands for value. Direct marketing is used by many companies to contact organizational and consumer buyers.

Companies have many options available for direct marketing to buyers. The methods include catalogs, direct mail, telemarketing, television, radio, magazines/newspapers, electronic shopping, and kiosk shopping. Developing a strategy for using each method includes selecting the market target(s), setting objectives, developing the communications strategy, implementing and managing the strategy, and evaluating results.

QUESTIONS FOR REVIEW AND DISCUSSION

1. What information does management require to analyze the selling situation?

2. Suppose an analysis of sales force size and selling effort deployment indicates that a company has a sales force of the right size but that the allocation of selling effort requires substantial adjustment in several territories. How should such deployment changes be implemented?

3. What questions would you want answered if you were trying to evaluate the effectiveness of a business unit's sales force strategy?

4. Discuss some of the advantages and limitations of recruiting salespeople by hiring the employees of companies with excellent training programs.

5. Is incentive compensation more important for salespeople than for product managers? Why?

6. Select a company and discuss how sales management should define the selling process.

7. Direct marketing is similar in many ways to advertising. Why is it important to view direct marketing as a specific group of promotion methods?

8. Discuss the reasons why many companies are interested in the marketing potential of the Internet.

9. Select one of the direct marketing methods and discuss the decisions that are necessary in developing a strategy for using the method.

10. Suppose you have been asked to evaluate whether a regional camera and consumer electronics retailer should obtain Internet space. What criteria should be used in the evaluation?

NOTES

1. Karen Padley, "Sullivan Dental's Robert Sullivan: Product Supplier Cleans Up by Covering All Sales Bases," *Investor's Business Daily,* December 21, 1992, pp. A1, A2.

2. James Brooke, "Avon Calls in Amazon Rain Forrest," *International Herald Tribune,* July 8–9, 1995, p. 9.

3. Gilbert A. Churchill, Jr., Neil M. Ford, and Orville C. Walker, Jr., *Sales Force Management,* 3rd ed. (Burr Ridge, IL: Richard D. Irwin, 1990), pp. 3–7.

4. Rahul Jacob, "The Struggle to Create an Organization for the 21st Century," *Fortune,* April 3, 1995, pp. 90–92, 94, 96, 98, and 99.

5. David W. Cravens, "The Changing Role of the Sales Force," *Marketing Management,* Fall 1995, pp. 48–57.

6. Churchill, Ford, and Walker, *Sales Force Management,* pp. 99–106.

7. Andy Cohen, "Starting Over," *Sales and Marketing Management,* September 1995, pp. 40–44.

8. Greg Burns, "Will So Many Ingredients Work Together?" *Business Week,* March 27, 1995, pp. 188 and 191.

9. Howard Sutton, *Rethinking Company's Selling and Distribution Channels,* Report No. 885 (New York: The Conference Board, Inc., 1986).

10. The following discussion is drawn from Raymond W. LaForge, David W. Cravens, and Thomas N. Ingram, "Evaluating Multiple Sales Channel Strategies," *Journal of Business and Industrial Marketing,* Summer/Fall 1991, pp. 37–48.

11. Jerome A. Colletti and Gary S. Tubridy, "Effective Major Account Management," *Journal of Personal Selling and Sales Management,* August 1987, pp. 1–10.
12. Ibid.
13. For an expanded discussion of sales force decision models, see David W. Cravens, "Sales Force Decision Models: A Comparative Assessment," in *Sales Management: New Developments from Behavioral and Decision Model Research,* ed. Richard P. Bagozzi (Cambridge, MA: Marketing Science Institute, 1979), pp. 310–24.
14. Raymond W. LaForge, David W. Cravens, and Clifford E. Young, "Improving Sales Force Productivity," *Business Horizons,* September/October 1985, pp. 50–59.
15. David W. Cravens, Thomas M. Ingram, Raymond W. LaForge, and Clifford E. Young, "Hallmarks of Effective Sales Organizations," *Marketing Management,* Winter 1992, pp. 56–67.
16. Churchill, Ford, and Walker, *Sales Force Management,* p. 400.
17. Churchill, Ford, and Walker, *Sales Force Management,* chap. 13.
18. David W. Cravens, Thomas M. Ingram, Raymond W. LaForge, and Clifford E. Young, "Behavior-Based and Outcome-Based Sales Force Control Systems," *Journal of Marketing,* October 1993, pp. 47–59.
19. Sandra Baker, "Mail Bonding," *Fort Worth Star-Telegram,* December 16, 1995, pp. B1 and B3.
20. Keith Fletcher, Colin Wheeter, and Julia Wright, "The Role and Status of U.K. Database Marketing," *Quarterly Review of Marketing,* Autumn 1990, pp. 7–14.
21. Bob Shaw and Merlin Stone, "Competitive Superiority through Database Marketing," *Long Range Planning,* October 1988, pp. 24–40.
22. Leslie Gornstein, "How Safe Is Cybershopping," *Fort Worth Star-Telegram,* August 27, 1995, pp. B1 and B8.

Cases for Part IV

CASE 4–1   Du Pont Company

From the creation of nylon during the Depression to the latest studies of exotic carbon molecules, the Du Pont Company has long been at the forefront of basic corporate research. It led the nation's chemical companies last year in U.S. patents applied for and granted.

But good science hasn't always been good for Du Pont shareholders. Despite spending more than $13 billion on chemical and related research over the past 10 years, Du Pont's 5,000 scientists and engineers were a technological black hole: They sucked in money but, company officials concede, didn't turn out a single all-new blockbuster product or even many major innovations. And only about 5 percent of Du Pont's own managers surveyed recently rate the company among the best U.S. or Japanese corporations in introducing new products.

"They've been like the space program: The technology is great, but where's the payoff?" says John Garcia, an industry analyst at Wertheim Schroder & Co.

But now Du Pont, one of the nation's most prolific inventors, is trying to reinvent itself. It is striving to create a new culture driven by profits, not just research prowess. It is betting that radical improvements in the way it develops new products, as well as the way it makes nylon and other mainstays, can yield huge savings. At the same time, it is trying to restructure a bloated bureaucracy.

Du Pont needs a top-to-bottom overhaul, says Edgar S. Woolard, Jr., its chief executive officer since 1989. He ticks off its shortcomings: The company takes too long to "convert research into products that can benefit our customers," he says. In major established products, it has lost ground to rivals that spend more on improving manufacturing (it was forced out of the Orlon fiber business for that reason). And years of paternalistic employment practices have made Du Pont a secure place to work, but "we have too much bureaucracy running these businesses," Mr. Woolard complains.

The deceptively soft-spoken, 58-year-old North Carolina native is forcing change on a corporate culture widely considered about as agile as one of the company's lumbering Conoco supertankers. Du Ponters were shocked out of their complacency last summer when Mr. Woolard announced a plan to slash annual costs by $1 billion within two years. The company also aims to increase pretax profit by another $2 billion within five years, mainly by improving its manufacturing efficiency and reducing its plants' turnaround time between processing runs.

Wilmington is still shaking from the initial jolt: 5,500 Du Pont employees here have already taken early retirement, and more cutbacks are expected. Du Pont has about 20,000 employees in the area and 133,000 worldwide.

Perhaps shielded by his Southern-gentleman manners, Mr. Woolard hasn't been blamed for Du Pont's problems, even though he has been part of top management since being named an executive vice president in 1983. Wall Street applauds the steps he is taking, but some complain that he is taking too long.

Mr. Woolard says he is moving as fast as he can. He says he wants to avoid short-term moves, such as being too quick to sell or close weak operations, that might someday damage the company.

If anything can scorch Mr. Woolard's Teflon coating, it may be the recession's effect on Du Pont's earnings. Last year, net income dropped nearly 40 percent to $1.4 billion. That plunge partly reflected lower oil revenues at Du Pont's Conoco unit as oil prices dropped after Operation Desert Storm ended quickly. Sales last year slipped 3 percent to $38.7 billion. Over the past 12 months, Du Pont's stock has traded between the mid-30s and 50½; it closed yesterday at $47.25, up 25 cents in New York Stock Exchange trading.

But even after the recovery kicks in, the heat isn't going to be off Du Pont or many other U.S. corporate giants. Companies ranging from Du Pont to International Business Machines Corporation and American Telephone & Telegraph Company are being forced by mounting competition to deliver both new and existing products faster and more efficiently. And a history of dominating an industry doesn't provide much of a competitive edge. In fact, it can be a hindrance, if, as at Du Pont, it spawned a somewhat sluggish and backward-looking culture.

Du Pont isn't used to such pressure. After diversifying away from its gunpowder and munitions businesses after World War I, it became, for decades, one of America's most innovative companies. It introduced synthetic fibers and rubber, new plastics and polymers. After World War II, with European and Japanese rivals leveled, Du Pont and other U.S. chemical makers reigned supreme in many areas for another 20 years.

But, obsessed with finding the next big breakthrough, many Du Pont scientists slighted minor advances, customer needs—and profitability. Joseph Miller, director of polymers research, notes a "mind-set that research's responsibility was to find another nylon.'' And the pursuit of what he calls Big Bangs led to some spectacular new-product busts. Among them:

- Kevlar, pound for pound stronger than steel, was the Superman of synthetic fibers when introduced in 1972. But it began to resemble Clark Kent when tire makers instead went for cheaper steel-belted radials. After nearly 20 years and $600 million of development and marketing costs, Kevlar recently turned a profit, having found niche markets such as bulletproof vests and army helmets.

- Synthetic silk is a product Du Pont would like to forget. Qiana, as it was known, cost about $200 million to develop and market. After a brief fling with high-fashion designers in the late 1960s and early 1970s, it was abandoned for natural fibers and died barely a decade later.

- Electronic-imaging businesses have cost Du Pont more than $600 million since the mid-1980s. The technological potential of things such as digital printing may seem dazzling, but all Du Pont has got out of it so far is a river of red ink.

- And pharmaceuticals, Du Pont officials admit after 10 years and $1 billion, take longer and cost more to bring to market than they anticipated. In 1990, Merck & Company was brought in as a partner in a joint venture to add marketing muscle.

With new-product development faltering, Du Pont has relied on "tweaking" existing products into slightly improved versions. Its Lycra spandex fiber, which was introduced more than 30 years ago to replace rubber in girdles, has expanded via modifications to dominate the active-wear market. And low-dose herbicides, invented in the mid-1970s, are selling well.

To focus "more intensity on customer needs," Mr. Woolard says Du Pont has shifted about 30 percent of its research budget, or more than $400 million a year, toward speeding new products to customers (Exhibit 1).

In the past, customers wanting to make changes in high-strength Zytel nylon-resin products used to have to wait as long as six months to get an answer out of Du Pont, says John Jack, Zytel global product manager. By that time, the customer, often an auto maker or one of its suppliers, may have taken the business elsewhere.

In response, Du Pont salespeople created an informal "skunkworks" with the aid of frustrated in-house researchers to go outside channels and push their pet projects. But those projects often didn't produce much profit, Mr. Jack says, and they may not have even been in the customer's best long-term interests.

A skunkworks antidote is being tried by several Du Pont departments and is supposed to be adopted throughout the company. To speed the new-product process, the departments have created small, interdisciplinary teams to field all new-product ideas. These teams, including research, manufacturing and sales representatives, get just two weeks to make a decision. If they decide to go ahead with the idea, they have two more weeks to form another team to carry it out. The elapsed time for a new, still-secret auto-safety product, from the idea to a prototype product, was just two months, Mr. Jack says.

Du Pont is also working more closely with customers. Fluorware Inc., a supplier to the semiconductor industry, wanted Du Pont to make a purer version of a Teflon basket

---

EXHIBIT 1

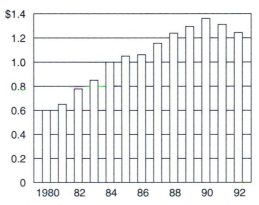

Heavy R&D Spending
Du Pont's annual research and development
spending, in billions*

*Excludes Conoco and energy products research.
1990–92 figures include share of R&D budget
for Du Pont-Merck joint venture.

---

that Fluorware uses to hold silicon wafers during production. The companies formed a joint team to find a solution, even though Fluorware's annual sales total only about $60 million. Last year, Du Pont brought out a commercial version of the product for sale to other companies. The Fluorware-Du Pont team now holds regular meetings, "which we hope will lead to breakthroughs in materials science," says John Goodman, the Minnesota company's senior director for corporate technology.

Another problem at Du Pont: bugs. Some divisions spend about three times as much money and effort on debugging new products—ironing out problems after the product is launched—than the top new-product development companies in the United States. That can send costs through the roof. Substantially cutting debugging time companywide could lift profit by more than $200 million a year, officials estimate.

"We need to shift the emphasis from investment in product development to improving our understanding of the processes used to manufacture our products," says Uma Chowdhry, an efficiency expert in Du Pont's microcircuits and component-materials business.

Some scientists studying nylon in the lab are doing just that. It might seem that Du Pont couldn't learn much more about nylon after making it for more than 50 years. Yet in recent months the scientists have, for the first time, devised a way to break down nylon into its raw materials without creating waste by-products.

"This is one of our high-risk, big-impact activities," says James Meyer, the project leader. The company could eventually recycle nylon and save tens of millions of dollars in raw materials if the process works on a commercial scale. It also would eliminate the cost of handling the waste byproduct—and perhaps a big environmental headache.

The potential profits from improving manufacturing at Du Pont's more than 100 plants worldwide are huge. Reducing the downtime between the dozens of processes at polymer plants is expected to raise profits by as much as $200 million a year within a few years, says Mr. Miller, the head of polymers research. With so much money at stake, it's no surprise that the polymers division now spends 60 percent of its research budget on improving its processing and only 40 percent on products. A few years ago, 70 percent of the budget went to products and only 30 percent to processing.

One of Du Pont's most efficient plants sits along the Delaware River not far from company headquarters in downtown Wilmington. Fixed costs to produce titanium dioxide, an opaque pigment used in paper and paint, have been flat since 1989 while productivity has jumped sharply, says Jack Kane, the plant manager. The efficiency gains came from shutting down one production line and reducing downtime between processing runs on the remaining line. The plant is running 22 hours a day, up from 18 hours just a few years ago.

Mr. Kane says many of the plant's productivity gains came from involving workers in the process. When he started working at the plant in 1956, he says, a supervisor answered one of his questions by saying, "You don't need to know that." Mr. Kane says that to get workers to think for themselves and identify with the company's goals, he "gives cost figures on any of our operations down to the newest guy on a maintenance team."

In a program started last year, plant management has paid about $18,000 to workers for actions that ended up saving Du Pont a multiple of that amount, says Cindy Coker, the assistant plant manager. Walt Zerbe, an employee, got a bonus of more than $1,000, for example; he rejected a contractor's bid to paint the plant's buildings and equipment, and the contractor came back a few days later with a bid 20 percent lower. "That wouldn't have happened even two years ago," Ms. Coker says.

Meanwhile, Mr. Woolard's back-to-basics sermon has led to inevitable strains between applied research directed at processing and fundamental research. Research managers say they think a lot harder before approving projects without an obvious payoff.

"The trickiest thing is to strike that balance between 'buckyballs' [a new form of pure carbon] and process technology," says Richard Quisenberry, head of central research. Buckyballs are being studied by a highly respected group of nearly 20 Du Pont scientists even though practical applications are probably years off.

Senior management's commitment to fundamental research remains strong, Mr. Quisenberry insists, despite all the talk about profits. He adds: "I still get notes from people written across the top of research proposals that say, 'This looks pretty applied. Are you sure we're taking care of our long-term interests?'"

Source: Scott McMurray, "Changing a Culture: Du Pont Tries to Make Its Research Wizardry Serve the Bottom Line," *The Wall Street Journal,* March 27, 1992, pp. A1, A4. Reprinted by permission of *The Wall Street Journal,* © 1992 by Dow Jones & Company, Inc. All Rights Reserved Worldwide.

CASE 4–2   American International Group, Inc.

Wu Chitung is a gold digger hoping to score with a little giant.

Briefcase in hand and smile on straight, he dodges through busy traffic to accost an electronics-shop owner idling in his own doorway. A few quick words, and he has lured the man inside. Some fast talk, and the slightly puzzled shop owner has become the newest customer of American International Group Inc. (AIG), the only foreign insurance company in China selling directly to Chinese citizens.

"I never believed in such things before," confesses Zhang Shengdong, the shopkeeper, as he pays his first year's life-insurance premium in cash. "I just decided to have a try—a new taste—to see what it's like."

That may be an odd reason for buying insurance, but it is good enough for AIG and its agent, Mr. Wu ("Jeffery" to foreigners). He is one of some 140 AIG representatives knocking on Shanghai doors for clients and commissions, and many seem to be successful "gold diggers"—ambitious workers, in local slang. In eight months, they have sold more than 12,000 policies—a small straight-life version called the little giant is popular—and AIG expects them to sell many, many more in a country with one-fifth the world's people and its fastest-growing economy.

"We are optimistic about the potential for AIG in China," says Maurice R. (Hank) Greenberg, the company's feisty chairman. "In the long term, China will be reaching out for what is commonplace elsewhere. The people will want to buy life, education, and all the other policies."

But AIG's presence in Shanghai has significance beyond the company's own prospects. It illustrates the Chinese economy's growing complexity. Foreign traders and manufacturers are already active; now, Beijing officials call AIG's presence an experiment to see whether service companies also can help China develop. They seem especially interested in companies that manage or otherwise deal with money. So, they are watching AIG closely; if pleased, they will extend its operating license beyond Shanghai to other growth cities. AIG has already asked for a license for Guangzhou (formerly Canton). Other service companies would probably follow quickly into China.

But if officials decide that insurance and other service companies take out more than they put in, they will slam the door—and please state-owned monopolies that don't want them here anyway. In fact, the main Chinese insurance company—People's Insurance Co. of China—fought hard to exclude AIG despite their close business relations since 1980; political leaders in Beijing ruled in favor of AIG. Chinese banks, freight forwarders, airlines, and other service companies are equally opposed to letting outsiders enter their home markets—though they also arrange joint ventures to gain toeholds overseas.

"If Chinese companies can do well, then there won't be so much of a role for foreigners," warns Wang Yuanzhi, a senior official of the powerful State Economic and Trade Commission in Beijing, a recently created economic-policy panel.

The Clinton administration, meanwhile, is pushing China to open service markets faster. It contends that China's rules unfairly hobble foreign companies. This matters because U.S. service industries are highly competitive in global markets, and their earnings partly offset America's huge deficits in merchandise trade. Since this year's trade deficit with China may reach $20 billion, Washington sees no reason for Beijing to keep reaping what one U.S. official calls high "monopoly rents" by protecting its service companies from competition.

However these market-access negotiations turn out, they show how fast China is changing. Not long ago, it would have seemed preposterous to contend that foreign stockbrokers, merchant bankers, accountants, and insurance people, among others, could play a direct role here. China was seen mainly as a source of cheap toys and textiles, offering little opportunity for sophisticated foreign operations.

In recent years, however, some 90,000 foreign companies have said they will invest $100 billion here, according to Beijing, to make everything from Volkswagen autos to AT&T telephone switches to NEC semiconductors. New factories spring up daily to make increasingly complex products.

The service industries are the latest wave of applicants. But AIG, in a sense, has merely come home again. Back in 1919, a wandering young American named Cornelius Vander Starr founded its predecessor company here, after previously running an ice-cream parlor in California and working as a shipping clerk in Yokohama. Unlike his stuffier, colonial-minded European rivals, he hired Chinese agents to sell to Chinese citizens, and his company prospered until the Communists forced it out in 1950 (its headquarters had moved to New York as World War II drew near). By then, it was a major global player; now, it is one of the world's largest, most profitable insurers.

Its competitors want a share of the Chinese market, too. For example, Aetna Life & Casualty sees a market if state factories have to take responsibility for employee pensions from the central government, which wants them off its books. "When that happens, they'll need outside expertise," an Aetna official says.

Meantime, accountants see their chance as Chinese industry enters global markets, seeks more private financing, and thus must lift its accounting methods to world standards. When Chinese companies raise capital, firms such as Merrill Lynch & Co. want to underwrite the offerings and sell shares directly to Chinese investors. And John Hart of Schenker & Co.'s Beijing office says his freight-forwarding company might even operate a domestic trucking line if the Chinese ever let foreigners in to compete.

"The idea of service as a product you sell doesn't quite register," Mr. Hart notes. China's state companies "tend to think that they're not selling you a service but doing you a favor."

It is no accident that foreign companies are focusing on Shanghai. China's largest city, with nearly 14 million people, it is out to become a regional commercial and financial center again; it once dwarfed Hong Kong and Singapore. It isn't as boisterous or tawdry as in prewar days, but some of the old verve is back now that the Maoists are gone. Its official assignment is to become "the head of the dragon" linking the serpentine Yangtze Valley, home to perhaps 300 million people, to the sea and beyond. "In particular, we will pay much attention to [developing] financial markets and money markets," says Hua Jianmin, chairman of the city's planning commission.

The city is flaunting new wealth. High-rise apartments, offices, and hotels—many of them joint ventures with foreigners—are sprouting up. Traffic jams seem constant even though trucks are banned during the day. Busy managers clutch beepers or cellular phones when out of their offices. Shops are well-stocked with food, clothing, cosmetics, and customers.

There is not a baggy Mao suit in sight. Women are rediscovering style in everything from short shorts to long dresses, from shops such as the Flying Bat Firm or Pierre Cardin. Many youngsters prefer T-shirts, though their English phrases are often rude or wrong. Some old hands say Shanghai reminds them of other developing Asian cities a few decades ago.

Already, 20 overseas banks have offices here; so do many other service companies. The roster at Shanghai Centre, a high-rise office, apartment, and hotel complex partly owned by AIG, lists such names as Merrill Lynch, Barclay's Bank, and Credit Lyonnais, among others. Most are so-called representative offices, which can deal only with expatriates, joint ventures, or their official state counterparts. Merrill Lynch, for example, can help underwrite Chinese companies' stock offerings overseas but can't sell shares locally. Foreign bankers must channel their foreign-exchange business through state banks rather than handle it themselves, and they can't engage in retail banking.

AIG is the exception; it sells directly to local citizens. And it hopes that China will account for 10 percent or 15 percent of its huge Asian life-insurance business in another decade or so. "We always had the aspiration to return," says Mr. Greenberg, who succeeded Mr. Starr as chairman in 1968.

The tough campaign to get back began with Mr. Greenberg's first China visit in 1975, not long after the U.S. resumed political ties with Beijing. After years of talking, AIG persuaded People's Insurance Co. in 1980 to enter a joint venture, its first with a foreign company, to insure cargoes moving between the countries. But that didn't get AIG on the inside.

So it set out to prove itself a long-term friend of China, not just a fast-buck operator. It invested in Shanghai Centre. It created an "International Business Leaders' Advisory Council for the Mayor of Shanghai," which, among other things, held a 1990 conference here (chaired by the president of the New York Federal Reserve Bank) so "world-class managers" could explain how financial companies might help Shanghai. It constantly touted its Shanghai heritage. It strongly advocated favorable U.S. tariff treatment for Chinese goods. It hired Henry Kissinger, a noted friend of China, as chairman of its international advisory board. And it is forming a $1 billion investment fund for Asian industrial and infrastructure projects with about half the money earmarked for China.

AIG got its license last September and quickly opened for business here. The company contends, not surprisingly, that "life insurance is essential for nation-building," in Mr. Greenberg's words, because insurers collect local funds and invest them productively.

AIG is collecting those premiums as fast as it can even though, because of start-up costs, profits seem more than five years away. "There's so much business in China," says Ernest Stempel, vice chairman for life insurance and a 55-year company veteran who has 70,000 agents elsewhere in Asia. "It's a young population, and so few are insured."

Work at AIG's Shanghai Centre offices begins with "morning call": Agents recite (in English) AIG's seven rules of selling—"don't be too serious," says one—and report (in Chinese) on the previous day. Managers from AIG's large Taiwan unit provide training and sales tips.

Then its men and women hit the street. Most agents are 25 to 35 years old and college-educated; three are doctors. According to Nysco Shu, the Taiwanese manager of life-insurance operations here, representing an American company is prestigious and helps close sales. ("I wouldn't sign up if this was a Japanese company," one new customer says.) But the lure of money is the main draw, even though agents must rely on commissions—something unknown in China for decades.

Jeffery Wu seems typical. He is a cheery 25-year-old with a degree in computer engineering—"but I'm not very good at it," he concedes. After a stint as a bartender, he joined AIG four months ago. In his first month, he made only 300 yuan ($30 at the street rate) but soon hit 3,000 yuan and dared tell his factory-engineer father and English-teacher mother where he works. Relying on commissions seems too precarious to older Chinese.

Some of his success is due to *kwangxi,* the personal connections on which all Chinese rely. But he does more than sell to friends. One recent afternoon, Mr. Wu revisited Friendly Neighbor State Farm Commercial Corp., a city-owned but prospering distributor of produce. Its manager had previously agreed to buy a health plan to supplement his state benefits.

The visit yielded a small bonanza; the manager bought policies for all 12 employees. The state system pays only five yuan a day toward hospital fees, half the cost; the AIG plan pays 60, partly toward lost compensation. So, the manager decided his staff needed extra protection. Mr. Wu collected a premium check for 4,732 yuan—he will keep 20 percent—and said he would return to discuss life insurance.

It wasn't a hard sell. "He wanted to sell, and we intended to buy, so our interests matched," one employee noted.

So, too, at the Purple Happiness audio shop, which provides equipment for discos and karaoke bars. Dai Meiping, the owner and a former manager in a missile factory, said she was signing up partly "to support this young man" and also "to enlarge my friendship network by taking part in this insurance company." She seemed a bit vague about the policy itself.

But cold calls aren't all so easy; Mr. Wu says 80 percent of his fail. Yet the novelty of his trade helps. Not for decades have insurance companies or door-to-door salesmen operated here, and there is little ingrained resistance against either. As a Friendly Neighbor office clerk explains: "Mr. Wu has a very good sense of public relations. He just knocked on our door even without an invitation, as an unexpected friend, and it was pleasant to meet him."

Source: Adapted from Robert Keatley, "A Boom in Asia: AIG Sells Insurance in Shanghai, Testing Service Firms' Role," *The Wall Street Journal,* July 21, 1993, pp. A1, A5. Reprinted by permission of *The Wall Street Journal,* © 1993 by Dow Jones & Company, Inc. All Rights Reserved Worldwide.

CASE 4–3 Kimbell Art Museum

In the year since the Barnes Collection exhibit lifted it to new levels of public awareness, the Kimbell Art Museum has further expanded its audience, membership, and program offerings—even as it has pursued winning programs and policies of long standing.

The one-time-only exhibit of French paintings drew a record-setting 430,000 people to the museum between April 24 and August 14, 1994. Since then, attendance at the Kimbell has climbed by about 25 percent, according to a recent poll of North Texas households.

The increase in attendance is "phenomenal," according to John Fullingim, director of Addison Marketing Group, which has conducted several market surveys for the museum. "That kind of increase would be a home run by any business standards. But considering they are in the museum world, it's just unheard of," he said.

The Barnes exhibition "didn't change our values," said Kimbell Director Ted Pillsbury. "But it solidified and expanded audience awareness and our membership."

Reenrollment of museum members who joined during the Barnes has been unusually successful, new members continue to be added, and many established members have increased their annual dues in order to join new levels of patronage.

The same poll—of 100 randomly selected North Texas households—also revealed that a stunning 100 percent of respondents knew about the Kimbell.

"The Kimbell has done an extraordinary job of marketing their treasures to the public," Fullingim said. "I've never seen anybody, for-profit or non-profit, even on the same page as the Kimbell."

Addison Marketing Group also has done studies and projects for the Fort Worth Museum of Science and History, the Dallas Opera, the Dallas Museum of Natural History, the Dallas Historical Society, and the St. Louis Science Museum, as well as a number of for-profit organizations.

The company's most recent random-sample poll for the Kimbell, conducted in July, indicated that 78 percent of respondents had attended the Kimbell—up from 62.9 percent in October 1993 (before the Barnes) and 69.4 percent in June 1994 (during the Barnes).

Responding to both the Barnes and market research, the Kimbell has developed a range of offerings for the general public and for members only. They include:

- Friday evening hours with dinner served in the museum's buffet, as well as free musical performances and lectures.

- Addition of a Director's Circle membership category, with annual dues of $500.

- Thursday-night receptions for Director's Circle members and Sustaining Patrons (dues of $250), in addition to Saturday-night openings for individual and Dual/Family Patrons (dues of $50 and $75).

- By-reservation, behind-the-scenes tours of the museum and a For Members Only series of meetings with Kimbell curators and art conservators, free and open to all membership categories.

- Sunday Family Hour activities and exhibit tours, also offered by reservation, but free and open to the general public.

- All-day Saturday exhibit previews for all members.

At the same time, the Kimbell has continued to attract high-caliber international shows—often as the sole U.S. venue or one of only two—and to organize thoughtful, ambitious exhibitions of its own.

A prime example of the former opens October 1: *Art and Empire: Treasures from Assyria in the British Museum* is the largest loan of art ever from that imperial treasure house. Its only other U.S. venue was New York's Metropolitan Museum of Art.

An exhibit co-organized by the Kimbell opens there on November 5: a survey of paintings by noted French genre artist Louis-Leopold Boilly. After showing in Fort Worth, the show will move to the National Gallery of Art in Washington, D.C., its only other venue.

Additionally, this fall the museum re-introduces its popular Artist's Eye series of talks by Texas artists, who will present informal auditorium lectures on loan shows as well as the permanent collection.

Not to be overlooked, however, is an exhibit that continues through September 3—of art from the Kimbell's collection.

Titled *The Art of Collecting: Thirty Years in Retrospect,* this show has proven a dazzling eye-opener. It is primarily composed of works familiar to museum visitors, but it leaves many viewers feeling they're seeing things for the first time—and appreciating the full significance of the Kimbell's achievements in building its collection.

At the same time, the Kimbell Art Foundation has continued to purchase stellar artworks for the museum. The foundation has an endowment of about $130 million; interest earned on the endowment goes to fund museum operations, making the Kimbell among the top-funded museums in the United States.

The Barnes exhibit also led to a near-tripling of Kimbell membership, said Jo Vecchio, the Kimbell's assistant director for membership and development.

Although membership is a source of income for many museums, for the Kimbell it means community outreach. "We like having people in the museum," Vecchio said.

Before people began anticipating the Barnes exhibition, membership stood at about 7,000 households. After the Barnes closed, it was about 17,000 households.

Typically, such membership boosts are only temporary, Vecchio said, noting that about 70 percent of the people who join museums because of blockbuster shows do not renew their memberships.

But the Kimbell so far can claim better than 50-percent reenrollment of first-time members. Even as Vecchio's three-person staff continues encouraging people to rejoin, they have also signed up more than 2,700 new members since last September—primarily people who visited the museum and registered their names and addresses.

"We just did our direct-mail campaign, so it will continue to rise, by about 1,000," Vecchio said, noting that current membership is about 14,500 households.

"The reason you lose the great majority of new members after a blockbuster is that most museums apply the wrong strategy," Fullingim said. "They sell membership based only on avoiding long lines and getting in for free."

The Kimbell used those perks to sell memberships during the Barnes, but the museum also asked Addison Marketing Group to identify what would bind new members to the institution.

"And one thing we find across the board is that people want to be closer to a cultural experience," Fullingim said. "They don't want to just stand behind the railing and look at a painting, or sit through an opera and not understand what is going on.

"They want the institution to make the experience compelling and real for them on a meaningful, emotional level," Fullingim said. That, he said, is the tie that binds.

Without taking away from its efforts to serve the general public, Pillsbury said, the Kimbell "is trying to build an audience of people who are interested, who care about the museum and wish to be given opportunities to participate.

"And the way to do that is through membership," Pillsbury said. "Those are the people who are most interested, who are your frequent fliers, if you wish."

Recent Acquisitions

Here is a list of artworks, valued at about $9 million, purchased by the Kimbell Art Museum since the opening of the Barnes Collection exhibit on April 24, 1994.

April 1994.
Pair of Maya onyx bowls, Guatemala (A.D. 300–500). Ife terra cotta head of a king, Nigeria (12th–14th century).

August 1994.
Piet Mondrian painting, *Composition No. 8,* Netherlands (1939–1942). Adam Elsheimer painting, *The Flight into Egypt,* Germany (circa 1605).

December 1994.
Western Han Dynasty equestrian figure, China (206 B.C.–A.D. 9). Northern Qi or Sui Dynasty jar, China (circa A.D. 550–618).

February 1995.
Jean-Baptiste-Camille Corot painting, *The Stonecutters,* France (circa 1872–74).

April 1995.
Western Han Dynasty painted jar, China (206 B.C.–A.D. 9). Eastern Han Dynasty figure of a dog, China (A.D. 23–200). Western Chou Period bronze bell, China (10th century B.C.).

June 1995.
Edgar Degas drawing, *After the Bath: Woman Drying Her Hair,* France (c. 1895).

July 1995.
Religious folk painting, Korea (late 17th century). Wooden door panel, Japan (early 17th century). Warring States Period ribbed stoneware jar, China (4th century B.C.). Southern Sung Dynasty porcelain bowl, China (12th century).

Source: Janet Tyson, "Opening the Barnes Door," *Fort Worth Star-Telegram,* August 22, 1995, pp. F1 and F4.

CASE 4–4   Genentech Inc.

Genentech Inc., maker of a drug to help short children grow taller, sells it to 14,000 patients in America. By a 1992 count, that may be as much as twice the number who are believed to have the condition for which the drug was designed and approved.

Marketing feats like this have helped make Genentech one of the few thriving biotechnology companies. Now the Swiss company that owns close to 70 percent of Genentech, Roche Holding Ltd., is nearing a deadline to decide whether to buy the rest of it. Genentech's rich pipeline of future drugs makes it a prize, but the other half of the company's formula—its aggressiveness in marketing—has lately become a more questionable asset.

Genentech's top sales executive is under indictment, charged with bribing a Minneapolis doctor to prescribe the growth hormone for more children. After numerous warnings, the Food and Drug Administration has begun a broad investigation of Genentech's marketing practices, citing evidence of "a continuing pattern of violative product promotion." One focus: complaints of Genentech's pitching approved drugs for nonapproved uses or at nonapproved dosages. In addition, the Federal Trade Commission is looking into certain Genentech marketing practices.

Prescription drugs differ from most merchandise in one key respect: The ways they may be promoted are rigorously circumscribed, by federal regulators and by the American Medical Association. Genentech tests these limits, inspired by a hard-charging chief executive officer, G. Kirk Raab, who built its sales force from scratch after a career that earlier took him close to the top of Abbott Laboratories. Jack Schuler, who succeeded Mr. Raab as Abbott's president, isn't surprised at the flak Mr. Raab's company is drawing. "Within the law," he says, "Kirk will take it as close to the edge as he can."

Mr. Raab agrees that "every aspect of this company has always been aggressive" but says any improprieties are isolated acts of misguided individuals that were corrected as soon as they were found out about. Last year, Mr. Raab says, Genentech tightened supervision of its 350-member sales force after getting a warning letter from the FDA. And he is putting a toll-free fax machine in his office so doctors can send any complaints straight to him.

"We wouldn't be where we are today if we didn't have extraordinarily high standards," Mr. Raab says. "I have always done my very best to instill in the organization that there are things I don't want to tolerate or accept."

What, then, has caught the attention of so many investigators? A look inside Genentech's marketing machine shows how the company wrung some $600 million of sales last year from just three main drugs, with limited advantages or markets—a heart-attack medicine that some studies found little better than a far cheaper competitor, plus drugs for the treatment of growth deficiency and cystic fibrosis that are targeted at small groups of people. It is estimated that Genentech's sales rose 20 percent last year and its earnings at least doubled.

Despite the limitations of its drugs, Genentech has prospered by using some resourceful techniques to grab market share from pharmaceutical giants, in the process triggering a backlash with its aggressive methods.

One thing Genentech does that other drug makers don't is compile an extensive registry of thousands of patients who have had a particular illness—such as a heart attack—listing how they were treated and with what outcome. The company pays nurses and doctor's assistants up to $50 for each patient form they fill out, then compiles and analyzes the result. Sales representatives thus can tell where to direct their efforts and also, as a talking point in their next call, can give hospitals and doctors customized analyses of their practices plus a nationwide summary for comparative purposes.

Such information can help hospitals spot trends in patient care and determine where improvement is needed. Because it is useful to them, more than 1,400 of the nation's

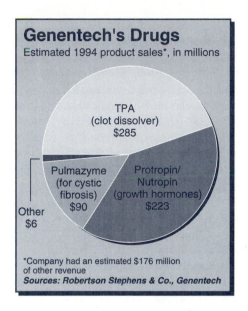

Genentech's Drugs
Estimated 1994 product sales*, in millions

TPA
(clot dissolver)
$285

Pulmazyme
(for cystic
fibrosis)
$90

Protropin/
Nutropin
(growth hormones)
$223

Other
$6

*Company had an estimated $176 million
of other revenue
Sources: Robertson Stephens & Co., Genentech

6,000 acute-care facilities contribute to the registry. The registry is a lot of trouble to compile but can give Genentech products an edge because it concentrates on patients taking the company's drugs. The heart-attack registry, for example, asks detailed questions about recipients of TPA, Genentech's bioengineered clot buster for heart-attack patients, but not about patients receiving other treatments. Despite this imbalance, the registry has the look and feel of science, and routinely gets cited at cardiology conferences.

The registry is just one of the strategies Genentech has used to dominate the market for cardiac clot dissolvers—even though its product costs 10 times as much as an older one sold by pharmaceutical giant Astra AB of Sweden and even though some studies showed scant difference in the drugs' effectiveness.

It was to address this last point—to try to prove the Genentech drug's superiority—that the company spent an almost unprecedented $55 million on a huge study of the two drugs, encompassing 41,000 heart-attack patients. The 1993 study yielded a small edge for TPA, showing it to save one additional life per 100, although it involved a higher risk that the patient would have a stroke.

Genentech rapidly converted that narrow advantage into a rout. It quickly faxed hospitals a news release, sales reps sent out "dear doctor" letters using words like "fastest" and "greatest." Within three months, Genentech had recaptured market share it had lost, and today it holds 70 percent of the market.

Richard Peto, an Oxford University professor of statistics who analyzes clinical-trial data, is critical of how Genentech has promoted the results of the study. "To convey the impression that one [clot buster] is definitely superior to the other is inappropriate, based on the totality of evidence," including two earlier trials, Dr. Peto says. "And the company has had too much influence in the whole way the thing is presented to doctors."

Replies Genentech's Mr. Raab: "If I can think every day that a thousand or two thousand people more will live in this country because of what we did . . . , I think that's wonderful."

The effort to get doctors to prefer TPA has even included raising the specter of legal liability. Last April, a malpractice attorney warned the staff at Hemet Medical Center outside Los Angeles that the public expects TPA to be used in heart attack victims despite its cost. Genentech underwrote the seminar, including the $750 fee of the attorney, William Ginsburg.

Mr. Raab says that such legal briefings were inappropriate and that Genentech halted them several months ago. Mr. Ginsburg, who says he gave the Genentech-sponsored speech at five hospitals, says the opinions he gave were his own and weren't influenced by Genentech.

Last February, a Genentech employee named David O'Connor gave a hospital presentation in which he denigrated a rival clot buster, telling his audience it was made from urine collected from portable toilets. (A version of the drug that is sold overseas is indeed made from urine, but not from such a source.) The FDA wrote a letter to Genentech saying the presentation, at Kennedy Memorial Hospital in Turnersville, New Jersey, was rife with misleading and unauthorized statements about Genentech drugs. (Mr. O'Connor also said Pulmozyme, a Genentech cystic-fibrosis drug, works against chronic bronchitis, a use not approved by the FDA.) Genentech says Mr. O'Connor no longer works for it. He didn't return calls seeking comment.

Another Genentech salesman, Steve Briseno, drew the ire of the pharmacy director at Saddleback Memorial Medical Center in Laguna Hills, California, by repeatedly entering restricted patient areas and scattering literature in his wake, says the pharmacy chief, Hugo Folli. "I threw him out of here a couple of times," Dr. Folli says. "He walked around like he owned the place. I felt he was undermining my ability to do the job." Genentech says Mr. Briseno "still has access to the hospital." The salesman denies he ever was thrown out.

In promoting TPA, Genentech has sometimes urged hospital pharmacies not to stock the rival clot dissolver, a lawsuit in Texas contends. Doing so would narrow physicians' choices—an effect that the suit suggests can have serious consequences.

When Elijio Uresti had a heart attack in December 1991, one of the first things emergency-room doctors at Alice (Texas) Physicians and Surgeons Hospital did was inject him with TPA. Within hours, Mr. Uresti suffered a stroke that caused severe brain damage. Studies have shown that the main rival to TPA, Astra's streptokinase, is significantly less likely than TPA to lead to stroke and is suitable for patients with high blood pressure like Mr. Uresti. A suit filed by Mr. Uresti's wife in Jim Wells County Court says a Genentech salesman had persuaded the hospital to exclude rival drugs by exaggerating TPA's benefits and glossing over its risks.

The hospital won't comment, and Mr. Raab says he can't discuss the case. But he does note that Genentech has faced "almost no" product-liability suits.

Genentech also gets its message into hospitals through their continuing medical-education programs. Like other drug makers, Genentech sponsors lots of these.

Among the speakers at seminars it has sponsored have been Allan Ross, an investigator in the big TPA study, and Eric Topol, the study's lead investigator. In October 1993,

Dr. Ross conducted an hour-long teleconference with 66 hospitals, earning $2,500. Another time, Dr. Topol did a teleconference and was paid $1,000.

Both men had pledged not to accept any payments from Genentech for a year after the study was done, and, in fact, Genentech didn't pay them for these teleconferences. But the organization that did, the University of Texas Health Science Center, paid the fees out of a $16,000 grant that Genentech provided.

Dr. Ross says that when he is invited to speak, he doesn't ask who is paying, and "I go and say what I believe, regardless of who is or isn't the sponsor. No company can buy my opinion." Dr. Topol says he would have refused to speak at the teleconference had he been aware of Genentech's sponsorship.

Dr. Topol adds: "I've done everything I can to distance myself from this company. Our good research is clouded by their marketing practices that I think are atrocious."

Genentech says hospitals chose the topics of their educational programs, selected the most knowledgeable speakers available, and paid them in a way that didn't violate the investigators' pledge.

Product information is apt to be more persuasive with doctors if it comes from a source other than a drug company, and Genentech is good at cultivating such sources. In the late 1980s, it recruited several hundred emergency-room nurses and gave them grants to train their colleagues in administering clot busters. But some nurses went further, second-guessing doctors and handing out literature promoting TPA, activities a physician at Stanford University hospital complained were "oppressive." Genentech says that the nurses had no sales role and that the program ended in 1991. A former Genentech executive says, "It was starting to smell bad and we dumped it."

Among the greatest sources of marketing controversy for Genentech has been its Protropin growth hormone. The Minneapolis indictment, handed up last August, accuses a Genentech executive of funneling $224,000 to a doctor—disguised as research grants and consulting fees—to prescribe more Protropin. (Both the doctor and the executive denied the charges; Genentech itself wasn't indicted.)

Now, federal investigators are looking at records of some other major prescribers of Protropin, including one whose patients bought $2 million of the drug a year and who advertised for patients on TV.

Meanwhile, the FTC is examining Genentech's role in funding two charities that screened schoolchildren and suggested a doctor's visit for those who were very short for their age. The Human Growth Foundation in Falls Church, Virginia, and the Magic Foundation in Oak Park, Illinois, derive a majority of their funding from Genentech, getting most of the rest from the maker of a competing growth hormone, Eli Lilly & Co. The corporate connection wasn't disclosed to school officials or to parents of short children who received follow-up letters from the charities offering information on medical help.

Because Genentech controls 70 percent of the growth-hormone market, it had much to gain from the programs. It maintains there is nothing wrong with screenings—that extending a hand to a child who may be growth-hormone-deficient can prevent a lifetime of suffering. But it has suspended financial support of screenings pending review by a National Academy of Sciences affiliate.

A National Institutes of Health study in 1992 concluded that "up to half" of children receiving growth hormones might not have the deficiencies for which the drugs may be prescribed, and thus have only cosmetic reasons for taking them. It isn't easy to tell for sure which short children are merely short and which have hormone deficiencies. Still, some critics say the figures indicate that Genentech is overpromoting its product and that doctors are overprescribing it. "Either Genentech violated [the drug's approved uses] or the doctors did," argues Jess Thoene, chairman of the National Organization of Rare Disorders.

Genentech disagrees with the NIH finding, saying its data show over 90 percent of Protropin patients are hormone deficient.

It isn't known what weight the flap over Genentech's marketing might carry in Roche's decision on whether to buy the last 30 percent of the biotech firm's stock. (Roche bought another 1 percent of the stock on the open market in December, regulatory filings show.) The Swiss company's option expires in June. One thing that makes Genentech an attractive target is its strong pipeline of new drugs and expanded uses for existing ones. Last June, for instance, Genentech apparently won a fierce biotech race by isolating a protein that spurs growth of cells vital to blood clotting. It also is neck-and-neck with Merck & Co. to develop a promising drug to halt tumor growth in the pancreas and colon. And several years of collaboration with Roche is bearing fruit in the form of a souped-up aspirin to treat heart attacks.

A rigorous discipline rules Genentech's research, with each drug assigned a success probability rating at every stage of development. Yet the company lets scientists devote one day a week to their own research, and it was this freedom that gave rise to Genentech's most recently approved product, the cystic-fibrosis drug Pulmozyme. Genentech also has been a pioneer in drug manufacturing, having invested in new production technologies such as ways to grow cells quickly and to purify substances precisely. It has become a contract manufacturer for drug companies that lack such expertise.

Mr. Raab remains confident that the company will come through the FDA matter and other difficulties without significant consequences, financial or otherwise. Questions about Genentech's marketing amount to "tidbits and sour grapes and practices that some people may not agree with," he says.

"I tell friends, 'Do you know that your doctor makes decisions often based on a salesman?' " Mr. Raab says. "They say, 'Can't be, not true.' People don't want to believe that."

Source: Ralph T. King, Jr., "Profit Prescription: In Marketing of Drugs, Genentech Tests Limits of What Is Acceptable," *The Wall Street Journal,* January 10, 1995, pp. A1, A4. Reprinted by permission of *The Wall Street Journal.* © 1995 by Dow Jones & Company, Inc. All Rights Reserved Worldwide.

IMPLEMENTING AND MANAGING MARKETING STRATEGY

Designing Effective Marketing Organizations

"In outfits as diverse as Eastman Kodak, Hallmark Cards, and General Electric—even the San Diego Zoo—the search for the organization perfectly designed for the 21st century is going ahead with the urgency of a scavenger hunt."[1] Several influences are impacting the design of organizations including: (1) the implementation of self-managing teams and other employee empowerment methods, (2) emphasis on managing and improving business processes using the concepts and methods of total quality management, and (3) the application of an array of impressive information technology. Organizational effectiveness is particularly important in marketing operations because of marketing's interaction with the external environment and its coordination between the various business functions.

The last decade was an unprecedented period of organizational change. Companies realigned their organizations to establish closer contact with customers, improve customer service, reduce unnecessary layers of management, decrease the time between decisions and results, and improve organizational effectiveness in other ways. Organizational changes include the use of information systems to reduce organizational layers and response time, use of multifunctional teams to design and produce new products, and creation of flexible organizational units to compete in turbulent business environments.

First we will look at several organization design issues, and then consider alternative designs and the features and limitations of each in different situational settings. Next, we will discuss selecting an organization design. Finally, we will consider several global aspects of organizations.

CONSIDERATIONS IN ORGANIZATION DESIGN

Several factors influence the design of marketing organizations. These include: (1) using independent organizations to perform marketing activities; (2) determining the vertical structure of the organization; (3) establishing horizontal relationships; (4) improving response time between decisions and results; and (5) understanding and managing the operating environment.

Internal and External Organizations

Marketing organization design includes consideration of the trade-offs between performing marketing functions within the organization and having external organizations perform the functions. The discussion of channel-of-distribution design, in Chapter 10, examined the use of intermediaries to perform various distribution functions. Contractual arrangements are often made for advertising and sales promotion services, marketing research, and telemarketing. Services are also available to perform marketing functions in international markets.

The importance of outsourcing various business functions expanded in the 1990s. This trend is likely to continue due to cost reduction pressures, availability of competent services, increased flexibility, and shared risk. There are various marketing functions that may be provided by independent suppliers. Examples include telemarketing, database marketing, logistics, information services, and personal selling.

Internal units provide more control of activities, easier access to other departments, and greater familiarity with company operations. The commitment of the people to the organization is often higher since they are part of the corporate culture. The limitations of internal units include difficulty in quickly expanding or contracting size, lack of experience in other business environments, and limited skills in specialized areas such as advertising, marketing research, and database management.

External organizations offer specialized skills, experience, and flexibility in adapting to changing conditions. These firms may have lower costs than an organization that performs the function(s) internally. But obtaining services outside the firm also has limitations, including loss of control, longer execution time, greater coordination requirements, and lack of familiarity with the organization's products and markets. Identifying core competencies, coordinating relationships, defining operating responsibilities, establishing good communications, and monitoring and evaluating performance are essential to gaining effective use of external organizations.

Vertical Structure

The vertical organization structure concerns the number of management levels and reporting relationships. Vertical design issues include determining reporting relationships, establishing departmental groupings, and creating vertical information linkages.[2] Reporting relationships indicate who reports to whom in the organizational hierarchy. Departmental grouping considers how sets of employees are assigned responsibilities. Groupings may be according to function, geography, product, market, or combinations of these factors. Vertical information linkages are necessary to aid communications among organizational participants. Various techniques help to move information through the organization, including approval of proposed actions, rules and procedures, plans and schedules, creation of additional levels or positions, and information systems.

Organizations today have fewer levels than traditional organizations and are beginning to be organized around processes such as order processing, new-product planning, and customer services. One estimate is that the typical large business in 2010 will have fewer than half the levels of management of its counterpart today.[3] These flat organizations will have no more than one-third the managers of today and will be information-based. Information storage, processing, and decision-support technology will move information swiftly up and down and across the organization. Levels of management can be eliminated since people at those levels function primarily as information relays rather than as decision makers and leaders. In many organizations, management is under pressure to reduce operating costs. You can reduce staff size by eliminating organizational levels and increasing the number of people supervised.

Horizontal Relationships

The traditional focus in organization design has been vertical structure, rather than spelling out how different organizational units coordinate their activities. Horizontal relationships are also very important in achieving organizational objectives.[4] The use of horizontal multifunction teams for new-product planning and other projects requires close working relationships. Coordination between organizational units such as research and development, finance, manufacturing, human resources, and marketing is accomplished by written communications, direct contact, liaison roles, task forces, full-time integrators (e.g., product manager), and teams (permanent task forces).

A major motivation in horizontal relationships is improving relationships with customers in the field. Many companies have restructured their sales and marketing organizations to move closer to their customers:

> An electrical products manufacturer, previously organized on a functional basis, has set up four separate operating divisions, each with its own sales and engineering units.
>
> A packaging company, following the successful revamping of its sales force along industry lines, is now reorganizing its warehousing and customer service activities on a geographic basis, so as to ensure more familiarity with customer by area.
>
> A manufacturer serving industrial markets has formed a special marketing group solely for support of its distribution network.[5]

These actions indicate marketing executives' continuing concern about organizational effectiveness. Organizational change will occur more frequently in the future as businesses respond to market turbulence and competitive pressures.

Multifunctional teamwork is critical to improving product and supporting-service quality. Union Pacific Railroad (UP) found that nearly one-fifth of its invoices contained errors.[6] Management formed a special team to analyze the problem. Statistical analysis identified 20 specific causes of the billing errors originating from several departments. A quality-improvement team was formed with the objective of reducing the errors to one-half the current level within a year for each of the 20 causes.

Speed of Response

The design of an organization affects its ability (and willingness) to respond quickly. The advantage of doing things faster than the competition is clearly established in various kinds of business. The Limited's skills in moving women's apparel from design to the store in weeks instead of months enables the retailer to market new designs ahead of its competition. Organizations that can do things faster are more competitive. General Electric reduced the time between order receipt and delivery for custom-made industrial circuit breaker boxes from three weeks to three days.[7] The company formed a team of manufacturing, design, and marketing experts with the responsibility of changing the manufacturing process.

Managing the Operating Environment

The environment influences an organization in several ways.[8] For example, as environmental complexity increases, management may expand the number of positions and departments to cope with the complexity. Uncertainties in the external environment are created by instability, variability, dispersion, turbulence, and resource constraints. Rapidly changing customer needs and wants require organizations to adapt to customers' requirements. One organization form may be more adaptable than another.

Environmental complexity and risk create new organizational challenges. Flexibility and adaptability in an organization are important capabilities. Responses to environmental uncertainty may include: (1) creating additional positions and departments; (2) performing buffering and boundary-spanning roles by units that work with environmental elements (e.g., placing a salesperson in the facility of a key customer); (3) performance of specialized functions within departments and intensified integration between departments; (4) adoption of looser, free-flowing, and adaptive internal organizations; (5) selection of structures, management processes, and strategies used by other industry members; and (6) expanded planning and environmental forecasting activities.[9]

Organizations are drastically altering traditional organization forms.[10] The changes are in response to new environmental threats and opportunities, relocating in new product-markets, countering competitive threats, and developing buffers to reduce the impact of environmental influences. One popular new organization form is the network where various business functions are performed by several independent organizations and individuals. Tommy Hilfiger, the men's apparel company, has fewer than 600 employees, while generating over $500 million in annual sales. The company's network consists of several manufacturing, distribution, and marketing organizations.

ORGANIZATIONAL DESIGN OPTIONS

Functional specialization is often one consideration in selecting an organizational design. Emphasis on functions may be less appropriate when trying to direct activities toward market targets, products, and field sales operations. When two or more targets and/or a mix of products are involved, companies often depart from functional organizational designs that place advertising, selling, research, and other supporting services into functional units (e.g., sales department). Similarly, the distribution channels used and sales force considerations may influence the organizational structure adopted by a firm. For example, the marketing of home entertainment products targeted to business buyers of employee incentives and promotional gifts might be placed in a unit separate from a unit marketing to consumer end-users. Geographical factors have a heavy influence on organization design because of the need to make the field supervisory structure correspond to how the sales force is assigned to customers.

Mary Kay Cosmetics, Inc., found an interesting opportunity when launching its sales organization in Russia in 1993.[11] Management used a geographical design similar to that used in the United States. Starting with 30 salespeople, the sales organization had 17,000 people at the end of 1995 and estimated sales over $30 million. Recruiting is not difficult due to the shortage of jobs for women in Russia and the earning opportunities. A really top sales representative earns $1,500 a month compared to the $112 average pay in Russia. Unlike the United States, job turnover is low in Mary Kay's Russian organization.

In this discussion we assume that the marketing organization is part of a strategic business unit. Companies with two or more business units may have corporate marketing organizations as well as business unit marketing organizations. Corporate involvement may range from a coordinating role to one in which the corporate staff has considerable influence on business unit marketing operations. Also, the chief marketing executive and staff may participate in varying degrees in strategic planning for the enterprise and the business unit.

We will first look at several traditional approaches to organizing marketing activities and assigning responsibilities, and we will examine the role of corporate marketing. This will be followed by a discussion of some new approaches in marketing organization design.

Traditional Designs

The major forms of marketing organizational designs are *functional, product, market,* and *matrix* designs.

Functional Organizational Design.   This design assigns departments, groups, or individuals responsibility for specific activities, such as advertising and sales promotion, pricing, sales, marketing research, and marketing planning and services. Depending on the size and scope of its operations, the marketing organization may include some or all of these activities. The functional approach is often used when a single product or a closely related line is marketed to one market target.

Product Organizational Design.   The product mix may require special attention in the organizational design. New products often do not receive the attention they need unless specific responsibility is assigned planning and coordination of the new-product activities. This problem may also occur with existing products when a business unit has several products and involves technical and/or application differences. Organizational schemes for managing products can be categorized according to whether they are temporary or

---

EXHIBIT 14–1   Organizational Approaches for Managing New and Existing Products

---

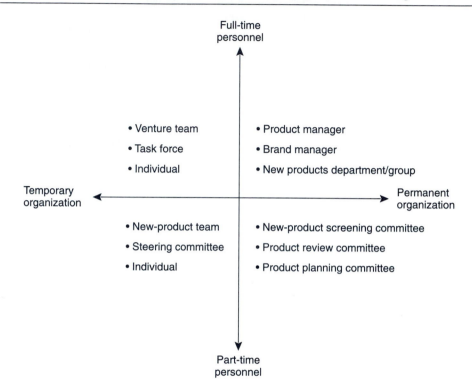

---

permanent and whether the people involved are assigned full-time or part-time.[12] Exhibit 14–1 shows the various approaches to product management. We will examine several of the approaches to organizing using a product focus.

The *new-products committee* is popular because it involves the various functional interests in new-product planning without creating an organizational unit.[13] It is quite flexible and can be used either as a coordinating mechanism for a particular project or on a continuing basis. Committees may be formed at the top management level for decision-making purposes or at operating levels for coordination or special-purpose assignments, such as screening new-product proposals.

By using the committee system, companies avoid creating a permanent, full-time organizational unit—a major advantage. Limitations of the committee include lack of authority, coordination difficulties, and lack of full-time monitoring. Key factors in the success of a new-product committee are the chairperson and the choice of members.

The *product/brand manager,* sometimes assisted by one or a few additional people, is responsible for planning and coordinating various business functions for the assigned products. Typically, the product manager does not have authority over all product-planning activities but may coordinate various product-related activities. The manager usually has background and experience in research and development, engineering, or marketing and is normally assigned to one of these departments. Product managers' titles and responsibilities vary widely across companies.

The *product department* places product-planning responsibility in a formal department. Two versions may be found: (1) a separate department to give new products attention, push, focus, and drive, as would occur if the chief operating executive were managing the product and (2) the product manager cluster, in which a manager is responsible for two or more product managers.[14] The departmental approach provides a strong base of support for new-product planning, but a separate department may also create internal frictions with other functional areas.

The *venture team* requires the creation of an organizational unit to perform some or all of the new-product-planning functions. This unit may be a separate division or company created specifically for new-product or new-business ideas and initiatives.[15] Examples of successful products planned by venture units include the Boeing 757 aircraft, the IBM personal computer line, and Xerox products other than photocopiers. Venture teams offer several advantages, including flexibility and quick response. They provide functional involvement and full-time commitment, and they can be disbanded when appropriate. Team members are motivated to participate on a project that offers possible job advancement opportunities.

The *new-product team* is similar to a task force in that the team consists of functional specialists working on a specific new-product development project.[16] However, the product team has a high degree of autonomy with the authority to select leaders, establish operating procedures, and resolve conflicts. The team is formed for a specific project, although it may be assigned subsequent projects.

Factors that often influence the choice of a product organization design are the kinds and scope of products offered, the amount of new-product development, the extent of coordination necessary among functional areas, and the management and technical problems previously encountered with new products and existing products. For example, a firm with an existing functional organizational structure may create a temporary team to manage and coordinate the development of a major new product. Before or soon after commercial introduction, the firm will shift responsibility for the product to the functional organization. The team's purpose is to allocate initial direction and effort to the new product so that it is properly launched.

Market Organizational Design.   This approach is used when a business unit serves more than one market target and when customer considerations are important in the design of the marketing organization. For example, the customer base often affects the structuring of the field sales organization. Some firms appoint market managers and have a field sales force that is specialized by type of customer. The market manager operates much like a product manager, with responsibility for market planning, research, advertising, and sales force coordination. Market-oriented field organizations may be deployed according to industry, customer size, type of product application, or in other

---

EXHIBIT 14–2   A Marketing Organization Based on a Combination of Functions and Products

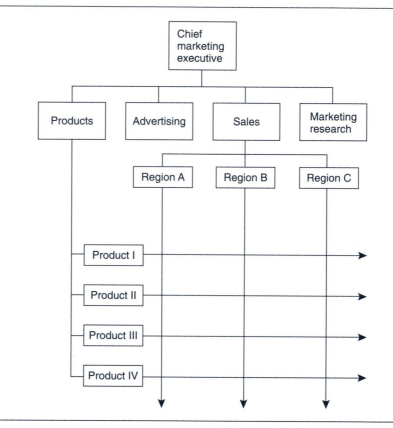

---

ways to achieve specialization by end-user groups. Conditions that suggest a market-oriented design are: (1) multiple market targets being served within a strategic business unit, (2) substantial differences in the customer requirements in a given target market, and/or (3) each customer or prospect purchases the product in large volume or dollar amounts.

Combination or Matrix Design.   This design utilizes a cross-classification approach to emphasize two different factors, such as products and marketing functions (Exhibit 14–2). Field sales coverage is determined by geography, whereas product emphasis is obtained using product managers. In addition to working with salespeople, product managers coordinate other marketing functions such as advertising and marketing research. Other matrix schemes are possible. For example, within the sales regions shown in Exhibit 14–2, salespeople may be organized by product type or customer group. Also, marketing functions may be broken down by product category, such as appointing an advertising coordinator for Product II.

The combination approaches are effective in responding to different influences on the organization and offer more flexibility than the other traditional approaches. A major difficulty with these designs is establishing lines of responsibility and authority. Product and market managers frequently complain that they lack control over all marketing functions even though they are held accountable for results. Nevertheless, the matrix approaches are popular, so their operational advantages must exceed their limitations.

Marketing's Corporate Role.   An important organizational issue in firms with two or more operating units is deciding whether a corporate marketing function should be established, and if so, what its role and scope should be. The Conference Board identifies three possible roles of corporate marketing:

1. Performing services for the company and/or its operating units.
2. Controlling or monitoring the performance of operating unit marketing activities.
3. Providing an advisory or consulting service to corporate management and/or operating units.[17]

Services may include media purchases, marketing research, planning assistance, and other supporting activities. Control may cover pricing policies, new-product planning, sales force compensation, and other monitoring/control actions. Advisory or consulting services provide professional marketing expertise such as market segmentation analyses, new-product planning, and marketing strategy.

Influenced by the trend toward decentralized management, corporations are moving marketing functions away from the corporate level to the business-unit level. Decentralized marketing activities are more likely to occur when:

Senior management is moving the company toward further diversification into areas having little or no relation to its present array of businesses.

New growth leads to added organizational complexities and to a further proliferation of the company's operating components.

Senior management makes no attempt to integrate newly acquired businesses into the company's existing corporate structure.

Senior management tends to focus on financial results and asset management.

Areas other than marketing are the principal sources of a company's strength, efficiency, and momentum.

Senior management strongly prefers decentralizing as much responsibility as possible to the company's operating units.

A company has to cut corporate staff to reduce costs.[18]

Thus, the corporate role of marketing is influenced by top management's approach to organizing the corporation as well as the nature and complexity of business operations. Typically, marketing strategy decisions are centered at the business-unit and product-market levels. Nevertheless, it is very important for the top management team to include strategic marketing professionals. The market-driven nature of business strategy requires the active participation of marketing professionals.

New Forms of Marketing Organizations

As we discussed early in the chapter, the use of self-managing employee teams, emphasis on business processes rather than activities, and the application of information technology are creating major changes in organization design. First, we will explore how these influences are altering the traditional vertical organization. Then, we will look at some new marketing organization designs.

Transforming Vertical Organizations. Transformation involves defining the business as a group of interrelated processes rather than as functions of research and development, manufacturing, marketing, and finance. Since most business processes involve several business functions, the basis of organization becomes the process rather than the function. Consider, for example, the process of "order generation and fulfillment."[19] The process owners are manufacturing and marketing. The process team responsible for defining, analyzing, and continually improving the process includes the workers that perform the various activities necessary to create the process outputs (completed orders delivered to customers).

The process concept of managing a business is a dramatic departure from traditional, functional organizational designs. The use of matrix and the team-oriented designs provides experience in coordinating the activities of multifunctional teams. For example, a large industrial-products company uses teams to develop and implement its marketing plans. Team membership includes product managers, research and development managers, manufacturing managers, sales management, finance executives, and top management. Nonetheless, making the transition to the true process-driven organization requires a major alteration in how the organization is designed and how it functions.

New Organization Forms. An example of one new concept of how to design an organization is the marketing coalition company shown in Exhibit 14–3.[20] This horizontally aligned organization is the control center for organizing a network of specialist firms. The core of this organization is a functionally specialized marketing capability that coordinates a network of independent functional units. They perform such functions as product technology, engineering, and manufacturing.

No pure forms of the marketing coalition company are known to exist. Several Japanese companies have certain of the characteristics of the coalition company. One U.S. retail chain, the Bombay Company, is organized in a similar form to the coalition design in its supplier network. Bombay has a global network of specialized suppliers of its home furnishings. Specific components (e.g., legs, top) of a table are produced by different manufacturers, shipped to Bombay's product-assembly faculty, and deployed through a national distribution system to Bombay's company-owned retail stores. While the Bombay design is not identical to Exhibit 14–3, there are striking similarities.

EXHIBIT 14–3 The Marketing Coalition Company

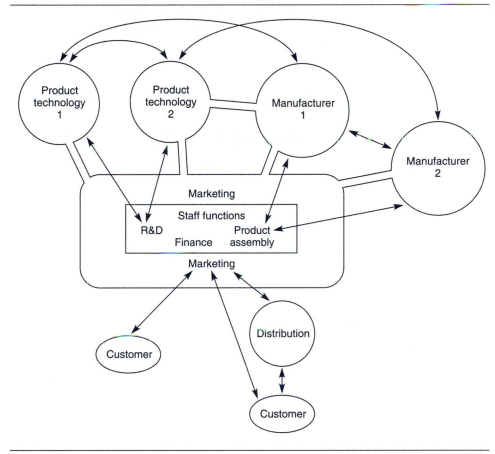

Source: Ravi S. Achrol, "Evolution of the Marketing Organization: New Forms for Turbulent Environments," *Journal of Marketing,* October 1991, p. 88.

SELECTING AN ORGANIZATION DESIGN

The design of the marketing organization is influenced by market and environmental factors, the characteristics of the organization, and the marketing strategy followed by the firm. A sound organizational scheme displays several characteristics:

The organization should correspond to the strategic marketing plan. For example, if the plan is structured around markets or products, then the marketing organizational structure should reflect this same emphasis.

Coordination of activities is essential to successful implementation of plans, both within the marketing function and with other company and business unit functions.

The more highly specialized that marketing functions become, the more likely coordination and communications will be hampered.

Specialization of marketing activities leads to greater efficiency in performing the functions. As an illustration, a central advertising department may be more cost-efficient than establishing an advertising unit for each product category. Specialization can also provide technical depth. For example, product or application specialization in a field sales force will enable salespeople to provide consultative-type assistance to customers.

The organization should be structured so that responsibility for results will correspond to a manager's influence on results. While this objective is often difficult to fully achieve, it is an important consideration in designing the marketing organization.

Finally, one of the real dangers in a highly structured and complex organization is the loss of flexibility. The organization should be adaptable to changing conditions.

Since some of these characteristics conflict with others, organizational design requires looking at priorities and balancing conflicting consequences.

Structure–Environment Match

Matching the organization design to its markets and competitive environment should contribute to organizational effectiveness. A framework for analyzing the structure–environment match is shown in Exhibit 14–4. It utilizes the dimensions of market/environmental complexity, and interconnectedness and predictability, and it indicates organizational designs for each contingency.[21] Interconnectedness refers to the degree to which the organization, intermediaries, and markets function as an organized and integrated system. A vertical marketing channel system has this characteristic. A predictable environment is one that does not change rapidly, marketing relationships with buyers are routinized, and the organization is in direct contact with the environment.

High environmental complexity coupled with a predictable environment suggest the use of a decentralized organization to gain organizational effectiveness (Cell I):

> Decentralization offers many benefits for coping with a complex multi-product-market environment. The unit managers can focus their entire efforts on a specific set of products and/or markets. They are task-oriented versus function-oriented. All of the resources to perform the marketing function are possessed by each decentralized unit. Thus, the need to compete for shared resources is eliminated. The unit managers in a decentralized organization assume some of the decision-making and coordination roles concentrated in the marketing manager of a functional organization. Thus, decisions are made more quickly. In effect, a complex environment has been divided up into a subset of simpler environments that can be effectively dealt with by the simple functional organizational form.
>
> The increase in effectiveness gained through decentralization is not costless. There is duplication of functional services across units and, thus, these specialized services may not be used to their full capacity. This duplication and potential underutilization may lead to a deterioration of in-depth competence. It may be difficult, for example, to attract an advertising specialist to work in a product group as opposed to an advertising department.[22]

EXHIBIT 14–4 Structure–Environment Match of the Marketing Organization

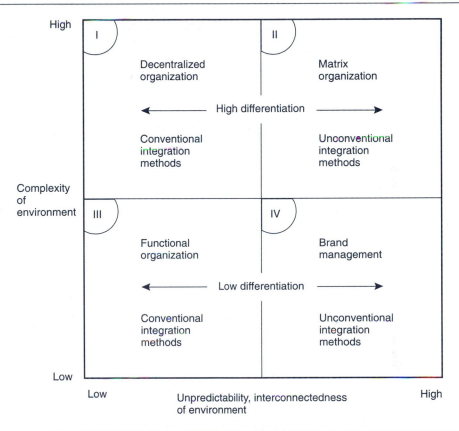

Source: Barton Weitz and Erin Anderson, "Organizing the Marketing Function," in *Review of Marketing 1981,* ed. Ben M. Enis and Kenneth J. Roering (Chicago: American Marketing Association, 1981), p. 137.

A decentralized marketing organization reduces the problems created by a large organization, as well as environmental complexity. Management's challenge is to coordinate and integrate the activities of the units. Organizational units (e.g., market, product) that have independent marketing activities are appropriate for a decentralized organizational design.[23]

Choosing the best design for each of the situations involves trade-offs. Exhibit 14–4 is a useful framework for analysis. When considered with other influences, such as corporate culture, available staff, and cost-benefits, the framework helps to select an effective organizational design.

Organizing Concepts

How marketing activities are organized affects strategy implementation. Consider, for example, the four organizing concepts shown in Exhibit 14–5. Note the usage context and performance characteristics of each structure. The organization structure adopted may

EXHIBIT 14–5 Four Archetypal Organizational Forms

	Market versus Hierarchical Organization	
	Internal Organization of Activity	*External Organization of Activity*

| Structural Characteristics | Centralized Formalized Nonspecialized | **Bureaucratic Form**

Appropriate usage context
• Conditions of market failure
• Low environmental uncertainty
• Tasks which are repetitive, easily assessed, requiring specialized assets
Performance characteristics
• Highly effective and efficient
• Less adaptive
Examples in marketing
• Functional organization
• Company or division sales force
• Corporate research staffs | **Transactional Form**

Appropriate usage context
• Under competitive market conditions
• Low environmental uncertainty
• Tasks which are repetitive, easily assessed, with no specialized investment
Performance characteristics
• Most efficient form
• Highly effective for appropriate tasks
• Less adaptive
Examples in marketing
• Contract purchase of advertising space
• Contract purchase of transportation of product
• Contract purchase of research field work |
| | Decentralized Nonformalized Specialized | **Organic Form**

Appropriate usage context
• Conditions of market failure
• High environmental uncertainty
• Tasks which are infrequent, difficult to assess, requiring highly specialized investment
Performance characteristics
• Highly adaptive
• Less efficient
Examples in marketing
• Product management organization
• Specialized sales force organization
• Research staffs organized by product groups | **Relational Form**

Appropriate usage context
• Under competitive market conditions
• High environmental uncertainty
• Tasks which are nonroutine, difficult to assess, requiring little specialized investment
Performance characteristics
• Highly adaptive
• Highly effective for nonroutine, specialized tasks
• Less efficient
Examples in marketing
• Long-term retainer contract with advertising agency
• Ongoing relationship with consulting firm |

Source: Robert W. Ruekert, Orville C. Walker, Jr., and Kenneth J. Roering, "The Organization of Marketing Activities: A Contingency Theory of Structure and Performance," *Journal of Marketing*, Winter 1985, p. 20.

facilitate the implementation of certain activities and tasks. For example, the bureaucratic form should facilitate the implementation of repetitive activities such as telephone processing of air travel reservations and ticketing. Once management analyzes the task(s) to be performed and the environment in which they will be done, it must determine its priorities. What is the objective to be? Performance and short-run efficiency or adaptability and longer-term effectiveness?

> Activities in different categories should be structured differently whenever feasible. Some firms appear to be moving in this direction, as shown by reports of cuts in corporate staff departments, the shifting of more planning and decision-making authority to individual business unit and product-market managers, and the increased use of ad hoc task forces to deal with specific markets or problems—all of which indicate a shift toward more decentralized and flexible structures.[24]

The corporate culture may also have an important influence on implementation. For example, implementing new strategies may be more difficult in highly structured, bureaucratic organizations. General Motors' difficulty in responding to the global competitive pressures during the last decade is illustrative. Management should consider its own management style, accepted practices, specific performance of executives, and other unique characteristics in deciding how to design the organization.

Organizing the Sales Force

In many companies, the sales force constitutes most of the marketing organization. Therefore, organizing the sales force is often a central part of the marketing organization design. We discussed the design of the sales organization in Chapter 13, which also presented designs that correspond to variations in product offering and customer needs. Some additional aspects of organizing the sales force are now examined.

Organizing Multiple Sales Channels.   Expanding the sales organization beyond the field sales force to include major-account programs, telemarketing, and/or electronic sales programs requires consideration as to how to organize the channel network. A key issue is whether to establish separate organizational units or instead to combine two or more channels into one unit. For example, should the national account salespeople be placed from a separate organizational unit or assigned to field sales units (e.g., regions or districts)?

When sales channel activities are relatively independent of the field sales force, a separate channel organization is appropriate. This occurs when major-account managers or telemarketing salespeople provide all contacts with assigned accounts. An example is the assignment of low-sales-volume accounts to telemarketing salespeople. A more likely situation is when contacts are made by both field personnel and other channels. These contacts require coordination between salespeople. The creation of independent sales-channel organizations complicates the coordination of selling activities.

Coordinating Major-Account Relationships.   A look at the alternatives for coordinating key account relationships highlights several multiple-channel issues. A major-account program requires assignment of account responsibility to account managers. When the customer has several purchasing locations, coordination of selling and service activities is necessary. Several alternatives are available, including (1) assigning key accounts to top sales executives (e.g., sales vice president), (2) creating a separate corporate division, and (3) establishing a separate major-accounts sales force.[25] Factors that influence the choice of an alternative include the number of major accounts served by the organization, the number of different geographical contacts with an account, the organizational level of contact (e.g., vice president versus maintenance supervisor), and the sales and service functions to be performed.

Marketing's Links to Other Functional Units

Marketing professionals often coordinate their activities with other functional areas of the business. Examples include new-product planning, distribution-channel coordination, pricing analysis, and strategic marketing alliances. Ruekert and Walker offer guidelines regarding these interactions.[26]

> Effectiveness is improved by developing organizational structures and processes to move resources faster across departments with strong resource dependencies.

> Promising coordination mechanisms are formalized operating rules and procedures and horizontal resolution of conflicts. However, resolving conflicts may decrease efficiency.

> Communications between functions appear to be enhanced by similarity in departmental tasks and objectives, and when formal operating rules and procedures are used.

> There is mixed support for the proposition that higher conflict occurs when higher levels of interaction or resource flows exist between marketing and other functional areas.

These research findings offer useful insights into marketing's horizontal organizational relationships. Additional research is needed to determine how applicable these preliminary findings are in different internal and external organizational environments.

GLOBAL DIMENSIONS OF ORGANIZATIONS

Implementing the global strategies of companies creates several important marketing organizational issues. The president of The Conference Board comments on managing in a competitive global environment.

> Finding that critical point where regional differentiation can give way to product standardization will spell success. In many instances your core product will be essentially the same in every market, but marketing will differ widely according to local tastes.[27]

Several issues in organizing global marketing strategies are examined, followed by a discussion of organizational concepts used to manage global marketing activities. Much of the earlier material in the chapter applies to international operations. This discussion highlights several additional considerations.

Issues in Organizing Global Marketing Strategies

The important distinction in marketing throughout the world is that buyers differ in their needs, preferences, and priorities. Since such differences exist *within* a national market, the variations between countries are likely to be greater. "What success would Swedish car makers or Italian pasta manufacturers have in the United States if they went after the same solid consumer of their home markets instead of appealing to affluent, trendy consumers of their products in this country."[28] Global market targeting and positioning strategies create several marketing organizational issues.

Variations in Business Functions.   Global decisions concerning products, finance, and research and development are often more feasible than making the marketing decisions that span these markets. Marketing strategies require sensitivity to cultural and linguistic differences. Foreign currencies, government regulations, and different product standards further complicate buyer–seller relationships. The important issue is recognizing when standardized marketing strategies can be used and when they must be modified. There is probably no better global marketer than Coca-Cola:

> It is far more patient than most companies. It spent 15 years and several million dollars in China before it began turning a profit there. . .
>
> And Coke deftly uses the same tricks abroad that have worked in the United States. Aiming to be ubiquitous, it is a staple at sporting events. The red and white logo shows up at bullfights in Spain, camel races in Australia, and sheep-shearing contests in New Zealand. . . .
>
> Coke does adjust a bit from country to country. In Spain, it is used heavily as a mixer—even for wine. In Italy, it is increasingly drunk with meals in place of wine or cappuccino. In China, it is a luxury item, served on silver trays at government functions.[29]

Organizational Considerations.   The marketing organization selected for competing in national markets is influenced by the market *scope* (e.g., single-country, multinational, or global strategy) and by the market *entry strategy* (export, licensing, joint venture, strategic alliance, or complete ownership). Recall the discussion of marketing strategies in global markets in Chapter 6. The adoption of a global strategy using joint ventures, alliances, and or complete ownership presents the most complex organizational challenge.

The marketing organization design in international operations may take one of three possible forms: (1) a global product division, (2) geographical divisions, each with product and functional responsibilities, or (3) matrix design incorporating (1) or (2) in combination with centralized functional support or instead a combination of area operations and global product management.[30] The global form corresponds to rapid-growth situations for firms that have a broad product portfolio. The geographic form is used to obtain a close relationship with national and local governments. The matrix form is utilized by companies reorganizing for global competition. Exhibit 14–6 shows an example of a combination organization design.

Coordination and Communication

Organizing marketing activities to serve international markets creates important coordination and communication requirements. Language and distance barriers complicate organizational relationships. Beech Aircraft Corporation uses an international team-marketing

---

EXHIBIT 14–6   Marketing Organization Plan Combining Product, Geographic, and Functional Approaches

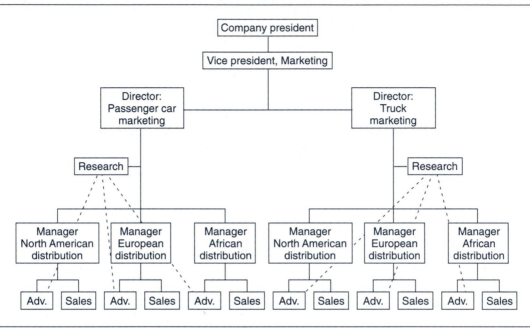

Source: Philip R. Cateora, *International Marketing,* 9th ed. (Burr Ridge, IL: Richard D. Irwin, 1996), p. 346.

approach to respond faster to market opportunities, manage budgets more effectively, and coordinate goals and objectives.[31] The world is divided into three geographic landmasses, with a marketing team assigned to each area. Previously, Beech utilized 10 independent regional managers to cover the world. The new teams are responsible for analyzing markets, planning strategy, presenting their recommendations to top management, and executing the strategy. The three teams make quarterly presentations to the president.

"Global teamwork approaches are now being tested by companies with vastly different organizational structures and varying levels of international involvement."[32] The Conference Board study of 30 major U.S. multinational companies indicates that global teamwork improves market and technological intelligence, contributes to more flexible business planning, leads to stronger commitment to corporate worldwide goals, and achieves closer coordination in implementing strategic actions.

Strategic Alliances.   The rate of formation of international strategic alliances escalated in the last decade.[33] Expanded use of alliances is expected in the 1990s. IBM has 40 active alliances, including major partnerships with Japan. The alliance relationship presents major interorganizational coordination and strategy implementation requirements. Peter Drucker offers several guidelines for improving strategic alliances:

Before the alliance is completed, all parties must think through their objectives and the objectives of the "child."

Equally important is advance agreement on how the joint enterprise should be run.

GLOBAL FEATURE   Developing Global Managers

Several companies are offering fast-track managers global management training. The core objective is to develop an internationally experienced cadre of executives. The programs are offered to managers early in their careers. Japanese and European companies are ahead of U.S. firms in implementing these programs. The training includes conducting business in foreign cultures and understanding differences in global customers' needs. Several programs are described in the chart. The typical participant in the Colgate-Palmolive Company's 24-month global marketing management program has an M.B.A. degree, speaks a foreign language, and has strong computer skills and prior business experience. They become associate product managers in the United States or abroad after completing the program. One-fourth are foreign nationals. More than 15,000 people apply for 15 positions in the program every year.

Learning the Ways of the World

Company	Program
American Express Co.'s Travel Related Services unit	Gives American business-school students summer jobs in which they work outside the United States for up to 10 weeks. Also transfers junior managers with at least two years' experience to other countries
Colgate-Palmolive Co.	Trains about 15 recent college graduates each year for 15 to 24 months prior to multiple overseas job stints
General Electric's aircraft-engine unit	Will expose selected midlevel engineers and managers to foreign language and cross-cultural training even though not all will live abroad
Honda of America Manufacturing Inc.	Has sent about 42 U.S. supervisors and managers to the parent company in Tokyo for up to three years, after preparing them with six months of Japanese language lessons, cultural training, and lifestyle orientation during work hours
PepsiCo's international beverage division	Brings about 25 young foreign managers a year to the United States for one-year assignments in bottling plants
Raychem Corp.	Assigns relatively inexperienced Asian employees (from clerks through middle managers) to the United States for six months to two years

Source: Joan L. Lublin, "Younger Managers Learn Global Skills," *The Wall Street Journal,* March 31, 1992, p. B1. Reprinted by permission of *The Wall Street Journal*, © 1992 Dow Jones & Company, Inc. All Rights Reserved Worldwide.

Next, there has to be careful thinking about who will manage the alliance.

Each partner needs to make provision in its own structure for the relationship to the joint enterprise and the other partners.

Finally, there has to be prior agreement on how to resolve disagreements.[34]

The effectiveness of the alliance depends on how well operating relationships are established and managed on an on-going basis and how well the partners can work together.

Executive Qualifications.   International experience will increasingly be required for executive advancement in the 21st century. (See Global Feature.) Managing international marketing operations requires knowledge of finance, distribution, manufacturing, and other business functions. The trend toward flat organizations with wide spans of control will make on-the-job executive development more difficult. Similarly, the qualifications for the chief executive's job will require experience in several areas. With creative financing techniques that turn financial decisions into marketing questions, manufacturing processes that are driven by computer technology, and product designs that depend on rapid market feedback, the chief executive will indeed need a varied background.[35]

SUMMARY

Differences in environmental situations create different organization design requirements. The design and adaptation of organizations to their environments involves consideration of several important issues for marketing organization design, including decisions regarding the use of internal and external organizations, designing the vertical structure, coordinating horizontal relationships, increasing speed of response, and analyzing environmental complexity and the forces of change.

Several traditional marketing organization designs may be used. The options include functional, product, market, and combination designs. Increasingly, market considerations are included in organization designs. The role and scope of corporate marketing is changing in many firms with multibusiness operations. The importance of corporate marketing appears to be declining, with marketing strategy emphasis instead being focused at the business level.

New forms of marketing organizations are developing, driven by the use of multifunction teams in organizations that manage business processes rather than functions, and by the use of powerful information technology. These influences are transforming vertical organizations into horizontal ones. An example is the marketing coalition company.

The choice of an organization design involves finding a good structure–environmental match. The match is influenced by the complexity of the environment and the unpredictability and interconnectedness of the environment. The design also involves selecting the best organizational form based on structural characteristics and the internal versus external orientation of marketing operations. The key role of the sales force in many organizations makes it a central part of marketing organization design. Marketing's interactions with other functional units is an important factor in organization design.

Finally, the global strategies of companies highlight several marketing organizational issues. These include recognizing the differences in business functions in international operations and the increased coordination and communication requirements in international markets. Strategic alliances, an expanding area of global activity, present complex management and coordination situations. Executive qualifications in marketing and other business functions increasingly include international experience.

QUESTIONS FOR REVIEW AND DISCUSSION

1. The chief executive of a manufacturer of fibers for use in carpets is interested in establishing a marketing organization in the firm. Sales to carpet tufters are handled by a manufacturer's agent, and advertising is planned and executed by an advertising agency. Other than the CEO, no one inside the firm is responsible for the marketing function. What factors should the CEO consider in designing a marketing organization?

2. Of the various approaches to marketing organization design, which one(s) offers the most flexibility in responding to changing conditions? Discuss.

3. Discuss the conditions where a matrix-type marketing organization would be appropriate, indicating important considerations and potential problems in using this organizational form.

4. Assume that you have been asked by the president of a major transportation services firm to recommend a marketing organizational design. What important factors should you consider in selecting the design?

5. Discuss some of the important issues related to integrating marketing into an organization such as a regional women's clothing chain compared to accomplishing the same task in The Limited Inc.

6. What are possible internal and external factors that may require changing the marketing organization design?

7. Is a trend toward more organic organizational forms likely in the future?

8. How will the expanded use of information and decision-support systems contribute to organizational effectiveness?

9. Discuss the important issues in establishing an effective strategic alliance between organizations.

10. What are the major approaches to organizing the marketing function for international operations? Discuss the factors that may affect the choice of a particular organization design.

NOTES

1. Thomas A. Stewart, "The Search for the Organization of Tomorrow," *Fortune,* May 18, 1992, pp. 93–98.

2. Richard L. Daft, *Organization Theory and Design,* 3rd ed. (St. Paul, MN: West Publishing, 1989), pp. 212–17.

3. Peter F. Drucker, "The Coming of the New Organization," *Harvard Business Review,* January–February 1988, pp. 45–53.

4. Daft, *Organization Theory and Design,* pp. 218–24.

5. Earl L. Bailey, *Getting Closer to the Customer,* Research Bulletin No. 229 (New York: The Conference Board, Inc., 1989), p. 5.

6. Brian Dumaine, "What the Leaders of Tomorrow See," *Fortune,* July 3, 1989, p. 51.

7. Brian Dumaine, "How Managers Can Succeed Through Speed," *Fortune,* February 13, 1989, pp. 54–59.

8. Daft, *Organization Theory and Design,* p. 55.

9. Ibid., pp. 55–62.

10. David W. Cravens, Nigel F. Piercy, and Shannon H. Shipp, "New Organization Forms for Competing in Highly Dynamic Environments, the Network Paradigm," *British Journal of Marketing,* in press.

11. Neela Banerjee, "For Mary Kay Sales Reps in Russia, Hottest Shade Is the Color of Money," *The Wall Street Journal,* August 30, 1995, p. A8.

12. George Benson and Joseph Chasin, *The Structure of New Product Organization* (New York: AMACOM, 1976), p. 10.

13. C. Merle Crawford, *New Products Management* (Burr Ridge, IL: Richard D. Irwin, 1983), pp. 169–70.

14. Crawford, *New Products Management,* pp. 174–75.

15. Christopher K. Bart, "New Venture Units: Use Them Wisely to Manage Innovation," *Sloan Management Review,* Summer 1988, p. 35.

16. Erick M. Olson, Orville C. Walker, Jr., and Robert W. Ruekert, "Organizing for Effective New Product Development: The Moderating Role of Product Innovativeness," *Journal of Marketing,* January 1995, pp. 48–62.

17. David S. Hopkins and Earl L. Bailey, *Organizing Corporate Marketing* (New York: The Conference Board, Inc., 1984), p. 23.

18. Ibid., p. 40.

19. Thomas A. Stewart, "The Search for the Organization of Tomorrow," p. 94.

20. Ravi S. Achrol, "Evolution of the Marketing Organization: New Forms for Turbulent Environments," *Journal of Marketing,* October 1991, pp. 77–93.

21. The following discussion is based on Barton Weitz and Erin Anderson, "Organizing the Marketing Function," in *Review of Marketing 1981,* ed. Ben M. Enis and Kenneth J. Roering (Chicago: American Marketing Association, 1981), pp. 134–42.

22. Ibid., p. 138.

23. Ibid., p. 139.

24. Quote from Robert W. Ruekert, Orville C. Walker, Jr., and Kenneth J. Roering, "The Organization of Marketing Activities: A Contingency Theory of Structure and Performance," *Journal of Marketing,* Winter 1985, pp. 23–24. See also Hopkins and Bailey, *Organizing Corporate*

Marketing, and "A New Era for Management," *Business Week,* April 25, 1983, pp. 50–67.

25. For an expanded discussion of this and other sales force organizational design issues, see Gilbert A. Churchill, Jr., Neil M. Ford, and Orville C. Walker, Jr., *Sales Force Management,* 4th ed. (Burr Ridge, IL: Richard D. Irwin, 1993), chap. 5.

26. Robert W. Ruekert and Orville C. Walker, Jr., "Marketing's Interaction with Other Functional Units: A Conceptual Framework and Empirical Evidence," *Journal of Marketing,* January 1987, pp. 1–10.

27. *The Conference Board's Management Briefing: Marketing,* (New York: The Conference Board, Inc., December 1989/January 1990), p. 5.

28. Ibid.

29. Michael J. McCarthy, "The Real Thing: Its a Global Marketer, Coke Excels by Being Tough and Consistent," *The Wall Street Journal,* December 19, 1989, pp. A1, and A6.

30. This discussion is based on Phillip R. Cateora, *International Marketing,* 9th ed. (Burr Ridge, IL: Richard D. Irwin, 1996), pp. 345–48.

31. *The Conference Board's Management Briefing: Marketing* (New York: The Conference Board, Inc., February/March, 1989), pp. 1–2.

32. Ibid; p. 2.

33. Jeremy Main, "The Winning Organization," *Fortune,* September 26, 1988, p. 52.

34. Peter F. Drucker, "From Dangerous Liaisons to Alliances for Progress," *The Wall Street Journal,* September 8, 1989, p. A8.

35. Amanda Bennett, "Going Global: The Chief Executives in Year 2000 Will Be Experienced," *The Wall Street Journal,* February 27, 1989, p. A1.

Marketing Strategy Implementation and Control

The ultimate performance of market targeting and positioning decisions rests on how well the marketing strategy is implemented and managed on a continuing basis. Placing the strategy into action and adjusting it to eliminate performance gaps are essential success factors.

During the 1990s many companies altered their strategies to improve performance. Germany's Lufthansa A.G. in 1992 began a major program to improve its competitive advantage in the global air travel market.[1] Cost cutting and higher customer satisfaction are major parts of Lufthansa's strategy for competing against its major competitors in Europe and the United States. The company was privatized in 1994, its first profitable year after major losses in 1989 through 1993. Lufthansa is the second largest international air carrier, with 18 million passengers compared to British Airways' 24 million passengers. The German carrier's cost cutting, involving 100 different areas, was very successful. It must continue to control costs while increasing revenues. Lufthansa has partnerships with United Airlines, Thai Airways, and Scandinavian Airlines System. New competition emerged in 1996 when the European Union allowed carriers to compete on domestic routes in other EU countries.

We will begin with an overview of the marketing plan, followed by a discussion of implementing the plan. Next, we will examine the development of a strategic evaluation and control program. Finally, the major evaluation activities will be discussed and illustrated. These include conducting the strategic marketing audit, selecting performance criteria and measures, determining information needs and analysis, evaluating performance, and taking needed actions to keep performance on track.

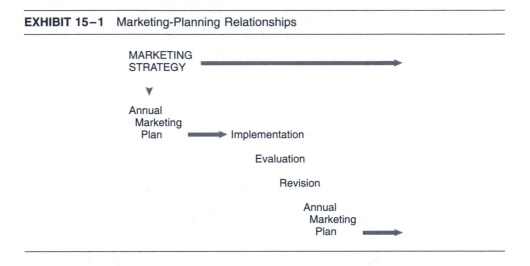

EXHIBIT 15–1   Marketing-Planning Relationships

MARKETING
STRATEGY

Annual
Marketing
Plan   Implementation

Evaluation

Revision

Annual
Marketing
Plan

THE MARKETING PLAN

The marketing plan guides implementation and control, indicating marketing objectives and the strategy and tactics for accomplishing the objectives. Since a step-by-step planning process was presented in Chapter 1, we will briefly consider several planning issues and offer examples of marketing planning activities.

How the Marketing Plan Guides Implementation

Exhibit 15–1 shows the relationships between marketing strategy and the annual plan. The planning cycle is continuous. Plans are developed, implemented, evaluated, and revised to keep the marketing strategy on target. Since a strategy extends beyond one year, typically, the annual plan is used to guide short-term marketing activities. The planning process is a series of annual plans guided by the marketing strategy. An annual planning period is necessary, since several of the activities shown require action within 12 months or less, and budgets also require annual planning.

A look at the marketing-planning process used by a large pharmaceutical company illustrates how planning is done. Product managers are responsible for coordinating the preparation of plans. A planning workshop is conducted midyear as the kickoff for the next year's plans. The workshop is attended by top management and product, research, sales, and finance managers. The firm's advertising agency also participates in the workshop. The current year's plans are reviewed, and each product manager presents the proposed marketing plan for next year. The workshop members critique each plan and suggest changes. The same group comes together 90 days later, and the revised plans are reviewed. At this meeting the plans are finalized and approved for implementation. Each product manager is responsible for coordinating and implementing the plan. Progress is reviewed throughout the plan year, and when necessary the plan is revised.

Contents of the Marketing Plan

An outline for developing the marketing plan was presented in Chapter 1, and many plans follow this general format. An executive summary can be used to provide an overview for top management and other executives not closely involved in implementation. The executive summary outlines the current situation, indicates marketing objectives, summarizes strategies, outlines action programs, and indicates financial expectations.[2]

Exhibit 15–2 shows the marketing plan outline for Sonesta Hotels. The activities include making the situation assessment, setting objectives, developing targeting and positioning strategies, deciding action programs for the marketing-mix components, and preparing supporting financial statements (budgets and profit-and-loss projections).

The typical planning process involves quite a bit of coordination and interaction among functional areas. Team-planning approaches like the pharmaceutical company's planning workshop are illustrative. Successful implementation of the marketing plan requires a broad consensus among various functional areas.[3] For example, a consensus between product managers and sales management is essential. Product managers must obtain a commitment from the sales department to provide sales effort for their products. Multiple products require negotiation in reaching agreement on the amount of sales force time devoted to various products. The Planning Feature provides a CEO's view of how marketing plans are developed by a consumer-products manufacturer.

IMPLEMENTING THE PLAN

Implementation determines the outcome of the marketing planning. Japanese companies have a reputation for the effective implementation of marketing strategies. Consider Japan's domination of the Chinese market even though anti-Japanese sentiment is strong and widespread in China.[4] Although the local reception of Japanese traders is often unfavorable, Japan holds a strong market position by using an extensive network of sales offices in China. The marketing strategy Japanese companies use includes selling initially at low prices to gain market position, later raising prices and making money on spare parts and services. A Japanese trading company adds value to the trading relationship by coordinating an entire project. Japanese traders understand and adapt to China's culture and customs, benefiting from a close location and cultural affinity. The Japanese understand and use the Chinese system called *guanxi*—a complex set of relationships whereby Chinese people become obligated to each other. Gifts help Japanese traders gain access to the system. The gifts are viewed as tokens of esteem rather than bribes. The Japanese government supports trade relations with China through loans.

Implementation

A good implementation process describes the activities to be implemented, who is responsible for implementation, the time and location of implementation, and how implementation

---

EXHIBIT 15–2   Sonesta Hotels: Marketing Plan Outline

Note: Please keep the plan concise—Maximum of 20 pages plus summary pages. Include title page and table of contents. Number all pages.

I. *Introduction.* Set the stage for the plan. Specifically identify marketing objectives such as "increase average rate," "more group business," "greater occupancy," or "penetrate new markets." Identify particular problems.

II. *Marketing Position.* Begin with a single statement that presents a consumer benefit in a way that distinguishes us from the competition.

III. *The Product.* Identify all facility and service changes that occurred this year and are planned for next year.

IV. *Marketplace Overview.* Briefly describe what is occurring in your marketplace that might impact on your business or marketing strategy, such as the economy, the competitive situation, etc.

V. *The Competition.* Briefly identify your primary competition (three or fewer) specifying number of rooms, what is new in their facilities, and marketing and pricing strategy.

VI. *Marketing Data*

    A. Identify top five geographic areas for transient business, with percentages of total room nights compared to the previous year.

    B. Briefly describe the guests at your hotel, considering age, sex, occupation, what they want, why they come, etc.

    C. Identify market segments with percentage of business achieved in each segment in current year (actual and projected) and projected for next year.

VII. *Strategy by Market Segment*

    A. Group

        1. *Objectives:* Identify what you specifically wish to achieve in this segment. (For example, more high-rated business, more weekend business, larger groups.)

        2. *Strategy:* Identify how sales, advertising, and public relations will work together to reach the objectives.

        3. *Sales Activities:* Divide by specific market segments.

            a. Corporate

            b. Association

            c. Incentives

            d. Travel agent

            e. Tours

            f. Other

        Under each category include a narrative description of specific sales activities geared toward each market segment, including geographically targeted areas, travel plans, group site inspections, correspondence, telephone solicitation, and trade shows. Be specific on action plans, and designate responsibility and target months.

        4. *Sales Materials:* Identify all items, so they will be budgeted.

        5. *Direct Mail:* Briefly describe the direct mail program planned, including objectives, message and content. Identify whether we will use existing material or create a new piece.

        6. *Research:* Indicate any research projects you plan to conduct in 1990 identifying what you wish to learn.

    B. Transient (the format here should be the same as group throughout)

        1. *Objective*

        2. *Strategy*

[handwritten margin note: SWOT / Porter's]

EXHIBIT 15–2   (*concluded*)

---

      3. *Sales Activities:* Divide by specific market segments.

        a. Consumer (rack rate)

        b. Corporate (prime and other)

        c. Travel agent: business, leisure, consortia

        d. Wholesale/Airline/Tour (foreign and domestic)

        e. Packages (specify names of packages)

        f. Government/Military/Education

        g. Special interest/Other

    4. *Sales Materials*

    5. *Direct Mail*

    6. *Research*

  C. Other Sonesta Hotels

  D. Local/Food and Beverage

    1. *Objectives*

    2. *Strategy*

    3. *Sales Activities:* Divide by specific market segments.

        a. Restaurant and Lounge, external promotion

        b. Restaurant and Lounge, internal promotion

        c. Catering

        d. Community Relation/Other

    4. *Sales Materials* (e.g., banquet menus, signage)

    5. *Direct Mail*

    6. *Research*

VIII. *Advertising*

  A. Subdivide advertising by market segment and campaign, paralleling the sales activities (group, transient, F&B).

  B. Describe objectives of each advertising campaign identifying whether it should be promotional (immediate bookings) or image (longer-term awareness).

  C. Briefly describe contents of advertising identifying key benefit to promote.

  D. Identify target media by location and type (newspaper, magazine, radio, etc.).

  E. Indicate percent of the advertising budget to be allocated to each market segment.

IX. *Public Relations*

  A. Describe objectives of public relations as it supports the sales and marketing priorities.

  B. Write a brief statement on overall goals by market segment paralleling the sales activities. Identify what proportion of your effort will be spent on each segment.

X. *Summary:* Close the plan with general statement concerning the major challenges you will face in the upcoming year and how you will overcome these challenges.

Source: Adapted from Howard Sutton, *The Marketing Plan in the 1990s* (New York: The Conference Board, Inc., 1990), pp. 34–35.

PLANNING FEATURE   Integrating Marketing Plans with Business Strategy

---

Our planning process begins with a half-day meeting to discuss strategic issues. The meeting includes just three people—the president of the division (me), the chairman of the board, and the president of the corporation. I have about three sheets of paper, maybe four, that talk about these things: What are the issues? What are the market dynamics, as I see them today and what do I see in the next three years? What should we be spending in terms of protecting our market share? Where is the market going, from a demographic standpoint?

This is a high-level strategic discussion. We just sit and talk about my business—not a lot of slides, not a lot of pictures, more informal than formal—to get a frame around what I think the strategic issues in the division are. I want to get agreement from them, the chairman and the president, that, yes, those are the issues they're concerned about as well, and that we need to develop plans around those issues.

What we agree to is that there are five or six strategic imperatives. In each case, we agree that a particular objective has to be successfully achieved or the division will not succeed in its business efforts, and we have a three-year horizon. The objectives might have to do with share, or new-product technologies, or management development, or organizational issues that need to be addressed.

Then I draw up a two-page response. It says, here's what we talked about, here's what we agreed to do. Then I go back to the division with this document in my hand. I say, "OK, here's what we're headed for, here's where we got strategic agreement from the corporation." Then we start developing a plan around that direction.

There isn't an awful lot of planning that goes into that first meeting. I mean, we get bunches of numbers, and we look at the most strategic spots, such as share, such as technology. But it's really an opportunity for one time during the year for the three of us to sit down and just talk. That's much better than having a bunch of people in the room, presenting and showing what they want us to see. The next step is to come back to the division and put together a team to prepare a plan based on the strategic plan. This book, which we call a marketing strategic plan, deals with marketing and the whole focus on what we're going to do, and what we're going to do different.

The preparation is typically done by the marketing department, supervised by the manager or director of marketing services and planning. He sort of heads up the committee that puts the book together. Then, once the book is done, we have a meeting at corporate headquarters. We go over very specific areas, with a 35- to 50-page report. That's basically the way it ends up. That seems to be a basic Marketing 101 kind of process, but it's amazing how much disagreement there can be. You have one idea of what your job is, and other people in the organization may have a different idea. I think the key is to get agreement on the mission: what are we really trying to accomplish?

—President of a division of a manufacturer
of consumer products

Source: Howard Sutton, *The Marketing Plan in the 1990s* (New York: The Conference Board, Inc., 1990), p. 20.

---

will be achieved (Exhibit 15–3). Let's evaluate the following statement from a product manager's marketing plan:

> Sales representatives should target all accounts now using a competitive product. A plan should be developed to convert 5 percent of these accounts to the company brand during the year. Account listings will be prepared and distributed by product management.

EXHIBIT 15–3   The Implementation Process

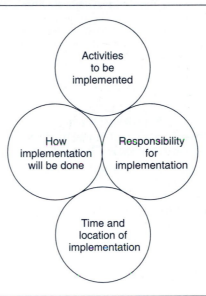

In this instance, the sales force is charged with implementation. An objective (5 percent conversion) is specified but very little information is provided as to *how* the accounts will be converted. A strategy is needed to penetrate the competitors' customer base. The sales force plan must translate the proposed actions and objective (5 percent conversion) into assigned salesperson responsibility (quotas), a timetable, and selling strategy guidelines. Training may be necessary to show the product advantages—and the competitors' product limitations—that will be useful in convincing the buyer to purchase the firm's brand.

The marketing plan can be used to identify the organizational units and managers that are responsible for implementing the various activities in the plan. Deadlines indicate the time available for implementation. In the case of the plan above, the sales manager is responsible for implementation through the sales force.

Improving Implementation

Managers are important facilitators in the implementation process, and some are better implementers than others. Good planners and implementers often have different strengths and weaknesses. An effective planner may not be good at implementing plans. Desirable implementation skills include:

- The ability to understand how others feel, and good bargaining skills.
- The strength to be tough and fair in putting people and resources where they will be most effective.
- Effectiveness in focusing on the critical aspects of performance in managing marketing activities.

• The ability to create a necessary informal organization or network to match each problem with which they are confronted.[5]

In addition to skillful implementers, several methods facilitate the process. These include *organizational designs, incentives,* and *effective communications.* The features of each method are highlighted.

Organizational Design.   Certain organizational designs aid implementation. For example, product managers and multifunctional coordination teams are useful implementation methods. Management may create implementation teams consisting of representatives from the business functions and/or marketing activities involved. The flat, flexible organization designs discussed in Chapter 14 offer several advantages in implementation, since they encourage interfunctional cooperation and communication. These designs are responsive to changing conditions.

Incentives.   Various rewards may help achieve successful implementation. For example, special incentives such as contests, recognition, and extra compensation are used to encourage salespeople to push a new product. Since implementation often involves teams of people, creation of team incentives may be necessary. Performance standards must be fair, and incentives should encourage something more than normal performance.

Communications.   Rapid and accurate movement of information through the organization is essential in implementation. Both vertical and horizontal communications are needed in linking together the people and activities involved in implementation. Meetings, status reports, and informal discussions help to transmit information throughout the organization. Computerized information and decision-support systems improve communications speed and effectiveness.

Problems often occur during implementation and may affect how fast and how well plans are put into action. Examples include competitors' actions, internal resistance between departments, loss of key personnel, delays affecting product availability (e.g., supply, production, and distribution problems), and changes in the business environment. Corrective actions may require appointing a person or team for troubleshooting the problem, increasing or shifting resources, or changing the original plan. Consider, for example, Gillette's experience in moving the Sensor razor to market in early 1990. Production and distribution were unable to meet initial demand for the new product. Management corrected the problem by speeding up production and delaying the introduction of Sensor in Europe.

Internal Strategy-Structure Fit

It is important that the organization's competitive and marketing strategy be compatible with the internal structure of the business and its policies, procedures, and resources.[6] Exhibit 15–4 shows several internal factors that may impact the implementation of marketing strategy. These factors include higher-level corporate and business strategies, SBU and corporate relationships (e.g., extent of autonomy), the SBU's internal organi-

EXHIBIT 15–4   Factors Affecting the Implementation of Business and Marketing Strategies

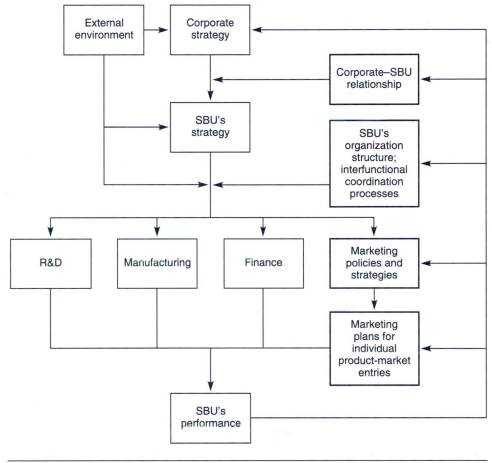

Source: Harper W. Boyd, Jr., and Orville C. Walker, Jr., *Marketing Management* (Burr Ridge, IL: Richard D. Irwin, 1990), p. 826.

zation structure and coordination mechanisms, and the specific actions programmed in the marketing plan.

Coping with the influence of these factors on implementation requires close coordination of the strategies at the four levels shown in Exhibit 15–4. The marketing plans must be compatible with this internal structure. Otherwise implementation and performance are constrained. For example, a major objective of the marketing-planning process of the pharmaceutical company, discussed earlier, is to communicate and respond to issues and concerns at these four levels. Similarly, the Planning Feature (page 458) highlights a CEO's methods of achieving a good strategy- structure fit.

Achieving a Market Orientation throughout the Organization

An important responsibility of marketing management is to encourage and facilitate a market orientation throughout the business. The chief executive officer of a large transportation services company states that the marketing and operations functions are the customer-service components of the firm, and that the role of accounting, finance, human resources, and information systems is to support the two operating components of the business. He emphasizes that the supporting functions are evaluated on the basis of how effectively they meet the needs of marketing and operations. Since the entire organization is concerned with delivering customer satisfaction, this CEO's operating philosophy encourages (and rewards) a customer-driven approach throughout the organization.

The Customer Is First.   A key issue in developing a market orientation throughout an organization is convincing every employee that customer satisfaction is his or her responsibility. Training programs are used to achieve this objective. The starting point is getting the entire management team to recognize its role and responsibility for market-oriented leadership. This philosophy is one of the key strengths of Japanese management systems. Customer advisory groups are sometimes used in developing an internal awareness about the importance of the marketplace. Multifunctional (e.g., finance, marketing, operations) task forces may also be helpful integrating methods.

Both the characteristics and culture of an organization affect the development of a market orientation. Small companies achieve this integration more easily than large, multilayered corporations. The corporate culture may aid or constrain integration. Managers of nonmarketing functions must be encouraged to recognize the importance of meeting customer needs through their activities. A strong commitment and active participation by the chief executive officer are essential to the integration of marketing into the thinking and actions of everyone in the firm.

The Role of External Organizations.   The implementation of marketing strategy is affected by external organizations such as marketing research firms, marketing consultants, advertising and public relations firms, channel members, and other organizations participating in the marketing effort. These outside organizations present a major coordination challenge when they actively participate in marketing activities. Their efforts should be identified in the marketing plan and their roles and responsibilities clearly established and communicated. There is a potential danger in not informing outside groups of planned actions, deadlines, and other implementation requirements. For example, the organization's advertising agency account executive and other agency staff members need to be familiar with all aspects of promotion strategy as well as the major aspects of marketing strategy (e.g., market targets, positioning strategy, and marketing-mix component strategies). Withholding information from participating firms hampers their efforts in strategy planning and implementation.

The development of collaborative relationships between suppliers and producers improves implementation. Total quality improvement programs encourage reducing the number of suppliers and building strong relationships (see Chapter 7). Companies that are effective in working with other organizations are likely to also do a good job with implementation inside the organization, since they have skills in developing effective working relationships. Total quality programs also encourage internal teamwork among functions.

STRATEGIC EVALUATION AND CONTROL

Marketing strategy has to be responsive to changing conditions. Evaluation and control keep the strategy on target and show when adjustments are needed. The competitive pressures on Japan Air Lines (JAL) highlight the importance of control.[7] JAL lost over 13 billion yen in fiscal 1992. Intense price competition and high operating costs squeezed out profits. JAL has the highest operating costs of all Asian airlines, and on a global basis the firm's costs are near the top. Staff reductions are used by other airlines to lower costs, but the company's six powerful unions and Japan's stable employment culture make layoffs difficult. JAL's chairman believes that the U.S. carriers are too powerful, and this places his company at a competitive disadvantage. Nevertheless, JAL faces major pressures to lower costs and develop strategies for competing in the 1990s. Other carriers have made substantial staff reductions, as well as establishing strategic alliances with other airlines. The relentless pursuit of cost reductions through strategy adjustments is a reality for competing in the 21st century.

Strategic evaluation requires information for gauging performance and taking the actions necessary to keep results on track. Marketing executives need to continually monitor performance and, when necessary, revise their strategies because of changing conditions. Strategic evaluation, the last stage in the marketing strategy process, is really the starting point. Strategic marketing planning requires information from ongoing monitoring and performance evaluation. We delayed discussion of strategic evaluation until now in order to first consider the strategic areas that require evaluation and to identify the kinds of information needed for assessing marketing performance. Thus, one objective of the first 14 chapters has been to establish an essential foundation for building a strategic evaluation program.

Overview of Evaluation Activities

Evaluation consumes a high proportion of marketing executives' time and energy. Evaluation may seek to (1) find new opportunities or avoid threats, (2) keep performance in line with management's expectations, and/or (3) solve specific problems that exist. Areas of evaluation include environmental scanning, product-market analysis, marketing program evaluation, and gauging the effectiveness of specific marketing-mix components such as advertising.

These are illustrations of the three types of evaluations. An example of a threat identified via product-market analysis is the shift away from wearing suits and more formal business attire toward sporty clothing. These changes in preferences are major threats for companies like Hartmarx, which produces several brands of men's suits. The Japan Air Lines example shows the importance of keeping performance on track. Evaluating the effectiveness of alternative TV commercials is an example of solving specific problems.

The major steps in establishing a strategic evaluation program are described in Exhibit 15–5. Strategic and short-term marketing plans set the direction and guidelines for the evaluation and control process. A strategic marketing audit is often conducted when setting up an evaluation program, and periodically thereafter. Next, performance stan-

---

EXHIBIT 15–5   Strategic Marketing Evaluation and Control

Conduct strategic
marketing audit

Select performance
criteria and measures

Obtain and
analyze information

Assess performance and
take necessary action

---

dards and measures are determined, followed by obtaining and analyzing information for the purpose of performance-gap identification. Actions are initiated to pursue opportunities or avoid threats, keep performance on track, or solve a particular decision-making problem.

Supermarket monitoring of buyers' purchases is an important information source for evaluating the marketing program effectiveness of food, health, beauty products. For example, sales data indicate that displays pay off for grocery marketers.[8] The use of frozen dinner displays increased sales by 245 percent during the 13 weeks ended in September 1992 (reported by Information Resources Inc.'s InfoScan service). Other products benefiting from display promotion include laundry detergent, snack foods, and soft drinks. Exhibit 15–6 shows the companies with large percentages of volume sold on display in 1992.

The Strategic Marketing Audit

A marketing audit is useful when initiating a strategic evaluation program. Since evaluation compares results with expectations, it is necessary to lay some groundwork before setting up a tracking program. This complete review and assessment of marketing operations is similar to the situation analysis discussed in Part II. However, the marketing audit goes beyond customer and competitive analysis to include all aspects of marketing operations. The audit is larger in scope than the situation analysis and is a more complete review of marketing strategy and performance. The audit can be used to initiate a formal strategic marketing planning program; it then may be repeated on a periodic basis. Normally, the situation analysis is part of the annual updating of marketing plans. The marketing audit is conducted less frequently. Auditing intervals may span three to five years.

A guide to conducting the strategic marketing audit is shown in Exhibit 15–7. It can be adapted to meet the needs of a particular firm. For example, if a company does not use indirect channels of distribution, this section of the audit guide will require adjustment. Likewise, if the sales force is the major part of a marketing program, then we expand this section

---

EXHIBIT 15–6 Manufacturers' Supermarket Volume Sold on Display (percentage of total unit sales during 52 weeks ending September 13, 1992)

	Percentage of Manufacturer's Volume Sold on Display
Pepsi-Cola	61.6%
Dr. Pepper/Seven-Up	48.8
Frito-Lay	36.8
Eagle Snacks	33.8
Keebler	32.6
Ft. Howard Paper	32.0
Nabisco Biscuit	30.1
Georgia-Pacific	29.7
Tetley	29.7
Ocean Spray Cranberries	28.2
Anheuser-Busch	27.8
Sunshine Biscuits	27.8
Miller Brewing	26.8
Coca-Cola	25.0
Mars	25.0

Source: Kathleen Devency, "Market Scam," *The Wall Street Journal,* October 15, 1992, pp. B1, B5. Reprinted by permission of *The Wall Street Journal,* © 1992 Dow Jones & Company, Inc. All Rights Reserved Worldwide. From Information Resources Inc.

to include other aspects of sales force strategy. The items included in the audit correspond to the strategic marketing plan because the main purpose of the audit is to appraise the effectiveness of the plan. The audit guide includes several questions about marketing performance. The answers to these questions are incorporated into the design of the strategic tracking program.

Beyond deciding what should be audited, other aspects of conducting the audit are important.[9]

- *Responsibility for the audit.* Some authorities advise the use of company personnel, while others suggest outside consultants. A combination approach offers the advantages of both company and external experience, capabilities, and perspectives. Objectivity and professional expertise are two key prerequisites in selecting an individual or team to plan and conduct the audit.

- *Planning the audit.* Depending on the size and scope of the business unit, attention needs to be given to planning the areas to be audited, defining the scope of audit operations, scheduling activities, coordinating participation, and indicating desired results. Auditing costs and expected benefits should be estimated and priorities set regarding various aspects of the audit program.

- *Using the findings.* The results of the audit should help improve performance. Opportunities and problems that are identified should be incorporated into strategic plans. If nothing happens as a result of the audit, it may not have been needed.

EXHIBIT 15–7 Guide to Conducting the Strategic Marketing Audit

---

I. CORPORATE MISSION AND OBJECTIVES

  A. Does the mission statement offer a clear guide to the product-markets of interest to the firm?

  B. Have objectives been established for the corporation?

  C. Is information available for the review of corporate progress toward objectives, and are the reviews conducted on a regular (quarterly, monthly, etc.) basis?

  D. Has corporate strategy been successful in meeting objectives?

  E. Are opportunities or problems pending that may require altering marketing strategy?

  F. What are the responsibilities of the chief marketing executive in corporate strategic planning?

II. BUSINESS COMPOSITION AND STRATEGIES

  A. What is the composition of the business (business segments, strategic planning units, and specific product-markets)?

  B. Have business strength and product-market attractiveness analyses been conducted for each planning unit? What are the results of the analyses?

  C. What is the corporate strategy for each planning unit (e.g., develop, stabilize, turnaround, or harvest)?

  D. What objectives are assigned to each planning unit?

  E. Does each unit have a strategic plan?

  F. For each unit what objectives and responsibilities have been assigned to marketing?

III. MARKETING STRATEGY (FOR EACH PLANNING UNIT)

  A. Strategic planning and marketing:

    1. Is marketing's role and responsibility in corporate strategic planning clearly specified?

    2. Are responsibility and authority for marketing strategy assigned to one executive?

    3. How well is the firm's marketing strategy working?

    4. Are changes likely to occur in the corporate/marketing environment that may affect the firm's marketing strategy?

    5. Are there major contingencies that should be included in the strategic marketing plan?

  B. Marketing planning and organizational structure:

    1. Are annual and longer range strategic marketing plans developed, and are they being used?

    2. Are the responsibilities of the various units in the marketing organization clearly specified?

    3. What are the strengths and limitations of the key members of the marketing organization? What is being done to develop people? What gaps in experience and capabilities exist on the marketing staff?

    4. Is the organizational structure for marketing effective for implementing marketing plans?

  C. Market target strategy:

    1. Has each market target been clearly defined and its importance to the firm established?

    2. Have demand, industry, and competition in each market target been analyzed and key trends, opportunities, and threats identified?

    3. Has the proper market target strategy been adopted?

    4. Should repositioning or exit from any product-market be considered?

  D. Objectives:

    1. Are objectives established for each market target, and are these consistent with planning unit objectives and the available resources? Are the objectives realistic?

    2. Are sales, cost, and other performance information available for monitoring the progress of planned performance against actual results?

EXHIBIT 15–7   (*continued*)

    3. Are regular appraisals made of marketing performance?

    4. Where do gaps exist between planned and actual results? What are the probable causes of the performance gaps?

  E. Marketing program positioning strategy:

    1. Does the firm have an integrated positioning strategy made up of product, channel, price, advertising, and sales force strategies? Is the role selected for each mix element consistent with the overall program objectives, and does it properly complement other mix elements?

    2. Are adequate resources available to carry out the marketing program? Are resources committed to market targets according to the importance of each?

    3. Are allocations to the various marketing mix components too low, too high, or about right in terms of what each is expected to accomplish?

    4. Is the effectiveness of the marketing program appraised on a regular basis?

IV. MARKETING PROGRAM ACTIVITIES

  A. Product strategy:

    1. Is the product mix geared to the needs and preferences that the firm wants to meet in each product-market?

    2. What branding strategy is being used?

    3. Are products properly positioned against competing brands?

    4. Does the firm have a sound approach to product planning and management, and is marketing involved in product decisions?

    5. Are additions to, modifications of, or deletions from the product mix needed to make the firm more competitive in the marketplace?

    6. Is the performance of each product evaluated on a regular basis?

  B. Channel of distribution strategy:

    1. Has the firm selected the type (conventional or vertically coordinated) and intensity of distribution appropriate for each of its product-markets?

    2. How well does each channel access its market target? Is an effective channel configuration being used?

    3. Are channel organizations carrying out their assigned functions properly?

    4. How is the channel of distribution being managed? What improvements are needed?

    5. Are desired customer service levels being reached, and are the costs of doing this acceptable?

  C. Price strategy:

    1. How responsive is each market target to price variations?

    2. What role and objectives does price have in the marketing mix?

    3. Should price play an active or passive role in program positioning strategy?

    4. How do the firm's price strategy and tactics compare to those of competition?

    5. Is a logical approach used to establish prices?

    6. Are there indications that changes may be needed in price strategy or tactics?

  D. Advertising and sales promotion strategies:

    1. Have a role and objectives been established for advertising and sales promotion in the marketing mix?

    2. Is the creative strategy consistent with the positioning strategy that is being used?

EXHIBIT 15–7 (concluded)

---

    3. Is the budget adequate to carry out the objectives assigned to advertising and sales promotion?

    4. Do the media and programming strategies represent the most cost-effective means of communicating with market targets?

    5. Do advertising copy and content effectively communicate the intended messages?

    6. How well does the advertising program measure up in meeting its objectives?

  E. Sales force strategy:

    1. Are the role and objectives of personal selling in the marketing program positioning strategy clearly specified and understood by the sales organization?

    2. Do the qualifications of salespeople correspond to their assigned roles?

    3. Is the sales force of the proper size to carry out its function, and is it efficiently deployed?

    4. Are sales force results in line with management's expectations?

    5. Is each salesperson assigned performance targets, and are incentives offered to reward performance?

    6. Are compensation levels and ranges competitive?

V. IMPLEMENTATION AND MANAGEMENT

  A. Have the causes of all performance gaps been identified?

  B. Is implementation of planned actions taking place as intended? Is implementation being hampered by marketing or other functional areas of the firm (e.g., operations, finance)?

  C. Has the strategic audit revealed areas requiring additional study before action is taken?

There are other reasons besides starting an evaluation program for conducting a strategic marketing audit. Corporate restructuring may bring about a complete review of strategic marketing operations. Major shifts in business activities such as entry into new product and market areas or acquisitions may require strategic marketing audits.

PERFORMANCE CRITERIA AND INFORMATION NEEDS

The next two stages in the evaluation and control process (Exhibit 15–5) are (1) selecting the performance criteria and the measures to be used for monitoring performance and (2) identifying the information management needs to perform various marketing control activities.

Selecting Performance Criteria and Measures

As the marketing plans are developed, performance criteria need to be selected to monitor performance. Specifying the information needed for marketing decision making is important and requires management's concentrated attention. In the past, marketing executives could develop and manage successful marketing strategies by relying on intuition, judgment, and experience. Successful executives of the 1990s are using judgment and experience with information and decision support systems. These information systems are becoming increasingly important in gaining a strategic edge in industries such as airline services, direct marketing, packaged foods, wholesaling, retailing, and financial services.

Objectives state the results that management is seeking and also serve as the basis for evaluating the strategy's success. Objectives set standards of performance. Progress toward the objectives in the strategic and short-term plans is monitored on a continuing basis. In addition to information on objectives, management requires other kinds of feedback for use in performance evaluation. Some of this information is incorporated into regular tracking activities (e.g., the effectiveness of advertising expenditures). Other information is obtained as the need arises, such as a special study of consumer preferences about different liquid-diet brands.

Examples of performance criteria are discussed in several chapters. They should be selected for the total plan and its important components. Illustrative criteria for total performance include sales, market share, profit, expense, and customer satisfaction targets. Brand-positioning analyses may also be useful in tracking position relative to key competitors. These measures can be used to gauge overall performance and for specific market targets. Performance criteria are also needed for the marketing-mix components. For example, new-customer and lost-customer tracking is often included in sales force performance monitoring. Pricing performance monitoring may include comparisons of actual to list prices, extent of discounting, and profit contribution. Many possible performance criteria can be selected. Management must identify the key measures that will show how the firm's marketing strategy is performing in its competitive environment and where changes are needed.

Obtain and Analyze Information

The costs of acquiring, processing, and analyzing information are high, so the potential benefits of needed information must be compared to costs. Normally, information falls into two categories: (1) information regularly supplied to marketing management from internal and external sources and (2) information obtained as needed for a particular problem or situation. Examples of the former are sales and cost analyses, market share measurements, and customer satisfaction surveys. Information from the latter category includes new-product concept tests, brand-preference studies, and studies of advertising effectiveness.

Several types of information are needed by management (see Chapter 5). Information for strategic planning and evaluation can be obtained from these sources:

1. The *internal information system* is the backbone of any strategic evaluation program. These systems range from primarily sales and cost reports to highly sophisticated computerized marketing information systems.

2. *Standardized information services* are available by subscription or on a one-time basis, often at a fraction of the cost of preparing such information for a single firm. Nevertheless, these services are expensive. Standardized services are available in both printed form and in data files for computer analysis. Nielsen's TV rating data service is an example.

3. Marketing managers may require *special research studies.* A study of distributor opinions concerning a manufacturer's services is an example.

4. The firm's *strategic intelligence system* is concerned with monitoring and forecasting external, uncontrollable factors that influence the firm's product-markets. These efforts range from formal information activities to informal surveillance of the marketing environment.

Standardized data services are important information sources in several product categories such as foods, drugs, and other packaged goods. Information Resources Inc. (IRI) is one of the leading suppliers of this information. An example of IRI's InfoScan service is shown in Exhibit 15–8. Interestingly, the sales of most liquid-diet brands declined significantly in 1992.[10] Dieters apparently became disillusioned with liquid meals, perhaps due to alternative foods for weight loss. For example, diet microwave food sales increased during the same period. In 1990 liquid diets were the top seller in weight control. Services like InfoScan track sales, market share, customer demographics, and other information on a regular basis during the year. IRI's information is obtained from 2,700 supermarkets, 500 drugstores, and 250 mass-merchandise outlets, selected to represent the national marketplace. Transactions are recorded by universal product code with scanners connected to cash registers. IRI monitors 45 million transactions each week.

A relevant part of strategic evaluation and control is protecting proprietary information. Nearly 75 percent of Fortune 1000 companies indicate that "theft or attempted theft by computers of customer information, trade secrets and new product plans has increased over the past five years."[11] The reasons cited for the increase in the theft of corporate secrets include computer technology and decline in worker loyalty. It is important, in supporting claims of corporate theft, to show that an organization has taken reasonable precautions to protect secret information.

PERFORMANCE ASSESSMENT AND ACTION

The last stage in the marketing evaluation and control process is determining how the actual results compare with planned results. When performance gaps are too large, corrective actions are taken. For example, the large decline in liquid-diet sales (Exhibit 15–8) triggered pricing cuts and advertising increases by the companies competing in this market.

Opportunities and Performance Gaps

Strategic evaluation activities seek (1) to identify opportunities or performance gaps and (2) to initiate actions to take advantage of the opportunities or to correct existing and pending problems. Strategic intelligence, internal reporting and analysis activities, standardized information services, and research studies supply the information needed by marketing decision makers.

The real test of the value of the marketing information system is whether it helps marketing management to identify problems. In monitoring, there are two critical factors to take into account:

EXHIBIT 15–8   Shrinking Liquid-Diet Brands

	Sales ($ million)	% Change vs. Year Earlier	Current Market Share
Ultra Slim-Fast	51.6	–45%	70.5%
Slim-Fast	9.6	–54	13.2
Ultra Slim-Fast Plus*	5.4	—	7.4
DynaTrim	2.8	–65	3.8
Figurine 100	1.4	–23	1.9
Carnation Slender	1.1	–28	1.6
Sego	0.6	–25	0.9
Total	73.3	–44%	100.0%

---

* New brand.

Note: Information is for sales and market shares in supermarkets, drugstores, and mass-merchandise outlets for the 13-week period ended September 20, 1992.

Source: Kathleen Deveny, "Market Scam," *The Wall Street Journal*, October 13, 1992, pp. B1, B10; from Information Resources Inc.

Problem/opportunity definition. Strategic analysis should lead to a clear explanation of an opportunity or problem since this will be needed to guide whatever strategic action may be taken. Often it is easy to confuse problem symptoms with problem causes.

Interpreting information. Management must also separate normal variations in performance from significant gaps in performance, since the latter are the ones that require strategic action. For example, how much of a drop in market share is necessary to signal a performance problem? Limits need to be set on the acceptable range of strategic performance.

No matter how extensive the information system may be, it cannot interpret the strategic importance of the information. This is the responsibility of management.

Exhibit 15–9 describes how the Metropolitan Life Insurance Company links the control function to planning. Management recognizes that gaps will occur between desired and actual results. The guidelines emphasize looking at the causes of variances. The description of the three primary control tools highlights what information is used for comparing performance with the plan. Finally, the role of performance reporting in the company's overall planning and control process is indicated.

Environmental concerns are ongoing areas of strategic evaluation. Companies must identify important areas of concern and implement strategies that take into account consumer, public policy, and organizational priorities. Surprisingly, European consumers appear to be changing their priorities about eco-friendly products.[12] Buyers are not willing to pay a premium for green detergents and cleaners. While in surveys people indicate high interest in eco-friendly products, sales of these items dropped substantially from 1993 to 1995. For example, in Britain green detergent sales declined 40 percent, and account for less than 1 percent of total sales. Several explanations are offered, including lower performance, higher prices, and environmentally responsible regular products.

EXHIBIT 15–9   Planning Guidelines, Metropolitan Life Insurance Company

---

COMPARING THE PERFORMANCE WITH THE PLAN

Each person, to do a satisfactory job, must achieve his or her portion of the plan. And this is where the concept of control fits in. This section discusses:

1. The general principles underlying the process of management control.

2. The Performance Reports we use to implement control.

THE PROCESS OF MANAGEMENT CONTROL

Simply defined, the process of management control consists of seeing that everything is being carried out in accordance with the plans that have been adopted. From this definition, it follows that the primary purpose of the control process is to isolate *variances* from plan so that they can be analyzed, to determine their significance, and to take corrective action as needed.

This does not mean that *variances* from plan are necessarily bad. It simply means that *variances* should be the basis for analysis to determine: (1) whether the *variance* should be accepted as a sound and desirable departure from our plan, (2) whether the *variance* is unavoidable and therefore should serve to sharpen future planning, or (3) whether a different course of action should be taken, such as refocusing of effort or increasing the amount of effort.

The three primary control tools

Control is exercised in a variety of ways, but there are three basic tools or mechanisms which underlie the process.

1. *Preapproval of proposed courses of action.* This form of control is implemented by the use of our marketing plan procedure. For example, one of the items we plan is the creation and abolishment of districts in various areas. The effect of such planning is to establish control over changes that will actually be made in the number and location of our districts.

2. *Direct observation.* This is the basic day-to-day control technique used at the district level. It takes the form of the face-to-face supervision and guidance that district management provides the field force.

3. *Analysis of formal performance reports and taking required action.* The key control tool of management is the set of performance reports that each manager receives indicating his/her subordinates' performance versus plan. These reports provide the basis for identifying and analyzing *variances* and for taking corrective action as required.

Performance reports

The primary purpose of performance reports are:

1. To show the *net effect* of many day-to-day decisions and developments.

2. To provide a check on the adequacy of front-line controls.

3. To provide a means of continuously motivating down-the-line personnel to take objectives and action programs seriously.

4. To serve as a further stimulus to continuous sharpening of the planning process.

From all of the above, it follows that performance reports by themselves represent only one aspect of the total control process. Nevertheless, they are an indispensable aspect of the control system, since they provide the basis for evaluating and planning management action.

Source: David S. Hopkins, *The Marketing Plan,* Report No. 801 (New York: The Conference Board, Inc., 1981), p. 127.

Determining Normal and Abnormal Variability

Operating results such as sales, market share, profits, order-processing time, and customer satisfaction display normal up-and-down fluctuations. The issue is determining whether these variations represent random variation or instead are due to special causes. For example, if a salesperson's sales over time remain within a normal band of variation, then the results are acceptable under the present operating conditions. Random high and low variations do not indicate unusually high or low performance. If this range of performance is *not* acceptable to management, then the system must be changed. This may require salesperson training, redesign of the territory, improvement in sales support, or other changes in the salesperson's operating system.

Statistical process-control concepts and methods are useful in determining when operating results are fluctuating normally or instead are out of control.[13] Quality-control charts can be used to analyze and improve results in marketing performance measures such as the number of orders processed, customer complaints, and territory sales. Control-chart analysis indicates when the process is experiencing normal variation and when the process is out of control.

The basic approach to control-chart analysis is to establish average and upper and lower control limits for the measure being evaluated. Examples of measures include order processing time, district sales, customer complaints, and market share. Control boundaries are set using historical data. Future measures are plotted on the chart to determine whether the results are under control or instead fall outside the acceptable performance band determined by the upper and lower control limits. The objective is to continually improving the process that determines the results.

Deciding What Actions to Take

Many corrective actions are possible, depending on the situation. One objective of this book is to provide a process for selecting strategic actions based upon the opportunity or problem at hand. Management's actions may include exiting from a product-market, new-product planning, changing the target-market strategy, adjusting marketing strategy, or improving efficiency.

An illustration shows how evaluation and control guide corrective action. Deere & Company, the giant farm equipment producer, had a strong performance record during the agriculture slump of the 1980s.[14] Management invested in product and process research, reduced employment, and cut costs. Monitoring of performance indicated the need to take further corrective action in 1989. The industry shakeout of the 1980s weakened farmers' brand loyalty and created two strong competitors. Deere was losing customers that had been buying the popular green farm equipment for three generations. The nation's 2.2 million farmers were making money and buying equipment, but Deere purchases had been drastically curtailed during the early 1980s.

The J. I. Case unit of Tenneco was the number two firm in the U.S. market, strengthened by acquisitions of International Harvester and Steiger Tractor. Case had 1989 global farm equipment sales of $2.9 billion compared to Deere's $4.1 billion. The number three competitor was the Ford Motor Company with sales of $2.3 billion. Both firms are fighting Deere for top position in the $8 billion-a-year domestic market. Farmers' purchases are heavily influenced by equipment quality, price, and dealer service. Competitors are beginning to penetrate Deere's loyal customer base with high-quality equipment, aggressive selling, and dealer support.

Deere has a reputation for high-quality products. Its greatest edge is its 1,700-dealer U.S. network. To strengthen its advantage, Deere's factory employees are phoning or visiting farmers who have purchased Deere products. Service teams are deployed to the field for troubleshooting during heavy equipment-usage periods such as harvesting.

Continued investment in new and improved products occurred in the 1990s. Competitors are challenging Deere with requests for equipment comparisons. This battle for position in farm equipment promises to be an interesting marketing challenge in the decade ahead.

Managing in a changing environment is what strategic marketing is all about. Keeping up with and even anticipating change is the essence of marketing evaluation and control. Executives develop innovative marketing strategies and monitor their effectiveness, altering the strategies as a result of changing conditions.

SUMMARY

Marketing strategy implementation and control are vital links in a series of strategic marketing activities. These actions emphasize the continuing process of planning, implementing, evaluating, and adjusting marketing strategies. Strategic evaluation of marketing performance is the first step in strategic marketing planning and the last step after launching a strategy. The objective is to develop an approach to strategic evaluation, building on the concepts, processes, and methods established in Chapters 1 through 14. Strategic evaluation is one of marketing management's most demanding and time-consuming responsibilities. While the activity lacks the glamour and excitement of new-strategy development, perceptive evaluation often separates the winners from the losers. The managers of successful companies anticipate and respond effectively to changing conditions and pressures. Regular strategic evaluation processes guide these responses.

Marketing strategy implementation and control are guided by the marketing plan and budget (Exhibit 15–1). The plan indicates the activities to be accomplished, how they are to be done, and the costs. The planning process moves into action through the annual marketing plan. It shows the activities to be implemented, responsibilities, deadlines, and expectations. Implementation (Exhibit 15–3) makes the plan happen.

Much of the actual work of managing involves strategic and tactical evaluation of marketing options. Yet performing this function depends greatly on management's understanding of the planning process and the decisions that form plans. Strategic evaluation is a continuing cycle of making plans, launching them, tracking performance, identifying performance gaps, and initiating problem-solving actions. In accomplishing strategic evaluation, management must select performance criteria and measures and then set up a tracking program to obtain the information needed to guide evaluation activities. As an initial step in the strategic evaluation program (and periodically thereafter), a strategic marketing audit provides a useful basis for developing the program.

It is so easy for practicing managers to become preoccupied with day-to-day activities, neglecting to step back and review overall operations. Regular audits and continuous monitoring of the market and competitive environment can prevent sudden shocks and can alert management to new opportunities. Building on findings from the strategic marketing audit, the chapter has examined the major steps in acquiring and using information for strategic analysis. While the execution of the steps varies by situation, they offer a useful framework for guiding a strategic evaluation program in any type of firm. An important part of this process is setting standards for gauging marketing performance. These standards help determine what information is needed to monitor performance.

QUESTIONS FOR REVIEW AND DISCUSSION

1. Discuss the similarities and differences between strategic marketing *planning* and *evaluation.*

2. Establishing a strategic evaluation program involves a series of activities. Beginning with selecting performance criteria and measures, indicate which executives (type of position) and marketing specialists should be responsible for each step.

3. Selecting the proper performance criteria for use in tracking results is a key part of a strategic evaluation program. Suggest performance criteria for use by a fast-food retail chain to monitor strategic marketing performance.

4. What justification is there for conducting a marketing audit in a business unit whose marketing performance has been very good? Discuss.

5. Examination of the various areas of a strategic marketing audit, shown in Exhibit 15–7, would be quite expensive and time-consuming. Are there any ways to limit the scope of the audit?

6. Several kinds of information are collected for a strategic marketing evaluation. Develop a list of information that would be useful for a strategic evaluation in a life insurance company.

7. One of the more difficult management control issues is determining whether a process is experiencing normal variation or is actually out of control. Discuss how management can resolve this issue.

8. How frequently should a marketing manager evaluate the market share of the firm's brands to determine if the brands are performing well against competition? Discuss.

NOTES

1. Greg Steinmetz, "Lufthansa Now on Its Own, Rebounds," *The Wall Street Journal,* August 25, 1995, p. A6; Brian Coleman, "Lufthansa's New Chairman Is Planning to Restructure Carrier, Seek Alliances," *The Wall Street Journal,* November 8, 1991, p. B3.

2. Donald R. Lehmann and Russell S. Winer, *Analysis for Marketing Planning,* 2nd ed. (Burr Ridge, IL: Richard D. Irwin, 1991), pp. 10–13.

3. Ibid., pp. 4–7.

4. This account is based on Barry Kramer, "Master Merchants: Japanese Dominate the Chinese Market with Savvy Trading," *The Wall Street Journal,* November 18, 1985, pp. 1 and 10.

5. Thomas V. Bonoma, "Making Your Marketing Strategy Work," *Harvard Business Review,* March–April 1984, p. 75.

6. This discussion is based on Harper W. Boyd, Jr. and Orville C. Walker, Jr., *Marketing Management* (Burr Ridge, IL: Richard D. Irwin, 1990), pp. 824–25.

7. Yumiko Ono and Susan Carey, "Japan Air Lines Is Struggling to Come Down to Earth," *The Wall Street Journal,* September 22, 1992, p. B4.

8. Kathleen Deveny, "Market Scam," *The Wall Street Journal,* October 15, 1992, pp. B1 and B5.

9. See, for example, Dr. Ernst A. Tirmann, "Should Your Marketing Be Audited?" *European Business,* Autumn 1971, pp. 49–56.

10. Deveny, "Market Scam," pp. B1 and B10.

11. Milo Geyelin, "Why Many Businesses Can't Keep Their Secrets," *The Wall Street Journal,* November 20, 1995, pp. B1 and B3.

12. Tara Parker-Pope, "Europeans' Environmental Concerns Don't Make It to the Shopping Basket," *The Wall Street Journal,* August 18, 1995, p. B3A.

13. Kaori Ishikawa, *Guide to Quality Control* (Tokyo: Asian Productivity Organization, 1982).

14. This account is based on Robert L. Rose, "Tougher Row: Deere Faces Challenge Just When Farmers Are Shopping Again," *The Wall Street Journal,* February 8, 1990, pp. A1 and A6.

Cases for Part V

CASE 5–1   Avon Products, Inc.

Alice Melcher is a big gun in Avon Products Inc.'s sales artillery. Some years, the Lemoyne, Ohio, mother of three has sold more than $500,000 of Avon cosmetics to friends and neighbors, pocketing 50 percent of her sales as commissions.

But Mrs. Melcher's success means she and a helper often must put in 14-hour days at her kitchen table, assembling as many as 7,000 separate orders for her customers. That is the Avon irony: A $4 billion international company's sales force propels what amounts to an enormous, labor-intensive cottage industry rooted in an era when housewives were home when the Avon lady came calling.

Most Avon sales still are made door to door, and the average purchase is $20 or less. But the U.S. customer base has been dwindling since the late 1970s, and Avon has tried to extend its reach by meshing an old-fashioned, yet still potent, selling apparatus with more modern marketing techniques. In doing so, the company instituted organizational changes that shocked Avon's paternalistic corporate culture and sharply divided the company's formerly close-knit ranks.

Some fault Chief Executive Officer James E. Preston for exacerbating the problem. A 30-year Avon veteran, Mr. Preston fended off a flurry of takeover attempts in the late 1980s and cleaned up Avon's debt-ridden balance sheet. Now the 60-year-old executive has an infinitely more complex task: gingerly navigating between Avon's past and its future.

Critics say Mr. Preston has lurched from one fix-it strategy to another. In a six-year period he has hired and then ousted three presidents of the U.S. unit, and recently installed a fourth. These executives pushed a succession of pet theories, including "professionalizing" Avon's sales force with more training and adding earning opportunities. As each left, his plans were dismantled or truncated.

Last year, Avon tried contacting consumers directly through mail-order catalogs and toll-free phone numbers publicized with a $34 million national advertising campaign, the largest in its history. To pay for its corporate makeover, Avon cut its sales representatives' commissions and incentives and let go scores of executives.

The speed and magnitude of the changes now generally are believed to have been misguided. Company insiders say the overhaul generated scant new business and hastened attrition in the sales ranks during the first three quarters of last year, while 1993 pretax profit from Avon's mature U.S. business fell 22 percent, not including a restructuring charge in 1992. Now, the company is projecting a first-quarter surge in U.S. pretax profits ranging from 23 percent to 35 percent, which it attributes mainly to the stronger economy and the phaseout of some of last year's unprofitable marketing ventures.

On Thursday, Avon's stock closed on the Big Board at $56.25, up $1.25, below its 52-week high of $62.375.

Mr. Preston stresses that to keep customers, "change we did, change we must, and change we will." He adds: "For 108 years, we've done business one way. Avon's a human company and a very paternalistic company. Because of this culture, change is even more difficult."

For most of his career, the avuncular Mr. Preston excelled at rallying the troops. He wasn't above donning a grass skirt and dancing the hula at sales meetings, and as president of the U.S. unit in 1985 even postponed honeymooning with his second wife to travel around the country attending sales pep rallies. "He was as passionate a direct-selling person as ever walked the halls of Avon," says Paul Markovits, head of the U.S. unit in 1988 and 1989.

After all, direct selling was Avon's game. The company's business structure has changed little since its founding in 1886, when former book salesman David H. McConnell enlisted a housewife named Mrs. P.F.E. Albee to peddle perfumes in Winchester, New Hampshire. Up through the 1950s, Avon grew by recruiting throngs of mostly homebound women looking for flexible hours and extra income. Today, Avon ladies earn commissions on gross sales ranging from 10 percent to a high of 50 percent for top producers, such as Mrs. Melcher, who sells over $32,750 annually.

The genius of the concept was quickly apparent. Avon ladies did more than ring doorbells; they made friends, who in turn became loyal customers. Even today, Avon managers say that when a representative quits or moves, her clients usually revert to buying cosmetics at stores. Some executives cite the "cookie jar" theory, which holds that customers feel obligated to set aside money to buy something during the Avon lady's regular visit rather than turn her away without a sale.

"The ding-dong lady brings a high-value, lifetime customer on board," says John Deighton, associate professor at the University of Chicago's business school. "The salesperson creates confidence in the brand, delivering much more than advertising is able to do."

Thus it became an article of faith at Avon that reaching and retaining customers was best accomplished through the sales representatives. While other cosmetics companies might spend millions on advertising to launch a new lipstick, Avon lavished its marketing dollars on commissions, trips, trophies and testimonial dinners for Avon ladies. But in the 1980s, as its U.S. business stagnated, some executives began to lose faith in the Avon lady as the company's sole provider.

An abortive attempt to diversify into health care had left the company in debt, making it an alluring takeover target. Mr. Preston became chief executive in September 1988 and was thrust into a period of defending Avon against unwanted suitors, including direct seller Amway Corp. and investor Irwin Jacobs.

It was during the takeover battles that Avon's management conceived of what came to be known as Avon Select, a program offering Avon's products to customers via direct-mail and toll-free numbers. When it was announced in 1991, Mr. Preston predicted Avon Select would grow into a $300 million to $500 million business in three to five years, mainly by attracting new customers who either didn't know an Avon lady or chose not to deal with one. Wall Street hailed it as long overdue.

Not everyone at Avon was sold on Select, particularly Everett "Rick" Goings, the head of Avon's U.S. business at the time. Mr. Goings declined to be interviewed, but former associates say he felt Avon should concentrate on motivating the sales force rather than becoming side-tracked with direct marketing.

So, while a small team at Avon's New York headquarters spearheaded Select in 1991 and 1992, Mr. Goings and his allies championed Leadership, a version of the "multilevel selling" strategies used by most direct sales companies. Under that strategy, representatives recruit and train other sales people in return for a percentage of the recruits' sales. The Goings camp was convinced they had identified Avon's fundamental problem: Selling Avon is a labor-intensive and relatively unremunerative job for all but an elite few.

For the hours they put in, "Avon ladies don't make any money, " says Alan Kennedy, a former Avon sales executive who now heads a direct sales company in Utah. Avon won't disclose the average earnings of its representatives, but says that over half its $1.4 billion U.S. revenue comes from just 17 percent of the 415,000 sales representatives—the 70,000 top-sellers.

The Goings camp concluded that Avon needed powerful new earnings incentives, not a new marketing concept. It was an awkward situation: dueling factions with radically different approaches. Mr. Preston seemed to support both in a "Darwinian strategy," says Virginia Gray, a former manager who worked on Select.

Mr. Preston insists that the programs represented "tests" that fit under Avon's larger strategy of updating its U.S. business. "There's been no change in strategy at all," he says. "I look at the last four to five years as a continuum. We needed to make changes."

By late 1991, Mr. Preston started to cool on Leadership, arguing that it created an unseemly, hard-sell environment. In an industry tainted by charges of high-pressure sales tactics, Avon always has enjoyed a spotless reputation.

"I was beginning to see some people coming into the program who gave me pause," Mr. Preston says. "They were not interested in the product and not interested in what Avon stands for."

But proponents of Mr. Goings's plan contend Leadership would have spurred growth—had it been given a chance. "We don't stick to anything," complains William

Roy, a former regional vice president. "We launch into a strategy, and in two years we run into another one."

In March 1992, Mr. Goings abruptly resigned; soon afterward, Leadership withered away in most sales districts.

To carry Avon Select forward, Mr. Preston hired Walker Lewis as Mr. Goings's successor. A Harvard-educated consultant, Mr. Lewis had spent his career turning around troubled companies. He was convinced Avon had to expand beyond the Avon lady. "Walker bet very heavily on direct marketing—he felt it was the answer," recalls a former Avon executive.

With Mr. Lewis at the helm, Avon's U.S. unit rolled out its national TV and print campaign last year. Some of the new customers declined to work with an Avon lady. For the first time ever, Avon had cut the representative out of a sale.

That policy raised eyebrows throughout the direct sales industry. In merging direct sales and direct marketing, "the key is not to undercut the field sales force," warns Neil Offen, president of the Direct Selling Association, a trade group.

Avon's closest rival, privately held Mary Kay Corp., also is testing a direct-mail catalog. But it carries different merchandise than that sold by its sales consultants, and if a new customer places an order directly with Mary Kay, the company forwards the commission to the Mary Kay representative in her area. Noting that Mary Kay's U.S. sales rose 20 percent last year, Curran Dandurand, senior vice president of global marketing, says, "We will never, ever have a gray area about competing with the sales force. It's the kiss of death."

While opening new channels to the customer, Avon chose last year to restructure commissions, requiring most Avon ladies to sell more to maintain earnings. Avon argues that it hadn't changed commissions in four years, and that sales of some new, pricier products should easily offset the tougher goals.

But it was losing their awards, trips, and other incentives that discouraged the top sellers. "I know it sounds picky, but I guess those things gave us the feeling we were being noticed," says Carmelita Caburet, an Avon lady in Detroit who sells more than $250,000 of merchandise annually.

At headquarters, Avon loyalists were shocked both by the marketing changes and a sweeping management reorganization. Early last year, for example, all executives in the marketing department were forced to reapply for redesigned jobs; a third failed to get the new positions. The turmoil sapped morale and ultimately spilled over to the bottom line.

Despite shedding 600 jobs and other cost-cutting steps, Avon's pretax profit in the United States sank 10 percent in the first quarter of 1993, 7 percent in the second quarter, 36 percent in the third quarter, and 29 percent in the fourth quarter. U.S. sales were off 1 percent for the year, though international business is booming.

Reflecting on last year, Mr. Preston now says: "Perhaps we did too much testing over a period of time that exacerbated a difficult sales climate." He adds: "We walk a fine line—a balance—between supporting the core representative business and testing new concepts. We got out of balance last year."

But marketing specialists say Avon blundered last year by forgetting its history and misreading its customers. When Avon tried its end run around the Avon lady, it did so without first building a brand image that could stand alone. Says Gerron Vartan, president of Aegis Partners Inc., a San Francisco marketing consulting firm: "When you take away that selling relationship, you're left with a brand that's relatively naked."

By last summer, associates say Mr. Preston's lack of confidence in Mr. Lewis had become apparent: The CEO took more personal control of the U.S. unit, down to the layouts of catalogs used by sales reps. Mr. Lewis resigned in November, after 18 months on the job. He declined to be interviewed for this article.

His successor, 46-year-old Christina Gold, was the head of Avon's Canadian operations and is the first female U.S. chief. She is considered an effective motivator of people who boosted sales and profits despite a recession in Canada.

"My No. 1 priority is to rebuild Avon's relationship with representatives," Ms. Gold vows, and even before her arrival in New York, Avon began to reinstate the representatives' birthday presents, anniversary plates, and annual pins. Ms. Gold recalls marshalling a phone blitz to the Canadian sales force and watching orders jump 1 percent in three weeks. "We just told them they're appreciated," she says.

Significantly, however, Avon hasn't abandoned its direct pitch to consumers. Mr. Preston describes Avon Select as "on plan," having generated about $45 million in sales last year, or 3.2 percent of Avon's U.S. revenue. But company insiders say it was a disappointment, and Wall Street analysts suspect much of Select's volume came from customers who would have ordered Avon anyway.

"Avon has no choice but to contemporize an antiquated U.S. distribution system," says Andrew Shore of PaineWebber Inc. "But [Select] just doesn't matter. It's too small."

Avon's recent decision to shrink its ad campaign puzzles some marketing specialists, who argue that refurbishing a brand takes years—not months—of advertising investment. Avon says it is continuing to update its image by introducing new vitamin and lingerie lines this year, and that as sales grow, so will ad budgets.

Avon stumbled last year when it attempted to diversify its product line. It recently ditched Galleries, a direct-mail catalog that carried higher-priced merchandise such as $220 beaded evening dresses. Avon, which manufactures all its beauty products, was ill-equipped to deal with the dozens of outside suppliers and unfamiliar products. Because of problems filling orders, Mr. Preston says, "it's difficult to ascribe much benefit at all" to Galleries. Avon's lingerie and vitamin ventures will involve few outside suppliers.

Mr. Preston says U.S. sales began to pick up almost upon Ms. Gold's arrival, which he attributes in part to better morale in Avon's U.S. sales force. "We see a much improved tone in the field," he says.

Based on focus groups with sales representatives around the country, Brian Connolly, director of national sales incentives, confirms this assessment. "They believe management will listen and respond—that's why they've stayed with us," he says. But as always, it appears they need tokens of corporate affection. When asked whether Avon should continue to bestow awards or offer them more practical business tools, the Avon ladies vote overwhelmingly for the awards. "It's part of the magic," Mr. Connolly says.

Source: Suein L. Hwang, "Ding-Dong: Updating Avon Means Respecting History Without Repeating It," *The Wall Street Journal* April 4, 1994, pp. A1, A4. Reprinted by permission of *The Wall Street Journal*, © 1994 by Dow Jones & Company, Inc. All Rights Reserved Worldwide.

CASE 5–2   United States Tobacco Co.

Travis Tippetts, an Orem, Utah, teenager, took up snuff last year after hearing his friends talk about a hot new brand, cherry Skoal Long Cut. Its sweet taste reminded him of cherry cough syrup, and Travis, then 16, liked the "little tobacco buzz." But two months later, the thrill was gone.

"Cherry wasn't satisfying me,"he says. "I wasn't getting enough nicotine." So he "moved up" to Copenhagen, a brand so powerful that it can make new users gag. Cherry Skoal, he says, "is a beginner's product" that "helped me gradually go up the ladder."

The tobacco industry emphatically denies that it doctors levels of nicotine, the chemical that makes tobacco addictive, in order to make some products stronger than others. No company has been more insistent in those denials than UST Inc.'s United States Tobacco Co. unit, maker of both cherry Skoal and Copenhagen. "U.S. Tobacco does not in any way manipulate or 'spike' the nicotine levels of its tobacco products," Joseph Taddeo, U.S. Tobacco's chief executive officer, testified before Congress in April.

But two former U.S. Tobacco chemists, speaking on the topic for the first time, say that while the company doesn't manipulate nicotine levels, it does manipulate the amount of nicotine that users *absorb*. U.S. Tobacco, they say, adds chemicals to boost the alkalinity of its snuff. The more alkaline the snuff is, they say, the more nicotine is released.

Their descriptions provide powerful support for allegations that the tobacco industry has spiked products to boost nicotine delivery. Two not-yet-released government studies appear to back that conclusion. U.S. Tobacco's manufacturing process also lays the groundwork for what critics allege is a "graduation" strategy: marketing lower-impact products such as cherry Skoal to first-time users, and then profiting as they move up the nicotine chain to ever more addictive brands such as Copenhagen.

U.S. Tobacco, the dominant player in the $1.1 billion snuff industry, refused to comment specifically on the manipulation of nicotine absorption. The company didn't make executives available for interviews, and asked for written questions, to which it responded in writing.

Quoting from Mr. Taddeo's congressional testimony, U.S. Tobacco said it doesn't "take any action to control the nicotine content of its tobacco products, before, during, or after the manufacturing process." In the testimony, Mr. Taddeo also denied a marketing strategy of "graduating" users from lower-nicotine to higher-nicotine products, saying that was a "fanciful concept." He added, "Like any tobacco products, our smokeless tobacco products vary in nicotine content."

Allegations of nicotine manipulation have emerged as a grave threat to the $22.5 billion U.S. tobacco industry. Food and Drug Administration Chief David A. Kessler has said he may use alleged nicotine manipulation as the basis to regulate tobacco as a drug. Congressional hearings last spring made much of cigarette makers' use of reconstituted tobacco—which involves removing nicotine and then adding it back later—but it was never established that this process raised nicotine levels; in fact, cigarette companies argued that the process lowers levels.

The hearings didn't focus on smokeless tobacco, an approximately $1.6 billion industry that includes both snuff and chewing tobacco. Yet U.S. Tobacco routinely adds chemicals to its snuff "to deliver the free nicotine faster and to make the product stronger," says Larry D. Story, a former company chemist who says he left voluntarily in 1982.

Snuff, which sometimes is confused with chewing tobacco, is shredded tobacco that users suck on, but don't chew. Users take a pinch, or "dip," and place it between the cheek and gum, shifting it about with their tongues and spitting occasionally. Snuff is the only segment of the tobacco industry that is growing, with U.S. volume up 3 percent in 1993, according to Sanford C. Bernstein & Co., an investment house.

It also is increasingly popular with children, by some measures. According to a 1992 Surgeon General report, the average age of initiation to snuff was just 9½ years. U.S. Tobacco says it markets its products only to adults. An estimated 7.5 million people in the U.S. use smokeless tobacco, mostly snuff, compared with 53.9 million who smoke cigarettes.

The nicotine level of snuff—as well as that of cigarettes and cigars—is determined by how different types of tobaccos are blended. Reflecting the nicotine-rich varieties U.S. Tobacco primarily uses, James C. Taft, a chemist who was the company's head of product development from 1972 to 1991, jokes that its products "all have enough nicotine to kill a horse."

But nicotine content is only part of the equation. The other crucial variable is the amount of nicotine that is free to get quickly absorbed into a user's bloodstream. In part, this so-called free nicotine is determined by the cut of the tobacco; finely chopped particles release nicotine faster than larger pieces. More important, though, is the alkalinity of the tobacco, as indicated by the pH level. Most tobaccos used in snuff start out with a pH of less than six, which means the snuff is acid, not alkaline; nicotine isn't readily absorbed until the pH tops seven, reflecting the shift to alkalinity, scientists say.

Two former U.S. Tobacco chemists, Mr. Taft and Mr. Story, say that while they were with the company, it used certain chemicals—especially sodium carbonate and ammonium carbonate—to increase the alkalinity of its tobaccos and, thus, their levels of free nicotine. The company added these chemicals during and after fermentation, the process that turns tobacco into snuff, they say. (Ammonia, primarily a byproduct of fermentation, also "really increases the pH," Mr. Story says.)

According to Mr. Taft, "The fermentation process involves adding chemicals and, at the end, you add some more chemicals which increase pH, too." Without increasing the pH, he says, "you couldn't get nicotine release."

U.S. Tobacco declined to comment on the fermentation process or pH levels. "We cannot discuss the intricacies of our manufacturing process due to proprietary reasons," a company spokesman said in a letter. "Scores of companies from Coca-Cola to KFC have gone to extraordinary lengths to keep its formulas a closely guarded secret. . . ."

Nevertheless, in 1986, the company's then-chairman, Louis F. Bantle, testified during a liability trial that pH plays a role in nicotine absorption; he said he was "not an expert in that" and wasn't asked to elaborate. Moreover, sodium carbonate and ammonium carbonate appeared on a list of 562 additives that the snuff industry released in May to a congressional subcommittee during hearings on the tobacco industry's manufacturing and research practices. The additives were described as ingredients in edibles such as baked goods.

Snuff makers may not be alone in boosting the pH levels of their products. The FDA's Dr. Kessler has alleged that cigarette companies add ammonia to their products to boost pH levels and to free up nicotine. Cigarette makers deny the charge. In any case, government health officials believe pH manipulation isn't as crucial for cigarettes as it is for snuff, because the lung is so much more efficient in drawing out nicotine than the mouth.

U.S. Tobacco has been tinkering with the pH of its products—and with their free-nicotine levels—at least since the late 1960s, according to Mr. Story. At the time, new users were scarce and the company's results were stagnant. The chemist, who joined U.S. Tobacco in 1967, says that during his tenure, each product occupied a specific rung on the nicotine-absorption ladder. U.S. Tobacco tried to control as precisely as possible the dose that each delivered, he says. "There used to be a saying at UST that 'There's a hook in every can,' " he says. "And that hook is nicotine."

For example, Mr. Story says that in his day, the company's bestselling Copenhagen brand would emerge from fermentation with a pH of about 7.4. Then, to make it a finished product, "it was brought up to a pH of 7.8, by adding more sodium carbonate and ammonium carbonate." (Copenhagen's fermentation continues in the can, which can raise its pH considerably higher, according to Mr. Story.) Original Fine Cut Skoal, U.S. Tobacco's second-most-potent product, was formulated to wind up with a pH of 7.4, he says.

Yet both Copenhagen and Fine Cut Skoal, the company's mainstay products through the 1970s, were difficult for beginners to get the hang of. Both are made of finely chopped tobacco that tends to float messily around the mouths of new users. And both are so strong they can make new users throw up. What was needed was a starter product with a lower pH.

So by the late 1970s, Mr. Story was helping develop products that would be more accessible. First, in 1983, came Skoal Bandits, a beginner product in which the tobacco remains in a tea-bag-like pouch. Bandits—introduced in ads as "easy to use, anywhere, anytime"—are "a lot weaker product, nicotine-wise," Mr. Story says. Also, "you don't have to expectorate—you don't have to spit."

Then, in 1984, U.S. Tobacco introduced Skoal Long Cut flavors, made from bigger pieces of tobacco that "pack" more easily, somewhat like chewing gum. The bigger pieces also don't release nicotine as fast as the tiny particles of Copenhagen and Fine Cut, Mr. Story says. The idea of Skoal Long Cut, he says, was in part to provide "a softer chew" for "younger men." Soon, the company was offering four different Long Cut flavors, including wintergreen.

Last year, the company introduced its even easier-on-the-palate cherry Skoal Long Cut, along with a new spearmint Long Cut flavor. Cherry took off, and is now emerging as the company's most successful new product in about a decade, some distributors say.

The company says it developed cherry "to appeal to adult consumers of other smokeless tobacco products," and notes that there are numerous cherry-flavored tobaccos on the market. It says the launch of both cherry and spearmint was based on research in which more than 60 percent of adult snuff users said they would purchase the two products. In a brochure, the company describes cherry Skoal's flavor as "fresh-tasting."

But to Kitch Hopkins, a skinny, blond-haired 11-year-old user from New Market, Alabama, it "tastes sweet, like a cherry pie." His 17-year-old brother Jackie, lingering outside Bud's Family Arcade, adds, "with cherry, when you swallow, it's more like sweet-tasting bubble gum."

A number of teens interviewed say cherry has become the starter brand of choice among underage users, a group estimated by some government officials to be more than one million strong. Darrell Janke, for example, tried snuff for the first time in the summer of 1993 and, upon entering fifth grade that fall, discovered that "just about everybody" was pulling the same red cans from their back jeans pockets. "Kids are definitely starting out with cherry," says the youngster, who by this summer was buying a can every three days at gas stations in his hometown of St. Maries, Idaho. "The regular kind doesn't taste as good or smell as good—they're aiming this at us."

Even some former employees have doubts about the company's objectives with cherry. Bob Beets, a sales representative at U.S. Tobacco until 1990, says, "Cherry Skoal is for somebody who likes the taste of candy, if you know what I'm saying."

The new products, and U.S. Tobacco's courtship of beginning users who may move up the line to more potent brands, have paid off: Today, U.S. Tobacco is the most profitable American tobacco company on the basis of profit margins, and controls 84 percent of the U.S. snuff market. Earlier this year, acclaimed investor Warren Buffett disclosed he had acquired a 2.8 percent stake in its parent company, which last year earned $349 million on sales of $1.1 billion.

U.S. Tobacco denies that it has a "graduation process" to ratchet users up the line to stronger brands, saying that "there is no set pattern of brand switching." However, the company itself used the term internally, and publicly alluded to it in the mid-1980s. "They talked about graduation all the time—in sales meetings, memos, and manuals for the college program. It was a mantra," says Ken Carlsen, a division manager in U.S. Tobacco's sales department, who worked at the company from 1979 until 1986.

"For people who haven't ever tasted [snuff], you'd of course begin them on a product that had a little tobacco taste, but wouldn't turn them off," explains Barry Nova, U.S. Tobacco's president until 1984. He adds: "The graduation is to a more tobacco-y product . . . to a stronger product."

The two recent laboratory tests, conducted by different government agencies, found that U.S. Tobacco's Copenhagen is capable of delivering more nicotine than the company's flavored brands. One analysis, completed last month by the National Institute on Drug Abuse following an inquiry by this newspaper, showed that a one-gram pinch of Copenhagen had an average pH of 8.6, making a huge 79 percent of its nicotine immediately free for absorption. Cherry Skoal Long Cut posted a pH of 7.5, making 22 percent of its nicotine immediately free to be absorbed. And in wintergreen Skoal Bandits, with a pH of 6.9, only 7 percent of its nicotine was instantly available, helping explain why even rookies often complain that this brand is too weak.

The second study, commissioned by the National Cancer Institute and completed in August, came up with similar results. (The two studies found different pH levels for some of the same brands, however; researchers say outside factors, such as how long a product sits on a shelf, also can change a product's pH.)

Jack Henningfield, chief of NIDA's clinical pharmacology branch, contends the research illustrates that U.S. Tobacco's products deliver four different nicotine doses: low, medium, high, and super. For those needing a heavy dose, Copenhagen is "the prescription," says the government scientist, who calls this brand "the heroin of smokeless tobacco." U.S. Tobacco says "that claim is without merit," and notes that Mr. Henningfield testified against the company as an expert witness in a 1986 liability trial.

Brian Woodard knows the progression well. Last July, the 14-year-old switched to cherry from popular wintergreen Skoal with the intent of weaning himself off snuff. But by the end of 1993, he was dipping more than ever—and was ready for a "whole new ballgame."

"Cherry kind of prepared me to go all the way up, though I wasn't planning on it preparing me," says the Danville, Alabama, youth, who now consumes a can of Copenhagen every day. "Cherry is like the kindergarten for Copenhagen."

According to the Centers for Disease Control and Prevention, snuff users are four times as likely to develop mouth cancer as nonusers. They are 50 times as likely to contract cancers of the gum and inner-cheek lining. Because of exposure to high levels of nicotine and nitrosamines, a chemical linked to cancer, dippers also may suffer tooth loss and gum lesions more frequently than nonusers.

Last year, there were 30,000 new cases of oral cancer in the U.S. and 8,000 deaths. CDC officials believe 75 percent of the deaths were attributable to cigarette smoking; they don't have figures on the mortality linked to smokeless tobacco.

The statistics don't include people like Sean McFarland, a Fort Worth, Texas, teenager who used to use three cans a week of Copenhagen. Last year, Mr. McFarland was diagnosed with receding gums and hyperkeratosis, or whitish lesions on his lower gums. After a skin-graft operation, the then-18-year-old briefly managed to kick the habit. But three weeks later, he was back to Copenhagen again—though he still had stitches in his mouth and couldn't eat solid food. Today, Mr. McFarland, who now uses five cans a week, has no expectation that he will ever quit.

"Dipping calms me," he says. "It eases me down."

U.S. Tobacco denies that snuff is addictive and disputes the CDC's statistics. It successfully argued that there isn't conclusive evidence linking snuff to cancer in the much-publicized 1986 wrongful-death trial of Sean Marsee. The mother of Mr. Marsee, a 19-year-old Oklahoma "dipper" who died of oral cancer six years after first receiving a free sample of Copenhagen at a rodeo, sued U.S. Tobacco in federal court in Oklahoma City. But the jury took less than a day to absolve the company of liability, and Mrs. Marsee's appeal was unsuccessful.

Negative publicity from the case prompted a 1986 federal law requiring the industry to place health-warning labels on snuff cans. Snuff makers also stopped TV advertising and curbed sampling activities. Yet snuff use among teens by some measures continued to rise, though there are conflicting reports. The CDC reported that 19 percent of high-school boys had used smokeless tobacco in 1991, up from 2 percent in 1970. U.S. Tobacco, on the other hand, cites a 1993 report by the Substance Abuse and Mental Health Services Administration saying that the figure had declined to 4.8 percent of 12- to 17-year-old boys in 1992.

Some teens say that U.S. Tobacco's marketing strategies, especially for its cherry Skoal Long Cut, play right to underage users. Though the company spends little on traditional advertising, its full-page ads have appeared recently in magazines, including Rolling Stone and Sport. "It's time you got the great taste of Skoal on us," the ads cajoled readers, offering free samples to those who sent in a perforated card. (The ads say the offer isn't available to minors.)

Even more than advertising, U.S. Tobacco spends millions each year doling out free products to woo new dippers, mostly white males from America's blue collar and rural locales, say former employees at Holland Mark Martin, U.S. Tobacco's direct-marketing firm. Consumer-marketing representatives work countless rodeos, car races, and fairs. It is here at the grass-roots level that U.S. Tobacco is probably most persuasive: Company sales representatives mix down-home folksiness with a hard sell. Mr. Carlsen, the former division manager, recalls seeing sales representatives "who weren't heavy [snuff] users actually getting sick because they had to keep putting the product in their own mouths."

At a Copenhagen/Skoal Pro Rodeo in New Market, Alabama, in late August, a team of U.S. Tobacco's sales reps stood in a green-awninged booth, doling out box after box of cherry and spearmint samples—and sometimes personally demonstrating snuff's appeal—to a steady stream of rodeo fans. Males who asked for it could get wintergreen Skoal Long Cut, and the infrequent female automatically was handed what company representatives billed as "ladylike" Bandits. But the largess had limits; there was nary a sign of either Original Fine Cut Skoal or Copenhagen, which holds a commanding 42 percent of the snuff market.

That's no mistake, say some veterans of U.S. Tobacco's sales force. They say U.S. Tobacco doesn't want to feed its existing customers—or alienate new ones—with its two most potent products. Snuff is a "tough sell," says Boyd Buergee, a division manager in U.S. Tobacco's sales department until 1987. "You need a product that is mild and good-tasting to get people used to it."

At the Alabama rodeo, a prominently placed sign proclaimed: "Absolutely no samples given to those under 19," and company representatives requested identification cards from a number of baby-faced boys. But some teens enlisted older friends or their relatives to stand in line. Others simply fibbed. "I went right up to them and they said, 'Here, have you some cherry,' " bragged 15-year-old Len Cox, triumphantly flashing his samples.

U.S. Tobacco lists numerous steps it takes to prevent youths from procuring its samples. The company's mail-in coupons say that giving false information, such as the wrong age, may be illegal. Samples come in envelopes addressed to the adult head of household. When U.S. Tobacco learns that a youth has falsified his age, he is dropped from its mailing list and a notification letter is sent to an adult resident. Sales representatives must sign a code that samples will be given only to adults.

The company also says it has devoted "substantial resources" to preventing retailers from selling its products to minors. Still, at the XTRA Mart convenience store in Ballston Spa, New York, store manager Jacqueline Ketchel contends that any store willing to peddle to minors will sell "tons" of cherry Skoal. Ms. Ketchel, who says she doesn't sell the product to underage users, claims: "With this flavor, the company was shooting for a younger audience just like R.J. Reynolds with Joe Camel."

Already, some of that younger audience says cherry Skoal Long Cut is suffering from a kiddie image; experienced teen dippers insist they have progressed beyond it.

"Doing cherry would make me feel like a wimp," says Marty White, a 15-year-old Copenhagen user in Fort Worth who began his habit at age 11 with Skoal Bandits and says he already has receding gums and mouth sores. Cherry, he adds, "is for little kids."

FEATURE   The Long Road to Cherry Skoal

With its popular new cherry Skoal Long Cut, U.S. Tobacco has achieved what once seemed almost impossible: making snuff fashionable, and making it appealing to beginners.

It has been a long road. In the late 1960s, the dipping habit was waning, and snuff was suffering from a decidedly low-brow reputation. With its future hanging in the balance, the UST Inc. unit set out to make snuff and its less savory aspects—like spitting and spittle about the lip line—palatable to a new generation. According to the minutes of a 1968 marketing meeting held in New York, Louis F. Bantle, then vice president for marketing, declared: "We must sell the use of tobacco in the mouth and appeal to young people . . . we hope to start a fad. " Mr. Bantle, who followed his father, Louis A. Bantle, as UST's chief executive in 1973 and retired last year, didn't return calls or respond to a letter seeking comment.

"We were looking for new users—younger people who, by reputation, wouldn't try the old products," recalls meeting attendee James Taft, who later became the company's head of product development.

U.S. Tobacco first tackled the development of a starter product, a task that required years of trial and error—often error. In the mid-1960s, for example, the company began marketing Happy Days, which Boston Red Sox catcher Carlton Fisk once touted in ads as "for you guys just starting out."

But Happy Days fell prey to a sissyish image among snuff's macho consumers—an image not helped by its treacly name. "We got a lot of feedback from the field that the name wasn't a hooker name like 'Skoal,' " recalls Thomas O'Grady, who served as UST's vice chairman until 1991. Perhaps an even bigger difficulty, recalls Mr. Taft, was that Happy Days, with flavors including raspberry, was the only U.S. Tobacco snuff product that wasn't fermented. As a result, its pH was "below seven, and too low for nicotine release."

Meanwhile, in an attempt to make snuff more acceptable, the company began using sports stars in ads. In 1973—after cigarette advertising was banned, but snuff advertising was left untouched—it took to the airwaves with ads starring football and rodeo star Walt Garrison. Through the 1970s, Mr. Garrison, who is still on the company's payroll, proclaimed in magazine spreads, "I love tobacco. I don't smoke."

In the early 1980s, endorser and baseball star Bobby Murcer even hit the country-music charts with "I'm a Skoal Dippin' Man." The chorus: "Just a pinch between my cheek and gum . . . makes me feel like a long home run." Mr. Murcer has since quit snuff, and today characterizes himself as a "huge antitobacco proponent."

Despite those efforts, a rival's starter product began drawing in younger users in a way that U.S. Tobacco's own products weren't. Introduced by Conwood Co. in 1979, the brand was called Hawken. In a memo dated January 21, 1980, A. H. Cameron, one of U.S. Tobacco's regional sales managers, reported this to the firm's national sales manager: "Retailers all agree that the majority of Hawken is being used by young kids and young adults. The age of the kids is from 9 years old and up." That, the sales manager continued, was "four or five years earlier than we have reached them in the past." (In his testimony during the Marsee trial, Mr. Bantle disputed the young starting age.)

"They were concerned Hawken would appeal to kids because it was sweeter than Original Fine Cut Skoal and used a coarser cut that didn't float as much," recalls Larry Story, who was a company chemist until 1982. U.S. Tobacco also feared, he says, that once initiated to Conwood's starter product, "the Hawken kids might graduate to [Conwood's stronger] Kodiac, rather than to Skoal."

(continued)

FEATURE *(concluded)*

So, as part of the effort to build up its base of young people, U.S. Tobacco in 1983 introduced its Skoal Bandits—a starter product, with the tobacco contained in a pouch like a tea bag, whose name wouldn't make a cowboy cringe.

The brand appeared to have its roots in the Lotus Project, an effort undertaken in the early 1970s by United Scandia International, a joint venture between UST and Swedish Tobacco Co. The mission: "To make it easier for a new user to use tobacco in the mouth," said one of the 1972 marketing documents detailing the project. Its target audience: "New users, mainly cigarette smokers, age group 15 to 35," according to one document.

Joseph Taddeo, U.S. Tobacco's chief executive officer, told Congress in April that this document was "written over 20 years ago, does not mention Skoal Bandits, was not created by U.S. Tobacco and does not reflect U.S. Tobacco policy." The company added in a statement that the docu-ment referred only to a marketing initiative in Sweden, by Swedish Tobacco.

The internal document suggests other-wise. According to the document—minutes from a meeting at the company's Greenwich, Conn., headquarters—Louis A. Bantle "de-clared that he wanted a Lotus product for the U.S. market as soon as possible." Soon after, U.S. Tobacco introduced a snuff product in a tea-bag-like pouch called Good Luck, which ultimately fizzled.

In the end, with Bandits and especially the flavored Skoal Long Cut brands introduced in 1984, U.S. Tobacco appears to have suc-ceeded in making starter products, making them fashionable—and making them lead up the nicotine chain. "A lot of people may start on the more flavored products," says Mr. O'Grady, the former UST vice chairman. "But ultimately, they'll come to Copenhagen."

CASE 5–3 Intuit Corporation

This past February, on the day postal rates jumped from a quarter to 29 cents, I visited my local post office. So did a lot of other people. Not that anything was different there. The clerks had still opened only one window out of a possible three, thus creating a line that was 10 deep. And the one guy on duty had run out of 4 cent stamps.

OK, so the post office hasn't yet discovered customer service. But every other organization seems to have gone nuts over it. Hotels virtually beg you to fill out those little cards telling them where they messed up. Retailers trumpet their money-back guarantees, manufacturers their toll-free numbers (Questions? Complaints? Call 1-800-WELOVE-U). Banks—banks!—stay open later and promise no-hassle loan applications. Or at least they did before they quit lending money.

Most companies, of course, stop right there. They want customers to feel fawned over, but they rarely seem to care whether those same customers actually go away happy. My health club, for example, uses the ubiquitous tell-us-how-we-can-do-better cards. But do the people who run it really need me to tell them the rowing machines are busted half the time? And if they cared about customer satisfaction, as opposed to the semblance of customer service, wouldn't they just fix the damn machines?

The fact is, the icons of customer service—800 numbers, guarantees, suggestion cards, and surveys—have become no more than a ticket of admission to today's marketplace. They no longer confer a competitive advantage; indeed, they may even be liabilities. (Customers who get curt responses from that toll-free line will be madder than if they had never called.) They cost money, and they don't deliver commensurate benefits.

And yet, as long as we're on the subject of customer service, let your imagination run wild. Suppose your company could *really* satisfy its customers. Suppose you could provide a product or service that was better than they expected, for less money than anybody else charged. Suppose that every time you brought out something new it was just what buyers wanted. Suppose your after-sale service was so good that customers with problems went away feeling better than before.

What would happen? Easy—you'd own your marketplace. People would buy from you over and over again, would relish the experience, would never even dream about doing business with anybody else. They would proselytize on your behalf, telling their friends and associates to buy from you. You'd hardly need salespeople.

Impossible, you say. Farfetched. Then again, you haven't met Scott Cook, and you probably don't know much about his company, Intuit Inc. All those statements apply to Intuit. Better yet, Cook has figured out how to build that kind of customer orientation into the organizational bricks and mortar of his company.

"Operating without a safety net," the 38-year-old president calls it. Or "the Toyota approach." Or simply "getting it right." Whatever—it's partly a matter of management techniques, partly a matter of fundamental philosophy. And it's what sets Cook's company way, way apart from the competition.

Intuit makes microcomputer software. Its flagship product is Quicken, a program that allows consumers and small businesses to write checks and keep track of their finances on a personal computer. Owning the marketplace? Quicken is probably the most successful personal-finance program ever written, holding a market share estimated at 60 percent. "It has become the brand-name product in what would otherwise be a commodity business," says Jeffrey Tarter, editor of the industry publication *Softletter.* "It's the Kleenex or Xerox of its market." Intuit, accordingly, has been exploding. It ranked number 15 on the 1990 *Inc.* 500. Revenues last year hit $33 million, up from $19 million the year before. After-tax earnings were into double digits.

Granted, the software industry has always been populated by hotshot fast-growth companies. But Intuit doesn't fit the conventional mold. Unlike, say, Lotus, it started without venture capital or other early advantages. (See box, "Wager: One Company.") Unlike VisiCorp or Wordstar, it has dominated its marketplace through several generations of software, beating back waves of would-be competitors. Consumers yank Quicken off the shelves virtually unbidden. Intuit sold close to a million units in 1990. Its product is carried by retailers all over the country, by Target stores and Wal-Marts as well as computer chains. Yet the company's sales force numbers exactly two.

So what moves the goods? Asked that question, founder and president Scott Cook peers mock—earnestly through his thick glasses, allowing only the hint of a grin to cross

---

FEATURE   Wager: One Company

Scott Cook's Year of Living Dangerously

May 1, 1985. Almost six years later, Scott Cook still remembers the date. "It was the worst day of my life," he says.

Who would disagree? His company, Intuit, was less than two years old. And he had to tell his seven employees he could no longer pay their salaries.

Cook knew he had a promising product, an easy-to-use check-writing program for personal computers. What he didn't have was money.

The dozens of venture capitalists he had approached scarcely gave him a second glance. The $350,000 he himself had sunk into Intuit, a sum pieced together from life savings and home-equity credit, from credit cards and loans from his father, was nearly gone. Without money, he had no distribution channels and no customers. What computer store would carry an unknown software product—unsupported by advertising?

Intuit's sales so far had been a kind of good-news/bad-news joke. The good news: Cook had persuaded a few banks to sell the program in their lobbies. Each one ordered several hundred copies for inventory when it signed up, generating a little cash. The bad news: banks were lousy at selling software, so reorders were slim. Knowing he had to get the program into computer stores, he scrambled to sell to just a few more banks.

By the summer of 1986 Cook's efforts had just barely paid off. The little company had $125,000, enough to start an ad campaign. By rights he and his colleagues should have done some tests. But there was no time, not if they wanted to catch the Christmas selling season. So early in the fall they took the $125,000—all of it—and spent it on one make-or-break ad campaign. Cook wrote the ad himself. If it didn't work . . . nah, better not to think too hard about that.

Well, Lady Luck was smiling that fall. Or maybe Cook's extraordinary efforts to create a product that would truly satisfy its buyers were on the money. Whatever the reason, the ad launched Intuit's program on what turned out to be a brilliant career.

"The company," says Cook, now president of a $33-million business, "grew a bunch."

his face. " Really," he says innocently, "we have hundreds of thousands of salespeople. They're our customers." Suddenly missionary—sober, he adds that he wants his customers to be "apostles" for Quicken. Intuit's mission is to "make the customer feel so good about the product they'll go and tell five friends to buy it."

And as to what would make a customer feel that good, which is to say better than most customers feel about any product or service—well, the only way to understand it may be to watch Cook and his company at work.

The year is 1984; the place Palo Alto, California, not far from Intuit's current hometown of Menlo Park. Cook and three colleagues are in a room with a bunch of computers and several well-dressed women. The women—members of the Palo Alto Junior League—are not what you'd call computer nuts; some have never even touched one of the machines before. But today, after croissants and orange juice, they are sitting at the keyboards, trying to use the computers to write checks. Cook and his colleagues watch but don't help.

Cook—a Harvard MBA, a Proctor & Gamble-trained marketer—is a bit on edge. In a way, his fledgling company depends on what he learns here.

His epiphany, a year or so earlier, was simplicity itself. More and more consumers and small businesses were buying PCs. All those computer buyers wrote checks and kept financial records. Outfitted with the right software, a computer should be able to automate such tasks. The only rub: a few dozen check-writing programs were already on the market, and Cook had no money to elbow them aside. If he wanted to start a software company—and he did—he would have to offer customers something his competitors didn't.

Wondering what that something might be, he and a newly hired assistant began placing telephone calls to middle- and upper-middle-income households. They didn't stop until the calls numbered in the hundreds—and until they began hearing the same responses over and over.

The vast majority of respondents said they did financial work every month, they didn't like spending so much time on it, and they would consider using a computer to do the work. But they couldn't be bothered with learning a complex program, and they certainly didn't want to spend more time on the chore than they were spending now. Curious, Cook assembled a panel of computer buffs to test the most popular programs then available, writing checks and keeping records first by computer and then by hand. Sure enough—in every case, the computer was slower.

Conclusion: there was a market out there, already big and undoubtedly growing bigger, a market capable of appealing to Cook's P&G-honed aspirations. But if he wanted to reach that potential mass market, his program had better be fast, cheap, hassle free, and above all easy to use, so easy that anyone could sit down at the computer and start writing checks.

So, now he's watching very intently as the Junior Leaguers stare at the unfamiliar keys. He and his chief programmer, a recent Stanford graduate named Tom Proulx (rhymes with true), have developed a prototype, and today's trial is one of many to see how well they've done. If the women flunk, so does the program.

For a while the test goes swimmingly. The women hunt and peck, but they don't have much trouble selecting "write checks" from a menu on the screen. The outline of a check appears, and the cursor jumps neatly from date to payee to amount. Anyone who has ever written a paper check, they discover, can write one with this new software. And the computer's check register looks just like an ordinary checkbook.

Then, alas, they go to print the checks they've written. Cook and the others have loaded up the printers with specially prepared checks, and the testers find "print checks" on the menu. But the first check prints too high, or maybe too low. To a woman they fumble with the printers; to a woman they make the problem worse. *What's the matter with this computer? The checks just won't line up right.*

Cook cringes. So does Proulx; so does Tom LeFevre, another colleague present at the creation.

"We knew one thing," recalls Proulx, now the company's vice president of product development. "If people had that much trouble the first time they used the program, they'd never use it again."

"Scott looked at Tom and me," adds LeFevre, also a vice president. "He said, 'You guys figure out a way to solve that problem.' His tone said, And don't come back until you do."

Jump cut: 1990. Proulx and LeFevre have long since resolved the alignment problem, developing a fancy bit of programming (patented and still unique in the industry) that makes the computer line the checks up automatically. And Quicken has long since been released, upgraded, and released again. It has climbed to the top of the best-seller charts; it has won industry awards. Intuit is making a lot of money selling not only the programs but upgrades, special checks, and other supplies.

Yet now Alex Young, a product-development manager for the next release of Quicken, is sitting in the home of a man he doesn't know, watching him open a shrink-wrapped box.

Maybe it was the P&G training, maybe the lesson of the Junior Leaguers, maybe just the impact of the original market research. Whatever the reason, figuring out how to satisfy customers has become Cook's, and Intuit's, obsession. The company runs an annual customer survey, asking which of Quicken's features buyers use and don't use, like and don't like. It polls dealers anonymously, asking what personal-finance programs they recommend and why. It compiles data from customers who call in with problems or write in with suggestions. It runs focus groups, usually consisting of people who aren't Quicken customers but (according to Intuit) ought to be. Information from all those sources flows directly to product-development teams (working on the next version of Quicken), to the documentation department (which regularly updates the manual), and to marketing.

The company also tests its programs relentlessly. And not just the so-called alpha and beta testing commonly practiced by most software companies—tests that are designed primarily to locate bugs in the programming—but tests at a much earlier stage of product development. Get in some experienced Quicken users—see if this new version is going to confuse them in any way. Get in some Junior League–style novices. What's their reaction to a certain screen? "You watch their eyebrows, where they hesitate, where they have a quizzical look," says Cook. "Every glitch, every momentary hesitation is our fault."

Enough, you might think. That'll do it, you might think. Not that all the research costs so much—only the big sample surveys represent much of a cash outlay, in the neighborhood of $150,000 a year. But surely Intuit has been finding out all it possibly can about its customers' experiences with the product?

Nope. "There's still a group of people we were missing," says product manager Mari Latterell. "People just setting the program up. In fact, we didn't really know how easy it was to get started with Quicken. When you survey customers, they've been using it for six months or a year and won't remember. When you bring in testers you have them in an artificial situation. They aren't entering their own data in their own homes."

Which is why Latterell, imbued with Cook's market-research mission, proposed the Follow-Me-Home program, in which Quicken buyers from local stores are asked to let an Intuit representative observe them when they first use Quicken. And why Alex Young, who volunteered to participate, is now watching his new acquaintance unwrap the shrink-wrapped Quicken box.

Today Young will spend five hours with his subject, longer than any of the dozen or so other employees who have so far followed customers home. Sitting behind the customer, he watches and listens. Customer confronts the program's main menu. (Confusion, notes Young: he thinks the word *register*, meaning the check register, has something to do with the product-registration card.) Customer begins to enter data from his checkbook. (Problem: he tries to enter a balance manually. You can't do that; once the opening balance is entered, the program calculates the balances automatically.) Customer tries to print checks. (He prints more samples than he needs to.) Finally, the day is done, and the customer is happy. As part of the deal, Young is now allowed to offer a little help and advice.

Young and Intuit, for their part, have their payoff: a thick sheaf of notes on the myriad ways that the next incarnation of Quicken, already the most popular program on the market, might be made just a tiny bit easier for first-time users.

"If people don't use the product," observes Tom LeFevre, "they won't tell their friends to use it, either."

Suna Kneisley, senior customer support specialist, can't quite believe the fax. A customer she has just spoken with wants to know how to put his various records onto Quicken and has just faxed her nine pages' worth of data. It's a Friday; no way she can go through it all today. Oh, well. She calls the customer and leaves a message; she'll take it home with her over the weekend and get back to him Monday. Monday, she has the answers he wants.

Technical-support reps such as Kneisley are Intuit's front-line employees, like waiters in a restaurant or reservation clerks at an airline. There are 40 of them, almost a quarter of the company's 175-person workforce. You've just bought a new printer, and you can't get it to work with Quicken? Call tech support. You've damaged a disk and lost some data? Call tech support. The response you get, of course, will define your attitude toward Quicken and Intuit, probably forever.

So ask yourself: How much is it worth to the company when a customer gets a response like Kneisley's—not only that she'll answer a request going well beyond the ordinary, but that she'll take it home and work on it *over the weekend?*

Kneisley, 24, has been at Intuit only five months when this particular request comes in. No matter—she has already absorbed the messages that Cook has somehow built into the very structure of his company. *Intuit stands or falls with what happens in tech support. Do whatever you need to do to satisfy the customer.* The messages are hammered home in several different ways:

- Thank-you letters from customers are read aloud, circulated throughout the company, and then framed and posted on the wall. Kneisley's colleague Debbie Peak gets a letter because she faxed a customer some printer information, then thought to call the next day to make sure it had arrived safely. Kneisley herself gets one from a woman who damaged four years' worth of data; working at home with a special data-recovery program, Kneisley salvaged it.

- Virtually everyone in the company, from Cook on down, spends a few hours each month working the customer service lines, underscoring by example the importance of what the department does. "I was hired in September," recalls Victor Gee, who started as a rep and is now a supervisor in tech support. "That same month Scott came by and started taking calls, too. I thought, What other company would have the president do the same thing I'm doing?" Every few months, moreover, each employee is taken to lunch by a top manager. Lunch with a Dork, employees have christened the program—but its message is not lost. "My last one was with Scott," says customer support specialist Dwight Joseph. "He had his notebook with him, and he writes down what you say, any ideas you might have. It's pretty gratifying."

- A torrent of statistics—daily write-ups, weekly summaries, hand-lettered charts covering a whole quarter—tracks the tech-support department's performance for all to see. How many callers have to wait longer than 60 seconds? How many give up? At the company's Monday morning meetings, says Cook, "the first four numbers we go through have to do with customer service. Even before we get to revenues. It creates real peer pressure to improve service—people see how we're doing each week."

At a lot of companies, pressure to improve customer service creates a white-collar sweatshop: harried managers browbeat supervisors; supervisors keep an iron grip on employees. Intuit, by contrast, is structured to encourage cooperation and to make improvements through innovation rather than through tighter controls. Greg Ceniceroz, recently promoted from tech-support rep to product specialist, is assigned the job of figuring out how to cut down on the average time spent with each customer. His first step toward a solution: a big loose-leaf reference binder containing answers to customers' most frequent questions, for every rep's desk. He encourages reps to submit questions and answers for inclusion in the binder and makes sure those who do get a public thank you.

Kneisley, meanwhile, notices that management is looking for a volunteer to chair a group dubbed the Innovative Ideas Committee, which has been charged with collating and following up on every product-improvement idea emanating from the tech-support department and from Quicken users. She writes a four-page proposal about what she thinks the group ought to do, and gets the job. "We worked with her to set the committee's ob-jectives," says Tom LeFevre, "since she had been here only a few months. But she was *very* interested. And the more interested someone is, the better job they'll do."

Involvement of that sort, of course, translates into a sense of ownership more valuable and more productive than any amount of iron-grip supervision. "Most of us work at least 50 hours a week," says Kneisley. "We don't get any extra compensation. But we do have a profit-sharing plan, and if Intuit does well, we will, too."

Scott Cook is showing me Intuit's latest ad campaign. I'm a little incredulous, but there it is: Send for a copy of Quicken. Pay only an $8 shipping-and-handling charge. If you don't think you're doing useful work within a few minutes, don't pay for the product. No, not "send it back for a refund." *Keep it.* Just don't pay for it.

Why would a company do this?

"It's like the Japanese," Cook says.

"Oh," I answer, trying to think of the last time a Japanese company offered me something virtually free. Fortunately, Cook elaborates.

"It's like the Japanese assembly lines, where they have only two hours' worth of inventory. There's no margin for error—they have to have super reliability from their suppliers." Cook goes to his bookshelf, pulling out a copy of *The Machine That Changed the World,* the new book about Toyota's "lean production" system. "What we're doing is the Toyota approach. We take away the safety net. If you do that, you have to get it right."

The more Cook talks, the more the scenes I have observed at Inuit begin to fall into place.

Tech support, for example. Here are 40 people answering all kinds of crazy questions—for free. Here is a $500,000 state-of-the-art telephone system, installed in late

1989 just so callers won't have to wait so long. This isn't normal: nearly all of Intuit's competitors put a limit on tech support, some charging for it and some curtailing it so many months after purchase. And nearly every company with an after-sale call-in line doesn't mind keeping customers waiting for a few minutes.

But then, those companies have a safety net. "Most software companies would go broke if they didn't charge for tech support," argues Cook. "We said, We're not going to charge. If our customers have problems, we pay. That makes us get the product right the first time."

Take the product itself. For $50 or less—sometimes as low as $20 on store-sponsored special sales—you can buy a copy of Quicken. In its latest form, you get a program capable not only of writing checks but of tracking investments, generating profit-and-loss statements, and doing a dozen other chores a small-business owner or financially sophisticated consumer might want to do on a computer. You also get a 460-page manual, the right to regular upgrades at modest cost, and access to unlimited help. Once again: abnormal. Quicken's chief competitor lists for three and a half times as much as Quicken, and Quicken's price could probably double before Intuit noticed much of a sales decline.

But that would be a safety net. "We sell an inexpensive product, and we offer free customer support," says Alex Young. "We have to make sure it's right when it goes out the door." Suddenly, refinements like the Follow-Me-Home program make perfect sense.

And finally, look at Intuit's marketing. The no-pay ad, for example. "We heard from our focus groups that people really didn't believe the product could be so easy to use," recalls Mari Latterell. "After all, software never is. So we did this big advertising campaign—'You'll be using Quicken in six minutes or it's free.' The goal was to put our money where our mouth is." Even the company's tiny sales force—two people—begins to seem comprehensible. Outside salespeople could maybe push more product into stores. But depending on pull-through marketing means the company can't survive without satisfying its customers. "When someone comes in and thanks a clerk for selling him Quicken," says marketing vice president John Monson, "there's nothing a salesperson could do that would come close to being as powerful a recommendation."

Funny that Monson should conjure up that image. When I return from my visit to Intuit, I call up the manager of the local Egghead Discount Software store and ask him about the product. "People love it," he says. "Someone actually came in here and thanked me for selling it to him. That doesn't happen too often."

By some reckonings, Intuit's approach to customer satisfaction is costly.

Technical support and other departments that have customer contact (the one taking orders for checks, for example) cost the company about 10 percent of revenues, or upward of $3 million a year. The testing, surveys, fancy telephone systems, focus groups, and other stay-close-to-the-customer expenses add another $1 million to $2 million. Imagine yourself a corporate raider concerned only with the next quarter's earnings; you'd buy up Intuit, cut back on all such expenditures, and boost profits anywhere from 50 percent to 100 percent.

"That," says Scott Cook, "is the advantage of owning the company. When you own the company, you take the long view."

In that long view, the payoff of the Intuit approach is far higher than the immediate cost. Quicken is likely to continue its utter domination of the market. Other products introduced by Intuit will be launched with a running start. Even now, fully one-third of Quicken customers say they bought the product because it was recommended by a friend. As they say in the trade, that's advertising money can't buy.

So is this: As I am working on this article, my friend Bruce stops by. "I hear you're writing about Intuit," he says. "I just bought its program, Quicken."

Bruce doesn't buy much software. A copy of Lotus 1-2-3 given to him by his sister-in-law sits on the shelf unopened. He uses his computer mostly for writing. But he bought Quicken because two different people urged him to. "You've got to get this program," they told him.

Now he has become an apostle himself. The reason: one day, while working on some financial records, he left the room. His two-and-a-half-year-old daughter, Emma, waltzed in and cheerfully turned off the computer. In panic, Bruce turned it back on and booted up Quicken. "Don't worry!" the screen cheerfully informed him. Quicken had saved all but the last little bits of data.

Somewhere, at some point, Scott Cook's engineers had put that capability and its comforting message into the program. Intuit, they knew, was depending on its customers to sell the product.

And customers, they knew, don't really want money-back guarantees or complaint forms or even 800 numbers. What they want is the product to be right.

Source: John Case, "Customer Service: The Last Word," *INC.*, April 1991, pp. 89–93.

INTUIT CORPORATION EPILOGUE

Intuit Inc.'s chairman plans to revolutionize the way people manage their finances. And he predicts the Justice Department won't stand in the way.

Speaking at a gathering of industry executives here, Scott Cook detailed his strategy to use Microsoft Corp.'s power and money to set up a new service that would give consumers more control over their finances.

Such a service would funnel information to personal computer users about potential investments, insurance policies, and retirement plans. With the right software, they could arrive at better decisions than they could by relying on advice from financial institutions biased toward their own products, Mr. Cook said.

Bringing Mr. Cook's plan to a global audience, however, hinges upon the Justice Department's evaluation of Microsoft's $1.5 billion acquisition offer for Intuit, a personal finance software company in Menlo Park, California.

Mr. Cook argued that the agency has no grounds to block the deal. "There is no legal case," he told reporters after his speech at the annual PC Forum conference. "They will approve it."

In the past, all actions to block mergers affected companies that were either competitors or suppliers, Mr. Cook maintained. Since Microsoft is spinning off its own personal-finance program to Novell Inc., neither relationship is applicable. He argued that legal precedents don't allow the Justice Department to file suit based on markets such as online services that companies may enter in the future, despite contrary theories advanced by rivals.

Nevertheless, Mr. Cook did say the Justice Department asked Intuit for papers that relate to online services, operating systems, and combinations of application programs, sometimes called suites.

The furor over the possible merger underscores the high stakes in electronic commerce. Much of the conference here focuses on obstacles to information-highway opportunities, including the difficulties of ensuring that transactions won't be attacked by hackers. Nonetheless, the possibilities have already inspired a flurry of alliances among major banks, communications companies, and software companies.

These giants are able to develop their own finance software for desktop computers or buy it from smaller companies, Mr. Cook said, and then give it away free as part of their service to customers. That trend will cause "a great transformation" in a business accustomed to getting paid for each program sold, he said.

Intuit and Microsoft won't be able to match banks' access to electronic payments systems or the trust placed in them by customers, Mr. Cook said. And such financial institutions will understandably try to control their customers' access to competing products, he predicted.

Mr. Cook wants to build, therefore, on customers' existing relationships with their financial institutions, while acting as a neutral broker to offer information about other products as well. Customers, for example, could compare the performance of thousands of mutual funds on their own PCs.

Desktop software to handle these functions would probably have to be given away, he said. Intuit and Microsoft would rely on some form of transaction fee as well as sell server software to manage such services, though Mr. Cook would not elaborate further.

His remarks follow a week in which Intuit was forced to apologize for technical bugs in its popular tax-preparation software. Mr. Cook said the company received 25,000 calls about the problem Friday; by Sunday, calls to Intuit's toll-free number had declined to 5,000. Only one-third to one-quarter of the consumers actually requested software to fix the problem, however.

Source: Don Clark, "Intuit's Cook Details Ambitious Plans to Change Way People Manage Money," *The Wall Street Journal,* March 7, 1995, p. B9. Reprinted by permission of *The Wall Street Journal,* © 1995 by Dow Jones & Company, Inc. All rights reserved worldwide.

CASE 5–4   Medco Containment Services Inc.

The Venetian blinds of the small, cramped room are drawn to keep out the sun. Still, sweat glazes Jack Diamond's brow as he paces between two desks, working a pair of telephones.

While holding on one call, he delivers a sales pitch on the other with a practiced urgency, then hangs up with a smile. "I just got a double," he proclaims to his bosses.

In a state renowned for its telemarketers, Mr. Diamond seems to be one of the best. But he isn't selling magazines or penny stocks. As a pharmacist employed by Merck & Co.'s newly acquired Medco Containment Services Inc., he is trying to persuade physicians to cancel prescriptions they have written for one drug and prescribe a drug he is promoting instead. The "double" he just scored was the switch of two prescriptions a doctor had written.

In call after call one recent afternoon, the bespectacled Mr. Diamond, clad in a white medical coat, talked nearly all of the doctors and nurses he contacted into changing their prescriptions to Medco-preferred drugs. Nine other pharmacists and assistants also work elbow-to-elbow in this tiny room, and among them they switch thousands of prescriptions each month.

That ability to directly influence physicians' prescribing decisions—and affect drug market share—is a big part of what Merck sought when it paid $6.6 billion last year for Medco. It is also a driving force behind the multi-billion-dollar scramble by other drug makers to acquire Medco's competitors. SmithKline Beecham PLC recently announced that it will buy United HealthCare Corp.'s Diversified Pharmaceutical Services for $2.3 billion. Pfizer Inc. plans to form close relationships with Value Health Inc. and Caremark International Inc. through strategic alliances. And Glaxo Holdings PLC is negotiating an alliance with McKesson Corp.'s PCS Health Systems Inc. subsidiary.

When Medco was independent, it developed the telemarketing and other tactics to control its customers' prescription drug costs by steering physicians to lower-cost branded and generic drugs. Almost overnight it disrupted the powerful and enormously profitable marketing link with physicians that drug companies like Merck had taken years to build. And by forcing drug companies to discount prices—or face losing market share to those that did—Medco and its competitors put enormous pressure on the industry's profits.

Now, with Medco under its control, Merck is turning that formerly damaging strategy to its advantage. While Merck's salespeople are still visiting physicians and leaving drug samples, the company has begun putting Medco's pharmacists to work, manning the telephones to sell Merck's products. Together, the combined Merck and Medco are revolutionizing the way pharmaceuticals are sold.

But the acquisition is controversial. Edward S. Curran, Jr., director of pharmacy at HMO Blue in Framingham, Massachusetts, a Medco customer, finds disturbing Merck's turning cost-control techniques into ways to sell pharmaceuticals. "It's putting the fox in charge of the henhouse," he says. Philip R. Alper, a Burlingame, California, physician, denigrates telemarketing pharmacists as "hucksters for the drug companies" and "totally unprofessional."

Regulators are beginning to scrutinize the drug companies' changing marketing strategies. The Food and Drug Administration is looking into the new marketing tactics to determine whether they violate laws on patient safety and disclosure. And now, the Health and Human Services Department has launched a criminal investigation of the Miles unit of Bayer AG over a program that paid pharmacists for counseling patients on use of a Miles drug.

"The market is changing radically, and delivery to this market is going to be very different in the future," says P. Roy Vagelos, Merck's chairman. Those new marketing tactics will be controversial, he concedes. But "that's always true of a new thing."

Merck-Medco will always offer the best medicines for the best patient health, combined with Medco's ability to contain drug costs, a spokesman said.

The acquisitions and alliances are controversial also because they give drug companies direct access to specific information about individual prescriptions through mail-order or claims-processing operations. Drug benefit management companies use such data to intervene in relationships among physicians, patients and pharmacists to influence drug selection and use. The patient information also gives drug companies a database to help them try to prove their drugs are more cost-effective than competing drugs or other treatments.

Some physicians complain the new marketing tactics by Medco and other managed-care institutions are coercive and disruptive. Glenn Littenberg, a Pasadena, California, internist, says he feels "badgered" by phone calls that interrupt his time with patients and that push him to use drugs that aren't his first choice.

Many retail pharmacists, already angry at Medco and its competitors for their low re-imbursement rates and, in some cases, for excluding them from health-plan networks, profoundly resent Merck for joining Medco's side. The NARD, an association of independent pharmacists, recently wrote Dr. Vagelos complaining that "Merck has increasingly initiated programs that will result in the demise of the independent retail pharmacist if not challenged." It added that it won't accept financial support from Merck anymore.

The new marketing tactics may be generating ill will, but they work. Medco's telemarketing pharmacists at its 11 facilities across the country expect to switch some 75,000 prescriptions a month, or nearly one million over the next year.

Merck just a few years ago resisted demands by managed-care organizations such as Medco to discount prices. But as managed care grew in size and power, Merck's salespeople weren't able to get into certain hospitals. And, even more disturbing, Merck drugs were excluded from institutions' formularies (lists of recommended drugs), Dr. Vagelos says.

How things have changed. Since taking over Medco, Merck has wasted no time in putting managed care to work for its own drugs. Medco is developing a program to put a package of Merck drugs into telemarketing and other switch programs, says Wayne T. Gattinella, Medco's marketing chief. The program will guarantee that the Merck drug is appropriate for the patient and that the health plan will pay less whenever a Merck drug is substituted for a competing product.

Merck drugs will soon benefit from handling such as Medco gives to the Upjohn Co. drug Colestid. Upjohn recently reformulated the anticholesterol drug, a powder that "tastes like Tang" when mixed with water, says Mr. Diamond.

Whenever a prescription for Bristol-Myers Squibb Co.'s competing drug Questran comes into Medco's huge mail-order facility here in Tampa, a computer redirects it to the telemarketing room. Mr. Diamond's assistants, Alice Smith and Vicki Knott, place a call to the prescribing physician's office, using techniques they have mastered for getting past receptionists. In a friendly voice, Ms. Smith tells the receptionist she is calling from a pharmacy, which is true, and she needs to talk to the doctor about a prescription he has written for a certain patient. (Physicians usually take a pharmacist's call concerning a prescription.)

When the doctor comes to the telephone, Ms. Smith waves to Mr. Diamond, who plugs into the call and, looking over Ms. Smith's shoulder, quickly scans the patient's computerized drug history. He tells the doctor that the patient's health plan has a cost-savings program and has asked whether the Questran prescription can be switched to Colestid. The flavor has been improved so the patient is more likely to take the drug regularly, he adds. "OK? Fine. Is that two times a day?" he asks.

Ms. Knott, sitting across the aisle from Ms. Smith, then signals Mr. Diamond to join another call in progress. In the course of an hour, Mr. Diamond completes the switch of 10 Questran prescriptions to Colestid, which could result in Colestid sales to those patients for years to come. Drug companies pay Medco rebates for switched prescriptions and other market-share increases. Medco shares those rebates with health plans. Moreover, telemarketing calls appear to predispose the physician to then prescribe the drug for other patients as well, says Mr. Gattinella, who is a former vice president of consumer marketing at MCI Communications Corp.

Medco has started a switch program for Merck drug Prilosec. In another Medco facility in Columbus, Ohio, pharmacist Claudia Ongaro sits at one of a roomful of small carrels, where she spends her day calling physicians about prescriptions that they have written for high doses of popular stomach medicines, an indication they are treating severe heartburn. During a call to a New Jersey gastroenterologist, she learns the patient also has an ulcer, and she concurs with the doctor's judgment that, in this case, Prilosec wouldn't be appropriate. But before hanging up, she still manages to get across that, when severe heartburn is the problem, the health plan recommends Prilosec because it is cheaper. The seed is planted.

Medco's telemarketing pharmacists are making obsolete Merck's 2,000 traditional foot soldiers, the detail men and women who make personal sales calls on physicians. Dennis Hansen, a pharmacist who oversees Medco's Tampa telemarketing operation, recalls his frustrating days as a detail man for Eli Lilly & Co. sitting in waiting rooms for hours to get maybe two minutes with doctors, he says.

Merck and Medco executives have assured the traditional Merck salespeople that they will still be needed to promote drugs. But it is clear that managed care's influence over prescription drugs is growing, and many Merck marketing employees have volunteered to move to the Medco operation to be part of the future action, Merck managers say.

Pharmacists who work the phones take a three-week telemarketing course and periodic refreshers. They also learn along the way to identify themselves as pharmacists, omitting mention of their connection with Medco unless they are specifically asked who employs them. That they happen to work for Medco is irrelevant, Medco managers say.

Medco soon will also pitch preferred drugs directly to patients when they call a toll-free number about their prescription order or when they have other questions, Mr. Gattinella says. The company gets 14 million patient calls each year, and every call is an opportunity to move prescriptions to preferred, lower-cost drugs.

And patients are encouraged to carry Medco's message to physicians. The company sends to patients a credit-card-sized pamphlet that identifies drugs to be avoided, suggests alternatives, and rates popular drugs by cost.

Medco is also giving retail pharmacists incentives to boost Merck's blood-pressure medication Prinivil over the competing product Zestril, sold by Zeneca Group PLC, which has its own incentive program. Under the Medco program, retail pharmacists can earn a rebate for increasing the share of prescriptions for Merck's products over Zeneca's.

(The drugs are identical. Indeed, Merck makes both of them, selling one as Prinivil and licensing the other to Zeneca, for a portion of the proceeds. Zeneca's version has a far larger share of the market.)

In addition, Medco pays pharmacists to counsel its health-plan patients about taking medicines properly—for example, the correct technique for using asthma inhalers. Such programs have won the endorsement of the American Pharmaceutical Association, a professional group. Lowell Anderson of St. Paul, Minnesota, a past president of the group, concedes that pharmacists could be seen as salespeople if they are in the pay of drug companies. But, he adds, "These are things we've been doing all along for free for the managed-care people. If someone wants it to be done, then we *should* be paid."

All the new marketing approaches are done under the banner of cost-containment. And many of the tactics are also used by managed-care organizations, including health-maintenance organizations. Clearly, the drug–benefit-management companies must demonstrate that they lower drug costs if they are to win business from health plans. But Medco is one of the most aggressive of the group, and it unabashedly claims its "proactive patient and physician communications" move the market share of preferred drugs. It always adds, however, that in all of its programs it will "always offer the best medicines" selected by an independent committee.

Besides pushing lower-cost branded products, Medco programs aggressively encourage substitution of generic drugs. Merck is developing a broad line of generics so that all of Medco's mail-order generic switches will go to its products by March 1995. Between 35 percent and 40 percent of the drugs Medco dispenses through its mail-order facility are generics, and the percentage is expected to rise as a number of big-selling branded drugs lose their 17-year patent protection.

All the prescribing pressure from Medco and other managed-care organizations makes some physicians yearn for the old days when all they had to contend with was detail men bearing free samples and other goodies. Dr. Alper says drug companies now compete with physicians for the authority to prescribe—and the companies have the advantage because "they have the leverage of manipulating the prices that the doctor doesn't have."

Employer health plans aren't opposed to the prescription switching programs so long as the physician has the final say, says Beth Ann Bird, a consultant at Hewitt Associates, which evaluates benefit management programs for employers.

Physicians can choose to ignore the pressure from Medco and other such organizations. In fact, Mr. Diamond's group usually fails to persuade about 40 percent of physicians called. But some doctors feel cowed. "At a certain point, you throw up your hands and say, 'Who am I to fight this?' " says Dr. Alper.

All the acquisitions and alliances, not just the Merck-Medco linkup, could backfire on the drug industry by creating credibility problems for the benefit management companies, says Alan L. Hillman, director of the center for health policy at the University of Pennsylvania. But, he adds, if Medco chooses to give Merck drugs preferential treatment and makes that strategy clear to its customers, "then caveat emptor."

Source: Elyse Tanouye, "Changing Minds: Owning Medco, Merck Takes Drug Marketing the Next Logical Step," *The Wall Street Journal,* May 31, 1994, pp. A1, A5. Reprinted by permission of *The Wall Street Journal,* © 1994 by Dow Jones & Company, Inc. All rights reserved worldwide.

PART
VI

COMPREHENSIVE CASES

Cases for Part VI

CASE 6–1   Coca-Cola (Japan) Company

It was October 1987. Arthur Grotz, brand manager, was pacing the floor in his Tokyo office. He was pondering whether he should recommend that Coca-Cola launch a ready-to-drink tea in Japan. Since 1981, four notable Japanese companies had entered the tea market. The decision needed to be made quickly and was critical to Grotz's career. For him it was "sink or swim." A success for Coca-Cola would mean career advancement; a failure could result in much more dire consequences.

Grotz's research and final suggestion would pass through many hands within the Coca-Cola company. Approval would have to come first from the president of Coca-Cola (Japan). Ultimate approval would come from corporate headquarters in Atlanta, Georgia (USA). Thus, the final decision would rest with Robert C. Goizueta, chairman of the Coca-Cola Company.

Grotz mused, "Should Coca-Cola enter the tea market in Japan?"

The Coca-Cola Company

The Coca-Cola empire was founded in 1886. This was the year that John C. Pemberton, an Atlanta, Georgia (USA) pharmacist, developed Coca-Cola, a carbonated soft drink. Following a strategy of national and international expansion, the company, by the late

This case was prepared by Laura Gow, MBA Student, under the supervision of Victoria L. Crittenden, associate professor of marketing, Boston College, as the basis for class discussion rather than to illustrate either effective or ineffective handling of a managerial situation. Information was derived from secondary sources. Pseudonyms are used.

1980s, was the world's largest producer and distributor of soft drink syrups and concentrates. The company's products were sold through bottlers, fountain wholesalers, and distributors in more than 155 countries. Soft drinks generated approximately 81 percent of operating revenues and 96 percent of operating income in 1987. Exhibit 1 provides summary revenue and income information from 1984 through 1987.

Japan

Japan, located in the Pacific Ocean, consists of four main islands covering 145,856 square miles: Honshu (mainland), Hokkaido, Kyushu, and Shikoku. It has a population of around 123 million, of which 75 percent are urban dwellers.

In the 1980s the Japanese economy had improved considerably and, consequently, more Japanese enjoyed a higher standard of living with an annual income of US$25,000. This led to a boom in consumer spending for both durable and nondurable goods. The yen had been appreciating in value from 1985 to 1987 (see Exhibit 2 for 1970–1987 yearly average yen–U.S. dollar exchange rates). Economists were positive about the future, but consumers were guarding their purse strings very carefully.

The 1980s' Japanese consumer was more concerned with health issues than ever before. This was due in part to an aging population interested in longevity and feeling well. Additionally, it was aided by a desire to be fit and trim. This health trend appeared to be continuing, and possibly gaining in popularity, into the late 1980s. Along with this consumer interest came a proliferation of nutritious food and beverage products.

Japanese Beverage Market.   The Japanese beverage industry was worth US$18 billion by 1987. The market consisted of the following segments:

Colas	10%
Other carbonated drinks	9%
Juices	26%
Teas	9%
Coffees	21%
Waters	16%
Sports drinks	9%

Japanese Tea Market.   Originating in the 15th and 16th centuries when leaders in China began to boil tea leaves in water, tea preparation traditionally has been considered an almost ceremonial event. The first canned tea (a green tea) was introduced in Japan in 1981. By this time, a canned oolong tea was already available in China.

The ready-to-drink tea segment was comprised of oolong (57 percent of the market), black (31 percent of the market), and green (12 percent of the market). From 1985 to 1987, oolong tea growth had averaged 42 percent annually and black tea growth had averaged 60 percent annually. Tea sold in cans (250 milliliters) for around ¥100 and also in larger PET containers (1,500 milliliters).

EXHIBIT 1   Total Operating Revenues and Income for Soft Drink Products

	Overall		International	
	Revenues (%)	*Income (%)*	*Revenues (%)*	*Income (%)*
1984	67	86	42	51
1985	67	86	42	50
1986	81	89	53	75
1987	81	96	55	74

Source: Coca Cola Company annual reports, 1984–1993.

Tea, along with other beverages, was sold through grocery stores, convenience stores, restaurants, and vending machines. Grocery stores had experienced an annual average growth rate of 5.1 percent by the middle 1980s (1985 grocery store sales of ¥4.8 million). Convenience stores had an annual average growth rate during this same period of 15.8 percent (1985 convenience store sales of ¥3.4 million). Vending machine sales, which accounted for approximately 50 percent of beverage sales, continued to grow. In fact, a well-placed machine was expected to sell about 10,000 cans of beverage per year, similar to a convenience store. Japan had about five million vending machines, with two million selling canned drinks. The average drink machine had 20 spots in 250 milliliter or 350 milliliter sizes.

In crowded urban areas, a consumer usually had a choice among many machines and alternative products. Aside from canned drinks, vending machines offered everything from flowers to comic books to lingerie. Companies competed not only on vending machine accessibility, but also on machine appearance and interactive capabilities—a talking or singing machine was not uncommon. A downside to vending machine distribution, however, was vandalism.

The Coca-Cola (Japan) Company

The Coca-Cola (Japan) Company Limited (CCJC) was established in Tokyo in 1957. Because trade regulations prohibited Coca-Cola from expanding to other Japanese locations, company executives focused their attention on making local connections, assessing the competitive environment, and gaining a solid understanding of Japanese culture. This information and knowledge provided a strong foundation for future growth. In 1961 when the Japanese government enacted trade deregulation policies, CCJC was ready to pursue expansion and unrestricted advertising.

A major part of CCJC's strategy was to form strategic alliances with powerful Japanese corporations. The three most notable partners were Mitsui, Mitsubishi, and Kikkoman. By forming strong relationships with these local bottlers, CCJC was able to reap immediate economies of scale and scope, as well as gain the Japanese consumer confidence and buy-in.

In the 1960s, Coca-Cola's sales in Japan soared, with revenues doubling every year, making Coca-Cola the best selling soft drink in Japan by 1965. By 1985, CCJC had solidified its dominance in the market, becoming the industry leader in improving quality

EXHIBIT 2 Yen–U.S. Dollar Exchange Rates (year average)

Year	Rate
1970	360
1975	297
1977	269
1980	227
1981	221
1982	249
1983	238
1984	238
1985	239
1986	169
1987	145

standards and introducing new products. To establish itself as an integral part of the Japanese lifestyle, CCJC actively promoted cultural, educational, and athletic activities.

CCJC Success. Two factors were thought to have contributed to the company's leadership position: (1) the company's direct marketing approach and (2) the company's distribution system of independent local franchisees. In addition to supplying bottlers with syrups and concentrates, the company provided support in distribution and the entire marketing effort—"from the TV set to the store shelf."

The Japanese market was divided into 17 regions which were serviced by 17 individual bottlers. See Exhibit 3 for a geographic view of the market and the company's bottlers. The direct sales concept (which was pioneered for Coca-Cola in its start-up operations in the United States) had encountered stiff resistance in Japan initially. Traditional Japanese business practices involved several wholesalers. However, the enthusiasm of the bottlers and strong sales of Coca-Cola eventually convinced local retailers of the benefits of the new system. A key element of the distribution system was that it generated activity in the local economy because CCJC's system established partnerships with local businesses. In principle, bottlers acted as independent corporations, sourcing their raw materials locally and completing all aspects of production on site. The CCJC unified this assembly of disparate players through a carefully crafted strategy of aggressively monitoring all regional operations, creating all market strategies, and initiating new-product development.

Although CCJC offered a variety of products (Exhibit 4), three products were Japan's favorites.

Hi-C. The Hi-C line of products with 50 percent fruit content was introduced in 1973. The product line opened the way for a new fruit juice drink market and, in the process, helped avert a crisis for Japanese citrus farmers. An overproduction of *mikan,* Japanese tangerines, had caused a serious problem for individual growers and agricultural co-

EXHIBIT 3 Individual Bottler Regions in Japan

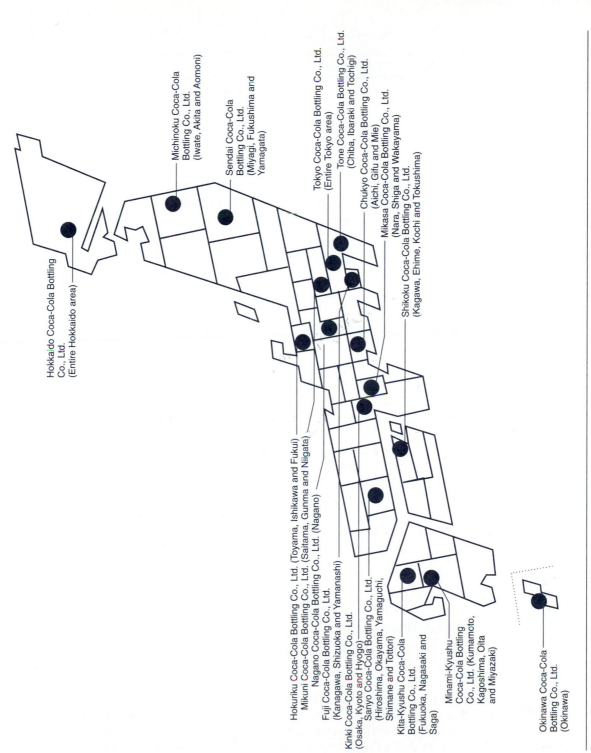

Michinoku Coca-Cola
Bottling Co., Ltd.
(Iwate, Akita and Aomoni)

Sendai Coca-Cola
Bottling Co., Ltd.
(Miyagi, Fukushima and
Yamagata)

Tokyo Coca-Cola Bottling Co., Ltd.
(Entire Tokyo area)

Tone Coca-Cola Bottling Co., Ltd.
(Chiba, Ibaraki and Tochigi)

Chukyo Coca-Cola Bottling Co., Ltd.
(Aichi, Gifu and Mie)

Mikasa Coca-Cola Bottling Co., Ltd.
(Nara, Shiga and Wakayama)

Shikoku Coca-Cola Bottling Co., Ltd.
(Kagawa, Ehime, Kochi and Tokushima)

Hokkaido Coca-Cola Bottling
Co., Ltd.
(Entire Hokkaido area)

Hokuriku Coca-Cola Bottling Co., Ltd. (Toyama, Ishikawa and Fukui)
Mikuni Coca-Cola Bottling Co., Ltd. (Saitama, Gunma and Niigata)
Nagano Coca-Cola Bottling Co., Ltd. (Nagano)
Fuji Coca-Cola Bottling Co., Ltd.
(Kanagawa, Shizuoka and Yamanashi)
Kinki Coca-Cola Bottling Co., Ltd.
(Osaka, Kyoto and Hyogo)
Sanyo Coca-Cola Bottling Co., Ltd.
(Hiroshima, Okayama, Yamaguchi,
Shimane and Tottori)
Kita-Kyushu Coca-Cola
Bottling Co., Ltd.
(Fukuoka, Nagasaki and
Saga)

Minami-Kyushu
Coca-Cola Bottling
Co., Ltd. (Kumamoto,
Kagoshima, Oita
and Miyazaki)

Okinawa Coca-Cola
Bottling Co., Ltd.
(Okinawa)

Source: Coca-Cola (Japan) Company, 1993.

EXHIBIT 4 CCJC Product Line

Coca-Cola
Coca-Cola Light
Fanta
Sprite
Hi-C
Aquarious
Ambassa Water
Georgia Coffee
Real Gold
Mello Yello

---

operatives. Coca-Cola had stepped in and bought the bumper crop for the production of its Hi-C products. This led to a lasting relationship between CCJC and the growers, as well as to the development of drinks tailored specifically to the tastes and preferences of the Japanese.

Georgia. In 1975, CCJC launched a ready-to-drink coffee, Georgia. The Georgia brand quickly became the leading brand in this very competitive market segment.

Aquarious. Soon after the 1983 introduction of the Aquarious line of isotonic drinks, it became as popular as Georgia and Hi-C. Touted as a health drink, it was ideal for replenishing fluid and electrolytes lost through perspiration.

CCJC commanded 90 percent of the cola market, slightly less than 60 percent of the noncola carbonated market, and approximately 10 percent of the remaining drink market. Coca-Cola beverage sales in Japan accounted for 21.5 percent of Coca-Cola worldwide profits, compared with 18 percent for the United States, with profit per gallon four times higher than in the United States. Gross sales in Japan were approximately US$195 million. CCJC owned and operated around 700,000 vending machines and distributed to approximately 1 million retail stores and food service outlets. See Exhibits 5 and 6 for selected financial information.

Competition

The soft drink industry was highly competitive with up to 1,000 new product introductions each year. Competitors included producers of other nationally and internationally advertised brands, as well as regional producers and private label suppliers. Other beverages competed with soft drinks. Advertising and sales promotional programs, the introduction of new packaging and new products, and brand and trademark development protection were important competitive factors. Ito En Ltd., Suntory Ltd., Kirin, and Hitachi Zosen Corp. were the leading competitors in the tea market.

EXHIBIT 5 Select Financial Data Summary of Operations (in US$ millions)

	1987	*1986*
Net operating revenues	$7,658	$6,977
Cost of goods sold	3,633	3,454
Gross profit	4,025	3,523
S, G, & A	2,665	2,446
Provisions for restructured operations and disinvestment	36	180
Operating income	1,324	897
Interest income	232	154
Interest expense	297	208
Equity income	113	152
Other income (deductions)—net	—	35
Gain on sale of stock by former subsidiaries	40	375
Income from continuing operations before income taxes	1,412	1,405
Income taxes	496	471
Income from continuing operations	$ 916	$ 934

Source: Coca-Cola annual reports, 1984–1993.

EXHIBIT 6 Net Operating Revenues and Operating Income (in US$ millions)

United States	*1987*	*1986*
Net operating revenues	$3,459.1	$3,277.9
Operating income	384.5	273.8
Latin America	*1987*	*1986*
Net operating revenues	$ 558.0	$ 555.5
Operating income	153.2	140.8
Europe & Africa	*1987*	*1986*
Net operating revenues	$1,709.5	$1,628.9
Operating income	508.1	354.6
Pacific & Canada	*1987*	*1986*
Net operating revenues	$1,917.0	$1,502.4
Operating income	453.3	352.4

Source: Coca-Cola annual reports, 1984–1993.

Ito En Ltd. was a leading Japanese tea leaf producer and wholesaler. The company initiated the canned tea boom in 1981 by marketing the first unsweetened tea in a can. In 1985, it introduced the first can of Japanese green tea, Ryokucha. Ito En spent months perfecting systems to manufacture and produce a canned Japanese tea that was free from oxidation and did not change color, taste, and aroma even when subjected to drastic temperature changes.

Suntory Ltd. was Japan's largest distiller. However, the company was gaining ground in its nonalcoholic divisions. In 1981, Suntory introduced a canned oolong tea called Tess. By 1987, Suntory held nearly 50 percent of the oolong tea market. Additionally, the company produced canned colas, green tea, and health tonics.

Kirin was the first to produce a canned black tea, called Afternoon Tea, in 1986. The fifth largest Japanese brewery, Kirin had 50 percent of the Japanese beer market. As well, the company was one of Japan's leading soft drink producers and marketers with canned soft drink sales of around US$1 billion. Kirin also produced fruit drinks, vitamin-enriched drinks, sports drinks, and coffee.

Hitachi Zosen Corp. was a "Big Five" shipbuilder in Japan that diversified into biotechnology and developed a new tea from the Chinese tochu tree. In 1987, it introduced this "healthy" unsweetened tea in cans and bottles. For centuries, the Chinese had used the bark of the tochu tree in herbal medicine to treat high blood pressure as well as liver and kidney ailments. The bark was also rich in calcium, iron, and magnesium.

The Tea Decision

In the early 1970s, a Japanese company first began marketing a canned ready-to-drink beverage that contained coffee, milk, sugar, and water. Served cold, it was considered a soft drink under Japanese food laws. For approximately 50 years, Coca-Cola had been looking into coffee-flavored technologies that would enable the canned coffee to be served hot or cold, depending on the season, from a vending machine. Despite the fact that the technology was available and a sales opportunity existed, seeing a sales opportunity in Japan, it took CCJC five years to arrive at the decision to enter the coffee market. It then took several years to capture a portion of the growing canned coffee market.

Would ready-to-drink tea, like coffee, be a success in the long term, or was it a passing fad? Would the Japanese truly embrace a canned version of their traditional beverage? For Arthur Grotz, this could make or break his career at Coca-Cola (Japan) Company. Should he recommend that Coca-Cola enter the ready-to-drink tea market? What were the pros and cons of this strategic move? He needed to present his recommendation to the vice president of marketing next week. What should he do?

SOURCES

Benjamin, Todd. "Ready-To-Drink Tea Catches On in Japan." *Cable News Network, Inc.,* October 13, 1992.

Beverage World. *Coke's First 100 Years.* Kentucky: Keller International Publishing Corporation, 1886.

"Breweries Beefing Up Soft Drinks Divisions." *Japan Economic Newswire,* March 8, 1991.

Casteel, Britt. "Japan's Taste for Canned Tea Growing." *The Daily Yomiuri,* January 6, 1991.

Coca-Cola Company. *Annual Reports, 1984–1993.*

———. *The Chronicle of Coca-Cola since 1886.*

Coca-Cola (Japan) Company, Limited. *The Coca-Cola Business in Japan.*

"Consumption of Upmarket Goods Booms in Japan." *Business Asia,* October 22, 1990.

"Drink Makers Read Tea Leaves, Discover Canned Teas Are Trend." *Nikkei Weekly,* August 29, 1994.

Fukui, Makiko. "At Your Convenience: 24-Hour Services Take Root in Urban Areas." *The Daily Yomiuri,* September 9, 1993.

Hideko, Taguchi. "Tea Reading." *Asia Inc.,* May 1994.

Hoover's Handbook of World Business. Kirin Brewery Company, Ltd. 1993.

"Japan: Canned Tea New Battleground in Japanese Food War." *Reuter News Service,* August 10, 1992.

"Japan: Canned Tea Sales Look Set to Rise Further." *Nikkei Weekly,* October 13, 1990.

"Japan: Green Tea Making Comeback in Cans." *Nikkei Weekly,* May 24, 1993.

"Japan: Marketing Weekly Spotlight on Marketing and Media Information." *Marketing Week,* April 11, 1991.

"Japan: Producers Banking on Strong Sales of Canned Coffee." *Nikkei Weekly,* September 21, 1992.

"Japan: Soft-Drink Makers Focus on Blended Tea in Push for Share." *Nikkei Weekly,* February 21, 1994.

"Japan: Sugar-Free Tea Enjoys Revival." *Marketing Week,* September 20, 1991.

Jean-Michel Bock, Vice President, Coca-Cola International, Pacific Group, P.O. Drawer 1734, Atlanta, GA 30301.

John Elwood, Assistant to President, Coca-Cola (Japan) Company, Limited, Shibuya P.O. Box 10, Tokyo 150 Japan.

Karassawa, Kazuo. "Canned Coffee Sales Regain Two-Digit Growth: Japanese Coffee Sales." *Tea & Coffee Trade Journal,* March 1991.

Kilburn, David. "Suntory Splashes in Softer Drinks." *Advertising Age,* March 25, 1991.

———. "Pepsi's Challenge: Double Japan Share." *Advertising Age,* December 10, 1990.

Killen, Patrick. "Business Talk: Coca-Cola Light Bubbles to No. 2 in Cola Market." *The Daily Yomiuri,* February 20, 1990.

———. "Coke Chief Sees Japan." *The Daily Yomiuri,* December 21, 1993.

Market Reports. "Japan—Health Foods." *1993 National Trade Data Bank,* October 15, 1993.

Mitari, Shin. "The Japanese Beverage Market." *Prepared Foods New Products Annual,* 1991.

Miyatake, Hisa. "Shipbuilder Berths in Tea Market and Sales Soar." *Japan Economic Newswire,* March 12, 1994.

Morris, Kathleen. "The Fizz Is Gone." *Financial World,* February 1, 1994.

Nomiyama, Chizu. "Fickle Public Makes Japan Soft Drinks Tough Market to Tap." *The Reuter Library Report,* January 29, 1991.

Pepper, Thomas; Merit Janow; and Jimmy Wheeler. *The Competition Dealing with Japan.* New York: Praeger, 1985.

"Rivals Thirst to Reduce Coca-Cola's Lead: Some Cautious, Others Bold—But All Challengers Are Still Far Behind." *The Japan Economic Journal,* April 27, 1991.

Stinchecum, Amanda. "The Where and Ware of Hagi." *The New York Times,* July 3, 1988.

Thomson, Robert. "Setting Out to Get the Coffee Market in the Can." *Financial Times,* December 10, 1990.

Tsukiji, Tatsuro. "Tea Brings in Wave of Beverage Market Profit." *The Japan Economic Journal,* January 19, 1991.

"Unsweetened Soft Drinks Soar on Health Fad." *Report from Japan, Inc.,* 1990.

Watters, Pat. *Coca-Cola.* New York: Doubleday, 1978.

CASE 6–2 Electro-Products Limited

Mr. Josef Novak, recently appointed manager of marketing and marketing analysis at Electro-Products Limited (EPL), is faced with a dilemma.[1] A number of marketing issues important to his firm have surfaced suddenly. Some of these issues relate directly to the role marketing needs to play in the future operations of the firm; others relate to the strategic question of survival. The issue that is most troublesome is EPL's relationship with a large European client.

EPL, located in a semirural area of Czechoslovakia, is a manufacturer of small home appliances. Currently, a significant portion of EPL's production is being exported under an exclusive agreement with a large European-based international electronics manufacturing and marketing firm (LIEM). Under this agreement, EPL is responsible for manufacturing handheld vacuum cleaners for LIEM. LIEM markets these products under its own brand name in Western markets. EPL has exclusive rights to market the products domestically under its own brand name ZETA.

The Czechoslovak economy is going through a major transition. A competitive domestic market is emerging. Domestic and foreign competitors are entering the market. Both EPL and LIEM have realized that the Czechoslovak market needs to be systematically reexamined in light of all the changes taking place. Not only is EPL looking for market opportunities in its own domestic market, but it is also concerned with survival in a rapidly changing economy—dealing with privatization, foreign ownership, and new consumer demand, among other strategic uncertainties.

Prior to the changes in Czechoslovakia that began in late 1989, LIEM had no interest in its internal market. Since the changes, however, LIEM is actively looking for market opportunities in EPL's domestic market. EPL's small marketing group is faced with several issues that may potentially evolve into major confrontations with LIEM.

This case was prepared by George Tesar, visiting professor, Uméa Business School, Uméa University, Uméa, Sweden, and Professor Marie Pribova, Czechoslovak Management Center, Celakovice, Czechoslovakia. At the time this case was written, Professor Tesar was on sabbatical leave from the University of Wisconsin, Whitewater.

[1]All names of individuals and firms, domestic or foreign, have been changed.

EPL realizes that its agreement with LIEM helps EPL understand product development efforts in the context of a large firm. It also helps EPL engineers comprehend the quality control requirements of Western markets. And, to a certain degree, the agreement assures EPL of future revenue. However, LIEM is a large international firm that views EPL as a captive supplier of a product whose attributes are set by LIEM's marketing personnel.

Mr. Novak would like to develop a cooperative relationship with LIEM. He is interested in working closely with LIEM's marketing personnel so that he and his staff can learn more about marketing practices in Western Europe. Mr. Novak is particularly curious about the entire product development process used by LIEM. He would like to know more about it. LIEM's management is not interested and is ignoring any such overtures from EPL.

EPL organized a small marketing group over two years ago. Until recently, this group did not play a significant role in EPL's strategic management. Under the current leadership of Mr. Novak, marketing concepts are slowly being recognized and accepted in the strategic development and growth of the firm. The marketing group is being asked to generate new opportunities for the entire firm. Plans and strategies are being developed as part of this new marketing effort.

The latest plans developed by the marketing group have three important objectives: (1) developing an effective and efficient domestic distribution and sales network for its products, (2) broadening its cooperation with foreign firms in areas of product development and cross-marketing arrangements, and (3) improving the overall image of its brand name ZETA in Western European markets.

According to Mr. Novak, these are realistic and strategically implementable objectives under normally operating market conditions. However, given the nature of the transitionary economy in Czechoslovakia today, these objectives present a complex combination of challenges, not only to the small marketing group, but also the entire firm.

Background Information

EPL has been manufacturing and exporting small home appliances since 1943. After the general nationalization in the late 1940s, it became the sole producer of small home appliances in Czechoslovakia, and since late 1989 it has been trying to become an important competitor in the international small home appliance industry.[2]

In the past, EPL produced a wide range of small home appliances and heating elements. Its current catalog lists the range of products available for domestic and export sales (Exhibit 1). However, before late 1989, approximately 43 percent of its total production was vacuum cleaners and 13 percent was steam and dry irons. These two product lines accounted for a total of 56 percent of EPL's production.

---

[2]EPL has a relatively long history among manufacturers in Czechoslovakia. Over the past 50 or more years its ownership has been in question. Between the late 1940s and November 1989 it held a monopoly on the manufacture of small home appliances and a variety of home and industrial electrical heating elements. EPL still makes most of these products; however, the overall contribution of these products to its operations and profits is not known.

EXHIBIT 1   List of Small Appliances Currently Produced by EPL

Blenders

Coffee grinders

Coffeemakers

Dry flat irons

Electric countertop units

Electric frying pans

Electric pans

Food mixers

Food processors

Hand-held food mixers

Heating elements (domestic use)

Heating elements (industrial use)

Plastic welding units

Portable electric plates

Portable grills

Portable space heaters

Roasting ovens

Steam irons

Vacuum cleaners

Warm air ventilators

EPL exported about one-quarter of its products to eastern and western European markets. Western European markets demanded higher quality and better-designed products from EPL. Quality was not an issue in eastern Europe due to general shortages of consumer products in these markets. Vacuum cleaners accounted for 68 percent of exports and dry irons for 24 percent; all remaining products produced by EPL accounted for only 8 percent (Exhibit 2).

The primary activity of EPL has been manufacturing vacuum cleaners. According to the marketing group, handheld vacuum cleaners represent the most lucrative and the most advanced product in EPL's product line. They believe that these products exemplify the level of quality found in most western European products intended for the demanding Western consumer.

From the overall perspective of EPL's management, the contract with LIEM enabled the technical and administrative staff of EPL to understand the dynamics of Western markets. It enabled EPL to raise its manufacturing standards to world-class production, and, consequently, EPL is in a better position to market its own products in world markets.

The marketing group, now under the leadership of Mr. Novak, was formed at the end of 1990. It is positioned too low in the organization to make any significant impact on top management's decision-making performance. Mr. Novak came to the group from

---

EXHIBIT 2 Production of Small Home Appliances and Domestic and Foreign Sales before 1989

		Sales		
Product Line	Production	Domestic	Foreign	Total
Vacuum cleaners	43%	32%	68%	100%
Steam and dry irons	13	76	24	100
Other	44	92	8	100
Total	100%			

Note: The above percentages are estimates only. Actual production figures are not available.

---

engineering; he was in charge of product design and development. Currently he and his group are developing promotional, retailing, and distribution strategies for EPL products in the domestic market.

Working with a Trading Company

In the past, EPL was represented exclusively by Alfa, a state-owned export trading company located in Prague. Alfa was responsible for all of EPL's exporting activities, including initiation of contacts, negotiation of sales agreements, and delivery of finished products. EPL's marketing personnel, or in the past the individuals responsible for product development and sales, had little or no direct contact with customers. Alfa was also responsible for all communications between EPL and its customers abroad.

This was not unusual prior to late 1989. State-owned export trading companies represented all Czechoslovak manufacturing firms and state-owned enterprises abroad. Management of many firms and enterprises had no direct contact with foreign customers or consumers. It was only in early 1990 that Czechoslovak firms and enterprises were free to conduct business abroad without the state-owned export trading companies. But even after these changes were made, the state-owned export trading companies retained important information about foreign contacts, clients, customers, and consumers. In other words, they withheld the export technology from the firms they had represented.

In some cases, the client firms were completely dependent on individuals within the export trading companies and could not operate without them. This dependency resulted from the structural inability to communicate with the outside world, lack of foreign language competency, and even the inability to travel to foreign markets.[3]

Consequently, EPL's top management, and the entire engineering, manufacturing, and purchasing staffs had little or no direct contact with their clients such as LIEM. They did not understand LIEM's consumers. Alfa served as a filter for all marketing and competitive information.

---

[3]Many of these situations were created by direct government policies. Individual manufacturing firms had no input into the creation or implementation of such policies.

EXHIBIT 3   Product Specifications for a Handheld Vacuum Cleaner

---

Dimensions and technical parameters
Physical design and color specifications
Number and type of models (economy, standard, and deluxe)
Purchase price of each model
Annual purchase schedule of each model for the next four years

---

The Agreement with LIEM

An agreement between EPL and LIEM to produce a new handheld vacuum cleaner was negotiated by Alfa during 1987. Before the November 1989 political changes in Czechoslovakia, LIEM had insisted that the agreement be kept secret. The agreement clearly defines the roles and responsibilities of each party. LIEM is responsible for the development of product specifications based on marketing information. The overall product specifications can be classified into several categories as shown in Exhibit 3.

These product specifications not only represent engineering specifications, but they also provide clear cost and expense guidelines. In other words, under this contract EPL became a captive fabricator and supplier of handheld vacuum cleaners to LIEM.

It was also agreed that during the engineering process, testing would be conducted by both parties separately. This included testing, verification, and documentation of each step in the engineering process. Any tooling, dies, or fixtures were subject to inspection and testing. The prototypes and products produced during pilot production runs would be subject to testing by both parties.

EPL was able to calculate the cost of engineering and manufacturing at the end of the pilot production of all models specified under the contract. It became apparent that EPL could not deliver any of the three models at the price specified by LIEM. After a series of negotiations, LIEM agreed to a price increase of 18 percent. At the same time the projected mix of models based on the original set of specifications was also changed as indicated in Exhibit 4.

An important factor in the arrangement between the two firms was the way in which the representatives of the two firms met to discuss important points during the engineering of the handheld vacuum cleaner. All meetings were scheduled by Alfa and were held five times during the product engineering process (Exhibit 5). Notes were taken during each meeting, the main points on which both sides agreed were recorded, new deadlines were set, and managers responsible for specific tasks were appointed.

EPL's representatives included the chief design engineer, the engineer directly responsible for the product, and the manager responsible for the pricing and delivery of the product. From the LIEM side the meetings were attended by the product manager, product designer, technical specialist, quality control specialist, and sales manager. Top management of EPL did not routinely meet with the product manager from LIEM, but held only informal discussions during trade fairs or industrial exhibitions.

Once the product-engineering process had been completed for the handheld vacuum cleaner, all the decisions regarding the production machinery, sourcing of raw material

---

EXHIBIT 4   The Original Purchase Schedule by LIEM Compared to the Final Purchase Schedule for 1991

	Model		
Purchase Schedule	Economy	Standard	Deluxe
Original	25%	55%	20%
Final	35	45	20

---

and components, and sourcing of packaging material were the responsibility of EPL. Product modifications during manufacturing were not allowed under the agreement. Only minor production changes, or changes that did not alter the cosmetic or functional characteristics of the product could be made without LIEM's approval.

Additional factors such as cosmetic modifications, including color changes, were incorporated into the engineering process as necessary. Color specifications were changed four times during the engineering process. Final performance and quality testing before commercialization was completed by LIEM. The final product was shown at two major exhibitions. Two months after the presentation of the product, the product was available for sale in retail outlets.

From the perspective of Mr. Novak, the agreement between EPL and LIEM has several problems:

1. EPL is not part of the marketing process managed by LIEM.
2. LIEM ignores requests by EPL for one or more of its managers to visit LIEM's operations.
3. EPL cannot communicate directly with LIEM due to the lack of language capabilities.

The language barrier presents the most important problem for EPL. Representatives from Alfa sit in on all meetings, including meetings that are strictly technical in nature, and serve as translators and interpreters. Recently, LIEM offered to work directly with EPL without involving Alfa, but EPL does not have marketing personnel with the language capabilities needed to conduct negotiations.

EPL's Marketing Perspective

The situation at EPL has been changing rapidly since late 1989. The marketing department wants to play a greater role in strategic management of the firm. According to Mr. Novak, EPL as a manufacturer has learned a great deal from cooperation with LIEM. EPL learned how to enter highly competitive foreign markets at the same time that its own domestic market is going through a major transition.

Cooperation with a large international firm that is consistently concerned about product quality in highly competitive markets offers an opportunity for EPL to learn what these markets demand so that in the future EPL can enter these markets on its own. From a marketing

---

EXHIBIT 5   Handheld Vacuum Cleaner: List of Individual Steps from the Time of Negotiations to Product Completion

Beginning of 1987	Negotiations between EPL and LIEM begin.
January 21, 1988	Product developed by LIEM.
March 15, 1988 Meeting	Product designed and engineering specifications completed by LIEM.
May 1, 1988 Meeting	Mutual agreement between EPL and LIEM on the final product design, engineering specifications, and cost structure.
August 1, 1988	Production of the first functional prototype by EPL.
November 1, 1988	Production of the final prototype by EPL.
December 1, 1988 Meeting	Testing and verification of the final prototype by LIEM.
February 1, 1989 Meeting	Product changes and modifications by EPL resulting from final prototype testing by LIEM.
February 1, 1990	Technical development and manufacturing engineering for mass production of the final product by EPL.
March 1, 1990	Delivery of manufactured products by EPL to LIEM for final testing and verifications. End of pilot production run for EPL.
May 1, 1990 Meeting	Testing completed by LIEM. Calculation of final costs by EPL completed.
July 1, 1990	Final product modifications completed by EPL.
October 1, 1990	LIEM's purchasing process begins.
December 1, 1990	Mass production begins by EPL.
January 15, 1991	First shipment left EPL's production facility.

---

perspective, this cooperation enables EPL, to a degree, to develop a fundamental understanding of the role marketing plays in the development and engineering of consumer products, and at the same time, realize how important quality standards are in competitive markets abroad.

EPL's management offered to cooperate with LIEM as part of the new marketing perspective. LIEM appears uninterested. The relationship with Alfa changed significantly after late 1989. Alfa's management established a new unit concerned only with export of EPL's products. Mr. Novak sees a strong potential for cooperation with this unit. EPL, with Alfa's assistance, also exports some of its vacuum cleaners to western Europe under brand names owned by various retail store chains.

LIEM is interested in entering the Czechoslovak market with its own brand name, even with products manufactured by EPL. The same products manufactured under LIEM's label and under EPL's label would compete side by side. EPL offered to represent LIEM in the Czechoslovak market, but LIEM declined the offer and opened offices for all its products in Prague and Bratislava. Recently, LIEM's unit dealing with small home appliances offered EPL the possibility to negotiate representation in the future.

As part of the new marketing effort at EPL, some of the marketing specialists suggest that perhaps EPL should improve the image of its own brand name ZETA and concentrate on sales and distribution of its own products in Western Europe.

EPL is at a crossroads for its manufacturing and marketing operations. It wants to become better known in its own domestic market. It also realizes that it needs to enter foreign markets to generate foreign capital for its operations. The agreement with LIEM is bothersome for EPL's marketing group. And, most significantly, EPL's business climate and the domestic market are progressing through rapid changes.

CASE 6–3   Wentworth Industrial Cleaning Supplies

Wentworth Industrial Cleaning Supplies (WICS), located in Lincoln, Nebraska, is experiencing a slowdown in growth; sales of all WICS products have leveled off far below the volume expected by management. Although total sales volume has increased for the industry, WICS's share of this growth has not kept pace. J. Randall Griffith, vice president of marketing, has been directed to determine what factors are stunting growth and to institute a program that will facilitate further expansion.

Company and Industry Background

WICS is a division of Wentworth International, competing in the janitorial maintenance chemical market. According to trade association estimates, the total market is roughly $2.5 billion in 1992. Exhibit 1 shows the nature of this market. Four segments comprise the institutional maintenance chemical market, which consists of approximately 2,000 manufacturers providing both national and private labels.

Total industry sales volume in dollars of janitorial supplies is approximately $1.3 billion. Exhibit 2 shows the breakdown by product type for the janitorial market. WICS addresses 75 percent of the market's product needs with a line of high-quality products. The composition of WICS's product line is as follows:

Special purpose cleaners	46%
Air fresheners	9
General purpose cleaners	16
Disinfectants	15
Other	14

The janitorial maintenance chemical market is highly fragmented; no one firm, including WICS, has more than 10 percent market share. Agate and Marshfield Chemical sell directly to the end-user, while Lynx, Lexington Labs, and WICS utilize a distributor network. Most of WICS's competitors utilize only one channel of distribution; only Organic Labs and Swanson sell both ways. Most private-label products move through distributors. Sanitary supply distributors (SSDs) deliver 65 percent of end-user dollars, while direct-to-end-user dollar sales are 35 percent (Exhibit 3).[1] The following shows the sales breakdown by target market by type of distribution:

Reprinted by permission from Gilbert A. Churchill, Jr., Neil M. Ford, and Orville C. Walker, Jr., *Sales Force Management,* 4th ed., Burr Ridge, IL: Richard D. Irwin, Inc., 1993, pp. 861–877.

[1]Includes paper supply distributors that carry janitorial supplies.

Distributor Sales	
Retail	20%
Industrial	18
Health care	18
Schools	11
Building supply contractors	10
Restaurants	3
Hotels	3
Other	17

Direct Sales	
Retail	47%
Building supply contractors	35
Health care	15
Hotels	2
Restaurants	1

Trade association data plus information from other sources estimate the number of SSDs to be between 5,000 and 6,000. The following shows the sales volume breakdown for the SSDs based on an average 5,500:

Size in Sales Volume	
Less than $100,000	1,210
$100,000–$500,000	2,475
$500,000–$1,000,000	1,375
More than $1,000,000	440
Total	5,500

According to a recent analysis of end-users, WICS provides cleaning supplies for approximately 20,000 customers. WICS's sales force is expected to call on these accounts as well as prospect for new business. These 20,000 end-users receive product from the SSDs who supply cleaning supplies manufactured by WICS and others as well. About one-third of the average SSD's total sales is accounted for by WICS's products. An exception is the paper supply distributor, where WICS's products account for an average of 10 percent of sales.

The typical SSD carries other related items. In fact, according to a survey conducted by an independent firm, SSDs almost always carry a private-label line of cleaning supplies plus one to two additional branded products besides the WICS line. This survey revealed that 60 percent of the SSDs carry a private-label line along with WICS and one other national brand. Forty percent carry two national labels and WICS and a private label. The private label may be a regional label or the SSD's own label.

WICS places almost total reliance on selling through the SSDs, although a small amount of sales (less than 10 percent) are made direct. WICS sells its janitorial

EXHIBIT 1   Institutional Maintenance Chemical Market

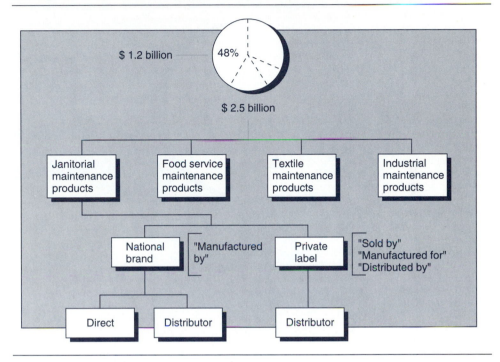

maintenance products through roughly 400 distributors, who in turn "see" 65 percent of the end-user dollar market. Thus, 65 percent of sales in the total janitorial maintenance market are made through SSDs (35 percent are direct sales); and the 400 SSDs used by WICS provided 65 percent coverage. The market seen by each distributor, referred to as his or her *window* on the market, is a function of the following:

Product lines carried (paper versus chemical).

Customer base (type and size).

Nature of business (specialization by market versus specialization by sales function).

The combination of these factors produces end-user market coverage of 42 percent (65 percent distributor sales × 65 percent coverage). WICS has very limited direct sales.

To reach its market, WICS uses a sales force of 135 area managers, 21 territory managers, and 4 regional managers (Exhibit 4). Regional managers are located in San Francisco, Denver, Chicago, and Boston. Although WICS is viewed as a giant in the industry, it does not produce a complete line of janitorial chemicals. Janitorial chemicals are rated based on their performance. WICS produces products that have average to premium performance ratings; WICS has no products in the economy class. Moreover, due to various factors, WICS's coverage in the average and premium classes is not complete. The emphasis on premium and average products results in providing only 75 percent of the market's product needs.

EXHIBIT 2   WICS "Served" Portion of the Janitorial Maintenance Chemical Market

---

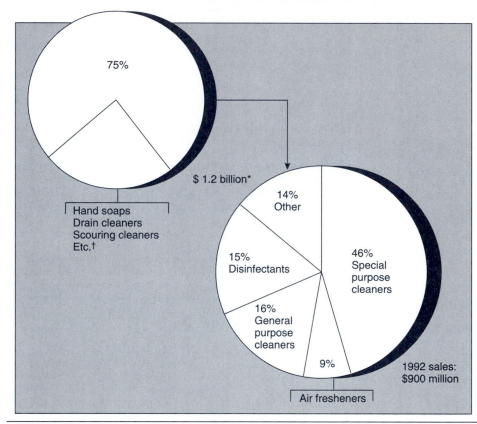

75%

Hand soaps
Drain cleaners
Scouring cleaners
Etc.†

$ 1.2 billion*

14%
Other

46%
Special
purpose
cleaners

15%
Disinfectants

16%
General
purpose
cleaners

9%

Air fresheners

1992 sales:
$900 million

---

* End-user dollars.
† Includes some general purpose cleaners and air fresheners that WICS does not manufacture.

To provide high distributor margins and extensive sales support, WICS charges premium prices. Recent estimates reveal that only 40 percent of the served market is willing to pay these premium prices. The impact of WICS's limited product line coupled with its premium prices is evident in Exhibit 5.

An overall description of WICS's marketing program shows that it has focused on market development. Distributors receive high margins (30 to 40 percent) and sales costs are high (10 to 15 percent) due to emphasis on selling technical benefits, demonstrations, and cold calls. Area managers call on prospective end-users to develop the market for the SSD. By comparison, WICS's competitors offer SSDs low margins (15 to 20 percent) and incur low sales costs (5 to 8 percent).

Griffith recently received a memo from Steve Shenken, WICS's national sales manager, reporting on a study of the effectiveness of SSDs. Territory managers evaluated

---

EXHIBIT 3   Janitorial Maintenance Chemical Market (end-user dollars)

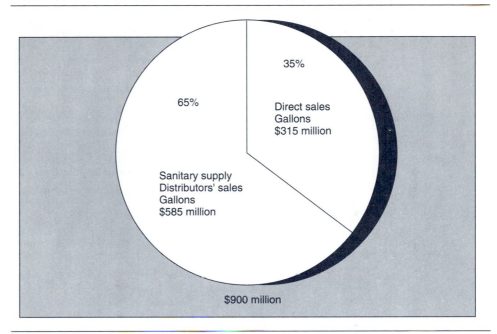

35%

65%

Direct sales
Gallons
$315 million

Sanitary supply
Distributors' sales
Gallons
$585 million

$900 million

---

each SSD in their respective regions on a basis of reach (advertising and promotional programs) and frequency of sales calls. The composite report indicated distributors as a whole were doing an excellent job servicing present accounts. In other words, 400 SSDs provide WICS with a sizable share of the market.

Area managers (AMs) represent WICS in distributor relations. The AMs' "prime focus is to sell and service existing key end-user accounts and selected new target accounts in their assigned territories." According to a recent study, maintenance of current accounts comprises approximately 80 percent of the AMs' time (Exhibit 6). In addition to handling old accounts, the AM makes cold calls on prospective distributors as directed by the territory manager. However, the number of cold calls made monthly has decreased substantially in the past year since the major SSDs now carry WICS products. A study of AM and SSD attitudes, conducted by MGH Associates, management consultants, is presented in Appendixes A and B. Some of the sales management staff question the use of AM time; however, there has been no indication that formal changes will be made in the future regarding sales force organization and directives. The AM job description has seen few revisions, if any, during the firm's past 10 years of rapid growth (Exhibit 7).

Area managers are compensated with a straight salary, enhanced periodically by various incentive programs and performance bonuses. Incentive programs generally require that AMs attain a certain sales level by a specified date. For example, the "Christmas Program" necessitated that AMs achieve fourth-quarter quotas by November 15; on completion of

---

EXHIBIT 4   WICS's Access to the Market

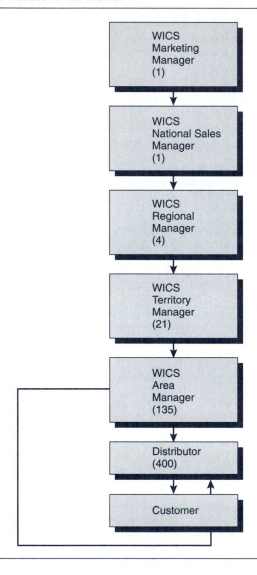

---

this objective, the AM received a gift of his or her choice, such as a color television. To date, management considers the Zone Glory Cup the most effective incentive program. The Glory Cup is an annual competition among areas within territories, which entails meeting or exceeding sales objectives by a specified date. An all-expense-paid vacation at a plush resort for area, territory, and regional managers and their "legal" spouses is the prize for the winning team. However, management at WICS believes that prestige is the prime motivator in this competition and the underlying reason for the program's success.

EXHIBIT 5   End-User Product Coverage

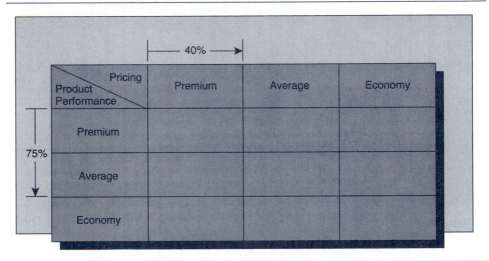

In a recent meeting, Terry Luther, executive vice president of the WICS division of Wentworth International, expressed his concern to Griffith about WICS's mediocre performance. Luther indicated corporate cash flow expectations from WICS were not being met and that a plan was needed from Griffith concerning how WICS could improve its overall operating performance. Griffith was quite aware that Wentworth International would make personnel changes to meet corporate objectives and that selling off divisions not able to meet corporate expectations was not unlikely. Griffith informed Luther that an action plan would be developed and be on his desk within 30 days.

Griffith's first step was to approve an earlier request made by Mike Toner, sales and distributor relations manager, for a study of sales force and distributor attitudes and opinions (Appendixes A and B). Next, the following memo was sent, discussing Griffith's assignment from Luther:

Intra-Office Memorandum

To: Steve Shenken, National Sales Manager
 Caitlin Smith, Manager—Sales Analysis
 Ryan Michaels, Manager—Sales Training
 Calla Hart, Manager—Special Sales Program
 Charlotte Webber, Senior Product Manager
 Mike Toner, Sales and Distributor Relations Manager

From: Randall Griffith, Vice President—Marketing

Subject: WICS Performance Review

 As you all know, our performance has not met corporate expectations. To rectify this situation, before we all lose our jobs, we need to meet to discuss ways for improving our market performance.
 At our next meeting, I want each of you to develop proposals for your areas of responsibility. These proposals need not be detailed at this time. For the moment, I am seeking ideas, not final solutions.

EXHIBIT 6   Allocation of Area Manager Duties*

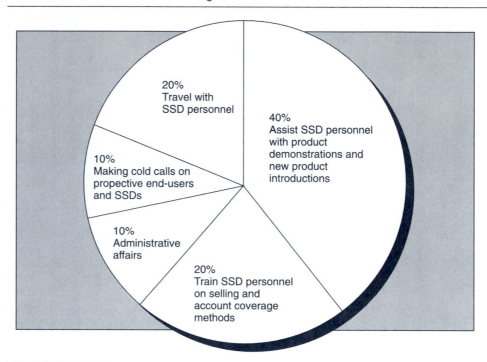

*Based on an analysis of call reports.

Staff reaction to Griffith's memo was one of frustration and anger. Several managers thought they had already complied with Griffith's request. One person commented, "I've told Randy numerous times what we need to do to turn the division around, and all he does is nod his head. Why go through this 'wheel-spinning' exercise again?" Another said, "The only time old J. R. listens to us is when the top brass leans on him for results." Despite staff reaction, the meeting would be held, and everybody would have suggestions for consideration.

To provide adequate time, Griffith scheduled an all-day meeting to be held at Wentworth's nearby lodge, located on Lake Woebegone. Griffith started the meeting by reviewing past performance. Next, he asked each manager to outline his or her proposal. First to speak was Steve Shenken, who indicated that Mike Toner would present a proposal combining both of their ideas. Shenken also said he would listen to all sales force proposals and try to combine the best parts into an overall plan.

Mike Toner's Proposal

Toner's proposal was rather basic. If improving market was WICS's objective, then more SSDs were needed in all territories. According to Toner:

Each area manager serves, on the average, four SSDs. Since we can only get so much business out of a SSD, then to increase sales we need more SSDs. I suggest that each area manager add

---

EXHIBIT 7 Wentworth Industrial Cleaning Supplies Position Description

---

Date: January 1, 1983	Position:	Area Manager, Maint. Prods.
Approved by: (1) _____	Incumbent:	135 Positions Nationally
(2) _____		
(3) _____	Division:	Janitorial Maintenance Products Division
		Reports to: Territory Manager, Janitorial Maintenance Products Division

POSITION PURPOSE:

To sell and service user accounts and authorized distributors in an assigned territory to assure that territory sales objectives are attained or exceeded.

DIMENSIONS:

Annual sales:	$300 M (average)
Number of distributors:	4 (average)
Number of distributor salesmen:	12 (average)
Annual expense budget:	$4.2 M (average)
Company assets controlled or affected:	$8 M (average)

NATURE AND SCOPE

This position reports to a territory manager, janitorial maintenance products. Each district is subdivided into sales territories that are either assigned to an individual member of the district or to a team effort, based on market and/or manpower requirements.

The janitorial maintenance products division is responsible for developing and marketing a broad line of chemical products for building maintenance purposes.

The incumbent's prime focus is to sell and service existing key user accounts and selected new target accounts in his assigned territory. He multiplies his personal sales results by spending a major portion of his time working with distributor sales personnel, selling WICS maintenance products and systems to key accounts such as commercial, industrial, institutional, governmental accounts, and contract cleaners. When working alone, he sells key user accounts through an authorized distributor as specified by the user customer.

The incumbent plans, schedules, and manages his selling time for maximum sales productivity. He interviews decision makers and/or people who influence the buying decision. He identifies and evaluates customer needs through careful observation, listening and questioning techniques to assure proper recommendations. He plans sales strategy to include long-term/quick-sell objectives and develops personalized user presentations to meet individual sales situations, utilizing product literature, manuals, spot demonstrations, and sales aids to reinforce presentations. This position sells systems of maintenance to major volume user accounts through the use of surveys and proposals, test programs, and other advanced sales techniques. He develops effective closing techniques for maximum sales effectiveness. This position trains custodial personnel in product usage techniques through the use of product demonstrations and/or audiovisual training to assure customer satisfaction. He follows up through the use of product demonstrations and/or audiovisual training to assure customer satisfaction. He follows up promptly on customer leads and inquiries. He services customer and distributor complaints or problems and provides technical support as required. On a predetermined frequency basis, he surveys and sells assigned local accounts currently being sold on national contract. He represents the division in local custodial clinics and trade shows as required. He maintains an adequate current supply of literature, forms, and samples and maintains assigned equipment and sales tools in a businesslike condition.

The incumbent is responsible for training, developing, and motivating distributor sales personnel. This is accomplished by frequent on-the-job training in areas of product knowledge, selling skills, and demonstration techniques. He sells distributor management and assists distributors to maintain an adequate and balanced inventory of the full product line. He introduces marketing plans and sells new products and sales promotions to distributor management. He participates in distributor sales meetings to launch new products or sales promotions, or for training and motivational purposes. He keeps abreast of pertinent competitive activities, product performance, new maintenance techniques, and other problems and opportunities in the territory. Periodically, he communicates Wentworth growth objectives versus distributor progress to distributor management (i.e., sales

---

EXHIBIT 7   *(concluded)*

---

coverage, volume and product sales, etc.). He assists the distributor to maintain a current and adequate supply of product literature, price lists, and sales aids.

The incumbent prepares daily sales reports, weekly reports, travel schedules, weekly expense reports, and the like, and maintains territory and customer records. He maintains close communication with his immediate supervisor concerning products, sales, distributor and shipping problems.

He controls travel and business expenses with economy and sound judgment. He handles and maintains assigned company equipment and territory records in a businesslike manner.

Major challenges to this position include maintaining established major users, selling prospective new target accounts, and strengthening distribution and sales coverage to attain or exceed sales objectives.

The incumbent operates within divisional policies, procedures, and objectives. He consults with his immediate supervisor for recommendations and/or approval concerning distributor additions or terminations, exceptions to approved selling procedures, and selling the headquarter's level of national or regional accounts.

Internally, he consults with the editing office concerning distributor shipments, credit, and so forth. Externally, he works closely with distributor personnel to increase sales and sales coverage and with user accounts to sell new or additional products.

The effectiveness of this position is measured by the ability of the incumbent to attain or exceed territory sales objectives.

This position requires an incumbent with an in-depth and professional knowledge of user account selling techniques, product line, and janitorial maintenance products distributors, and a minimum of supervision.

PRINCIPAL ACCOUNTABILITIES

1. Sell and service key user accounts to assure attainment of territory sales objectives.
2. Sell, train, develop, and motivate assigned distributors to assure attainment of product sales, distribution, and sales coverage objectives.
3. Plan, schedule, and manage personal selling efforts to assure maximum sales productivity.
4. Plan and develop professional sales techniques to assure maximum effectiveness.
5. Train custodial personnel in the use of Wentworth products and systems to assure customer satisfaction.
6. Maintain a close awareness of territory and market activities to keep the immediate supervisor abreast of problems and opportunities.
7. Perform administrative responsibilities to conduct an efficient territory operation.
8. Control travel and selling expenses to contribute toward profitable territory operation.

---

two more distributors. Of course, this move will require that we either add more area managers or that we hire and train a special group to call on new end-users and new distributors. It's difficult to attract new SSDs unless we show them a group of prospective end-users who are ready to buy WICS's products. Now, I have not made any estimates of how many more people are needed, but we do know that present AMs do not have enough time to adequately seek new business.

After Toner presented this proposal, Griffith asked if the existing AMs could not be motivated to apply more effort toward securing new business. Calla Hart thought the AMs could do more and that her proposal, if adopted, would alleviate the need for expansion of the AMs and SSDs.

Calla Hart's Proposal

As expected, Hart's proposal revolved around her extensive experience with WICS's incentive programs. This satisfactory experience led Calla to suggest the following:

If I thought that the AMs and the SSDs were working at full capacity, I would not propose more incentive programs. But they are not! We can motivate the AMs to secure more new business, and we can get more new business from our distributors. We all know that the SSDs are content to sit back and wait for the AMs to hand them new business. Well, let's make it worthwhile to the SSDs by including them in our incentive programs. For the AMs I suggest that we provide quarterly incentives much like our Christmas Program. AMs who achieve their quotas by the 15th of the second month of the quarter would receive a gift.

In addition, we need to develop a program for recognizing new end-user sales. Paying bonuses for obtaining new end-user accounts would be one approach. For example, let's reward the AM from each territory who secures the highest percentage increase in new end-user accounts. At the same time, we need to reward the distributor from each territory who achieves the highest percentage increase in new end-user sales dollars. And let's recognize these top producers each quarter and at year-end as well. Our incentive programs work. We know that, so let's expand their application to new sales.

Finally, on a different note, I support establishing quotas for our distributors. We have quotas for our sales force, and we enforce them. AMs who do not make quotas do not stay around very long. Why not the same procedures for some of our SSDs? We all know that there are some distributors who need to be replaced. Likewise, I have not made any cost estimates but feel that we are just searching for new ideas.

Griffith thanked Hart for her comments. He wondered whether applying more pressure to the distributors was the most suitable approach. He agreed with Hart that WICS's incentive programs seemed to be very popular but questioned if other techniques might not work. Griffith then asked Ryan Michaels for his comments.

Ryan Michaels's Proposal

During his short time with WICS, Michaels has gained respect as being very thorough and analytical. He is not willing to accept as evidence such comments as "We know it works" as a reason for doing something. Determining the value of sales training, Michaels's area of assignment, has caused him considerable concern. He knows it is useful, but how useful is the question he is trying to answer. According to Michaels, WICS needs to examine the basic selling duties of the area managers:

Before we recruit more AMs and SSDs, or try to motivate them to obtain more new business with incentive programs, we need to examine their job activities. I favor doing a job analysis of the area manager. Some evidence that I have seen indicates that job descriptions are outmoded. AMs do not perform the activities detailed in the job descriptions. For example, most AMs spend very little time calling on prospective end-users. Accompanying distributor sales reps on daily calls does not lead to new end-user business. Possibly the AMs could better spend their time doing new-account development work. But before we make any decisions concerning time allocation, we need to conduct a job analysis. And, while we are collecting data, let's ask the AMs what rewards are important to them. How do they value promotions, pay increases, recognition, and so forth? Maybe the AMs do not want more contests.

Griffith agreed that the job descriptions were out of date. He also contended this is typical and nothing to be concerned about in the short run. The idea of finding out what rewards AMs value intrigued Griffith. Next, Griffith asked Charlotte Webber for her reactions to WICS's market share problem.

Charlotte Webber's Proposal

Webber's proposal was more strategic in nature than the previous suggestions. Her experience as a product manager led her to consider product-oriented solutions and to suggest the following:

> I think we can increase market share and sales volume through the expansion of current lines and the addition of a full line of economy-based products. We can expand our present premium and average lines to cover 100 percent of the product class by adding air fresheners and general purpose cleaners. In addition we must introduce the economy-based products to counter competition.
>
> The proposed plan would not be costly because we could use our existing distributor network. If additional SSDs are necessary, we can select those in the $500,000 to $1,000,000 sales volume range. I feel that through these extensions and an increased number of SSDs we can address 75 percent of the SSD end-user dollars.

Griffith agreed that line extensions were a viable means of achieving some corporate goals. He expressed concern over entry into the low-quality segment of the market due to WICS's present customer perceptions of the company as a high-quality producer. Griffith turned to Caitlin Smith for additional suggestions on how to increase market share.

Caitlin Smith's Proposal

Smith's proposal came as no surprise to those attending the meeting. Her position in sales analysis made her critically aware of WICS's high cost of sales. It was only recently, however, that she developed a plan incorporating market share and cost of sales. Her views were accurate, but often given little weight due to her inexperience. According to Smith:

> Our cost of sales are currently running at 10 to 15 percent, while our competitors' costs average 5 to 8 percent. As many of you know I am in favor of changing the job description of the area manager and the sales presentation. These changes are necessary due to our products' stage in the life cycle and customer service level preferences. Recently I have become convinced that there is another means of reducing sales costs. By reducing prices we could increase sales volume and reduce the cost of sales. This strategy would also increase penetration and market share.

Griffith conceded that price reductions were a possibility but expressed concern over the possibility of weakening consumer perceptions of WICS as a high-quality manufacturer. He also questioned Smith's assumption that the industrial cleaning supplies industry was presently in the mature stage of the product life cycle.

Following these comments, Griffith thanked the participants for their input and adjourned the meeting. On retiring to his room, he reflected on the suggestions presented during the meeting and his own beliefs. He knew he must begin to formulate an action plan immediately since the 30-day deadline was drawing near.

APPENDIX A

Conclusions of Study of Area Manager Attitudes

MGH Associates, management consultants, was retained by WICS to investigate attitudes and opinions of field personnel and sanitary supply distributors. Initially, MGH conducted lengthy interviews with selected individuals, followed by the administration of a comprehensive question-naire. The results below identify role expectations and attitudes toward their reasonableness.

Territory Manager's Role Expectations

MGH Associates's interviews included territory managers because the territory manager is really the only management level contact the distributor has.

The territory manager interprets his or her role to be that of an overseer, to assure that WICS objectives are achieved, and that quotas are met.

The territory manager interprets his or her role to include:

- Training the area managers to
   Sell WICS products.
   Train and motivate the distributor sales force.
- Coordinating area manager activities with headquarters in Lincoln.
- Hiring and firing area managers.
- Striving for new product commitments from the distributors.
- Acting as "referee" for competition between distributors.
- "Building the book" for the adding or deleting of distributors.
- Submitting the "study" to the regional manager, who writes a proposal based on the territory manager's "study." It is submitted to corporate management where the final decision is made.

Area Manager's Role Expectations

The following is the area manager's view of the role he or she believes WICS management expects to be performed:

- Multiply sales effort through distributor's sales force (listed first because it was consistently mentioned first).
- Teach and motivate the distributor's sales force to sell WICS products.
- Introduce new products to the market through
   Direct calls on end-users.
   Distributors.
- Keep margins high to keep distributors happy. If they are happy, they will push WICS.
- Follow through on direct sales responsibilities.

- Collect information for management.
- Fulfill responsibilities relating to incentives.
  New gallon sales.
  Repeat gallon sales.
  Demonstrations.
  30, 35, 40? calls/week.
  Major account calls.
  Cold calls—"to develop business the distributor is reluctant to go after."

Area Manager's Role Problems

The area manager's perception of what management expects does not imply that the area manager feels that management's approach is working. In general, the sales force appears frustrated by a sales role they see as ineffective:

- A sales role that stresses:
  New gallon sales.
  Cold calls on end-users.
  Product demonstrations.
  New product introduction.
- "Checking the boxes" rather than being "creatively productive."
  15 demos.
  10 cold calls.
  5 distributor training sessions.
- Incentives stress selling techniques that may not be the most productive ways to sell. Emphasis is on new gallon sales over repeat gallon sales. Incentives weigh new gallons over repeat gallons (two to one).
  Emphasis to "demonstrate as often as possible" for the points. Demonstrate to show you are a "regular guy" who gets his or her hands dirty, not necessarily to show product benefits.
- Bonus incentives appear to be a "carrot" only for those who don't regularly make bonus, that is, "hit 106 for maximum bonus and minimum quota increase."
- The sales role gives the area manager little ability to impact his or her own success to
  Change distribution.
  Move distributor outside his or her window.
- The area manager describes his or her role as:
  A "lackey."
  A "chauffeur."
  A "caretaker of old business."

Area Manager's Role: Making Cold Calls

One of the causes of area manager frustration is the general ineffectiveness of their cold calls sales role:

- The area manager makes cold calls on end-users not presently sold by the WICS distributor, with the difficult objective of moving these accounts to the WICS distributor.
- If the area manager succeeds in moving this account over to WICS products, chances are small that the distributor will keep the business. Without a major portion of the account's

total purchases, the distributor cannot afford to continue to call on the account.
Distributor sales rep is on commission.
After five calls, will stop calling if purchases have not begun to increase.

- The distributor that lost the account will try extremely hard to get back the business. This may mean giving the product away to keep control of the account—maintain majority of the account's purchases. Past experience indicates it is very difficult to move distributors outside their "window."

APPENDIX B

Conclusions of Study of WICS Sanitary Supply Distributor Attitudes

WICS DISTRIBUTOR'S ROLE EXPECTATIONS

The following is the WICS distributor's role as outlined by WICS management and sales force.

- Act as an extension of the WICS sales force.
- Push and promote WICS product line in a *specified area.*
  Sell WICS over other brands.
  Always sell the premium benefits of WICS products to the end-user, instead of distributor's private label.
  Be aware that the WICS line could be lost if private label sales grow too large.
- Actively market new WICS products.

Distributor's Role Problems

Distributors have been angered by WICS's attempt to run their businesses ("WICS is trying to tell me what to do").

- WICS makes demands—"uses pressure tactics."
  Distributors say they are told "our way or no way."
  Distributors feel they are forced to carry products they don't want.
  High minimum buy-ins.
  "Won't see area manager if we don't carry the new product."
  Distributors say WICS management doesn't "realize we make
  our living selling all our products—not just WICS."
- Communication is poor with WICS management.
  One way—"Our opinions never reach Lincoln."
- "WICS uses the distributor as a testing ground for new products."
  Distributor is not told what to expect.
  After 14-week blitz, "You never hear about the product again."
  The distributor sales force is not trained to sell to, and cannot afford to call on, certain segments of the market.

- Growth takes the distributor into new geographical market areas, and WICS may elect not to go/grow with the distributor.
  New branch in different city.
  Growth may take distributor sales personnel out of area manager's district.
  Receives no support from WICS.
  Worst case—distributor sales rep's territory is completely outside district.
  No WICS representative at any accounts.
  Prefer to sell other than WICS.

- WICS does not realize that a distributor's total business extends beyond "its own backyard" in many markets.

Distributor's Role Selling Costs

Distributors have shown concern over the high cost of selling WICS products. Sales costs are approximately 45 percent of the total operating costs.

- "WICS products are basically no better than anyone else's."

- Yet WICS asks distributors to switch competitor's accounts over to WICS products.
  Price advantage is very rare.
  A problem must exist.
  A demonstration is required.

- All these make the "problem-solving" sale time-consuming and costly.

- Result: When WICS product is sold, it is easy for competitive WICS distributors to cut price to try to get the business.
  They have very low sales costs.

- Required action: Original distributor must cut margin to keep the business.
  This frustrates distributor salespeople.
  Causes them to sell private label.

CASE 6–4   Rollerblade, Inc.

 Mary Horwath, vice president of marketing services at Rollerblade, Inc., summarized Rollerblade's success as a function of introducing a product along with the simultaneous creation of a sport. As the No. 1 leader in in-line skate sales in the 1990s, however, Horwath cringed when she heard people say that they were going "Rollerblading" on non-Rollerblade skates.

With at least 30 competitors in the in-line skate market, Rollerblade had to begin focusing on brand recognition for Rollerblade skates. One of Horwath's major objectives was to make the Rollerblade skate distinct from the competition's products, all the while keeping "Rollerblade" from becoming a generic household term as in what happened to

This case was prepared by Victoria L. Crittenden, associate professor of marketing at Boston College, as the basis for class discussion rather than to illustrate either effective or ineffective handling of a managerial situation. Research assistance was provided by Jennifer Fraser, MBA student, Boston College. All material was from secondary sources.

brands such as Aspirin, Thermos, Yo-Yo, Shredded Wheat, and Lanolin. Building brand recognition in a market that could reach $1 billion by the late 1990s was critical for Rollerblade, Inc.

The Company

As a 19-year-old goaltender for a minor league hockey team, Scott Olson divined a simple idea which soon led him to multimillionaire status. The simple idea was ice skates that worked without ice.

In 1979, Olson came across a pair of roller skates where the wheels were arranged in a single row rather than two-by-two. This "in-line" skate originated in the Netherlands in the 1700s and was said to be the first roller skate.[1] Although slow and clumsy, the skate provided the feel of skating on ice. As a hockey player himself, Olson knew that a skate targeted toward hockey players that could simulate the feel of ice skating, but allow the hockey player to perform off the ice and during the off-season, had outstanding potential.

After locating the manufacturer of the in-line skate and buying up back stock (the manufacturer had quit making the skate by then), Olson proceeded to refine the skate (via good skate boots and better wheels for a faster, smoother ride) and began building them in his basement. In 1983, Olson's company, Rollerblade, Inc., based in Minnesota, became the only manufacturer of in-line skates. Olson soon sold most of his holdings in Rollerblade, Inc., to Robert O. Naegele, Jr., and in 1985, Olson left Rollerblade after a business dispute.[2]

The success of the company continued through the late 1980s and into the 1990s with Rollerblade, Inc., maintaining its No. 1 position in a growing market which was experiencing increased competitive activity. In 1991, Rollerblade, Inc., embarked on a partnership with Nordica Sportsystem (Italy). Nordica, a division of Edizione Holding (controlled by the Benetton family) and the world's No. 1 ski boot maker, purchased 50 percent of Rollerblade, Inc., for an undisclosed sum.[3] Edizione Holding's product lines, under the Benetton Sportsystem umbrella, also included Prince tennis rackets, Asolo mountain boots, and Kastle Skis.

In-Line Skating

By 1990, sales of in-line skates were around $120 million, with Rollerblade capturing approximately 70 percent of the market. By 1993, the in-line skate market had become a $300 million industry with Rollerblade still the market leader, accounting for 60 percent

---

[1]In-line skating was a fad in the 1860s.

[2]Olson introduced Switch-It skates in 1985. These skates had interchangeable ice and in-line blades. Fifty percent of this business was sold in 1990 and Olson went on to start two more new businesses. Nuskate Inc. focused on a product that married in-line skates to a cross-country ski track exerciser. O.S. Designs sold other of Olson's sporting goods designs, such as a lightweight golf bag with wheels and built-in pull handle.

[3]Both Nordica ski boots and Rollerblade in-line skates were made from the same basic plastic composite material. Machines at the Nordica production plant in Italy could switch easily between components for the ski boot and the Rollerblade skate shell. Plans were for up to 50 percent of Rollerblade production to take place at Nordica plants. In the United States, Rollerblade operated out of its Minnesota facility and Nordica out of its Vermont facility.

EXHIBIT 1   Wholesale Shipments of Sports/Recreation Equipment Percentage of
Growth Estimates (1988–1991) and 1991 Wholesale Market Size

Category	Percentage of Growth 1988–1991	Market Size (wholesale) 1991*
In-line/roller skates	184%	$ 185
Volleyball	63	75
Billiards	38	156
Exercise	36	1,155
Camping	33	1,065
Ice/hockey skates	32	113
Tennis	26	328
Archery	24	210
Basketball	23	117
Golf	21	1,400

*In millions of dollars.

Source: Glen Macnow, "New Ideas Get a Sporting Chance," *Nation's Business,* December 1992, pp. 62–63.

---

of the market. Estimates were that in-line skates were used by over 3.5 million people (primarily in the United States). Worldwide, in-line skate sales were projected to peak around $1 billion by 1998.

By 1993, there were an estimated 30 competitors in the in-line skate market. Rollerblade held about 60 percent of the market, with First Team Sports, Inc., ranking second with 20 percent of the market. While the remainder of the market consisted of knockoff versions, Bauer Precision In-Line Skates was considered a possible No. 3 in the market. Olson's Switch-It skate (owned by Innovative Sport Systems, Inc.) was a rival, as was Fisher-Price with its size-adjustable kids' skates. Taiwanese knockoffs were capturing a large percentage of the low end of the market. The basic in-line skate was not difficult to copy. Rollerskate, ice skate, and/or boot manufacturers generally possessed the capabilities to manufacture some form of in-line skate.

Sports/Recreation Market.   Around 5,000 new sports and recreation products entered the market annually. Annual sales in this market totaled around $31 billion. The U.S. economy during the early 1990s was said to be the cause of a downturn in sales of high-cost sports equipment for skiing and boating. However, this same downturn led to fast growth in areas such as camping, tennis, and all types of personal fitness products.

While not the most prominent outdoor sport activity at the beginning of the 1990s, one survey placed in-line skating second only to family camping in terms of growth expectations for the first half of 1990. In-line skating had become prominent enough to have its own industry association, the International In-Line Skate Association. Skating (both in-line and roller) experienced the largest percentage of growth in wholesale shipments of sports/recreation equipment from 1988 to 1991. Exhibit 1 provides percentage-of-growth estimates for the sport/recreation equipment marketplace during this time period.

The marketing effort for many new sports and recreation products began, traditionally, in February of each year at the Super Show in Atlanta, Georgia. The show was a convention of around 90,000 buyers and sellers of sports and recreation equipment. Held in a garage sale environment, the New Products Show took up an entire convention hall at the Super Show. In a typical year, around 2,000 new products were introduced at the New Products Show.

Rollerblade's Marketing Strategy

Mary Horwath joined Rollerblade, Inc., in 1987 as director of promotion. At that time, the company had 16 employees, annual sales of less than $3 million, and hockey players as customers. Horwath's challenge was to grow the company. To do this, she had to reposition the skate in order to attract a wider range of customers—with a marketing plan budget of $200,000.

Initial Marketing Strategy.   Horwath relied on "guerrilla marketing" tactics to reposition Rollerblade products. Horwath described these tactics as aggressive, unorthodox methods which were fairly cheap but attracted positive publicity quickly. She determined the primary U.S. market for Rollerblade skates to be 46 million active adults, primarily between the ages of 18 and 35 years.

To get people talking about Rollerblade skates, Horwath gave the product to high-profile people such as cyclists, skiers, runners, walkers, football players, surfers, ice skaters, journalists, and celebrities. The publicity generated by these giveaways was worth about $250,000 in advertising. Many of the people were seen on television or in magazines wearing their Rollerblades.

The next step involved cross-promotional tie-ins with other companies targeting the same audience. A joint promotion sweepstakes in 1987 with General Mills' Golden Graham cereal resulted in Rollerblade giving away 1,000 pairs of skates in return for Rollerblade products displayed on 6 million cereal boxes. Also in 1987, Rollerblade skates were included in a feature-length film on action sports sponsored by Swatch. The film appeared on 40 college campuses across the United States. Rollerblade had to pay for additional filming and sponsorship rights only. Free exposure also occurred when Procter & Gamble and Pepsi featured Rollerblade skates in commercials.

Horwath then redesigned Rollerblade's packages and displays to better depict the company's mission of "fun." Also, she created videos for in-store displays. Twelve demonstration vans were then sent to community events targeting sports-minded people (such as the Los Angeles Marathon) to let people try the skates for free.

Finally, Horwath created Team Rollerblade. Team Rollerblade was a group of elite demonstration skaters who traveled around the United States appearing at top sporting events. The Team displayed the sporty, exciting, healthy, and fun components of in-line skating. Early on, the Team performed at the Super Bowl half-time and the opening ceremonies of the Winter Olympics in France.

The guerrilla marketing strategy worked better than expected. Rollerblade's sales skyrocketed between 1989 and 1991 (from less than $20 million to just under $90 million), and the in-line skate market expanded dramatically. Additionally, Rollerblade skates received "product of the year" status from both *Time* and *Fortune* in 1990.

In sum, Horwath's "Cheap Skate Strategies" focused upon four points:[4]

1. Give your product away to celebrities and athletes who attract media attention.

2. Team up with other companies to promote your product, but make sure the product you're affiliated with is used by the people you want to reach.

3. Demonstrate the product in places or at events where your prime target audience gathers.

4. Create related projects, like teams, books, and videos—anything that will catch consumers' eyes.

Product Line.   Rollerblade's products were positioned in the higher-price segment of the market. Rollerblade's prices ranged from $100 to $400 and were not available through mass merchandising stores such as Woolworths, Ames, Target, or Wal-Mart. Rollerblade's strategy was to distribute their products through sports stores and in-line skating specialty stores.

While Horwath described Rollerblade's target market as the 46 million active adults between 18 and 35 years of age, she recognized diversity in this large group. Different market segments were defined based upon use: street hockey, exercise, transportation, racing, complex acrobatics, and fun.

Examples of in-line designs targeted toward specific use segments included the *Metroblade* for transportation, the *Problade* for racing, the *Mondoblade* for the first-time skater, and the *Microblade* for kids.

Rollerblade also offered in-line skate apparel called *Bladegear* and a complete line of skating accessories such as kneepads, wristguards, and helmets. As well, Rollerblade spearheaded in-line skating safety campaigns, including the use of proper equipment.[5]

Rollerblade's Marketing Strategy, 1991–1993.   Rollerblade's guerrilla marketing strategy led it to success both in creating the in-line skate market and in attaining the No. 1 spot in the market. After such a successful start, the company did not want to veer too far from the strategy. However, the rapid growth market of the 1990s was bringing in many new competitors and if and when there was an industry shakeout, Howarth wanted Rollerblade to come out on top. Therefore, Rollerblade's marketing plan maintained many of the guerrilla tactics that had helped Rollerblade get to its 1991 No. 1 position, while adding tactics that could help the company battle competitors directly and create brand recognition for Rollerblade skates.

Partnering became a prominent theme of Rollerblade's marketing strategy during the 1990s. Rollerblade and Procter & Gamble's Sunny Delight juice drink joined together for a joint communications campaign. There were coupon tie-ins and television spot-airings on MTV. Rollerblade teamed with Coca-Cola Foods' Hi-C to co-sponsor a 10-city "Rollerblade America Tour," which featured in-line skating races and demonstrations. Hi-C's input into the co-sponsorship included extensive on-site signage and sampling. Mattel launched a Rollerblade Barbie and Friends line. The Rollerblade trademark

---

[4]Found in " 'How I Did It'—Guerrilla Marketing 101," *Working Woman,* December 1991, pp. 23–24.
[5]In-line skates can reach speeds as high as 30 miles per hour.

appeared on the box, with Rollerblade coupons inside. Tie-ins for 1993 and 1994 were expected with Northwest Airlines and Warner Brothers. Since safety was such an important issue with in-line skating, Rollerblade expected its long-term relationship with Benetton to prove beneficial in its expansion into accessories such as kneepads.

By 1991, Rollerblade had expanded into a little conventional print advertising. One ad featured a skater rolling down a mountain highway. The caption read, "It's kinda like running a marathon. It's kinda like eating a hot-fudge sundae. Rollerblade." In 1992, measured media spending was just under $1 million. By 1993, the company was planning its first-ever television commercial which would be provided to its distributors for use in local markets. The 30-second spot was filmed in New Zealand. It depicted an in-line skater passing a carriage transporting an Amish girl. The skater and the girl exchanged glances before a voice-over said, "There are but a few ways to separate yourself from this hectic world. Rollerblade—let yourself go."

Team Rollerblade, featuring 25 skaters in black and neon-colored attire, was also an important element of the marketing strategy in the 1990s. The Team traveled, annually, around the United States performing stunts and skate dancing at festivals, theme parks, fairs, college campuses, and playgrounds. The tours were called "Rock 'N' Rollerblade Tours."

Rollerblade's most popular skates retailed for $139 to $199. However, in an effort to combat competition at the low end, Rollerblade was planning to introduce the *Blade-Runner* family of in-line skates. These skates would be available at mass merchandisers for under $100.

Trying to position Rollerblade as a lifestyle, rather than just a product, Rollerblade planned to continue offering its *Bladegear* line of sportswear. The line included bright-colored lycra and nylon ensembles and T-shirts. The T-shirts were emblazoned with helpful hints such as "Skate Smart" and "Don't Skate Naked." There were plans to open Rollerblade boutiques in some sporting goods stores around the United States.

A Competitor on the Move

First Team Sports, Inc., was founded in 1985 by golfing partners John Egart and David Soderquist. Both Egart and Soderquist were sales representatives in Minnesota for internationally based firms. Egart sold shoes and equipment for Adidas (a German company). Soderquist sold hockey skates for Amer Sport (a Finnish company).

Egart and Soderquist's interactions with sporting goods buyers led them to discover that in-line skating was a sport with a future and that Rollerblade, Inc., was falling behind in deliveries as well as raising prices arbitrarily (at least from the buyer's perspective). After taking out second mortgages on their homes, raising $380,000 in start-up capital, and enlisting a Taiwanese manufacturer to make their Ultra-Wheel skate, the two friends started First Team Sports, Inc.

Sales of the Ultra-Wheels line began in early 1986. The company, however, had a stormy start. By the beginning of 1987, the company lost about $20,000 monthly on sales of $65,000. In October 1987, 70 percent of First Team Sports was sold to the public for $2.6 million. Interactions surrounding the sale eventually led to a proxy fight which could have ousted Egart and Soderquist. Spending $60,000 in legal fees and five months, the two owners finally won the battle and began promoting the Ultra-Wheels line intensely.

The company sold a full-line of Ultra-Wheels in-line skates through mass retailers such as Dayton-Hudson's Target Stores. Prices of $79 to $349 were just below price points for similar Rollerblade models. While catering to all levels of in-line skaters, Ultra-Wheels aggressively pursued the street hockey market with its Street King line of skates, sticks, and related equipment. First Team Sports signed Wayne Gretzky, a hockey "great" with the Los Angeles Kings, to endorse the Ultra-Wheels line.[6] By 1992, hockey star Bret Hull and Olympic figure skating gold medalist Katerina Witt had accepted endorsement deals as well.

By mid-1993, the company had negotiated deals with distributors in Europe and Asia to sell the company's in-line skates internationally. The company's goal was to be in every continent by 1998.

In 1993, First Team Sports, Inc., captured the No. 2 market position behind Rollerblade, Inc., with 20 percent of the U.S. market. Fiscal 1993 sales were $38.2 million, with profits of $3 million. First Team Sports was number 15 on *Business Week*'s 1993 Hot Growth List. The company expected to grow 25 percent annually through the late 1990s.

The Future

With the in-line skate market expected to peak by 1998, Rollerblade, Inc., knew that it needed (1) to build brand recognition for the Rollerblade name and (2) to continue expanding its product offerings. Horwath wondered, too, if now was the time for Rollerblade to begin a shift away from the company's traditional "pull" strategy to more of a "push" approach.

Random House Webster's College Dictionary had plans to include Rollerblade as a word in its next edition. While the name would be recognized as a trademark with the first letter in uppercase, there was still uncertainty as to whether the verb form (rollerblading) and the shorter form (blading) would be included and, if so, whether they would be listed as trademarks. Horwath knew that loss of the Rollerblade name to the dreaded "genericide" would be horrible for the company.[7]

With concerns about market saturation, Rollerblade needed to expand its product offerings to encompass the total skater and to increase the number of new participants. The youth and roller hockey markets seemed to hold promise. The pending merger of the World Roller Hockey League and Roller Hockey International could help the sport attain increased television coverage.

Yet another fear lodged itself in the back of Horwath's head. Rollerblade, Inc., and other in-line skate manufacturers had stolen the roller skate cash cow. Was there a new technology that could preempt in-line skating? Horwath knew that Rollerblade could not sit back with the "We've got it made" attitude.

---

[6]Gretzky, who made up to $500,000 a year per endorsement, agreed to endorse Ultra-Wheels for $100,000 a year in cash, plus options to buy 100,000 shares of First Team stock (trading at $1.12 a share at the time), plus a small percentage of sales of his signature line.

[7]First Team Sports had said that it would never call itself Ultra-Wheels rollerblades even if the name became generic.

SOURCES

Bultmeyer, Suzanne. "Lining Up Skaters." *Sporting Goods Business,* January 1994, pp. 65–66.

Comte, Elizabeth. "Blade Runner." *Forbes,* October 12, 1992, pp. 114–17.

Fahey, Alison, and Scott Hume. "Marketers Team in Time of Trouble." *Advertising Age,* February 18, 1991, p. 36.

"The Future Is Already Here." *Across the Board,* January 1994, pp. 22–25.

Goerne, Carrie. "Rollerblade Reminds Everyone That Its Success Is Not Generic." *Marketing News,* March 2, 1992, pp. 1–2.

Greising, David. "First Team Sports: A Fleet No. 2 in the Rollerblade Derby." *Business Week,* May 24, 1993, pp. 67–68.

" 'How I Did It'—Guerrilla Marketing 101." *Working Woman,* December 1991, pp. 23–24.

Jensen, Jeff. "Rollerblade Teams with Hi-C, Warner in Summer Tie-Ins." *Advertising Age,* June 14, 1993.

Macnow, Glen. "New Ideas for a Sporting Chance." *Nation's Business,* December 1992, pp. 62–63.

Marcial, Gene. "The Picks of a Pro Whose List Gained 18 Percent Last Year." *Business Week,* January 25, 1993, p. 82.

"Synergy Standouts." *Sporting Goods Business,* February 1994, p. 74.

Therrien, Lois. "Rollerblade Is Skating in Heavier Traffic." *Business Week,* June 24, 1991, pp. 114–15.

CASE 6–5 Highlights for Children, Inc.

Elmer C. Meider, president of Highlights for Children, Inc., had just completed a lengthy meeting involving several of his managers. Each manager had been assigned the task of preparing recommendations that would allow Highlights for Children to more effectively utilize the three marketing channels currently being used. Meider felt that the company had not been taking full advantage of the capabilities of direct mail, telemarketing, and direct sales in terms of prospecting, lead distribution, current and new product sales, and overall profitability. Moreover, Meider contends that Highlights for Children needs to capitalize on the continuity of direct mail, the rapid follow-up possible via telemarketing, and the value of face-to-face customer contact available through direct sales.

Although Meider knew he had the authority to eliminate the direct sales force operation, he felt this would not be in the best interests of Highlights. Rumors were abundant about possible legal restrictions on telemarketing programs. In fact, several states were considering legislation that would greatly restrict when telephone calls could be made for sales purposes. One such law would limit telephone calls to specified times and no later than 7:00 P.M. Meider knew that such a limit would sharply curtail Highlights's successful telemarketing program. Moreover, the threat of increases in postal rates caused Meider concern about the future of Highlights' successful direct-mail program. These possible environmental changes provided support for Meider's position to keep the direct sales arm intact. Company experience revealed that the direct sales force was in a better position to learn about and resolve customer problems and concerns than either telemarketing or direct mail.

Managers from each of the three distribution methods had been asked to prepare recommendations concerning changes they would implement to improve the overall sales and profitability picture. Meider's task would be to review the various recommendations and prepare a final report to present to Garry C. Myers III, chief executive officer, who was present at the meeting. Also present at the meeting were Richard H. Bell, chairman of the board; Lynn Wearsch, national rep sales service manager; Chuck Rout, vice president—telemarketing; and Gayle Ruwe, mail marketing manager.

Of the various recommendations, the one that provoked the most discussion was that Highlights for Children rely exclusively on telemarketing and direct-mail distribution and that the company eliminate the direct sales force. Richard Bell, responding to this suggestion, pointed out that it was the direct sales force that got the company started, and would keep the company going well into the future. He commented, "Highlights for Children might as well close its doors if the direct sales force is eliminated." One manager's response to Bell's defense of the direct sales force consisted of referring to the relative sales contributions from each source and how telemarketing and direct mail have grown faster. This manager noted the following:

> Telemarketing and direct sales are in a competitive position from a lead utilization standpoint. Profitability is greatly enhanced when leads are sent directly to telemarketing rather than to the direct sales force. Sure, representatives can sell a bigger package and a longer-term subscription than the other marketing arms, but the reps rely solely on company-generated leads and are not using referrals generated from customers, nor are they doing any local prospecting. The resources assigned to the direct sales force could be more profitably used by telemarketing and direct mail. Our opportunity costs, or losses, have been rising as a result of sending leads to the direct sales group. They cannot handle all of the leads, and by the time telemarketing receives them they are stale and of little value.

Bell agreed in part with these observations but was quick to note that the size of the direct sales force had dropped from an all-time high of 750 to the current level of 265 independent sales reps, which includes 65 area managers. "We need to be more effective recruiting new sales reps. Just doubling the direct sales force would produce significant benefits," noted Bell in his rejoinder. After this interchange, Garry Myers suggested that Elmer would take all proposals into consideration and attempt to arrive at a recommendation that would combine the best of everything.

The Company

General Information.   Begun in 1946 as a children's publication, Highlights for Children, Inc., has become a multidivisional company, selling not only magazines but also textbooks, newsletters, criterion referenced tests, and other materials. The consumers include children, parents, and teachers.

The Mission Statement of Highlights for Children states:

Highlights for Children, Inc.'s, mission is to create, publish, produce, or distribute on a profitable basis quality products and services uniquely designed for the educational development of children, their parents and teachers, and others with specific educational needs.

Each of the current divisions or subsidiaries operates within these guidelines.

Highlights emphasizes the fair and courteous treatment of its customers. Promotional offers are closely reviewed to ensure prospective customers are not being misled. Highlights is committed to maintaining a "pure" image in the marketplace in terms of marketing efforts as well as quality of its product.

Highlights for Children magazine is circulated to approximately 2 million subscribers. It is marketed through direct selling (via independent contractors), telephone marketing, and direct mail. Parents, teachers, doctors, and gift donors are targeted by the different marketing arms. In addition, Highlights sells various educational products that have been promoted through the introductory-offer school programs.

History.   Dr. Garry C. Myers, Jr., and Caroline C. Myers founded Highlights for Children, Inc., in 1946 in Honesdale, Pennsylvania. Based on the belief that learning must begin early in order to fully develop a child's learning ability, the magazine was geared to challenge children's creative thinking and abilities. Today, the editorial offices are still in Honesdale, although the corporate headquarters are located in Columbus, Ohio, and the magazine is printed in Nashville, Tennessee.

At the time *Highlights for Children* was founded, magazines were sold almost exclusively by door-to-door salesmen. *Highlights for Children* followed suit. Today, Highlights continues to use direct selling in conjunction with telephone marketing and direct mail to market the magazine.

In 1955, Myers hit upon the idea of putting *Highlights for Children* in doctors' offices with lead cards. At about the same time, his wife came up with the introductory-offer program to be marketed to parents through the schools. This was the beginning of marketing *Highlights for Children* by mail. Both programs met with immediate and resounding success.

Magazine Content

Highlights for Children targets and services a diverse age group from 2 to 12. The material in the magazine ranges from easy to advanced. This conforms to the philosophy of challenging children: Rather than having material graded and directed to a particular age child, children are allowed to work at their own rate and are "encouraged" to achieve and understand more.

The tag line of *Highlights for Children* is "Fun with a Purpose." The *purpose* of the magazine is to educate and instruct, not merely entertain. The magazine is positioned as supplemental material to be used in the home, rather than in the classroom.

Highlights for Children likes to maintain the image of an educational magazine. No cut-outs or mark-ups are included in the magazine content, enhancing the idea of *lasting* quality. There is no paid advertising in *Highlights for Children,* which is in line with the educational image. Throughout the years, advertising has been considered at various times. Management continues to feel the magazine is more salable as an educational supplement

EXHIBIT 1 Highlights for Children, Inc., Organization Chart

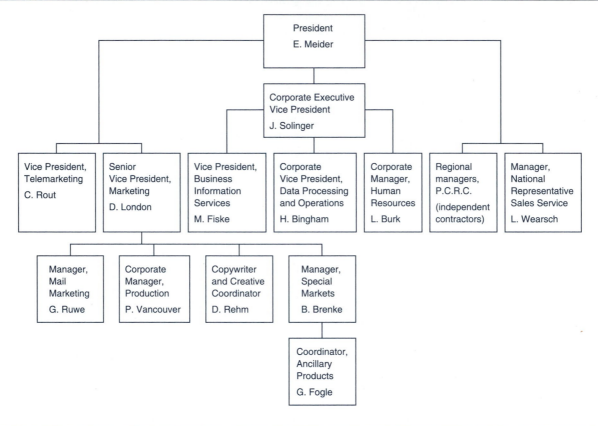

without advertising. Highlights also believes that children are already subjected to more than enough advertising pressure through other sources, much of which is resented by parents and teachers. Recently, President Elmer Meider raised the advertising issue and suggested that advertising revenues might be a way to improve *Highlights'* profit performance.

The Marketing Program

Highlights for Children uses three different marketing arms to sell its products: direct selling, telephone marketing, and mail marketing. Each type is discussed in following sections. Exhibit 1 shows the current organization.

Direct Selling.   The direct selling organization has two kinds of representatives: the school representatives and regular representatives. Almost all reps receive company-generated leads; however, school reps make most of their sales from self-generated "school drop" leads.

School Representatives.   Reps make their initial presentation to a school principal or superintendent. The object of the presentation is to gain permission to leave sample copies of *Highlights for Children* in grades K–4. If the school agrees to participate, a sample copy, along with a lead card, is sent home with each child. The child is instructed to return the card to the school if the parents are interested in ordering *Highlights*. Reps then pick up the lead cards from the schools. A school rep usually visits a particular school once every two to three years. Currently *Highlights for Children* has about 70 school reps.

Regular Reps.   Regular reps contact the following company-generated leads:

1. *Parent inquiries* (PI) and *doctor inquiries* (DI). These people have not had a subscription but have sent in a card indicating interest.
2. *Introductory-offer renewals* (IO). These people have been sold the 6-month introductory offer through the school and are now up for renewal.
3. *Regular renewals* (RR). These people have had a regular subscription (11 issues or more) and are up for renewal.
4. *Donor renewals* (DR). These people have given a gift subscription (11 issues or more) and are up for renewal.

A rep has a set amount of time to work the leads (depending on the type). At the end of that time period, the lead automatically goes to either phone or mail representatives for follow-up. Reps send back the leads marked "no contact" or "no sale" once they have been worked, so the other departments can follow up quickly.

Reps call on parents at home. The increasing number of women working and higher gasoline prices have made the rep's job more difficult over the years. When reps do find someone at home, their presentation hits mainly on what *Highlights for Children* is, how to use it, and its educational value. The rep can sell, on average, a 2.8-year term subscription.

There is a management structure in the regular rep program. Not all reps are under a manager; none reports directly to the home office. Managers receive an override on all area sales (personal and representative's sales).

The current rep structure is composed of about 265 active reps, of which about 65 are managers. The Columbus, Ohio, office has seven employees who are assigned to the direct selling arm. Reps are independent contractors and as such are not paid a salary; rather, they earn a commission on their sales. Their commission is calculated by commission level times sales units. Units are determined by term sold: (five-year subscription = 1.4 units; three-year subscription = 1.0 unit; two-year subscription = 0.7 unit; and one-year subscription = 0.3 unit). *Highlights for Children* subscription rates are $49.95 for 33 issues (three years) and $79.95 for 55 issues (five years). For example, the commission for a three-year subscription is $24.97 (1.0 unit = 0.50; $49.95 × 0.50 = $24.97).

Telephone Marketing.   Started over 10 years ago in response to the energy crisis and the possibility of the greatly reduced mobility of the representative selling arm, telephone marketing has grown and flourished from a staff of 3 to 190 telemarketing reps, all paid on a commission basis. Telemarketing commissions are about one-half (23 percent) of direct-sales commissions. Commissions are not paid for sales that are canceled or never paid by the customers. These reps are located in Columbus along with 25 staff employees.

Basically, telemarketing receives three types of leads: parent and doctor inquiries, introductory-offer renewals, and regular renewals. Telemarketing reps have a specified time period in which to contact and sell their leads before they go to mail marketing for follow-up. They attempt to contact leads, all types, 10 times before giving up. In one day's time, they can make up to four attempts. On average, telemarketing sells a 2.3-year term.

Mail Marketing.   The Mail Marketing Department consists of three primary areas: creative, production/analysis, and list rental. Currently, 10 employees work in the mail marketing department. Major responsibilities, in addition to list rental, include acquiring *new customers* (through efforts such as the Christmas mailing and school teacher introductory-offer mailing), acquiring *new leads* (through the doctors' offices, doctor inquiries, and parent inquiries mailings), and converting leads (these leads may be new or renewals) to customers (typically after regular reps and/or phone reps have tried to convert). All activities are conducted through direct mail.

More specifically, all promotion packages (to acquire either a lead or a customer), space ads, package inserts, billing stuffers, preprinted computer forms, and so forth, are created and produced through the efforts of this department. The actual mail production (merge/purge, lettershop, etc.) is also coordinated here. Finally, the analysis of the results is performed here as well.

Christmas Program.   The Christmas program is a multimedia effort to acquire one-year subscriptions targeting a donor. The mail program consists of over 5 million names, mailed from mid-September to mid-October.

Additionally, the Christmas program includes card inserts in the October, November, and December issues of *Highlights for Children* magazine, statement stuffers, approximately 2 million package inserts in outside packages (*Drawing Board, Current,* etc.) and space ads (*The Wall Street Journal, The New York Times, Christian Science Monitor,* etc.).

Introductory-Offer Program.   A mailing is made to teachers who hand out "take-home" slips on which the parents can subscribe. The subscription offer to the parents is for six months of *Highlights for Children,* an "introductory offer."

Parent Inquiry/Doctor Inquiry Program.   Several times a year, *Highlights for Children* purchases doctor lists for an outside mailing to produce doctor inquiries. General practitioners, pediatricians, dentists, any doctors who have children, and/or parents visiting their offices and waiting rooms are targeted. Doctors who subscribe are especially valuable because they provide a vehicle to reach parents, and the primary purpose of the doctor mailing is to eventually reach parents. Highlights for Children can send the magazine, complete with parent inquiry cards, into a doctor subscriber's office on a *monthly* basis, potentially reaching many parents.

Marketing Arm Effectiveness

Background information revealed that mail marketing produced the most revenue for the last seven years. In 1983, telemarketing surpassed direct marketing in terms of revenue. Exhibit

EXHIBIT 2 Highlights for Children, Inc.: Annual Gross Sales by Source, 1976–1985 ($000)

Year	Reps	Telephone	Mail
1976	11,400	860	10,700
1977	11,800	1,500	11,300
1978	12,100	2,300	12,100
1979	10,300	3,300	14,400
1980	10,400	6,400	16,300
1981	11,100	8,400	16,400
1982	12,400	9,000	21,400
1983	12,300	13,400	28,000
1984	10,800	20,400	36,000
1985	10,200	23,800	46,000

2 shows sales by marketing arm since 1976. Order-per-lead ratios by marketing arm are as follows:

Telemarketing: over 30 percent.

Direct sales: over 20 percent.

Mail: over 5 percent.

Normally, order-per-lead ratios are higher for direct sales. In fact, for a given number of leads, say 50, the direct sales group will produce more orders than the telemarketing group. However, since the reps are asking for more leads than they can possibly handle, many end up wasted and are not viable by the time they are received by telemarketing and direct mail.

The decline in the number of independent contractors has been of some concern for several years. Various programs have been initiated over the years to increase the number of reps. These programs have not met with much success as evidenced by the size of the direct sales force. Selling low-ticket items, however, limits how much a regular rep can earn. About one-half of the regular reps worked part-time. Earnings range from as low as $1,000 a year for some reps to as high as six figures for those reps who are managers. Managers earn overrides on the sales of those reps that they have recruited into the sales organization, a common practice in direct selling programs. Exhibit 3 is typical of the literature used by Highlights to recruit new reps.

Meider and others are aware that this is a problem that others in direct selling have faced. Giants in the direct selling industry such as Avon, Tupperware, Mary Kay, Amway, and so forth, have all confronted this problem and have adopted various techniques to alleviate the negative impact that fewer reps have had on sales. A major contributing factor has been the dramatic increase in the number of working mothers who are no longer home during the day.

The ability of people in direct selling to earn a reasonable level of income has been inhibited due to these trends. Many companies have adopted party plan selling programs in an attempt to increase the income earning opportunities of the reps. Other companies

---

EXHIBIT 3   Sales Opportunity Fact Sheet

Highlights for Children is an educational magazine for children ages 2 through 12. There are 11 issues published each year, and the December issue includes an annual Resource Index, which turns that year's books into a home reference library for the whole family.

Highlights is available by enrollment only. It is not sold on any newstand, contains no advertising, and is created primarily for family use. The vast majority of its subscribers are parents. *Highlights* contains a wide range of fiction, nonfiction, thinking and reasoning features, contributions from readers, and things to make and do. The high-interest articles include humor, mystery, sports, folk tales, history, arts, animal stories, crafts, quizzes, recipes, action rhymes, poems, and riddles.

Dr. Garry Cleveland Myers and Caroline Myers founded *Highlights for Children* in 1946 as the outcome of years of professional work in child psychology, family life, education, and publishing for children. *Highlights* has grown from a first issue circulation of 22,000 to over 1,500,000 in 1982 and is the world's most honored book for children.

Noted educator, psychologist, and author, Dr. Walter B. Barbe, is the editor-in-chief of *Highlights*. Dr. Barbe's books and professional publications have made him nationally renowned in education and in demand as an international speaker. The ongoing production of each issue is coordinated by a talented staff of educators, most of whom are parents. The editorial offices are located in Honesdale, Pennsylvania. The marketing arm for *Highlights for Children* is Parent and Child Resource Center, Inc., and the administrative offices are centered in Columbus, Ohio, where a dedicated representative sales staff plans and directs the business of selling and delivering *Highlights* all around the world.

Highlights for Children is sold nationally by authorized independent representatives directly to families, teachers, preschools, daycare centers, doctors' offices, and to any other person or place interested in the welfare and development of children. This is a direct, person-to-person sales opportunity.

As an independent contractor selling *Highlights'* products, you are free to work the hours you want and earn as much commission as possible. You are in business for yourself with exclusive leads and virtually no product competition. There is no investment required, and you are provided with the information and instruction you need to grow in skill, experience, and earnings. Your business will grow in proportion to the time, skill, and resourcefulness you use in presenting the values of *Highlights* to families, individuals, or groups in your community. Your job is to visit with prospective customers, show them how *Highlights* will benefit their children, and write up the order. Statistics show that one out of three contacts will enroll.

You will find that selling *Highlights'* products is enjoyable, pleasant, and profitable. The only qualifications necessary are that you enjoy meeting people and have a sincere interest in children.

There is no limit to your earnings. Every home with children aged 2 through 12 is a potential customer. You retain a liberal commission on every enrollment at the time of the sale, plus additional commissions as your sales record grows. You receive bonuses for the quantity of sales you report, bonuses for the quality of the sale you make, and bonuses for recommending others as representatives. Your sales can also make you eligible to win incentive contests with case and/or merchandise prizes.

If you are interested in a sales career, complete the enclosed Confidential Information form and mail it today!

---

have expanded their product lines in order to provide their direct sales reps with more commission opportunities. Exhibit 4, a fact sheet published by the Direct Selling Association, provides a summary of the 1985 direct selling industry.

Meider, on the other hand, feels that despite these trends the direct sales reps are not working as hard as they should and are not following prescribed and proven methods of selling. Reps are supposed to ask customers who have ordered a subscription to

---

EXHIBIT 4   Fact Sheet

Summary: 1985 Direct Selling Industry Survey

Total retail sales: $8,360,000

Percent of sales by major product group:

Personal care products	34.8%
Home/family care products	50.0
Leisure/educational products	9.4
Services/other	5.8

Sales approach (method used to generate sales reported as a parent of sales dollars):

One-on-one contact	81.0%
Group sales/party plan	19.0
In the home	77.0
In a workplace	11.8
At a public event*	2.5
Over the phone	6.9
Other	1.8

Total salespeople: 2,967,887

Demographics of salespeople:

Independent	97.9%
Employed	2.1
Full-time (30+ hours per week)	11.7
Part-time	88.3
Male	22.0
Female	78.0

---

*Such as a fair, exhibition, shopping mall, theme part, etc.
Source: Direct Selling Association, Washington, D.C.

Highlights for Children for the names of others who might be interested in subscribing. Since the reps knew that they could secure company-generated leads free, there was no financial incentive for them to ask for referrals. This referral process has been the mainstay method of direct selling not only for *Highlights for Children* but other direct selling companies as well. Reps are expected to engage in local prospecting, which involves locating residential areas occupied by parents of young children. These activities have been neglected, and reps today rely solely on company-generated leads.

Sales reps continually ask for more leads than they can process, resulting in lost opportunities. By the time the leads are sent back to Columbus, they are of limited value. Meider was particularly distressed to learn that several reps had established their own telemarketing operations to enhance their earnings opportunities. As a result of this practice, Highlights was paying the reps a commission that was twice the amount normally paid for telemarketing sales. A report prepared by Marilyn Fisk, vice president of business information services, added further to Meider's concern. Her report contained the following points:

- Telemarketing sales in general are for the magazine only; sales of other products are very limited.
- Telemarketing sales do not involve a down payment, hence there are more cancellations.
- Recruiting of additional direct sales reps has declined, especially in those situations where the reps, with the assistance or blessing of their managers, have started their own telemarketing operations.

Meider's reaction to Fisk's report further solidified his decision that changes are needed. He could understand why the managers would favor telemarketing conducted by their direct reps. Each subscription netted a $4 override for the manager regardless of how it was secured, although suggestions had been made that the $4 override was not adequate. And the direct reps received their usual commission. He had attempted at an earlier date to persuade the former national sales manager to do something about this practice only to be told that the direct reps were independent and would view this as interference. Besides, as the national sales manager indicated, "The reps view the annual Christmas mailing as a direct threat and want the program to be eliminated or at least share in the commissions on sales from their territories."

Sometime later, the national sales manager left Highlights for Children, due to a reorganization that eliminated the position. Meider hired two regional sales managers who work in the field and can provide closer supervision of the direct sales reps and their managers. Meider divided the United States into two regions, east and west. This move greatly reduced the span of control problems experienced by the former national sales manager.

Meider discussed these problems with Garry Myers III and asked for his reactions. Myers noted that it should not be surprising that reps rely totally on company-generated leads. As Myers stated, "Our reps want to make the most sales, and the best avenue is to call on people who have taken the effort to complete a card and mail it in to Highlights. Reps know that these leads are more likely to produce sales than what they are likely to obtain using the referral process." Myers likened the referral process to "cold-call selling" and company-generated leads as "warm-call selling." Regardless, Highlights for Children is losing profits as a result of these practices, and Myers hoped that Meider's report would be available soon.

Meider indicated that his initial report would contain a series of alternative recommendations that would be used to generate discussion. For example, Meider suggested that one alternative would be to eliminate company-generated leads. Another possibility, suggested by Meider, would place a limit on the number of company-generated leads that a rep could receive each month. The number received might be a function of previous referral sales or some other factor. Meider also suggested charging the managers and/or the reps for each company-generated lead. To offset these additional charges, one likely counter-suggestion would be to increase commissions paid to the reps. The Fisk report prompted another option: reducing the commission paid to reps for orders received without a down payment. This might curtail the use of telemarketing by the reps, a practice Meider wanted to stop. Finally, one manager suggested that the school reps be charged a small fee for all of the sample copies that are left at schools for K–4 distribution. The manager said, "If the regular reps are wasteful of the excessive leads that they receive, then the school reps may be just as guilty when they give away too many free samples."

Eliminating the independent reps is one alternative, as is increasing the number of reps. Meider did not agree with Bell that more reps was the best solution, although he did think that it was an alternative to consider. Expanding the product line to give the reps more items to sell and more commission opportunities was another alternative suggested to Meider. Currently, a three-year subscription at $49.95 produces a commission of $24.97. Meider knew that no one would suggest replacing the direct sales force with a company sales force. Such a move would increase overhead expenses by at least 15 percent to cover fringe benefits costs plus staff additions needed for purposes of governmental reporting. Eliminating the direct selling arm would be a better solution than creating a company sales force.

Myers thought that Meider's suggestions would indeed produce much discussion among his management team. At this juncture, he felt that Meider should narrow the alternatives down to a final set of recommendations.

CASE 6–6   Wind Technology

Kevin Cage, general manager of Wind Technology, sat in his office on a Friday afternoon watching the snow fall outside his window. It was January 1991 and he knew that during the month ahead he would have to make some difficult decisions regarding the future of his firm, Wind Technology. The market for the wind profiling radar systems that his company designed had been developing at a much slower rate than he had anticipated.

Wind Technology

During Wind Technology's 10-year history, the company had produced a variety of weather-related radar and instrumentation. In 1986, the company condensed its product mix to include only wind-profiling radar systems. Commonly referred to as wind profilers, these products measure wind and atmospheric turbulence for weather forecasting, detection of wind direction at NASA launch sites, and other meteorological applications (i.e., at universities and other scientific monitoring stations). Kevin had felt that this consolidation would position the company as a leader in what he anticipated to be a high-growth market with little competition.

This case was prepared by Ken Manning, Gonzaga University, and Jakki Mohr, University of Colorado at Boulder. This case is intended for use as a basis for class discussion rather than to illustrate either effective or ineffective administrative decision making. Some data are disguised. Copyright © by Jakki Mohr 1990. All rights reserved.

Wind Technology's advantages over Unisys, the only other key player in the wind-profiling market, included the following: (1) The company adhered stringently to specifications and quality production. (2) Wind Technology had the technical expertise to provide full system integration. This allowed customers to order either basic components or a full system, including software support. (3) Wind Technology's staff of meteorologists and atmospheric scientists provided the customer with sophisticated support, including operation and maintenance training and field assistance. (4) Finally, Wind Technology had devoted all of its resources to its wind-profiling business. Kevin believed that the market would perceive this as an advantage over a large conglomerate like Unisys.

Wind Technology customized each product for individual customers as the need arose; the total system could cost a customer from $400,000 to $5 million. Various governmental entities, such as the Department of Defense, NASA, and state universities, had consistently accounted for about 90 percent of Wind Technology's sales. In lieu of a field sales force, Wind Technology relied on top management and a team of engineers to call on prospective and current customers. Approximately $105,000 of their annual salaries was charged to a direct selling expense.

The Problem

The consolidation strategy that the company had undertaken in 1986 was partly due to the company's being purchased by Vaitra, a high-technology European firm. Wind Technology's ability to focus on the wind-profiling business had been made possible by Vaitra's financial support. However, since 1986 Wind Technology had shown little commercial success, and due to low sales levels, the company was experiencing severe cash flow problems. Kevin knew that Wind Technology could not continue to meet payroll much longer. Also, he had been informed that Vaitra was not willing to pour more money into Wind Technology. Kevin estimated that he had from 9 to 12 months (until the end of 1991) in which to implement a new strategy with the potential to improve the company's cash flow. The new strategy was necessary to enable Wind Technology to survive until the wind-profiler market matured. Kevin and other industry experts anticipated that it would be two years until the wind-profiling market achieved the high growth levels that the company had initially anticipated.

One survival strategy that Kevin had in mind was to spin off and market component parts used in making wind profilers. Initial research indicated that, of all the wind-profiling system's component parts, the high-voltage power supply (HVPS) had the greatest potential for commercial success. Furthermore, Kevin's staff on the HVPS product had demonstrated knowledge of the market. Kevin felt that by marketing the HVPS, Wind Technology could reap incremental revenues, with very little addition to fixed costs. (Variable costs would include the costs of making and marketing the HVPS. The accounting department had estimated that production costs would run approximately 70 percent of the selling price, and that 10 percent of other expenses—such as top management direct-selling expenses—should be charged to the HVPS.)

High-Voltage Power Supplies

For a vast number of consumer and industrial products that require electricity, the available voltage level must be transformed to different levels and types of output. The three primary types of power supplies include linears, switchers, and converters. Each type manipulates electrical current in terms of the type of current (AC or DC) and/or the level of output (voltage). Some HVPS manufacturers focus on producing a standardized line of power supplies, while others specialize in customizing power supplies to the user's specifications.

High-voltage power supplies vary significantly in size and level of output. Small power supplies with relatively low levels of output (under 3 kV)[1] are used in communications equipment. Medium-sized power supplies that produce an output between 3 and 10 kV are used in a wide range of products, including radars and lasers. Power supplies that produce output greater than 10 kV are used in a variety of applications, such as high-powered X rays and plasma-etching systems.

Background on Wind Technology's HVPS

One of Wind Technology's corporate strategies was to control the critical technology (major component parts) of its wind-profiling products. Management felt that this control was important since the company was part of a high-technology industry in which confidentiality and innovation were critical to each competitor's success. This strategy also gave Wind Technology a differential advantage over its major competitors, all of whom depended on a variety of manufacturers for component parts. Wind Technology had successfully developed almost all of the major component parts and the software for the wind profiler, yet the development of the power supply had been problematic.

To adhere to the policy of controlling critical technology in product design (rather than purchasing an HVPS from an outside supplier), Wind Technology management had hired Anne Ladwig and her staff of HVPS technicians to develop a power supply for the company's wind-profiling systems. Within six months of joining Wind Technology, Anne and her staff had completed development of a versatile power supply which could be adapted for use with a wide variety of equipment. Some of the company's wind-profiling systems required up to 10 power supplies, each modified slightly to carry out its role in the system.

Kevin Cage had delegated the responsibility of investigating the sales potential of the company's HVPS to Anne Ladwig since she was very familiar with the technical aspects of the product and had received formal business training while pursuing an MBA. Anne had determined that Wind Technology's HVPS could be modified to produce levels of output between 3 and 10 kV. Thus, it seemed natural that if the product was brought to market, Wind Technology should focus on applications in this range of output. Wind Technology also did not have the production capabilities to compete in the high-volume, low-voltage segment of the market, nor did the company have the resources and technical expertise to compete in the high-output (+ 10 kV) segment.

---

[1]V (kilovolt): 1,000 volts.

The Potential Customer

Power supplies in the 3–10 kV range could be used to conduct research, to produce other products, or to place as a component into other products such as lasers. Thus, potential customers could include research labs, large end-users, OEMs, or distributors. Research labs each used an average of three power supplies; other types of customers ordered a widely varying quantity.

HVPS users were demanding increasing levels of reliability, quality, customization, and system integration. *System integration* refers to the degree to which other parts of a system are dependent upon the HVPS for proper functioning, and the extent to which these parts are combined into a single unit or piece of machinery.

Anne had considered entering several HVPS market segments in which Wind Technology could reasonably compete. She had estimated the domestic market potential of these segments at $237 million. To evaluate these segments, Anne had compiled growth forecasts for the year ahead and had evaluated each segment in terms of the anticipated level of customization and system integration demanded by the market. Anne felt that the level of synergy between Wind Technology and the various segments was also an important consideration in selecting a target market. Exhibit 1 summarizes this information. Anne believed that if the product was produced, Wind Technology's interests would be best served by selecting only one target market on which to concentrate initially.

Competition

To gather competitive information, Anne contacted five HVPS manufacturers. She found that the manufacturers varied significantly in terms of size and marketing strategy (see Exhibit 2). Each listed a price in the $5,500–$6,500 range on power supplies with the same features and output levels as the HVPS that had been developed for Wind Technology. After she spoke with these firms, Anne had the feeling that Wind Technology could offer the HVPS market superior levels of quality, reliability, technical expertise, and customer support. She optimistically believed that a one-half percent market share objective could be achieved the first year.

Promotion

If Wind Technology entered the HVPS market, they would require a hard-hitting, thorough promotional campaign to reach the selected target market. Three factors made the selection of elements in the promotion mix especially important to Wind Technology: (1) Wind Technology's poor cash flow, (2) the lack of a well-developed marketing department, and (3) the need to generate incremental revenue from sales of the HVPS at a minimum cost. In fact, a rule of thumb used by Wind Technology was that all marketing expenditures should be about 9 to 10 percent of sales. Kevin and Anne were contemplating the use of the following elements:

EXHIBIT 1   HVPS Market Segments in the 3–10 kV Range

Application	Forecasted Annual Growth (%)	Level of Customization/ Level of System Integration*	Synergy Rating**	Percentage of $237 Million Power Supply Market***
General/Univ. laboratory	5.40	Medium/medium	3	8%
Lasers	11.00	Low/medium	4	10
Medical equipment	10.00	Medium/medium	3	5
Microwave	12.00	Medium/high	4	7
Power modulators	3.00	Low/low	4	25
Radar systems	11.70	Low/medium	5	12
Semiconductor	10.10	Low/low	3	23
X-ray systems	8.60	Medium/high	3	10

*The level of customization and system integration generally in demand within each of the applications is defined as low, medium, or high.

**Synergy ratings are based on a scale of 1 to 5; 1 is equivalent to a very low level of synergy and 5 is equivalent to a very high level of synergy. These subjective ratings are based on the amount of similarities between the wind-profiling industry and each application.

***Percentages total 100 percent of the $237 million market in which Wind Technology anticipated it could compete.

Note: This list of applications is not all-inclusive.

1. Collateral Material.   Sales literature, brochures, and data sheets are necessary to communicate the product benefits and features to potential customers. These materials are designed to be (1) mailed to customers as part of direct-mail campaigns or in response to customer requests, (2) given away at trade shows, and (3) left behind after sales presentations.

Because no one in Wind Technology was an experienced copywriter, Anne and Kevin considered hiring a marketing communications agency to write the copy and to design the layout of the brochures. This agency would also complete the graphics (photographs and artwork) for the collateral material. The cost for 5,000 pieces (including the 10 percent markup for the agency) was estimated to be $5.50 each.

2. Public Relations.   Kevin and Anne realized that one very cost-efficient tool of promotion is publicity. They contemplated sending out new-product announcements to a variety of trade journals whose readers were part of Wind Technology's new target market. By using this tool, interested readers could call or write to Wind Technology, and the company could then send the prospective customers collateral material. The drawback of relying too heavily on this element was very obvious to Kevin and Anne—the editors of the trade journals could choose not to print Wind Technology's product announcements if their new product was not deemed newsworthy.

The cost of using this tool would include the time necessary to write the press release and the expense of mailing the release to the editors. Direct costs were estimated by Wind Technology to be $500.

EXHIBIT 2 Competitor Profile (3–10 kV range)

Company	Gamma	Glassman	Kaiser	Maxwell*	Spellman
Approximate annual sales	$2 million	$7.5 million	$3 million		$7 million
Market share	1.00%	3.00%	1.50%		2.90%
Price**	$5,830	$5,590	$6,210	$5,000–$6,000	$6,360
Delivery	12 weeks	10 weeks	10 weeks	8 weeks	12 weeks
Product customization	No	Medium	Low	Medium	Low
System integration experience	Low	Low	Low	Medium	Low
Customer targets	Gen. lab.	Laser	Laser	Radar	Capacitors
	Space	Medical	Medical	Power mod.	Gen. lab.
	Univ. lab.	X ray	Microwave	X ray	Microwave
			Semiconductor	Medical equip.	X ray

*Maxwell was in the final stages of product development and stated that the product would be available in the spring. Maxwell anticipated that the product would call in the $5,000–$6,000 range.
**Price quoted for an HVPS with the same specification as the "standard" model developed by Wind Technology.

3. Direct Mail. Kevin and Anne were also contemplating a direct-mail campaign. The major expenditure for this option would be buying a list of prospects to whom the collateral material would be mailed. Such lists usually cost around $5,000, depending upon the number of names and the list quality. Other costs would include postage and the materials mailed. These costs were estimated to be $7,500 for a mailing of 1,500.

4. Trade Shows. The electronics industry had several annual trade shows. If they chose to exhibit at one of these trade shows, Wind Technology would incur the cost of a booth, the space at the show, and the travel and incidental costs of the people attending the show to staff the booth. Kevin and Anne estimated these costs at approximately $50,000 for the exhibit, space, and materials, and $50,000 for a staff of five people to attend.

5. Trade Journal Advertising. Kevin and Anne also contemplated running a series of ads in trade journals. Several journals they considered are listed in Exhibit 3, along with circulation, readership, and cost information.

6. Personal Selling.

    a. Telemarketing (Inbound/Inside Sales).[2] Kevin and Anne also considered hiring a technical salesperson to respond to HVPS product inquiries generated by product announcements, direct mail, and advertising. This person's responsibilities would

---

[2]*Inbound* refers to calls that potential customers make to Wind Technology, rather than *outbound,* in which Wind Technology calls potential customers (i.e., solicits sales).

EXHIBIT 3 Trade Publications

Trade Publication	Editorial	Cost per Color Insertion (1 page)	Circulation
Electrical manufacturing	For purchasers and users of power supplies, transformers, and other electrical products.	$4,077	35,168 nonpaid
Electronic component news	For electronics OEMs. Products addressed include work stations, power sources, chips, etc.	$6,395	110,151 nonpaid
Electronic manufacturing news	For OEMs in the industry of providing manufacturing and contracting of components, circuits, and systems.	$5,075	25,000 nonpaid
Design news	For design OEMs covering components, systems, and materials.	$8,120	170,033 nonpaid
Weatherwise	For meteorologists covering imaging, radar, etc.	$1,040	10,186 paid

Note: This is a partial list of applicable trade publications. Standard Rate and Data Service lists other possible publications.

---

include answering phone calls, prospecting, sending out collateral material, and following up with potential customers. The salary and benefits for one individual would be about $50,000.

b. Field Sales. The closing of sales for the HVPS might require some personal selling at the customer's location, especially if Wind Technology pursued the customized option. Kevin and Anne realized that potentially this would provide them with the most incremental revenue, but it also had the potential to be the most costly tool. Issues such as how many salespeople to hire, where to position them in the field (geographically), and so on, were major concerns. Salary plus expenses and benefits for an outside salesperson were estimated to be about $80,000.

Decisions

As Kevin sat in his office and perused the various facts and figures, he knew that he would have to make some quick decisions. He sensed that the decision about whether or not to proceed with the HVPS spin-off was risky, but he felt that to not do something to improve the firm's cash flow was equally risky. Kevin also knew that if he decided to proceed with the HVPS, there were a number of segments in that market in which Wind Technology could position its HVPS. He mulled over which segment appeared to be a good fit for Wind Technology's abilities (given Anne's recommendation that a choice of one segment would be best). Finally, Kevin was concerned that if they entered the HVPS market, that promotion for their product would be costly, further exacerbating the cash flow situation. He knew that promotion would be necessary, but the exact mix of elements would have to be designed with financial constraints in mind.

CASE 6–7   Amtech Corporation

In 1992, Amtech Corporation, leader in advanced electronics to improve the U.S. transportation system, had reached a critical point in its relatively young life (Amtech went public in 1989). Amtech Corporation, based in Dallas, Texas, was a $60 million company operating in two areas of transportation electronics. The company was a pioneer in the Intelligent Vehicle Highway Systems (IVHS) market. This market included electronic toll and traffic management systems. The company also operated in the transportation market. The transportation market included Automatic Equipment Identification (AEI) for the rail, intermodal, shipping, and fleet market segments. Prior to 1992, most of Amtech's revenues had come from the IVHS market. In 1992, however, the transportation segments (AEI) accounted for 62 percent of Amtech's revenues, with the IVHS market holding the remaining 38 percent of revenue accountability.

G. Russell Mortenson, Amtech's president, thought Amtech should focus on the transportation segment of the market. The dollar potential in this market was large. Mortenson felt that toll tags in the IVHS were only an "appetizer" for Amtech.

Mr. Mortenson needed to provide direction to Amtech workers. He needed to let them know whether Amtech would continue in both the AEI and IVHS markets. He also needed to work with his management in determining which segments (of either or both of these markets) Amtech should target.

Amtech Corporation

Amtech Corporation, a leader in IVHS and AEI, had come a long way from the origination of its name—Animal Management Technology. Originally a product used to monitor livestock, Amtech got its start in 1983 when the U.S. Agriculture Department released the patents on an 11-year-old radio beam system. David Cook and Kenneth Anderson (Blockbuster Entertainment co-founders) were convinced of the commercial viability of radio frequency technology. Cook and Anderson put up the seed money for the venture, with Texas billionaire Ross Perot later joining the Blockbuster duo. American President (a shipping concern) and Mitsubishi invested in Amtech as well.

Initial use of the technology was in inventory management as an electronic bill of lading (AEI). A radio frequency tag was developed to track equipment movement of rail and shipping containers. The technology had been adopted by many trucking companies and, by 1992, railroads had adopted the technology in all their 1.4 million rail cars.

A byproduct of Amtech's AEI project was toll-road tags (IVHS). With this system, commuters had a credit-card-size tag on their car that emitted a signal at the tollgate. Transceivers, installed at toll plazas, bounced radio beams off these tags. Instantly, the tag identified the motorist, and his or her toll account was debited for the toll charge.

This case was prepared by Victoria L. Crittenden, associate professor of marketing, Boston College, as the basis for class discussion rather than to illustrate either effective or ineffective handling of a managerial situation. Research assistance was provided by Stephanie Hillstrom. All information was derived from secondary sources.

EXHIBIT 1   Five-Year Financial Summary ($ thousands, except per share data)

	Year Ended December 31				
	1992	*1991*	*1990*	*1989*	*1988*
Statement of Operations Data					
Sales	$39,856	$18,748	$14,770	$ 6,017	$ 1,383
Operating costs and expenses:					
Cost of sales	20,190	11,563	10,123	4,012	1,021
Research and development	2,562	1,963	2,835	2,714	2,750
Marketing, general and administrative	10,960	10,640	10,654	6,976	4,348
	33,712	24,166	23,612	13,702	8,119
Operating income (loss)	6,144	(5,418)	(8,842)	(7,685)	(6,736)
Interest income	1,261	433	1,181	421	281
Contract settlement	—	—	687	—	—
Provision for income taxes	132	—	—	—	—
Net income (loss)	$ 7,273	$(4,985)	$(6,974)	$(7,264)	$ (6,455)
Earnings (loss) per share	$ 0.64	$ (0.50)	$(0.71)	$ (1.02)	$ (1.21)
Shares used in computing earnings (loss) per share	11,359	9,927	9,760	7,121	5,343
Balance Sheet Data					
Working capital	$38,030	$13,554	$13,566	$21,163	$ 3,982
Total assets	57,445	22,991	22,269	27,191	7,459
Total stockholders' equity*	48,821	15,965	18,925	25,524	6,266
Stockholders' equity per share	4.25	1.57	1.95	2.65	1.37

*The company completed an initial public offering in November 1989 by selling 2,760,000 shares of common stock for net proceeds of $21,522,000. Additionally, in May 1992, the company completed a follow-on public offering of 1,250,000 common shares for net proceeds of $24,884,000.

Source: Amtech Corporation, *1992 Annual Report*.

At the beginning of 1992, Amtech ranked No. 2 in the top 100 fastest-growing international companies.[1] Exhibit 1 provides a five-year financial summary for Amtech. Exhibit 2 provides Amtech's mission statement.

Amtech was involved in a joint venture in Europe with Alcatel AVI S.A. in which Amtech products were marketed and serviced. (Named Alcatel Amtech S.A., ownership was 51 percent Alcatel AVI S.A. and 49 percent Amtech.) Mitsubishi Corp., which owned a 5 percent share of Amtech, marketed Amtech products in Asia. In the United States, Amtech and Motorola Inc. were involved in a joint venture to develop technology for the traffic management and electronic toll collection (IVHS) markets.

While the public's perception of Amtech was centered upon the IVHS market, by 1992, Amtech's revenue stream had shifted to the AEI market. Amtech referred to the AEI market as the transportation segments.

---

[1]*International Business,* "The Top 100 Fastest-Growing International Companies," December 1991.

EXHIBIT 2   Mission Statement

It is the mission of Amtech Corporation to establish and maintain unparalleled technology, product, and customer satisfaction leadership in the provision of radio frequency identification systems for transportation and intelligent vehicle highway systems (IVHS) applications worldwide. We will establish this leadership while creating an open and participative work environment. We will encourage innovation, reward performance and provide the opportunity for growth for all employees.

Amtech Quality Strategy Committee
August 10, 1992

Source: Amtech Corporation, *1992 Annual Report.*

Automatic Equipment Identification

The Automatic Equipment Identification system was a scanning system for capturing cargo location information from all vehicles and sending this information directly to a mainframe computer. The bottom line was that a customer (and the shipper) would always know where the shipment was in the transit process. The AEI system eliminated the manual recording of identification numbers. The AEI provided continuous monitoring of rolling stock by sensors that scanned electronic tags containing identification information. The tags, which could be written on as well as read, allowed for locating where a container was in the shipping process, as well as identifying what was in the container. As most cargo involved some interchange (different carriers handling the cargo before it reached its final destination), an AEI system virtually eliminated "lost" cargo.

AEI tags were electronic transponders that emitted radio signals. The tags could be attached to rolling stock containers (such as rail cars or trucks) and to every piece of equipment handling the container. For example, if a crane placed the wrong container on the wrong carrier, the computer would signal the crane operator to remove the container.[2] Basically, the transponder was coded with a serial number that corresponded with a cargo container. The transponders were interpreted by a transceiver using radio frequency waves. The serial number was transmitted when the device was polled by the transceiver, and the data was routed from the transceiver to a processor that collected the data (a mainframe computer). Exhibit 3 diagrams the AEI process.

Rail. The AEI[3] had been sanctioned by the American Association of Railroads as a mandated standard reporting method. It was felt that AEI usage would offer the following four major benefits to railway users.

   1. *Customer satisfaction* would be higher due to reduced cost in shipment tracing/ expediting, real-time exception reporting (deviations from train schedule), reduced billing errors, reduced claim filing, reporting accuracy, enhanced electronic data interchange capability, scheduling, enhanced rail competitiveness, seamless transportation (carrier interchange would not matter), and support for shipper quality

---

[2]Error rates for the AEI system were predicted to be one in 800 million.
[3]Tests showed accurate readings at up to 180 miles per hour, with tags read as far away as 100 feet. Additionally, the system was reliable in harsh conditions such as snow, rain, and extreme dirt and dust.

EXHIBIT 3   The AEI Process

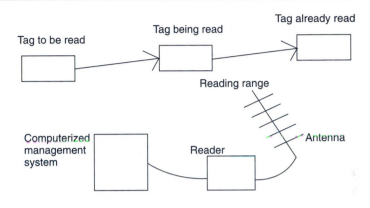

programs. Regarding inventory control, there would be reduced inventory carrying cost,[4] support for just-in-time capability, improved production scheduling, reduced need for premium transportation, accurate and timely reporting of weights, and real-time control.

2. *Equipment and other asset productivity gains* would be realized from private fleet size reduction (due to improved productivity of every car), improvement of utilization, management, control and operation of assigned cars and private fleets, and reduced facility requirements for storage, tracks, tanks, and warehouses.

3. *Information systems benefits* would result from worldwide standardization, support for service measurement in quality programs, minimized clerical rework and audit, support for a paperless environment, and improved data quality on private fleet mileage payments.

4. *Safety* would be enhanced, particularly in regards to the movement of hazardous materials.

Dollar-wise, estimates were that railway companies could save from $56 million to $75 million annually in fuel, maintenance, and personnel costs.

The Association of American Railroads' mandate required all rolling stock in North America to be equipped with electronic tags.[5] The mandate covered 1.4 million railcars, locomotives, and other equipment in Canada, the United States, and Mexico. Tagging was to begin January 1992 and be completed by January 1995. By 1993, Amtech had sold 800,000 tags to the railroads through its rail distributors. Additionally, there were 400 installed reader sites throughout North America, with estimates that the reader site

---

[4]One study indicated a cycle time reduction of 4 to 5 percent, generating inventory cost savings in excess of the tagging costs.

[5]European railroads endorsed the system in 1993.

EXHIBIT 4 Top 20 Common General Freight Fleet Carriers

1992 Rank	*Carrier*	*Location*
1	United Parcel Service, Inc. (OHIO)	Atlanta, GA
2	United Parcel Service, Inc. (NY)	Atlanta, GA
3	Yellow Freight System, Inc.	Overland Park, KS
4	Roadway Express, Inc.	Akron, OH
5	Consolidated Freightways Corp.	Portland, OR
6	Schneider National Carriers, Inc.	Green Bay, WI
7	J. B. Hunt Transport, Inc.	Lowell, AR
8	Overnite Transportation Co.	Richmond, VA
9	ABF Freight System, Inc.	Fort Smith, AR
10	Con-Way Transportation Services	Portland, OR
11	Carolina Freight Carriers Corp.	Cherryville, NC
12	Ryder Dedicated Logistics, Inc.	Miami, FL
13	Werner Enterprises, Inc.	Omaha, NE
14	Missouri Nebraska Express (MNX)	St. Joseph, MO
15	TNT Holland Motor Express, Inc.	Holland, MI
16	Watkins Motor Lines, Inc.	Lakeland, FL
17	Preston Trucking Company, Inc.	Preston, MO
18	Nationsway Transport Service	Commerce City, CO
19	American Freightways, Inc.	Harrison, AR
20	Central Transport, Inc.	Warren, MI

Sources: *Commercial Carrier Journal,* August 1994; Transportation Technical Services, Fredericksburg, VA.

---

network would increase to between 3,000 and 5,000 sites. The Association's mandate standards were adopted as the European standard, affecting 32 railroads across the width of the continent. The European railroad market was estimated to be five times bigger than the U.S. market.

Railway usage of AEI opened up the need for complementary new products. Such potential products included: tags that could interface with on-board devices such as fuel, temperature gauges in refrigerated rail cars, and fluid levels; portable readers that would allow a person to retrieve and display data from individual tags (such as special handling instructions on a hazardous shipment); and improved tag programmers to make field programming of tags more efficient.

Fleet. Trucking was another area of use for the AEI system. Trucking companies were more numerous, but smaller in size. Trucking firms received $100 billion of the $130 billion spent annually in the U.S. on the transportation of goods. Exhibit 4 provides a listing of the top 20 "Common General Freight" truck carriers.

Better fleet asset management could result from usage of the AEI system as drivers would not have to stop and call the dispatch center to report status or receive instructions, and trucks equipped with IVHS would benefit from nonstop trips on toll roads which would reduce cycle time. As well, many truck and trailer fleets ended up as piggy-back traffic on railroads. Basically, the same advantages found with rail usage would result with fleet usage.

Trucking companies were also evaluating another technology. Satellite-based networks forged data links between dispatch centers and terminals located in truck cabs. Two vendors were vying for this market: Geostar Corp. of Washington, D.C., and Qualcomm, Inc., of San Diego, California.

Intermodal.   Intermodal shippers were the largest customers of the railroad.[6] Several million intermodal containers traveled North America annually. AEI-tagged containers would be advantageous for intermodal shipping containers as more and more North American railroad reader systems were installed.

Security Access Market.   Another market that opened up for AEI was not part of the traditional transportation segment. The security market, particularly regarding walled communities, was a strong candidate for AEI.[7] The same concept as with transportation segments applied in the security market. An antenna would send out radio signals near the property entrance. As a vehicle approached the gate, the signal reflected off the tag. The computer-based system immediately looked up at the tag's vehicle information in the community's database. Residents would be allowed to drive through security. Others, such as contractors, visitors, and service providers would have to stop. The system allowed for monitoring the movement of contractors and service people around the community (as the contractor/service providers would be provided a temporary transponder while on the site).

Intelligent Vehicles and Highway Systems

Traffic congestion costs American businesses around $100 billion in lost productivity annually. This $100 billion estimate does not include costs associated with the billions of gallons of fuel wasted and the tons of pollutants spewed while sitting in traffic jams. Nor does the $100 billion include the $70 billion annual cost of traffic accidents which would be reduced if traffic congestion were decreased.

The U.S. Intelligent Vehicles and Highway Systems was a public-private research project with the objective of improving the U.S. road-based transportation system. The key IVHS products and services were transportation management, traveler information systems, productivity enhancements, and safety and driver assistance. The overall market for IVHS technologies was estimated to total $210 billion from 1992 through 2011. However, estimates were that more than $450 billion would be spent during this time period for R&D and test development. IVHS American was the nonprofit, scientific organization that served as the IVHS advisor to the U.S. Department of Transportation.

---

[6]Intermodal shipping took place when more than one type of carrier was used to deliver the product. For example, a container might arrive via water travel and then be transported via rail.

[7]Walled communities were those communities that log traffic in and out in order to control access to the facility within the secured area (e.g., apartment complexes, specific neighborhoods within larger cities, country clubs, military installations, corporate R&D labs).

EXHIBIT 5   Sales by Geographic Region

	Year Ended December 31		
	1992	*1991*	*1990*
North America	$34,053,000	$14,317,000	$10,509,000
Far East	911,000	555,000	857,000
Europe	4,892,000	3,876,000	3,404,000

Source: Amtech Corporation, *1992 Annual Report.*

There were several foreign programs similar to the IVHS. The Program for European Traffic with Highest Efficiency and Unprecedented Safety (Prometheus) was a safety research project supported by the automotive companies in Europe and 50 research institutes. Japan had its Road Automotive Communications Systems and the Advanced Mobile Traffic Information System. At least 400,000 cars in Japan had navigation systems in place. In England, Trafficmaster was used to notify drivers of accidents, construction problems, or other traffic delays. Additionally, the European DRIVE (Dedicated Road Infrastructure for Vehicle Safety in Europe) project had 70 different initiatives directed toward integrating the road transport environment.

Through the development, testing, and deployment of advanced electronics using computers, communication, positioning, and automation technologies, IVHS contained five applications: Advanced Traffic Management Systems (ATMS), Advanced Traveler Information Systems (ATIS), Advanced Vehicle Control Systems (AVCS), Advanced Public Transportation Systems (APTS), and Commercial Vehicle Operations (CVO). Each of these five applications is described in the appendix at the end of this case.

Customers

In 1992, Amtech had four major customers who accounted for 21 percent, 13 percent, 12 percent, and 10 percent of sales. (In 1991, one customer accounted for 34 percent of sales. In 1990, two customers accounted for 28 percent and 13 percent of sales.) Export sales were $10,983,000 (1992), $4,896,000 (1991), and $4,402,000 (1990). Exhibit 5 shows Amtech sales by geographic region for a three-year period.

Prices for both the railway and electronic tolls started at $2,600. Prices varied depending upon the customer's specifications. The tags for both systems ranged from $18 to $250 each, with the price dependent upon the sophistication of the tag. The $18 tag, used for gate access applications, typically, complimented the $2,600 system and was the least sophisticated tag. The $250 tag was almost like a minicomputer. However, most tag sales were in the $35 to $60 range.

The electronic toll systems were sold to the toll authorities. These toll authorities then leased tags to patrons at tag stores which were owned by the toll authority. At the tag store, the patron opened an account for tag usage and received a tag. When the tag was used (when it went through a toll booth), the toll charge was deducted from the patron's account.

EXHIBIT 6 IVHS/ATMS Toll Collection Process

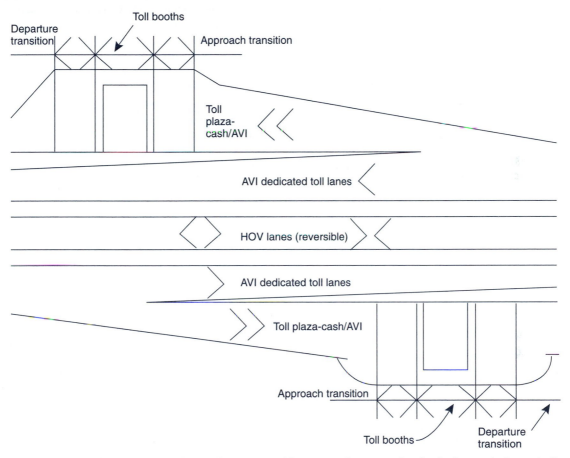

AVI dedicated lanes allow nonstop, high-speed passage, while patrons for conventional toll plaza exit the main line to a parallel roadway to pay.

The IVHS market at Amtech was almost synonymous with automated toll plazas. (Exhibit 6 diagrams a toll area using IVHS/ATMS technology.) Amtech expected an increased number of toll roads in the future. This was based on the belief that states would not have the money to continue funding road construction at the demanded level and that the U.S. government would not have the support funding needed either. Both the North Dallas Tollway and the entire Oklahoma turnpike system used Amtech technology. Oklahoma's 561 mile system resulted in the purchase of more than 100,000 transporter tags. The North Dallas Tollway, with 15,000 issued tags, had been the largest in terms of number of transponders prior to the Oklahoma project. Amtech also operated its toll systems in parts of Louisiana and Georgia in the United States and in Mexico, France,

Spain, and the United Kingdom. U.S. toll roads expected to decide upon IVHS technology included California and a group of seven toll-road agencies in the Northeast serving New York, New Jersey, and Pennsylvania. Internationally, Amtech was certain to obtain a contract in Hong Kong for the Aberdeen Tunnel.

The toll tags, scanners, and related equipment market was expected to total $5 billion to $10 billion by the year 2000. Most of the systems would be sold in Europe and the Far East where toll roads were more common than in the United States.

Amtech received a major boost when the Association of American Railroads gave final approval for automatic equipment identification (AEI). This $100 million revenue opportunity required that all 1.4 million rail freight cars in interchange service have identification tags (two tags per car) compatible with Amtech technology by the beginning of 1995.

By the middle of 1992, orders for tags totaled about 750,000.[8] Amtech was producing 100,000+ tags per month at its Santa Fe, New Mexico, facility. The company, reportedly, had trouble keeping up with demand because railroads were mounting the tags faster than expected. While slower than anticipated, 500 to 600 readers were expected to be installed by the end of 1992. Complete reader installation was expected to range from 3,000 to 5,000 readers.

The first international, intermodal carrier to begin outfitting its container fleet with AEI was American President Companies. American President expected to invest $15 million to $20 million in the installation of Amtech AEI tags on its domestic and international fleets and reader systems at 130 facilities in North America, Asia, and the Middle East.[9]

Amtech's Canadian distributor was working on a joint effort with a Canadian carrier, Sultran, to adapt the company's AEI technology to Sultran's requirements. Sultran was a highly specialized company that moved 5 million tons of dry-formed sulphur for 22 owners. The company worked from 17 origins which fed into two terminals in Vancouver. Sultran owned or leased over 1,500 freight cars.

Also in the AEI market, the truckload carrier J. B. Hunt began installing Amtech tags in its 5,800 unit tractor fleet in 1992. The installation would allow J. B. Hunt rigs to participate in the New Mexico Port of Entry inspection bypass and weigh-in-motion program. The system also allowed the rigs to participate in the Oklahoma Turnpike automatic toll system (IVHS).

Competition

The IVHS market was not lacking in competitors for Amtech. Many large companies from the cutback-ridden defense industry and several key members of the Fortune 500 were entering the IVHS market. As well, several alliances were formed that contributed

---

[8]One rail company, the Santa Fe, had problems with its tagging systems. Cars tagged in Kansas City were showing up in California with no-read tags. Information had been destroyed. Amtech worked with Santa Fe and located the problem as ground radar interference from a Texas airport. The Texas radar was an old FAA installation that was scheduled for replacement anyway. The problem, which was reported in the industry, did not slow orders for Amtech's technology. The Santa Fe served 12 western and midwestern states, from Chicago to California and the Gulf of Mexico. The company operated 1,600 locomotives and 31,000 freight cars. With around 15,000 customers, it handled 1.6 million carloads of freight each year, traveling over more than 9,000 miles of track.

[9]This included containers, chassis, tractors, railcars, and other equipment.

to the strength of even the already powerful companies. Examples of such ventures included alliances between American Telephone & Telegraph (AT&T) and Mark IV Industries, Lockheed and AT&T, and Texas Instruments and MFS Network Technologies.

Regarding *electronic tolls,* Mark IV Industries Inc. (an Amherst, New York, maker of electronic industrial equipment) and AT&T had formed a joint venture to compete in this market. The venture was thought to be a strong competitor for Amtech for seven toll-road agencies' contracts in the Northeast. Other entrants in this market included General Motors Corp.'s Hughes Aircraft unit and AT/Comm Inc. (hardware and software system supplier who distributed its equipment either directly to the end-user or through contractors such as Westinghouse, Cubic Corp., or Kiewit Technologies). Both Hughes and AT/Comm were competing for the $2 million system that would eliminate weigh station waits along Interstate 75 between Florida and Ontario, Canada. Additionally, Rockwell International had announced its intention to focus upon new markets in automated road and public transportation systems.

In other areas, Lockheed Corp. (a company already involved in electronic toll collection systems in some states) and AT&T had joined to create new *traffic-management systems.* Hughes, Westinghouse, and TRW were hoping to supply everything from *digital maps to collision-avoidance radars.* Texas Instruments and the MFS Network Technologies subsidiary of Peter Kiewit Sons Inc. had signed a co-development agreement to *integrate telecommunications and highways systems.* Etak Inc. (a Menlo Park, California, company that made digital maps for navigation systems) was working on *electronic yellow pages for car computers.* As well, the three major U.S. auto manufacturers were entering the competition by bidding on a federally sponsored automated-highway test project. (See Exhibit 7 for a listing of each of these competitors.)

In the AEI market, Amtech was the only company producing equipment that met the Association of American Railroads mandated standard. The American Trucking Association was studying the railroad's standardization effort. The group was working with the railroads and maritime shippers to ensure that all could agree upon a standard that trucking, rail, and maritime industries could use for intermodal purposes.

The Situation

By 1992, Amtech had moved from a company with operating losses to a company with a high-volume of operations, and revenue and earnings growth. Russell Mortenson was poised to move Amtech into the year 2000. Should he concentrate his (and the company's) efforts in the transportation (AEI) markets or in the IVHS markets? Could he continue in both markets? Should he be a mass marketer in either or both of these markets? Or should he target particular segments of each or both? Many of Amtech's competitors could call upon extensive corporate resources, so Mortenson knew he had no time to spare in making these decisions.

Competitors were nipping at Amtech's heels. The debate was raging on whose technology was best. Yet another issue was nagging at the back of Mr. Mortenson's mind. As contracts were won and lost, the company's stock would go up and down. Would Amtech make a nice fit for a much larger company?

EXHIBIT 7 IVHS Competitors

Electronic toll market

    Mark IV Industries Inc. and American Telephone & Telegraph (AT&T)

    General Motors Corp.'s Hughes Aircraft unit

    AT/Comm Inc.

New markets in road and public transportation systems

(also involved in the FAST-TRAC project)

    Rockwell International

Traffic management systems

    Lockheed Corp. and AT&T

Everything from digital maps to collision-avoidance radars

    Hughes

    Westinghouse

    TRW

Work toward integrating telecommunications and highway systems

    Texas Instruments and MFS Network Technologies

Electronic yellow pages for car computers

    Etak Inc.

Federally sponsored automated-highway test project

    General Motors, Ford, Chrysler

(GM was a sponsor in the TravTek project)

APPENDIX

IVHS Applications

Advanced Traffic Management Systems (ATMS). ATMS comprised methods for integrating the management of various roadway functions. These functions included freeway surveillance and incident detection, changeable message signs, electronic toll collection, and the coordination of traffic signal timing over wide areas in response to real-time conditions. Additionally, real-time data from ATMS could be used as input to the ATIS.

Combining ATMS and Advanced Traveler Information Systems (ATIS), FAST-TRAC[10] involved coordinating 1,000 intersections in Oakland County, Michigan. Infra-red beacons were used to provide real-time traffic and route guidance information. And electronic toll collection was a growing trend in the ATMS realm of activity, with systems in Texas, Oklahoma, and the northeastern United States. Exhibit 6 diagrams a toll area using ATMS technology.

---

[10]Rockwell International designed the traffic operations center for FAST-TRAC.

System operators in Canada, using ATMS technology, monitored traffic flow via sensors or detectors embedded in the pavement and television cameras installed along highways. The central computers continuously ran an incident detection algorithm. When the computer alarm indicated a problem, the operator analyzed the situation via the computer readings. The system allowed operators to control road signs to inform motorists of problem areas.

A growing trend in the ATMS segment of IVHS was the adoption of regional technology specifications. In 1992, California set a statewide specification for the technology (modulated-backscatter technology) to be used in electronic toll collection. Another regional trend was the formation of toll agency coalitions which selected a technology for a specific region/area (as with seven toll agencies in the northeastern United States).

Advanced Traveler Information Systems (ATIS). ATIS was a system designed to aid the individual driver. An ATIS system could assist the private vehicle or public transit in reaching specific destinations without encountering long traffic delays. Recommended routes would be adjusted via the on-board navigation system, based on input from the ATMS regarding accident locations, weather conditions, road conditions, or lane restrictions.

"TravTek" and "ADVANCE" were ATIS research projects.[11] TravTek involved 100 Oldsmobile Toronados in the Orlando, Florida, area equipped with a communications system for receiving traffic data and conveying vehicle information, as well as an on-board computer loaded with Orlando-area tourist information. ADVANCE, evaluated in the Chicago, Illinois, area, involved 5,000 vehicles equipped with navigation and route guidance systems that provided real-time traffic information to a traffic information center.

Advanced Vehicle Control Systems (AVCS). AVCS was created to assist drivers with vehicle control. This would help avoid accidents and could lead, ultimately, to fully automated chauffeuring capabilities. Inventions in this area included the anti-lock braking system, collision warning devices, and intelligent cruise controls that would automatically adjust speed according to distance and speed of the vehicle being followed.

Anti-lock braking systems were available in some automobiles: Other AVCS programs were to be developed in three stages over the 1992–2011 time period: (1) advice and warning systems, (2) support systems, and (3) automatic control systems.

Advanced Public Transportation Systems (APTS). APTS was aimed at users of high-occupancy vehicles such as car pools and transit buses. A key behind APTS was the lack of exchange of cash. Such usage would allow consumers to board transit vehicles without paying cash. Additionally, APTS was designed to allow transit vehicles to pay tolls and parking fees without cash. ATIS was a part of the APTS system as well.

Commercial Vehicle Operations (CVO). The CVO system was designed for commercial vehicle fleets. CVO would eliminate truck stoppage for weight measurements or state border inspections. As well, automated vehicle identification systems would allow

---

[11]TravTek was sponsored by General Motors, the Federal Highway Administration, the Automobile Association of America, the Florida Transportation Department, and the city of Orlando. The Federal Highway Administration, the Illinois Department of Transportation, and Motorola were sponsors of ADVANCE.

automated toll collection for fleets, and automated vehicle location systems would allow dispatchers to locate vehicles immediately.

CVO programs included trucks equipped with electronic locator systems and two-way digital satellite communications systems that linked drivers and dispatchers and trucks traveling the Interstate 75 corridor from Florida to Ontario, Canada, equipped with transponders that allowed them to bypass weight stations and state border inspection stations.

SOURCES

"APC Will Equip Its Fleet with AEI." *Railway Age,* April 1993, p. 25.

"Automatic Equipment Identification—A Rail Industry Quality Improvement Program." July 1991, pp. 1–17.

Bary, Andrew. "Not-So-Fast-Lane: A Few Potholes for Maker of High-Tech Toll Device." *Barron's,* December 7, 1992, pp. 22–28.

Bergoffen, Gene S. "A New Agenda For Private Fleets." *Transportation & Distribution,* April 1991, pp. T4–T8.

Carey, Patricia M. "The Top 100 Fastest-Growing International Companies." *International Business,* December 1991, pp. 35–48.

Cullen, David. "Traveling the Electronic Road." *Fleet Owner,* February 1993, pp. 38–42.

Desmond, Paul. "Advanced Networks Keep Freight Industry Moving." *Network World,* August 14, 1989, pp. 1, 26–30, 34.

Eaton, Leslie. "Know Your Stocks." *Barron's,* September 28, 1992, pp. 12–14.

French, Robert. "Transportation Comes of Age." *American City & County,* December 1992, p. 10.

Gerlin, Andrea. "Amtech, a Hot Technology Stock, Encounters Glitches." *Boston Globe,* June 22, 1993.

———. "Mark IV's Toll Plan Is Backed: Amtech's Stock Falls 34.2%." *Boston Globe,* March 22, 1994.

Hartje, Ronald L. "Tomorrow's Toll Road." *Civil Engineering,* February 1991, pp. 60–61.

Herst, Eric R. "AEI Adds Accuracy to JIT Logistics." *Global Trade & Transportation,* November 1993, p. 58.

Koelper, Jim A. "Railroad Streamlines Operation with CTI and IVR." *Communication News,* January 1994, pp. 25–27.

"Network with Shortlines." *Transportation & Distribution,* January 1993, p. 15.

"Officers Know Who's Coming with Auto ID." *Security,* September 1992, pp. 20–21.

"One Mystery, No Panic." *Railway Age,* August 1992, pp. 91–93.

Ridings, Richard L., and Stephen Quinn. "Life in the Fast Track." *Civil Engineering,* April 1992, pp. 46–49.

Riley, Kristyn. "Selling Automation to Toll Collectors." *New England Business,* April 1992, pp. 44–45.

Rourke, John. "Radio That Can Read—and Write." *Communications,* December 1992, pp. 24–25.

Sager, Ira. "The Great Equalizer." *Business Week* (The Information Revolution 1994), pp. 100–107.

Schine, Eric. "Here Comes the Thinking Car." *Business Week,* May 25, 1992, pp. 84, 87.

"Selling Automation to Toll Collectors." *New England Business,* April 1992, pp. 44–45.

Sheeline, William E. "Ten Ways to Bet Your Mad Money." *Fortune* (1993 Investor's Guide), pp. 72–76.

"Smart Highways . . . Slow Governments." *Distribution,* December 1993, pp. 18, 20.

Studt, Tim. "Smart Vehicles, Smart Highways Roaring Down the Pike." *R&D Magazine,* October 25, 1993, pp. 14–18.

Sullivan, R. Lee. "Fast Lane." *Forbes,* July 4, 1994, pp. 112, 114.

"Tags Hold Data and a Glimpse of the Future." *Distribution,* May 1993, p. 16.

Weber, James. "Ministry Turns to Visuals in Attempt to Help Motorists." *Computing Canada,* April 25, 1991, pp. 17–18.

Wexler, Joanie M. "Conrail Revamps Architectures." *Computerworld,* May 25, 1992, p. 6.

Zipser, Andy. "Positive Identification." *Barron's,* December 2, 1991.

———. "Watch the Steak, Not the Sizzle." *Barron's,* November 8, 1993.

CASE 6–8   Barro Stickney, Inc.

Introduction

With four people and sales of $5.5 million, Barro Stickney, Inc. (BSI), had become a successful and profitable manufacturers' representative firm. It enjoyed a reputation for outstanding sales results and friendly, thorough service to both its customers and principals. In addition, BSI was considered a great place to work. The office was comfortable and the atmosphere relaxed but professional. All members of the group had come to value the close, friendly working relationships that had grown with the organization.

Success had brought with it increased profits as well as the inevitable decision regarding further growth. Recent requests from two principals, Franklin Key Electronics and R. D. Ocean, had forced BSI to focus its attention on the question of expansion. It was not to be an easy decision, for expansion offered both risk and opportunity.

Company Background

John Barro and Bill Stickney established their small manufacturers' representative agency, Barro Stickney, Inc., 10 years ago. Both men were close friends who left different manufacturers' representative firms to join as partners in their own "rep" agency. The two worked very well together, and their talents complemented each other.

John Barro was energetic and gregarious. He enjoyed meeting new people and taking on new challenges. It was mainly through John's efforts that many of BSI's eight principals had signed on with BSI. Even after producing $1.75 million in sales this past year, John still made an effort to contribute much of his free time to community organizations in addition to perfecting his golf score.

This case was prepared by Tony Langan, B. Jane Stewart, and Lawrence M. Stratton, Jr., under the supervision of Professor Erin Anderson of the Wharton School, University of Pennsylvania. The writing of the case was sponsored by the Manufacturers' Representatives Educational Research Foundation. The cooperation of the Mid-Atlantic Chapter of the Electronic Representatives Association (ERA) is greatly appreciated.

Bill Stickney liked to think of himself as someone a person could count on. He was thoughtful and thorough. He liked to figure how things could get done, and how they could be better. Much of the administrative work of the agency, such as resource allocation and territory assignments, was handled by Bill. In addition to his contribution of $1.5 million to total company sales, Bill also had a Boy Scout troop and was interested in gourmet cooking. In fact, he often prepared specialties to share with his fellow workers.

A few years later, as the business grew, J. Todd Smith (J. T.) joined as an additional salesperson. J. T. had worked for a nationally known corporation, and he brought his experience dealing with large customers with him. He and his family loved the Harrisburg area, and J. T. was very happy when he was asked to join BSI just as his firm was ready to transfer him to Chicago. John and Bill had worked with J. T. in connection with a hospital fund-raising project, and they were impressed with his tenacity and enthusiasm. Because he had produced sales of over $2 million this past year, J. T. was now considered eligible to buy a partnership share of BSI.

Soon after J. T. joined BSI, Elizabeth Lee, a school friend of John's older sister, was hired as office manager. She was cheerful and put as much effort into her work as she did coaching the local swim team. The three salespeople knew they could rely on her to keep track of orders and schedules, and she was very helpful when customers and principals called with requests or problems.

Most principals in the industry assigned their reps exclusive territories, and BSI's ranged over the Pennsylvania, New Jersey, and Delaware area. The partners purchased a small house and converted it into their present office located in Camp Hill, a suburb of Harrisburg, the state capitol of Pennsylvania. The converted home contributed to the familylike atmosphere and attitude that was promoted and prevalent throughout the agency.

Over the years, in addition to local interests, BSI and its people had made an effort to participate in and support the efforts of the Electronics Representative Association (ERA). A wall of the company library was covered with awards and letters of appreciation. BSI had made many friends and important contacts through the organization. Just last year, BSI received a recommendation from Chuck Goodman, a Chicago manufacturers' rep who knew a principal in need of representation in the Philadelphia area. The principal's line worked well with BSI's existing portfolio, and customer response had been quite favorable. BSI planned to continue active participation in the ERA.

Each week, BSI held a 5 o'clock meeting in the office library where all members of the company shared their experiences of the week. It was a time when new ideas were encouraged and everyone was brought up to date. For example, many customer problems were solved here, and principals' and members' suggestions were discussed. An established agenda enabled members to prepare. Most meetings took about 60 to 90 minutes, with emphasis placed on group consensus. It was during this group meeting that BSI would discuss the future of the company.

Opportunities for Expansion

R. D. Ocean was BSI's largest principal, and it accounted for 32 percent of BSI's revenues. Ocean had just promoted James Innve as new sales manager, and he felt an additional salesperson was needed for BSI to achieve the new sales projections. Innve expressed the opinion that BSI's large commission checks justified the additional effort, and he further commented that J. T.'s expensive new car was proof that BSI could afford it.

BSI was not sure an additional salesperson was necessary, but it did not want to lose the goodwill of R. D. Ocean or its business. Also, while it was customary for all principals to meet and tacitly approve new representatives, BSI wanted to be very sure that any new salesperson would fit into the close-knit BSI organization.

Franklin Key Electronics was BSI's initial principal and had remained a consistent contributor of approximately 15 percent of BSI's revenues. BSI felt its customer base was well suited to the Franklin line, and it had worked hard to establish the Franklin Key name with these customers. As a consequence, BSI now considered Franklin Key relatively easy to sell.

A few days previously, Mark Heil, Franklin's representative from Virginia, perished when his private plane crashed, leaving Franklin Key without representation in its D.C./Virginia territory. Franklin did not want to jeopardize its sales of over $800,000 and was desperate to replace Heil before its customers found other sources. Franklin offered the territory to BSI and was anxious to hear the decision within one week.

BSI was not familiar with the territory, but it did understand that there were many military accounts. This meant there was a potential for sizable orders, although a different and specialized sales approach would be required. Military customers are known to have their own unique approach to purchase decisions.

Because of the distance and the size of the territory, serious consideration was needed as to whether a branch office would be necessary. A branch office would mean less interaction with and a greater independence from the main BSI office. None of the current BSI members seemed eager to move there, but it might be possible to hire someone who was familiar with the territory. There was, of course, always the risk that any successful salesperson might leave and start his or her own rep firm.

In addition to possibilities of expanding its territory and its sales force, BSI also wanted to consider whether it should increase or maintain its number of principals. BSI's established customer base and its valued reputation put it in a strong position to approach potential principals. If, however, BSI had too many principals, it might not be able to offer them all the attention and service they might require.

Preparation for the Meeting

Each member received an agenda and supporting data for the upcoming meeting asking them to consider the issue of expansion. They would be asked whether BSI should or should not expand its territory, its sales force, and/or its number of principals. In preparation, they were each asked to take a good hard look at the current BSI portfolio and to consider all possibilities for growth, including the effect any changes would have on the company's profits, its reputation, and its work environment.

It was an ambitious agenda: one that would determine the future of the company. It would take even more time than usual to discuss everything and reach consensus. Consequently, this week's meeting was set to occur over the weekend at Bill Stickney's vacation lodge in the Poconos starting with a gourmet dinner served at 7 PM sharp.

EXHIBIT 1 Return versus Difficulty in Selling

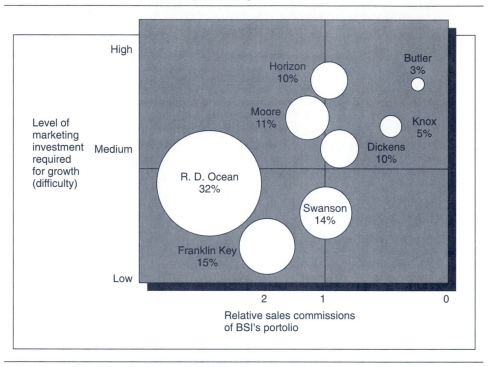

Before the meeting, Bill Stickney examined the sources of BSI's revenue and the firm's income for the previous year. He also estimated the future prospects for each of BSI's lines, considering each line's market potential and BSI's level of saturation in each market. Finally, he estimated the costs of hiring a new employee both in the current sales territory and in the Washington/Virginia area. Immediately before the meeting, Elizabeth finished compiling Bill's data into four exhibits (see Exhibits 2–4).

Exhibit 1 evaluates the amount of sales effort (difficulty in selling) necessary to achieve a certain percentage of sales in BSI's portfolio (return). Difficulty in selling is measured by the level of marketing investment required for growth. Stickney's estimate is shown on the vertical axis. Return for this investment is measured by the relative sales commissions as a percent of BSI's portfolio, shown on the horizontal axis. If BSI's time were evenly divided among its eight principals, each would receive 12.5 percent of the agency's time. The X axis shows each principal's time allocation as a proportion of 12.5 percent, the "par" time allocation. The area of each ellipse reflects each principal's share of BSI's commission revenue.

Bill Stickney presented the following additional comments as a result of his research:

1. Swanson's products are being replaced by the competition's computerized electronic equipment, a product category the firm has ignored. As a result, the company is losing its once prominent market position.

EXHIBIT 2 Barro Stickney, Inc., Estimation of Cost of Additional Sales Representative

Compensation Costs for New Sales Representative

Depending on the new sales representative's level of experience, BSI would pay a base salary of $15,000–$25,000 with the following bonus schedule:

  0% firm's commission revenue up to $500,000 in sales

20% firm's commission revenue first $.5 million in sales over $500,000

25% firm's commission revenue for the next $.5 million in sales

30% firm's commission for the next $.5 million in sales

40% firm's commission sales above $2 million

Estimate of Support Costs[1] for New Representative[2]

Search applicant pool, psychological testing, hiring, training,[3] flying final choice to principals for approval.[4]	$28,000
Automobile expenses, telephone costs, business cards, entertainment promotion.	$22,000
Insurance, payroll taxes (social security, unemployment compensation)	$16,000
Total expenses	$66,000

Incremental Expenses for New Territory

Transportation (additional mileage from Camp Hill to Virginia)	$ 2,000
Office equipment and rent (same regardless of headquarter's location)	$ 4,000
Cost of hiring office manager[5]	$18,000
Total incremental expenses	$24,000

[1]Rounded to the nearest thousand.
[2]In current territory.
[3]Excludes the lost revenue from selling instead of engaging in this activity (opportunity cost).
[4]Although rep agencies are not legally required to show prospective employees to principals, it is generally held to be good business practice.
[5]Discretionary.

EXHIBIT 3 Barro Stickney, Inc., Statement of Revenue Total Sales Revenue 1991, $5.5 million

Principal	Estimated Market Saturation	Product Type	Sales/ Commission Rate	Share of BSI's Portfolio	Commission Revenue
R. D. Ocean	High	Components	5%	32%	$96,756
Franklin Key	High	Components	5	15	45,354
Butler	Low	Technical/computer	12	3	9,070
Dickens	Low	Components	5	10	30,236
Horizon	Medium	Components	5.5	10	30,237
Swanson	High	Components	5.25	14	42,331
Moore	Medium	Consumer/electronics	5.25	11	33,260
Knox	Low	Technical/communications	8.5	5	15,118

EXHIBIT 4 Barro Stickney, Inc., Statement of Income (for the year ending December 31, 1991)

Revenue	
Commission income	$302,362
Expenses	
Salaries for sales and bonuses (includes Barro Stickney)	130,250
Office manager's salary	20,000
Total nonpersonnel expenses[1]	128,279
Total expenses	$278,529
New income[2]	**$ 23,833 (7.9% of revenue)**

---

[1]Includes travel, advertising, taxes, office supplies, retirement, automobile expenses, communications, office equipment, and miscellaneous expenses.

[2]Currently held in negotiable certificates of deposits in a Harrisburg bank.

2. Although small amounts of effort are required to promote Ocean's product line to customers in the current sales territory, Ocean is extremely demanding of both BSI and other manufacturers' representative firms.

3. According to a seminar at the last ERA meeting, the maximum safe proportion of a rep firm's commissions from a single principal should be 25 to 30 percent. Also, at the meeting, one speaker indicated that if a firm commands 80 percent of a market, it should focus on another product or expand its territory rather than attempt to obtain the remainder of the market.

4. The revenue for investment for the manufacturers' representative firm comes from one or more of several sources. These sources include reduced forthcoming commission income, retained previous income, and borrowed money from a financial institution. Most successful firms expand their sales force or sales territory when they experience income growth and use of the investment as a tax write-off.

CASE 6–9   Konark Television India

On 1 December, 1990, Mr. Ashok Bhalla began to prepare for a meeting scheduled for the next week with his boss, Mr. Atul Singh. The meeting would focus on distribution strategy for Konark Television Ltd., a medium-sized manufacturer of television sets in India. At issue was the nature of immediate actions to be taken as well as long-range planning. Mr. Bhalla was managing director of Konark, responsible for a variety of activities, including marketing. Mr. Singh was president.

This case was written by Fulbright Lecturer and Associate Professor James E. Nelson, University of Colorado at Boulder, and Dr. Piyush K. Sinha, associate professor, Xavier Institute of Management, Bhubaneswar, India. The authors thank Professor Roger A. Kerin, Southern Methodist University, for his helpful comments in writing this case. The case is intended for educational purposes rather than to illustrate either effective or ineffective decision making. Some data in the case are disguised. © 1991 by James E. Nelson.

TV Industry in India

The television industry in India started in late 1959 with the Indian government using a UNESCO grant to build a small transmitter in New Delhi. The station soon began to broadcast short programs promoting education, health, and family planning. Daily transmissions were limited to 20 minutes. In 1965, the station began broadcasting variety and entertainment programs and expanded its programming to one hour per day. Programming increased to three hours per day in 1970 and to four hours per day by 1976, when commercials were first permitted. The number of transmission centers in the country grew slowly but steadily during this period as well.

In July 1982, the Indian government announced a special expansion plan, providing 680 million rupees (Rs) for extending its television network to cover about 70 percent of India's population. By early 1988, the 245 TV transmitters in operation were estimated to have met this goal. The government then authorized construction of 417 new transmitters which would raise network coverage to over 80 percent of India's population. By late 1990, daily programming averaged almost 11 hours per day, making television the most popular medium of information, entertainment, and education in India. The network itself consisted of one channel except in large metropolitan areas where a second channel was also available. Both television channels were owned and operated by the government.

Despite the huge increase in network coverage, many in the TV industry would still describe the Indian government's attitude toward television as conservative. In fact, some would say that it was only the pressure of TV broadcasts from neighboring Sri Lanka and Pakistan that forced India's rapid expansion. Current policy was to view the industry as a luxury industry capable of bearing heavy taxes. Thus, the government charged Indian manufacturers high import duties on foreign manufactured components that they purchased plus heavy excise duties on sets that they assembled; in addition, state governments charged consumers sales taxes that ranged from 1 to 17 percent. The result was that duties and taxes accounted for almost one-half of the retail price of a color TV set and about one-third of the retail price of a black and white set. Retail prices of TV sets in India were estimated at almost double the prevalent world prices.

Such high prices limited demand. The number of sets in use in 1990 was estimated at about only 25 million. This number provided coverage to about 15 percent of the country's population, assuming five viewers per set. To increase coverage to 80 percent of the population would require over 100 million additional TV sets, again assuming five viewers per set. This figure represented a huge latent demand, almost 16 years of production at 1989 levels (see Exhibit 1). Many in the industry expected production and sales of TV sets would grow rapidly if only prices were reduced.

Indian Consumers

The population of India was estimated at approximately 850 million people. The majority lived in rural areas and small villages. The gross domestic product per capita was estimated at only $450 for 1990.

In sharp contrast to the masses, however, the television market concentrated among the affluent middle and upper social classes, variously estimated at some 12 percent to 25

EXHIBIT 1 Production of TV Sets in India (00,000 omitted)

Year	Black & White		Color	Total
	36 cm*	*51cm**	*Color*	*Total*
1980	—	3.1	—	3.1
1981	—	3.7	—	3.7
1982	—	4.4	—	4.4
1983	—	5.7	0.7	6.4
1984	1.8	6.6	2.8	11.2
1985	4.4	13.6	6.9	24.9
1986	8.2	13.3	9.0	30.5
1987	17.0	14.0	12.0	43.0
1988	28.0	16.0	13.0	57.0
1989	32.0**	18.0**	13.0**	63.0**

*Diagonal screen measurement.
**Estimated.

percent of the total population. Members of this segment exhibited a distinctly urban lifestyle. They owned video-cassette recorders, portable radio-cassette players, motor scooters, and compact cars. They earned MBA degrees, exercised in health spas, and traveled abroad. They lived in dual income households, sent their children to private schools, and practiced family planning. In short, members of the segment exhibited tastes and purchase behaviors much like their middle class, professional counterparts in the United States and Europe.

While there was no formal marketing research available, Mr. Bhalla thought he knew the consumer fairly well. "The typical purchase probably represents a joint decision by the husband and wife to buy. After all, they will be spending over one month's salary for our most popular color model." That model was now priced at retail at Rs 11,300, slightly less than retail prices of many national brands. However, a majority in the target segment probably did not perceive a price advantage for Konark. Indeed, the segment seemed somewhat insensitive to differentials in the range of Rs 10,000 to Rs 14,000, considering their TV sets to be valued possessions that added to the furnishing of their drawing rooms. Rather than price, most consumers seemed more influenced by promotion and by dealer activities.

TV Manufacturers in India

Approximately 140 different companies manufactured TV sets in India in 1989. However, many produced fewer than 1,000 sets per year and could not be considered major competitors. Further, Mr. Bhalla expected that many would not survive 1990—the trend definitely was toward a competition between 20 or 30 large firms. Most manufacturers sold in India only, although a few had begun the export of sets (mostly black and white) to nearby countries.

Most competitors were private companies whose actions ultimately were evaluated by a board of directors and shareholders. Typical of this group was Videocon. The company was formed in 1983, yet it was thought to be India's largest producer of color sets. A recent trade journal article had attributed Videocon's success to a strategy that combined higher dealer margins (2 percent higher than industry norms), attractive dealer incentives (Singapore trips, etc.), a reasonably good dealer network (about 200 dealers in 18 of India's 25 states), an excellent price range (from Rs 7,000 to Rs 18,000), and an advertising campaign that featured Indian film star Sridevi dressed in a Japanese kimono. Onida, the other leader in color, took a different approach. Its margins were slightly below industry standards; its prices were higher (Rs 13,000 to Rs 15,000); its advertising strategy was the most aggressive in the industry. Many consumers seemed sold on Onida before they ever visited a retailer.

Major competitors in the black and white market were considered by Mr. Bhalla to be Crown, Salora, Bush, and Dyanora. These four companies distributed black and white sets to most major markets in the country. (Crown and Bush manufactured color sets as well.) Strengths of these competitors were considered to be high brand recognition and strong dealer networks. In addition, several Indian states had one or two brands such as Konark or Uptron whose local success depended greatly on tax shelters provided by state governments.

All TV sets produced by the different manufacturers could be classified into two basic sizes, 51 centimeters and 36 centimeters. The larger size was a console model while the smaller was designed as a portable. Black and white sets differed little in styling. Differences in picture quality and chassis reliability were present; however, these differences tended to be difficult for most consumers to distinguish and evaluate. In contrast, differences in product features were more noticeable. Black and white sets came with and without handles, built-in voltage regulators, built-in antennas, electronic tuners, audio and video tape sockets, and on-screen displays. Warranties differed in terms of coverages and time periods. Retail prices for black and white sets across India ranged from about Rs 2,000 to Rs 3,500, with the average thought by Mr. Bhalla to be around Rs 2,600.

Differences between competing color sets seemed more pronounced. Styling was more distinctive, with manufacturers supplying a variety of cabinet designs, cabinet finishes, and control arrangements. Konark and a few other manufacturers had recently introduced a portable color set in hopes of stimulating demand. Quality and performance variations were again difficult for most consumers to recognize. Differences in features were substantial. Some color sets featured automatic contrast and brightness controls, on-screen displays of channel tuning and time, sockets for video recorders and external computers, remote control devices, high fidelity speakers, cable TV capabilities, and flat-screen picture tubes. Retail prices were estimated to range from about Rs 7,000 (for a small-screen portable) to Rs 19,000 (large-screen console), with an average around Rs 12,000.

Advertising practices varied considerably among manufacturers. Many smaller manufacturers used only newspaper advertisements that tended to be small in size. Larger manufacturers, including Konark, advertised also in newspapers, but used quarter-page or larger advertisements. Larger manufacturers also spent substantial amounts on magazine, outdoor, and television advertising. Videocon, for example, was thought to have spent about Rs 25 million or about 4 percent of its sales revenue on advertising in 1989. Onida's percentage might be as much as twice this amount. Most advertisements for TV sets tended to stress product features and product quality although a few were based primarily on whimsy and fantasy. Most ads would not mention price. Perhaps 10 percent of the newspaper advertising appeared in the form of cooperative advertising, featuring the product prominently in the ad and listing local dealers. Manufacturers would design and place cooperative ads and pay upwards of 80 percent of media costs.

Konark Television Ltd.

Konark Television Ltd. began operations in 1973 with the objective of manufacturing and marketing small black and white TV sets to the Orissa state market. Orissa is located on the east coast of India, directly below the state of West Bengal and Calcutta. Early years of operation found production leveling at about 5,000 sets per year. However, in 1982 the company adopted a more aggressive strategy when it became clear that the national market for TV sets was going to grow rapidly. At the same time, the state government invested Rs 1.5 million in Konark in order to produce color sets. Konark also began expanding its dealer network to nearby Indian states and to more distant, large metropolitan areas. Sales revenues in 1982 were approximately Rs 80 million.

The number of Konark models produced grew rapidly to 10, evenly divided between color and black and white sets. (Exhibit 2 presents a sales brochure describing Konark's top-of-the-line color model.) Sales revenues increased as well, to Rs 640 million for 1989, based on sales of 290,000 units. For 1990, sales revenues and unit volume were expected to increase by 25 percent and 15 percent, respectively, while gross margin was expected to remain at 20 percent of revenues. In early 1990, the state government added another Rs 2.5 million to strengthen Konark's equity base, despite an expectation that the company would barely break even for 1990. Employment in late 1990 was almost 700 people. Company headquarters remained in Bhubaneswar, the state capital.

Manufacturing facilities were located also in Bhubaneswar except for some assembly performed by three independent distributors. Assembly activity was done to save state sales taxes and to lower the prices paid by consumers; that is, many Indian states charged two levels of sales taxes depending upon whether or not the set was produced within the state. The state of Maharashtra (containing Bombay), for example, charged a sales tax of 4 percent for TV sets produced within the state and 16.5 percent for sets produced outside the state. Sales taxes for West Bengal (Calcutta) were 6 percent and 16.5 percent while rates for Uttar Pradesh (New Delhi) were 0 percent and 12.5 percent. State governments were indifferent as to whether assembly was performed by an independent distributor or by Konark, as long as the activity took place inside state borders. Present manufacturing capacity at Konark was around 400,000 units per year. Capacity could easily be expanded by 80 percent with the addition of a second shift.

The Konark line of TV sets was designed by engineers at Grundig, Gmbh., a German manufacturer known for quality electronic products. This technical collaboration saved Konark a great deal of effort each year in designing and developing new products. And

EXHIBIT 2 Konark Sales Brochure

Presenting the amazing new colour TV 'Galaxy Plus'

EXHIBIT 2   *(concluded)*

The New Colour TV from Konark. 'Galaxy Plus'. Incorporating <u>all</u> the sophisticated features likely to be introduced in the next few years.

Superior German technology. That's what sets the new 'Galaxy Plus' apart from all other colour TVS.

One of the latest models of GRUNDIG (W. Germany), world leaders in entertainment electronics. Brought to you by Konark Television Limited.

A symbol of German perfection

The Galaxy Plus combines the best of everything: World-famous German circuitry and components. The latest international TV technology. And the most demanding standards of picture and sound quality.

All of which make it more sophisticated. More dependable.

Features that are a connoisseur's delight.

The Galaxy Plus has several advanced features which offer you an extraordinary audio-visual experience, the like of which you will probably not feel with any other make.

What the Galaxy Plus offers you that other TVs don't

Never-before picture quality

Through the world's latest Colour Transient Improvement (CTI) technology. Which reduces picture distortion. And improves colour sharpness. Giving you a crystal-clear picture and more natural colours.

Programmes from all over the world

The Galaxy Plus is capable of bringing you the best of international TV networks. Thanks to satellite dish antenna, a unique 7-system versatility, and 99 channels with memory.

These features of the Galaxy Plus also help it play all types of Video Cassettes. Without any picture or sound distortion.

Simultaneous connection with external devices

An exclusive 20 pin Euro AV socket helps you connect the Galaxy Plus simultaneously with all external audio/video devices: Computers, VCRs, Video games. And cable TV.

While its automatic colour and brightness tuning save you the bother of frequent knob-fiddling.

Catch all your favourite programmes. Always.

You can preset the Galaxy Plus to switch itself on and off for your favourite programmes. Or, for worry-free operation by your children, in your absence.

Your own musical alarm clock

An on-screen time display reminds you of an important programme or appointment. While a built-in chimer wakes you up every day. Pleasantly.

Automatic pre-selection and operation

Select specific stations or external functions, code them in the 39+AV programme memory of the Galaxy Plus. And then, get them at the touch of a button. On the full-function Remote Control.

Handles wide voltage fluctuation

From a heart-stopping low of 140V. To a shocking high of 260V. The Galaxy Plus performs merrily through such a large range.

Richer, better TV sound

A higher audio output (8W) brings you all the beauty and power of full-bodied sound and clarity.

Saves power and money

Unlike other TVs, the Galaxy Plus uses only 60W. Besides, it also switches to the stand-by-mode automatically, when there is no TV signal for over 10 minutes.

Both features help you save precious electricity and money.

From Konark Television Limited

The futuristic Galaxy Plus is brought to you by Konark Television Limited. Through its nationwide network of over 500 sales outlets. Each of which also provide you prompt after-sales service. Should you ever need it.

The revolutionary new Galaxy Plus. See it in action at your nearest dealer. Compare it with every other make available in the local market.

And see how, feature by advanced feature, the Galaxy Plus is truly years ahead of its time. And the competition.

A marvel of German Technology

Konark Television Limited
(A Government of Orissa Enterprise)
Electronic Bhawan, Bhubaneswar 751 010. Phone: 53441 Telex: 0675-271

the resulting product line was considered by many in the industry to be of higher quality than the lines of many competitors. Circuitry was well designed and production engineers at the factory paid close attention to quality control. In addition, each Konark set was operated for 24 hours as a test of reliability before being shipped. The entire line reflected Konark's strategy of attempting to provide the market with a quality product at prices below the competition. In retail stores in Orissa, the lowest priced black and white model marketed by Konark sold to consumers for about Rs 2,200 while its most expensive color set sold for about Rs 15,000. Sales of the latter model had been disappointing to date. The premium market for color sets was quite small and seemed dominated by three national manufacturers.

Konark had a well-established network of more than 500 dealers located in 12 Indian states. In eight states, Konark sold its products directly to dealers through branch offices (Exhibit 3) operated by a Konark area manager. Each branch office also contained two or three salesmen who were assigned specific sales territories. Together, branch offices were expected to account for about 30 percent of Konark's sales revenues and cost Konark about Rs 10 million in fixed and variable expenses for 1990. In three states, Konark used instead the services of independent distributors to sell to dealers. The three distributors carried only Konark TV sets and earned a margin of 3 percent (based on cost) for all their activities, including assembly. All dealers and distributors were authorized to service Konark sets. The branch offices monitored all service activities.

In the state of Orissa, Konark used a large branch office to sell to approximately 250 dealers. In addition, Konark used company-owned showrooms as a second channel of distribution. Konark would lease space for showrooms at one or two locations in larger cities and display the complete line. The total cost of operating a showroom was estimated at about Rs 100,000 per year. Prospective customers often preferred to visit a showroom because they could easily compare different models and talk directly to a Konark employee. However, they seldom purchased—only about 5 percent of Orissa's unit sales came from the 10 showrooms in the state. Buyers preferred instead to purchase from dealers because dealers were known to bargain and sell at a discount from the list price. In contrast, Konark showrooms were under strict orders to sell all units at list price. About half of Konark's 1990 revenues would come from Orissa.

The appointment of dealers either by Konark or its distributors was made under certain conditions (Exhibit 4). Essential among them was the dealer's possession of a suitable showroom for the display and sale of TV sets. Dealers were also expected to sell Konark TV sets to the best of their ability, at fixed prices, and in specified market areas. Dealers were not permitted to sell sets made by other manufacturers. Dealers earned a margin ranging from Rs 100 (small black and white model) to Rs 900 (large color model) for every TV set they sold. Mr. Bhalla estimated that the average margin for 1990 would be about Rs 320 per set.

The Crisis

The year 1990 seemed to represent a turning point in the Indian TV industry. Unit demand for TV sets was expected to grow at only 10 percent, compared to almost 40 percent for 1989 and 1988. Industry experts attributed the slowing growth rate to a substantial hike in consumer prices. The blame was laid almost entirely on increases in

EXHIBIT 3   Branch Offices and Distributors for Konark Television India

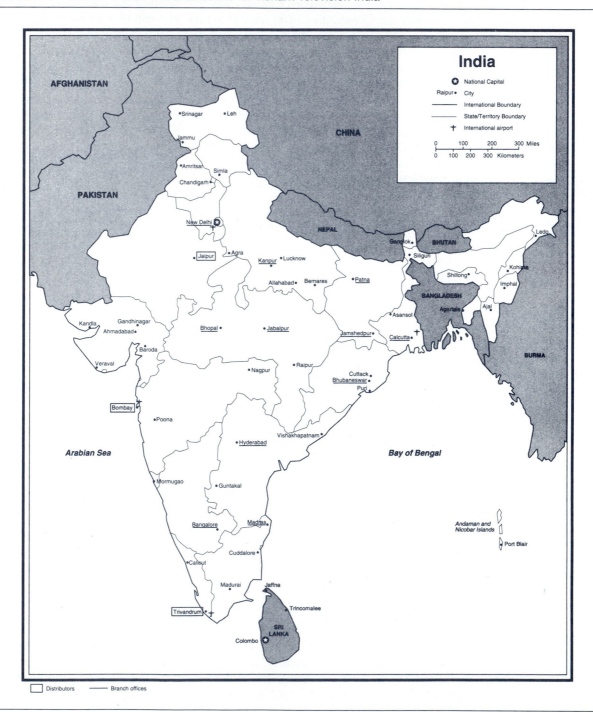

EXHIBIT 4   Terms and Conditions for Dealers of Konark TV Products

---

1. The Dealer shall canvass for, secure orders, and effect sales of Konark Television sets to the best of his ability and experience and he will guarantee sale of a minimum of sets during a calendar month.

2. The Company shall arrange for proper advertisement in the said area and shall give publicity of their product through newspapers, magazines, cinema slides, or by any other media and shall indicate, wherever feasible, the Dealer's name as their Selling Agents. The cost of such advertisements may be shared by the Company and the Dealer as may be mutually agreed to.

3. The appointment shall be confirmed after three months and initially be in force for a period of one year and can be renewed every year by mutual consent.

4. The company reserves the right to evaluate the performance of a Dealer.

5. This appointment may be terminated with a notice of one month on either side.

6. The Company shall deliver the Konark Television sets to the Dealer at the price agreed upon on cash payment at the factory at Bhubaneswar. On such delivery, the title to the goods would pass on to the Dealer and it will be the responsibility of the Dealer for the transportation of the sets to their place at their cost and expenses.

7. The Company may, however, at their discretion allow a credit of 30 (thirty) days subject to furnishing a Bank Guarantee or letter of credit or security deposit toward the price of Konark Television sets to be lifted by the Dealer at any time.

8. The Company shall not be responsible for any damage or defect occurring to the sets after delivery of the same to the Dealer or during transit.

9. The Dealer shall undertake to sell the sets to customers at prices fixed by the Company for different models. Dealer margins will be added to wholesale prices while fixing the customer's price of the television sets.

10. The Dealer will not act and deal with similar products of any other company so long as his appointment with Konark Television continues.

11. The Dealer shall not encroach into areas allotted to any other Dealer.

12. Any dispute or difference arising from or related to the appointment of the Dealership shall be settled mutually and, failing amicable settlement, shall be settled by an Arbitrator to be appointed by the Chairman of the Company whose decision shall be final and binding upon the parties. The place of arbitration shall be within the State of Orissa and the Court in Bhubaneswar (Orissa) only shall have jurisdiction to entertain any application, suit, or claim arising out of the appointment. All disputes shall be deemed to have arisen within the jurisdiction of the Court of Bhubaneswar.

13. Essential requirements to be fulfilled before getting Dealership:
    a. The Dealer must have a good showroom for display and sale of television sets.
    b. The Dealer shall have sufficient experience in dealing with electronics products (consumer goods).

---

import duties, excise taxes, and sales taxes, plus devaluation of the rupee—despite election year promises by government officials to offer TV sets at affordable prices! In addition, Konark was about to be affected by the Orissa government's decision to revoke the company's sales tax exemption beginning 1 January 1991. "Right now we are the clear choice, as Konark is the cheapest brand with a superior quality. But with the withdrawal of the exemption, we will be in the same price range as the 'big boys' and it will be a real run for the money to sell our brand," remarked Mr. Bhalla.

Mr. Bhalla was also concerned about some dealer activities that he thought were damaging to Konark. He knew that many dealers would play with the assigned margin and offer the same Konark product at differing prices to different customers. Or, equally damaging, different dealers might quote different prices for the same product to a single customer. Some dealers recently had gone so far as to buy large quantities of TV sets from Konark and sell them to unauthorized dealers in Bhubaneswar or in neighboring districts. This problem was particularly vexing because the offending dealers—while small in number—often were quite large and important to Konark's overall performance. Perhaps as much as 40 percent of Konark's sales revenues came from "problem" dealers.

Early in 1990, Mr. Bhalla thought that an increase in margins that Konark allowed its dealers was all that was needed to solve the problem. However, a modest change in dealer compensation had resulted in several national competitors raising their dealer margins even higher—without an increase in their retail prices. The result was that prices of Konark's models became even closer to those of national competitors and Konark's decline in market share had actually steepened. By late 1990, Konark's unit share of the Orissa market had fallen from 80 percent to just over 60 percent. "Unless something is done soon," Mr. Bhalla thought, "we'll soon be below 50 percent."

The Decision

Some immediate actions were needed to improve dealer relations and stimulate greater sales activity. An example was Konark's quarterly "Incentive Scheme" which had begun in April 1989. The program was a rebate arrangement based on points earned for a dealer's purchases of Konark TV sets. Reaction was lukewarm when the program was first announced. However, a revision in August 1989 greatly increased participation. Other actions yet to be formulated could be announced at a dealers' conference that Mr. Bhalla had scheduled for next month.

All such actions would have to be consistent with Konark's long-term distribution strategy. The problem was that this strategy had not yet been formulated. Mr. Bhalla saw this void as his most pressing responsibility, as well as a topic of great interest to Mr. Singh. Mr. Bhalla hoped to have major aspects of a distribution strategy ready for discussion for next week's meeting. Elements of the strategy would include recommendations on channel structure—branch offices or independent distributors, company showrooms or independent dealers—in existing markets as well as in markets identified for expansion. The latter markets included Bombay, Jaipur, and Trivandrum, areas that contained some 2 million consumers in the target segment. Most importantly, the strategy would have to address actions to combat the loss of the sales tax exemption in Orissa.

CASE 6–10   Optical Fiber Corporation

Introduction

The business year had just ended and Edward Porter, president and CEO of Optical Fiber Corporation (OFC), was reviewing the financial results with pleasure and concern. It had been a successful year with record sales and earnings and the addition of 30 percent more

---

manufacturing capacity. The expansion was timely because the sales report that accompanied the financial statements indicated that the order backlog for the company's optical glass fiber products had already reached $20 million and was steadily increasing. Yet, Porter was concerned about the ability of the company to continue its successful growth. Several years ago OFC had entered the fiber optics industry by obtaining patent licenses that allowed it to manufacture and market optical fiber and cable. In return, the license agreement obligated OFC to pay royalties to the patent holders based on its sales of the licensed products. Beginning in 1989 and continuing into 1997, some of the basic patents on the optical fiber technology would begin to expire, enabling the entry of new competition to manufacture and market some of the same products that OFC was successfully marketing.

The threat of new competition caused Porter to reflect on how OFC should be strategically positioned for the next five years. Several opportunities were under review by Porter and Paul Harriman, the vice president of marketing:

1. Over the past two years, OFC had been successful in developing optical glass fibers for a number of small specialized markets. They included medical, military and commercial aircraft, aerospace, and specially coated fibers for installation in severe environments. Additional product development and marketing would enable OFC to expand its sales of fibers to specialty markets.

2. Recently, engineers had been successful in reducing the costs to manufacture OFC optical fibers. Improvements in technology and manufacturing had made it possible to lower the costs on several important OFC products. With continuing expenditures for research and development (R&D), it was likely that further cost reductions could be achieved.

3. Historically, OFC's expertise has been in the production of multimode optical glass fiber for short-distance, high-speed data communications. Recently, the company had been contacted by prospective customers interested in a source for singlemode fiber to be used in long-distance communications systems.* OFC believed it had the expertise to manufacture singlemode fiber and was considering the development of a product line.

4. Although OFC had obtained the necessary patent licenses to produce fiber-optic cable from strands of optical fibers, it had chosen not to do so. Instead, it had pursued the strategy of selling optical fibers to the companies that assembled them into cables. Some executives believed that OFC should integrate forward and begin selling cable in addition to glass fiber.

Each opportunity was being carefully considered by the company and, hopefully, one or more would eventually make sense. However, it was not entirely clear to management which opportunities would place the company in the strongest competitive position. A number of factors would need to be considered as the company attempted to develop a corporate marketing strategy for the future.

Singlemode: an optical fiber that allows only one light to travel through the fiber. Singlemode fibers have very small cores (diameters) and are widely used in long-distance communications. *Multimode:* an optical fiber that allows several light rays to travel through the fiber simultaneously. Multimode fibers have larger cores and wide application in data communications networks that connect electronic equipment.

History and Development of Optical Fiber Corporation

OFC was founded in 1980 by four engineers to participate in the fast-growing fiber optics industry. The founders had been successful in negotiating patent licenses that enabled OFC to manufacture and market optical glass fiber subject to restrictions on production volume. For a few years, the company struggled to survive because the optical fiber and the electronic equipment necessary to make it work were too expensive for most businesses to consider. But as fiber prices dropped and communication systems became more data intensive, the economics of optical glass fiber began to be competitive with other means of transporting information such as copper wire cable, microwave transmission, and satellite. Initially, the company focused its resources on developing a product line of multimode optical fibers for use in data communications. Although the data communications market was substantially smaller than the telecommunications market, it was growing rapidly and enabled OFC to avoid competing with the larger companies that specialized in manufacturing optical fiber for telecommunications applications. The company was successful with its strategy and within eight years, sales had increased to more than $20 million and employment had grown to 110. OFC markets included military, aerospace, communications, computers, and process control.

In 1989, OFC moved into a larger facility in a new industrial district of Minneapolis to accommodate its expanding engineering and manufacturing operations. At the same time, OFC began to pursue R&D to reduce manufacturing costs and achieve technical breakthroughs that would lead to new products. The R&D commitment, which amounted to about 2.0 percent of sales was quite successful, and by 1990, the company had applied for seven patents covering the development of special performance optical fibers and fiber coatings for use in a variety of emerging specialty markets. Management was confident that the patents would be awarded over the next few years.

In 1991, OFC was successful in extending the earlier license agreements which had enabled the company to enter the market. The new licenses provided for an immediate increase in the quantities of optical fiber licensed for manufacture and also provided for annual increases through the year 2000. In return for the extended license, the company agreed to pay an additional $3.0 million in 1993 for the license as well as a royalty fee of 9.0 percent of net sales of OFC products manufactured under the agreements. Approximately 85 percent of the company's sales were subject to the license agreement.

During 1992, OFC expanded its manufacturing capacity and extended its line of multimode fiber optics products with three specialty optical fibers used in military missile guidance systems, nuclear power plants, and other military applications. Additionally, the data communications markets were strong reflecting the growth in computers, peripheral equipment, and local area networks. OFC sold multimode fibers to these markets through cable manufacturers who assembled the optical fibers into cables jacketed with a protective covering and resold them to original equipment manufacturers and cable distributors. The three largest cable companies that OFC supplied with optical fiber accounted for over 70 percent of the company's revenues. By the end of 1992, OFC sales had reached $48.8 million and the company had 250 employees in manufacturing, marketing, administration, R&D, and quality assurance. Additionally, OFC generated

---

TABLE 1 Income Statement (year ending 12–31–92)

Net sales	$48,764,000
Cost of sales	30,475,000
Gross profits	18,289,000
Marketing and administrative expenses	7,575,000
Research and development costs	975,000
Income (loss) from operations	9,739,000
Other income (expense):	
Interest income	737,000
Interest expense	(245,000)
Income (loss before taxes)	10,231,000
Income tax	4,092,000
Net income (loss)	$ 6,139,000

---

over $8.0 million in cash flow from operations during 1992, up substantially from the prior year. Tables 1 and 2 contain the financial statements for the year ending December 31, 1992.

Fiber Optics Technology

Fiber optics is a new technology that uses rays of light instead of electricity to transmit information over optical fibers at very high speeds. The optical fibers are usually thin strands of glass that are combined into cables and used to send information and computer data in the form of pulses of light. The optical fibers provide much clearer and faster transmission than conventional copper cable and satellite links.

An optical fiber consists of a core of high-purity glass encased in a coating of optical cladding to reduce signal loss through the side walls of the fiber. The information to be transmitted is converted from electrical impulses into light waves by a laser or light emitting diode. At the point of reception, the light waves are converted back into electrical impulses by a photo-detector. Figure 1 shows a basic fiber-optic system connecting two electronic circuits.

Communication by means of light waves guided through glass fibers offers a number of advantages over other methods of communication. Signals of equal strength can be transmitted over longer distances through optical fibers than through metallic conductors such as copper wire cables. Fiber-optic cables are substantially smaller and lighter than metallic cables of the same capacity, they can be installed more rapidly and used in confined spaces, and they are often less expensive. Optical fibers also have other advantages over satellite and line-of-sight transmissions such as microwave. Fiber-optic cables provide interference-free communications that offer a high degree of security.

Optical fibers are manufactured using expensive, precisely engineered equipment. Gaseous vapors of varying chemical composition are introduced into a glass tube in a clean, controlled environment. The glass tube, which will form the optical cladding, and

---

TABLE 2　Balance Sheet (year ending 12–31–92)

Assets

Current assets:

Cash	$11,894,000
Marketable securities	4,574,000
Accounts receivable	7,392,000
Inventories	6,656,000
Prepaid expenses	506,000
Total current assets	31,022,000

Property, plant and equipment:

Land	991,000
Buildings	7,042,000
Machinery and equipment	25,349,000
Less accumulated depreciation	13,352,000

Other assets:

License agreements	5,424,000
Total assets	56,476,000

Liabilities and Stockholders' Equity

Current liabilities:

Long-term debt	2,310,000
License for payable	3,000,000
Accounts payable	1,149,000
Income taxes payable	1,405,000
Accrued liabilities	4,629,000
Total liabilities	12,493,000

Stockholders' equity:

Common stock	1,500,000
Paid-in capital	50,153,000
Retained earnings (deficit)	(7,670,000)
Total stockholders' equity	43,983,000
Total liabilities and stockholders' equity	$56,476,000

---

the vapors are heated; and the oxide particles, which are formed through a reaction of chemical vapors with oxygen, are deposited on the inside of the tube. As the particles attach to the tube wall, they are fused to create a layer of high-purity glass. Succeeding layers of glass are deposited in this fashion to permit the transmission of light in accordance with the desired specifications. The glass tube is then collapsed into a rod consisting of a deposited core and the optical cladding. The glass rod, called a *preform,* is placed at the top of a fiber drawing tower and heated until it softens, after which it is drawn into a fiber of predetermined diameter. Figure 2 illustrates the core and cladding of singlemode and multimode glass fiber.

FIGURE 1   Fiber-Optic Transmission

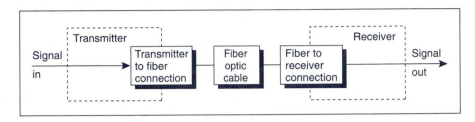

Before an optical fiber can be used, it must be converted into a cable by a manufacturing process called *cabling* to apply an outer protective covering around the fiber to protect it during installation and use. Important characteristics of optical cables are strength, flexibility, environmental resistance, and appearance. The importance of these features depends on how the cable will be used. An outside telephone cable, for example, must endure extremes of temperature, ice deposits that cause it to sag on a utility pole, high winds that buffet it, and rodents that chew on it underground. Similarly a cable running under an office carpet has different requirements than a cable running within the walls of an office. Cable design and construction can be simple or complex, depending on the cable's intended use and desired performance. Aerial cables that are strung between buildings may contain only one or two optical fibers, while other cables may carry several dozen fibers if they are used in local area networks. About 20 companies are involved in the manufacture of optical cable in the United States. It is a highly competitive industry requiring sophisticated design and engineering capabilities. And, as the market for optical fiber expands, copper cable manufacturers will extend their product lines to include fiber-optic cable. Facing increasing competition, these cable companies will prefer extremely responsive optical fiber suppliers. The ability of OFC to provide excellent customer service has enabled it to establish business relationships with some copper cable manufacturers.

An Example Application of Fiber Optics

Local area networks which connect office computers, factory workstations, and peripheral equipment are an example of an important application for optical fiber cables. Such cable networks improve productivity and quality by enhancing the speed, accuracy, and capacity of data transmission.

In a business involving multiple locations, there are three applications for optical fiber links. Optical cables designed for aerial or underground installation are used between buildings to connect main distribution panels, sometimes as replacements for copper wire cables.

Individual workstations on a particular floor within a building may also be connected by fiber-optic cable. Here, networks employing optical fiber cable connect workstations to a central processing unit and to other stations through a communications panel.

FIGURE 2   Singlemode and Multimode Optical Fiber

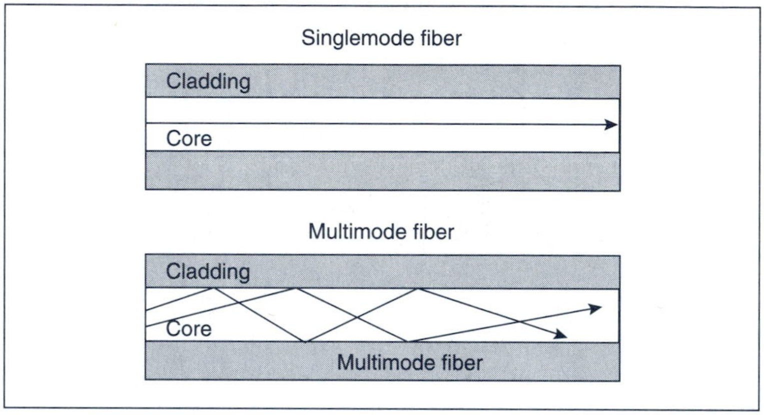

In the third application, the communications panel on each floor is linked with the main building distribution center using multiple vertical cable runs through elevator or other shafts forming the communications backbone of the building. The information capacity and resistance to electrical interference provided by optical transmission are distinct advantages in this application. Fiber-optic cable designs for office-floor and between-floor connections meet building safety codes, so the optical cable for these applications will often replace conventional copper wire cables.

Local area networks present a significant long-term opportunity for OFC. It is estimated that more than 50 million workstations are now installed in the United States, and continued growth and rapid technological change is expected. Many companies are increasing productivity by networking individual workstations, while others are converting existing systems from copper to fiber-optic cables. Although the market for optical communications systems has been growing over the past several years, the majority of optical cable penetration of local area networks has yet to be realized. OFC has about a 30 percent share of the U.S. market for optical fiber installed in local area networks.

The Market for Optical Fiber and Cable

The world market for optical fiber continues to grow rapidly, with shipments increasing 14 percent from an estimated 7.0 million kilometers of fiber in 1990 to approximately 8.0 million in 1991. The United States enjoys a 40 percent share of the world market and a surplus in the international trade of optical fiber and fiber-optic cable. In 1992 the trade surplus amounted to $303 million, a 43 percent increase from the previous year. However, some foreign-based companies produce fiber, cable, and fiber-optic components in U.S.

FIGURE 3   U.S. Multimode Cabled Fiber Market

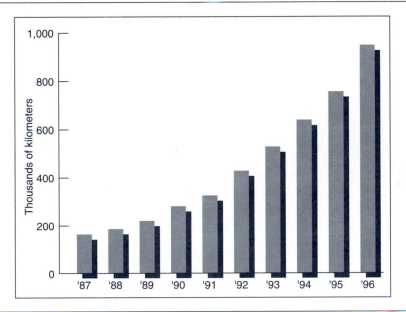

facilities, which increases the competition faced by OFC and other domestic businesses in the industry.

In the United States, the total 1991 optical fiber market has been estimated at 3.5 million kilometers, comprised of approximately 3.2 million kilometers of single-mode fiber valued at $320 million and 330 thousand kilometers of multimode fiber valued at approximately $65 million. This represents a growth in demand for multimode fiber in the United States in excess of 20 percent from 1990 to 1991. As shown in Figure 3, the demand for multimode fiber is predicted to continue to expand through the mid-1990s, with some market analysts indicating that 15 to 20 percent annual growth over the next three years is reasonable. Strong demand is expected for singlemode and multimode fiber to be used in cables for local area networks, telecommunications, cable television (CATV), and transoceanic fiber-optic systems.

Local Area Networks.   The local-area-network segment of the U.S. fiber optics market is expected to grow 20 percent annually through the first half of the 1990s. Ease of connection, compatibility with cost-effective electronics, and multimedia applications that combine text, voice, and video at a workstation make multimode fiber attractive for local area networks. Industry analysts expect new installations to continue to drive the growth of multimode fiber in data communication markets such as business, banking and financial services, government facilities, universities and hospitals, and other industries with high-volume data or security requirements.

Telecommunications. Telecommunications companies such as AT&T, Sprint Corporation, and MCI Communications Corporation are still installing fiber-optic cable throughout their long-distance systems. Presently, about 80 percent of the long-distance network is fiber-optic cable and 60 percent of the network between the long-distance system and local telephone offices is cabled with optical fiber.

Strong interest by the federal government in constructing a telecommunications network that will enhance the nation's ability to compete with foreign countries is expected to stimulate the development of fiber-optic telecommunications. A goal of achieving a nationwide fiber-optic network by the year 2015 has been mentioned by government sources. Singlemode optical fiber is usually preferred because it can transmit signals at very high rates over long distances without regeneration. This information-carrying capacity and low signal-loss make singlemode fiber well suited to very-high-speed, long-distance applications.

Recently, attention has turned to fiber-optic installation from the local telephone office to the residential customer where less than 5 percent is fiber-optic cable. For these "fiber-to-the-home" and "fiber-to-the-curb" applications cost is still an issue. While fiber optics is competitive with copper cable on a technical basis, it is still not economical to install fiber in all cases. That economic "cross-over" point should be achieved by the mid-1990s. It is expected that these shorter-distance communications applications will be served with singlemode and multimode cable.

Cable Television (CATV). An area of dramatic growth for fiber optics in the United States is cable television. The market is growing rapidly because cable television companies are installing new fiber-optic CATV systems to increase channel capacity and to upgrade existing systems to provide consumers with more sophisticated two-way services, including telecommunications. The National Cable Television Association estimates that the CATV operator's use of fiber optics has increased 400 percent since 1988 and will continue to increase by 25 percent annually through the 1990s. Industry plans call for spending $18 billion during the next 10 years to upgrade plant and equipment and rebuild more than 60 percent of existing systems. As Figure 4 illustrates, the installed base of fiber-optic cable in the cable television industry is estimated to be 40 thousand miles in 1993. Both singlemode and multimode fibers will be used to produce the cables needed by this industry. Some cable producers have established separate divisions specifically dedicated to the needs of CATV customers.

Undersea Cable Systems. The next several years could see an explosion of capacity for international communication if the transoceanic fiber-optic systems being planned during 1991 and 1992 are constructed. Many of the plans involve linking or extending international fiber-optic cable systems. Most are expected to be completed between 1993 and 1998 and they will link the United States with Europe, Asia, and South America. Transoceanic systems will feature transmission speeds up to 5 billion bits per second using both singlemode and multimode fiber-optic cable. The total investment in currently installed and planned undersea fiber-optic cable may exceed $12 billion by the time of its completion in the late 1990s.

FIGURE 4   Installed Base of Fiber-Optic Cable in the CATV Industry

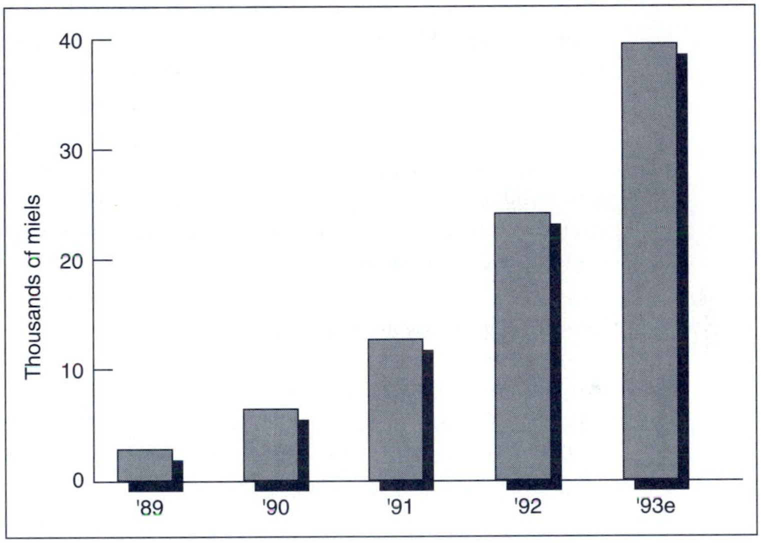

Marketing Strategy and Product Lines

OFC primarily markets its optical fibers through direct sales made by a small sales and marketing staff located at the corporate offices in Minneapolis. The company also advertises in trade publications, distributes product brochures and other technical material to its mailing list of potential customers, and demonstrates its products at technical conferences and trade shows. All of its present customers are cable manufacturers that purchase optical fibers and assemble them into fiber-optic cables for resale to manufacturers, distributors, and other customers such as government and military facilities, colleges and universities, CATV, and telecommunications and broadcasting firms. In 1992, approximately 70 percent of the company's sales were made to three large cable manufacturing companies, one of which was a firm that was licensing OFC to produce and market optical glass fibers.

Standard Multimode Optical Fibers.   OFC specializes in multimode fiber for data communications and telecommunications markets. The markets are extremely competitive and OFC's main rivals are the two licensors to whom it pays royalties. Each has substantially greater resources and operating experience. To date, OFC has been successful because of the licensing requirements that limit competition and because of its competitive advantages of outstanding customer service, product performance, and competitive pricing.

The multimode product line is very profitable and accounts for most of the firm's profits. It consists of six products, each designed for specific communications requirements. Four products, OFGI-100, OFGI-110, OFGI-120, and OFGI-130, are optical fibers with different core diameters designed for telecommunications and local area networks requiring high-speed data transmission. Two products, OFSI-200 and OFSI-210, have other uses such as short-distance data links, electronic instrumentation, and process control. Technological change in fiber optics is rapid, so improvement in the performance characteristics of multimode fiber is a frequent occurrence. Both OFC and its competitors offer product revisions and line extensions that improve the performance of multimode fibers in customer applications. OFC, for example, has recently developed a process to apply a metallized coating to the end of its multimode fiber so it could be soldered to a semiconductor laser light source and other electronic components. To keep abreast of changing technology and competition, OFC was required to maintain an expensive, ongoing R&D program.

Product quality was also essential to the success of OFC's multimode optical fibers. Quality control programs were designed to maintain strict tolerances during the manufacturing process and to assure compliance with the customer's requirements. Each product was 100 percent tested for quality and performance using standard industry test procedures before it was shipped. Careful attention to product quality was an important factor in establishing OFC as a major supplier to three of the leading manufacturers of optical cable.

Specialty Optical Fiber.   During 1992, OFC was successful in the development and introductory marketing of three optical fibers for application in niche markets. OFC-SF100 was a radiation-resistant optical fiber designed for cables that would be installed in radioactive environments such as nuclear power plants, missile silos, and naval vessels. A hermetically sealed optical fiber, OFC-SF200, was specially coated to withstand air, moisture, and water for cables to be used in underwater and harsh outdoor environments. OFC-SF300 was a coated fiber developed for cables used in high-temperature environments such as heating ducts and other locations where fire was a threat. Table 3 summarizes the standard and specialty optical fibers marketed by OFC during 1992.

Specialty fibers were an attractive marketing opportunity for OFC because the sales of these products were frequently not covered by the patent licenses. Although the markets were usually small and the fibers required marketing research and product development, the profit margins were substantially larger than those for the standard multimode products. OFC was regularly contacted by manufacturers' representatives and cable companies requesting special fibers for cables to be installed in severe environments around chemical and petroleum plants, military installations, and in equipment for the defense and space programs.

Recently, OFC had successfully experimented with a fiber capable of transmitting ultraviolet light and another fiber made of fluoride glass that had promise in laser surgery and other medical and scientific applications. However, if OFC were to continue to pursue optical fibers for niche markets, an additional annual R&D expenditure of $400,000 would be required and several organizational changes would be necessary. The present marketing staff was not adequate to conduct the market research needed to identify prospective customers, define their special needs, and complete the sales process. Paul

---

TABLE 3   OFC Fiber-Optic Products

Product	Type	Recommended Application
OFGI-100	Multimode	Telecommunications and local area networks
OFGI-110		
OFGI-120		
OFGI-130		
OFSI-200	Multimode	Electronic instrumentation, data links, process control
OFSI-210		
OFC-SF100	Multimode	Radioactive environments
OFC-SF200		High moisture and wet environments
OFC-300		High temperature environments

Harriman estimated that OFC would need a sales manager, a product manager, and a marketing assistant. Experienced sales managers were paid an annual salary of $140,000, typically, while product managers with experience earned around $110,000 a year. One or more marketing assistants were usually employed to assist product management, and trained personnel expected a salary of $75,000 a year.

The marketing organization would also have to be restructured so the specialty optical fiber products would receive the necessary attention. Whatever organizational changes were made, it would be necessary to make some arrangement for sales personnel to represent the product line. Consideration was being given to using salaried employees as either sales representatives or manufacturers' representatives. Recently, OFC had been contacted by a business in Oakland, California, about representing the specialty fiber products in the western region of the United States. The company employed four salespeople and specialized in selling the optical and electronic components of manufacturers for a sales commission of 10 percent. Paul Harriman believed that until the necessary marketing organization and strategy were formalized for the products, additional product development expenditures could not be justified.

Product Development of Singlemode Optical Fibers.   Recent improvements in the technology for producing singlemode fibers has made it possible to produce them as economically as multimode fibers. In applications involving the transmission of information over short distances, both fibers were acceptable substitutes. However, because of their desirable optical properties and high transmission rates, it was expected that the next generation of fiber-optic cable for the CATV and long-distance telephone industry would be made using single-mode fibers. Although the change would occur slowly, it would be significant because these industries were the largest users of fiber-optic cable.

During 1992, OFC was contacted by cable companies and requested to become an alternate supplier of singlemode fiber. OFC had not responded to the opportunities because it had not developed singlemode fibers for marketing. Management estimated that if OFC were to market singlemode fiber, two products would be necessary. Product development would require a year and an expenditure in R&D of $2,500,000. In addition, new manufacturing equipment would be needed to produce the smaller diameter fibers to the exacting specifications of the cable producers. New equipment would take a year to install and test before acceptable fiber could be produced for marketing. A capital investment of $4 million (not including the R&D expenditure) would be necessary to enter the market.

The marketing strategy and personnel presently used to market the standard multimode fibers could also be used for singlemode fiber products. Direct sales by the existing OFC corporate marketing staff would be made to the cable producers. Still, the market would be very competitive because one of the OFC licensors owned a large subsidiary that produced singlemode cable for the long-distance telephone industry and was a leading supplier. Management reasoned that OFC could be successful as a secondary supplier of singlemode fiber and eventually sell a large quantity at modest profit margins.

Vertical Integration.   Several times over the past few years, management had considered the possibility of producing optical cable with its fibers. Two of the company founders had been previously employed in the optical cable industry, and they believed that OFC should diversify its business by forward integration. They persuasively argued that since most of the OFC multimode fiber business was with three cable companies, it would be possible to expand the sales of optical fiber by producing cables for OEM's and cable distributors. They also noted that the patent licenses recently negotiated authorized not only the production of optical fiber, but also the conversion of the fiber into optical cable. It was the opinion of some that forward integration into cable production would enable OFC to add more value to its products and enhance the profitability of the company. Two strategic approaches were being evaluated by OFC management.

One strategy was to enter the optical cable business through internal product development. In this instance, OFC would expand its R&D department to develop a line of optical cable products. Management estimated that ongoing R&D costs would increase by $500,000 annually when the necessary personnel and prototype equipment were added to conduct the development and testing. OFC planned to focus initially on developing cable products that used its specialty optical fiber. This approach was considered attractive because royalties would not have to be paid on the cable produced with the specialty fibers and they would be protected from competition if the OFC patents were awarded. About two years would be needed to develop and test the products. If the development effort was successful, equipment would have to be purchased to manufacture the optical cable. It was estimated that a capital investment of $5 million would have to be made in manufacturing equipment and facilities. Management believed that the optical cables produced with the specialty fibers could initially be sold by the corporate marketing staff to OEM's and military installations and through optical cable distributors to other users. As the cable business expanded, OFC would add marketing staff as necessary.

A second integration strategy under consideration was the acquisition of an optical cable manufacturer for cash. Management was confident that an excellent business could be located which would permit OFC to quickly enter the cable market with products and the necessary manufacturing and marketing capability. Rapid expansion of the cable industry over the past several years and a weak economy had resulted in a temporary oversupply of cable. As a result, a number of good businesses were looking for buyers to avoid bankruptcy or liquidation. Some executives favored an acquisition as the avenue for growth because it was likely that a producer of both singlemode and multimode cable could be purchased which would enable OFC to completely integrate its business if it desired to do so. Others argued against the acquisition because it would immediately place OFC in competition with its existing cable customers.

If OFC were to proceed with an acquisition, 18 months would be needed to locate an acceptable company, borrow the money and complete the negotiations, and combine the business operations. Industry experts estimated the cost to acquire a cable manufacturer at between $10 million and $15 million. Of course the price would probably increase as the economy recovered and the supply of fiber-optic cable came back into balance with demand.

Developing a Corporate Marketing Strategy

As Edward Porter and Paul Harriman considered the future marketing strategy, they were reminded once again of the importance of protecting OFC's enviable market position. Success had not come easily and it had only been achieved with the dedication of loyal employees and carefully planned and executed strategic decisions. Yet, expiration of the basic fiber optics patents over the next several years posed a serious threat. It would certainly mean new businesses offering comparable fiber-optic products and competing for the same customers. Both executives wondered what OFC could do to continue to differentiate its products and preserve its competitive advantage in the marketplace.

Continued growth was also an important priority of management. However, selecting the most desirable combination of marketing opportunities was somewhat complicated because of a recent regulatory development. In 1992, a landmark decision by the FCC allowed CATV operators to provide telecommunications services, bringing them into direct competition with the telephone companies. The decision was expected to encourage CATV operators to upgrade and build fiber-optic networks to handle telecommunications. In response, the telephone companies were acquiring CATV systems as a way of offering video services to preserve and expand their market position. Most industry experts, including Harriman, thought that in a few years, after the acquisitions, joint ventures, and strategic alliances were completed, little distinction would exist between the companies in the two industries.

Porter and Harriman strongly believed that in addition to protecting its existing business, OFC must carefully select new marketing opportunities that would enable it to continue to achieve record levels of sales and profits without exposing the company to unnecessary risk. Because resources were limited, the selection of an inferior marketing strategy would have serious consequences for OFC's ability to remain an industry leader. Porter wasn't even willing to consider this as a possibility.

CASE 6–11   Golden Valley Microwave Foods, Inc.

Jim Watkins and his company, Golden Valley Microwave Foods, was in a market where repeat business was key. Consumers would buy novelty microwavable items; however, the key was getting these consumers to continue to buy the products. The challenge to Golden Valley was to link technology, quality, convenience, and price into a product which consumers would buy on a regular basis.

The company had been successful with its Act II microwavable popcorn. However, success had not come as readily with the company's Morning line offering of microwavable breakfast items. And the jury was still out regarding the company's move into microwavable french fries.

Watkins knew that he could not sit back and watch his company's success. The microwave food market had experienced ups and down. To remain successful, Golden Valley had to continue to introduce new products into its current markets, while at the same time educating new markets to the notion of microwavable food items.

The Company

Jim Watkins was the founder and largest shareholder (17 percent) of Golden Valley Microwave Foods, Inc. (GVMF). Watkins worked for Pillsbury from 1971 to 1978 as a member of a research team developing foods for microwave ovens. Pillsbury was not as enthusiastic about microwave oven foods as the team and Watkins would have liked. Watkins quit Pillsbury when the company refused to focus efforts on the microwave food market. Watkins started the Edina, Minnesota, based Golden Valley Microwave Foods with $250,000 in venture capital in 1978.[1] GVMF was founded upon Watkins's strong belief that every family in the United States wanted to cook entire meals in a few minutes.

Watkins felt certain that the microwave market was a lucrative market. By the end of the 1970s, only 12 percent of U.S. households owned microwave ovens.[2] By the mid-1980s, this number had risen to 40 percent, with projections for rapid growth. Aspiring to pioneer in this high-tech market, Watkins set out to sell microwavable frozen, ready-to-eat dinners through supermarket chains. An outside firm was hired to make dinners under the Golden Valley label in 1980. Watkins met with difficulty. GVMF was a new company with minimal marketing or business clout, a new unrecognized product, and no formal channels of distribution. The new-product introduction failed.

Watkins decided that the product failure was not solely with the product and market, but also in the mode of distributing the product. Supermarkets were in a highly competitive arena that GVMF was not able to penetrate. Watkins then began to pursue vending machines

This case was prepared by Victoria L. Crittenden, associate professor of marketing at Boston College, as the basis for class discussion rather than to illustrate either effective or ineffective handling of a managerial situation. Research assistance was provided by Jennifer Fraser, MBA student, Boston College. All material was from secondary sources.
[1]The company went public in 1986.
[2]One percent represented approximately 800,000 homes.

as a way to distribute microwave food items.[3] Microwave ovens had started to appear in cafeterias and office suites next to vending machines stocked with ready-to-heat foods.

Watkins thought distributors should be ripe for more snack items to place in vending machines. Deciding the popcorn market was a great microwave food opportunity, Watkins hired five people to find the best kernels and develop bags that would actually pop all of the kernels. Golden Valley microwavable popcorn was born. In 1983, one year after introduction, Golden Valley had almost $7 million in popcorn sales. The initial popcorn product was a frozen version. The shelf-stable popcorn was introduced in 1984. GVMF concentrated its efforts on vending machines and mass merchandisers. The company licensed its packaging technology to General Mills to use in the grocery store market.

By the beginning of the 1990s, approximately 90 percent of GVMF's $140 million in revenues came from the sale of its microwave popcorn. The remaining 10 percent of revenues were from the company's Microwave Morning line of waffles, pancakes, and french toast.

The Snack Food Market

The snack food industry was comprised of many different types of products, with an estimated market size ranging from $10 billion to $15 billion.[4] Major categories included in these estimates were chocolate candies, nonchocolate candies, gum, nuts, granola, salted snacks, meat snacks, ice bars, fruit snacks, and baked snacks. However, the range on market size was indicative of the fact that the snack food market was ill-defined in that many different products could possibly be included in some estimates but not in others (e.g., drinks such as beer, colas/noncolas, and wine were included in some estimates). Needless to say, the snack market was a sizable market in the 1990s.

American consumers were reported to have consumed 5 billion pounds of snacks in 1991. Per capita consumption of packaged savory snacks in the United States was around 20 pounds in 1991. Potato chips accounted for 32 percent of the market share in pound volume, tortilla chips had 21 percent, popcorn (in various forms) held 14 percent, and pretzels and nuts captured 8 percent. Projections were for growth in low-fat and lightly salted snacks. Pretzels were predicted to outpace the growth of most other snack foods (pretzels saw a growth rate of 12 percent in 1990).

The size and continued growth of the snack food market resulted in the introduction of around 500 new snack products (including reformulations) each year. Companies were capitalizing on the health-conscious trend and introduced many new products that were low-sodium, low-fat, and/or low-calorie. Gourmet snack foods were also in vogue.

Keebler Co. introduced eight new products in the early 1990s, including cookies, pretzels, and additional varieties in its well-established lines such as Town House Crackers and Club Crackers. Frito-Lay (estimated to have over 40 percent of the salty

---

[3]No reliable estimates of vending machine market size were available.
[4]The buying power of children was thought to have a strong impact on consumption of snacks in the future. There were 33 million children between the ages of 4 and 12 in the U.S. at the beginning of 1990. The most popular expenditure for children's wealth (valued at $9 billion), aside from saving about 30 percent of this money, was snack food at a rate of about $2 billion per year.

snack market) invested heavily in its Rold Gold brand of pretzels, while buying out the SunChips brand of multigrain chips.[5] Terra Chips sold an estimated $10 million in the early 1990s of its chip made from taro and flavored with beet juice, yucca, sweet potato, batata, and parsnip. Other new chip flavorings included jalapeno, cheddar, and chile cheese. Party mixes (premixed batches of assorted snacks) and the snack cracker/chip (baked instead of fried) were two other growth areas. The one product category that experienced flat growth was nuts.

Popcorn.   Popcorn had moved from junk food status to health food, which was low in calories and high in fiber. Per capita consumption of popcorn in the United States was approximately 50 quarts at the beginning of the 1990s.[6] Excluding movie sales of popcorn, Americans were spending $1 billion for popcorn annually. U.S. retail sales of popped and unpopped popcorn had experienced annual growth rates of 25 percent. Some industry experts predicted that the microwave popcorn market was matured, resulting in a plateauing of sales for the future. Contrary to this prediction, Golden Valley believed that it would see annual growth rates of 15 percent.

The global market was open to popcorn as a snack. However, the international version of popcorn was not the butter and salt version found in the United States. The Swedes liked their popcorn very buttery, the Germans and French sprinkled sugar on their popcorn, Europeans had a strong preference for goat cheese on their popcorn, and Mexicans liked jalapeno-flavored popcorn. The British, however, perceived popcorn as child's food or candy rather than a salty snack product.

Although not a big competitor in the United States due to company size, a player in the global popcorn market was Ramsey Popcorn. A 50-year-old, $14 million, family-run business, Ramsey was based in Indiana and began global operations in 1990. Twenty-five percent of its business was abroad. The company's strategy was to link with local foodservice firms and adjust the product's taste to meet local market demands. However, 40 percent of the company's export sales came from its six varieties of branded microwave popcorn.

Much of the growth in popcorn consumption was attributed to the increased use of microwave ovens to make popcorn. By the 1990s, the microwave popcorn market was estimated to be around $600 million. Segmentation had begun occurring in the microwave popcorn market through flavored and light product offerings.

Microwave Ovens

Microwave oven penetration of the U.S. home market soared from 0.1 percent in 1971 to 85 percent by 1993.[7] As consumers became used to microwave ovens in their homes, usage extended to the away-from-home market. As such, microwave ovens smaller in size than those found in the home began appearing in cafeterias, workplaces, dormitory rooms, and any other place a person might spend time away from their primary place of

---

[5]Multigrain chips were derived from rice, corn, wheat, and oats. Some industry experts predicted that these chips had the potential to be a $300 million to $400 million annual business by the end of the 1990s.
[6]This was equivalent to almost 13 billion quarts.
[7]One study reported that almost 92 percent of mature consumers (ages 55+) used a microwave oven.

residence. By the beginning of the 1990s, microwave ovens were being used more for warming up food than for cooking food.

Internationally, microwave ovens were found in approximately 40 percent of Japanese homes and 30 percent of homes in the United Kingdom. Microwave ovens were the fastest-growing home appliance in Western Europe.

Microwave Oven Foods. Americans tended to search continually for a convenient meal. By the early 1990s, the fast-food market was estimated to be around $55 billion. Of this, around 75 percent was fast-food consumed in the home (such as carryout and delivery items). This was a 55 percent increase over fast-food consumption in the 1980s. This search for convenience led to an increased use of the microwave oven,[8] which in turn led food manufacturers to provide microwave-ready food items. However, by the beginning of the 1990s, average yearly household expenditures for food designed specifically for the microwave were only $15. Microwaves were not utilized as supermarkets would have liked. According to the Supermarket Business's 1990 Consumer Expenditures Study, a large percentage of microwave food sales came from snacks and occasion foods. Sales of unpopped popcorn increased almost 10 percent in grocery outlets, double the growth for frozen dinners and entrées. Single-serve microwave meals for children represented a growing segment of the market by the 1990s.

Microwave food items introduced included dessert mixes, instant potatoes, frozen pizza, frozen pies, bacon, popcorn, vegetables, cake mixes, sandwiches, and french fries. Most of these products were considered "under performers" compared to other products in their product categories. A major problem that specifically occurred in the microwave food market was product quality. Novelty tended to fascinate consumers enough to purchase the food item initially. However, repeat purchase failed to materialize because the products did not meet consumers' expectations. Yet with repeat business a must, microwave foods tended to experience increased quality problems as production levels increased.

Examples of companies that introduced products into the microwave market included Pillsbury (cake mixes), Pitaria Products Co. (sandwiches), J. R. Simplot Co. (sandwiches), Geo. A. Hormel & Co. (sandwiches, single-serve meals, french fries), Quaker Oats Co. (sandwiches), General Mills (popcorn), Hershey Foods Corp. (pasta), Dial Corp. (single-serve meals), and Golden Valley Microwave Foods (popcorn, french fries, pancakes).

Not every product was microwavable (bagels, for example). Development of microwavable products that tasted good, did not pick up any packaging odors, and cooked evenly was difficult. The key to preparing food in the microwave tended to rest with the packaging of the product.

Packaging. Microwavable containers were a hot topic among packaging experts. Package forms range from traditional plates/bowls/cups, to pouches/bags, to boards, to packages with visual indicators for doneness. Materials included plastic, paperboard, and molder pulp. There was concern in the industry, however, that food packagers and package suppliers were not working together to make the proper package for the designed type of food.

---

[8]The barbecue grill had experienced usage as well. By 1992, 32 percent of U.S. households used their grill for at least one meal during a two-week period. This compared to 22 percent in 1984.

Two major issues focused upon taste and technology arose surrounding packaging. First, the package material and form had to be such that the food cooked properly (thoroughly, crispy, browning, crunchy). Second, the packaging had to be safe for the consumer. Serious burns had occurred from collapsing packages and from the eruption of superheated liquids. Additionally, food packages had to be made of such material that they would not ignite in the oven during the cooking cycle. Environmental concerns also were directed toward the type of material used in microwavable products. Clear labeling of cooking directions was a must on the microwave package.

Golden Valley's Marketing Strategy

Golden Valley's marketing strategy was twofold. First, the company wanted to find new markets for its current products. Second, the company knew that it would have to develop new products for its current and future markets. Management felt that the key to growth was to offer products for low-wattage microwave ovens.[9] The challenge was to use technology to produce microwave products that were convenient, of high quality, and priced appropriately.

Microwave popcorn was at the heart of Golden Valley's success, accounting for 90 percent of revenue. Packaging and distribution were critical to this success. Golden Valley researchers had developed an innovative package, using laminated paper that focused microwave energy, which was the source of Act II's competitive edge. Consumers had complained that microwave popcorn left too many unpopped kernels. Golden Valley's package allowed more complete popping of the kernels. The company held 13 patents on the packaging. The popcorn was distributed through vending machines and discount stores (representing around 50 percent of the nongrocery popcorn market and around 90 percent of the microwave popcorn market).

To grow without being solely dependent upon popcorn, Golden Valley introduced its second product line in the late 1980s: microwave pancakes, waffles, and french toast. Upon introducing the Morning line of microwave items, Golden Valley began work immediately on its third product: single-serve, microwave french fries. Traditionally, less than 50 percent of french fry volume went through grocery stores. French fries were largely a restaurant item.

Microwave french fries represented a $60 million market at the beginning of 1990. Two contenders (J. R. Simplot, a privately held Boise, Idaho, potato processor, and the Ore-Ida division of Heinz) owned most of the microwavable french fry market share. Another entrant, Geo. A. Hormel, was expected to begin test-marketing its New Traditions line of microwave fries. To help produce and distribute its french fries, Golden Valley formed a joint venture with ConAgra[10] to acquire a major processor of frozen potatoes.

French fries raised some distinctly different issues as a product offering than had popcorn or breakfast items. One issue was the healthy-snack perception consumers had

---

[9]Low-wattage microwave ovens were the smaller ovens found, typically, in offices, dormitories, and cafeterias (away-from-home locations).
[10]ConAgra was known for its Healthy Choice and Kids Choice frozen food items and its Orville Redenbacher popcorn line.

regarding popcorn. French fries did not carry the same healthy image. Additionally, popcorn was a shelf-stable product, whereas french fries were not. Golden Valley planned to distribute its french fries through refrigerated vending machines. The third issue surrounded the packaging of the french fry. The FDA had addressed concerns regarding the migration of packaging components into the food item. Golden Valley felt certain that their package placed a "food-safe" barrier between the packaging technology and the french fries. The bottom line was that Golden Valley sought to give consumers the gold standard for french fries: that which typically comes from a deep fryer—a shoestring, lightly browned, crispy french fry about four inches long. Providing this type of product required complex packaging.

Watkins knew that popcorn, breakfast items, and french fries were not enough. To continue growing, should GVMF develop more new products and open new markets? Ramsey Popcorn had been successful in the international market. Should Golden Valley move in that direction? Given its successful packaging technology, should it focus most of its attention on developing new microwavable products? Jim Watkins needed a growth strategy that would take his company into the year 2000.

SOURCES

Balzer, Harry. "The Ultimate Cooking Appliance." *American Demographics,* July 1993, pp. 40–44.

Berman, Bonnie. "Candy & Tobacco Supplement: Holidays Are Happy Times for Candy Industry/Value-Priced Cigarettes Capture Industry Attention." *Discount Merchandiser,* September 1987, pp. 69–77.

Doyle, Kevin. "Snack Makers Feel the Crunch." *Incentive,* November 1991, pp. 50–52.

Duff, Mike. "Making More out of the Microwave." *Supermarket Business,* April 1991, pp. 45–48, 89.

Dwyer, Steve. " 'Healthy' or Traditional, Snacks Maintain Their Customer Appeal." *National Petroleum News,* July 1992, pp. 38–41.

Erickson, Greg. "For One on the Run." *Packaging,* March 1991, pp. 26–28.

Forest, Stephanie Anderson. "Chipping Away at Frito-Lay." *Business Week,* July 22, 1991, p. 26.

Larson, Melissa. "Microwave Packaging Cooks Up Conflict." *Packaging,* October 1988, pp. 60–62A.

———. "Microwave Technology Heats Up." *Packaging,* June 1988, pp. 66–69.

———. "Taste and Value Drive Microwave Foods." *Packaging,* February 1991, pp. 32–36.

Liesse, Julie. "Microwave-Only Food Market Loses Steam." *Advertising Age,* July 16, 1990, pp. 3, 40.

Lubove, Seth. "Report from the Front." *Forbes,* September 13, 1993, p. 220.

Madonia, Moira. "Snack Foods." *Supermarket Business,* September 1992, pp. 134–35.

McNeal, James. "Children as Customers." *American Demographics,* September 1990, pp. 36–39.

Remich, Norman. "High Tech Wins Vote of Mature Consumers." *Appliance Manufacturer,* March 1991, pp. 62–63.

Riell, Howard. "Consumer Expenditures Study: Snack Foods." *Supermarket Business,* September 1991, pp. 172–73.

Roman, Mark. "Renegades of the Year 1987." *Success,* January/February 1988, pp. 43–49.

Savitz, Eric J. "This Spud's for You? Or, Are French Fries the New Popcorn?" *Barron's,* October 23, 1989, pp. 20, 51–53.

Scarpa, James. "Piece Meal: Munching Madness." *Restaurant Business,* July 20, 1992, pp. 127–28.

Tierney, Robin. "Pop Culture." *World Trade,* October 1993, p. 20.

Wold, Marjorie. "Nuts Can't Crack the Snack Market." *Progressive Grocer,* May 1992, pp. 179–80.

Zbytniewski, Jo-Ann. "A Snack Food Free-for-All." *Progressive Grocer,* September 1992, pp. 121–22.

CASE 6–12 TenderCare Disposable Diapers

Tom Cagan watched as his secretary poured six ounces of water onto each of two disposable diapers lying on his desk. The diaper on the left was a new, improved Pampers, introduced in the summer of 1985 by Procter & Gamble. The new, improved design was supposed to be drier than the preceding Pampers. It was the most recent development in a sequence of designs that traced back to the original Pampers, introduced to the market in 1965. The diaper on his right was a TenderCare™ diaper, manufactured by a potential supplier for testing and approval by Cagan's company, Rocky Mountain Medical Corporation (RMM). The outward appearance of both diapers was identical.

Yet the TenderCare diaper was different. Just under its liner (the surface next to the baby's skin) was a wicking fabric that drew moisture from the surface around a soft, waterproof shield to an absorbent reservoir of filler. Pampers and all other disposable diapers on the market kept moisture nearer to the liner and, consequently, the baby's skin. A patent attorney had examined the TenderCare design, concluding that the wicking fabric and shield arrangement should be granted a patent. However, it would be many months before results of the patent application process could be known.

As soon as the empty beakers were placed back on the desk, Cagan and his secretary touched the liners of both diapers. They agreed that there was no noticeable difference, and Cagan noted the time. They repeated their "touch test" after one minute and again noted no difference. However, after two minutes, both thought the TenderCare diaper to be drier. At three minutes, they were certain. By five minutes, the TenderCare diaper surface seemed almost dry to the touch, even when a finger was pressed deep into the diaper. In contrast, the Pampers diaper showed little improvement in dryness from three to five minutes and tended to produce a puddle when pressed.

These results were not unexpected. Over the past three months, Cagan and other RMM executives had compared TenderCare's performance with 10 brands of disposable diapers available in the Denver market. TenderCare diapers had always felt drier within a two- to

This case was written by Professor James E. Nelson, University of Colorado. Some data are disguised. © 1986 by the Business Research Division, College of Business and Administration and the Graduate School of Business Administration, University of Colorado, Boulder, Colorado 80309-0419.

four-minute interval after wetting. However, these results were considered tentative because all tests had used TenderCare diapers made by RMM personnel by hand. Today's test was the first made with diapers produced by a supplier under mass manufacturing conditions.

Rocky Mountain Medical Corporation

RMM was incorporated in Denver, Colorado, in late 1982 by Robert Morrison, M.D. Sales had grown from about $400,000 in 1983 to $2.4 million in 1984 and were expected to reach $3.4 million in 1985. The firm would show a small profit for 1985, as it had each previous year.

Management personnel as of September 1985 included six executives. Cagan served as president and director, positions held since joining RMM in April 1984. Prior to that time he had worked for several high-technology companies in the areas of product design and development, production management, sales management, and general management. His undergraduate studies were in engineering and psychology; he took an MBA in 1981. Dr. Morrison currently served as chairman of the board and vice president for research and development. He had completed his M.D. in 1976 and had been board certified to practice pediatrics in the state of Colorado since 1978. John Bosch served as vice president of manufacturing, a position held since joining RMM in late 1983. Lawrence Bennett was vice president of marketing, having primary responsibilities for marketing TenderCare and RMM's two lines of phototherapy products since joining the firm in 1984. Bennett's background included an MBA received in 1981 and three years' experience in groceries product management at General Mills. Two other executives had also joined RMM in 1984. One served as vice president of personnel, the other as controller.

Phototherapy Products. RMM's two lines of phototherapy products were used to treat infant jaundice, a condition experienced by some 5 to 10 percent of all newborn babies. One line was marketed to hospitals under the trademark Alpha-Lite. Bennett felt that the Alpha-Lite phototherapy unit was superior to competing products because it gave the baby 360-degree exposure to the therapeutic light. Competing products gave less-complete exposure, with the result that the Alpha-Lite unit treated more severe cases and produced quicker recoveries. Apart from the Alpha-Lite unit itself, the hospital line of phototherapy products included a light meter, a photo-mask that protected the baby's eyes while undergoing treatment, and a "baby bikini" that diapered the baby and yet facilitated exposure to the light.

The home phototherapy line of products was marketed under the trademark Baby-Lite. The phototherapy unit was portable, weighing about 40 pounds, and was foldable for easy transport. The unit when assembled was 33 inches long, 20 inches wide, and 24 inches high. The line also included photo-masks, a thermometer, and a short booklet telling parents about home phototherapy. Parents could rent the unit and purchase related products from a local pharmacy or a durable-medical-equipment dealer for about $75 per day. This was considerably less than the cost of hospital treatment. Another company, Acquitron, Inc., had entered the home phototherapy market in early 1985 and was expected to offer stiff competition. A third competitor was rumored to be entering the market in 1986.

Bennett's responsibilities for all phototherapy products included developing marketing plans and making final decisions about product design, promotion, pricing, and distribution. He directly supervised two product managers, one responsible for Alpha-Lite and the other for Baby-Lite. He occasionally made sales calls with the product managers, visiting hospitals, health maintenance organizations, and insurers.

TenderCare Marketing

Right now most of Bennett's time was spent on TenderCare. Bennett recognized that TenderCare would be marketed much differently than the phototherapy products. TenderCare would be sold to wholesalers, who in turn would sell to supermarkets, drugstores, and mass merchandisers. TenderCare would compete either directly or indirectly with two giant consumer-goods manufacturers, Procter & Gamble and Kimberly-Clark. TenderCare represented considerable risk to RMM.

Because of the uncertainty surrounding the marketing of TenderCare, Bennett and Cagan had recently sought the advice of several marketing consultants. They reached formal agreement with one, a Los Angeles consultant named Alan Anderson. Anderson had extensive experience in advertising at J. Walter Thompson. He had also had responsibility for marketing and sales at Mattel and Teledyne, specifically for the marketing of such products as IntelliVision™, the Shower Massage™, and the Water Pik™. Anderson currently worked as an independent marketing consultant to several firms. His contract with RMM specified that he would devote 25 percent of his time to TenderCare the first year and about 12 percent the following two years. During this time, RMM would hire, train, and place its own marketing personnel. One of these people would be a product manager for TenderCare.

Bennett and Cagan also could employ the services of a local marketing consultant who served on RMM's advisory board. (The board consisted of 12 business and medical experts who were available to answer questions and provide direction.) This consultant had spent over 25 years in marketing consumer products at several large corporations. His specialty was developing and launching new products, particularly health and beauty aids. He had worked closely with RMM in selecting the name TenderCare, and had done a great deal of work summarizing market characteristics and analyzing competitors.

Market Characteristics

The market for babies' disposable diapers could be identified as children, primarily below age 3, who use the diapers, and their mothers, primarily between ages of 18 and 49, who decide on the brand and usually make the purchase. Bennett estimated there were about 11 million such children in 1985, living in about 9 million households. The average number of disposable diapers consumed in these households was thought to range from 0 to 15 per day and to average about 7.

The consumption of disposable diapers is tied closely to birth rates and populations. However, two prominent trends also influence consumption. One is the disposable diaper's steadily increasing share of total diaper usage by babies. Bennett estimated that disposable diapers would increase their share of total diaper usage from 75 percent currently to 90 percent by 1990. The other trend is toward the purchase of higher quality disposable diapers. Bennett thought the average retail price of disposable diapers would rise about twice as fast as the price of materials used in their construction. Total dollar sales of disposable diapers at retail in 1985 were expected to be about $3 billion, or about 15 billion units. Growth rates were thought to be about 14 percent per year for dollar sales and about 8 percent for units.

Foreign markets for disposable diapers would add to these figures. Canada, for example, currently consumed about $0.25 billion at retail, with an expected growth rate of 20 percent per year until 1990. The U.K. market was about twice this size and growing at the same rate.

The U.S. market for disposable diapers was clearly quite large and growing. However, Bennett felt that domestic growth rates could not be maintained much longer because fewer and fewer consumers were available to switch from cloth to disposable diapers. In fact, by 1995, growth rates for disposable diapers would begin to approach growth rates for births, and unit sales of disposable diapers would become directly proportional to numbers of infants using diapers. A consequence of this pronounced slowing of growth would be increased competition.

Competition

Competition between manufacturers of disposable diapers was already intense. Two well-managed giants—Procter & Gamble and Kimberly-Clark—accounted for about 80 percent of the market in 1984 and 1985. Bennett estimated market shares as follows:

	1984	1985
Pampers	32%	28%
Huggies	24	28
Luvs	20	20
Other brands	24	24
	100%	100%

Procter & Gamble was clearly the dominant competitor with its Pampers and Luvs brands. However, Procter & Gamble's market share had been declining, from 70 percent in 1981 to about 50 percent today. The company had introduced its thicker Blue Ribbon™ Pampers recently in an effort to halt the share decline. It had invested over $500 million in new equipment to produce the product. Procter & Gamble spent approximately $40 million to advertise its two brands in 1984. Kimberly-Clark spent about $19 million to advertise Huggies in 1984.

The 24 percent market share held by other brands was up by some 3 percentage points from 1983. Weyerhaeuser and Johnson & Johnson manufactured most of these diapers, supplying private-label brands for Wards, Penneys, Target, Kmart, and other retailers. Generic disposable diapers and private brands were also included here, as well as a number of very small, specialized brands that were distributed only to local markets. Some of these brands positioned themselves as low-cost alternatives to national brands; others occupied premium ("designer") niches with premium prices. As examples, Universal Converter entered the northern Wisconsin market in 1984 with two brands priced at 78 and 87 percent of Pampers' case price. Riegel Textile Corporation's Cabbage Patch™ diapers illustrated the premium end, with higher prices and attractive print designs. Riegel spent $1 million to introduce Cabbage Patch diapers to the market in late 1984.

Additional evidence of intense competition in the disposable diaper industry was the major change of strategy by Johnson & Johnson in 1981. The company took its own brand off the U.S. market, opting instead to produce private-label diapers for major retailers. The company had held about 8 percent of the national market at the time and decided that this simply was not enough to compete effectively. Johnson & Johnson's disposable diaper was the first to be positioned in the industry as a premium product. Sales at one point totaled about 12 percent of the market but began to fall when Luvs and Huggies (with similar premium features) were introduced. Johnson & Johnson's advertising expenditures for disposable diapers in 1980 were about $8 million. The company still competed with its own brand in the international market.

Marketing Strategies for TenderCare

Over the past month, Bennett and his consultants had spent considerable time formulating potential marketing strategies for TenderCare. One strategy that already had been discarded was simply licensing the design to another firm. Under a license arrangement, RMM would receive a negotiated royalty based on the licensee's sales of RMM's diaper. However, this strategy was unattractive on several grounds. RMM would have no control over resources devoted to the marketing of TenderCare: The licensee would decide on levels of sales and advertising support, prices, and distribution. The licensee would control advertising content, packaging, and even the choice of brand name. Licensing also meant that RMM would develop little marketing expertise, no image or even awareness among consumers, and no experience in dealing with packaged-goods channels of distribution. The net result would be that RMM would be hitching its future with respect to TenderCare (and any related products) to that of the licensee. Three other strategies seemed more appropriate.

The "Diaper Rash" Strategy. The first strategy involved positioning the product as an aid in the treatment of diaper rash. Diaper rash is a common ailment, thought to affect most infants at some point in their diapered lives. The affliction usually lasted two to three weeks before being cured. Some infants are more disposed to diaper rash than others. The ailment is caused by "a reaction to prolonged contact with urine and feces, retained soaps and topical preparations, and friction and maceration" (Nelson's *Text of Pediatrics,* 1979, p. 1884). Recommended treatment includes careful washing of the affected areas with warm water and without irritating soaps. Treatment also includes the application of protective ointments and powders (sold either by prescription or over the counter).

The diaper rash strategy would target physicians and nurses in either family- or general-practice and physicians and nurses specializing either in pediatrics or dermatology. Bennett's estimates of the numbers of general or family practitioners in 1985 was approximately 65,000. He thought that about 45,000 pediatricians and dermatologists were practicing in 1985. The numbers of nurses attending all these physicians was estimated at about 290,000. All 400,000 individuals would be the eventual focus of TenderCare marketing efforts. However, the diaper rash strategy would begin (like the other two strategies) where approximately 11 percent of the target market was located—California. Bennett and his consultants agreed that RMM lacked resources sufficient to begin in any larger market. California would provide a good test for TenderCare because the state often set consumption trends for the rest of the U.S. market. California also showed fairly typical levels of competitive activity.

Promotion activities would emphasize either direct mail and free samples or in-office demonstrations to the target market. Mailing lists of most physicians and some nurses in the target market could be purchased at a cost of about $60 per 1,000 names. The cost to print and mail a brochure, cover letter, and return postcard was about $250 per 1,000. To include a single TenderCare disposable diaper would add another $400 per thousand. In-office demonstrations would use registered nurses (employed on a part-time basis) to show TenderCare's superior dryness. The nurses could be quickly trained and compensated on a per-demonstration basis. The typical demonstration would be given to groups of two or three physicians and nurses and would cost RMM about $6. The California market could be used to investigate the relative performance of direct mail versus demonstrations.

RMM would also advertise in trade journals such as the *Journal of Family Practice, Journal of Pediatrics, Pediatrics,* and *Pediatrics Digest.* However, a problem with such advertisements was waste coverage because none of the trade journals published regional editions. A half-page advertisement (one insertion) would cost about $1,000 for each journal. This cost would be reduced to about $700 if RMM placed several advertisements in the same journal during a one-year period. RMM would also promote TenderCare at local and state medical conventions in California. Costs per convention were thought to be about $3,000. The entire promotion budget, as well as amounts allocated to direct mail, free samples, advertisements, and medical conventions, had yet to be decided.

Prices were planned to produce a retail price per package of 12 TenderCare diapers at around $3.80. This was some 8 to 10 percent higher than the price for a package of 18 Huggies or Luvs. Bennett thought that consumers would pay the premium price because of TenderCare's position: The pennies-per-day differential simply would not matter if a physician prescribed or recommended TenderCare as part of a treatment for diaper rash. "Besides," he noted, "in-store shelf placement of TenderCare under this strategy would be among diaper rash products, not with standard diapers. This will make price comparisons by consumers even more unlikely." The $3.80 package price for 12 TenderCare diapers would produce a contribution margin for RMM of about 9 cents per diaper. It would give retailers a per-diaper margin some 30 percent higher than that for Huggies or Luvs.

The Special-Occasions Strategy.   The second strategy centered around a "special-occasions" position that emphasized TenderCare's use in situations where changing the baby would be difficult. One such situation was whenever diapered infants traveled for any length of time. Another occurred daily at some 10,000 day-care centers that accepted infants wearing diapers. Yet another came every evening in each of the 9 million market households when babies were diapered at bedtime.

The special-occasions strategy would target mothers in these 9 million households. Initially, of course, the target would be only the estimated 1 million mothers living in California. Promotion would aim particularly at first-time mothers, using such magazines as *American Baby* and *Baby Talk*. Per-issue insertion costs for one full-color, half-page advertisement in such magazines would average about $20,000. However, most baby magazines published regional editions where single insertion costs averaged about half that amount. Black-and-white advertisements could also be considered; their costs would be about 75 percent of the full-color rates. Inserting several ads per year in the same magazine would allow quantity discounts and reduce the average insertion cost by about one-third.

Lately, Bennett had begun to wonder if direct-mail promotion could instead be used to reach mothers of recently born babies. Mailing lists of some 1 to 3 million names could be obtained at a cost of around $50 per 1,000. Other costs to produce and mail promotional materials would be the same as those for physicians and nurses. "I suppose the real issue is, just how much more effective is direct mail over advertising? We'd spend at least $250,000 in baby magazines to cover California while the cost of direct mail would probably be between $300,000 and $700,000, depending on whether or not we gave away a diaper." Regardless of Bennett's decision on consumer promotion, he knew RMM would also direct some promotion activities toward physicians and nurses as part of the special-occasions strategy. Budget details were yet to be worked out.

Distribution under the special-occasions strategy would have TenderCare stocked on store shelves along with competing diapers. Still at issue was whether the package should contain 12 or 18 diapers (like Huggies and Luvs) and how much of a premium price TenderCare could command. Bennett considered the packaging and pricing decisions interrelated. A package of 12 TenderCare diapers with per-unit retail prices some 40 percent higher than Huggies or Luvs might work just fine. Such a packaging/pricing strategy would produce a contribution margin to RMM of about 6 cents per diaper. However, the same pricing strategy for a package of 18 diapers probably would not work. "Still," he thought, "good things often come in small packages, and most mothers probably associate higher quality with higher price. One thing is for sure—whichever way we go, we'll need a superior package.'' Physical dimensions for a TenderCare package of either 12 or 18 diapers could be made similar to the size of the Huggies or Luvs package of 18.

The Head-On Strategy.   The third strategy under consideration met major competitors in a direct, frontal attack. The strategy would position TenderCare as a noticeably drier diaper that any mother would prefer to use anytime her baby needed changing. Promotion activities would stress mass advertising to mothers, using television and magazines. However, at least two magazines would include a dollar-off coupon to stimulate trial of a package of TenderCare diapers during the product's first three months on the market. Some in-store demonstrations to mothers using "touch tests" might also be employed. Although no budget for California had yet been set, Bennett thought the allocation would be roughly 60:30:10 for television, magazines, and other promotion activities, respectively.

   Pricing under this strategy would be competitive with Luvs and Huggies, with the per-diaper price for TenderCare expected to be some 9 percent higher at retail. This differential was needed to cover additional manufacturing costs associated with Tender-Care's design. TenderCare's package could contain only 16 diapers and show a lower price than either Huggies or Luvs with their 18-count packages. Alternatively, the package could contain 18 diapers and carry the 9 percent higher price. Bennett wondered if he really wasn't putting too fine a point on the pricing/packaging relationship. "After all," he had said to Anderson, "we've no assurance that retailers or wholesalers would pass along any price advantage TenderCare might have due to a smaller package. Either one or both might instead price TenderCare near the package price for our competitors and simply pocket the increased margin!" The only thing that was reasonably certain was TenderCare's package price to the wholesaler. That price was planned to produce about a 3-cent contribution margin to RMM per diaper, regardless of package count.

Summary of the Three Strategies.   When viewed together, the three strategies seemed so complex and so diverse as to defy analysis. Partly the problem was one of developing criteria against which the strategies could be compared. Risk was obviously one such criterion; so were company fit and competitive reaction. However, Bennett felt that some additional thought on his part would produce more criteria against which the strategies could be compared. He hoped this effort would produce no more strategies; three were plenty.

   The other part of the problem was simply uncertainty. Strengths, weaknesses, and implications of each strategy had yet to be given much thought. Moreover, each strategy seemed likely to have associated with it some surprises. An example illustrating the problem was the recent realization that the Food and Drug Administration (FDA) must approve any direct claims RMM might make about TenderCare's efficacy in treating diaper rash. The chance of receiving this federal agency's approval was thought to be reasonably high; yet it was unclear just what sort of testing and what results were needed. The worst-case scenario would have the FDA requiring lengthy consumer tests that eventually would produce inconclusive results. The best case could have the FDA giving permission based on TenderCare's superior dryness and on results of a small-scale field test recently completed by Dr. Morrison. It would be probably a month before the FDA's position could be known.

"The delay *was* unfortunate—and unnecessary," Bennett thought, "especially if we eventually settle on either of the other two strategies." In fact, FDA approval was not even needed for the diaper rash strategy if RMM simply claimed (1) that TenderCare diapers were drier than competing diapers and (2) that dryness helps treat diaper rash. Still, a single-statement, direct-claim position was thought to be more effective with mothers and more difficult to copy by any other manufacturer. And yet Bennett did want to move quickly on TenderCare. Every month of delay meant deferred revenue and other postponed benefits that would derive from a successful introduction. Delay also meant the chance that an existing (or other) competitor might develop its own drier diaper and effectively block RMM from reaping the fruits of its development efforts. Speed was of the essence.

Financial Implications

Bennett recognized that each marketing strategy held immediate as well as long-term financial implications. He was particularly concerned with finance requirements for start-up costs associated with the California entry. Cagan and the other RMM executives had agreed that a stock issue represented the best option to meet these requirements. Accordingly, RMM had begun preparation for a sale of common stock through a brokerage firm that would underwrite and market the issue. Management at the firm felt that RMM could generate between $1 and $3 million, depending on the offering price per share and the number of shares issued.

Proceeds from the sale of stock had to be sufficient to fund the California entry and leave a comfortable margin remaining for contingencies. Proceeds would be used for marketing and other operating expenses as well as for investments in cash, inventory, and accounts receivable assets. It was hoped that TenderCare would generate a profit by the end of the first year in the California market and show a strong contribution to the bottom line thereafter. California profits would contribute to expenses associated with entering additional markets and to the success of any additional stock offerings.

Operating profits and proceeds from the sale of equity would fund additional research and development activities that would extend RMM's diaper technology to other markets. Dr. Morrison and Bennett saw almost immediate application of the technology to the adult incontinence diaper market, currently estimated at about $300 million per year at retail. Underpads for beds constituted at least another $50 million annual market. However, both of these uses were greatly dwarfed by another application, the sanitary napkin market. Finally, the technology could almost certainly be applied to numerous industrial products and processes, many of which promised great potential. All these opportunities made the TenderCare situation that much more crucial to the firm; making a major mistake here would affect the firm for years.

CASE 6–13 The Bacova Guild, Ltd. (A)

Introduction

As the director of marketing for the hardware division of the Bacova Guild, Ltd., John Walters was facing some decisions on new products that were not meeting expected sales. The disappointing sales were of concern to senior management because the firm's growth was driven by the successful development and marketing of new products. The Bacova Guild was an innovative company, winning two *Inc.* awards in the 1980s as one of the 500 fastest-growing small companies in the United States. The firm had expanded operations to accommodate the sales growth and it now faced a situation of having to successfully develop and market a steady stream of new products to cover a higher level of overhead and maintain profitability.

John Walters knew he faced a challenge. Product life cycles were getting shorter as competitors copied the Bacova products. In addition, the product categories that Bacova had entered with new products were proving to be susceptible to changing consumer tastes and economic conditions.

The hardware division, which had been very successful marketing decorative mailboxes, was also experiencing some problems with maturing markets. Division sales had fallen from $5.3 million in 1989 to $3.6 million in 1990. In response to the declining sales, the hardware division marketing group was beginning to market two new products designed to extend an existing line of outdoor decorative products for homeowners.

Postmaster, marketed in late 1989, was a complete mailbox system that could be purchased in one location to simplify the task of installing a rural mailbox. SignMaster, the newest product and the subject of this case study, is shown in Figure 1. It was a decorative house sign that could be used to identify a residence. Constructed of plastic in different shapes and decorative designs, it was sold with SignMaster house numbers made of peel-and-stick outdoor vinyl that the customer purchased separately and installed on the sign. Introduced during the National Hardware Show in August 1990, the product had received favorable reviews from the trade. Later in 1990, it was market-tested by a mass merchandiser and a home center store. The consumer sales had proven to be disappointing.

Bacova management believed that it was necessary to review SignMaster and its marketing strategy. Certainly changes would be made, but what was needed was not clear. Some Bacova employees believed that SignMaster had been priced improperly, while

This case was written by Lawrence W. Lamont, Timothy J. Halloran, and Thomas D. Lowell, all of Washington and Lee University.

Property of the Department of Management, Washington and Lee University. Case material is prepared as a basis for class discussion and not designed to present illustrations of either effective or ineffective handling of administrative problems. Copyright © 1992 by Washington and Lee University.

The authors gratefully acknowledge the cooperation and assistance of Mr. Ben Johns and Mr. Patrick Haynes, senior management of The Bacova Guild, Mr. John Walters, director of marketing for the Hardware Division, and the employees of The Bacova Guild, Ltd.

Postmaster™, SignMaster™, and Accentbox™ are registered trademarks of The Bacova Guild, Ltd., Bacova, Virginia.

FIGURE 1 The SignMaster™ Decorative House Sign

Shown: (top left to right) Ivy, Cardinal Chickadee, and Decoy; (bottom left to right) Floral, Classic Border, and Country House.

others felt that the packaging for the product did not have strong enough appeal for a self-service environment. Walters reflected that SignMaster had been introduced without trade or consumer promotion. With the end of 1991 approaching, Bacova management knew that decisions had to be made to finalize the marketing strategy and determine the role of SignMaster in the company's future.

History of The Bacova Guild, Ltd.

The Bacova Guild, Ltd., traces its origins back to 1963, when Grace Gilmore and her husband, William, began a small company known as Gilmore Designs, in New Bern, North Carolina. Grace was an artist and the business centered around silk-screening her wildlife drawings onto paper which was laminated between fiberglass surfaces to form a flexible decorative panel. The panels were then used for TV trays, card tables, and other gift items.

In 1957, Malcolm Hirsh, a retired businessman from New Jersey, purchased a "company town" located in the Allegheny Mountains of Virginia. The town was named Bacova, an acronym for Bath County, Virginia. Later, in 1964, Hirsh purchased Gilmore Designs, relocated the business to Bacova, and renamed it The Bacova Guild, Ltd.

FIGURE 2   The Classic Bacova Mailbox

Source: The Bacova Guild, Ltd.

Hirsh transformed Gilmore Designs from a mom-and-pop operation into a small company that found its niche selling to retail gift shops and mail-order companies. In the late 1960s he recognized that the fiberglass panels, originally used for indoor products, would also withstand the outdoor environment. This discovery led to the development of the Classic Bacova Mailbox, a product that would eventually become the cornerstone of the business. The Bacova Guild mailboxes were constructed with fiberglass covers attached to standard rural mailboxes. They utilized the original Gilmore wildlife designs and could be personalized with the name and address of the purchaser. Figure 2 shows the Classic Bacova Mailbox.

Financial difficulties led Hirsh to put The Bacova Guild up for sale in 1980. The Guild was sold in 1981 to Patrick R. Haynes, Jr., and Benjamin I. Johns, Jr., two former tennis professionals looking for a business opportunity. At the time of the purchase, there were 25 employees, a small building, and 900 customers.

The business was unprofitable in 1980, losing $40,000 on sales of $550,000. To become profitable, the partners aggressively pursued market penetration and product and market development. Bacova marketed ice buckets, waste baskets, utility barrels, and outdoor window thermometers using the wildlife designs and the fiberglass lamination process that worked with the mailboxes. Haynes and Johns also developed additional customers through increased participation in gift trade shows and dealer recruitment. The firm achieved profitability in 1982, and by 1983 sales had grown to $1.7 million, while earnings reached $98,016.

In 1984, Bacova diversified into the textile industry. The firm developed inks and a printing process that enabled it to print the same traditional wildlife designs on indoor/outdoor doormats. The mats were an instant success with gift shops and mail order businesses that sold them with the decorative mailboxes.

The success with wildlife designs printed on doormats led Bacova to develop a line of products for mass merchandisers. The new line, branded Accentmats, used similar wildlife designs, but the mats were smaller and priced for a market of lower income consumers. Within a short time, the sales of Accentmats made it the leading product line. A similar strategy was followed with mailboxes. In 1986, Bacova was successful in developing an inexpensive decorative mailbox that could be sold through the same retail outlets at prices considerably lower than the price of the original Bacova Classic Mailbox. The new mailbox line was branded with the name Accentbox. Like the doormats, the product was very successful and Bacova discovered the enormous sales and profit potential of distribution channels that reached the majority of American consumers.

Sales and profits grew rapidly and employment and production capacity was expanded to meet the growing demand for Bacova products. The original Bacova facility was doubled in size, a new manufacturing facility was constructed across the street, additional production capacity was leased in a nearby village, and a small carpet plant was opened in Dalton, Georgia. At the end of 1987, sales reached $19 million, profits stood at $1.8 million and about 200 people were employed at Bacova.

Bacova's success drew the attention of competitors and they quickly copied its designs and products. During 1989 through 1990, sales declined as Bacova faced a slowing economy, maturing markets, and aggressive price competition in both hardware and textile products. The firm responded with new-product development and added a product line of printed cotton throw rugs, molded plastic mailboxes, decorative mailbox cover kits that could be applied to existing mailboxes, Postmaster post kits and accessories, and SignMaster house signs. The new products helped, but as the sales and profit history in Table 1 indicates, the problems persisted. For the 1990 business year, Bacova's sales had fallen to $13.4 million and the firm reported a profit of $39,539. Tables 2 and 3 contain the financial statements for the year ending December 31, 1990.

Bacova Marketing and Product Lines

The textile and hardware divisions of The Bacova Guild market the product lines which account for a majority of company sales. Additionally, Bacova has a gift line that includes some hardware and textile products marketed to retail gift shops and mail-order

TABLE 1   Sales and Profit History

Sales and Net Income, 1981–1990

Year	Sales	Net Income
1990	$13,371,093	$ 39,539
1989	14,380,456	(301,914)
1988	15,766,699	866,314
1987	19,090,441	1,821,085
1986	9,599,765	807,943
1985	3,808,209	242,569
1984	2,420,683	150,197
1983	1,681,189	98,016
1982	1,116,058	64,637
1981	776,282	(10,840)

Source: The Bacova Guild, Ltd.

TABLE 2   Income Statement Year Ending December 31, 1990

Net Sales	$13,371,093
Cost of sales	9,537,692
Gross profit	$ 3,833,401
Selling, general, and administrative	3,486,321
Operating income	347,080
Other income (expense)	
Interest expense	(338,585)
Interest income	13,556
Other, net	17,488
Net income	$ 39,539

Source: The Bacova Guild, Ltd.

companies at higher prices. However, management responsibility for the gift line falls within either the textile division or the hardware division depending on the product.

The textile product lines include floor mats and rugs for indoor and outdoor use, while the emphasis of the hardware line is on outdoor products such as mailboxes. In 1990, the textile division accounted for 55.3 percent of Bacova sales, while the hardware division's sales were 28.1 percent. Sales of hardware and textile products to the gift and mail-order trade were 16.6 percent of total sales. Table 4 provides a percentage breakdown of textile, hardware, and gift sales by product line.

Product development is conducted in Bacova, Virginia, where the firm maintains a design facility and support staff. When appropriate, Bacova also contracts with other firms for assistance with market research, product design, packaging, and the preparation of promotional materials.

TABLE 3 Balance Sheet, Year Ending December 31, 1990

Assets	
Cash	$1,131,840
Accounts receivable	2,173,248
Inventories	1,437,035
Prepaid expenses	64,886
Total current assets	$4,807,009
Net fixed assets	2,518,282
Total assets	7,325,291

Liabilities and Equity	
Current installments	315,546
Accounts payable	590,413
Accrued expenses	139,221
Current liabilities	1,045,180
Long-term liabilities	2,151,792
Total liabilities	3,196,972
Stock	12,000
Paid-in capital	396,049
Retained earnings	3,720,270
Total equity	4,128,319
Total liabilities and equity	7,325,291

Source: The Bacova Guild, Ltd.

Approximately 31 manufacturer's representative firms with a total of 75 salespeople sell Bacova products to mass merchandisers, home center stores, hardware stores, do-it-yourself lumber yards, department stores, retail gift shops, and mail-order firms. Manufacturer's representatives earn sales commissions averaging 5.0 percent on sales of Bacova products. They are managed out of Bacova's New York sales office and showroom by a vice president of marketing and sales with assistance from three sales managers located in the Eastern, Midwestern, and Western regions of the United States. Bacova also directs promotional literature, catalogs, and sales promotion to middlemen and is regularly represented at the major trade shows attended by its customers. Historically, Bacova has used trade shows to introduce new products such as SignMaster.

Textile Products. The textile division markets decorative indoor/outdoor mats, and cotton, braided, and berber rugs. The products are usually printed with attractive wildlife and contemporary designs and purchased as a decorator item. The textile business is quite seasonal, and the majority of sales occur in the last quarter of the year. Popular designs are quickly imitated by competitors, and aggressive pricing is important to success. Bacova believes that its success in the textile market also depends on its design capability,

TABLE 4   1990 Sales by Product Line

Hardware Product Lines	*Percentage of Sales*
Accentbox	4.2%
Postmaster	15.3
Hearth Mat	6.6
Auto Mat	0.9
SignMaster	0.1
Other	1.0
Total	28.1%
Textile Product Lines	
Accentmat	33.2%
All American Rug	19.5
Braided Rug	1.2
Other	1.4
Total	55.3%
Gift and Mail Order	
Classic Mail Box	5.0%
Bacova Guild Mat	7.3
Other	4.3
Total	16.6%

Source: The Bacova Guild, Ltd.

printing technology, and ability to respond quickly to changes in consumer tastes. These unique strengths have enabled Bacova to market superior products at competitive prices.

Product Lines.   Accentmats, the best-selling product line in the company, are decorative doormats featuring the original Bacova designs printed on the mat. They are targeted to lower- and middle-income consumers looking for attractive prices. Distribution is through mass merchandisers, home center stores, and retail hardware stores.

The "All American" cotton rug is a line of indoor rugs printed with a variety of original Bacova designs. Available in four popular sizes, the rugs are made of 100 percent cotton with a nonskid backing so they can be used in a kitchen, bathroom, or hallway. The cotton rugs have been on the market since 1989 and are distributed through department stores and gift shops.

Two other product lines are the braided rugs and berber rugs. Braided rugs are made of 100 percent cotton, oval shaped, and available printed with Bacova designs or unprinted. The berber rug is a new line made of synthetic fibers. It is also available with Bacova designs and a nonskid backing.

Hardware Products.   The hardware division markets mailboxes and accessories, specialty mats for automobiles and fireplace hearths, and house signs. With the exception of the mats, most of the products are used as outdoor accents for residences. The specialty mats are marketed by the hardware division because the buyers for these products purchase primarily hardware items.

Mailboxes and accessories are the hardware division products accounting for the majority of sales. Bacova competes with three competitors whose products have low prices, comparable designs, and widespread retail distribution. Bacova believes it retains a competitive advantage because of the quality of its mailboxes, but competition has been successful in penetrating the market for decorative mailboxes. Bacova is moving to strengthen its position by marketing a full line of mailboxes and accessories.

Product Lines. Accentbox is a line of metal mailboxes with a decorative plastic panel permanently attached to the cover. Fifteen decorative designs are available for the Accentbox and personalization is available by special order. The Accentbox line is distributed through gift shops and specialty stores to consumers preferring an inexpensive decorative mailbox.

Postmaster is the newest line of mailboxes in the hardware division. The line includes plastic mailboxes with and without decorative covers, snap-on mailbox cover kits to enable the purchaser to select and change the design on the mailbox, mounting plates, plastic posts, and an easy-mount stake that eliminates the need to dig a posthole. Postmaster is designed to be merchandised as a complete modular system and is distributed through mass merchandisers, home center stores, and hardware stores.

Hearth and automobile mats complete the product lines of the hardware division. Hearthmats are used to protect surfaces in front of fireplaces and doorways. Automats are sold in sets of two and are designed to fit most automobile floorboards. The products are constructed of synthetic fibers and are available in sporting, wildlife, and designer motifs.

Retail Gift Store and Mail-Order Products. Historically, sales to retail gift shops and mail-order companies were the foundation of the Bacova customer franchise. As new products were developed and distribution channels were expanded, the gift market became a smaller part of the firm's business. However, Bacova continues to market mailboxes and indoor/outdoor doormats to consumers interested in purchasing higher quality, more expensive products through retail gift shops and mail-order catalogs. The business is attractive because of the higher profit margins available through these distribution channels.

Product Lines. The Classic Bacova Mailbox and the Bacova Guild Mat line are the most important product lines marketed as gifts. The Classic Bacova Mailbox has a handcrafted decorative fiberglass cover permanently applied to a sturdy steel mailbox. About 35 different decorative designs featuring animals, wildlife scenes, birds, flowers, and sports motifs are available to consumers. The Bacova Guild Decorative Doormats are large rugged indoor/outdoor carpets with a nonskid rubber backing. The mats are available in different colors with a variety of attractive designs. If desired, the mailboxes and doormats can be personalized with the purchaser's name, address, or other message and drop shipped from the Bacova facility in Virginia to the consumer after the retailer has made the sale.

The mailboxes and doormats have strong appeal as gifts where consumers are looking for top quality and price is not a major consideration. Both products are distributed through retail gift shops and mail-order firms.

SignMaster—a New Bacova Product

The most recent addition to the hardware division is SignMaster, a home identification product that enables consumers to identify residences with house numbers mounted on a decorative sign. SignMaster house signs are available in rectangular, oval, and tavern shapes with three Bacova designs for each shape. Three-inch house sign numbers made of weather-resistant peel-and-stick vinyl are displayed with the signs and selected at the time of purchase. Enclosed in the package is an alignment guide and directions to assist in applying the numbers to the sign. The house sign is ⅛-inch thick and is attached to the residence by using the double-sided adhesive mounting tape included in the package. Figure 3 illustrates a SignMaster Classic Border installed at a residence.

Development of SignMaster began in the spring of 1990 when management was looking for new products to extend the hardware division's line of outdoor accents. Following a three-month period involving a collaborative effort between the hardware division marketing group and a firm contracted to provide product development assistance, SignMaster was ready for marketing in August 1990.

SignMaster offered a new approach to identifying a residence. Decorative house signs were generally not available to consumers except through a few mail-order catalogs. The closest competitive products were the plastic, wood, aluminum, and brass numbers which consumers attached individually to their residence. The inexpensive plastic numbers were available individually or in packages of 25 or more, while the wood, aluminum, and brass numbers could generally be purchased individually from a point-of-purchase display. A consumer using the conventional method of numbering a residence with three numbers could expect to invest between $1.20 and $18 in house numbers depending on the size and type of product selected.

Pricing and promotion of SignMaster house sign and numbers were important decisions. Bacova management reasoned that if the price of SignMaster to retailers was lower than it needed to be, Bacova would receive a low profit margin and fail to maximize the profits on the product. On the other hand, if a high price was established, there was a risk that it would not be acceptable to consumers and the product would not sell. Complicating the decision was the retail markup that the retailers in the distribution channels would apply to the product. Previous experience indicated that hardware chains, home center stores, and mass merchandisers usually used markups of about 40 percent.

Consumer behavior would also influence the pricing decision. Consumers purchasing the product at retail were required to make two purchasing decisions. First, the consumer had to select the preferred shape and decorative design, and then one to four numbers depending upon the residence address. Thus, the cost to the consumer for the house sign and numbers was the total of the two purchase decisions. A second consideration centered around the fact that comparable products did not exist in the channels being considered for SignMaster. It was not clear whether consumers would simply compare the cost of installing SignMaster with the conventional approaches to numbering a residence or whether the product would be perceived as an entirely new and better solution to the problem. If the product was viewed as new, then it was likely that consumer promotion would be necessary to develop an understanding of what SignMaster was before it would sell.

FIGURE 3   SignMaster Installed at a Consumer Residence

Shown in Rectangular—Classic Border.

Costs would also be a factor in arriving at Bacova's selling price. Based on minimum production runs, the total cost for the house sign was $3.15, comprised of $2.60 variable costs and $0.55 fixed overhead. The house numbers had a cost of $.109 each, including variable costs of $.096 and fixed overhead of $.013. Management believed that these costs would remain unchanged over the next few years, unless substantial changes were made in product design or packaging.

SignMaster was introduced without consumer or trade promotion in August 1990, at the National Hardware Show in Chicago. Bacova priced the house sign at $8.50 and the numbers at $0.50 each. Initial distribution was achieved in 10 Target stores, a discount department store chain owned by Dayton-Hudson, and in one Lowe's store, a specialty retailer pursuing the home-center do-it-yourself business. Sales for the period September–December 1990, were $14,000. Consumers purchased an average of three numbers with each house sign.

Retail pricing was believed to be partly responsible for the disappointing sales. Pricing for SignMaster at the Target Stores was approximately $15.95, while Lowe's priced the product at $13.47. The house numbers were priced at $0.79. Late in 1990, both retailers reduced the price of the house sign to $9.95 in an attempt to stimulate sales.

Review of SignMaster Marketing Strategy

In January of 1991, management decided to review SignMaster and its marketing strategy. After reflecting that consumer research had not been conducted prior to market introduction, management decided to retain an independent marketing research organization to survey consumers and determine their reaction to the new product. At the same time, management moved to address the pricing issue by using the research organization to assist the hardware division marketing group in the design and implementation of a test market. SignMaster was placed in retail hardware stores located in six Virginia cities where three prices could be tested for consumer acceptance. The consumer survey research was completed by March. The sales results from the test market became available in November of 1991.

Research Methodology for Consumer Research. A sample of 79 homeowners consisting of married couples and singles representing 46 different homes in 13 states was surveyed using personal interviews. The average age of survey respondents was 46, and the median market value of the homes was $140,000. After respondents had examined the house sign and numbers, they were asked a series of open-ended questions.

Survey Results.   The research confirmed that most consumers viewed SignMaster as a new product. Only 23 percent of the sample had ever seen a similar product. Most respondents believed that SignMaster would be purchased primarily by a female, although as indicated in Table 5, it was also cited as a product that might be purchased by a male, jointly, or given as a gift. When asked to name the retail stores where they would expect to find SignMaster, respondents mentioned hardware stores, home-center stores, and mass merchandisers most often as indicated in Table 6. After examining the house sign in its package and the house numbers, respondents were asked what retail prices they

TABLE 5 Expected Purchaser of SignMaster

Purchaser	Number	Percent
Female	44	60.3
Male	15	20.5
Joint	10	13.7
For others as gift	4	5.5
Total	73	100.0

Source: Independent market research.

TABLE 6 Expected Retail Outlets for SignMaster

Retail Outlet	Number	Percent
Hardware store	42	31.3
Home-center store	30	22.4
Mass merchandiser	27	20.1
Gift shop	13	9.7
Department store	6	4.5
Mail-order catalog	5	3.7
Craft store	3	2.2
Lumberyard	3	2.2
Other	6	4.5
Total	134	100.0

Multiple response: Totals may not equal 100% due to rounding.
Source: Independent market research.

TABLE 7 Expected Retail Price (median) of SignMaster House Sign and Numbers

	Respondents		
Product	Male	Female	Combined
House sign	$7.99	$10.99	$10.00
House numbers	0.59	0.79	0.69

Source: Independent market research.

would expect for each item. Table 7 summarizes the responses for the survey sample. The significant difference in the expected price between male and female respondents was quite remarkable.

Preferred sign shapes and decorative designs were also examined in the survey research. Consumers were asked to express a preference for the shapes and decorative designs available for each shape. The most popular items were oval-Decoy, oval-Floral, tavern–

TABLE 8 Advertising Media Mentioned for SignMaster House Sign and Numbers

	Respondents		
Advertising Media	*Male*	*Female*	*Total*
Magazines	39.1%	38.7%	38.9%
Mail-order catalog	13.0	16.1	14.8
Direct-mail flier	15.2	11.3	13.0
Newspaper supplement	10.9	8.0	9.3
Newspaper print	6.5	9.7	8.3
Television	6.5	9.7	8.3
Point of purchase	8.7	6.5	7.4
Total	100.0%	100.0%	100.0%
Number of responses	46	62	108

Multiple response: Totals may not equal 100% due to rounding.
Source: Independent market research.

Country House, and the rectangle-Classic Border. Less preference was expressed for the other combinations, although some had sold well during the market introduction in 1990.

In an effort to identify promotion opportunities, consumers were asked where they would expect to find advertising for SignMaster. Magazines were cited most frequently by both female and male respondents, although direct-mail and newspaper advertising was also mentioned. The responses are shown in Table 8.

At the end of the interview, survey respondents were asked to remove the house sign from its package and carefully examine the product and instructions. Once again, consumers were asked to provide an expected retail price for SignMaster house sign. The median price changed, with males now reporting $7.95 and females $10. In short, the perceived value of the product declined after the product was removed from the package and carefully inspected. Upon further questioning, respondents expressed concern about the strength of the adhesive mounting tape used to attach the sign to the residence, the complicated instructions and multiple-step procedure for attaching the numbers, the durability of the product, and the time and patience required for installation. Respondents even suggested that the house numbers be included in the house-sign package to simplify the purchasing process. Management acknowledged that this would be possible, but to do so would require the inclusion of many more numbers than would be needed to identify a residence.

Some survey respondents also reacted negatively to the packaging used for the house sign. They asserted that it concealed the product and restricted the ability of a purchaser to determine the material used in construction and its thickness. Others felt that the light gray color of the package did not enhance the image of the product and would not be visually appealing at the point of sale.

The research was successful in identifying target markets for SignMaster. Although the findings are preliminary, three possibilities emerged when consumers were asked who they believed would purchase the product. First, young low-income couples who were

TABLE 9 Population Characteristics of Test Market Cities

	Covington	Waynesboro	Harrisonburg	Buena Vista	Staunton	Lexington
Population (in thousands)	7.6	18.1	29.5	6.5	22.7	6.8
Median Age	38.2	36.6	27.8	34.1	37.6	24.6
Age distribution (%)						
18–24 years	9.7	9.3	30.2	10.2	10.9	39.0
25–34 years	14.8	15.3	14.5	16.0	15.6	10.2
35–49 years	18.4	21.8	15.6	22.4	21.3	13.4
50 and over	35.7	30.7	23.9	26.1	32.5	24.2
Median household income	$20,113	$26,028	$20,047	$23,493	$24,726	$24,053
Income distr. (%)						
$10,000–19,999	28.7	22.5	28.0	24.6	22.9	22.4
20,000–34,999	29.8	30.5	24.6	35.4	28.6	24.2
35,000–49,999	13.9	17.4	13.9	17.2	17.7	13.3
50,000 and over	6.6	15.9	11.8	7.6	14.4	21.5

Source: Sales and Marketing Management, 1989 Survey of Buying Power, August 13, 1990.

owners or renters of inexpensive residences in suburban locations were mentioned as attractive prospects. Second, older retired middle-income couples living in traditional country homes in rural areas and small communities were mentioned as likely to be interested in SignMaster. Finally, the product was viewed as a decorative accent for second residences such as cottages, chalets, beach houses, townhouses, and condominiums located in vacation and recreational areas.

The SignMaster Test Market. In March 1991, John Walters decided to incorporate some of the consumer research findings into the design of an attractive display that would hold up to 12 house signs and allow consumers to visually inspect SignMaster prior to purchase. The point-of-purchase display, shown in Figure 4, was designed to display a house sign with the numbers installed and feature three popular shapes and decorative designs. It was loaded with 12 SignMaster house signs and 100 house numbers and market tested in six hardware stores located in small- and medium-sized cities in the state of Virginia. The test was designed to determine the sales response to three different SignMaster retail prices and the acceptability of the display as a point-of-purchase merchandiser in hardware stores. Table 9 summarizes the demographic characteristics of the test market cities and Table 10 describes the experimental design used to test retail prices of $8.95, $9.95, and $10.95 for the house sign and $0.69 for the numbers. The market test began in May 1991 and lasted six months. Each SignMaster price was tested in each store for a two-month period and the sales made at each retail price were recorded.

Test Market Results. The test market for the SignMaster conducted in retail hardware stores was reasonably successful. The new product sold best during the July–August test period when consumers were likely to be making exterior home improvements. Table 11

FIGURE 4   SignMaster Point-of-Purchase Display

Source: The Bacova Guild, Ltd.

TABLE 10   Retail Pricing of SignMaster in Test Market Cities

Test Period	Covington	Waynesboro	Harrisonburg	Buena Vista	Staunton	Lexington
May–June	$10.95	$10.95	$ 9.95	$ 9.95	$ 8.95	$ 8.95
July–August	8.95	8.95	10.95	10.95	9.95	9.95
September–October	9.95	9.95	8.95	8.95	10.95	10.95

House numbers priced at $0.69 each during entire test market.

summarizes the results for each two-month period of the test. The Country House was the most popular sign in the display and a $9.95 retail price resulted in the most sales. Seventy-seven percent of the consumer purchases were made in the communities of Buena Vista, Covington, and Waynesboro, cities in which the economic base was primarily manufacturing and blue-collar employment.

Looking Ahead—1991 and Beyond

As John Walters and the hardware division marketing group pondered the future of SignMaster, they reflected on the brief history of the new Bacova product. In many ways, substantial progress had been made. SignMaster had achieved retail distribution and even though the 1990 sales had proven to be disappointing, the trade had reacted favorably to the product. The consumer research, although conducted after the product had been introduced to the market, had been useful in developing a display that responded to some of the consumer questions at point of purchase. The market test, conducted during the middle of 1991, seemed to indicate that the product would sell in a retail hardware store if it was properly priced and displayed. Yet to be considered was the desirability of offering retailers advertising allowances to build consumer awareness of SignMaster prior to the retail shopping experience. If management decided to add this promotional enhancement to the marketing strategy for SignMaster, the costs would result in a lower before-tax profit margin on sales for the product. The display (excluding house signs and numbers) cost Bacova $7.52, while advertising allowances of $1.15 per sign would probably be necessary to motivate retailers to advertise the product.

Most of the information had now been collected, and it was time to reconsider the marketing strategy for the balance of 1991 and beyond. John Walters reflected that the market research would be helpful in improving the marketing strategy. It was obvious that some changes were needed because the 1991 SignMaster sales forecast of $250,000 (30,000 signs) would be difficult to achieve. Through the first nine months of 1991, sales were approximately $100,000 (11,338 signs).

Pricing was an important decision that needed to be finalized. The marketing group had to decide on an acceptable trade price for the house sign and numbers that would result in an attractive retail price for consumers. Promotion was another area of special concern. Research indicated that a point-of-purchase display was helpful, but it also seemed that some consumer promotion prior to the shopping experience would be

---

TABLE 11 SignMaster Sales in Test Market Cities

Retail Price	May–June	July–August	September–October	Sales (Units)
	Unit Sales in Test Period			
$ 8.95	0	5	2	7
9.95	3	3	5	11
10.95	5	3	0	8
	8	11	7	26

Source: Independent market research.

---

desirable. Advertising allowances for retailers were one possibility, and if necessary, they could be combined with the point-of-purchase display that had proven successful in the market test. Whatever pricing and promotion methods were used, they had to be carefully considered because management was concerned that the house sign and numbers provide a profit margin on sales of at least 30 percent.

Packaging for the house sign was also a troubling issue. The consumer survey research seemed to indicate that improvements could be made to enhance the visual appeal of the product and simplify the application of the numbers. On the other hand, the market test results indicated that the product would sell at retail if it was properly priced and displayed.

Regardless of the marketing decisions on SignMaster, the hardware division marketing group knew that new products would be needed to meet the division's goals for sales and profitability. Experience with SignMaster seemed to indicate that a different approach to product development might be appropriate to assure success in the future.

CASE 6–14 Navistar International Transportation Corporation

A truck is a capital good. It's purchased to do a job. It's not purchased for esoteric reasons, it's only purchased to create value for the user. The buyer is a very professional person or company. They are looking for something that's going to create a return for them. [Our job] is understanding the needs of each one of those customers.

Gary E. Dewel, senior vice president of sales and marketing at Navistar, reflected upon the strategic intent that had been a major factor in the Fortune 500 company's turnaround. A descendant of International Harvester Corporation, Navistar was on the brink of bankruptcy in 1982. Heavy debt, rising interest rates, and a struggling agricultural

---

This case was prepared by Victoria L. Crittenden, associate professor of marketing, Boston College and John DeVoy, MBA student, Boston College as the basis for class discussion rather than to illustrate effective or ineffective handling of a managerial situation. All information was derived from secondary sources.

business resulted in the loss of $3.4 billion between 1980 and 1985. New management, facing the task of transforming the stifling bureaucracy into a flexible organization with the ability to compete in an increasingly competitive trucking industry, had chosen to focus on reducing costs and increasing customer service. Management felt that a greater familiarity with the customer would result in a competitive advantage that had been lacking in Navistar's history. Management knew, however, that a customer orientation would have to go hand in hand with new avenues for cutting costs.

The Company

History. In 1831, Cyrus H. McCormick pioneered the first mechanical grain reaper, providing the foundation for International Harvester—a company specializing in the production of farm machinery. Trucks became part of Harvester's core business in the 1920s, as the soldiers returning from World War I continued the industrialization of the United States. Perhaps beginning Harvester's troubles, Fowler McCormick, grandson of the late Cyrus, led the company into an era of haphazard expansion in the late 1940s, culminating in a devastating battle to dethrone Caterpillar's leadership of the construction machinery industry.

In the 20 years that followed Fowler's 1951 ousting, Harvester was hindered by an unmanageable variety of truck models. Attempting to provide such a wide product offering, Harvester ignored both production capabilities and marketing difficulties. At the same time a lack of customer awareness, resulting in gross underestimation of tractor demand, severely limited Harvester's main business. Costs soared and profit margins disappeared.

The agricultural boom of the 1960s and 1970s provided cover for Harvester's rigid structure and rising cost base. The series of strikes and concessions to the United Auto Workers (UAW) that lasted through the early 1980s resulted in the establishment of operating inefficiencies throughout the corporation. Capital spending, aimed at the modernization of aging factories, was increased modestly, but barely offset administrative inefficiencies. The most agonizing union battle came at the start of the 1980 recession, resulting in a six month strike. Lost sales, rising interest rates, and a growing debt left the company struggling for survival. Trying to keep the company afloat, Archie McCardell, who began leading the company in 1978, sold the company's profitable Solar Turbines unit to Caterpillar in 1981 and disposed of several smaller businesses, including the company's unprofitable steel mill.

New management was brought in by early 1982. Donald Lennox (on the verge of retirement from International Harvester) began presiding over the company. Unfortunately, his tenure began at the start of four of the worst years in the company's history. Saddled with tremendous debt and outdated product lines, Lennox was forced to do everything possible just to keep the company from hemorrhaging cash.

With the sale of its losing agricultural business to Tenneco in 1985—along with the rights to the Harvester name—the company adopted the name "Navistar" and began to focus exclusively on manufacturing trucks.

Navistar International Corporation. Navistar International Corporation was a holding company. Its principal operating subsidiary was Navistar International Transportation Corporation. Navistar International Transportation Corporation manufactured and marketed medium and heavy trucks and parts in North America. The products were sold to distributors in certain export markets. The company had financial services subsidiaries that provided wholesale, retail, and lease financing, and commercial physical damage and liability insurance. Dealers and retail customers comprised the majority of the financial services customers.

In 1986, led by James C. Cotting (CFO), the company posted its first full-year profit since 1979, earning $2 million on sales of $3.4 billion. Cotting maneuvered the company through a vast restructuring during the mid-1980s and became chief executive officer in 1987.

Cotting's long-range plan was for half of Navistar's revenue to come from new businesses by 1997. These new businesses were to come from acquisitions related to Navistar's core truck business. While simultaneously seeking acquisitions, Cotting began cutting costs internally. For example, the plan was to trim 450 white collar jobs and add more medical copayments on employee insurance by 1990.

Navistar International Transportation Corporation. The transportation subsidiary of Navistar operated in one principal industry segment—the manufacture and marketing of medium and heavy trucks. This included school bus chassis, mid-range diesel engines, and service parts.

Led by Neil A. Springer and based in Chicago, Illinois, the company had introduced 22 new models by 1989. These models replaced S-Series units that were introduced in 1977 and 1978. Additionally, the company began partnering with its customers and its suppliers.

In late 1987, when U-Haul International wanted to revamp its medium-sized rental truck, it could not, initially, find a supplier who would agree to make the requested design changes. No one was interested because U-Haul was requesting some nontraditional ideas. However, Navistar began working with U-Haul and the final result was that Navistar won an order for 5,400 trucks. U-Haul received a prototype five months after an agreement was reached with Navistar. Dana Corporation, Navistar's frame supplier and partner, brought the truckmaker and U-Haul together.

Started in 1986, the Navistar/Dana Corporation vertical partnership was one of the oldest and most fully developed partnerships between two companies.[1] Both companies felt that combining Dana Corporation's component design expertise and manufacturing capability with Navistar's ability to put the total system together and manage distribution would be an advantage for each firm. The success of the partnership led to partnering between Navistar and Goodyear and Navistar and Caterpillar. As such, when Navistar introduced two dozen new models in late 1988, the product display included drive trains composed of Caterpillar engines, transmissions, clutches, drivelines, and axles plus Goodyear tires.

---

[1] Interestingly, the partnership did not include a written contract between Navistar and Dana. The deal was consummated on a handshake and a lot of trust.

In 1987, top management supported a major cost-cutting proposal—electronic data interchange (EDI). In its simplest form, EDI involved the electronic exchange of business documents over a standard telephone line using computer information systems. Prior to EDI, Navistar's monthly needs were mailed to suppliers and daily production requirements were phoned in. With EDI in place, Navistar was able to instantaneously transmit and receive documents that had previously taken up to a week of processing time. The result was that inventories were reduced from 33 days supply to an average of 6 days, and as little as four hours inventory in some instances. Navistar was able to reduce its inventory by $167 million (33 percent) in the first 18 months of EDI implementation.[2]

The U.S. Truck Marketplace

The beginning of the 1990s was not an easy time for truck manufacturers. The trucking industry was reeling from a business recession (which began for truckers around the middle of 1989) that meant both rising fleet expenses and sluggish freight traffic. The economy had posted a 1 percent decline from the third quarter of 1990 through the second quarter of 1991. Predictions were that the economy would begin working itself out of that decline, but the outlook was not good with growth rates maybe around 2 percent. This translated into expected "sluggishness" in the trucking marketplace.

Truck Class.   Several classes of trucks existed in the truck marketplace. Classes 1 and 2 were considered *light duty trucks*. A rise in sales for *Class 1* (under 6,000 lb. GVW)[3] trucks was predicted at the beginning of 1990. *Class 2* (6,001 to 10,000 lb. GVW) sales were thought to have peaked in 1990, and declines were projected for the early 1990s. Vehicles sold for straight commercial-fleet applications were expected to account for slightly over 10 percent of combined Classes 1 and 2 sales.

The emerging segment of the *commercial* market was Classes 3 and 4. *Class 3* (10,001 to 14,000 lb. GVW) was the only vehicle class to show growth in the early 1990s. *Class 4* (14,001 to 16,000 lb. GVW) showed signs of growth and the outlook was positive. The smallest commercial market class in annual sales, *Class 5* (16,001 to 19,500 lb. GVW) had peaked in sales in 1985 when over 8,000 units were sold.

The *medium-duty* trucks encompassed Classes 6 and 7. *Class 6* (19,501 to 26,000 lb. GVW) and *Class 7* (26,001 to 33,000 lb. GVW) showed signs of growth. Medium-duty truck sales were predicated on wholesale and retail traffic. Other factors had begun affecting sales in this category as well. One, there was a large number of late-model used trucks in this range. Two, fleets had begun stretching replacement cycles due to increases in warranty mileage coverage.

Heavy-trucks made up the *Class 8* (over 33,000 lb. GVW) market. The market for Class 8 trucks had been declining. Projections were that this market would not see an increase until 1992. There was concern that 1991 would be the worst year since the 1982–1983 recession. The industry's replacement-demand pattern was being reshaped

---

[2]Prior to EDI, a one-day reduction in inventory was the largest reduction the company had been able to achieve.
[3]GVW refers to gross vehicle weight.

EXHIBIT 1 Example of Fleet Owner Specifications

Category	Percent of Total Items Ordered
Standard to manufacturer	27%
Improved maintenance	35
Operational requirements	11
Improved safety	8
Increased driver comfort	7
Improved appearance	7
Fuel economy	5

Source: "Spec'ed or Standard," *Fleet Equipment,* June 1989, pp. 38–42.

---

due to more productive trucks and an increase in warranty mileage. The trend in the heavy truck market was toward trucks designed specifically for a single vocation.[4]

The outlook for the mid-1990s was better than for the beginning of the 1990s. The expected economic recovery would be further along, and carriers would begin replacing older trucks with newer technology vehicles. Vocational or job-specific trucks[5] were increasingly being considered by buyers and sellers in Classes 3 through 8. Another trend was toward automatic transmissions. By the early 1990s, around 70 percent of Class 3 trucks sold were automatics.

Buying Behavior. Fleet managers were bombarded daily with trade magazines[6] and factory mailings regarding product offerings. Additionally, OEMs and suppliers would often bring their product directly to the offices of larger fleets. The annual International Trucking Show, however, was the premier show where truck manufacturers and truck users would interact. The show offered a hands-on introduction to the newest in trucks and refinements to existing trucks. Another show in which suppliers of trucking equipment and OEMs exhibited was the beverage industry's premier show, the InterBev.

Order specifications from a fleet owner were very detailed and could fill several pages and include as many as 200 line items. Exhibit 1 provides an example of the types of specifications requested by a fleet owner. A large percentage of items might require a specific manufacturer's part. Additionally, there was some concern that many standard parts had not been tested sufficiently prior to becoming standard. In 1989, estimates were that 60 percent of fleets operating fewer than 10 trucks had Class 8 trucks built to order. The number increased steadily by fleet size, with 94 percent of fleets operating over 100 Class 8 trucks requesting built-to-order trucks. This was a 35 percent increase in built-to-order, compared to 1985.

---

[4]Some industry experts doubted that there would ever be the time when a *standard* model Class 8 truck would be popular.

[5]These were trucks tailored as much as possible to the job requirements of specific vocational applications in given market segments.

[6]Examples include *Fleet Equipment, Fleet Owner, Distribution,* and *Equipment Management.*

Many truck manufacturers had begun focusing upon ways in which they could help the transportation industry address some of its most pressing concerns. A major industry concern was the turnover rate of drivers. It was not uncommon to hear of 80 percent, 100 percent, 110 percent, and 200 percent as annual turnover rates among the U.S. private fleet owners. The turnover rate problem was compounded by an increasing driver shortage. A driver shortage was attributed primarily to low pay, long hours away from home, and uncomfortable equipment.[7] Another major industry concern was holding down costs for the fleet owner.

To address the driver shortage/turnover rate problem, truck makers were concentrating on improving the driver "environment." Manufacturers were providing high-tech features for comfort, maneuverability, safety, fuel economy, vehicle operation, and maintenance. Manufacturers of Classes 7 and 8 trucks were paying increased attention to driveability, ergonomics, and creature comforts.[8] Both truck manufacturers and fleet owners felt that a driver would treat the truck better if he or she was treated well.

To help fleet owners keep costs down, manufacturers were offering tremendous engineering advances with introductions of new aerodynamic and fuel-efficient designs. As well, durability had improved, with proper maintenance and repowering delaying capital expenditures for equipment replacement. There was even talk of the 1,000,000 mile truck.[9]

Industry Competitors

There were seven leading manufacturers in the medium and heavy truck categories (principally Classes 7 and 8). These were Ford, Freightliner, Mack, Volvo, GM, Peterbilt, Kenworth, and Navistar.

Ford. Ford was the manufacturer of a complete line of light-duty through Class 8 trucks. They produced both diesel and gasoline-powered vehicles. Ford had traditionally been the industry leader in Class 7 trucks. Their major plant in Kentucky was dedicated to medium and heavy trucks. This facility operated a rapid scheduling system for special orders. An $18 million computer system allowed Ford to save weeks of special engineering by comparing current and historical orders as a way of utilizing existing designs to speed vehicle delivery time. The company operated 28 field locations in the United States. In 1990, Ford planned to spend three times as much money on its heavy-duty truck line as it had in the previous five years. The plans were to upgrade every piece of equipment by 1995.

---

[7]The driver shortage problem was expected to be made worse, in the short-term, by the Commercial Driver's License (CDL), which was to be phased in nationwide by 1991. The CDL would provide one national license instead of several state licenses for truck drivers. The short-term impact was expected to be a decrease in the number of drivers (both good and bad). The longer-term impact was expected to be an improved quality of truck driver.

[8]Ergonomics is the scientific study of human factors in relation to working environments and equipment design. Examples include dashboard layout, support and seating adjustments, and outside visibility. An example of a creature comfort is an oversized sleeper cab.

[9]The 1,000,000 mile truck would go 1,000,000 miles with good routine maintenance and without rebuilding major components.

Ford offered a long line of Classes 7 and 8 trucks. The LTLS-9000 was designed for the heaviest applications. The most appropriate Ford truck for longhaul cargo applications was the LTL-9000. Ford's L-Series included a broad range of other heavy-duty trucks. In 1991, Ford was to offer its new AeroMax series. This aerodynamic series was focused upon fuel efficiency. Additionally, Ford planned to offer 24-hour emergency road service for the AeroMax.

Ford had conducted driver surveys at truck stops across North America. These surveys focused upon driver comfort issues. As a result of the information gathered in these surveys, Ford had plans to offer convenience items such as a dash-mounted cup holder, lumbar support in the driver's seat, an innerspring mattress, and a television package.

Freightliner. Freightliner offered the broadest range of Class 8 equipment of the seven leading heavy-truck manufacturers. In 1990, Freightliner began offering five new glider kits to complement its line of trucks. The glider kits provided an economical means for fleet owners to upgrade existing vehicles. The kits included the frame, finished cab, front axle with wheels, fuel tanks, steering systems, and electrical, cooling, and exhaust components. Basically, the kits allowed owners to turn an older truck into a new, customized truck with the high-tech features of Freightliner's new trucks.

Freightliner planned to introduce a new design that focused on interior comfort. Features to be included were an interior that would allow occupants to stand anywhere in the forward compartment, a wide-open sleeper, and multiple shelves and storage units/closets in the sleeper. This new offering would provide an improved ride inside a lighter-weight, aerodynamically designed truck.

The company's production was 17,000 units in 1986 and had remained relatively stable at 23,000–24,000 units during 1987 through 1991.

Mack. "Built like a Mack truck" was a popular American saying. Trying to continue this tradition, Mack promoted its durability and technological innovation, particularly in its Class 8 CH600 series. The CH600 series, launched in 1990, was Mack's premier truck. The series introduced Mack's V-MAC electronics system.

V-MAC, an acronym for Vehicle Management and Control, was a fully integrated, all-vehicle electronic control system that aimed to optimize vehicle performance and driver efficiency. Mack believed that its V-MAC was the start of total vehicle management, which would provide consistent vehicle performance through precise electronic control of fuel delivery and engine timing. The V-MAC offered several programmable options that would enable owners to adapt the truck to their particular needs and applications. The programmable options included cruise control, engine shutdown, idle shutdown, and variable engine speed limit. Mack felt that the V-MAC addressed the current and future needs of the industry.

Regarding "creature comforts," Mack boasted that its Class 8 CH600 had the most comfortable ride of Class 8 trucks in the industry. This was attributed to its unique air-suspended cab/sleeper combination. The CH600 was also the roomiest and quietest model Mack had ever produced. Standard in the truck were a tilt-telescoping steering wheel and a two-piece, wraparound windshield. Options included power windows and door locks and a high-rise sleeper-cab configuration.

Mack's production had increased steadily from 1986 to 1988 (from 17,000 units in 1986 to 23,000 units in 1988). However, production had tapered off to 15,000 units in 1990 and 10,000 units in 1991. The company expected production to increase for 1992.

Volvo GM. During the late 1980s, Volvo and General Motors (GM) formed a new company, Volvo GM, to develop Class 8 trucks. Volvo owned 76 percent and GM owned 24 percent of the new company. Volvo GM accounted for 34 percent of Volvo Truck Corporation's 1990 worldwide sales. Volvo's two product lines introduced in 1986, the FE Series Class 7 and Class 8 trucks, remained its two major lines at the beginning of the 1990s.

Both the Class 7 and Class 8 trucks featured dashboards, seating, and steering wheels designed to improve driver comfort and performance. The Class 8 models were designed to provide a high degree of fuel efficiency through advanced aerodynamics.

To better meet customer demands of flexibility and to appeal to a wider base of customers, Volvo began assembling its FE Series Class 7 trucks in its Ohio plant in 1991. The trucks had been assembled in its Belgium plant. In another move to push the company closer to the customer, Karl-Erling Trogen (president of Volvo GM) had plans to improve parts availability, increase training, enhance literature offerings, improve computer systems, and improve communications (via satellite) between headquarters and the company's 200 dealers. Trogen's goal was to increase the penetration of Volvo components in American trucks.

Peterbilt. Peterbilt, a division of PACCAR, offered a wide range of models in its Classes 7 and 8. Safety and driver concerns were major factors in the design of Peterbilt's newer models. To provide smoother ride quality, Peterbilt introduced its first front air suspension in 1990. To address safety concerns, the company provided a Bendix BPR-1 bobtail proportioning system as an option on its trucks. The Bendix BPR-1 was designed to prevent rear axle lock-up. This, in turn, reduced stopping distances and decreased uneven wear on the truck's rear tires.

Peterbilt's Class 7 line of trucks shared the same name with its sister company, Kenworth. This Mid-Ranger series was designed for ease of maintenance, better visibility and maneuverability, and a tighter curb-to-curb turning circle than a conventional Class 7 truck.

Kenworth. The PACCAR division selling Classes 7 and 8 trucks along with Peterbilt, Kenworth offered several models in its Class 8 line. The models offered improved aerodynamics which boosted fuel economy. Kenworth attempted to target its Class 8 truck models to particular market segments. For example, its T400A was marketed to fleets transporting various consumer and business-to-business products such as general freight, petroleum, food, and lumber. Its K100E was targeted toward moving companies, truckload carriers, and private fleets. The company's Class 7, Mid-Ranger series mirrored that of Peterbilt's.

Navistar. With production averaging around 75,000 units a year from 1986 through 1991, Navistar was the nation's largest truck manufacturer.[10] The focus of the company's truck design at the beginning of the 1990s was ergonomics. The manufacturer planned to increase driver

---

[10]Production peaked in 1988 at 85,000 units, with a low of 63,000 units in 1991.

comfort through a new axle that was designed to improve driver maneuverability and increase aerodynamics and driver visibility, plus new interiors and more electronic controls (such as cruise control). The plan was to update 65 percent of the company's product line by the end of 1992.

Customer support also was the center of attention at Navistar. As part of the company's greatly expanded parts program, a new service maintenance kit for truck air conditioning systems was introduced in 1990. The kit contained all of the parts needed for the annual preventive maintenance of all makes of its International trucks. The kit was made available through Navistar's network of 900 North American dealers.

Many of Navistar's trucks carried the International name. However, the company also offered its 8000 (Class 7) and 9000 (Class 8) series. Like Peterbilt, Navistar was strong on glider kits in 1990, with the kits available for its 8000 and 9000 series models. By the beginning of the 1990s, the company had introduced 22 new truck models that replaced models brought to the market in the late 1970s. Plans were to introduce a limited edition model[11] that would focus on the very best in driver comfort.

The International Truck Marketplace

South America and Mexico were potentially large markets for truck manufacturers. Projections for 1992 were that the South American commercial vehicle market would be around 6,500 new trucks (4,000 heavy-duty trucks and 2,500 medium trucks). In 1991, around 31 percent of Classes 6, 7, and 8 trucks shipped out of North America by U.S. producers were sold in South America. The relatively sound economy in Chile offered truck exporters a solid base from which to spread into nearby countries.[12] Additionally, Chile had no vehicle import restrictions, and there was no Chilean truck manufacturing industry.

U.S. companies that had entered Chile by the early 1990s were Ford, General Motors, Navistar, Kenworth, Mack, and Freightliner. There were also manufacturers from Europe, Asia, Scandinavia, and Russia. Russia's Kamaz truck had become the best selling truck (medium-duty). The Kamaz had edged out Mercedes-Benz, which had truck assembly operations in Argentina and Brazil.

Mexico also was perceived as a lucrative market. The Mexican truck fleet was very large with an estimated 550,000 trucks in operation at the beginning of the 1990s. The trucks had an estimated average age of 12 years, which was nearly twice the average for the U.S. truck fleet. Mathematically, industry sales would have to exceed 45,800 trucks a year to prevent further aging of Mexico's fleet.[13] Approximately 85 percent of total freight tonnage in Mexico was transported by truck.

Industrialization and rapid GDP growth in Mexico had led to a sharp increase in medium and heavy truck sales (Classes 6 through 8). In 1988, there were around 6,500 trucks sold, with predictions of close to 33,000 by 1992. A Mexican company, Grupo Dina, dominated

---

[11] Only 250 units would be produced. The cabs would feature air-suspended, high-back leather seats with dual armrests, an easy-to-read instrument panel accented by genuine rosewood trim, and an upgraded stereo system.

[12] Peru was seen as the country to enter after establishing in Chile.

[13] Douglas Laughlin, "Automotive—Heavy Trucks: A Sunshine Industry in Mexico," *Institutional Investor* (June 1993), p. SS8.

the Mexican truck market with close to 50 percent of the medium and heavy truck market. Other truck manufacturers in Mexico included Daimler Benz, KenMex, and Chrysler.

A Customer Orientation

Navistar was the largest truck manufacturer in the United States. But could it remain in that position long, given the customer-oriented actions taken by its competitors? Dewel knew a customer focus was necessary to survive in the highly competitive truck marketplace. But how could he implement this customer focus when he also had a mandate to cut costs? Weren't the two goals contradictory?

SOURCES

Birkland, Carol. "Gasoline Engine Update." *Fleet Equipment,* April 1992, pp. 14–17.

Burr, Barry, B. "Navistar Joins Electronic Pay Age." *Pensions & Investment Age,* April 6, 1987, pp. 37–38.

Byrne, Harlan S. "They Almost Bought the Farm, but Navistar and Varity Are on the Road to Recovery." *Barron's,* May 2, 1988, pp. 6–7, 32–34.

Cullen, David. "Building Working Assets." *Fleet Owner,* August 1991, pp. 55–58.

———. "The Long Pull Ahead." *Fleet Owner,* January 1992, pp. 30–36.

Deierlein, Bob. "The Next Best Thing." *Beverage World,* September 1992, pp. 92–96.

Deierlein, Bob, and Tom Gelinas. "Spec'ed or Standard." *Fleet Equipment,* June 1989, pp. 38–42.

Deveny, Kathleen. "Can the Man Who Saved Navistar Run It, Too?" *Business Week,* March 9, 1987, p. 88.

Dumaine, Brian. "How Managers Can Succeed through Speed." *Fortune,* February 13, 1989, pp. 54–59.

Duncan, Thomas W. "Adding Muscle to Light-Duty Trucks." *Fleet Owner,* August 1988, pp. 77–82.

———. "Chile Emerging as Export Prize." *Fleet Owner,* December 1992, p. 12.

Gage, Theodore Justin. "Cash Makes a Comeback in Navistar Financing." *Cash Flow,* December 1987, pp. 53, 58.

Gonze, Josh. "EDI Users Anticipate X.12 Boost." *Network World,* November 30, 1987, pp. 2, 45.

Green, Larry. "Building the Best Business Partnership." *Equipment Management,* April 1991, pp. 18–23.

———. "Staying Power." *Equipment Management,* June 1991, pp. 25–30.

"Highway Tractors: Accent on the Creature Comforts!" *Traffic Management,* November 1992, pp. 49–52.

Laughlin, Douglas K. "Automotive—Heavy Trucks: A Sunshine Industry in Mexico." *Institutional Investor,* June 1993, p. SS8.

Martin, James D. "Attention Returns to Heavy-Duty Trucks." *Distribution,* November 1990, pp. 54–62.

Mele, Jim. "The 1,000,000 Mile Truck." *Fleet Owner,* April 1994, pp. 77–83.

Milbrandt, Ben. "EDI: A More Efficient Way to Operate." *Corporate Cashflow,* August 1990, pp. 34–35.

———. "Making EDI Pay Off." *Corporate Cashflow,* December 1988, pp. 24–28.

Moore, Thomas L. "Forging Partnerships." *Fleet Owner,* May 1992, p. 4.

———. "New Volvo GM Head Pushes Customer Focus." *Fleet Owner,* February 1, 1992, p. 96.

Najlepszy, Frank. "Turnaround in Truck Design." *Machine Design,* April 7, 1988, pp. 40–48.

Navistar 1993 Annual Report.

"Navistar's New Lines of Medium-, Heavy-Duty Conventionals Replace S-Series Models." *Fleet Owner,* January 1989, pp. 58–61.

Stavro, Barry. "A Surfeit of Equity." *Forbes,* December 29, 1986, pp. 62, 64.

"Supplier Partnerships . . . Who Benefits?" *Fleet Equipment,* July 1989, pp. 43–45.

Teresko, John. "Speeding the Product Development Cycle." *Industry Week,* July 18, 1988, pp. 40–42.

"Truck Makers Feature Safety, Driver Comfort." *Traffic Management,* October 1991, pp. 73–77.

CASE 6–15   Ohmeda Monitoring Systems

Looking out his office window at the magnificant Front Range of the Colorado Rockies, Joseph W. Pepper, general manager of Ohmeda Monitoring Systems, was deep in thought concerning the future of Finapres®, a relatively new Ohmeda product. Introduced in 1987, the product had not lived up to its expectations. Now, in mid-June 1990, Pepper was considering a number of options. His choice, he knew, would have a significant impact on Ohmeda Monitoring Systems.

Background

Finapres (the name was derived from its use of finger arterial pressure) was the product on the market providing *continuous noninvasive blood pressure monitoring* (CNIBP). As such, it was the only unique product that Ohmeda could offer in 1990.

Originally introduced to the market in 1987, initial results had been disappointing. Its introduction in the United States had been generally unsuccessful. Results in Europe, and internationally, had been somewhat better but still had failed to meet the firm's expectations. Concerns about the product had led Ohmeda to stop shipments on May 1, 1990, pending a review of product problems and the overall situation.

At an all-day meeting on May 23, 1990, marketing research, field sales, and R&D had presented information on the status of Finapres. In particular, R&D had given its

---

This case was prepared by Professor H. Michael Hayes and Research Assistant Brice Henderson as a basis for class discussion, rather than to illustrate either effective or ineffective handling of an administrative situation. Copyright © 1993 by University of Colorado at Denver.

assessment as to the likelihood that proposed product changes and improvements would solve some of the product's shortcomings.

The specter of the disappointing initial introduction, and the uncertainty that R&D could improve the product sufficiently to satisfy all the concerns, hung over the decision to commit more funds to the product. An unsuccessful reintroduction would further hurt Ohmeda's credibility, both with customers and with the field sales force. On the other hand, successful reintroduction of Finapres would ensure a strong, and possibly dominant, position in the noninvasive blood pressure monitoring market, plus the possibility of increased sales of other monitoring products, as Finapres was combined with other Ohmeda products into packaged systems.

Subsequently, Pepper had many discussions with his key managers regarding their views of Finapres. In early June he visited a number of Ohmeda customers and distributors in Japan, many of whom were very interested in Finapres. Although there were several unanswered questions, it was up to Pepper to make the key decisions concerning Finapres.

BOC/Ohmeda

Ohmeda Monitoring Systems was a business unit of The BOC Group, a multinational firm, headquartered in Windlesham, Surrey, England. The Group had an international portfolio of what it described as "world-competitive" businesses, principally industrial gases, health care products and services, and high-vacuum technology. The Group operated in some 60 countries and employed nearly 40,000 people.

Health care products and services were provided by BOC Health Care for critical care in the hospital and in the home. Their equipment, therapies, and pharmaceuticals were used in operating rooms (OR), recovery rooms (PACU), intensive care (ICU), and cardiac care (CCU) units throughout the world. Divisions of BOC Health Care were organized around *pharmaceuticals, home health care, intravascular devices,* and *equipment and systems.*

Ohmeda Health Care, providing equipment and systems, was an autonomous division of BOC Health Care. It was made up of five major business units, plus a field operations unit. The five business units manufactured products for *suction therapy, infant care, respiratory therapy, anesthesia,* and *monitoring systems.* Field operations provided field sales and sales support, worldwide, on a pooled basis to all the business units. (See Exhibit 1 for a partial organization chart of Field Operations.)

A 1985 reorganization had put all business decisions in the hands of the business general managers, and established profit of the business unit as a major performance measure. In 1990, the managers of the business units, and the manager of field operations, reported to the president of Ohmeda Health Care, Richard Leazer, who, in turn, reported to the managing director of BOC Health Care, W. Dekle Rountree.

Ohmeda Monitoring Systems. Ohmeda Monitoring Systems (headquartered in Louisville, Colorado) designed, manufactured, and sold (through the field operations unit)

EXHIBIT 1   Ohmeda Monitoring Systems Partial Organization Chart—Field Operations

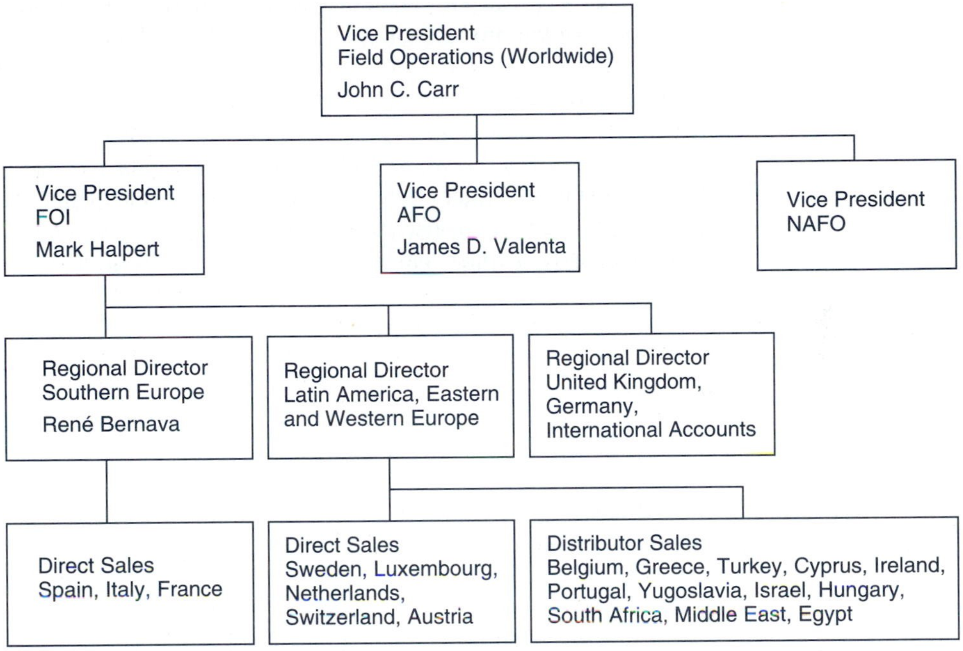

```
                    ┌─────────────────────────────┐
                    │ Vice President              │
                    │ Field Operations (Worldwide)│
                    │ John C. Carr                │
                    └─────────────────────────────┘
         ┌───────────────────┼───────────────────────┐
┌──────────────────┐ ┌──────────────────┐ ┌──────────────────┐
│ Vice President   │ │ Vice President   │ │ Vice President   │
│ FOI              │ │ AFO              │ │ NAFO             │
│ Mark Halpert     │ │ James D. Valenta │ │                  │
└──────────────────┘ └──────────────────┘ └──────────────────┘
```

Regional Director Southern Europe René Bernava	Regional Director Latin America, Eastern and Western Europe	Regional Director United Kingdom, Germany, International Accounts

Direct Sales Spain, Italy, France	Direct Sales Sweden, Luxembourg, Netherlands, Switzerland, Austria	Distributor Sales Belgium, Greece, Turkey, Cyprus, Ireland, Portugal, Yugoslavia, Israel, Hungary, South Africa, Middle East, Egypt

monitoring equipment for a number of segments of the health care industry. It focused its business activities on three classes of products:

- Oximetry products, used to measure oxygen content in arterial blood.
- Gas analysis products, used to measure a patient's respiratory gas levels.
- Noninvasive blood pressure measurement products.

Applications for these products were found in a wide variety of departments within hospitals and other health care facilities. Products were usually sold to the health care facility, either directly by the field sales force or by a distributor. Some products, however, were also sold to original equipment manufacturers (OEMs) for incorporation in a larger measurement package.

Most Ohmeda oximetry and Finapres products consisted of a "box," containing the hardware, software, and a display unit, and a probe or cuff, to allow a noninvasive way to measure the parameter of interest. These were of two types, disposable or reusable, and were designed to be attached to the patient's toe, foot, finger, hand, or ear, depending on the application.

Ohmeda had access to Finapres technology by virtue of a worldwide exclusive license, obtained from Research Unit Biomedical Instrumentation TNO (Amsterdam, the

Netherlands). Many other technologies had also been acquired, either by license or outright purchase.

Ohmeda estimated the noninvasive monitoring market was $1.2 billion worldwide, with 60 percent of the market in the United States. Overall, its market share was some 15 percent of those segments it served. In selected categories, however, its market share was considerably higher. With considerable variation by country and specific product, Ohmeda estimated the growth rate of its served market at 5–10 percent per year.

The competitive picture for Ohmeda was complex. Its main competitors were U.S.-based firms. Many of its products, however, faced strong competition from European firms. In oximetry there were an estimated 25 competitors, although only 4 had significant shares. Major competitors and estimated market shares were:

Nellcor (U.S.)	50%
Ohmeda (U.S.)	30%
Criticare (U.S.)	10%
Novametrix (U.S.)	8%

In respiratory gases there were an estimated 12 competitors. Major competitors and estimated market shares were:

Datex (Finland)	16%
Ohmeda	15%
Siemens (West Germany)	14%
Hewlett-Packard (U.S.)	12%

In blood pressure measurement only five companies competed. With an 80 percent share, Critikon (U.S.) dominated the noninvasive market with its oscillometric, or noncontinuous, product. Ohmeda's sales of its noninvasive products represented just 2 percent of this market.[1]

Based on pretax operating profits in 1989, Ohmeda's financial situation appeared to be very healthy. There were concerns, however. As Pepper observed:

> We tend to be more financially driven than market driven. Also, we have not been investing heavily in R&D. As a result, our product line is relatively mature and I don't know how much longer we can count on present products for high contribution margins.
>
> Finapres is the only major new product that is close to ready to go. Perfecting Finapres, and successfully reintroducing it, would not only produce direct sales but its uniqueness could also benefit our other monitoring businesses, through integrated packages that included a technology available nowhere else. The sales force in Europe, and also in Asia, is very excited about the product, even with its present deficiencies, and believes that with reasonable improvement it could become a major contributor to sales and profits. In the United States there is not the

---

[1] Market shares were for the U.S. market.

same excitement. There is agreement that if all the product deficiencies could be corrected we would have a real winner, but R&D can't give us any guarantees.

Field Operations.   Following the 1985 reorganization of Ohmeda Health Care from a functional organization to the five therapy units, the firm had considered how to organize its field sales operations. Given the complexity of the five product lines, and some desire on the part of the therapy unit managers to have more direct control over the sales forces that represented them, there was considerable support to establish specialized sales forces. There was also support for direct sales, as opposed to extensive use of distributors or dealers. Selling anesthesia equipment, it was argued, was very different than selling patient monitors and other Ohmeda products, because of product differences and customer buying procedures. Many of Ohmeda's competitors (e.g., Siemens and Hewlett-Packard) relied heavily on direct sales, feeling that distributors or dealers could not provide the required level of technical knowledge and service.

Arguing against specialized selling was the belief that it was far more efficient, in terms of time, travel expense, and customer knowledge, to have one salesperson calling on a hospital, rather than three, as was contemplated in one proposed form of organization. Still further, there was great concern about the consequences of terminating distributors or dealers, some of whom had been associated with Ohmeda (or its predecessor companies) for over 70 years. Finally, Ohmeda was aware that Baxter-Travenol, the largest medical supplies and equipment company in the world, had specialized its sales force in 1981 but had subsequently gone back to a general sales organization.

After extensive study, it was decided to continue with a pooled form of sales organization, together with pooled product service, customer service, and finance, all reporting to the vice president of field operations. As of early 1990, field operations had three principal regional components: NAFO, responsible for sales and service in North America (the U.S. and Canada); FOI, responsible for sales and service in Europe, the Middle East, and Latin America; and AFO, responsible for sales and service in Asia, including Japan. Depending on the particular country, sales were all direct, a combination of direct and dealer, or totally through dealers.

Ohmeda recognized the need for making specialized product knowledge, beyond the expertise of the local salesperson, available quickly to the customer. In NAFO, it was assumed that such specialized knowledge could be provided by specialists from manufacturing locations. In FOI and AFO, it was deemed impractical for specialists to travel from the United States, and product champions were appointed in the major countries. Paid principally on salary (as opposed to the salespeople who were paid on a salary and commission basis), the product champions supported the sales force for their assigned products in a variety of ways. They were available to call on customers with the salespeople. They held product seminars, either for salespeople or for customer groups. In some instances they acted as missionary salespeople, soliciting orders from new customers. In all instances, they provided a focused communication channel between the field and headquarters marketing. It was Ohmeda's view that the product champions had played a major role in assisting the introduction of Finapres in Europe. There was also some concern that not enough manpower was available from headquarters to provide similar support to the field sales force in the United States and Canada.

EXHIBIT 2 Ohmeda Monitoring Systems U.S. Market Size (sales potential in units, 1990–1992)

Segment	Potential Sites*	Oximetry	Gas Analysis	Blood Pressure	Saturation
OR/PACU	60,000	26,000	31,000	15,000	HI
ICU/NICU/CCU	78,000	20,000	15,500	9,750	HI
L&D	57,000	10,000	0	4,000	MED
Floors	800,000	15,000	0	2,000	LO
Nonhospital	65,000	10,500	0	200	MED

*Number of physical locations.

Health Care Markets

The health care industry was one of the largest, and most rapidly growing, segments of the world economy. While growth was occurring worldwide, the potential for Ohmeda products was greatest in the United States, Europe, Japan, and, generally, in the developed countries of the world. With certain exceptions, the United States tended to lead the world in the development and use of technologically sophisticated health care products. U.S. manufacturers of such products generally felt that the rest of the world followed the U.S. lead in acceptance and use, with countries in Europe following in as little as six months but with longer delays in other parts of the world.

Hospitals were the principal buyers of Ohmeda products. With some variation, due mainly to government regulations, purchasing practices were very similar in the developed countries of the world. All purchases of medical equipment required budgetary approval of the hospital administration. Their purchasing influence, however, was generally inversely related to the complexity of the item. Purchase decisions of disposable supplies and gases, for instance, were generally made solely by the hospital purchasing agent, based on the lowest price. By contrast, capital equipment was invariably selected by the hospital's medical specialists and clinical area end-users. Because any machine malfunction was potentially life-threatening, medical specialists were especially concerned with precision, reliability, and safety. In addition, both the sophistication of clinical procedures and the technical expertise and interest of medical specialists were increasing. As a result, the product and clinical knowledge required to sell medical equipment was also increasing.

Ohmeda segmented its market by hospital department or application, as follows:

OR/PACU (operating room/post anesthetic care unit, or recovery room).

ICU/NICU/CCU (intensive care unit/neonatal intensive care unit/coronary care unit).

L&D (labor and delivery).

Floors (basically patients' rooms in hospital wards).

Nonhospital (the growing nonhospital segment, which included ambulances, surgicenters, physicians' offices, dental and home care, for oximetry and blood pressure products).

EXHIBIT 3 Ohmeda Monitoring Systems Buying Influences

	OR	ICU	NICU	PACU	CCU	Floors	L&D
Probes	P	NTM	NT	NT	NTM	NTM	NT
Blood pressure	P	PNM	PN	PN	PNM	PNM	PN
Gas analysis	P	PTM	PT	PT	—	—	PT
Oximetry	P	NTM	NT	NT	NTM	PNTM	NT

Legend:

P = physician   OR = operating room
N = nurse   ICU = intensive care unit
T = technician   NICU = neonatal intensive care unit
A = administrator   PACU = post anesthetic care unit
F = financial officer   CCU = coronary care unit
M = materials (purchasing)   L&D = labor and delivery

Sales potential varied substantially, depending on the particular segment and the product (Exhibit 2). Segments outside the United States generally had lower saturation levels than in the United States. As was pointed out, however, saturation levels were not always the best indicator of sales potential. In many instances the replacement markets offered high potential as well.

In the operating room the physician (generally the anesthetist) was the key buying influence for all products. In all other segments decision making was a shared responsibility, as indicated in Exhibit 3. Key buying influences were thought to be influenced by different factors, in order of importance as indicated below:

Physician	Nurse	Technician
Technology	Ergonomics	Serviceability
Ergonomics	Relationship	Technology
Relationship	In-service	
Price/value	Technology	

Administrator	Financial Officer	Material (Purchasing)
Company reputation	Leasing options	Price/value
Price/value	Total package cost	Total package cost
Revenue generation	Reimbursement	Serviceability

Personal contact with key buying influences by direct sales representatives or distributors was an essential ingredient to securing an order. Key to success, however, were favorable results from experimental trials, particularly of new products, as reported in medical journals. Manufacturers worked closely with the medical community worldwide to identify opinion leaders interested in equipment who were willing to experiment with it and then publish their results in scholarly journals. Most such experiments were reported in English-language journals, but these were widely read in non-English-speaking countries.

Finapres

Modern medicine viewed measurement of arterial blood pressure as essential in the monitoring of patients, both during and after surgery. Traditional monitoring techniques have included both invasive and noninvasive methods. Arterial line monitoring provided continuous measurement, but invasion (meaning surgical insertion of a long, small-bore catheter into the radial or femoral arteries) involved the risk of thrombosis, embolism, infections, and nerve injuries. These risks were acceptable when arterial blood samples had to be taken regularly, but otherwise were to be avoided.

An oscillometric monitor, such as Criticon's Dinamap, was noninvasive. As commonly used, such a device provided readings automatically every three to five minutes, or on demand. It could provide readings more frequently, but this involved considerable patient pain or discomfort. As normally used, therefore, it could miss vital data due to the time lag of the readings. (Ohmeda sold a noninvasive blood pressure monitor of this type, manufactured for them, but had not promoted it heavily.) Manual methods were noninvasive but were highly dependent on the skill of the clinician and the application of the correct size arm cuff and involved even more time lag.

Finapres Technology.   In 1967 a Czech physiologist, Dr. Jan Peñaz, patented a method with which it was possible to measure finger arterial pressure noninvasively. (See Exhibit 4 for a detailed description of the method.) In 1973 the device was demonstrated at the 10th International Conference on Medical and Biological Engineering at Dresden. Subsequently, a group of engineers at the Research Unit Biomedical Instrumentation TNO in the Netherlands became interested in the technology and constructed, first, a laboratory model, and then a model that they felt was clinically and experimentally useful and commercially viable. In 1983 Ohmeda acquired an exclusive license for the Finapres technology.

Finapres and Ohmeda.   Although TNO had produced a working model of Finapres, Ohmeda had invested between $2 and $3 million in R&D in order to develop a manufacturable box and cuff and to recode the software to conform to Ohmeda protocols. The resultant design could be built largely on existing equipment, although some $100,000 was required for tooling the cuff. Prior to commercial introduction, extensive work was done with opinion leaders to establish the credibility of the product. Favorable test results of clinical studies of Finapres were reported in medical journals and were widely distributed to the medical profession. Cost of this work, and other market development expenditures, was roughly equivalent to the cost of R&D.

Ohmeda introduced a commercial design of Finapres in 1987 in the United States and in 1988 in Europe and other world markets. The initial offering consisted of a box, a patient interface module that attached to the patient's hand, and three reusable cuffs. It was positioned to compete against invasive measuring products. Although it was expected it would ultimately be offered to the OEM market, it was originally introduced directly to the OR market. Priced at approximately $9,500, it was expected to return a contribution margin in excess of 70 percent (generally typical for new and unique products in the health equipment industry). Some price resistance was experienced and the U.S. price was reduced to $8,500, six months after introduction. Disappointingly, U.S. sales through 1989 totaled only 200 units.

EXHIBIT 4 Ohmeda Monitoring Systems Principles of Operation

Arteries transport blood under high pressure to the tissues. The artery walls are strong and elastic; that is, they stretch during systole (when blood is forced onward by contraction of the heart) and recoil during diastole (dilation of the heart when its chambers are filling with blood). This prevents arterial pressure from rising or falling to extremes during the cardiac cycle, thus maintaining a continuous uninterrupted flow of blood to the tissues. The volume of blood inside the artery increases when it expands and decreases when it contracts. This change in volume is the key phenomenon on which the Peñaz/Finapres technology was based.

In the Finapres system, a cuff with an inflatable bladder was wrapped around the finger (see diagram below). A light source (LED) was directed through the finger and monitored by a detector on the other side. This light was absorbed by the internal structures according to their various densities. The emitted light was an indication of blood volume in the artery. Through a complex servomechanism system, the cuff was inflated, or deflated, to maintain the artery size at a constant level. Thus, cuff pressure constantly equaled arterial pressure and was displayed on the monitor as an arterial waveform and also digitally.

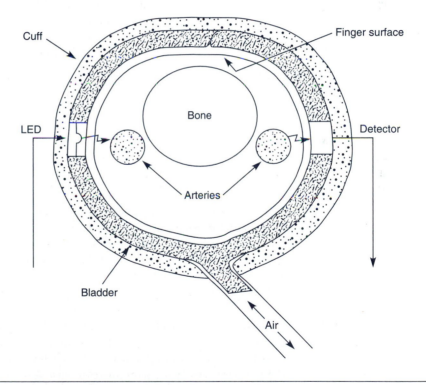

In 1988 the product was introduced internationally, at a U.S. equivalent price of $9,600. In contrast to the U.S. introduction, the product was targeted, for direct sale, at a number of segments in hospitals. As in the United States, price resistance was encountered and by 1989 the price had been reduced to approximately the U.S. equivalent of $5,000.

To some extent low sales in the United States were blamed on tactical marketing errors, such as the positioning and price of the product at introduction. There were also some technical problems with the system. Some were cosmetic in nature and easily fixed. Others were more serious, both for the clinicians using the equipment and for Ohmeda. Major problems were the difficulty in applying the cuff properly in order to get an accurate reading, and drift in readings that occurred after several hours of continuous use, a particularly serious problem in OR. Another problem was the inability of the equipment to accurately monitor patients with poor blood circulation.

Results were more promising in Europe. The European medical community had been anxious to get access to Finapres. Much had been written about the Peñaz methodology and the system developed by TNO in the European medical press. The noninvasive aspect of Finapres was particularly attractive. European doctors were less comfortable with arterial line methodology than were their American counterparts. In addition, they tended to be more willing to invest time and effort to learn new technologies, and there was less preoccupation with patient throughput than in the United States.

News of the problems experienced in the ORs in the United States had made penetration of the OR segment in Europe difficult. With its broader contacts, the sales force was able to introduce the product to other segments, particularly in CCU and physiology in teaching hospitals, where stability over long periods of time was either not as critical as in OR or where continuous blood pressure monitoring was of paramount importance. With this approach, supported by the willingness of the sales force to train medical personnel in application of the cuff, the company experienced much greater success, selling a total of 700 units in these markets through 1989.

Commenting on results through 1989, Melvyn Dickinson, international marketing manager observed:

> There are significant differences between the hospital markets in the United States and Europe, and in how our sales forces sell to them. In the United States, for example, anesthetic machines, made by one of our sister therapy units, are sold by the same field sales force that sells our monitoring equipment. The U.S. machines are made to more stringent requirements and are much more expensive than those sold in Europe. In addition, they tend to be replaced on a 5-year cycle, compared to 10–15 years in, say, Italy. As a result, our sales force in the United States tends to really concentrate on the OR market, whereas in Europe the sales force takes a broader approach.
>
> It's also important to recognize that the key influence for OR purchases is an anesthesiologist, for whom blood pressure is just one of many concerns. In other segments of the hospital, the situation is very different. In the CCU, or the cardiac operating theater, blood pressure is of paramount importance. Not all procedures are lengthy, and even where they are many cardiologists saw value in CNIBP, even though there was drift. For physiological measurements in research hospitals, or in hypertension units, there were even fewer drawbacks, plus the clinicians in these situations were much more inclined to take extra care with application of the cuff.
>
> Beyond these differences, we misread the market in general. It had been our assumption that arterial lines [the term for invasive systems] were the major competitors for Finapres. We priced and positioned Finapres accordingly. Unfortunately, our promotion didn't get this position established in the minds of our customers. As it turned out, many customers viewed the oscillometric machines as our major competitor. For these customers, our original price involved too large a premium, versus the less expensive oscillometric machines. Now there is some real question about going back to the original positioning strategy.

The two years following the introduction of Finapres were characterized by indecision about its future and lack of significant support for the product. Once introduced, Ohmeda required it to be self-supporting, with product improvements made on an ongoing basis financed out of current revenues. When the sales force began to report complaints from the clinicians in the field, it was felt that the major problems were cosmetic, concerning the size of the box and the readability of the screen. Complaints regarding inaccurate readings were thought to result from misapplication of the cuff. Despite some modifications, complaints continued and sales declined. As 1990 began, it was apparent that decisions as to the future of Finapres needed to be made.

Reassessment. Reassessment of Finapres had started with the development of the five year plan for Ohmeda Monitoring Systems. Subsequently, concerns on the part of the sales force about the commitment to Finapres indicated the desirability of a meeting involving sales force management, product management, and R&D. On May 23, 1990, Joe Pepper convened a meeting of representatives of all three groups, as well as headquarters marketing. The main points that emerged from the meeting were as follows:

- There was general agreement that the market potential for CNIBP was large. There was, however, considerable disagreement as to its exact size. Some estimates of the U.S. market were as large as 7,740 units per year. International estimates were considerably lower. There was general agreement that the largest market segments for Finapres were OR and ICU/CCU. It was the view of Ohmeda's product managers, however, that the focus of the NAFO sales force on the OR market made selling to the ICU/CCU segment difficult.

- It was emphasized that the diffusion of innovation in many instances took a long time. Acceptance of some currently standard medical equipment came only after a number of years. Oximetry, for example, took 14 years, echocardiography took 10 years and, as it was emphasized, capnometry (CO_2 gas analysis) took 40 years to become accepted. However, if Finapres was to ultimately succeed, investment was necessary not only in technological development, but in market development as well.

- The following reasons for lack of success to date were identified:

  Drift in readings over time.
  Not accurate for average clinician.
  Not easy to use.
  Inadequate alert for misapplied cuff.
  No alerts for problems with poor circulation.
  No toe/pediatric/neonatal thumb cuffs.

- Concerns were expressed about:

  Lack of a research culture.
  Bottom-line/short-term focus.
  R&D research shortage.

- R&D gave its assessment of time and cost to develop fixes and their likelihood of success:

The cause of drift was not certain, but there was a high probability that the problem could be fixed with changes in software, probably in 1990. If this fix worked, the cost would be relatively modest.

Assessing the present cuff as offering 30 percent of ideal requirements, currently contemplated modifications could be expected to improve performance to 40 percent by January 1991, again with relatively modest cost. With a more substantial effort it was expected performance could be improved to 80 percent in two years.

- Noninvasive oscillometric blood pressure machines were not likely to be "thrown out" in favor of Finapres. It was more likely they would be replaced on a normal schedule.

- On the positive side a number of strengths were identified:

> Patents lasting past the year 2000 (except United Kingdom and Germany).
> Strong distribution, particularly in OR.
> Technical expertise.
> Head start over competition.

After extensive discussion, four options were presented:

1. Stay on the present course. Make sufficient modifications to make it possible to carefully reintroduce the product in selected markets. This approach was estimated to cost $307,000 in R&D expense, generate sales of 820 units through 1994, and have a net present value of $30,000.

2. Stop the project. Taking into account writing off current inventory costs and possible return costs, this approach was estimated to have a negative NPV of $160,000.

3. Make a significant investment in R&D and marketing (including going forward with a mini-Fini, a much smaller version of Finapres that would be targeted at the OEM market). This contemplated a 50 percent penetration of the OR market by 1995, a 50 percent penetration of the ICU market by 1998, and significant penetration of the OEM market. Cumulative sales estimates for this approach were 7,700 units in the United States and 4,000 internationally (through 1995). With projected revenues of $40 million, investment in R&D of $2 million, investment in marketing of $1.2 million, the net present value of this approach through 1995 was estimated to be $2,200,000.

4. Sell the business. There was considerable discussion of this option, but the general view was that it was not likely Ohmeda could find a buyer willing to pay any significant amount for the business. In any event, it was unlikely that top management at BOC would approve such a step.

Management Views.   Subsequent to the May 23 meeting a number of views were expressed by Ohmeda managers. As John Carr, vice president of field operations saw it:

The international experience with Finapres was more successful for a variety of reasons. The original technology was developed by a European company (TNO) so the European medical community was familiar with the concept. The sales force is more balanced in its approach to the market. Hence, it was able to exploit niche markets where the device worked very well. The initial sales built confidence. The real key was the use of product champions. The product was given support and attention that it did not receive in the States.

Finapres represented a once-in-5-to-10-years type of opportunity. It was a significant new technology which didn't seem to fit Ohmeda's culture or annual financial cycle. If the initial effort had been followed by product enhancements, Finapres would have been successful. From here, the only two decisions I see are sell or go.

Similar views were expressed by James Valenta, vice president for Asia (AFO):

Finapres is a great product, which, from my view in the Asian markets, has significant customer appeal. It seems that things were stacked against the product from the beginning. Soon after Finapres was purchased, Ohmeda reorganized. The individual who had pushed to buy the technology moved on to other assignments, which resulted in some lost momentum. Finapres never really had a home, which compounded the problems with the system itself. Had there been a quicker response to feedback from the international sales force, most of what was discussed at the meeting today, the drift issue and the cuff, could have been resolved some time ago. Ohmeda had trouble accepting the fact that there was a problem. The feedback domestically was focused more on cosmetic rather than substantive issues. Changes were made without knowledge of the impact to other parts of the system.

Japan is more technologically oriented; they grasped the idea of the system quickly and easily. Maybe it's just that invasive technology isn't as advanced overseas as in the United States. The doctors in Japan seem more interested in learning about new technology than in the States.

If Ohmeda doesn't want to continue with Finapres, I'll buy it and produce it. I believe in the product that much.

A somewhat different perspective was given by René Bernava, regional director for southern Europe:

Europe was ready for Finapres. The medical community, especially in Germany, was excited about the studies and papers written about the product. As a whole, European doctors were much less comfortable with arterial monitoring than their American counterparts. Finapres should have been a dazzling success in Europe, but there were problems, both with the product and the way it was marketed.

The technology for Finapres was purchased but not improved. The early version did not work. The project had software problems and lacked leadership. The original plan was to make an inexpensive disposable cuff. With this focus, a cuff that really worked regardless of cost was never developed. Also, the product was introduced at a premium price. That philosophy did not work.

The international sales force felt we had the top technology and wanted to go ahead. The meeting today occurred because we were the most vocal. I went to Dekle (President Dekle Rountree) some time ago and asked him to investigate the product, renew agreements with TNO, and put some money into the project. Some money was forthcoming but it wasn't a continuing process.

As Mark Halpert, vice president for FOI, saw the situation:

There are several reasons Finapres was more successful in Europe and overseas than in the United States. The sales force in Europe sells many products whereas in the United States the sales force only sells Ohmeda products. With the large product line, we developed customer expertise. We know what the customer wants, and we use technical support to help conclude the transactions.

NAME INDEX

SUBJECT INDEX